1896-1996

Celebrating
100 Years of Proud History

hatever hard experience had pushed them, it was an act of faith—and a vision—which led them.

That it was the right time is proved by the fact that the Union has lived and thrived. It survived an infancy of hard and bitter times; it struggled through a turbulent adolescence wherein the waywardness of some officers later required stricter internal discipline; finally it grew into robust manhood.

The Union developed in maturity to what it is today: a vital and constructive component of the American Labor Movement and of our two nations as a whole. The International Association of Bridge, Structural and Ornamental Ironworkers, AFL-CIO is a source of pride to our membership and it presents a challenge to our stewardship now and in the future.

This history is dedicated, with gratitude, to our founders and to those who guided our Union from its inception. We are in their debt—they made our opportunity and challenge possible.

With the commitment and strength of our membership, we will meet that challenge head on and maintain our rightful place in the "Life of North America."

Jake West
General President

FIRST EDITION

The Pittsburg Leader.

ONE CENT

THIS WEEK

THURSDAY, FEBRUARY 6, 1896.

THE SHOWER OF MONEY

THE PITTSBURG LEADER, THURSDAY, FEBRUARY 6, 1896

THE WAGE SCALE

STRUCTURAL IRON WORKERS ARE NOW DISCUSSING IT.

PITTSBURG MEN RECEIVING THE HIGHEST
RATES JUST NOW - AN EFFORT
TO BRING OTHER CITIES INTO LINE -
FATE OF "TRUE UNIFORMITY"
NOW IN THE HANDS OF THE COMMITTEE
OF TEM. OTHER LABOR NEWS.

The delegates attending the structural iron workers' convention in Moorhead's hall will likely have more or less trouble before the basis of a wage scale is agreed upon. This morning's session was largely devoted to a consideration of the subject. No definite conclusions have been reached as yet.

The hitch occurs by reason of the differences in the wage and hours of work in the various cities affected by the organization just formed. In Pittsburg the men receive $2.75 per day for nine hours' work, and it transpires that in cities like Buffalo and Cleveland, but $2.50 a day is being paid. Many delegates favor demanding $3 for a eight hour work day, but the question is whether in view of rates in other cities, this demand can be carried but.

The Pittsburg workers do not care to come down to the basis that exist elsewhere, hence the discussion. It is altogether likely that men in other cities will support the Pittsburgers in upholding wages.

The convention will probably remain in session another day, as there are many other important questions awaiting action.

At yesterday afternoon's session the organization was formally perfected. The Bridge Builders and Structural Iron Workers of America is the name given to it. The following officers were chosen:

Edward Ryan, of Boston, President; J.W. Brady, New York, and G.H. Hanna, Cleveland, vice presidents; James G. Crowley, of Chicago, secretary and treasurer; George W. Geary, of Chicago, national organizer; Edward Ryan, J.W. Kelly of New York, P.J. Dalton of Chicago, David McKelvey, of Pittsburg, M.O. Treeter, of Cleveland, and P.J. McIntyre, of Buffalo, executive committee.

LAST EDITION.

THE PITTSBURG PRESS.

TEN PA

VOL. 13. NO. 35.   PITTSBURG, WEDNESDAY EVENING FEBRUARY 5, 1896

Pittsburgh Press, February 5, 1886:

FORMING A UNION.

Structural Iron Workers Here to Discuss an Organization

The structural workers of the country met in this city yesterday to form a national union. The meeting was called originally for the last week in January, but as the Press outlined at the time, a postponement until yesterday was decided upon.

Chicago was represented by Secretary P.J. Dalton, George W. Geary and James G. Crowley. Cleveland by James and Robert Teeter and Samuel Brasy. Buffalo by J.T. Rutter, P.J. McIntyre and Michael Hanna. New York by John Brady, William Barry and J.W. Kelly. Boston, Edward Ryan. The Pittsburg delegates were M. Cronin, President David McKelvey and William Mullin.

At the preliminary session President M. Garland, of the Amalgamated association, addressed the delegates on the advantages of organization and gave some helpful suggestions. It is probable the new association will become attached to the American Federation of Labor. The delegates reported the strength of their respective organization as follows: New York, 1,500; Chicago, 700; Cleveland, 350; Buffalo, 300; Boston, 500; Pittsburg, 300. The Chicago delegates reported that their members receive $3 a day for eight hours work. The delegates expect to be in Pittsburg until next Saturday. The committee on constitution and by-laws will report to-day."

It all began on Tuesday, February 4, 1896 when delegates from Boston, Chicago, Buffalo, New York City, Pittsburgh and Cleveland, met at Moorhead's Hall at the corner of Second and Grant Streets in Pittsburgh. Many of the delegates stayed at the nearby St. Charles Hotel at the corner of Third and Wood Streets.

They had originally planned to begin their meeting the last week of January, but certainly the weather and traveling conditions at that time must have partly accounted for the delay.

Although our Union was founded on that day the story of the struggle of workers in North America and in the world has been a long one. Let's examine that struggle in order to understand the problems we face today.

St. Charles Hotel, 3rd & Wood Streets, Pittsburgh, where delegates to the founding Convention stayed on February 4, 1896.

Moorhead Hall, Second & Grant Streets where delegates met.

Printed in the United States of America on Union Made Paper
Graphic Design, Layout, Electronic Pre-Press and Printing by Affiliated Graphics

Waterless
Printing Process™

Acknowledgements

I would like to thank General Vice President Raymond J. Robertson who wrote the history of the Iron Workers Union with the assistance of numerous individuals that did research and provided valuable information which enabled this book to be completed.

Jake West
General President
IABSOIW

When General President Jake West asked me to write the 100 year history of the Iron Workers Union, I knew it would be a tremendous undertaking. I would like to single out a few of the people who provided research and other help to me as we brought this book through the long process of publication. I would like to thank Martin T. Byrne, Editor of *the Ironworker Magazine* and Executive Assistant to General President Jake West. Also, General Organizers Mike White and George Cross who did a lot of the digging that formed the framework of the book. Brother Cross was particularly helpful in providing information on our Shopmen. A special thanks to William "Red" Collins, retired member and officer of Pittsburgh Locals No. 818 and 3, who unearthed a great deal of early history and some historic photographs of our founding convention in Pittsburgh.

I would also like to thank William Adelman, an American labor historian and Professor emeritus at the University of Illinois for the many hours he worked doing research. In addition, we owe thanks to James J. Clarke, who did some of the basic historical research for the book. And, last but not least, I wish to extend my thanks and gratitude to many of our local unions and some of the "old timers" who provided historical information that made this book possible. Because of the assistance these individuals gave, I was confident that the book would be finished in time for the 39th International Convention celebrating the Centennial of the International Association of Bridge, Structural and Ornamental Iron Workers, AFL-CIO.

Raymond J. Robertson
General Vice President
IABSOIW

Contents

The text of the centennial history of the Iron Workers Union includes rare photos and engravings of our union and the American labor movement as they developed together over the last century. The illustrations accompany the text, as it tells the day-by-day events and issues that formed our International Association.

Chapter One

Setting The Stage

A Historical Perspective Leading Up To The Birth of Our Union

In the last few years we have all heard people say, "Unions were all right in the past, but we don't need them today." However, from the earliest times workers have organized, demanded training in needed skills and their democratic rights on the job. As long as selfishness and greed exist in this world unions will always be needed.

It is also true that the history of the Ironworker goes back to even biblical times. In Genesis, Chapter 4, 22, one of the descendants of Adam named Tubal-Cain is described as the instructor of workers in brass and iron. This would make him the very first ironworker apprenticeship instructor.

An article on apprenticeship written by General President Jake West in the May, 1993 issue of *The Ironworker* mentioned the following:

> "The world's first written code of law, the 'Code of Hammurabi,' named after the King of Babylon in the 18th century B.C. included the formalization of the training which we identify today as apprenticeship."

Among the Greeks and Romans, Vulcan was the god of fire and iron. He was often portrayed as a blacksmith standing by his anvil. Due to their resistance to corrosion, objects of utility and decoration, fashioned from brass, bronze, gold, silver, etc., are still in existence as records of the early civilization which produced them. The iron works of ancient peoples, however, have long rusted away, but we know from the earliest written records that iron was in common use.

The earliest known labor-management agreement dates back to 459 A.D. and is known as the Sardis Building Trades Agreement. An American archeologist, W.H. Buckler, while digging at the site of the ancient city of Sardis in what is now modern Turkey, discovered a very large gray marble slab with an inscription on it. When Buckler translated the inscription he was surprised to find it was a collective bargaining agreement between the local Roman pro-consul and the Sardis Building Trades Crafts. This marble slab was hardly the kind of contract that you would carry around in your pocket.

It seems that the city of Sardis was experiencing a building boom, and contractors were finding that there was a shortage of labor. This put construction workers in the position of being able to demand higher wages as they moved from one contractor to another. The Roman pro-consul then negotiated a collective bargaining agreement.

Although this is the earliest agreement that has been found certainly even earlier agreements must have existed between workers and employers.

With the collapse of the Roman Empire new means of protecting workers developed during the Middle Ages. This new system was the "Craft Guilds."

Everyone in a particular field in a town or district belonged to a guild. Ornamental ironworkers had such an organization. The members drew up the statutes of the guild, elected their own officers, and paid dues. Once a guild was orga-

Ornamental Ironworkers belonging to the Craft Guilds designed and fabricated wrought-iron window grilles in the 15th Century.

The Iron Bridge. The first bridge in the world to use iron as the basic construction material, was built in 1779.

However, after the 14th century the masters gained control of the guilds and refused to allow journeymen to join the ranks of the masters. The journeymen then formed "journeymen guilds" and they engaged in strikes in order to gain higher wages. Thus was born the prototype of our modern trade unions.

Former General President John H. Lyons Jr., wrote the following in the September, 1975 issue of *The Ironworker.*

> *"One very important early American was the Iron Worker, whether he was known as a Bridgeman, Blacksmith, 'Mechanic', Rigger, or Housesmith...They erected bridges of heavy wooden timbers, using primarily rigging skills with ropes, blocks, rollers and skids as their tools. We know, for example, the first ironworks was built in 1619 north of Jamestown and continued in operation until the workers were killed in an Indian raid."*

The first iron bridge was built by Abraham Darby in 1779. It crosses the Severn at Coalbrookdale, Shropshire, England, and has a span of about 100 feet, rising to a height of 50 feet. It is built of cast-iron ribs hinged at the springs and the crown. Even with this development, iron remained unsuitable for general bridge construction. Not only was it difficult to obtain a reliable enough supply of cast iron, but the brittle quality of the material precluded its use in tension. The only form in which cast iron could be used successfully was in the form of an arch, which is always in compression. This Iron Bridge is a national monument in Great Britain.

American workers would not have the industry or skill for such iron construction, and at this time bridges in the colonies were built of either wood or stone. Even a wealthy planter like George Washington could not get the skilled carpenters to build his home. Mount

nized only its members could work in that field. Members included the master, the apprentices, and the journeyman. The theory was that after years in a trade a journeyman would become a master.

An article in *The Ironworker* described the way the system worked:

> *"In medieval England, apprenticeship agreements called indentures were made between master and apprentice. The English word 'pretence' or 'apprentice' came into use during this time; it derives from the latin word apprehendere, 'to lay hold of.'*
>
> *The relationship between master and apprentice was much like parent and child, with the master's authority extending to every phase of the apprentice's life; the master provided food, clothing, housing and tools. He taught the trade and instructed in ethics, morals and proper behavior, usually for a period of seven years.*
>
> *At the end of training, the apprentice had to develop a 'masterpiece' as a final exam. If he passed he became a 'journeyman.' When he could pay the necessary fees and could set-up his own shop, he became a master."*

The first cast iron bridge located in Brownsville, Fayette County, Pennsylvania was completed in 1836.

Once an apprentice finished his training he would become a member of his craft guild. At their height, the guilds performed many of the same functions that unions perform in America today. They engaged in political action to secure liberties for their members and the community. They regulated trade and industry and provided education for their members. They helped sick members and provided them with a decent funeral. They were involved in both the artistic and religious life of their communities.

The colonial iron industry, long restricted by British regulations, quickly geared up and produced vital products for the American cause. Large foundries and small workshops employed many skilled workers doing a variety of tasks.

Vernon is actually a "prefab". All the sections were constructed in England and then shipped to America.

The colonial iron industry, long restricted by British regulations, produced vital products for the American cause. Large foundries and small workshops employed many skilled workers doing a variety of tasks. These workers were actually some of the first Shop Ironworkers. At Fredericksburg (Virginia), production began very quickly. Thousands of new muskets were made and others repaired between 1775 and 1782.

The Westham foundry, near Richmond, was larger and took longer to begin operations. By March 1779, the Shop Ironworkers began to turn out mill gudgeons, flat irons, sledge hammers, spikes and nails. Production of cannon balls, grape and canister shot began in April. By September, cannons were being cast.

The war's demand of military hardware sparked a flurry of investment in new plants and stiff competition for scarce labor. The boom, however, lasted only as long as the war. Within a year after hostilities ended, all the major ironworks in Virginia and others throughout the nation had shut down.

By 1786, workers' organizations were beginning to spring up. In New York, printers organized. Philadelphia printers engaged in the first organized strike in the history of the new nation, and they gained a minimum wage of $6 a week. In 1794, during the middle of Washington's term, the Federal Society of Journeymen Cordwainers of Philadelphia, an organization of shoemakers, was formed. Twelve years later this union was tried for criminal conspiracy after they dared to go on strike. The charges were (1) combination to raise wages and (2) combination to injure others. The union was found guilty and fined. The union became bankrupt and disbanded. This court decision established a precedent that was used against other unions in the years to come.

It should be noted that no permanent union could be established in America because British common law still prevailed, and unions were regarded as *"conspiracies in restraint of trade."* Workers were still denied the right to vote in most states even though they were citizens. You had to own a certain amount of property, pay a certain amount of taxes or have so much money in the bank.

In the spring of 1828, the first labor party in America was founded in Philadelphia by the Mechanics Union. They ran workers for public office, and they referred to them as "Worky" candidates. In that same year, General Andrew Jackson, "Old Hickory", was elected

President of the United States.

When Van Buren became president in 1837 he faced a difficult four years because of the depression. He was pro-worker and while working as a lawyer in New York State he had fought to end imprisonment for debt, and he was a champion of universal suffrage. He also got his home state to pass a Mechanics' lien law and reform the militia system.

On March 31, 1840, President Van Buren issued an executive order establishing a ten-hour day for federal employees working on public projects. He also ordered that they should receive no reduction in pay. This idea had been suggested to him by various groups of mechanics and laborers. Conservatives attacked Van Buren for establishing a dangerous precedent. But Van Buren replied that workers needed more money to *"enable him to provide comfortably for himself and his (family) and to educate his children."*

The first all metal bridge built in America was a modest cast iron arch with a span of eighty feet consisting of five tubular arch rings. It replaced a suspension bridge built by James Finley around 1807-10. The new bridge, designed by Captain Richard Delafield to carry the National Road across Dunlap's Creek at Brownsville, Fayette County, Pennsylvania, was completed in 1836 and, quite remarkably, has survived until the present. Although it has been strengthened, the original bridge castings, which carry the busy main street of the town, can still be found beneath the roadway.

John Augustus Roebling
(1806-1869)

The Introduction of Wire Rope to America

John Augustus Roebling who would later promote and design the Brooklyn Bridge, was born in Mulhausen, Germany in 1806. He studied civil engineering at the Berlin Polytechnic Institute. Roebling came to America in 1831 where he tried farming for six years but in 1837 he went to work for the Pennsylvania Canal Company. Canal barges crossed the mountains on inclined planes like cable tramcars. They were pulled up and down by hemp ropes 6 to 9 inches in circumference. These ropes were a mile long and cost $3,000 each. The problem was that these ropes often frayed and broke. Roebling witnessed one of them breaking and causing the death of two men.

Roebling remembered that wire ropes were being used in Europe. In 1842, he developed such rope and received a U.S. patent for the "Methods of Manufacture

Making of Wire Rope.

was brought in to rebuild it. In that same year, Ellet was awarded a contract to build a span of 750 feet at Niagara Falls, New York. By flying a kite he finally got two cables across the span. He then covered them with planking, and got his name in the paper by riding a horse across. He went into the business of charging people a toll to walk across, and pocketed $5,000. This was not the kind of bridge his employer wanted, and they sued him. Eventually, John Roebling got the job and in 1855 he built the Niagara Bridge. This was the first suspension bridge to carry train traffic.

A key factor in American prosperity would be faster and faster means of transportation. Ironworkers and other trades would be the ones that provided this. The following figures show how travel time was shortened:

Philadelphia to Pittsburgh	Type of Transport	Time
1812	Stagecoach	6 Days
1834	Canal Boat	3 Days, 19 Hrs.
1854	Train	15 Hours

of Wire Rope". Now the farming community of Saxonburg, Pennsylvania became an industrial town with the founding of Roebling & Son. In 1849, Roebling would move his factory to Trenton, New Jersey. Wire ropes from this company would be used by our members in the 1930's during the construction of the Golden Gate Bridge.

Roebling would eventually become exclusively a bridge builder. Since he worked for a canal company at this time, he built suspension aqueducts that carried barges across mountain valleys. When the canal era ended he would go on to build other types of bridges.

Railroads and New Types of Bridge Construction

Soon the railroads were replacing the canals, since they were faster, cheaper, and could be used year round. By 1860 there would be a total of 30,793 miles of track laid. New types of bridge construction were required for these heavy trains, and early Ironworkers would build them!

The three leading bridge engineers of this period were Charles Ellet, Jr., Captain James B. Eads, who would build the Eads Bridge in St. Louis, and John Roebling, whom we have already discussed.

Probably the least effective engineer, but the most colorful was Charles Ellet, Jr., who studied in France. He was particularly interested in French suspension bridges. In 1840, he would build a suspension bridge at Fairmont, Pennsylvania. It was 357 feet long, but it had no stiffening girder and vibrated in the wind. However, it did remain in service until it was replaced in 1874.

In 1847 Ellet built a 1,011 foot span at Wheeling, West Virginia but it later collapsed and John Roebling

Cast Iron Used As Building Material

Cast iron construction is recognized today not only as the forerunner of the steel framed skyscraper, but also as an early example of prefabrication and modular design. The use of cast iron for bridges led some architects to see what could be done to utilize this material in building construction.

The first person who used iron as a building material for the exterior was Daniel D. Badger. In the year 1842, Mr. Badger erect-

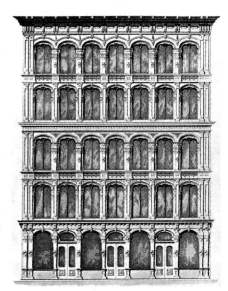

One of Badger's cast-iron building fronts erected in Albany, New York for J. Kidd Construction Company in the 1850's.

ed, in the city of Boston, the first structure of iron ever seen in America. He also erected cast iron buildings in Albany, New York. Most of the cast iron was used only for the fronts of the buildings.

James Bogardus was another individual who designed cast iron buildings. Although there is some controversy regarding his claims, it is said that Bogardus invented the first complete cast iron edifice ever erected in America, or in the world. His patent was for the *"construction of the frame, roof and floor of iron buildings."* In 1850, Bogardus built a factory completely out of cast iron. Cast iron buildings were usually limited to five stories due to the weight of the material and at that time the elevator had not been invented.

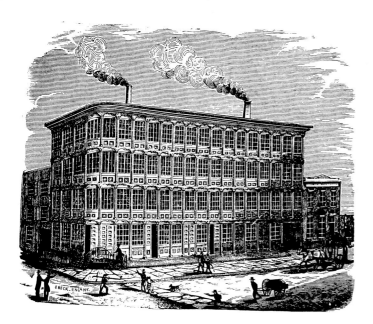

The factory of James Bogardus, inventor and patentee of cast iron buildings. It is the first building ever erected completely from cast iron.

The Early Production of Iron and Steel

Like cast iron, steel was used as a structural material for bridges before it was used for buildings. The objection against steel for bridges appeared to rise more from a lack of knowledge on how to use the material than from any deficiency in its quality.

Cast iron, though a marvelous material, has one great disadvantage. It is very brittle - it will hardly bend at all without cracking, therefore, this clearly limited its uses. Since very early days men had been aware of the comparative advantages of wrought iron and steel, but the making of steel in particular had always been a lengthy process. This changed in 1855 when the Englishman Henry Bessemer patented a process for making steel cheaply and in quantity.

While Bessemer was developing his invention, William Siemens was at work on the so-called open-hearth method of making steel. Siemens, working with his brother, developed the regenerative furnace in which the hot gasses of combustion were used over again to heat the air blast. Steel

One of Bessemer's early steel converters.

was produced satisfactorily and more economically by the open hearth method after Siemens teamed up with a Frenchman, Pierre Emile Martin. The Siemens-Martin process, as it is known, soon became the favored method and has remained the basis for the modern steel industry.

Bridge Construction After the Civil War

Bridge builders like Charles Ellet, Jr., Captain James B. Eads, General Sooy Smith and John Roebling gained experience prior to the Civil War. Sadly, many workers would die from some of the mistakes that were made. Many of these early bridges were canal aqueducts, but by 1861 the era of canals was ending. Also, steel was replacing iron as the material for construction.

Captain James B. Eads would build one of the three steel bridges that was built between 1874 and 1883. He would build the steel arched Eads Bridge in St. Louis

The Eads Bridge over the Mississippi River in St. Louis, Missouri, completed in 1874.

which was completed in 1874. This double-decked structure took five years to complete. The bridge was 520 ft. over the Mississippi River with approach spans of 502 ft. on both the Missouri and Illinois sides of the river. Eads would support the bridge by sinking huge caissons into the river bed. Little was known about the dangers of doing this and on March 19, 1870, an Ironworker died as a result of "caisson disease", which is known today as the "bends".

Although the Eads Bridge was built in part with steel, the first truly all steel bridge would be built by General Sooy Smith in 1879 in Glasgow, Missouri. It was built for the Chicago and Alton Railroad over the Missouri River. At first there was a great reluctance to use steel. Iron had earlier replaced timber as a construction material, but there was fear of using this new lighter material known as steel. Engineers at first thought it might crack or be too brittle and break in the cold weather. But General Sooy Smith used this material, and the Glasgow, Missouri bridge became the first to be entirely built of steel. This bridge would remain until 1902 when it was replaced because of the need for a wider span to deal with the heavier railroad traffic.

The Building of the Brooklyn Bridge

It would be the Brooklyn Bridge that would stand out as one of the great engineering achievements of the 19th Century. Also, many of the men and their sons who worked on this bridge would become charter members of Local No. 2 in New York City.

It would be the genius of John Augustus Roebling that would promote and design this bridge. But it would be his son, Washington Roebling, who would make this bridge possible.

In 1867, John Roebling successfully completed a bridge at Cincinnati across the Ohio River. He also would build, about this time, the Sixth Street Bridge in Pittsburgh across the Allegheny River. But his great dream was to build a bridge over the East River to connect New York City to the then separate City of Brooklyn.

At this time the City of New York felt they had no need of such a bridge to Brooklyn. However, the officials of the small City of Brooklyn felt it was vital to their future growth. Brooklyn at this time was a very wealthy and very religious community. Many of the citizens did not want to pay higher taxes or to be connected with what they considered the urban evil present in New York City.

However, the winter of 1866-67 changed the minds of people on both sides of the river. The East River froze and no ferry boat could cross. All commerce came to a

Founding of the Knights of Labor

A lithograph showing Knights leaders grouped around a portrait of Uriah S. Stephens, founder of the organization. **Left to right** are William Cook, James Wright, Robert Maculey, James Hilsee, Robert Keen, and Joseph Kennedy.

After the Civil War white northern workers found that their situation was little better than the former slave laborers that they had fought to free. Things did not get better when a recession hit the country from 1866 to 1868. When garment workers in Philadelphia spoke up and tried to improve their conditions they were fired and black-listed by their employer.

The leader of the Philadelphia garment workers, Uriah Stephens, a former minister, felt that a new labor organization needed to be established. Because workers could be black-listed by their employers if they knew they were union members, Stephens felt that membership should be kept secret.

In December of 1869, Stephens created "Local Assembly 1" with the high sounding name of the Noble Order of the Knights of Labor. Stephens knew Greek and had been a member of the Masons. Like the Masonic Orders, Stephens created for the Knights a number of secret rituals which the perspective member had to learn. This included a secret handshake, passwords, and countersigns. Members were never to refer to the organization by name. They called it the Five Stars. All meetings were announced by symbols chalked on sidewalks or fences. Members promised to defend the life, interest, reputation, and the family of all other members and never to reveal the name of the organization or the names of fellow members.

The cardinal principal was "to form a union of all wage-workers irrespective of race, creed or color". Even housewives could be members of the Knights but not...

"..lawyers, bankers, stock brokers, dealers in intoxicating liquors, and professional gamblers."

The membership grew slowly at first. The structure was in "Local" and "District Assemblies." Like the later C.I.O., members could be in a variety of trades both skilled and unskilled.

At first skilled craft unions did not come in together and have their own Assembly, but this changed in 1879 when the Window Glass Workers of America joined and became Local Assembly 300. This local gained control of almost the entire window glass industry in the United States. The local even sent organizers to Great Britain and Belgium to organize. The Union lobbied in Congress successfully for the passage of the Foran Act of 1885 to stop the importation of contract labor. Sadly, this law provided halt. Now even the State of New York saw the need for a bridge. The New York Bridge Company was set up in September of 1867 with the State of New York providing some of the funding. The original cost was to be seven million dollars with completion by 1870. But some state officials and engineers did not have faith in John Roebling's design and final approval was not given until 1869.

John Roebling was standing on some pilings near the Fulton Ferry docks, waiting for a signal to fix the position of the Brooklyn Tower of the bridge. He was concentrating so hard on his work that he failed to notice that a ferry boat was about to crash into the pilings. He lost his balance and his right foot was crushed between the pilings he was standing on. An incompetent doctor amputated his toes without using the proper anesthetic, and he developed tetanus. John Roebling died on July 22, 1869.

Brooklyn Bridge

for no federal inspector and was therefore not enforced.

Three issues would create dissension with the Knights of Labor. The **first** was the secrecy. It had helped the organization in the beginning, but it back-fired on them after the "Molly Maguires" incident, another supposedly secret organization which was verified in the conservative newspapers. Also, the Catholic Church at first condemned the Knights because there appeared to be some religious elements in their secret ceremonies. However, in 1881, Stephens was replaced as Grand Master Workman by Terence Powderly, a Catholic and the son of Irish immigrants. Powderly ended many of the secret rituals, and the Vatican and the Catholic Church in the United States and Canada in 1887 finally favored recognition of the Knights.

The Knights grew rapidly after the abandonment of the secret rituals. By 1884, there were 52,000 members and two years later 700,000 with many waiting to join. However, a **second issue** divided the membership. What should be the organization's role in regard to "political action"? Powderly approved completely of all political activities. He had been active in the Greenback-Labor Party and had been elected Mayor of Scranton, Pennsylvania for three two-year terms. But many of the skilled trade unions, that would later form the American Federation of Labor, supported the idea of work place action for wage increases and shorter hours with no political involvement either local or national.

The **third issue** that divided the membership within the Knights was the use of strike action by trade unions to achieve their goals. Powderly believed that strikes for wages and shorter hours were not the real problem facing American and Canadian workers. Powderly believed workers must form "producer cooperatives" that they would own. Then the problems of apprenticeship training, justice on

Women were welcomed into the Knights as members of separate assemblies. About 200 of these groups were affiliated when this picture was taken at a national meeting in 1886.

the job, shorter hours and higher wages, and child labor would be solved by the workers themselves.

However, the Knights found themselves involved in a number of strikes for wage increases and shorter hours. Some were won but most of them were lost. In 1882, Chicago bricklayers, who were affiliated with the Knights, went on strike and they won. However, the following year 4,000 telegraph workers that were members of the Knights lost their strike.

The downfall of the Knights would begin in 1886 with the movement for the Eight-Hour-Day. Powderly did not support a general nation-wide strike on May 1, 1886. Then, when the Haymarket bombing and the infamous trial took place, Powderly washed his hands of the entire incident. Samuel Gompers and the newly formed American Federation of Labor would support the nation-wide strike and supported the Haymarket Martyrs. Ironically, the Knights were blamed by the press for the Haymarket Affair even though they had nothing to do with it.

More and more workers would leave the Knights because of Powderly's indifference. This was especially true of the craft union members. By 1893, the membership of the Knights had dropped to only 75,000. Powderly resigned as Grand Master Workman and in 1896 he supported the Republican Party and its candidate for president, William McKinley. President McKinley rewarded Powderly in 1897 by appointing him United States Commissioner General of Immigration.

Washington Roebling Takes Over

After the death of his father, Washington Roebling became "Chief Engineer" of the Brooklyn Bridge. He was only 32 years old at the time but well qualified to carry on his father's work. He was born in Saxonburg, Pennsylvania in 1837. After his father's company moved to Trenton, New Jersey he attended school there. He studied engineering at our nation's best school at the time, the Rensselaer Polytechnic Institute. During the Civil War, Washington Roebling served in the New Jersey Militia building military bridges. After the war, he and his wife, Emily, went to Europe where he studied the new uses of steel as well as pneumatic caissons. When he returned, he worked with his father on the bridge over the Ohio at Cincinnati. When he took over his father's project he brought with him new ideas. He would modify considerably his father's design of stiffening girders for future traffic, and he favored an all steel design.

Washington A. Roebling (1837-1926)

Washington Roebling was concerned about the Iron-workers and other laborers that worked on the bridge. The big problem was the caissons that had to be sunk into the river beds for the two bridge towers, one on the New York side and the other the Brooklyn side. The caissons for the New York tower had to be sunk 78 feet below water level. The men working on this project were getting the same "caisson disease" that the workers on the Eads Bridge at St. Louis had experienced. Three men died sinking the caissons and 107 had to be given medical care. Washington Roebling went down with the workers, and he too was stricken and crippled for life!

During the early stages of construction, Roebling & Sons wire rope was used for walkways, travellers, and other preparatory work. By April of 1877, the first of the suspen-

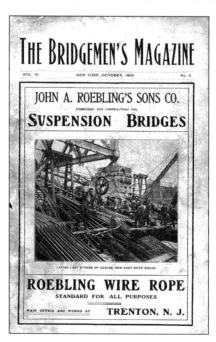

Bridgemen's Magazine October, 1903

The Molly Maguires and the Plight of the Miners

Our Union has always been interested in the plight of American miners. The early copies of *The Bridgemen's Magazine* were filled with articles about the low wages, long hours, unsafe conditions, and the use of child labor in the mines.

It is understandable that our Union would be interested in the miners, since they mined the coal, that would be turned into coke, that would be used to produce the steel, that would go into the bridges and skyscrapers that we would build. Another reason our members were interested was the fact that eventually the mines would be owned by the same businessmen that owned the steel mills and companies like American Bridge that were tying to lower our wages and destroy our Union.

Miners began organizing in the anthracite coal field as early as the 1850's. In 1862, during the Civil War, Irish miners in Pennsylvania organized. Their organization was known as the Ancient Order of Hibernians. Like the early Knights of Labor, membership was kept secret because of the hostility of the mine owners.

When the Civil War was over the mine owners decided to break every union in the anthracite coal fields, especially those in Pennsylvania. Anti-union newspapers suddenly began to print stories about a secret organization called "The Molly Maguires" that was terrorizing the mine owners. Such an organization did exist in Ireland. "Mollies" organized to stop the encroachment

continued on page 10

sion wires had been strung from anchorage to anchorage over tops of the towers and the wide expanse of the river. Wire by wire, the cables grew until the last wire was added in October of the following year. They seemed like giants, the four great cables each measuring almost sixteen inches in diameter. Though they look tiny beside the much greater cables of recent bridges, the Brooklyn Bridge cables represented one of the greatest advances in bridge engineering history.

The New York anchorage of the Brooklyn Bridge with two bridge towers in the background.

They carried a much longer span than any that had been previously built, and they also stand as the first example of the application of steel wire to bridge construction. The wire cables of earlier bridges had been made of iron wires, however, for the first time galvanizing was used on the bridge suspension steel wires of this bridge as a means of protecting the wire.

After 13 years the bridge was finished. Some authorities said that between 30 to 40 workers had been killed, but surprisingly no statistics were kept at that time. Newspapers reported the death of over twenty workers so we are sure of that number. Two workers were killed when one of the wire cable strands broke loose from the New York City side tower.

By 1883, the two stone towers of the bridge dwarfed the other buildings of New York City. They stood 275 feet above the high water mark. The

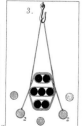
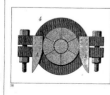

Ironworkers making cable for the Brooklyn Bridge (1878). As the wires were bound together into strands and lowered into place, the strands were, in turn, bound together to form manageable bundles. Eventually, all 19 strands would be joined, but the first step was to bind up what was called the core - the seven middle strands.

bridge's single span was 1,595 1/2 feet long and clearance above the water was 133 feet.

The official opening day was May 14, 1883 and on that day 150,000 people walked across the bridge. President Chester Arthur spoke at the dedication. The President then took the entire dedication committee to the apartment of Washington Roebling to honor him and his wife, Emily, for their achievements. A plaque was placed on the bridge giving credit to Emily Roebling for her work, as well as, that of her husband. Unfortunately, no plaque lists the names of the many workers who built this bridge or the names of those who died on the job!

A walk on the promenade of the Brooklyn Bridge became one of New York's favorite pastimes.

The Homestead Strike of 1892 and How It Affected Ironworkers

Five years after the execution of the Haymarket Martyrs, another event took place in the Pittsburgh area only four years before the founding of our Union....The "Battle of Homestead".

Ironically, the same steel companies that would later try to break our Union were involved in the destruction of the Amalgamated Association of Iron and Steel Workers (AAISW), which had organized many of the workers in Andrew Carnegie's Homestead Mills.

The Amalgamated Association was founded in August of 1876 by the merger of three existing unions: The United Sons of Vulcan, that were iron puddlers; the Associated Brotherhood of Iron and Steel Heaters, Rollers, and Roughers; and the Iron and Steel Roll Hands of the United States. When they were founded they only had 3,775 members, but by 1891 they had grown to 25,000 members in 290 lodges making them one of the most powerful unions in the country.

Both Andrew Carnegie and his business partner and chief lieutenant, Henry Clay Frick, wanted to get rid of unions in all their steel plants. Although Carnegie had allowed the union to exist at Homestead for many years, he now gave the go ahead to Frick to lock out all the union workers on June 29, 1892, one day before the union contract expired. The men were paid by the tonnage produced. Frick demanded that the price be set at $22 dollars a ton and not the $25 that the union requested. Although the company claimed that workers earned as much as $12 to $14 dollars a day, in reality at the time of the strike 1,177 workers averaged $1.68 to $2.50 a day, and another 1,625 averaged $1.40 or less a day. The company claimed they had the right to make an additional 15% profit, and they should get a greater profit based on the new machinery that they had installed.

Frick feared that the workers might storm the plant and take it over, so he erected a three mile long wooden fence topped with barbed wire around the plant. He also built sentry towers at strategic points for sharpshooters.

Frick contacted the Pinkerton Detective Agency in

Chicago for 300 private guards. Ironically, a number of students at Northwestern University, just north of Chicago, saw Pinkerton's newspaper ad for summer jobs and signed up not realizing what was in store for them!

The 300 Pinkertons, armed with Winchester rifles, were taken by train to McKees Rocks on the Ohio River just below Pittsburgh. On July 5th, they were put on two steel company barges and floated up the Ohio River, then to the Monongahela River, and on to Homestead.

*Andrew Carnegie
(1837-1919)*

Aware of their coming, a crowd of about 5,000 including Hugh O'Donnell, one of the union leaders, and even John McLuckie, the Mayor of Homestead, took over the plant. Then they gathered along the river bank as the barges approached early on the morning of July 6th. A battle took place and by 5 p.m. 13 had been mortally wounded. The Pinkertons finally displayed a white flag agreeing to surrender their weapons in exchange for safe passage.

However, the feeling of the crowd of men and women of Homestead was bitter because of the death of seven men. As the Pinkertons came ashore they had to walk up the hill to the railroad station through a gauntlet of townspeople. Women and children armed with sticks, umbrellas, and rocks attacked the Pinkertons. Some children threw mud. Some of the Pinkertons later stated that this gauntlet was more terrifying than the earlier battle.

The workers were now in control of both the plant and their town. However, six days later Frick convinced the Governor of Pennsylvania to declare martial law and send in the state militia. Union leaders were brought to trial because of the attack on the Pinkertons. Scabs were brought in, and the plant was reopened with military protection. By the end of 1892, 2,000 strikebreakers had been hired, the union had been destroyed, and only 800 of the original 3,800 employees were rehired.

The Homestead Strike ended unionism in the steel industry for the next 44 years. Although our Union would try again and again to organize workers in steel plants, it would not be until Roosevelt's New Deal in the 1930's and the passage of the Wagner Act that steelworkers in the mills would finally organize under the C.I.O.

Unionism Grows In Chicago

Chicago continued to be a strong union town even after the Haymarket Affair. At one time 25% of organized workers in America could be found in the Chicago area. One of the early groups to organize would be the structural and architectural ironworkers.

Many factors contributed to unionism among ironworkers in Chicago; for example, the Chicago River which passed through the central city and then broke into North and South Branches required wooden and

The Molly Maguires and the Plight of the Miners, *continued*

in Ireland of Protestant landlords. It was part of the century old conflict between Catholics and Protestants. American mine owners saw this as a convenient label to give to the militant union miners.

One of the most anti-union mine owners was Franklin B. Gowen, president of the Philadelphia and Reading Railroad and its subsidiary, the Philadelphia and Reading Coal and Iron Company. Gowen hired James McParlan, a Pinkerton detective, to infiltrate the union and find out the names of their members.

Certainly there was some violence in the mine fields, but most of these incidents took place after the Pinkerton detectives arrived. Many of the actual victims of the violence were not mine owners but union leaders and ordinary miners.

In the fall of 1875, twenty-four men, most of them actually members of the Miners' and Laborers' Benevolent Association were brought to trial. The evidence presented against them was totally fabricated. This trial was not unlike the McNamara Trial that was used by business to try to destroy our Union in 1911. Many of the men who testified against the Union were Pinkertons, like James McParlan, or criminals who were given immunity for their own crimes. The evidence was confusing and contradictory, but 14 of the men were sent to jail and 10 were hanged.

One of the men that was hanged was John (Jack) Kehoe, a leader of the Workmen's Benevolent Society. He was kept in solitary confinement for two years and then executed on Dec. 18, 1878. One hundred years later in January of 1979, Governor Milton Shapp of Pennsylvania would sign a bill posthumously pardoning Kehoe. The pardon was based on new historical evidence proving that he was innocent. The evidence showed he was framed by the mine owners in order to stop the growth of the union movement among their workers.

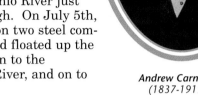

Founding of the American Federation of Labor

These men were the Executive Council of the Federation of Organized Trades and Labor Unions, predecessor of the American Federation of Labor. **Left to right** are Charles Burgman, Samuel Gompers, Richard Powers, William H. Foster, and Alexander Rankin. Rankin was the president of the powerful Iron Molders Union.

The American Federation of Labor was originally called the Federation of Organized Trades and Labor Unions or FOTLU for short. It was founded in 1881. After a series of small discussion meetings in the summer of 1881, a convention was held on November 15, 1881 in Pittsburgh. It would be in this same city 15 years later that the Iron Workers Union would be founded.

Attending was a total of 107 delegates of various craft unions such as the Printers, the Amalgamated Association of Iron and Steel Workers, the Molders, Glass Workers, Cigar Makers, Carpenters, and various delegates from local assemblies of the Knights of Labor. The opening paragraph of the call for the convention read as follows:

"Fellow-workingmen: The time has now arrived for a more perfect combination of Labor—one that will concentrate our forces so as to more successfully cope with concentrated capital."

Samuel Gompers of the Cigar Makers Union was elected chairman of the Committee on Organization. Gompers' committee suggested that the new organization be limited only to skilled workers of the United States and Canada. Gompers' committee wanted to change the name of the organization to the Federation of Organized Trade Unions and drop the word "Labor".

After the vote the name remained unchanged. However, at another convention in Columbus, Ohio in December of 1886, the name was changed to the American Federation of Labor. It was at that time that Samuel Gompers was elected president. However, they agreed to recognize their founding date as November 15, 1881, based on the date of the establishment of FOTLU. This is why the Centennial of the AFL-CIO was celebrated in 1981 and not in 1986.

Samuel Gompers -
President of the
American Federation of Labor.

Our Union and the entire American labor movement have been responsible for so many of the things that Americans today take for granted. They do not realize how long and hard we struggled to achieve some of these reforms. The original Platform of FOTLU in 1881 called for the following reforms:

1. Compulsory education of children;
2. Prohibition of child labor under age 14;
3. Uniform apprenticeship laws;
4. Enforcement of the National Eight-Hour Law;
5. Prohibition of convict contract labor;
6. A mechanics' lien law to guarantee you would be paid;
7. Repeal of conspiracy laws against unions;
8. Establishment of a Bureau of Labor Statistics;
9. Government regulation of railroads and telegraph companies;
10. Reclaim lands given by the government to the railroads that were not used for that purpose; and
11. Prevent importation of foreign contract laborers.

All of the above seemed revolutionary ideas at the time but eventually most of them became a reality. Today attempts are being made to turn-back-the-clock, and take away some of the protection that labor has won.

Although the AFL was in some ways similar to the Knights of Labor, it would differ in that it was made up of skilled trade unions. Gompers, as president, fought for shorter hours and more pay within the capitalistic system. The Knights wanted more workers to engage in cooperative ventures and to be more involved in politics.

AFL buttons, then and now, have the name of the union very large at the top and AFL-CIO (after 1955) very small at the bottom. Those of the Knights of Labor would have the organization's name very large at the top and the union...Mechanics, Molders, etc.... very small at the bottom.

Under the AFL more of the power was in the hands of the specific union and less in the hands of the national or international organization.

later iron and steel bridges to connect the various parts of the expanding city.

The first horse car lines were laid out in a "loop" which is now the downtown area of Chicago. As the land value increased in this area, the only way to go was up, and therefore the *"skyscraper"* and *"steel skeletal"* construction would begin here. In addition, the invention of the elevator made it possible to build buildings higher and higher.

Another factor was the Great Chicago Fire of October 1871. Any type of wooden construction would not be allowed in the downtown area and for some distance outside of it. This meant that new types of fireproof construction had to be developed to prevent future fires. The law required iron, and later steel, construction.

The first building to use the new type of fireproof construction was the Home Insurance Building built between 1884-85. It was designed by William Le

William LeBaron Jenney
In 1884 he started an important era of architectural vitality by designing the first metal skeleton skyscraper, the Home Insurance Building at LaSalle and Monroe Streets in Chicago.

Baron Jenney who developed this type of construction. When Jenney died in 1907 an article about him and this building appeared in the July, 1907 issue of *The Bridgemen's Magazine*, pointing out the importance of this pioneer structure to the growth of the union. Part of the article read as follows:

"Mr. Jenney's first important work as an architect was the application of the skeleton construction now in general use throughout this country. In the fall of 1883 he was appointed architect for an insurance company of New York City and instructed to prepare designs for a tall, fire-proof office building to be located on the northeast corner of LaSalle and Monroe Streets, Chicago, Illinois. The requirements were of such a nature that it was necessary to depart from

THE HAYMARKET AFFAIR:

Probably no single event has done more to influence the history of labor in the United States and even the world. It all began with a simple rally on May 4, 1886, but the consequences are still being felt today.

To understand what happened in Haymarket Square in Chicago on May 4, 1886 it is necessary to go back to the fall of 1884 when the Federation of Trades and Labor Unions (FOTLU), the predecessor of the A.F. of L., met in Chicago and called for May 1, 1886 to be the beginning of a nationwide strike for the eight-hour day. This was not a particularly radical idea since the State of Illinois and Federal employees were supposed to be covered by an eight-hour-day law since 1867. The problem was that the federal government failed to enforce its own law and, in Illinois, employers forced workers to sign waivers of the law as conditions of employment.

With two years to plan, organized labor in Chicago and throughout the nation sent out questionnaires to employers to see how they felt about shorter hours, piecework, child labor, and other issues. Although perhaps a simplistic solution to unemployment and low wages, the "Eight-Hour-Day Movement" caught the imagination of workers across the country.

In 1886, the City of Chicago had one of the strongest labor movements in the country. Chicago had a large German population and many of them had been socialists in the old country. Also, many Chicago workers had fled the eastern cities when their unions were broken and they were "black listed." Once in Chicago they were ready to fight rather than move again.

On Saturday, May 1, 1886, reportedly 80,000 workers marched up Chicago's Michigan Avenue, arm-in-arm, singing and carrying the banners of their unions. The unions most strongly represented were the building trades, and among them certainly were the Bridge Builder's Mutual

"We are peaceful," Samuel Fielden reportedly told the police a few minutes before the Haymarket explosion. During his trial, however, it was asserted that he urged workers to attack the police.

Association and various ethnic iron worker unions of that day. This solidarity shocked some employers, who feared a workers' revolution, while others quickly signed agreements for shorter hours at the same pay.

On Monday, May 3, the peaceful scene turned violent when the Chicago Police Department attacked and killed picketing workers at the McCormick Reaper Plant on the city's southwest side. It was this attack that provoked a protest meeting which was planned for Haymarket Square on the evening of Tuesday, May 4.

While the events of May 1 had been well planned, the events of the evening of May 4th were not. Most of the speakers failed to appear. Instead of starting at 7:30 pm, the meeting was the usual arrangements that were in style in building construction at that time. To meet all these new and untried propositions Mr. Jenney decided to substitute iron and steel for brick and stone, and the structural steel building of today is the result of his fertile brain."

The columns in the building were of cast iron. The riveted columns of plates and angles were thought to be too expensive. It was in this building that the first Bessemer steel beams were used. They were manufactured by the Carnegie-Phipps Company, who stated that these beams were the first to be used in building construction. This departure from old methods not only introduced steel skeleton construction to the world

The Home Insurance Building constructed in 1884. Note: The two upper floors were added in 1890.

but made possible the formation of our International Association.

This pioneer steel structure, the Home Insurance Building was torn down in 1931 to make way for the Field Building, which is now known as 135 S. LaSalle Building. The Field Building would also be built by our Union and completed in 1934. In 1995, of the ten tallest buildings in the world, seven are located in Chicago.

A final factor in the growth of unions in Chicago was the development of the railroads and the fact that Chicago was a transportation center. This meant there was a need for the construction of numerous viaducts and railway bridges of unique types that would not interfere with the river traffic.

The Eight-Hour Day Movement

delayed for about an hour. Instead of the expected 20,000 people, fewer than 2,500 attended.

Although Mayor Harrison who attended the meeting had told the police to leave, the minute he was out of sight, the crowd now numbering only about 200 was attacked by 176 policemen carrying Colt Lightning revolvers. Then someone, unknown to this day, threw the first dynamite bomb ever used in peacetime in the history of the world.

The police panicked, and in the darkness many shot at their own men. Eventually seven policemen died, only one directly accountable to the bomb. At least four workers were killed, but there may have been more since bodies were dragged away in fear of police harassment. Hundreds of labor leaders were arrested and all union newspapers were closed down.

Eventually eight men, representing a cross section of the labor movement, were selected and brought to trial. Only two of the men were at the Haymarket Square that night. Three of the men were sent to Joliet State Penitentiary and five were condemned to be hanged. On November 11, 1887 four of the men were hanged. One had died in jail prior to the execution.

Two years later the Haymarket Affair would take on world-wide dimensions. In Paris, France in July of 1889, Samuel Gompers and the American Federation of Labor sent a delegate to the World's Fair held in that city to celebrate the centennial of the French Revolution. It was at that time that the 934 foot Eiffel Tower was built, proving the possibilities for iron and steel construc-

The law vindicated - four of the Chicago anarchists pay the penalty of their crime.

tion. The A.F.of L. delegate recommended that a day be set aside to honor the Haymarket Martyrs, and the day that was selected was May 1st. Today, almost all the major industrial nations of the world, including Great Britain, Germany, Japan, Sweden, Norway, Israel and all the nations of Central and South America have May 1st as their "Labor Day". Only in the United States and English speaking Canada is this day not honored on May 1st.

After the Haymarket Affair, unions throughout the country found themselves under attack. Management used the Haymarket bombing to stereotype all union members as wild-eyed bomb throwers. Even the meaning of the word "anarchist" was changed from the original ideas of Plato and Socrates, of a world without armies, or police ...a kind of "Utopia." The new meaning became "someone who wanted to destroy everything through violence."

Although the Knights of Labor continued, its days were numbered. The fact that Terence Powderly had turned his back on the Haymarket Martyrs, and failed to support the "Eight-Hour-Day Movement" had disillusioned many workers with that organization. And the fact that Gompers had come to Springfield, Illinois to plead with Governor Ogelsby for the lives of the Martyrs, gave great credibility to the craft unions and the new American Federation of Labor.

Chapter Two

The Birth Of Our Union

In the late 1880's, steel had virtually replaced wood and stone as the primary load-carrying material in the erection of bridges and buildings. This abrupt change in structural materials brought about a demand for a new type of skill required of the working man. Practically overnight, bridge carpenters became "bridgemen" and blacksmiths became "housesmiths" and "architectural iron workers." As soon as American historian Frederick Jackson Turner proclaimed the end of an era for the American Frontier, Ironworkers became known as "cowboys of the skies", sharing the adventure and excitement which frontiersmen and explorers had enjoyed previously.

But the glamour and the appeal of the new skill had its drawbacks for the young man looking for a stable and secure profession. For one thing, natural death was looked upon with suspicion. For about $2.10 a day for ten hours work, the Ironworker in 1890 was expected to climb narrow steel beams six, sometimes seven days a week in all kinds of weather conditions. The accident and mortality rates were higher than in any other trade at the time, resulting in a high turnover of workers on any one job.

Since steel erection attracted only the most daring of independent men, little or no thought was given to the need for formation of an effective union for their protection. Nevertheless, many of these eligible bachelors, admired from a distance below by the "wholesome young girls" of the Gay Nineties for their feats

"Cowboys of the Skies "

of courage and strength, later gave thought to such things as provisions for sickness, injury, or death to protect their families. Primarily for these reasons, delegates from independent unions in the major cities met in Pittsburgh, and on February 4, 1896, the International Association of Bridge and Structural Iron Workers of America was established. After a few years of fierce struggle, our Union was fully recognized and took its rightful place among the older and prominent trade unions in America.

However, the formation of the International Union is only part of the early story of the Ironworkers. The fact that the independent unions had been in existence for some time was, indeed, an interesting part of that story. A closer look at two of these, one in Chicago and the other in New York, will illustrate some of the complexities involved.

Because of the danger of their work, many Ironworkers lost their lives, therefore as early as the 1880's Chicago Ironworkers formed the Bridge Builder's Mutual Association. The Association consisted of a loose federation of 20 men interested in giving each other a decent burial in the event of death on the job, and supporting one another in times of sickness and injury. As they began to see the need for defending workingmen's rights against the encroachments of sometimes ruthless contractors, this mutual aid federation was no longer adequate. Also at this time a demand was created for structural Ironworkers, and many of the old bridgemen answered the call since they would employ essentially the same skills on buildings as they would on bridges.

Therefore, in 1890 our Association became known as the *"Bridge and Construction Men's Union."* One of these men, George W. Geary, who later became known as the *"Father of the Ironworkers,"* spearheaded this Union. He stated:

> *"A State charter was procured and we sailed out in the waters of Trade Unionism, determined to protect the rights of each member of the craft, do justice to the Employers and control the industry."*

However, as has happened so many times in American labor history, workers were fighting each other. Another association known as the "Architectural Iron Workers", working not only in shops but also on the new skyscrapers, was in competition with Geary's union. For two years they fought each other.

George W. Geary said:

> *"..it finally dawned upon the members of the craft of both sides that while we were fighting each other, the Employers were realizing the benefits of the quarrel and the members were paying the cost."*

George W. Geary
The Father of the Bridgemen's Union

Finally in 1892, the Bridge and Construction Men's Union was dissolved and became the "Bridge and Structural Iron Workers Union" consisting of 2,700 members. Today that group is Local No. 1 of the present day International Union.

The Architectural Iron Workers Union was still a separate organization. In 1890 they were made up of three separate ethnic locals...a German branch with 279 members, an English branch with 198 members, and a Bohemian branch with 102 members. As skilled workers they had some of the lowest wages in Chicago when they were organized on June 5, 1890. They ranged from 17 1/2 cents to 25 cents an hour for a ten-hour day.

In 1891, with a membership of 1,500, the Architectural Ironworkers went on strike for higher wages and shorter hours. But they were defeated. They again went on strike during construction of the Chicago World's Columbian Exposition in 1893, and this time they won the eight-hour day. However, hard times followed the Exposition and until 1896, few men, engaging in architectural ironwork, remained in the union.

The Architectural Iron Workers Union of Chicago would loose members over the next few years. On December 27, 1900, they became Local No. 14 of the United Metal Workers International, but finally their President, O.H. Hill, would bring them into the Iron Workers International in 1903 as Local No. 63.

Samuel Gompers was one of the speakers on the first day of the Exposition. The topic of his speech was "What Does Labor Want?" Gompers stated that labor wanted the eight-hour day and perhaps even shorter hours in the future, better pay, and better educational opportunities. Labor wanted "more schools and less jails, more learning and less vice, more leisure and less greed."

His remarks were well received.

Minutes of the
Architectural Iron Workers - April 23, 1893.

Organizing In New York City and Other Eastern Cities

In April of 1886, 10 years before they would help to organize our International Association, a small group of German-American Ironworkers assembled in Herzog's Hall on East Fifth Street in New York City and organized the Locksmith and Railing Makers' Union. All business was transacted in the German language. By June of that same year a branch of the local was started in Brooklyn. By 1889, they achieved a membership of 120, and they affiliated with the "Eight Hour League" of the A.F. of L..

In March of 1890, the name of the organization was changed to the Architectural Iron Workers' Progressive Union (AIWPU). An English speaking branch and Jewish branch were organized with a total membership of 400. This was followed by another German branch in Hoboken, New Jersey.

Like their fellow workers in Chicago before them, they struck in 1891 for the eight-hour day, but they were crushed. The AIWPU and the Housesmiths' Union were both dissolved. Management used new immigrants as strikebreakers, and it became difficult to organize. Neither group of workers had the strength to get together and apply for a new state charter until 1893.

Shortly after each was reorganized, "Fighting Sam Parks" assumed leadership of the Housesmiths. In 1895 both took a militant stand against the Employers and held out once more for the eight-hour day. Although both unions stood united in their last-ditch effort against the employers, the Housesmiths, five months later, sought to strengthen its hand and became the Housesmiths' and Bridgemen's Local No. 2 of the International.

When Parks first arrived in New York he found that Ironworkers were receiving only $2 per day, and many were signing year-long contracts that turned them into slave labor. Under Parks leadership he would double the daily rate to $4, and restore the strength of the union despite attempts by big business to destroy him and his reputation.

The Architectural Iron Workers Union of New York did not affiliate and remained separate. On June 28, 1900, 300 of their members were locked out by the Architectural Iron Workers Employers' Association. At that time they had a treasury that by today's standards would be considered quite substantial. Nevertheless, six months later they were in debt.

The Employers' Association apparently was able to obtain the use of the State Militia and other military organizations, because in July of 1901 a resolution was passed not to take such men into the union. A year later the predominately German union adopted English as the official business language, and again, like their Chicago tradesmen, chose a different direction and became Local No. 50 of the United Metal Workers' International. This proved ineffective and finally, to protect their existence in the shops, the Architectural Iron Workers Union drew up an agreement with the

Sam Parks
and his dog, "Arbitrator."

Ferris Wheel-1893 Columbian Exposition erected by Ironworkers. in Chicago Illinois.

View of the shaft and hub of the Ferris Wheel during dismantling in 1894. 1, Frank Steel; 2, James McCabe; 3, Tom Downs; 4, W.J. McCain; 5, Assistant Engineer; 6, Deli Goodsell.

Ironworkers who dismantled Ferris Wheel in 1894 in Chicago.

Housesmiths of Local No. 2 of the International, promising not to do outside work. This led on November 11, 1902 for them to become Local No. 42 of the International Association of Bridge and Structural Iron Workers of America.

Our Founding Convention

Ironworkers were also organizing at this time in Pittsburgh, Boston, Buffalo, Cleveland, Detroit, and Philadelphia. They began to communicate with each other and decided to meet in Pittsburgh the last week of January 1896, but this was later postponed until the following week, perhaps because of weather conditions at that time of the year.

The choice of Pittsburgh as the founding convention city was not only practical (centrally located) but it was symbolic as well. Where would be a better place to build a national or international brigemen's union than in the City of Bridges? One of the local papers *(The Leader)* reported the day before the convention that "more bridge builders are employed here than in any city in the country." The story further reported that Geary would try to establish headquarters in Chicago (but) "the choice is between Pittsburg and Chicago."

Representatives from six cities answered the call to convene at **Moorhead Hall** in Pittsburgh on Tuesday, February 4, 1896 to organize an International Association of Bridge and Structural Iron Workers. The following day, the *Pittsburg Press* reported that sixteen delegates from Boston,

Buffalo, Chicago, Cleveland, New York City and Pittsburgh assembled. Later, the Pittsburgh *Leader* stated that delegates had been expected from Detroit and Philadelphia as well, for the five-day meeting.

The *Pittsburg Press* listed the sixteen delegates who attended the organizational convention as: Ed Ryan of Boston; John T. Butler, Daniel F. McIntyre, M. Hanna of Buffalo; George W. Geary, James G. Crowley, Patrick J. Dalton of Chicago; Emil and Edward Treter, and Cornelius Brady of Cleveland; John Brady, William Barry and James W. Kelly of New York; David McKelvey, Michael Cronin and William Mullin of Pittsburgh.

Moorhead Hall in Pittsburgh where first Convention was held in 1896.

18

The out-of-town delegates stayed at the nearby St. Charles Hotel at the corner of Third and Wood Streets. On Tuesday, February 4, 1896 they gathered at Moorhead Hall at the corner of Second and Grant Streets to begin the founding of the International Association of Bridge and Structural Iron Workers of America.

On the first day of the convention the delegates selected David McKelvey, president of the Pittsburgh local as president of the convention.

St. Charles Hotel, Pittsburgh where delegates stayed during the first convention.

Patrick Dalton, of Chicago, was selected as secretary. Each of the delegations reported their "estimated" membership, as follows: Boston, 500; Buffalo, 300; Chicago, 700; Cleveland, 350; New York, 1500; and Pittsburgh, 350. (The rounded figures suggest the delegates guessed at short term potential membership).

At the opening session President M. M. Garland, of the Amalgamated Association of Iron, Steel and Tin Workers, offered congratulations to the new Bridge and Structural Iron Workers Union. President Garland stressed the advantages of organization and recommended that the new organization affiliate as soon as possible with the American Federation of Labor. This would give the new organization additional strength as well as solidarity with the union brothers in the building trades.

On the second day the permanent officers were selected. Edward J. Ryan of Boston became our Union's first President, and John Brady was elected First Vice-President. M. Hanna became Second Vice-President, and James G. Crowley, Secretary-Treasurer. George Geary became the National Organizer. Chosen as Executive Board members were David McKelvey, James W. Kelly, Daniel F. McIntyre and Emil Treter. It seems that at the end of the first day the Cleveland delegation returned home because their local had gone out on strike.

During the next three days many issues were discussed by the delegates. One of these issues was the possibility of establishing a uniform wage rate for all the locals, but this proved impossible. While Pittsburgh Ironworkers received $2.75 for a nine-hour day, Buffalo and Cleveland received only $2.50. Workers in Chicago worked eight hour days. They decided to drop, for now, the idea of a uniform wage scale, and work for the eight-hour day that the Haymarket Martyrs had died for and concentrate on organizing.

Various obstacles faced their organizing effort. The employers, particularly the large contractors, did not like having their Ironworkers organized and there was a shortage of steel shapes that often delayed jobs. In addition, the International officers were not full-time paid officials. Very little time and energy remained after the officers put in their full day's work on the steel. If they had not lost their will and strength to run a union at night or on Sundays, they certainly didn't have the financial means for the necessary communication and transportation.

A 25 cent per capita tax was levied each month, but most locals did not have the funds to pay into the International, nor was there an established headquarters. Each year the International Headquarters moved to the home of the elected Secretary-Treasurer, and if he would move, so would the headquarters. All this while the local union's major concern was with their individual incessant struggles with various employers' associations. In its first four years of existence the International barely survived.

Who Were Some Of The Delegates That Attended The Founding Convention?

Let's look at some of the 16 delegates who attended our founding convention and what happened to some of them in the years to come.

Edward John Ryan, president and charter member of Local No. 7, Boston, Massachusetts, was elected as the **First International President** in 1896 by delegates attending the **First International Convention** in Pittsburgh. President Ryan was born in 1860 in Fredericton, New Brunswick, Canada. He migrated to Massachusetts, settling in Boston, where he worked as a blacksmith and later an Ironworker. He was International President until 1899. President Ryan died in Boston in 1921. As the International reached its 100th Anniversary, we learned that Eleanor Ryan Mulhern, daughter of Edward Ryan, was still living. She provided Local No. 7 with some of the history concerning her father.

Charter Members - February 4, 1896. **Top Row:** *P.J. Dalton; James G. Crowley (Secretary-Treasurer); John Brady (First V.P.);* **Bottom Row:** *John T. Butler; J.W. Pryle; George W. Geary (First National Organizer); Ed J. Ryan (First International President.)*

Edward John Ryan
First International President (Pictured as he began his Ironworking career)

Daniel F. McIntyre from Buffalo. In 1901 he was elected Secretary-Treasurer of the International.

John T. Butler of Buffalo was one of the prime movers in pushing for the meeting in Pittsburgh. He was a charter member of Local No. 6 in Buffalo. He would become General President of the International in 1899. He would remain active in the International and later serve as a delegate to the Building Trades Department of the A.F. of L.

Daniel F. McIntyre from Buffalo, New York became connected with the Housesmiths' Union in 1895 and became Recording Secretary of that organization, plus he was a delegate to the Central Labor Body of Buffalo. In 1896 he was elected as one of the delegates to represent Buffalo at our founding convention. At this time he was a member of the Executive Board of the Buffalo local. While at the convention he

was elected Chairman of the International Executive Board and he would hold that position for two years.

M. Hanna of Buffalo was a member of the Executive Board of that local. He was elected Second Vice-President of the International at the time of the founding convention.

George W. Geary of Chicago, would later write a column for The *Bridgemen's Magazine*. He would be known as "The Father of the Iron Workers Union." At the time of the founding convention he was an organizer for the Chicago local. At the founding convention he was elected as an organizer for the International. Later, he wrote about the efforts

One of the first banners in 1896.

The Bridgemen's Magazine

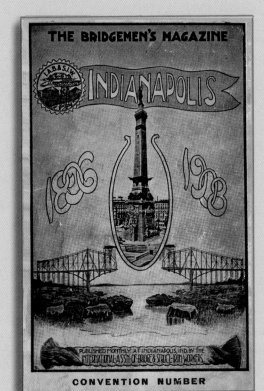

In July 1901, James L. Kelly, a member of Local 3 and a bridge inspector for the Wabash Railroad, published the first issue of *The Bridgemen's Magazine* at 625-631 Second Avenue in Pittsburgh, with the blessing of the International's Executive Board. The original subscription price was $1.00 per year - in advance. "Magazine" Kelly was a trusting soul, but he liked his money up front. Just three months later, the price rose to $1.25 per year.

The magazine's instant popularity and subscription sale surprised Kelly and his partners. Six weeks after the first issue, the publishers claimed its circulation had surpassed several of the contemporary labor magazines. The second issue was not published until the second week in September, 1901, and was marked Volume 1, Number 2. The Resolutions Committee at the Convention mandated that the journal be printed by union labor and only union advertisements inserted.

The magazine's masthead proclaimed it "the official Journal of the International Association of Bridge and Structural Iron Workers," although it was not owned by the International - rather, it was Kelly's property. His folksy style pleased the Union membership for the one and one-half years he edited the journal. The format Kelly established was continued for some years after the International assumed ownership and operation of the publication.

General President Frank Buchanan decided correctly that the magazine was the responsibility of the Union and foresaw the

political, economic and social advantages of International control and ownership. He recommended to the delegates of the 1902 Convention in Milwaukee that the International be empowered to purchase the magazine from Kelly and to begin publication with the January, 1903 issue. The delegates concurred. The International Executive Board at its meeting in New York in November, 1902, decided to leave in the hands of the Secretary-Treasurer the details of transferring ownership of the journal from the publishing company to the International. The shift was accomplished within a month.

The subscription price was reduced to the original charge of one dollar per year - also in advance, or 10 cents per copy. The delegates voted that henceforth the magazine would be managed and edited by the International's incumbent Secretary-Treasurer, a policy which prevailed for the ensuing twenty-six years. The delegates at the 1928 Convention unanimously supported General President Paul Morrin's recommendation to create a new position of general editor to be appointed by the General President the following year.

William "Billy" McCain, of Kansas City Local 10, served as an International officer for almost two decades when he was tapped by Morrin to replace the expelled Harry Jones as Secretary-Treasurer in April, 1925. McCain at the time was first Vice-President of the International Association. He decided early on that his new position, as the General Secretary and the chief financial officer, which also included handling the chores of editor of *The Bridgemen's Magazine*, was more of a three-man job than a one-man job. He conceived the idea of the Chicago Federation of Labor to pass legislation that after July 1, 1904, Illinois would not use convict labor in the production of goods.

James G. Crowley of Chicago was the Secretary-Treasurer of the local at the time of the founding convention.

Patrick J. Dalton of Chicago was a member of the Executive Board when he was sent to the founding convention.

Emil and Edward Treter and **Cornelius Brady** represented the Cleveland local, but it seems they had to leave early because of problems at home. However, Emil was chosen to be on the first Executive Board of the International.

John Brady of New York was later elected four times to be the president of his local. At the time of the founding convention he was vice president of the New York local and he was elected by his local to be a delegate. He would attend two additional International Conventions and be elected First Vice President in 1901. Earlier, when his local was suspended in 1900, he worked hard to straighten things out and to bring Local No. 2 back into favor.

David McKelvey was president of the Pittsburgh local, and was elected president of the convention on the first day of our founding convention. On the second day of the founding convention he was elected to the Executive Board.

The Second International Convention was held in Buffalo, New York in 1897. Ed Ryan was reelected General President and New York's William Barry was elected Secretary-Treasurer. **The Third International Convention** was postponed until 1899 when the delegates met at the St. Charles Hotel in Pittsburgh. John T. Butler, of Buffalo, was elected President and J.W. Pryale of Pittsburgh was chosen as Secretary-Treasurer. No Executive Board was elected.

The Fourth International Convention in 1900 was held in Pittsburgh. John T. Butler was reelected President. John Brady, Edward John Ryan, J.G. Morrison, George Boyd, John Kingsley and M.J. Reynolds were elected members of the Executive Board.

---

that the duties of his office be separated into two distinct positions of Secretary and Treasurer and that the Union should hire a competent full-time editor. His plan, of course, would require convention action. McCain easily convinced Morrin, who in turn persuaded the Executive Council and then successfully urged the delegates at the 1928 Convention to approve McCain's structural changes.

Since that time, six men have served as editor of the magazine: John J. Keegan, Julian Meyer, James J. Clarke, John Holmes, William Lawbaugh and the present editor, Martin T. Byrne, who is also Executive Assistant to the General President. Mr. Byrne's knowledge of the trade, having been an Apprentice, Journeyman and Business Agent, has made *The Ironworker* magazine a success resulting in several awards for "EXCELLENCE."

Between the tenures of Holmes and Lawbaugh, an editorial committee of International Union officials with Executive Director J.W. Hardesty as Chairman and General Organizers Raymond J. Robertson and Calvin Walker as two of the committee members, managed the journal.

The *Bridgemen's Magazine* continued to be published by the International Association solely under that name until January, 1959 when General President John H. Lyons, Sr. introduced the secondary title, *The Ironworker*. Lyons wrote an article for that issue entitled, *Presenting The Ironworker* in which he stated the International was presenting "a new, modern and streamlined version of *The Bridgemen's Magazine*, which shall

READ IN ALL PARTS OF THE WORLD

THE BRIDGEMEN'S MAGAZINE

henceforth be known under the pen name, *The Ironworker*." He also pointed out that the new title was more appropriate "and one that more clearly describes the work of all the men of our trade."

The delegates at the 1956 Convention officially changed the legal title of the journal from The *Bridgemen's Magazine* to *The Ironworker*, effective with the November issue of that year. Beginning with the July, 1957, issue the overall size of the publication was increased from 6 x 9 inches to 9 x 12 inches with a reduction in the number of pages. At the same time Lyons decided to have the magazine printed by sheet-fed offset presses in two colors, which he described in his June, 1957 President's letter "a very decided improvement." And it was; the new format proved to be more appealing to the membership and more readable.

Beginning with the January, 1971 issue, General President John H. Lyons, Jr. and the magazine's editorial committee agreed to modify slightly the size of *The Ironworker* to a handier 8-1/2 x 11 inches. The change was made not only for economic reasons but, as President Lyons noted, to conform with "what has now become a national standard in magazine page dimensions. We anticipate that this standardization will help the Postal Service in making deliveries...." During the last several months of 1970, Bill Hardesty, Ray Robertson, Calvin Walker and the rest of the committee completed the redesign of the magazine including its scope and format. Lyons also ordered a four-color process to be used on the covers while maintaining a two-color format for the inside text, and to be printed instead on a web offset press.

*James L. Kelly,
Founder of The
Bridgemen's Magazine
in July, 1901.*

The table listing the conventions and names of the officers elected at each previous convention printed in the October 1909 issue of *The Bridgemen's Magazine* states that J.W. Kelly was elected Secretary-Treasurer at the 1900 convention. The minutes of the fifth Convention held in Boston in 1901 states that J.W. Pryale was Secretary-Treasurer when the Convention was opened by President John T. Butler. Therefore, Pryale, who was first elected Secretary-Treasurer at the convention in 1899, must have been reelected at the next convention in 1900.

John T. Butler
elected 2nd International President in 1899

The year 1901 was the best year for the Iron Workers International since 1896, percentage wise at least. Membership swelled to 6,000, and by September there was over $2,000 in the International treasury. The number of locals receiving charters more than doubled that year.

National General Organizer George Geary, the first man to hold that position in the Union, resigned in the summer of 1901, when he was named superintendent of the Free Employment Agency of the State of Illinois. His office was in his hometown of Chicago. Geary was succeeded as National Organizer for the International Association by Thomas McGovern, business agent of Buffalo, Local No. 6.

Thomas McGovern,
National Organizer

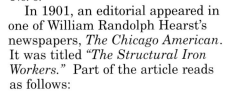

"Did you ever give a thought to these men? They build our skyscrapers, bridges and trestle work. They fasten together the steel beams and girders that form the bones and muscles of our high buildings."

In 1901, an editorial appeared in one of William Randolph Hearst's newspapers, *The Chicago American.* It was titled *"The Structural Iron Workers."* Part of the article reads as follows:

"Did you ever give a thought to these men? They build our skyscrapers, bridges and trestle work. They fasten together the steel beams and girders that form the bones and muscles of our high buildings. They wear no uniform. No band of music plays when they go to work. Not one of them has ever received a medal or stripe upon his sleeve. No editorial writer probably ever has commended them as patriotic citizens. The city has never given a banquet in their honor or even passed a vote of thanks for their services. And yet these structural Ironworkers risk their lives every weekday in the year for their country's sake. Several hundreds of them were killed or disabled in this state last year. The average length of time they live after beginning their work is ten years. The motto of their craft is, 'We do not die; we are killed'."

Local unions were chartered by the "International Association of Bridge and Structural Iron Workers of America" in 1896, however, in 1901 the words "of America" were dropped from the title. The first printed charter was issued to Local Union No. 1, Chicago on February 1, 1901. Also, in July of 1901, the first issue of *The Bridgemen's Magazine* was published in Pittsburg.

The Buchanan Presidency

The Fifth International Convention was held in Paine Memorial Hall, Boston, September 23 through October 3, 1901. President J. T. Butler was in the chair at the opening of the Convention, and Secretary-Treasurer J. W. Pryale was at his side. The reading of the credentials showed that Local Unions No. 21 through 27 were represented by delegates and proxy votes. It was ruled that Local No. 9 (then in Pittsburgh) had received its charter unconstitutionally and was therefore not entitled to a seat at the Convention. Local No. 14 (which apparently at that time was a railway bridgemen's local based in Pittsburgh) was granted a seat but no vote and its delegates withdrew from the Convention. The Convention further decided that Local Union No.'s 21, 22, 24, 25, 26, and 27, who were represented by proxy, were not entitled to representation because they had not paid per capita tax during the preceding year.

Frank Buchanan
3rd International President elected in 1901

During the 1901 Convention it was reported that Secretary-Treasurer J. W. Pryale had left Boston, which caused suspicion and concern. A committee was named and instructed to contact Pryale and request he turn over all monies, books and papers dealing with business of the International. General President Butler tendered his resignation when he learned of Pryale's departure, but upon request agreed to continue in office until the evening of September 30th. The Convention adopted *The Bridgemen's Magazine* as the official journal of the

Delegates to the Fifth International Convention in 1901

International Association and adopted a new constitution to become effective January 1, 1902.

Two-thirds of the delegates at the 1901 Convention were unhappy with the International's affiliation with the AFL, as this excerpt from the Convention minutes shows:

> *"As considerable dissatisfaction seemed to exist with reference to the manner in which we became affiliated with the A.F. of L., the matter was taken up for discussion and it was finally moved and seconded that we withdraw from the A.F. of L. It was moved and seconded in amendment that the matter be referred back to the different locals for referendum vote. The amendment lost by a vote of 27 to 26. The original motion was put and carried by a vote of 35 to 19."*

Ironworker members of Local Numbers 3, 20 and 17 on jobsite in December, 1900 at Benwood, West Virginia.

Agreement Reached In 1902

The following is a copy of the Agreement between the National Association of Manufacturers and Erectors of Structural Steel and Iron Work, and the International Association of Bridge and Structural Ironworkers:

1. Eight hours shall constitute a day's work in localities where it is now the prevailing custom to work eight hours. In other localities nine hours shall constitute a day's work; this, however, may be subject to arbitration.

2. Time and a half-time will be allowed for time worked in excess of the hours fixed upon as constituting a day's work for one shift, except as follows:

   a. On Sundays throughout the year, Decoration Day, Fourth of July, Thanksgiving Day, Christmas Day, or the days observed as these holidays, double time will be allowed for any time worked within the twenty-four hours constituting a calendar day. No work shall be performed on Labor Day except in case of dire necessity when the property of the employer is in jeopardy and the service of the men is required to place the same in a safe condition; double time will be paid for any time worked Labor Day. Only straight time will be allowed for time worked on Saturday afternoon, but a half-holiday Saturday afternoon without pay may be granted by arrangement between the employer and workman.

   b. When two separate shifts are employed on the same piece of work, each shift will be paid the regular prevailing rate of wages per hour. Hours of each shift may be arranged between the employer and workman as may be most advantageous, but the hours of employment of each shift will not be less than the hours fixed upon as constituting a day's work.

3. Workmen will be paid every two weeks upon pay days to be fixed by the employer, except in localities where it is required by law and where it is the prevailing custom to pay weekly.

4. It will be the general custom to withhold not more than one week's time, to enable the employer to prepare the rolls, etc.

5. When any workman is discharged or laid off, he shall be paid in full within twenty-four hours.

6. When a workman leaves the services of an employer of his own accord, he will receive the pay due him at the next regular pay day.

7. There shall be no restrictions or discrimination on the part of the workman as to the handling of any materials entering into construction of the work upon which they are employed.

8. There shall be no limitation upon the amount of work to be performed by any workman during working hours. There shall be no restriction as to the use of machinery or tools, or as to the number of men employed in the operation of same.

9. There shall be no restriction whatever as to the employment of foremen.

10. There shall be no sympathetic strikes called on account of trades' disputes.

11. No persons other than those authorized by the employer shall interfere with workmen during working hours.

12. The employer may employ or discharge, through his representative, any workman as he may see fit; but no workman is to be discriminated against on account of his connection with a labor organization.

13. There shall be no discrimination against, interference with, or fines imposed upon foremen who have been in the service of the employer during the time of strike.

14. Apprentices to learn the trade may be employed in proportion of one apprentice to every seven Bridgemen and such apprentices shall serve on erection work for a period of not less than six months before receiving the rates of wages agreed upon for members of such organization. No man shall be employed as an apprentice whose age is over thirty years. The Apprentices shall perform such duties as may be assigned to them by the Foreman-in-charge.

15. Laborers may be employed for unloading and handling materials in yards and storage points and for removing materials from such yards or storage points to the site of the work.

16. Such work as the framing of false work and travelers, the framing and placing of wooden decks (ties and guard-rails) and all woodwork on mill buildings, painting of structural steel and iron work, and placing and adjusting of operating machinery in draw bridges and machinery in other structures may be performed by such men as the employer may select.

17. In cases where misunderstanding or disputes arise between the employer and workmen, the matter in question shall be submitted to arbitration locally, without strikes, lockouts or the stoppage of work, pending the decision of the arbitrators.

Effective to January 1, 1905
(signed)

H. F. Lofland	Frank Buchanan
Daniel Scanlan	H. F. Donnelly
J. W. Johnston	Robert E. Neidig

The disaffiliation was short-lived, however. Frank Buchanan, who would assume the office of General President in October, 1901, immediately after the Convention, realized that separation would harm the International. He strongly favored affiliation with the A.F.L., but he bided his time and on September 30, 1903, the delegates at the Seventh Convention in Kansas City concurred with Buchanan's recommendation to return to the fold. One week later on October 6th, the International Association was granted another charter by A.F.L. President Samuel Gompers.

The records are not clear about the exact date the International affiliated with the A.F.L. the first time. The 1901 A.F.L. Convention Proceedings state that seven national unions had been issued charters during the preceding year and among them, the International Association of Bridge and Structural Iron Workers.

The following officers were elected at the 1901 Convention in Boston: President Frank Buchanan, Local 1, Chicago, who defeated George Boyd, Local 3, Pittsburgh; First Vice-President John Brady, Local 2, New York; Second Vice-President C. F. Lyons, Local 17, Cleveland; Secretary-Treasurer D. F. McIntyre, Local 3, Pittsburgh; Executive Board members William McIwaine, Local 13, Philadelphia; James Trainor, Local 18, St. Louis; J. F. Carr, Local 7, Boston; George Flairs, Local 19, Minneapolis; John McCabe, Local 3, Pittsburgh.

The Convention voted to send three provisional delegates to the Convention of the National Building Trades Council of America

First Charter - issued to Local Union No. 1 February 1, 1901 and signed by President Butler.

and later in 1901, the Iron Workers International Association became affiliated with that organization. The A.F.L. refused to endorse the National Building Trades Council because it "sometimes assumed an attitude of rivalry and hostility, not only to the American Federation of Labor, but often to unions connected with the regular organizations of the crafts, going so far as to charter and recognize independent unions frequently organized for the purpose of antagonizing existing organizations." The National Building Trades Council should not be confused with the Building and Construction Trades Department of the A.F.L. which was organized in February 1908, with the sanction and approval of the 1907 A.F.L. Convention.

There were many able men among the early stalwarts of the International Association, none more outstanding than Frank Buchanan. He possessed a vision beyond immediate interests. This extended sometimes farther than some local officers were able or willing to see. He also had a patience in his leadership that demonstrated his foresight.

Frank Buchanan was the third man to hold the office of General President. He served the International Association for four years. He was reelected in 1902, 1903 and 1904, and later was elected to the United States Congress. The Biographical Directory of the U. S. Congress (Bicentennial Edition) states he was born June 14, 1862 on a farm near Madison, Indiana (bordering on the Ohio River). He went to the rural county schools, worked on the family farm — or as the Congressional directory puts it "engaged in agricultural pursuits at home."

Frank left home as a young man, went forty miles down river to Louisville, Kentucky to learn the bridgeman's trade. In 1894, he moved to Chicago and there joined the recently organized and chartered Bridge and Structural Iron Workers. Within a few years he was elected business agent. He also aided George Geary, Pat Dalton, and James Crowley in their efforts to establish an International Association.

Seven weeks after Buchanan was elected to his first term as General President, one of his first official actions was to arrange a meeting in November with Joshua Hatfield, President of the American Bridge Company, to discuss his plan of making a national agreement with the nation's biggest bridge builder. As Buchanan put it, he wanted "to prepare a general or uniform agreement for all locals." Buchanan and Hatfield set up a conference to be held in January, 1902.

At the conference held at Pencoyd, near

Executive Board Elected at the Fifth International Convention in 1901.

Philadelphia, January 17, 1902, American Bridge was represented by H. F. Lofland, Erection Manager, and S. P. Mitchell, Chief Engineer. The International was represented by President Frank Buchanan and Secretary-Treasurer McIntyre.

A tentative National Agreement was reached which provided that the company would employ only members of the Union on all its erection work within the United States and in territory outside of the United States preference would be given to members of the Union.

The jurisdiction claims of the International, which at that time were disputed by other unions, were fully recognized by American Bridge and set forth in Section 11 of the Agreement. Section 33 provided, "When the Company is the original contractor and sublets the work to another firm or company, the sub-contractor shall be subject to all of the terms and conditions of this agreement."

Section 19 of the proposed Agreement provided that there would be no strikes or lockouts, pending a decision of the Board of Referees, and other sections established a rather elaborate plan of arbitration for the settlement of differences that might arise over the interpretation of any clause in the contract, or any differences to, specifically covered. Section 29 provided, "A sympathetic strike ordered by other trades, or by one of the central bodies, where it is necessary to take part to protect Union principles, shall not be considered a violation of this agreement."

The Agreement also contained provisions for employment of apprentices at a ratio of one apprentice to every ten bridgemen or structural Ironworkers. The term of apprenticeship was established at not less than eighteen (18) months.

President Buchanan and Executive Board members realized the importance of such a contract, as American Bridge was by far the largest employer of Ironworkers at that time and other large firms probably would have accepted the same Agreement. It would have resulted in completely organizing the trade at a time when it was not well organized outside of the larger cities, most in the East or Midwest. The Agreement was submitted to the Locals for a referendum vote of the membership. The *Bridgemen's Magazine* of April 1902 reported:

Quarterly Working Card 1902.

American Federation of Labor Affiliation Charter issued to the International Association of Bridge and Structural Iron Workers on October 6, 1903 and signed by AFL President Samuel Gompers.

"The referendum vote of the Locals of the International Association of Bridge and Structural Iron Workers as to the adoption of the universal scale proposed by the American Bridge Company has been received with exception of the votes of the Locals of St. Louis and New York. D. F. McIntyre, General Secretary-Treasurer said: 'Generally speaking, the votes favored the adoption of the universal scale. There are 32 articles, however, to the Agreement and I do not know of a local that adopted the scale in toto. This will mean much work for the general officers'."

There was a difference of opinion between the members and the officers of the locals on the matter of a uniform national wage scale and a national agreement. Some were strongly in favor of such a proposition, while others were in favor of a uniform national agreement with wage scales to be negotiated by each local. Still others believed all negotiations should be conducted by the individual local without International interference except International financial aid in case of a strike. This difference of opinion resulted in some locals giving very little consideration to the proposed Agreement with American Bridge when it was submitted for a referendum vote in the early part of 1902.

Charles Massey, a business agent of New York Local No. 2, pointed out that Sam Parks, chief business agent and the influential power in the Local, said the agreement should be thrown in the waste basket, and it was. Parks said that he wasn't interested in anything Lofland (of American Bridge) was interested in. Only later did the locals realize what they rejected.

Sam Parks had made a name for himself, among Ironworkers and other building tradesmen in New York, even before the founding of the International by establishing rates and working conditions much better than employers were originally willing to approve. He pushed them beyond their stated limit. Most employers didn't like that and even fewer liked him - but he wasn't interested in the "Mr. Congeniality" award. The New York contractors vowed to get him and they did finally, when Parks slipped, which will be discussed later in this chapter.

Although disappointed that the local unions did not accept the proposed contract, President Buchanan continued his efforts to bring about national action to organize the trade. Plans were made to organize some of the large non-union jobs by striking the work of the same contractor in other cities where they were operating union. Philadelphia was the center of a struggle causing sympathetic strikes elsewhere.

In a letter published in the June 1902 issue of the magazine, President Buchanan stated: "The Locals in Pittsburg, Buffalo, Cleveland, Albany, Boston and Philadelphia have made one of the most gallant fights in the history of organized labor. They were battling against one of the most powerful adversaries in the country and with exception of the local in Philadelphia, their efforts have been crowned with success, but all the

Rankin Bridge near Pittsburgh erected by members of Local No. 3 working for American Bridge in 1901.

signs point to the fact that the local of Philadelphia will likewise gain a victory in the near future."

The Philadelphia local demanded an eight-hour day and a ten cent per hour raise to 50 cents to become effective May 1, 1902. All structural steel companies doing work in that city agreed - except Pennsylvania Steel Company and American Bridge Company. Local 13's strike against them was not effective in stopping work. Two months later, General President Frank Buchanan arrived in Philadelphia from Chicago to work on a new skyscraper and was asked by the local officers for International assistance in their struggle against the two companies. He arranged with locals in New York, Pittsburgh, Buffalo and Albany to strike American Bridge in those cities. This moved American Bridge's President Hatfield to meet with Buchanan. They met in New York and reached a satisfactory agreement on August 13.

The American Bridge Company had about 400 non-union ironworkers in its employ, most of whom had been imported from other cities. The settlement provided

An Ironworker's Pride Showed...

The Ironworkers as well as all union members participated in Labor Day parades. The badges served two purposes-the colorful side was worn during parades and the black side was worn during funerals.

Group of popular members of Local 1, 1902.

that all of those men who desired to join the Union should be permitted to do so and the rest should be discharged. About two-thirds of the number joined the Union. The settlement of this strike was looked upon as a complete victory for the Union.

President Buchanan met early in 1902 with C.O. Sherman, a leader of the United Metal Workers' Organization. This union, which was formed in 1900, was working in a dual capacity by claiming all the work of the Bridge and Structural Iron Workers. At the meeting, Buchanan proposed that the United Metal Workers confine themselves "to the organization of the inside shop workmen" and the Outside Iron Workers would assist them whenever possible. Sherman agreed to consider the proposal.

In June of 1902, Local No. 26 of Cincinnati, Ohio, which was an Outside Structural Local, went on strike against the Architectural Iron League of Cincinnati for an increase in wages and reduction of hours. This organization of bosses conspired with the United Metal Workers to take the place of the Structural Iron Workers for half the wages. At that point, Buchanan felt there was no place for the United Metal Workers International Union. The common reference in the magazine was that it was a "catch-as-catch-can organization" or the "Tin Can Union."

As a result, Buchanan decided that for the "protection of the men who are erecting the structural iron work, as well as those who are working on the material in the shop, we have concluded that it has become necessary to use our efforts to organize inside men.."

The beginning of the Shop Division and Shopmen Local Unions had its birth in the summer and fall of 1902, just six years after the International was formed. The first local was Local No. 40 in Newark, N.J., which was designated as "Inside Architectural Bridge and Structural Iron Workers."

A gang of Local Union No. 10 members, working for Phoenix Bridge Co., at Jefferson City, Missouri went on strike for $3.50 per day on May 5, 1902. They were out only 5 hours when the company agreed to the scale wages asked for. Local No. 10 Business Agent W.J. McCain is in center sitting down.

...In Triumph And Tragedy

From time to time in this book the reader will note that the number of certain local unions changed, for example, Local No. 18 of St. Louis became Local No. 396. The reason is due to the Local Union losing its charter for a period of time. Possibly they did not pay their per capita or were placed under supervision. When the Local Union was reinstated, they were issued the next charter and Local Union number in sequence. In some cases numbers for locals were recycled during the early years, so that a number for a particular local in a city might again appear in another city at a later date. That is what occurred with Local No. 40. After the charter was revoked sometime in early 1904 and Local No. 2's charter was revoked about the same time, the International issued the number again to charter a new Outside Local in New York City.

Original Iron Workers logo

The Sixth International Convention

was held in Milwaukee, Wisconsin, September 13-22, 1902. In his annual report to the Convention, President Buchanan stated "One year ago our membership was in round numbers, about 6,000. Today, it is about 10,000 and if, during the coming year, we will actively advance the interests of our Association, there is no reason to doubt but that we will succeed in organizing the men working at our craft." President Buchanan's report indi-

cated that he had spent a considerable amount of time traveling from place to place, organizing and assisting local unions in adjusting their grievances and negotiating agreements.

Buchanan had better luck at the Milwaukee Convention than he did with his American Bridge Agreement. He recommended that (1) the President and Secretary-Treasurer be placed on fixed salaries and devote full time to the International; (2) authority be granted to the President to solve Union problems without waiting for approval of the Executive Board; (3) a contingent fund be set aside for the use of the President, so he could move quickly to any city where his services were needed; (4) a uniform road scale in areas outside the jurisdiction of established local unions; (5) ownership and control of *The Bridgemen's Magazine;* (6) establishment of an apprenticeship system throughout the International; and (7) affiliation with the A.F. of L.

The Convention delegates adopted all his recommendations except the one dealing with apprenticeship, which they decided to hold over to the next convention. There were sixty delegates in attendance at the Convention representing 28 local unions.

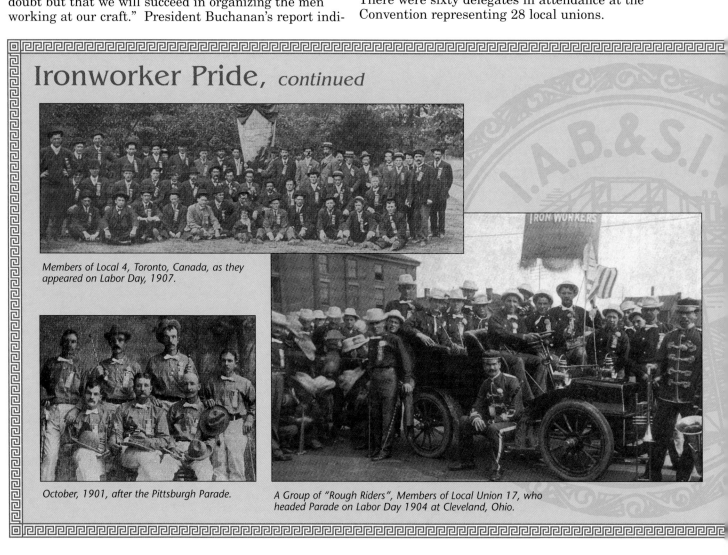

Ironworker Pride, *continued*

Members of Local 4, Toronto, Canada, as they appeared on Labor Day, 1907.

October, 1901, after the Pittsburgh Parade.

A Group of "Rough Riders", Members of Local Union 17, who headed Parade on Labor Day 1904 at Cleveland, Ohio.

The delegates voted to place the offices of President and Secretary-Treasurer on a salary basis, increase the per capita tax from 25 cents to 40 cents per month and establish a death benefit assessment of 10 cents per member per month. The Convention also adopted Buchanan's recommendation to take over publication of *The Bridgemen's Magazine* under the supervision of the International Secretary-Treasurer beginning January 1, 1903, and that the magazine be furnished at $1.00 per year to all subscribers, or 10 cents per single copy. Beginning with John W. Johnston, the incumbent Secretary-Treasurer would edit the magazine for the following twenty-six years.

Buchanan realized much more than most the political, economic and social value of Union ownership and control of *The Bridgemen's Magazine*. He knew that an informative monthly journal would keep the membership abreast of the officers' activities and make them aware of the International's efforts to improve wages, working conditions, and job safety for the rank and file Ironworker. This would provide for a more knowledgeable membership and a more cohesive Union.

The following International officers were elected at the 1902 Convention: President Frank Buchanan, Local 1, Chicago; 1st Vice President John T. Butler, Local 6,

J.W. Johnson
Local No. 2, elected Secretary-Treasurer of the International at the Sixth Convention in 1902.

Buffalo; 2nd Vice President E. L. Warden, Local 15, New Haven; Secretary-Treasurer J. W. Johnston, Local 2, New York; Executive Board Members: John McCabe, Local 3, Pittsburgh; Peter L. Beck, Local 24, Denver: H. F. Donnelly, Local 12, Albany; John H. Barry, Local 18, St. Louis; and Robert E. Neidig, Local 2, New York.

At a meeting of the International Executive Board held in New York City, November 24 through November 29, 1902, it was decided to recommend to each local union that they adopt an apprenticeship system to meet their local requirements with no more than one apprentice to seven journeymen. It was further decided to continue to grant charters to shop locals, but that shop locals would not work on erection work except with permission of the erection local union where the work was to be performed.

The Executive Board also gave authority to the International President to appoint District Organizers. The Executive Board adopted a motion to recommend to all locals that no men be shipped outside of their jurisdiction after May 1, 1902 for less than $3.50 per nine hours. This is believed to be the first uniform "road scale" ever approved by the International.

The four years following the 1902 Convention were very eventful and had great effect on the future of the

Members of Local Union No. 20, Wheeling, West Virginia who made a hit Labor Day, 1905.

Minneapolis, 1901.

Members of Local Union No. 10, of Kansas City, Missouri after the Parade on Labor Day, 1905.

International Association and its members. The progress made in organizing and obtaining increases in wages and, in some cases, signed agreements, was outstanding. Most local understandings and agreements were reached without strikes, or, if there was a strike, it usually was short.

The first General Presidents, Edward Ryan, John Butler and Frank Buchanan, grappled with basic issues, growing pains of the fledgling union, organizing, trying to get enough money for paid officers, and locating a headquarters somewhere other than the Secretary-Treasurer's basement or attic.

As early officers of the Iron Workers wrestled with these problems, the overriding problem only slowly real-

Snapshot of the officers of the Housemaids' Protective Association No. 1, of Buffalo, New York, organized by the members of the International Board during a meeting held in that city in 1903.

1903 Per Capita Tax Card of the United Housesmiths & Bridgemen's Union, Local No.2 of New York and Vicinity.

ized - and first by Frank Buchanan - was whether the International Association was to be a confederation of autonomous locals or a strong, indivisible union. On this score Buchanan would have to do battle with New York's Sam Parks and other stubborn, like-minded powerful local union leaders.

Buchanan knew that a strong International Association was the only means to give Ironworkers a fighting chance against employers who were forming their own organization. He was aware that steel companies, led by U.S. Steel, were pushing the open shop policy in the mills and realized that fabrication and steel construction companies could follow along the same path, especially those which were subsidiaries of U.S. Steel.

In early 1903, the American Bridge Company was working under signed agreements with Iron Worker local unions in localities where circumstances made that

Ironworker Pride, *continued*

At the wake, it was common to have flower arrangements designed like bridges and derricks. When a member was killed on the job, almost all of the members of the local union attended the funeral.

OBITUARY

In Memoriam
LOCAL No. 396
INTERNATIONAL ASSOCIATION
BRIDGE
AND
STRUCTURAL
IRON WORKERS
ST. LOUIS, MO.

expedient. In other localities where the Ironworkers were not well organized, American Bridge appears to have had little regard for union rules and regulations and this resulted in much friction.

In January of 1903, Secretary-Treasurer J.W. Johnston reported that twelve new charters had been issued during the last quarter of 1902. The shop or inside charters that were issued during that period were entitled: "Inside Architectural Bridge and Structural Iron Workers."

In June of 1903, Bernard J. Markle, Recording Secretary of Local No. 4 in Toronto, Canada, and Robert E. Neidig, President and Business Agent in New York City, organized Local No. 66, Inside Architectural Iron Workers.

In his report to the delegates attending the **Seventh International Convention** held in Kansas City in September, 1903, President Buchanan, who was reelected, stated "he had found that the locals at Buffalo, Pittsburgh, Philadelphia, Jersey City and Albany had suffered grievances at the hands of the American Bridge Company and that this company had refused to adjust them." The International Executive Board called a general strike on all of the American Bridge Company's jobs effective

1903 delegates badge worn at the Seventh International Convention in Kansas City.

March 12, 1903.

After the general strike had been in effect for about three weeks, President Buchanan secured an audience with financier J. Pierpont Morgan, at his residence in New York. The meeting was arranged through the influence of the officials of the National Civic Federation. After President Buchanan had outlined the Union's position, Mr. Morgan is reported to have said that while he did not approve of closed shop and certain other features of unionism, he was in sympathy generally with labor organizations and would see what he could do in the matter. After a three day meeting with representatives from the American Bridge Company, the National Association of Manufacturers and Erectors of Structural Steel and Iron Work and the International, an agreement was reached which became effective May 1, 1903 and was to continue in force until January 1, 1905.

President Buchanan in his report to the members in the May 1903 issue of *The Bridgemen's Magazine* pointed out that certain clauses of the agreement were not completely satisfactory to the Union Committee, but that the employers had made the largest concessions and that an

Delegates to the Seventh Annual Convention of the Iron Workers International at Kansas City, Missouri., in 1903.

immediate settlement was important. He also requested the members to live up to the spirit, as well as the letter, of the Agreement. The Agreement did not provide for a union shop, nor did it permit sympathetic strikes ordered by other trades as did the proposed Agreement with the American Bridge Company in 1902.

After the signing of the National Agreement, the New York contractors mobilized to force a compulsory arbitration plan on the city's construction unions, different from the arbitration clause contained in the National Agreement. The contractors formed a company union of Ironworkers, locked out Local No. 2 members, and threatened to lock out members of other construction unions. The New York Local No. 2 Ironworkers were getting clobbered, with no relief in sight. Within a few months, the fan was whirling out of control, throwing stuff in every direction.

In September, 1903 at the International Convention in Kansas City, Buchanan reported to the delegates with pride on the success (outside of New York) of the Agreement with the Erectors' Association. With good reason he was pleased; he reminded his fellow members that they had a contract with "the principal structural iron manufacturers and erectors in this country...(and) by the largest and most powerful association of employers that heretofore had been formed."

But the dispute in New York between the building trades and the contractors was the key issue for Buchanan and most of the delegates. They wanted it settled because of its potential national ramifications (even though some viewed it as just a local problem).

Immediately prior to the Convention, fighting Sam Parks, of Local No. 2, was in deep trouble. He was convicted of extorting money from contractors and was lit-

erally sent up the river to Sing-Sing. Then he was released temporarily pending a hearing on a motion for a new trial. In the interim, Parks went off to Kansas City as a delegate to his last convention.

At the Convention a resolution was adopted to support Local No. 2 members in its fight with the New York contractors. Earlier, the delegates voted to help Local No. 2, financially, with a $1,000 loan. However, the days of Local No. 2 and Parks were numbered.

Following the Convention, Buchanan and Executive Board members journeyed to New York to help settle the draining problem. After several meetings between the New York contractors group and the International officers, the contractors agreed to terminate the dual union

Members of Local No. 2 in New York City erecting the Manhattan Valley Viaduct connecting the Rapid Transit Tunnel between 125th and 135th streets, on Broadway in 1903.

(which had received a state charter through the political influence of the contractors). In turn, the International agreed to revoke the charter of one of its founding locals, Local No. 2, in February, 1904. The contractors wanted Parks' power base eliminated.

By this time, Parks' appeal for a new trial had been heard and denied. He was returned to prison - gone from the New York labor scene, but certainly not forgotten. He died in prison several months after the demise of his old local. Whatever might be said of Sam Parks, he was a man of his time, who was dedicated to the well-being of his fellow New York Ironworkers. He may have wanted a full wallet for himself, but he wanted his friends to earn sufficient wages to take care of their families adequately. Parks had many friends outside the ironworking trade as well. Newspaper accounts of the day report that more than 10,000 admirers lined the streets to view his funeral cortege as it wound its way to the cemetery.

The International then established four new locals: two in Manhattan (Locals 40 and 52) and one in Brooklyn (Local 35) and one in Jersey City (Local 45). Local No. 2's members were transferred to the new locals. The contractors recognized the new locals and agreed to employ union Ironworkers exclusively.

At the Convention, President Buchanan reported on the "inside shop men." There was opposition by some outside members. He recommended that before outside workers become involved in a controversy involving inside men, that the question should be presented to the rank and file for referendum vote and, likewise, if the outside requires the assistance of the inside men, that the question be submitted to the locals for a referendum vote by the rank and file. He further recommended that the inside and structural locals remain apart and separate with an agreement between them that neither local is to infringe upon another's work. During the Convention, it was regularly moved and seconded that the "Inside Iron Workers be considered part and parcel of this International Association." The motion was passed.

A new section in the Constitution, Article 21, governing the Inside Iron Workers was adopted.

By the end of 1903, fifteen Inside Architectural Iron Worker locals had been organized.

Wabash Bridge over the Monongahela River in Pittsburgh after wreck in 1903. On the morning of October 19, at 8:30 am, after the men had been at work one and one-half hours, the jib of the traveler gave away. Just below the jib were some men on a scaffold getting ready to drive a 10-1/2-inch pin. Ten men lost their lives and four were injured. Three of the men were members of Local No. 3.

At the **Eighth International Convention** held in Toronto, Canada in September, 1904, Buchanan was reelected President and John Joseph McNamara of Local No. 17, Cleveland was elected Secretary-Treasurer in a run-off with James Crowley, of Local No. 1. The incumbent Secretary-Treasurer, John Johnston, of New York, had been eliminated in the first ballot. With McNamara's election, the headquarters moved from New York to Cleveland. The International's headquarters in its first decade of existence was always the home town of the Secretary-Treasurer. (Two more years would pass before the International felt financially secure enough to establish headquarters in Indianapolis).

This Convention, the first held outside the United States, clearly established the international aspect that the founders desired. The Toronto local had been chartered as Local No. 4, just two years earlier, on September 15, 1902. Canadians since have been staunch and loyal members of the International Association.

A prime concern at the Toronto Convention was safety in the work

Delegates to the Eighth Annual Convention, held at Toronto, Canada, September 19-30, 1904.

Wilbur Bridge erected in 1904 by members of Local Union No. 12 at Kingston, New York, for American Bridge Company.

John J. McNamara
of Local 17, Cleveland, elected International Secretary-Treasurer at the Toronto convention in 1904.

place, as the high number of job fatalities continued unabated.

Buchanan had earlier put employers on notice that the rate of injuries and fatalities on the job was intolerable.

The following January, the National Agreement between the Iron Workers and the manufacturers and structural steel erectors expired. The two groups were unable to reach a new agreement or to extend the old one. There was some dissatisfaction on both sides over the original Agreement, and to make matters worse, some contractors were becoming more interested in, and enamored with, the open shop policy.

In September of 1904, the Executive Council of the American Federation of Labor ruled that the jurisdiction claims of "Structural Iron and Ornamental Assembling Shops" belonged to the Iron Workers International. The dispute between the United Metal Workers and Iron Workers International was finally settled and Buchanan wrote in *The Bridgemen's Magazine* that: "it is plain to me that it is to the interests of the men who work on the erection work to have the men who work in the assembly shops as members of this great organization."

Charter issued to the International Association by the Structural Building Trades Alliance of America on September 1, 1904.

On September 1, 1904 the International Association was issued a charter from the Structural Building Trades Alliance of America. This organization was eventually dissolved; however at the time it played a useful role in helping the International and its local unions in a variety of ways.

At the **Ninth International Convention** held in Philadelphia, Pennsylvania, September 18-30, 1905, President Frank Buchanan, despite having the support of his views by a large majority of the local unions, and having been elected President of the Building Trades Alliance (a forerunner of our present A.F. of L. Building Trades Department) and by having been selected to deliver an address on labor relations to the second session of the 57th Congress of the United States, surprised everyone with his decision to retire from his office as President. In 1906 Buchanan decided to run for Congress. He was defeated. He ran again in 1908 and again was unsuccessful. The third time was a charm, however, and in 1910 he made it. He served three terms as the Democratic Representative from the Seventh District of Illinois.

Frank M. Ryan, also of Chicago and a member of Local Union No. 1, was elected to take his place. Originally from Providence, Rhode Island, he moved to Chicago and became an active member of Local No. 1, which he served as president and business agent when elected to the International presidency. John J. McNamara was reelected to his second term as Secretary-Treasurer.

The Convention indeed became one of the most significant bodies in the short history of our organization. Shortly after accepting the decision of President Buchanan not to seek further office, the delegates proceeded to practically tie the new officers' hands.

In endorsing the nation-

Frank M. Ryan
of Local No. 1 elected International President at the Ninth Convention in 1905.

Delegates to the Ninth Annual Convention held at Philadelphia, September 18-29, 1905.

A watch fob carried by Frank Ryan until his death.

al strike against the large steel companies the delegates adopted a resolution which contained a clause that instructed the International Officers "not to call this strike off until every existing grievance is settled satisfactory to our affiliated locals." This inflexible resolution made it virtually impossible for International Officers to negotiate for a fair settlement of the issues that brought about the strike.

The delegates also passed Resolution No. 4, reaffirming action taken at the Toronto Convention; that is, the apprentice system may be established when agreed on by any local union and their employers, but in no case shall there be more than one apprentice to seven mechanics.

An interesting note - Resolution No. 13 recommended a more durable membership book. It was a practice for each Ironworker to check his fellow Ironworker's membership book on the job to make sure that he had paid his dues and the current stamps were properly displayed. This practice is still followed today with the

membership dues receipts. As the Ironworkers erected steel, moved iron and sweated all day, they found that their membership books became soiled and torn. After this resolution was passed, the International issued

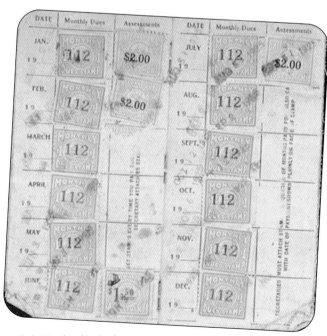

Cloth Membership Book.

35

Members of Local No. 1 working on the Lake Shore elevator at Whiting, Indiana, 1905.

Ironworkers hoisting telescope rotating mechanism with gears at the Yerkes Observatory, Rockford, Illinois, in 1896.

A bunch of Delegates to the Ninth Convention who spent Sunday, September 24, on the beach at Atlantic City, New Jersey.

"cloth" membership books. These books would not rip and water (sweat) did not affect them. Many of the members made special cases to hold the books primarily to protect them from fire (oxyacetylene burning and from cigarettes).

At the 1905 Convention, there were changes made in the Constitution. The following changes to Article XVI, Section 7 were made: *"The per capita tax of all inside Ironworkers shall be 15 cents per month per member, payable monthly. The Secretary-Treasurer shall issue a special dues stamp to distinguish all inside Ironworkers from structural Ironworkers. Stamps to be paid for at the above valuation."*

Members Badge (exact size)

THE BADGE

Shown herein is an actual size reproduction.
(exact size) Price 60c each

MATCH SAFES

Front
design

Reverse
design

A handy article every member
should carry. **Price 25c each**

If every member would wear a
button, dont you know it would
be a great influence for good?
The upper half of the gold and enamel emblem
illustrateed above is of dark blue enamel and
the lower half is of olive green   Lettering and
design in gold. **Price 50c each**

All orders must be accompanied by P. O. Order
or Draft, which should be made payable to

J. J. McNAMARA

No. 517 Superior Bldg.,   Cleveland, Ohio

July, 1905 Bridgeman's Magazine advertisement.

Chapter Three

The Turbulent Years— 1906 Through 1912

President Ryan and McNamara ran into difficulties immediately after assuming office in October, 1905. Ryan and American Bridge's S. P. Mitchell discussed the strike then in progress. Mitchell offered to employ only union Ironworkers on American Bridge's own erection work, but would not give that guarantee for work sub-let by American Bridge. Ryan decided to strike all jobs considered to have been sub-let by American Bridge. In his hometown of Chicago, he wanted work stopped on two jobs and the majority of the Local No. 1 members agreed. Frank Buchanan was one of the dissenters.

Cleveland Local No. 17 refused to call off its members from jobs sub-let by American Bridge and McNamara caused his own local to be temporarily suspended. Ryan also ran into trouble over the Tube Mill job being erected non-union, by National Tube Company, at McKeesport, Pennsylvania, within the jurisdiction of Pittsburgh, Local No. 3. National Tube and American Bridge were both subsidiaries of U. S. Steel Corporation; however, the Union's few friends at American Bridge couldn't order National Tube to use union Ironworkers, such interference being contrary to the parent company's established policy. Local No. 3 officers were adamant in their demand for union Ironworkers on the Tube Mill job, however the work continued non-union.

The American Bridge Company President, August Ziesing, decided to make Ryan an offer he couldn't refuse. In the presence of U. S. Steel officials, Ziesing proposed to Ryan that his company would use union Ironworkers exclusively on direct contract work and work done under sub-contract. He did not offer a signed agreement, but would put his offer in writing to hire and employ union men to work the uniform number of hours for the recognized wages. The Union would have to waive the claim to the work at McKeesport.

President Ryan tried to convince Local No. 3 to change its position on the Tube Mill job. The Local offi-

cers wouldn't budge. Ryan decided he then had to turn down American Bridge's offer, since the Local wouldn't waive its claim. Luke Grant, in *American Labor: From Conspiracy to Collective Bargaining*, recalls in an interview with AFL President Samuel Gompers circa 1915: Gompers considered "...this mistake one of the three most costly blunders made in recent years in the American labor movement."

This event was closely followed by the Post and McCord strike in New York, which Ryan insisted be called, though the local business agent said it would be fruitless. Ryan believed that Post and McCord and the American Bridge Company were the same entity, although that was denied by both firms. Luke Grant states that there is no "reliable information that Post and McCord ever was a part of the American Bridge Company." The Ironworkers struck Post and McCord on November 1, 1905.

"Roller Lift," being built by the Santa Fe R.R. across Channel Street at Third, San Francisco, California by members of Local Union No. 31.

Buildings after the San Francisco earthquake.

Members of Local No. 31, who cleared up part of the San Francisco ruins.

In part of his February, 1906 report to the Officers and members of affiliated local unions, President Ryan said: "In an effort to extend the benefits of our organization we have become involved in a strike that extends throughout the country, and was called on August 10, 1905, practically six months ago. This gang of conspirators, known as the United States Steel Corporation, have, during all that time used every despicable method to break the ranks of our organization through slander and bribery, and through their spy system they have worked every process that unprincipled men could invent to make criminals of honest men, that they might use them to do their nefarious work. So far they have failed to accomplish their object; the poor dupes they have in their employ as spies would soon be out of a job if they could succeed in disrupting our organization. They (the American Bridge Company) and their cohorts, have recently declared for the open shop, they would have us believe that it was a new policy they were adopting; on the contrary it has always been their policy, while at one time they had agreed to a closed shop, true to their natural instincts for dishonesty, they did not carry it out except through force of circumstances our organization compelled them to do so."

The National Erectors Association, under their new director, Walter Drew, formally declared for the open shop policy on May 1, 1906. American Bridge had been an open shop firm since the strike and other member firms fell in line for the open shop principle. However, the firms were pragmatic: they would employ union members

if any were willing to work for them and they would sublet to union contractors, if advantageous - for example, if a union firm was the lowest bidder. When it came to profit, the open shop companies had no principle.

The open shop policy of employers would prove costly to the Union and present a constant immovable barrier to growth. This was a time of sharp tensions and a hardening of confrontations between the International Association and a militant, well financed group of open shop employers. The Union seemed headed for a dark interlude.

Although problems existed due to the strike, a great deal of work was being erected throughout the United States and Canada in 1906. Safety continued to be a big factor to our members. Loss of life continued to rise. Local No. 1, Chicago, reported that in 1905, 23 of their members were killed on the job, 17 totally disabled, and 83 suffered from injury. The membership of Local No. 1 was 880. It was determined that three men in every group of twenty-two workers will be killed or injured every twelve months.

In the June issue of the 1906 *The Bridgemen's Magazine* an article titled **"STEEL CITY WILL RISE ABOVE RUINS":** April 20, 1906 - Wednesday's frightful earthquake shocks demonstrated the utility of the steel frame buildings in this country. When San Francisco is rebuilt brick and stone will be rejected in favor of the steel skeleton building. Many such buildings are in ruins, but they have been destroyed by fire and not by the shaking of the earth.

Throughout the early hours of the day, while other buildings were toppling into the streets, the steel frame buildings remained intact. They swayed and swung on their foundations, but the bolted steel beams and girders hung together. The steel skeletons preserved their form, although tested to the utmost limit of flexibility.

It was interesting to note that cutting of structural steel beams and girders by the electric arc was used to clear the

Delegates to the Tenth Annual Convention.

wreckage and debris caused by the San Francisco fires. A 15-inch I-beam could be cut in 20 minutes, whereas to cut a beam of this size with a hacksaw would have required several hours.

The Tenth International Convention was held in Detroit, Michigan, September 17-27, 1906. Frank M. Ryan and J.J. McNamara were reelected. There were many issues and resolutions presented at the Convention. Locals in Canada and several in the United States requested Organizers be assigned to their jurisdictions in order to help organize non-union companies. There were a number of local unions that wanted to expand their territory which met with opposition from those local unions already controlling the area. Several resolutions requested increases in their scale of wages from 45 cents to 50 cents per hour and an 8-hour day rather than the 9-hour day most members worked.

It was decided to issue an Initiation stamp at a cost of 50 cents. It was felt that this would help in keeping better records on members, i.e., when they started as an Ironworker. Another resolution was passed to move International Headquarters from Cleveland to Indianapolis. The main reason was due to the fact that most of the other International Unions were located in that city.

The Eleventh International Convention was held September 16-25, 1907 in Indianapolis, Indiana which is the city where our headquarters was located. Frank M. Ryan was reelected President and J.J. McNamara was reelected Secretary-Treasurer. The Convention dealt with many resolutions and issues. The delegates adopted the following Memorial:

WHEREAS, it is with sincere regret that the International Association of Bridge and Structural Iron Workers learns of the death of fifty of its members in what is known as the "Quebec Bridge Disaster;" and

WHEREAS, by this appalling accident, consternation and dismay has been visited upon the relatives and friends of our departed brothers, and one of our Canadian Locals almost wiped out of existence; therefore, be it

1907 badge worn by delegates to the 11th Annual Convention.

The Quebec Bridge Disaster of 1907

On Thursday, August 29, 1907 the Quebec Railroad Bridge collapsed. A 20,000 ton section of the bridge fell 300 feet into the St. Lawrence River. A total of fifty Ironworkers and 36 other workers were killed.

D. B. Haley wrote a letter to *The Bridgemen's Magazine* about what happened and it was published in the October, 1907 issue. Haley was lucky he only had his legs and ankles badly sprained in his fall into the river. Haley had come from Wheeling, West Virginia in June of 1907 to work on the bridge. The work was being done by Local No. 87. The bridge was being built for Canada's transcontinental railroad about seven miles above Quebec City. It was to be the largest bridge of its kind in the world, designed to set a record for a steel cantilever span of 1,800 feet.

Construction was being done by the Phoenix Bridge Company. They hired men at 50 cents an hour from all over the United States and Canada. The company would have preferred only non-union men but they found they needed skilled workers for this job. However, many of the workers became dissatisfied. When a man quit, the company would deduct from his wages the amount they had paid for his transportation to and from the work site. On August 6th, almost two weeks before the collapse, many of the men had gone on strike because of the poor working conditions. By a vote of 40 to 36 they decided to go

View of Quebec Bridge just prior to collapse.

Wreckage of Bridge on August 29, 1907.

back to work on August 10th.

Engineers inspected the bridge on August 26th and 27th and noticed that some of the cantilever arms were buckling. None of the men were told about the problem in order to keep them from leaving the job. The general foremen disregarded the orders of the engineers and told the men to continue working.

On Thursday, August 29 the crash came without a moment's notice. Among those killed were 33 Canadian Ironworker Indian members. The Indians were members of the Caughnawaga Indian Reserve. They left 25 widows and numerous fatherless children behind. Six apprentices were also killed, along with some management personnel.

An investigation was conducted by a Royal Commission appointed by the Canadian government and published on March 14, 1908. It was very confusing, placing some blame on the engineers' design, the policies of the Phoenix Bridge Company, and the Quebec Bridge and Railway Company. As a result none of the wives were able to sue for damages.

A new bridge was designed. The central span also collapsed while being put in place in 1916. Fortunately no lives were lost at this time. The bridge finally was completed and opened for traffic in August of 1918. But the tragedy of 1907 ranks as one of the worst losses of life in the history of our Union.

1906-07 International Executive Board.

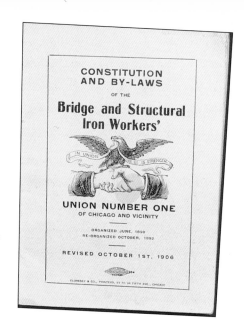

Local No. 1 Constitution and By-Laws revised October 1, 1906.

RESOLVED, that the International Association of Bridge and Structural Iron Workers in convention assembled deeply deplores the loss of so many of its members and extends to the parents, relatives and friends of our deceased brothers heartfelt sympathy in this their hour of sorrow and great grief; and, be it further

RESOLVED, that as a mark of the esteem in which we hold our departed brethren, one page of the official proceedings of this convention be set aside as a suitable memorial to the memory of the victims of the Quebec Bridge Disaster.

The Twelfth International Convention was held September 21-29, 1908 in Indianapolis, Indiana. Frank M. Ryan who was reelected President received a letter from Samuel Gompers, President, A.F. of L. It read as follows: "In the name of our great Trade Union movement, the movement for the uplift of American toilers, I send fraternal greetings to you and your assembled delegates. It was my hope to commission an organizer to attend your convention, but the proceedings to send Mitchell, Morrison and myself to jail for contempt of the VanCleave Buck Stove and Range Company's injunction made the performance of that and many other duties impossible. But despite their bitter and relentless antagonism, labor will triumph. The future is ours." J.J. McNamara was reelected Secretary-Treasurer.

Resolution 30 introduced at the Convention changed Section 11 of the Constitution by substituting the following language: "Representation shall be based upon the average number of monthly dues stamps purchased." The committee recommended the adoption of the amendment with the addition of the words, "during the fiscal year" after the word "purchased."

At the 1908 Convention, President Ryan, Vice-President Barry and delegate Butler, having received the highest number of votes, were

Elks' Building and Temple Theater, Detroit, Michigan. 1906 Convention was held in Elk's building which appears on the right of the picture.

declared duly elected to serve as delegates to the next convention of the American Federation of Labor.

Earlier in the year, February 10, 1908, the Building and Construction Trades Department was founded and on March 20, 1908 the AFL issued the formal charter to the seven founding members of the Department which included Ironworkers President, Frank M. Ryan.

The Thirteenth International Convention was held September 20-30, 1909 in Minneapolis, Minnesota. Once again, Frank M. Ryan was elected President and J.J. McNamara was elected Secretary-Treasurer. In his report, President Ryan reminded the delegates that four years and two months had passed since the general strike was inaugurated. He reported that the International and its affiliates had successfully withstood all efforts made to reduce wages, and in several instances had succeeded in increasing wages and improving working conditions.

Many of the issues discussed at the 1909 Convention dealt with agreements with the Boilermakers, Carpenters, Sheet Metal Workers and the Wood, Wire and Metal Lathers unions. A Resolution to have International Conventions every two years was defeated.

The Fourteenth International Convention was held September 19-26, 1910 in Rochester, New York. Both President Frank M. Ryan and Secretary-Treasurer J.J. McNamara were reelected. It was reported that many of the affiliate local unions increased their wages in 1910; for example, Local No. 1 increased their hourly rate from 62-1/2 cents per hour to 65 cents. The average increase for most of the local unions was 5 cents per hour.

Frank Buchanan, former International President and member of Local Union No. 1, was elected on the Democratic ticket to represent the Seventh Illinois district in Congress.

Delegates to the Eleventh Annual Convention held in Indianapolis, Indiana, September, 1907.

How the delegates of Local No. 31 were entertained in Kansas City on their way back to Frisco. From left to right, Thomas Stack, No. 31; W.J. McCain, No. 10; E.P. Ryan, No. 10; J.W. Thompson, No. 10, driver, and D.F. Dwyer, No. 31.

A bunch from Local No. 8, who are erecting building for Charles Volkmann & Company

International Headquarters in Indianapolis.

Complete pile-driving outfit used as a float in the Labor Day parade by Local No. 77 of San Francisco, California.

Members of Local No. 24, Denver, erecting Auditorium where the Democratic Convention was held in 1908.

California delegation to Indianapolis Convention.

The baseball team of Local No. 31, San Francisco.

768 members of Local No. 31, San Francisco as they appeared in the Labor Day Parade.

43

International Executive Board, 1908-09. **Left to right:** J.H. Barry, F.C. Webb, E.A. Claney, J.T. Butler, F.M. Ryan, J.J. McNamara, H.S. Hockin, H.W. Legleitner.

Charter issued to the International from the Building Trades Department, AFL on May 1, 1908.

Delegates badge worn at the 13th Annual Convention in Minneapolis, Minnesota.

STRUCTURAL IRON WORKER'S HALL.

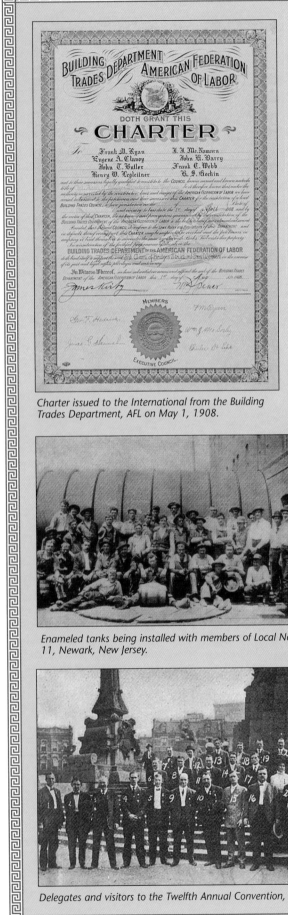

Enameled tanks being installed with members of Local No. 11, Newark, New Jersey.

Badge worn by a member of Local No. 13, Philadelphia to the 12th Annual International Convention in 1908.

Local No. 22 Union Hall where 1908 Convention was held.

Delegates and visitors to the Twelfth Annual Convention, Indianapolis, Indiana, September, 1908.

Delegates to the Thirteenth Annual Convention held in Minneapolis in 1909.

The McNamara Case

Probably no event has affected the history of our Iron Workers Union and the entire American Labor movement more than the McNamara Case. It was called "The Crime of the Century" by the conservative, anti-labor papers of the day, although it only took place during the first decade of this century. Before we can understand the importance of this event it is necessary to examine the reasons why it took place.

As pointed out earlier, the U.S. Steel Company was totally opposed to unionism. In March of 1903, U.S. Steel, the American Bridge Company, and all the other companies involved in the erection of structural steel, banded together to form the National Erectors' Association (NEA). The aim of the NEA was to destroy all the unions involved in the building trades including carpenters, bricklayers, masons, and especially ironworkers. Article III of the Constitution of the NEA read:

John J. McNamara
Secretary-Treasurer

"The aim of the association shall be the institution and maintenance of the Open Shop principal in the employment of labor in the erection of steel and iron bridges and buildings and other structural and iron work."

Although U.S.Steel and the NEA were able to crush many of the unions engaged in the fabrication, manufacturing, and transportation of steel, they were not able to crush the Iron Workers Union. Our International organized a nation-wide strike which totally frustrated the NEA and the American Bridge Company forcing them to sign a closed-shop agreement with our Union from May l, 1903 until January 1, 1905. But in July of 1905, seven months after the agreement had expired, the American Bridge Company, which was owned by U.S.Steel, along with other members of the NEA, decided to break our International by not hiring any union Ironworkers. The NEA hired Walter Drew, an

Richmond Hall, where the Convention was held in 1909.

exponent of the open shop, to co-ordinate a campaign against Ironworkers. Drew set up a network of spies, detectives, thugs, and provocateurs to carry out the task of breaking our Union.

By 1906, a "Labor War" had developed between Drews' NEA and our Union. The NEA convinced judges to issue injunctions against strikes. The police and thugs were paid to break up picket lines, and hand-billing and mass meetings were outlawed. These were rights that should have been protected by our nation's Constitution and its Bill of Rights.

NEA contractors continued to try to crush our Union and this was especially hard on men who risked their lives on scaffolds, atop bridges and buildings without life nets to save them from falls onto the cement or into rivers hundreds of feet below. At this time over one hundred structural Ironworkers were killed on the job each year. This represented approximately one out of every hundred members of the Union. Even Secretary-Treasurer John J. McNamara saw a member of his family die. He said:

"We work with a man one week and the next we read of his falling to his death. We become so accustomed to it that I've never realized what it meant until I sat by my own brother's deathbed last year."

This was war! Workers killed on the job, beaten by the police and thugs, and denied their rights to have a democratic union of their choice. All this was happening at a time when Ironworkers were paid only $2.50 a day, and the NEA wanted to even cut this lowly wage.

Between the years 1908 and 1911, eighty-seven to one hundred and fifty bombings took place at work sites. Perhaps some of these were set by

Delegate's badge worn at the Annual Convention in 1910, Rochester, New York.

management themselves in order to create propaganda against unions. Perhaps some were set by individual union members disgusted with the treatment they were receiving. At some 70 sites where explosions took place companies quickly gave the Ironworkers Union recognition. No one was ever killed in any of these explosions and the average loss of property was about one thousand dollars.

Despite all the vicious attacks by U.S. Steel and the NEA to destroy our unions, the membership of the Iron Workers Union grew to 12,230 by 1911 and our members went from being the lowest paid workers in the building trades to one of the highest at $4.30 for an eight-hour day. The militancy of the Iron Workers Union became a thorn in the side of the NEA and U.S. Steel!

Non-union workers were quickly imported from the Midwest and private detectives were hired to spy on strike leaders and assist the regular police force in an effort to crush the unions. But the unions stood firm. Pickets were orderly and no violence occurred until July 16, 1910, when the City Council passed its infamous anti-picketing ordinance.

The ordinance was strict enough to satisfy even the most militant of anti-union workers as "class legislation." Union pickets naturally defied the ordinance which ran counter to their constitutional principles. Fights broke out between strikers, strike-breakers, police, hired detectives, and professional sluggers. In such a blood-bath only the pickets were arrested, but as each defendant requested a jury trial, the court calendars were filled up until early the next year.

The arrested pickets received legal assistance from various organizations in San Francisco, where wages were about 30% higher, hours about 20% shorter, and labor conditions peaceful. The General Campaign Strike Committee, with headquarters in San Francisco, was requested to send lawyers down to Los Angeles to investigate claims of espionage, unlawful beatings, false arrests, unlawful detention, and third-degree treatment. The San Francisco Labor Council appealed to labor organizations all across the country for funds, and the executive council of the California State Federation of

Convention Headquarters, Hotel Eggleston, Rochester, New York in 1910.

Labor felt it necessary to order a special organizer to the Los Angeles area.

The strikers responded enthusiastically to the outside help. By the end of September, 1910, although every strike was thus far unsuccessful, the internal growth of the unions was phenomenal. Since the beginning of 1910 the Central Labor Council had nearly a 50% increase in strength: from 6,000 members of 62 unions in January to 9,500 members of 85 unions in September. Trade unionism was clearly on the rise in Los Angeles, and at that crucial time only some atrocious act could discredit the movement and ruin the cause for organized labor.

The Los Angeles Times Explosion

Then it happened at 1 A.M. on the morning of October 1, 1910-- the so-called "Crime of the Century." An explosion ripped through the printing plant of the Los Angeles *Times*. As a result of the explosion and fire that followed, twenty *Times* employees were killed and many others injured. Although there was no evidence at the time that labor was in any way involved, the headline the next day read, **"UNIONIST BOMBS WRECK THE TIMES"**.

The City of Los Angeles and the *Times* newspaper were completely controlled at the time by a man named Harrison Gray Otis, who loved to be called "General". Otis had fought in the Civil War and the Spanish American War and saw himself as "A General" fighting another war in Los Angeles against organized labor. Otis referred to unions as "...a tyranny--one of the most monstrous tyrannies that the world has ever seen."

Otis was determined to drive every sign of unionism from Los Angeles, and he was able to mobilize 85% of the city businessmen into the Merchants and Manufacturers Association (M & M). If any Los Angeles merchant hired union workers or declared for the eight-hour day, his business was no longer able to get credit from the banks or receive shipment of his goods.

Because of what he had done to the workers of Los Angeles, "General" Otis was so afraid for his life that he

First union job in San Diego, California for the Ironworkers, in 1910.

Delegates and visitors to the Fourteenth Annual Convention in Rochester, New York in 1910.

drove around town in a car with an operable cannon on the hood. Los Angeles became known as "Otistown of the Open Shop." One writer described Otis as "..the most unfair, unscrupulous and malignant enemy of organized labor in America."

Between 1910 and 1912, Otis had several reasons to be fearful. One was that the people of Los Angeles were becoming disgusted with one man rule. It looked like Job Harrison, the Socialist candidate for Mayor, might win the next election. This would mean the end of Otis' control of the city. Also, the Los Angeles Metal Trades Council decided to go on strike for recognition.

While unions were fighting for recognition in Los Angeles, to the north in San Francisco unionism was strong. One observer said:

> "...not a hammer was lifted, or a brick laid, or a pipe fitted, or wall plastered or painted, or papered without the sanction of the unions."

Because wages and working conditions were so different in Los Angeles and San Francisco it was making it difficult for San Francisco workers to keep their good conditions unless equally good wages and hours existed in Los Angeles. Therefore, this is why the Los Angeles Metal Trades Council called a strike to begin on June 1, 1910. The demands included union recognition, the eight-hour day, and a minimum wage of four dollars a day. All of these things were happening in Los Angeles when the explosion took place at Otis' *Times* printing plant on October 1, 1910.

Rivet gang at work.

What Caused the Explosion?

For weeks before the explosion there were reports of a gas leak in the area around the *Times* building. Because of this the insurance company had raised the rates on the old printing plant; Otis had already moved his business papers out of the old building. A satellite printing plant had been established, and even after the explosion occurred the paper was able to print the morning edition, as if nothing had happened.

Supposedly sixteen sticks of dynamite were placed in the *Times* alleyway, known as "ink alley" near drums of highly inflammable materials. Later, James B. McNamara, brother of Iron Workers Secretary-Treasurer John J. McNamara, and Ortie McManigal would be blamed for the bombing. There are many unanswered questions about the cause of the explosion. The dynamite could never have caused the kind of explosion that destroyed the entire block. Ironically, both "General" Otis and his son-in-law and future heir, Harry Chandler, were in the building that evening and left only a short time before the explosion. If it was negligence on the part of Otis in not correcting the gas leak, Otis could have faced criminal charges and would not have been able to collect a half million dollars in insurance money. Could blaming it all on the union have been his way of covering up his own negligence? Also, it is difficult to understand why the police did not see someone entering "ink alley" to place dynamite charges there since the alley was clearly visible from the Los Angeles Police Department Headquarters directly across the street!

The Investigation and the Arrest of John J. McNamara

Ironically, William J. Burns, head of the Chicago based Burns Detective Agency, arrived in Los Angeles the same morning as the bombing. Up to this point Burns had been a friend of the Progressive Movement and men such as Lincoln Steffens, who had exposed corruption all over the country. Several years before, Burns had exposed corporate graft in San Francisco and illegal take-overs of federal forest lands. "General" Otis did not like Burns at the time he first came to Los Angeles.

However, Burns was now in the employ of the National Erectors' Association. He would also be hired by the Mayor of Los Angeles, George B. Alexander, to find the perpetrators of the *Times* bombing. Mayor Alexander offered Burns a reward of $100,000.

The labor movement in California was disgusted with the fact that without any evidence, Otis had immediately blamed the unions for the explosion. Therefore, the California State Federation of Labor asked a distinguished panel to look into the cause of

John J. McNamara
Secretary-Treasurer

the bombing. This panel found no evidence that the explosion was caused by a bomb, and concluded that it was caused by the gas leak.

Then another bomb exploded in Los Angeles on Christmas Day at the anti-union Llewellyn Iron Works. This was set by Ortie McManigal, who would later become the star witness against our International Union. The Llewellyn bomb caused $25,000 damage and the nation became even more aroused.

There were reports, although not confirmed, that Ortie McManigal developed his dynamiting skills working in a quarry before his Ironworker career. McManigal was supposedly recruited by Herbert S. Hockin, of Detroit Local No. 25 and an International Executive Board member, and paid $125 and expenses for each job. Hockin used their mutual memberships in the Knights of Pythias to bring in McManigal - "do it for a lodge brother", as the saying goes. McManigal had difficulty finding and holding a job. Hockin figured correctly that McManigal was perfect for the kind of work he had in mind. McManigal was a better dynamiter than an Ironworker. Hockin had his man.

William Burns seemed to disappear from January to April of 1911, and the public was beginning to see the *Times* explosion as just a terrible tragedy. In March, Mayor Alexander even stopped paying Burns. Could Burns have then decided to combine the interests of several of his employers? The National Erectors' Association would forever be indebted to Burns if he could blame the International Bridge and Structural Iron Workers Union for the Llewellyn Iron Works bombings as well as all the others between 1906 and 1911. If he could find the culprits who bombed the *Times* he would receive the $100,000 reward from the businessmen of Los Angeles. The enemies he had made when he was fighting with the muckrakers and progressives, such as Otis and other corporate interests throughout the United States, would now see him as the friend of big business instead of its enemy. There certainly was a great deal more money to be made if, like the Pinkerton Detective Agency, he fought unionism.

Then on Saturday, April 22, 1911 at 5:30 p.m., Burns and a squad of police burst into a meeting of the General Executive Board of our International at our headquarters in the American Central Life Building in Indianapolis. The Superintendent of Police requested that John J. McNamara, our Secretary-Treasurer, and General Executive Board Member Herbert Hockin accompany them to police headquarters. Both agreed willingly to go with the police. John McNamara closed the office safe before leaving with the officers.

International President Frank M. Ryan then tried to continue the Executive Board meeting, but the police and Burns refused to leave. When President Ryan tried to adjourn the meeting the police refused to allow anyone to leave. When Herbert Hockin returned alone, he

Membership Book in 1911 with a picture of Secretary-Treasurer J.J. McNamara on the "Assessment" stamps. This member worked in Locals No. 51, 86 and 29 in 1911. Closeup at right.

informed the Executive Board that Secretary-Treasurer John J. McNamara had been kidnapped. McNamara was very popular with the membership and the labor movement in general, therefore, it is logical that he would be the target of Burns. Starting in October, 1911 all the "assessment" stamps issued to the local unions had a picture of McNamara.

The Kidnapping of John J. McNamara

What actually happened was that John J. McNamara was handcuffed, allowed no bail or trial, and rushed by car to Terra Haute, Indiana. The seven-passenger Owen Motor Car that could travel 75 miles an hour held John McNamara and several detectives.

At Terra Haute, John McNamara and the detectives boarded the 1:40 A.M. *Pennsylvania Flyer* which stopped at St. Louis. Here they had a very public breakfast in front of all the reporters. They let reporters see them buying tickets for another train, but they then re-boarded the *Pennsylvania Flyer* and traveled to Kansas City and then to Holsington, Kansas where another car was waiting. They then traveled across wild country to catch a local at Dodge City. At Dodge City they checked into a hotel where they waited for the *California Limited,* the fastest train into Los Angeles.

John J. McNamara did not know that his brother, James, was aboard the same train, but the entire nation knew it. Also aboard was Ortie McManigal, who was prepared to betray the Iron Workers.

Burns saw to it that this cross country race to Los Angeles was well publicized. At the same time Burns claimed that the train might be blown up and that someone might help the McNamara brothers to escape, therefore secrecy was needed.

Actually, all of this secrecy was because the entire abduction of John J. McNamara was illegal. There should have been a proper court hearing in Indiana before he could be removed from the state. Neither a judge nor even the Governor of Indiana had the right to sign extradition papers in this case. According to Indiana law, John J. McNamara would have had to have committed a crime in California and then fled to Indiana. Then the Governor could have ordered his immediate extradition without a hearing. But John J. McNamara had never been in Los Angeles at the time of the explosion.

Another story that came up during the case, probably from McManigal, was that James McNamara claimed to have invented an "infernal machine", which he used to time the explosion of charges; a simple, cheap alarm clock wired with a battery so that when the alarm was set to strike, it would close an electrical circuit that would discharge a blasting cap. This impressed McManigal, who had timed explosives by splicing fuses to burn up to thirty minutes or so. But McNamara's "infernal machine" provided hours of delay and permitted the setter to be miles away, even in an adjoining state, when the explosion occurred. The new device would now be their preferred technology.

What Happened at the International Offices?

Meanwhile, on the evening when John J. McNamara was first kidnapped, the police illegally broke into the Union's safe and removed papers as well as over $400 which was never returned.

At the time the police entered the International's office, President Ryan noticed a mysterious figure who began searching through the Union's file and papers. This person turned out to be Walter Drew, Commissioner of the National Erectors Association. Totally disgusted with the police and their violation of the law, the officers of the Executive Board tried to call the Union attorney, Leo Rappaport. Since it was a weekend and very late and many of the Executive Board members were from out of town, they did not know how to reach their attorney. Finally, they were able to get in touch with him and Attorney Rappaport arrived around 2 A.M..

Not content with just searching the offices of the International's headquarters, Burns supposedly had a tip that John J. McNamara had rented a barn outside of town. Burns and some men, as well as a group of reporters, left to search it. They returned claiming they had found two quart cans of nitroglycerin and fifteen sticks of dynamite in a piano box.

Burns then returned to the offices of the International in the American Central Life Building demanding a key to a vault in the basement. Burns went into the basement followed by reporters and sup-

In line for tickets at Indianapolis, Indiana for the movie "A Martyr to His Cause"

posedly found seven packages of dynamite weighing 200 pounds along with percussion caps and many yards of fuse, plus a dozen small alarm clocks.

What Was the Attitude of the Public?

Union members and even a large segment of the general public all over the United States felt that the entire event looked staged. It was discovered that after Burns' salary was cut off by the Mayor of Los Angeles, he borrowed $10,000 from friends and would only be able to repay it if he was able to get the $100,000 reward. Many Americans saw this as another frame-up similar to the Haymarket Affair, Debs' trial after the Pullman Strike, and the Haywood-Moyer-Pettibone Case of 1907. This latter case involved "Big Bill" Haywood and two other members of the Western Federation of Miners who were accused of a murder in Idaho. They were kidnapped from Colorado by Pinkerton detectives, handcuffed, and taken in a special train to Boise, Idaho to stand trial. Clarence Darrow, who had defended Debs after the Pullman Strike, was regarded as the lawyer of the oppressed. He successfully defended Haywood and the other two defendants and saved them from hanging.

Trade unionists and the general public throughout the country had an opportunity to witness the production of a motion picture titled **"A Martyr to His Cause"** which was produced to raise money for the McNamara brothers' defense and to show the public how a citizen was dragged from his home and friends and spirited to a distant part of the nation contrary to law and the traditions of the United States.

Clarence Darrow Hired to Defend the McNamaras

Samuel Gompers and other union leaders in the American Federation of Labor felt that Clarence Darrow would be the ideal lawyer to defend the McNamara brothers. But Darrow, now in his early 50's, was exhausted. His wife, Ruby, had made him promise her that in the future he would only take on easy cases. At first Darrow refused pleas from Gompers and Ryan to take on the case. Then he received the following telegram from Gompers:

"There is no other advocate in the whole United States who holds such a commanding post before the people and in whom labor has such entire confidence. You owe it to yourself and to the cause of labor to appear as the advocate of those men so unjustly accused."

Darrow finally agreed to take the case under the following conditions: The labor movement would raise $200,000 out of which Darrow would receive a fee of $50,000 after expenses. The union movement agreed to his terms and our Union began a fund raising effort to help defray the costs of the trial. McNamara buttons, stamps for the backs of letters were sold. The following appeared in the September, 1911 issue of *The Bridgemen's Magazine*.

Clarence Darrow

IMPORTANT NOTICE
"Are you wearing a McNamara button and are you using McNamara stamps on the backs of your envelopes? Also look into your membership book and see if the McNamara assessment stamps are in it for the months of May and June."

Darrow arrived in Los Angeles at 9:15 A.M. on May 14, 1911 surrounded by reporters. He went directly to the jail where the McNamara brothers were being held. He then went to see John Harrington, who had been representing the McNamaras up to this point and would continue to assist Darrow. John Harrington was also a candidate on the Socialist Party ticket for Mayor of Los Angeles. His election looked certain, but it all hinged on the outcome of this case.

It did not take Darrow long to realize that the evidence, whether true or false, against the brothers was overwhelming and it would be impossible to get a fair trial in Los Angeles' "Otistown".

Lincoln Steffens Enters the Scene

Lincoln Steffens was the most famous of the muckrakers of his day. He was from a wealthy California family, whose former home is to this day the Executive Mansion of the Governor of California. He was a close friend of President Teddy Roosevelt and his magazine articles on important Progressives like "Fighting Bob" LaFollette of Wisconsin had made them into national figures. His book *Shame of the Cities* had helped to rid many communities of their corrupt mayors and city councils. In 1911, Steffens would come to Los Angeles on behalf of a newspaper syndicate in the East to report on why the McNamaras had bombed the *Times*.

Steffens believed that the brothers were guilty but wanted the nation to understand why men had resorted to such means to bring about change. He thought he

could settle the case by appealing to Otis, Chandler, District Attorney John Fredericks, and twenty businessmen as "Christian men."

Darrow began to realize that the McNamara brothers could never get a fair trial in Los Angeles, and both of them would be given the death penalty. Throughout Darrow's life he opposed the death penalty. He often stated that no client of his had ever been executed, no matter how hideous the crime. Therefore, Darrow began to listen to Lincoln Steffens' proposal. It would be as follows:

1. Both of the McNamara brothers would change their plea from not guilty to "guilty" on December 1, 1911.

2. John J. McNamara would be set free but his brother James B. would be imprisoned for life.

3. The pursuit of other Ironworkers would be abandoned and the cases against President Ryan and other officers of the Executive Board would be dropped.

4. Labor and Los Angeles businessmen would meet in a city-wide conference to discuss their problems and restore good labor-management relations to the city.

The Plea Bargain Is Violated

A plea bargain was reached but it was never put in writing. The businessmen refused to allow John J. McNamara to go free and insisted on a ten year jail sentence. The defense agreed to this but later the judge refused and increased John's sentence to 15 years.

The joint labor-management meeting in Los Angeles never took place. Because of his role as a lawyer for the defense, John Harrington lost the mayoral election. A "Good Government" slate backed by "General" Otis and the Merchants and Manufacturers' Association won the election, and the union movement in Los Angeles suffered.

McNamara Defense Fund Certificate issued to Local No. 112, Peoria, Illinois. Every Ironworker had an opportunity to contribute to the Fund.

Not satisfied with their victory over the unions, Otis and his friends went after Clarence Darrow, who was brought to trial on bribery charges. Bert Franklin, who had been hired by Darrow, was supposed to have bribed a juror in the McNamara case for Darrow. Franklin turned out to be a former Los Angeles detective and a friend of the prosecutor, District Attorney John Fredericks. After two years in Los Angeles, Darrow was finally found not guilty. He returned to Chicago financially ruined. He would never again return to California.

The American Federation of Labor as well as every union member was crushed when they read about the guilty plea made by the McNamara brothers. This case would have the effect of making the American labor movement more and more conservative in order to be acceptable to the general public. Immediately the A.F. of L. and its many individual unions would try to distance themselves from this case. Clarence Darrow would never again work for any union. "General" Otis and the *Times* as well as conservative papers across the country had won.

Were They Guilty?

As you can see, there were many loopholes in this case. No one seemed to pay any attention to the earlier report that the gas leak had caused the explosion. Why had Otis and his son-in-law, Chandler, moved all their papers out of this location earlier and prepared a second printing site? Why would the Ironworkers be interested in bombing this site which employed none of their workers? The staging of the kidnapping of our Secretary-Treasurer was certainly illegal. The entire case served to keep Los Angeles in the control of Otis and gave the National Erectors' Association what it had wanted for years...a chance to try to break the only remaining union in the steel industry.

The chief prosecution witness in both Los Angeles and Indianapolis, Ortie E. McManigal, would write a book titled *The National Dynamite Plot,* published by the Neale Company of Los Angeles. He called it "...the authentic account of the attempts of Union Labor to destroy the Structural Iron Industry." Like a similar book published to promote the Pinkerton Detective Agency after the Haymarket Affair, this book helped to promote the Burns Detective Agency in its union busting efforts. It is interesting that all the private McNamara papers of both "General" Otis and his son-in-law, Harry Chandler, were destroyed. What an interesting story they might have told!

Certainly there were bombings on some job sites, but no lives were lost and the damage was small. After the guilty plea by the brothers, Eugene Debs wrote the following to a friend:

> "Every floor in every skyscraper represents a workingman killed in its erection. It is easy enough for a gentleman of education and refinement to sit at his typewriter and point out the crimes of the workers. But let him be one of them himself, reared in poverty, denied education, thrown into the brute struggle for existence from childhood, oppressed, exploited, forced to strike, clubbed by police, jailed while his family is evicted, and his wife and children are hungry, and he will hesitate to condemn these as criminals who fight against the crimes of which they are the victims of such savage methods as have been forced upon them by their masters."

While J.J. McNamara was in jail and the case was being processed, the International Association and its affiliates had to carry on the day-to-day business. Many articles from labor leaders and business men appeared in *The Bridgemen's Magazine* supporting Secretary-Treasurer McNamara.

Although 1911 was a bad year for the International, many jobs were being erected in the United States and Canada.

The Fifteenth International Convention was held September 18-25, 1911 in Milwaukee, Wisconsin. As can be expected, a great deal of the Convention business dealt with the McNamara case. The delegates reelected Frank M. Ryan as President (no opposition). President Ryan requested that he be permitted to place in nomination for the office of Secretary-Treasurer, the

St. Charles Hotel where 1911 Convention was held.

Delegates and visitors to the Fifteenth Annual Convention held in Milwaukee, Wisconsin in 1911.

International Association
—— OF ——
Bridge and Structural Iron Workers

GENERAL MEMBERSHIP CARD

I.A.B.&S.I.W.

*Name*_____

*Formerly of*_____

*Admitted Gen. Member*_____

*Date of Initiation*_____ *Age*_____

*No. Card*_____ *Ledger Page*_____

Gen'l Sec'y-Treas.

Members holding a General Membership Card and failing to deposit same after going to work in any town or city where a union exists, will be suspended and deprived of all the rights and privileges of the International Association.

Membership Card

Members of Local No. 1, Chicago, working on the Peoples Gas Light and Coke Co. building.

name of J.J. McNamara. The nomination was seconded by Delegate Cunnane and several other delegates, after which Delegate Pohlman moved that the election be made unanimous by a rising vote of the delegates.

The vote was called for, and all the delegates arose, and J.J. McNamara was declared reelected as Secretary-Treasurer, after which three cheers were given by all the delegates for the absent brother.

The year 1912, despite all of the trials, troubles and tribulations through which our International Association had passed, was one of unexcelled progress and prosperity, in so far as an abundance of good union work throughout the entire United States and Canada was concerned, together with the excellent working conditions enjoyed by the entire membership. During 1912, charters were granted to nine new locals, bringing into the ranks over five hundred new members. In addition to this, existing locals throughout North America brought into the International about 420 new members. The members of four locals, amounting to 2,100 men, received a wage increase of 15 to 20 per cent. On a sad note, 123 members lost their lives - 66 being accidental, 56 natural and 1 suicide.

768 members of Local No. 31, San Francisco as they appeared in the Labor Day Parade.

Two views of work being erected at Columbus, Ohio in 1906 by members of Local No. 17.

Members of Local No. 4, Toronto, Canada who are erecting work at the gas plant for the Dominion Bridge Company.

Members of Local No. 86, Seattle, Washington.

Ironworkers wrapping the cables of the Manhattan Bridge.

The Manhattan Bridge being erected in 1909 before the floor system was put in place.

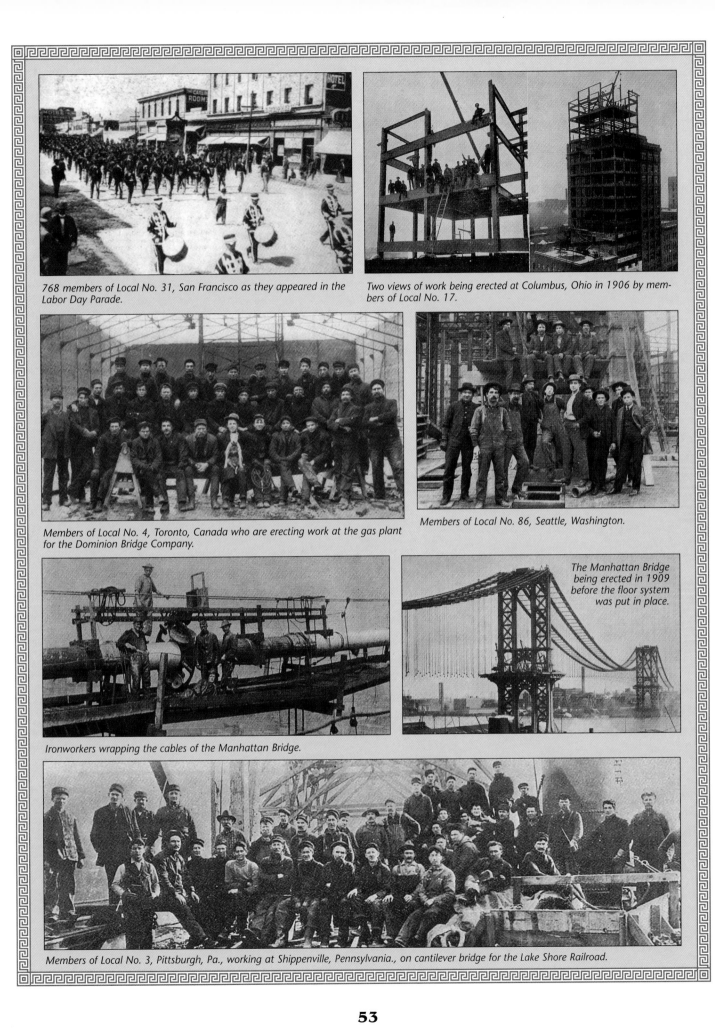

Members of Local No. 3, Pittsburgh, Pa., working at Shippenville, Pennsylvania., on cantilever bridge for the Lake Shore Railroad.

Chapter Four

The Conspiracy Trials and Aftermath

The **Sixteenth Annual Convention** of the International Association originally scheduled for Peoria in September, 1912, was postponed for six months. Difficulties stemming from the indictments on dynamite transport conspiracy charges against forty-six International and local union officials precluded a convention at that time. The conspiracy indictments of several men from other trade unions kept the trial from being strictly an Iron Worker event.

Other union men accused were California Building Trades officials Olaf Tveitmoe and Anton Johannsen; two United Brotherhood of Carpenters officials of Indiana, Spurgeon P. Meadows and Hiram Cline; Clarence Dowd, Machinists Union, Syracuse; and William K. Benson, president of the Detroit Building Trades. Confessed dynamiter Ortie McManigal, who had been hidden away in the Los Angeles area and guarded by local law enforcement officers, and the McNamara brothers, who were serving their sentences at San Quentin, were also named as conspirators on the long list of Federal indictments. The Federal Government consolidated all indictments into one proceeding.

General President Frank Ryan, acting Secretary-Treasurer Herbert S. Hockin, International Executive Board members and many of the most dedicated and diligent local officers were among the forty-six Ironworkers charged. The list of those indicted included a past, present, and a future General President of the Iron Workers.

Early indictments were issued on December 30, 1911, against two Ironworker officials, Eugene A. Clancy, of San Francisco and James E. Munsey, of Salt Lake City, as well as California labor officials Olaf A. Tveitmoe and Anton Johannsen for "conspiracy to transport dynamite over Federal territory," according to the *Los Angeles Record* of December 31, 1911. *The Indianapolis News* of the same date reported that the indictments were "returned under United States laws controlling transportation of explosives in interstate

commerce." Indictments at this time were also issued for Ortie McManigal, James B. McNamara and John J. McNamara. This was just the beginning. These seven men would be included in the sweeping Federal indictments five weeks later.

Detective William J. Burns, the structural steel employers' hired hand, responsible for the McNamara and McManigal arrests, still maintained a wrong-headed belief that A.F. of L. President Samuel Gompers was involved in the conspiracy. He based his inane judgment on the fact that Olaf Tveitmoe and Gompers were friends--guilt by association. He also believed Tveitmoe to be the instigator and planner of the *Los Angeles Times* bombing. Burns and his open shop sponsors wanted desperately to entangle Gompers in the conspiracy. If they were successful in their efforts to enmesh America's most respected trade unionist, they would cause irreparable damage to the labor movement. Burns unethically tried to persuade the Government

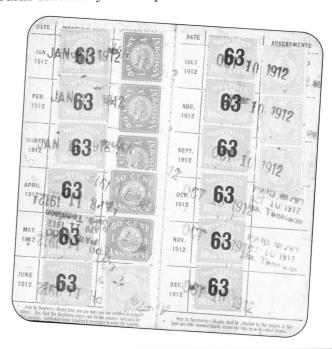

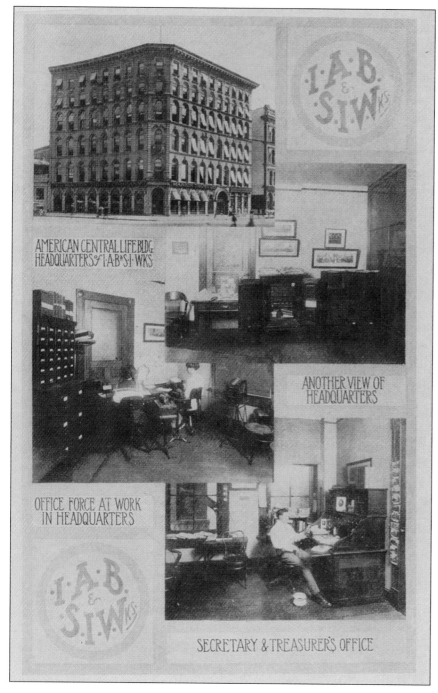

View of International Headquarters in 1912 and various offices in Indianapolis.

as International officers since 1906." Ryan also wrote that the executive director of the National Erectors Association, Walter Drew, "is reported to have said that he expected to break us financially before this case is finished."

Ryan, Hockin, and John T. Butler, First Vice President (and former General President) were arrested at headquarters in Indianapolis on St. Valentine's Day, February 14, 1912. As Butler put it, he "received a valentine in the form of a warrant from...a United States Marshall." They made bond that day. The bonding companies in town, however, wanted only cash surety for the $10,000 bonds for International officers. The Union also was to provide bonds for all indicted members. Some Indiana firms threatened to withdraw their business from any companies providing bond money to the International. Only one company, the Southern Surety Co., of St. Louis, would accept the Union's real estate worth to secure bonds. The excessive cash amount for bonds, the legal fees, and the cost of a protracted trial made Walter Drew's expectation and hope likely to become a reality.

The men indicted were arraigned on March 12, 1912, in Indianapolis, before Federal District Court Judge A. B. Anderson. To a man, they pleaded "not guilty." Some observers and newspaper publishers and editors were surprised by the pleas, having expected guilty pleas. Judge Anderson set the trial date for October 1, 1912.

Forty-six men, lined fifteen abreast, banked three deep, with one lonesome end, stood in the Federal Court room in Indianapolis to hear the charges against them. The group included forty-two Ironworkers. Several indictments had been dismissed.

The trial sparked great interest, coming just one year after the McNamaras' trial for the "Crime of the Century," as the newspaper tabloids called it. The conspiracy trial was not as sensational as the earlier trial. The public, however, was curious about, and were amazed by, the men who reportedly rode in rocking railroad cars with cases of dynamite and nitroglycerine they steadied with the balls of their feet, as they transported explosives to chosen sites.

To bolster its case against the defendants, the Government brought Ortie McManigal under heavy guard from California. His affirmation in this trial was quite similar to his confession which implicated the McNamara brothers; however, he broadened his testimony to include several indicted Ironworkers about whom he had information. McManigal especially zeroed in on his old "control" and fleecer, International Secretary-Treasurer Herbert Hockin, with a vengeance. It was payback time.

prosecutor to grant immunity to Tveitmoe, if he were to implicate Gompers. Tveitmoe would not lie about his friend to walk free, and was convicted. Later, the Appellate Court overturned his conviction. The decision against Olaf A. Tveitmoe was reversed, as W. W. Robinson writes, "...because, it was stated, part of the Pacific Coast file [relating to Tveitmoe] was missing from the files impounded at Indianapolis." No one could account as to how the file "was missing," however, there was much conjecture as to why it "was missing."

After the Federal Grand Jury in Indianapolis returned the fifty-four indictments on February 6, 1912, Ryan reported to the Iron Worker membership that the indictment list named "nearly all those who have served

Members of Local No. 70, Louisville, Kentucky., working for the Louisville Bridge and Iron Company at Nashville, Tennessee .

During the trial, Herbert Hockin was forced to resign as acting Secretary-Treasurer "by reason of the surrender of his bond in the case pending in the United States District Court," according to the Executive Board minutes. Hockin could not retain his financial office without bond; he resigned on November 28, 1912. The Board immediately appointed International Executive Board member Joseph E. McClory, of Local 17, Cleveland, to fill the position until the next convention, in March, 1913, when Harry Jones of New York was elected Secretary-Treasurer.

Philip Taft in his labor history book *The A.F. of L. In The Time of Gompers* points out, "A member of the Executive Board, H. S. Hockin, testified against his colleagues." Since Hockin had been a prime player in the dynamite campaign from the beginning, he knew all the players involved - who did what, and when, and how.

L. L. Jewell, erecting manager of McClintic-Marshall Construction Company, was a prosecution witness during the dynamite conspiracy trial. He electrified the courtroom with his testimony that Hockin had informed him of several planned explosions during the last half of 1910 and early 1911. Only with Jewell's testimony did the Iron Worker officials positively learn what some had suspected, that they had an informant in their midst.

Cases against some of the local officers who went on trial were dismissed; however, on New Year's Eve of 1912, thirty-nine men were found guilty and sentenced, including Herbert Hockin whose testimony against his fellow Ironworkers did not win him acquittal. Five men received suspended sentences, other sentences ranged from one year to six years, except for General President Frank Ryan, one of the oldest men. Judge Anderson levied the stiffest sentence against Ryan–seven years. All time was to be served at

the Federal Penitentiary in Leavenworth, Kansas. Union attorneys immediately filed appeals of their convictions.

Although these were trying times, the International continued to function. A charter was granted to the Ironworkers of Lincoln, Nebraska. It was Local No. 123 and was composed of both "inside" and "outside" men. On November 22, 1912, Local No. 97, Vancouver, British Columbia, was granted permission to open their charter to take in reinforcing Ironworkers. At that time, the business agent of Local No. 97 was only appointed two weeks at a time. Also, in 1912, architectural and ornamental Local No. 119 was chartered in Montreal, Quebec.

In the same year, Local No. 78, San Francisco, which was a local that had shopmen in addition to outside men, reported that they had demanded an eight-hour day for their shopmen inasmuch as the outside men and the other iron trades were working an eight-hour day. The other issues were: the ratio of one apprentice to every four mechanics; the rate of pay for shopmen who

Tug-of-War team of Local No. 97, Vancouver, B.C.

worked on the outside on three-days or less jobs (the employers took the stand that the shop rate was paid); and only allowing the business agent to visit the shops during the lunch hour. All the issues were resolved to the satisfaction of Local No. 78, except the eight-hour day. Three new Shopmen locals were organized in Chicago, Illinois. They were organized along ethnic and language lines, a practice quite common during this period. They were Local No. 132 (English), Local No. 133 (German) and Local No. 134 (Bohemian).

Three months after the trial, the International Association called the postponed **Sixteenth International Convention** from February 4 through March 6, 1913, in Indianapolis. The loyal delegates exhibited a rock-hard "semper fi" stance and reelected Ryan as General President, in the face of his conviction.

A riveting gang at work on the bridge being erected across the Illinois River at Peoria, Illinois, by members of Local No. 112 .

Harry Jones, Local No. 40, New York, N.Y. was elected Secretary-Treasurer. J.E. McClory, Local No. 17, Cleveland, was elected First Vice President.

AFL President Samuel Gompers addressed the delegates on February 27, 1913. He said among other things that "The Bridge and Structural Iron Workers are hard-working men, who are doing wonderful service to society; who are taking their lives in their own hands every

Members of Local No. 86, Seattle, Washington, on the 36th story of the Smith Building.

Members of Local No. 127, Savannah, Georgia.

Members of Local No. 44, Cincinnati, Ohio, working on the new ball park.

Members of Local No. 229, San Diego, California.

Work being erected by members of Local No. 48, Oklahoma City, Oklahoma.

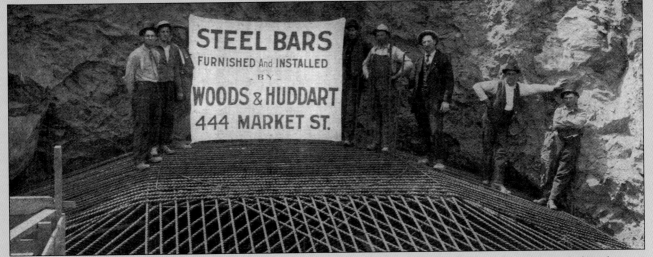

STEEL BARS
FURNISHED And INSTALLED
- BY -
WOODS & HUDDART
444 MARKET ST.

Rod work erected by members of Local 78, San Francisco, for pumping plant at the foot of Van Ness Avenue, San Francisco overlooking the Golden Gate Bridge. Among those pictured are: F. Ginsberg, superintendent, J. Bowman, F. DeMartini, H. Hogan, G. Linberg, T. Clancy.

Delegates to the 32nd Annual Convention of the American Federation of Labor, Rochester, New York November 11 to 23, 1912.

F.E. Thoman, J.E. McClory, D.J. O'Shea, delegates to the 32nd Annual AF of L Convention and Building Trades Department.

day and every hour of the day they work. Without them, and without that service, modern industrial and commercial structures would be an impossibility." He also said in reference to the trials of the International and local union officers that "I am not in position to constitute myself the censor of their judges, or of men, nor am I in position to say that these men are innocent, and I am not going to say that they are guilty; but there is one thing which was evident to every fair-minded observer, and that is the entire case was conducted with a prejudice and bitter partiality against the men, that it raises the question of an honest doubt in the minds of honest men, and it was my pleasure, as I felt it was my duty, when the opportune moment came, the time to appear before the Judiciary Committee of the United States Senate, to set forth my views as to who was responsible after all."

Five men were granted new trials by the Appellate Court, two decisions were reversed but the other convictions were upheld. The convicted men took their cases to the United States Supreme Court, which refused to review them. The Union appealed to President Woodrow Wilson on behalf of the men who were still out on bond. President Wilson pardoned four men. The remaining Union men including General President Frank M. Ryan, John T. Butler, a former General President, and Second Vice President Paul J. Morrin, a future General President, had to report to Leavenworth on June 25, 1914, to serve their sentences ordered by Judge Anderson on December 31, 1912.

For present day Ironworkers, the dynamite conspiracy and the bombings are neither a point of pride nor a reason for guilt. The Iron Worker leadership had

Delegates badge to the Sixteenth Annual Iron Workers Convention held in 1913.

President Frank M. Ryan, reelected for the eighth consecutive time.

no real option other than to succumb in the open shop battle, which was unacceptable to them. In the context of the times, their behavior can be understood, if not condoned. (After all, Thomas Jefferson bought and sold slaves.) An immoral act is not relative; its nature cannot be changed by custom or circumstance. Trend or times can merely help explain such an act, not excuse it. McNamara, Ryan, Clancy, Butler, Morrin and the others may have done what they thought they had to do to preserve the International Association. And despite other consequences of the dynamite campaign, they did save the Union. The International officers stretched the limits of zeal in a righteous cause. Their strategy and tactics suffered--not the cause or validity of trade unionism.

At the **Sixteenth International Convention,** the delegates amended Section 19 of the Constitution which increased the number of Officers of the International. The International Officers shall consist of a President, First, Second, Third, Fourth, Fifth and Sixth Vice Presidents and a Secretary-Treasurer. Prior to this there were only two Vice Presidents. It was voted that the Executive Board would consist of the President and all the Vice Presidents.

Frank Ryan resigned as General President when he entered Leavenworth Federal Prison. The International Executive Board members then convened and appointed First Vice President Joseph McClory as acting General President effective July 1, 1914, to serve until the upcoming convention. McClory was elected unanimously as General President two and a half months later by the delegates at the **Seventeenth International Convention** held September 21-30, 1914 in Peoria, Illinois.

There was a great deal of discussion at the Convention regarding the "Inside Workers or Shopmen." The International granted new charters to several locals of shopmen. It was agreed by the delegates that the work of organizing this class of workmen should continue wherever possible.

A very important resolution was introduced at the Seventeenth International Convention by Delegates Thoman and Clark, Local No. 63 and several other delegates.

Delegates to the Sixteenth Annual Iron Workers Convention held in Indianapolis, Indiana, February 24 to March 6, 1913.

"Whereas, In our official title a very component part of our trade does not receive the recognition it is rightfully entitled to, therefore be it
*Resolved, That we change the title of our Association to - International Association of Bridge, Structural and **Ornamental Iron Workers.**"*

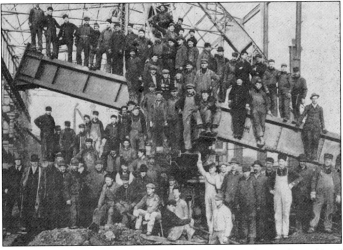

Work being erected at Lima, Ohio, for Worden Allen Co., by members of Local No. 55, Toledo, Ohio.

An amendment to the resolution was made to include the word *"Piledrivers"* to the title. The resolution and the amendment passed and the new title of the Association was *"The International Association of Bridge, Structural and **Ornamental Iron Workers and Piledrivers.**"* This title remained in effect until the end of 1917 when the International lost the Piledriver local unions over a problem with the AFL and Carpenters. If you are looking at an old badge or button with the International logo, you can determine approximately what period of time the badge represented; for example, if it had the lettering I.A.B.& S.I.W. it is before 1914. I.A.B.S.& O.I.W. & P.D. on a badge or button covered the period between 1914 through November, 1917. Beginning December, 1918, and up to the present day, the title of the Association is the **"International**

Association of Bridge, Structural and Ornamental Iron Workers (I.A.B.S.& O.I.W)." The logo, not the wording, of the International was changed in January, 1950.

McClory was subsequently reelected at the **Eighteenth International Convention** held September 20-30, 1915 in San Francisco and the **Nineteenth International Convention** held in New Orleans in 1916. He offered to step down at this time; however, the delegates wouldn't hear of it. They convinced him to reconsider and reelected him to a two year term, since the 1916 Convention was the last scheduled annual conclave. The delegates decided the Union was mature enough to meet every other year, rather than annually. There was also some fear expressed of America being dragged into World War I.

Joseph McClory was a native New Yorker; his family, however, moved to Cleveland several years after his birth in 1877. His father was lured by a better job. Young Joe was educated by the nuns at St. Malachi's School, and they taught him well. In his late teens, he was attracted to ironwork, and on March 12, 1898, was enrolled as a charter member of Local 17.

Six weeks later, while McClory was working on the Victoria Bridge over the St. Lawrence River, Spain declared war on the United States. McClory, an adventurous and a patriotic soul, as well, informed his foreman that he wanted to return home to enlist in the U. S. Army. He did, and served honorably, as did a number of his fellow Ironworkers. (Since record keeping was somewhat casual in those days, no precise figure is available, just that "many Ironworkers...volunteered" for service during the short war.)

After his discharge from the Army, McClory joined the Gold Rush to the Klondike which had started two years previously. The luck of the Irish eluded him, however, and he decided to go home again. His misfortune in

J.E. McClory,
elected General President
at the 17th & 18th
International Conventions
held in 1914 and 1915.

Members of Local No. 84, Houston, Texas, who erected the 13 story Texas Oil Company Building in Houston, Texas.

Members of Local No. 12, Albany, New York on Labor Day, 1913.

Gang on job of Snead Architectural Iron Works at Nashville, Tennessee, in 1913.

Members of Local No. 92, Birmingham, Alabama, starting for their Fourth of July Picnic.

Members of Local No. 129, working on the McLeod Building, Edmonton, Alberta, Canada.

Wife of Brother J.N. Johnson taking a ten story trip at the Tutwiler Hotel in Birmingham, Alabama, July 25, 1913.

Members of Local No. 14, Spokane, Washington.

Some of the underground bridgemen at work on the Rapid Transit Subway, New York City. Harry Kelly, Local No. 40, at the forge.

Members of Local No. 81, Anaconda, Montana, at their Annual Ball in 1913.

1914 Ironworkers delegate's badge worn at the 17th Annual Convention in Peoria, Illinois.

not finding gold proved to be good fortune for the International Association. Back in Cleveland, he resumed his craft, became active in his local, and also in affairs of the International Association.

At the San Francisco Convention in 1915, after his first full year as President, McClory wired fraternal greetings to John J. McNamara at San Quentin and Frank Ryan, Eugene Clancy and the other Ironworkers at Leavenworth. Three days later, Ryan sent a telegram to McClory to read to the delegates expressing gratitude and appreciation from all sixteen Ironworkers in the Federal prison.

During McClory's years in office, he kept in touch with the Union men at Leavenworth through personal visits and letters and always through Second Vice President William J. McCain, of Kansas City. (McCain had been business agent of

Kansas City Local 10 and was indicted in the dynamite transport conspiracy case. Since there was no real evidence against the mild-mannered McCain, he was found not guilty). Other International and local union officers visited the men, and brought tobacco and fruit.

The visitors reported that at all times the Ironworker inmates were of good cheer, but from time to time John Butler and Henry Legleitner, of Pittsburgh, were confined to the hospital because of health problems.

As evidence of their good spirits, the men formed Federal Iron Workers Local 1, of Leavenworth, with John Butler as business agent. Frank Higgins in a letter to the International in September, 1914, advised boomers and floaters "not to come this way looking for work just now."

McClory was a huge man with a heart to match. He helped prepare a resolution to provide weekly payments of $25.00 to Mrs. Mary McNamara, the mother of John J. and James B. He also appointed many of the men as part-time organizers, as they were released from prison beginning in 1915, thus helping them get a fresh start after they paid their debt to society. Some men stayed with the International a relatively short time. Others such as former General President John T. "Jack" Butler,

Delegates to the 17th Annual Convention held September 21-30, 1914.

At the 17th Annual Convention, delegate **F.E. Thoman** of Local No. 63 presented the resolution that changed the title of the Association to the International Association of Bridge, Structural and Ornamental Iron Workers. The resolution was amended to add the words "and Pile Drivers."

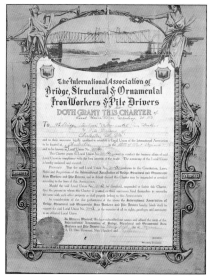

Charter with title that included "Pile Driver" issued to Local No. 20A, Charleston, West Virginia.

Headquarters of Local No. 77, 457 Bryant Street, San Francisco, California. This building was owned by Local No. 77.

Delegates and visitors at the 18th Annual Convention held September 20-30, 1915 in San Francisco during the Panama Pacific Exposition.

who was not in the best of health, remained for a couple of years. Stalwarts John H. Barry, of St. Louis, and James E. Munsey, of Salt Lake City, also stayed for extended periods. McClory looked forward to Frank Ryan's release; he wanted Ryan's assistance on keeping pile drivers in the International Association. This was not viewed as charity since the International could well use the expertise of the old hands and benefit from their experience.

In 1915, Shopmen's Local No. 164, New York City, reported on the success of their strike during the month of July. They increased their membership to over 1,000, increased wages by 75 percent, and reduced working hours by over 10 percent. They also negotiated a clause in the agreement where no inside men are to go to work on the outside. This was reported as being very helpful to Finishers Local No. 52.

Pile Drivers and Suspension of the Iron Workers From the AF of L

As pointed out previously, the title of the Association was changed to the "*International Association of Bridge, Structural and Ornamental Iron Workers and Pile Drivers*" in 1914. This title eventually led to the Iron Workers' temporary suspension from the American Federation of Labor and the Building Trades Department. Indeed, the change in title threatened the Iron Workers' existence as a union for a brief but crucial period.

As the A.F. of L. moved into the second decade of this century, it was still a relatively young organization, slightly over 30 years of age. It was exclusively made up of craft or trade unions. That is, each national or international union affiliated with the A.F. of L. was

made up of local unions with a membership which followed a particular trade or a specific craft. There were no such things as industrial unions, as we know them today. This was also a time of rapid technological change and industrial growth.

During this period, the A.F. of L. granted individual charters to each international union as they were created by a group of local unions getting together. Various Iron Worker local unions in 1896 did this very thing. The A.F. of L. also followed another procedure of granting charters to independent local unions in anticipation, at some later time, of merging such independent unions into the appropriate international union or to create a new international union from a group of independently chartered local unions.

Brothers Sweetman, Ryan and Anderson, delegates to the 18th Annual Convention from Local No. 63, Chicago, Illinois.

The A.F. of L., in granting charters of affiliation to the international unions, specifically spelled out in the charter grant what work the members of that international union performed by way of their trade or craft. Such identification or charter grant became commonly known as the work jurisdiction of the particular union. In granting charters, the A.F. of L. paid particular attention, as best they could, to drawing lines of demarcation so that no two international unions were granted

Pile Driver crew and members of Port Commission at Municipal Grain Elevator, New Orleans, Louisiana, in 1915.

a charter covering similar jurisdiction. The object, of course, was to stabilize and develop uniformity in wage rates and working conditions for people who followed the same trade or craft.

It was not too many years before the inevitable problems of such a procedure began to arise. And we still have them with us today. Technology changes and work operations, which were once recognized within the jurisdiction of a particular trade, gradually shifted and became more compatible to another trade. During this process, innumerable jurisdictional disputes arose. As these problems became more numerous and more serious, the A.F. of L., as the organization which originally granted the charter, accepted unto itself the responsibility of resolving the disputes.

It was within this framework and background that a significant technological change took place involving Ironworkers. It developed that piling of wood, which was part of the recognized jurisdiction of the

Delegates to the 19th Annual Convention held at New Orleans, Louisiana, September 18-25, 1916.

64

Carpenters, began to change from wood to steel H-beams and to reinforced concrete. As these changes in technology took place, many contractors, who had never been involved in the driving of wood piling, were able to purchase the H-beams and reinforced concrete piling and do the driving themselves in connection with their structural steel bridges or building projects. In so doing, these contractors merely used the available crews of Ironworkers. Gradually more Ironworkers were part-time, and some steadily engaged in the driving of steel and concrete piling.

The jurisdictional problems that this development would ultimately create began to crystalize in 1915. At this time, there was an independent local union of Dock Builders in New York City that was a direct affiliate local union of the A.F. of L. In February of that year, the A.F. of L. ordered the independent local of Dock Builders to affiliate with the Brotherhood of Carpenters. The Dock Builders, many of whom were actually Ironworkers laid off of other New York jobs and engaged primarily in the driving of steel and concrete piling, voted to reject the instructions to affiliate. Shortly thereafter, the A.F. of L. removed the charter of the New York Dock Builders.

In July of 1915, the Dock Builders were on strike and felt a need for established support. They turned to the Iron Workers International which granted them a charter. They became known as Pile Drivers Local No. 177 of this International Association. The strike was won and a three-year agreement signed on August 10, 1915 with the Contracting Dock Builders Association for "all water front improvements and pile driving on foundation work."

At the San Francisco Convention of the A.F. of L. in November, a resolution in protest was introduced. The delegates voted to have President Samuel Gompers appoint a committee on the problems involving all Dock Workers in New York City. The committee met after the convention. They issued a report that said in part: "The chartering of the Municipal Dock Builders by the Iron Workers has brought about a state of chaos, and the tearing down of well established conditions in the industry, and is making for dissatisfaction and a feeling akin to bitterness throughout the labor movement in New York City." The committee further recommended that the A. F. of L. instruct the Iron Workers to revoke Local No. 177's charter, and finally that such local then affiliate with Local No. 1456 of the Carpenters. On January 29, 1916, Iron Worker President McClory wrote Gompers and claimed that the committee report was "from the very outset...one-sided and favorable to the Carpenters." In February, the Iron Worker Executive Council backed McClory's position and voted to hold meetings between the involved international unions to seek a solution. On March 20, 1916, a meeting of Iron Workers, Carpenters and Longshoremen failed to reach a compromise.

The pile-driving dispute was thus moved along unsettled to become a topic of heated debate at the November A. F. of L. Convention in Baltimore, later in 1916. Despite the fact that the Dock Builders and their employers were well-satisfied and there were no specific problems, the convention ruled that the Iron Workers must revoke Local No. 177's Charter before April 1,

Members of New York and Vicinity locals employed on the 7th Avenue Subway.

Three members of Local No. 5 on the Muncy Building in Washington, D.C.

Members of Local No. 45, Jersey City, New Jersey employed on Ore Dumper for the Lehigh Valley Railroad at Bayonne, New Jersey.

Lincoln Memorial, Washington, D.C. Erection of derricks and steel work being done by members of Local No. 5.

Members of Local No. 33, Rochester, New York, on job for the Genesee Bridge Company.

Members of Local No. 25, Detroit, Michigan, employed at Hastings, Michigan, for the Morava Construction Company.

Reinforcing rod work being installed by members of Local No. 115, of Fresno, California.

1917, or suffer suspension from the Federation. Under the pressure of such a mandate, the Charter for Local No. 177 was revoked.

However, the New York Dock Builders refused to affiliate with the Carpenters. Instead, they tried to remain in the Iron Workers' organization and requested Iron Worker Local No. 189 of Jersey City be made a sub-local. The request was granted. In turn, the A. F. of L. Executive Council on June 27 ordered that Local No. 189's Charter be revoked by July 1, again threatening the Iron Workers International with suspension. President McClory felt that he could not take the steps needed to carry out the order in the next few days allowed by the AF of L, since the matter involved Local

Members of Local No. 6, Buffalo, New York working on bridge job in Buffalo.

established that their current difficulties were going to be used to divide up the jurisdiction of the Iron Workers. The resolutions adopted by the Building Trades Department were then passed on to the A. F. of L. Convention which was to meet in a few days for action at that Convention which, if passed, would then take that work from the jurisdiction of the Iron Workers.

The International immediately sought ways to be quickly re-admitted to the A. F. of L., so they could speak against approval of those resolutions on the floor of the A. F. of L Convention. Their predicament was indeed precarious. The International, at that time, was in dire need of the financial and organizational strength of the A. F. of L. which they had intended to seek at the convention.

However, instead of being in a position to seek help from the A. F. of L., they were suspended and without any representation. Not only would they be unable to seek help in the open-shop war with the large steel corporations; they instead were sitting on the outside while decisions were going to be made on whether or not their existing organization was going to be carved up by the

> "Ironworkers, instead of being in a position to seek help from the A. F. of L., were suspended and without any representation. Not only would they be unable to seek help in the open-shop war with the large steel corporations; they instead were sitting on the outside while decisions were going to be made on whether or not their existing organization was going to be carved up by the labor movement itself."

No. 189 and its sub-local, not the International. In addition, he was bedridden in very serious condition at the time of the order. As a result, the A. F. of L. officially suspended the Iron Workers on July 14, 1917.

While the Iron Workers were suspended, the A. F. of L. Building Trades Department, generally recognized at the time as "the most militant part of the labor movement," took an unprecedented action. It held its annual Convention before, rather than after the A. F. of L. Convention, contrary to the Constitutions of both the A. F. of L. and the Building Trades Department. At that November Convention, the Building Trades Department received and adopted two resolutions by the Lathers and Carpenters requesting annulment of a 1909 decision which granted reinforced concrete construction to the Iron Workers and a 1913 decision which granted the installation of solid steel and metal window frames to Iron Workers.

The suspended Iron Workers were astounded and furious at the passage of these resolutions. This clearly

AF of L Headquarters in Washington, D.C. in 1917.

Members of Local No. 197, New York City, at their annual outing and games at Duer's Pavilion, Whitestone, Long Island, New York in 1917.

labor movement itself. Unquestionably, the combination of the existing fight with the employers and a new fight against the other Building Trades Unions and the A. F. of L. for the right to represent workers on reinforcing rods and ornamental ironwork shortly would lead to the demise of the Iron Workers as an effective and meaningful International Union. The Iron Workers indeed were on the brink of destruction.

On November 13, 1917, the second day of the A. F. of L. Convention in Buffalo, the Iron Workers announced that they had revoked the charters of Jersey City Local 189 and its sub-local. They would relinquish all claims to dock building in New York City. The Iron Worker

delegates were immediately seated in the convention and were in a position to request the help of the Federation in the growing open-shop war against the Iron Workers.

President McClory told the delegates that the large steel corporations and the erectors associations were stepping up their efforts to crush the Union. He illustrated the outrageous situation by citing the fact that 75 percent of all men who followed the trade were members of this Union, not withstanding the steel employers refusing to negotiate with or to enter into any agreements with the International Association or any of its local unions. He pointed to the financial plight brought

Two hundred and fifty Ironworkers from Locals No. 189 and 189A of New York, New York and Jersey City, New Jersey somewhere in France to build docks and piers for the U.S. Government.

67

about by the decline in membership resulting from the enlistment in a short period of time of over 6 percent of the members into the armed forces and the loss of 1,200 members in the New York pile-driving dispute.

He stressed that the financial pressure of this loss in membership was magnified by the fact that the Iron Workers Union paid substantial death benefits because of the hazardous nature of the trade. These benefits were paid out of the general fund and in 1917 the benefit level had been doubled. Because of the high rate of accidental deaths, this had almost depleted the general fund. Although they were in the process of leveling the first general assessment since 1910, the treasury would be in dire straits before the effects of the assessment would be felt. The convention supported the appeal and adopted resolutions to urge the Secretary of War, the Secretary of the Navy, and the Council of National Defense to put pressure on the steel corporations and the erectors associations who had been refusing to recognize the Iron Workers Union.

In addition, the Iron Worker delegates were successful in having the convention not support the Building Trades resolutions to take **reinforcing and ornamental** ironwork from the Iron Workers. The records of the convention would indicate, although the A. F. of L. Convention did not support the resolutions, the resolutions were not voted down and apparently still a subject for future consideration. The action of President McClory in obtaining quick readmission into the A. F. of

Members of Local No. 1, Chicago, Illinois, burning and wrecking the Commonwealth Edison Power House in Chicago for the Oxweld Acetylene Company.

L. had indeed brought desirable results. The financial and organizational support of the A. F. of L. was obtained and the jurisdictional issue was not finalized.

Notwithstanding the fact that the A. F. of L. Convention refused to support the Building Trades resolutions, the Building Trades, nevertheless, proceeded to support the establishment of reinforcing rod local unions by the Lathers, as well as the efforts of the Carpenters to negotiate agreements with employers covering the erection of steel windows and ornamental metal work. They proceeded under the premise that action had been authorized by the previous Building Trades Convention and not reversed by the A. F. of L. Convention. It was then evident that the only course of action was to bring the question back to the next convention of the A. F. of L.

In December, 1917, McClory dispatched Vice President Ben Osborne to open a Washington office to represent the interests of the International Association during World War I. Osborne had to deal with eight different Government bureaus and boards involving construction, labor policy, wage adjustment, Navy Yard riggers and other matters. He also had jurisdictional disputes with the International Longshoremen's Association, which wanted the Iron Workers' shipyard riggers. McClory had the foresight to see that an office in Washington had to be established to protect the Union, and he had the good sense to send a man of Osborne's caliber.

In the year between conventions, the International received additional moral and physical support. On April 10, 1918 President Wilson, notwithstanding his almost total preoccupation with the affairs of World War I, took the time and interest

Having received requests from some Financial Secretaries for information regarding the way stamps should be affixed for the months where it requires three stamps in the one month, we herewith submit sample page of the 1917 Dues Book, showing how stamps should be placed in the books. MEMBERS SHOULD SEE THAT ALL STAMPS, AS SHOWN IN THE ABOVE CUT, ARE PLACED IN THEIR DUES BOOKS, FOR IF ANY STAMPS ARE OMITTED, THEY WILL NOT BE CONSIDERED IN GOOD STANDING.

It was a practice for Local No. 10, Kansas City to welcome and give a party to all the Ironworkers being released from Leavenworth. Below is Nipper Anderson, Local No. 17, returning to Cleveland from Leavenworth. He is welcomed by a group of Ironworker members and officers from Local No. 17.

to commute the sentence of former Iron Worker President Frank M. Ryan. This action indeed boosted the morale of the Iron Workers' leadership. It had the effect of saying, from the highest office in the land, that the Iron Workers in their fight to represent their members were indeed being persecuted.

When former President Ryan returned to Chicago, he was welcomed back by hundreds of local and national labor leaders in one of the most impressive receptions ever witnessed, in view of all of the events which had taken place. It was a reception that heightened the spirits and bolstered the energies of those who were fighting so devotedly in the interests of the working man. President McClory immediately obtained the help of Ryan in his efforts to resolve the pile driving issue and the other jurisdictional questions at the next A. F. of L. Convention.

A few months later, McClory and Ryan presented a brief to the A. F. of L. Convention held in St. Paul, Minnesota. The brief aimed itself at the actions of the convention of the Building Trades Department, which had annulled the 1909 and 1913 decisions. It was scholarly and effective. It pointed out the various violations of the A. F. of L. Constitution, which had taken place in the passage of resolutions aimed at taking established work jurisdiction from the Iron Workers.

The same brief was presented to the Building Trades Convention. The delegates of each convention voted concurrence that the Iron Workers had been dealt with unfairly and had not been given the protection afforded by the Constitutions of both the A. F. of L. and the Building Trades Department. Accordingly, the question was referred to the A. F. of L. Executive Council for action.

In a few months it became clear that the A. F. of L. Executive Council was not going to act on the illegality of the action until the Iron Workers were willing to make certain concessions. McClory was discouraged and disenchanted.

In 1917, George Kelly, Recording Secretary of Local No. 201 (Reinforcing Local), Washington, D.C., reported that Organizer P.J. Morrin organized Local No. 205 (Shopmen) in Washington, D.C. A District Council was formed at the same time, which was comprised of Locals No. 5, 201, and 205.

136 I.P.E.U.

Chapter Five

The Beginning of the Morrin Era

The **First Biennial Convention** and the **Twentieth International Convention** of the Iron Workers was held at the Adolphus Hotel in Dallas, Texas September 16-24, 1918. This marked General President Joseph E. McClory's swan song and the election of **Paul J. Morrin**. Morrin was known by his nickname **"Paddy"** to all his fellow Ironworkers and to other trade unionists, as well. One month after the convention, Morrin's wife, Stella, died of pneumonia, a complication of influenza she had contracted while nursing her husband, felled by the current epidemic. The stricken Morrin was bed ridden and his doctor ordered him not to attend his beloved wife's funeral. The bereaved and deathly ill Morrin, unaccustomed to taking orders, had no option but to acquiesce. The physician was as tough as Morrin - he told him to follow orders or Paddy could find himself another doctor. Morrin needed to heed his physician and fully regain his strength - he faced two years of rigorous and exhausting negotiations with other crafts, and a vigorous organizing campaign in the steel industry.

Morrin, like many early Ironworkers, was not originally an urban man. One of eight children, he was born on a farm in Iowa County, in southeastern Iowa on August 21, 1879. In most large Irish Catholic families years ago, it was hoped that one son would enter the priesthood and his parents entertained that idea about their son, Paul. Morrin always stayed close to his church; however, he decided not to become a priest. At nineteen years of age, he migrated two hundred miles to St. Louis. Within a year he got into ironwork. He served a two year apprenticeship in St. Louis Local No. 18 and was classified as a journeyman Ironworker on November 18, 1901.

He worked diligently at the trade and also applied himself on behalf of the local union. His active union interest was rewarded by election to several local offices including president, secretary-treasurer and business agent. As a delegate representing Local No. 18, he was immersed in affairs of the International during conventions. He served as a General Vice President prior to being chosen as the sixth man to head the International.

On December 14, 1918, two and a half months after his election as General President, Paul J. Morrin wrote to John J. McNamara at San Quentin, a friendly letter (they were good friends). Morrin offered help and that of the International Association in securing McNamara's and his brother's liberty. Morrin was troubled by what

he, and others in and outside of the trade union movement considered the excessive sentences handed the brothers, especially since the deaths caused by the *Los Angeles Times* explosion were accidental and not premeditated.

McNamara was delighted and moved by Morrin's thoughtful and warm letter. His response dated December 30, 1918 informed Morrin that a few friends and some well-meaning meddlers were planning to hire Clarence Darrow and attorneys of Darrow's choice to sue for McNamara's release. McNamara did not want Darrow to be involved. McNamara, ever direct, wrote Morrin, "My position is that if our officials are capable of paying the freight, they are capable of choosing the persons to whom it is to be paid. Can you see anything wrong with that attitude?"

In the meantime, other indictments may have been pending against McNamara in California as Morrin indicated in a letter to his friend on April 7, 1919. He also tried to comfort him and reminded McNamara, "I know that these delays are aggravating to you, as I understand from personal experience how you feel." (A reference to the time Morrin spent in Leavenworth for his conviction in the dynamite

P.J. "Paddy" Morrin
International President

transport conspiracy).

Morrin and former Secretary-Treasurer John J. McNamara continued to correspond until McNamara's release from San Quentin prison was imminent. McNamara served less than ten years of his fifteen year sentence. He was granted freedom on May 10, 1921, at forty-four years of age.

His brother, James B., was not so fortunate. His sentence was never commuted. He spent the last thirty years of his life behind bars, except for five years, all in San Quentin. In 1936, he was transferred to Folsom prison, a place without adequate medical care for his cancer-wracked body. State officials finally returned him to San Quentin three weeks before he died. God commuted Jim McNamara's life sentence on March 8, 1941 - he had done his penance.

General President McClory had served the International Association well as General President for four years, as Vice President for three years, and Acting Secretary-Treasurer for four months. The difficult years took their toll, and he was ready to relinquish the reins, to "turn over to some one else at this convention the burdens, responsibilities and onerous duties of this office."

McClory, as previously noted, was President during very trying times following the convictions of, and appeals losses by, former President Frank Ryan and other International officers on their dynamite conspiracy charges, in the wake of the sentencing of the McNamara brothers. He kept the Union alive and growing through World War I, and he even increased the membership

Members of Local No. 112, Peoria, Riveting Gang.

rolls fighting the good fight against the open shop policy of the National Erectors Association.

At the Dallas Convention, he did have some good news to report: "Our efforts in organizing the shopmen during the past six months have been more satisfactory than at any other period in recent years." At the end of the fiscal year, the International had eight shop local unions with a total of over 2,000 members. Since the last convention, the paid up membership showed an increase of 4,393 for a total of 18,607.

World War I saw 1,467 Ironworkers drop their spud wrenches and pick up rifles to defeat Germany - not quite 10% of the total membership of over 17,000 at the end of the war. (Americans served through nineteen months of combat to "the eleventh hour of the eleventh

Statue of "Kaiserin," taken off the Germania Life Building, St. Paul, by members of Local No. 94.

day of the eleventh month" of 1918. Most of the heavy American casualties totaling 224,089 men resulted from the fierce, relentless fighting of the brutal last 200 days of the war, from April to November). *The Bridgemen's Magazine* issues of the era, show that members of the Union served their country willingly and well.

Paul J. "Paddy" Morrin was destined to hold the office of General President for three decades. He recognized that if the Iron Workers were ever to win their fight against the big steel employers, they had to first solve their jurisdictional arguments inside the house of labor. He immediately set up committees to meet with the various trades. After a few months, negotiations with the Carpenters on the question of shipyard rigging was resolved, however all other issues remained stalemated. He sought to obtain a united front with all trades involved in bridge building in an effort to obtain greater strength in the fight with the employers. As this program was being assembled, it soon became evident that such an alliance was floundering on the issue of pile driving. There was no question that the dispute had to be settled.

Not only had the pile driving dispute become an issue that prevented the Iron Workers from resolving many of the major problems they faced, it was evident that at the next convention of the Building Trades Department, further jurisdictional resolutions were to be introduced. The question was of major importance, far beyond the question of the New York dock builders that had brought it to a head. In the ensuing years from the introduction of steel H-beams and reinforced concrete piling, every Iron Workers local was performing substantial pile driving.

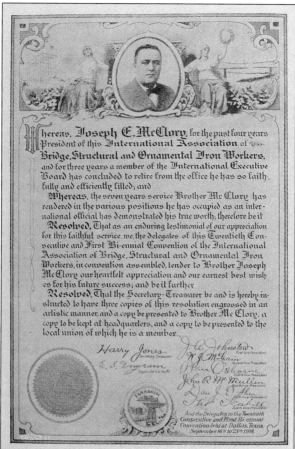

In fact, numerous local unions were made up exclusively of pile drivers. In the face of these facts, President Morrin took the only course open and reached an agreement conceding to the Carpenters all pile driving, except that done in connection with the erection of bridges. Such a settlement, in view of the substantial number of Ironworkers engaged in pile driving, was understandably received with indignation and outrage. President Morrin took the question to the membership. In local after local, he told them that "the fight with the Carpenters was suicidal." After a few months, concurrence was obtained. Local by local the Iron Workers relinquished their pile driving membership to the Carpenters and instructed their employers that no longer would they negotiate agreements covering pile driving.

The related parts of the agreements were shortly finalized at the following convention of the Building Trades Department. The resolutions voiding the 1909 and 1913 jurisdictional decisions were recognized and accepted as being illegal and the jurisdiction again recognized as to be that of the Iron Workers. The Lathers who, in the interim of years chartered many locals of reinforcing rodmen, were ordered to turn over all such members to the Iron Workers at the conclusion of every collective bargaining agreement which was in existence and not to seek to bargain for reinforced rodmen beyond the expiration of those agreements.

The Lathers, who had devoted much time and energy in taking over the vacated Iron Workers jurisdiction, nevertheless saw the uselessness in becoming involved in the type of fight with the Building Trades Department and the A. F. of L. that the Iron Workers had just come through. One local, however, saw a loophole in the order. Prior to the expiration of the agreement between the

Membership book (1918-1919) with World War I Service Stamps.

Brother Matthew Martin, better known as "Moon," a member of Local No. 63 who served in France. In 1931, "Moon" became Business Agent of Local No. 63 and remained in office for 38 years.

Lathers in New York City and the employers covering rodmen, the agreement was reopened and extended. Each agreement thereafter was reopened before the expiration date and extended in a procedure that was to continue year after year until the arguments on the question became academic. It is for this reason that the reinforcing rodmen in New York City were members of

Members of Pile Drive and Dock Workers Local No. 226, New Orleans, LA, 1919.

the Lathers International Union until 1979 when all Lather locals merged with the Carpenters except for Lathers Local No. 46, New York City, which became Ironworkers Local Union No. 46L.

When the fury of the pile driving dispute simmered down, the Building Trades Department was once again unified and sought to proceed under the strength of joint action. However, the alliance of Building Trades Unions in the construction of bridges, which President Morrin was unable to put together because of the pile driving dispute, nevertheless failed to materialize once the dispute was settled.

The Great Steel Strike of 1919

The Iron Workers and the entire A.F. of L. were behind the plan to organize all the steel companies at the end of World War I. John Fitzpatrick, President of the Chicago Federation of Labor, and Samuel Gompers, met at the Morrison Hotel in Chicago to map out the strategy.

William Z. Foster, who had successfully organized workers in the Stockyards during the war, was put in charge of the organizing campaign. The Iron Workers saw the opportunity of organizing the fabricating plants and assisting the Amalgamated Association of Iron, Steel, and Tin Workers in their efforts to again organize steel after their defeat at Homestead in 1892.

The strike began on September 22, 1919 with half a million workers across the country walking out. In the Calumet area of Illinois and Indiana almost 90% of the 87,000 workers in that area went out on strike. At this time the average worker was working over a 12-hour day for only 42 cents an hour.

After the "Great Steel Strike" of 1919, which ended in complete failure to organize the steel industry, it appeared that the struggle for union recognition of the Iron Workers was forever lost. A year after the strike, work slowed down.

On January 11, 1919 the International Association became affiliated with the Metal Trades Department of the AF of L. By 1920, there were seventy shop local unions organized. Practically all of the trades engaged in the various iron shops throughout the country were affiliated nationally with the Metal Trades Department.

Since 1918, in just two years, the International Association made greater progress both from a financial and membership standpoint than it had from 1896 through 1917. This was accomplished without any International assessment being levied upon the membership.

The **Second Biennial Convention** and the **Twenty-First International Convention** was held September 20-29, 1920 in Cleveland, Ohio. P.J. Morrin was reelected General President and Harry Jones was reelected Secretary-Treasurer. In President Morrin's report to the delegates he spoke on the progress made relative to the shop local unions. The shopmen were making forty- four dollars per week and after December of 1920 would be making three dollars more per week based on a forty-four hour week.

It was reported at the 1920 Iron Workers Convention that at the AF of L Convention held in St. Paul, May 18, 1919 an agreement was reached between the Carpenters, Laborers, Sheetmetal Workers, Boilermakers and Iron Workers that all rigging in shipyards, equipment and installation plants and yards in the construction and repairing of ships shall belong to the Iron Workers.

Members of Local No. 285, Wichita Falls, Texas on Labor Day, 1919.

Delegates to the Twenty-First Consecutive and Second Biennial Convention, held at Cleveland, Ohio, September 20-29, 1920. This Convention was the largest ever held by the Iron Workers.

General President Morrin came along at the right moment; it was an advantageous time for change for the Iron Workers. The dynamite conspiracy problems were behind them, the convicted men released from Leavenworth, the armistice ending World War I had been signed, and construction firms were preparing for the coming building boom. All this, plus a significant shift in the attitude and thinking of the members was occurring; they began to realize that they needed a strong International Association, as well as a strong leader. Morrin's predecessors during the past decade and a half, Buchanan, Ryan and McClory, were strong men but their powers were circumscribed by

First Annual Conference of Navy Yard Riggers at Washington, D.C., week of January 6, 1919. **P.J. Morrin** is seated 2nd from left.

convention delegates who for years preferred muscular local unions and a limited International Union. Morrin's timing was perfect. At long last, the Sam Parks syndrome was cured. (During his days as the power of New York Local No. 2, Sam Parks was the most strident advocate of strong locals and a restricted International Association.)

The International Union Constitution, adopted at the founding convention, was modified at subsequent conventions. Before his election as General President, Paul J. Morrin decided that the existing Constitution was a patchwork document, inadequate for an ascendant trade union like the Iron Workers. He planned to make changes he deemed appropriate and proper as soon as he took office in 1918.

General President Morrin engaged Frank P. Walsh, America's premier labor attorney, to counsel him and the general officers on a revised and strengthened Constitution. This was the same Frank Walsh whose brilliant legal mind and persuasive personality had

been recognized by President Woodrow Wilson five years earlier, when he appointed him Chairman of the United States Commission on Industrial Relations. Later, during World War I, President Wilson appointed Walsh

International Executive Board, 1919-1920: **Top row, right to left:** Thomas Scahill, 6th VP; Harry Jones, Secretary-Treasurer; Ben Osborne, 3rd VP; D.H. O'Shea, 5th VP; John R. McMullen, 4th VP - **Bottom row:** W.J. McCain, 2nd VP; P.J. Morrin, President; J.A. Johnston, 1st VP.

Chairman of the War Labor Board. Walsh's counsel was invaluable to the President of the United States, as well as to the General President of the Iron Workers.

A resolution passed at the Cleveland Convention empowered Morrin to appoint a fifteen-member committee "for the purpose of rewriting the Constitution to conform with present day needs." Although much of the plan for the new Constitution had been already prepared by General Counsel Frank Walsh, it was important that a group of local union and district council officers approve his ideas and provide other ideas, revisions and amendments.

The General Constitution Committee, whose members represented all branches of the trade and every section of North America, convened at Headquarters in Indianapolis on January 24, 1921. The members were: Messrs. J.T. Fitzpatrick, Local 10, Kansas City; Michael J. Cunnane, Local 13, Philadelphia; M.J. Louden, Local 15, New Haven; John O'Brien, Local 17, Cleveland; Theodore M. Brandle, Local 45, Jersey City; John Snyder, Local 52, New York; A.G. Dentler, Local 86, Seattle; T.H. Giblin, Local 89, Cedar Rapids; Michael Artery, Local 136, Chicago; George Baubach, Local 227, Mobile; Thomas A. Wood, Local 228, Portsmouth; F.J. Carlson, Local 229, San Diego; James McDonnell, Local 263, Fort Worth; Peter L. Arci, Local 274, Brooklyn; Daniel J. Brophy, Local 280, Montreal. The committee worked long hours and diligently for two

Vol. XX   September, 1920   No 9.

The BRIDGEMEN'S Magazine

Cleveland Convention Number

1896   1920

Soldiers and Sailors Monument Cleveland

Published Monthly by the International Association of Bridge, Structural and Ornamental Iron Workers

straight weeks and the new Constitution was approved and adopted on February 7, 1921.

General President Morrin sought broader powers for the General President as the Union's leader and a central role for the General Executive Board. He got both. He knew it was essential to have a potent International headed by a strong General President instead of a loose confederation of local unions and a limited General Presidency, if the Union was to succeed in organizing the non-union iron-workers and to stake out its proper place in the construction industry.

President Morrin hailed the new Constitution as a great benefit to the Union; the addition of three General Vice Presidents, a trimmed Executive Board, International approval of local agreements and work rules and tightening relationships with local unions by writing a uniform constitution for all locals, among other provisions.

Frank Walsh declared "the new Constitution should mark a most important epoch in the history of the International Association of Bridge, Structural and Ornamental Iron Workers. It is the most ambitious effort...looking to a solution to the greatest problem which confronts modern trade unionism, namely, to preserve the essentials of democracy while at the same time lodging the necessary power in the hands of chosen representatives to meet successfully the manifold problems which daily confront the organization... Also benevolent elements, which is the corner stone of true trade unionism must ever be considered. (Its) history is not only of individuals but of whole organizations making monumental sacrifices to aid their struggling fellow workers. Happily, under the new Constitution all that is sacred, so far as democracy is concerned, is preserved inviolate."

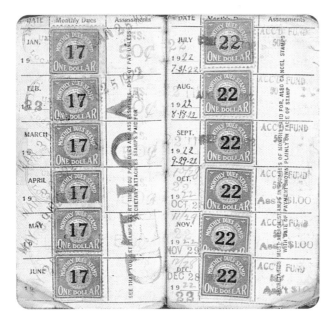

Cloth Membership Book (1920-1927)

General Counsel Walsh pointed out that local union and International funds were safeguarded in conformity with the rules of modern business and finance. He was also proud that stability was now assured in contracts with fair employers. He closed his praise for the new Constitution stating: "Under it the organization should go forward to a higher development and increasingly serve its members, the State and humanity."

In 1921 a brief economic collapse resulted in a loss of 5,000 Ironworkers' jobs. If the Iron Workers were in a desperate situation in 1921, their foes certainly were not. That same year nearly 200 open shop associations met in Chicago and renamed their drive to crush the unions "The American Plan."* Their motto read: "Every man to work out his own salvation and not to be bound by the shackles of organization to his own detriment." In reality, "The American Plan" meant the annihilation of organized labor, and indeed a few long-standing trade unions were dissolved at this time. In fact, organized labor felt that anti-union activities were condoned by the Harding Administration, including those who were later implicated in the Teapot Dome scandal. In 1921, Federal Judge Kenesaw Mountain Landis in Chicago arbitrated a building trades strike, ordering a 25 percent wage reduction from the 1914 level (much lower than employers had agreed to pay), and even formed a committee to enforce his own "Landis Decision" with private detectives. Meanwhile, barely one out of every 10 workers was earning $2,000 a year which was considered necessary for a "minimum" health and decency budget.

In 1921, the General Executive Board revoked the charter of Local Union No. 3 of Pittsburgh, for its persis-

*Similar to the "Right-to-Work" committee of today

President Morrin in 1920 at Caughnawaga Indian Reservation, Caughnawaga, Quebec, Canada, just after being conferred the title of Chief "Big Smoke" of the Caughnawaga Indians.

Members of Shopmen Local No. 275, New York, New York, employed in the shop of the Harris Uris Iron Works.

Members of Local No. 29, Portland, Oregon, employed on the Montgomery Ward job at Portland, Oregon for the Wells Brothers Construction Company.

One of the sections of the christening party arriving for the ceremony in connection with the christening of the only Union baby sponsored by Local No. 58 of New Orleans, Louisiana. The view is a magnificent one above the roofs of New Orleans skyscrapers.

tent refusal to carry out instructions of the International officials which were issued them by the Executive Council. After the revocation of the charter, Vice-President Johnston was detailed to stay in Pittsburgh to register all members of former Local No. 3, who wished to go along with the policy of the International. About 95 percent registered. On March 21, 1921 a new charter was granted Pittsburgh to take the place of Local Union No. 3, the new local being known as Local Union No. 371. None of the former officers of Local Union No. 3 were eligible to hold office in Local No. 371 for a period of one year. The records indicate that in September of 1922, Pittsburgh was reissued their Local No. 3 charter.

Early in 1922, to counteract the economic impact on Ironworkers of the lost strike of 1919 and to bring back into membership the thousands of members who had dropped their membership books through lack of employment in the slowdown of the twenties, President Morrin launched a national organizing program. Although the program was nationwide in scope, it was concentrated in the New York Metropolitan area. It was the theory of the Executive Council that if the New York Metropolitan area could be successfully organized, it would be both a launching point and an inspiration for organizing efforts elsewhere in the nation. Many of the non-union steel erectors in New York operated in many parts of the country.

"If we are successful in our efforts in the New York district," said Iron Worker President P. J. Morrin, "it would greatly aid us in establishing union conditions elsewhere, as it has been our determined intentions to extend our activities in this direction in other cities just as soon as we had succeeded in the Metropolitan district." Ironworkers across the country seem to have felt the same way: union recognition in New York would mean recognition everywhere in the U. S. and Canada. What these early Ironworkers did not calculate, however, was the massive implications of such a struggle. Unionizing New York at that time meant battling the entire steel industry that was the heart of the open-shop operation. The 1922 Lockwood Senatorial Investigation of the Steel Industry for the State of New York pointed out, "an intensive effort had been instituted by the steel manufacturers to break organized labor and to award all work to non-union erectors."

To carry out a successful organizing plan in New York City in the face of the obstacles, President Morrin issued instructions to all New York Metropolitan local unions that all union members should seek employment and work for all contractors, whether they be union or open-shop . This technique was fantastically successful in getting Ironworkers employed on construction projects. There was plenty of work created by the nation's hungry demands for new massive structures. Much of

Members of Local No. 27, Salt Lake City, who are erecting the Bannock Hotel, Pocatello, Idaho.

this work, however, was in the employment of open-shop contractors. In shortly over two years of this organizing program, 98 percent of all employees engaged in the erection of structural steel, in the New York Metropolitan area, were members of the International Association. It was then concluded that the Ironworkers had achieved the strength needed to fight the massive forces of the steel industry.

On May 1, 1924, a mass meeting was held at the Cooper Union in New York City where President Morrin issued the call for a strike to obtain a wage increase from $10 to $12 per day, and for all work to be done in accordance with signed agreements between the local unions and all steel employers. Immediately, all employers, including the open-shop employers, agreed to the wage increase. However, the open-shop contractors refused to sign an agreement by which they would both recognize the Union and commit themselves to operate 100 percent union. The strike was on.

Members of Local No. 1 who erected two buildings for the Live Poultry Transit Company at 48th Street and Hoyne Avenue, in Chicago.

President Morrin, in addressing the 4,000 Ironworkers on Sunday, May 4 had urged "a clean and honorable fight" and pledged the assistance of the International Association throughout the nation. Members throughout the country answered the call, and contributions of a day's pay started to flow in. It appeared the fight was going to be won, and a victory would be shortly obtained against the interest of big steel in the area they were at their strongest.

As the strike dragged on, week after week, the picture began to change. The fourteen large firms, constituting the open-shop employers in their association known as the "Iron League," took two courses of action. One was to institute the litigation that was to drag on for years. The second was to try to open up their shops and commence erecting structural steel with non-union ironworkers. The combined dual action tied up all of the International and local officers in court activities while the employers shipped non-union workers into the New York area by the hundreds. Although, indeed, New York became a strike torn area, one by one the non-

union jobs commenced operating. The war then was spread to those contractors who had signed the union agreement. Curiously enough, the fair contractors began to experience a shortage of steel to fabricate and erect.

Accordingly, more and more Ironworkers, working for the union contractors, were laid off because of lack of work. Ironworker pickets claimed hired operators were attempting to incite violence and dissension on the picket lines. However, notwithstanding the source, the support by other unions for the Ironworker strike began to dwindle. The antagonism of the past disputes was being rekindled by the violence. In this set of circumstances, many of the members who had joined the Union in the two years of the organizing program began having doubts. They dropped their books and returned to the open-shop jobs. The 4,000 Ironworkers who had assembled on May 4, numbered only about 1,500 by the first of October.

While these conditions were developing on the job site, the litigation instituted in July proceeded. The open-shop employers sought an injunction for $5 million in damages against the local unions involved, as well as the International and all of the officers. The litigation on the question of the injunction alone went all the way to the Supreme Court, which finally denied the efforts to obtain a restraining order against the strike. When the litigation commenced, the Iron Workers countered by seeking an injunction against the Iron League in its effort to destroy the Union, and sought $10 million in damages. They also failed in their injunction efforts. This ended only the earlier injunctive efforts of the litigation which drew on for over nine years.

Near the end of 1923 and the first part of 1924, Local

*Brother **James G. Crowley** of Local No. 124, Tacoma, Washington, who died July 14, 1921. Brother Crowley was the first Secretary-Treasurer of the International being elected at Pittsburgh, Pennsylvania, in 1896 when the International was organized.*

Members of Local No. 20, Wheeling, West Virginia employed on Round House at Mingo Junction for the George A. Fuller Company.

Harry Jones
General Secretary-Treasurer

Union No.1 of Chicago was charged by the International Association of violating the International Constitution, therefore their charter was revoked. However, after several meetings which took a few months, Local No. 1 came to an agreement with the International to abide by the International Constitution. Accordingly, Local No. 1's charter was reinstated. Because only a few months lapsed, Local No. 1 did not loose their charter or their local number.

The **Twenty-Second International Convention** was held September 15-20, 1924 at the Hotel McAlpin in New York City. General President P. J. Morrin was reelected. Secretary-Treasurer Harry Jones was also reelected. All but two of the Nine Vice-Presidents were reelected without opposition. The other two were reelected after a run off election. George Ashley of Local 347, Windsor, Canada was elected Seventh Vice-President. George McTague of San Francisco was elect-

Members of Local No. 331, Clarkdale, Arizona who are erecting work there for the Kansas City Structural Steel Company.

ed Third Vice-President.

There were many issues confronting the delegates at the convention such as jurisdictional disputes, Old Age and Disability Pension, safety scaffold and building code laws, the New York strike, changes in the constitution, I.W.W. activities and the Ku Klux Klan. The delegates condemned the K.K.K. and passed a resolution to insert wording in the constitution that those members who are members of such organizations will be fined and then expelled.

William Green
elected President of the American Federation of Labor after the death of Samuel Gompers

On December 13, 1924, Samuel Gompers, President of the American Federation of Labor for a period of 41 years, died at 4:05 a.m. in San Antonio, Texas. He was interred in Sleepy Hollow Cemetery, Tarrytown, 25 miles north of New York. Gompers was born in London, England, on January 27, 1850. William Green, age 51 and Secretary of the United Mine Workers of America, was selected by the A.F. of L Executive Council to succeed the late Samuel Gompers as President of the A.F. of L. A new record in building construction totaling $5,750,000,000 was set in 1924.

On April 9, 1925, General President P. J. Morrin, acting under the Constitution and laws of the International suspended General Secretary-Treasurer Harry Jones for being delinquent and derelict in his official duties. As a result, Harry Jones was expelled from membership in the International. General Vice-President William J. McCain was appointed Acting General Secretary-Treasurer.

On April 8, 1927, Acting Secretary-Treasurer McCain sent **Circular Letter No. 421** to all affiliated local unions of the International Association regarding a

Hotel McAlpin, 33rd and 34th Streets, 6th Avenue and Broadway, New York which is Convention Headquarters.

Delegates to the Twenty-Second Convention, September, 1924 in New York City.

24th AF of L
Convention Badge
1924.

Members of Local No. 16 erected the Columbia Graphophone Building at Baltimore, Md. January, 1921.

Members of Locals No. 11, 30, 45 and 361, erecting Loew's State Theater, 48th Street and Broadway, New York, New York.

number of changes made by the General Executive Council. Some of these changes were as follows:

"That all ex-members who were members of any local union of our International Association on April 30, 1924, can be reinstated in any of our local unions upon application being made and upon the payment of all back dues and assessments, without the payment of a new initiation fee, with the exception of aggravated cases of ex-members, which cases shall be referred to the General Executive Board for their action and decision. This shall also apply to anyone who became a member since April 30, 1924, and who has permitted his membership to lapse."

"The standard initiation fee to all applicants of $25.00, as provided for in our International Constitution, shall prevail in all of our local unions without exception, plus an examining fee of not to exceed $2.50."

"No officer of any local union can issue a permit to a new member or member seeking reinstatement until applicant has appeared before the Examining Board, made application and qualified for membership."

"No member under the influence of intoxicants shall be allowed to attend any meeting of any of our local unions, and that any president, chairman or presiding officer who permitted an intoxicated member to attend or remain in the meeting of any of our local unions or District Councils, shall be fined the sum of $25.00; and that any member who persisted in attending or disturbing any of our meetings in an intoxicated condition, shall likewise be fined $25.00."

On October 14, 1927 former General President Frank M. Ryan died from a cerebral hemorrhage. At the time of Brother Ryan's death, President Morrin was in Los Angeles attending the A.F. of L. Convention and was unable to attend the funeral, however, he assigned several of the Vice-Presidents to attend. Local No. 1 draped their charter for the period of 30 days in recognition of Brother Ryan who was a charter member of that local.

While most of the International's energies were concentrated in the New York area, the International Workers of the World (I.W.W., called Wobblies) and "One Big Union" advocates were gaining strength on the west coast. A dual organization, known as the United Association of Bridge and

Frank M. Ryan,
fourth General President, who
died on October 14, 1927
from a cerebral hemorrhage.

Clockwise, from top: Vestibule for vault in New Federal Reserve Bank, Richmond, Va., installed by members of Local No. 28; Members of Local No. 292, South Bend, Ind., who are installing Truscon Steel Sash, and operators on the new Studebaker Foundry Building, South Bend, Indiana;"Just getting back up from lunch"; Members of Local No. 3 on West Virginia Paper Company Plant at Tyrone, Pa., in 1924; Members of Local No. 147, Fort Wayne, Ind., and job being done by the Forest City Steel Company. Business Agent Ora Gilliland is standing next to column on right.

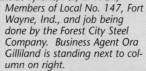

Structural Ironworkers, tried to take over the San Francisco Bay area just as the country was recovering from the depression and unemployment of the early 1920's. This organization sprang up after the International Executive Board was forced to revoke three charters in San Francisco and Oakland, as many other International Unions did to combat a wave of union radicalism. Before the charters were revoked, however, a handful of local leaders auctioned off the local unions' property, furniture, automobile, and a cemetery plot, valued at several thousand dollars, and sold them for one dollar. Within a few months the locals were reorganized, the dual union dissolved, and outlaw members reinstated. The division was settled, for a short time at least.

Farther up the Pacific Coast, shortly after the New York strike situation gathered momentum in 1924, new forces of dissension were stirring. Wobbly leaders took over a Seattle local of Ironworkers, and the so-called "Western District Council" was formed. This outlaw organization sought jurisdiction and control of all local unions in the West, and even endeavored to extend as far east as Montreal, Canada. Infiltration into other locals in the West was easy, for at that time a transfer card was equivalent to a passport into any Iron Worker local. The movement thus spread up and down the West Coast, and these workers soon became known as "White Card Ironworkers."

At the request of Seattle Ironworkers, who wished to remain loyal to the International, the Iron Worker Executive Council took the secession matter to court in order to protect the interest of the membership, their property, and their rights. The Seattle court not only ruled in favor of the International, but also rendered judgment against the secessionists. A former business agent of the Seattle Local was found in default of more than $8,000 to the Union. He was also the first President of the "Western District Council." Court action also proved effective in gaining back for Local 118 in Sacramento, its property, and its finances.

For several years, the "White Card Ironworkers" continued to operate along the West Coast. In April of

John H. Lyons, Local No. 17, elected First General Treasurer of the International Association, and his 1927-1937 membership book. Later he would be elected General Secretary and then General President.

1928, a conference of all the business agents of the Western local unions was held in San Francisco to work out plans and policies for the rehabilitation of the Union where outlaws had invaded the ranks. "A lenient and forgiving attitude" was adopted toward the "well-meaning but ill-advised former members," unlike the harsher attitudes of other International Unions who were also combating dual secessionist movements in their ranks. Later that year, 1928, the A. F. of L., the Building Trades Department, and the Metal Trades Department met in Los Angeles and decided to carry on an aggressive organizing effort up and down the West Coast, but especially in the San Francisco Bay District.

Within a year, most of the "White Card Ironworkers" were reinstated, and the gravest threat to Ironworker unity was dissolved.

W.J. McCain, Local No. 10, elected First General Secretary of the International Association

The **Twenty-Third International Convention** was held September 17-22, 1928 at the Hotel Missouri in St. Louis, P. J. "Paddy" Morrin was reelected General President. William J. McCain was elected to be the first **General Secretary** of the International Association (up to 1928 the International always had a Secretary-Treasurer). General Organizer John H. Lyons of Local No. 17 was elected to be the first **General Treasurer** of the International Association. **Later on, John H. Lyons Sr. would be elected General Secretary and then General President making him the only person to hold all three offices in the history of the International Association.**

At the convention the delegates upheld the action of the General Executive Board to expel J. J. McNamara, former Secretary-Treasurer of the International Association and up to June of 1927 he was the business agent and financial secretary of Local No. 22, Indianapolis, for submitting false audit reports. J. J. McNamara was supposed to appeal to the convention, however, he never appeared.

Members of Local No. 377 of San Francisco on Labor Day, 1925.

Delegates and visitors of the Twenty-Third Annual Convention, September 17-22, 1928 at St. Louis, Missouri.

International Officers, elected at the twenty-third convention. Standing, left to right, Vice Presidents John T. Fitzpatrick, Ben C. Pitts, B.J. Hiscock, Wm. H. Pope, J.A. Evensen, John M. Schilling, George McTague. Sitting, left to right: Vice President M.C. Artery, General Treasurer John H. Lyons, General President P.J. Morrin, General Secretary W.J. McCain and Vice President D.J. O'Shea.

Apprentices

Attention to Financial Secretaries

The attention of Local Union Financial Secretaries is called to Article 22 of the International Constitution, which is the article governing "APPRENTICES."

You will note that all apprentices must be registered at headquarters, and that they pay one-half the initiation fee paid by journeymen. The names of all apprentices should be sent to headquarters at once, and for each man a remittance of 10 per cent of the amount of their initiation fee sent in for their Initiation Stamp, also 30 cents for each member's book. The apprentices shall pay the same per capita tax as journeymen, have the same membership book, but it should be marked plainly "APPRENTICE," and the same monthly dues stamp must be used for them as is used for journeymen. Apprentices will be fully beneficial for death benefits as set forth in Article 16 of the International Constitution.

LABOR DAY, 1925

LABOR TOWERS ABOVE ALL

Note: The 1928 Convention had called for a big organizing campaign, which never took place because Morrin was injured on the day before Xmas in a train wreck and he was incapacitated for a long period. They tried to protect the little work they had by continuing to have organizers on the road. Also, an injunction was brought in the New York district in 1924 which prevented the International and its officers from soliciting contractors to sublet their steel erection to union concerns, and building owners were powerless to take action against contractors who were subletting their steel to non-union erectors in the New York district. Finally, an appeal was made and in August of 1932 the injunction was reversed. During the time of the injunction even the officers of the Union were subject to harassment and constant contempt proceedings and hearings which they always won.

Members of Local No. 81, Anaconda, Montana, at their annual banquet, held at Hotel Anaconda, January 10, 1925.

As outlaw Ironworkers were returning to the fold on the West Coast, and slow progress was being made in the unionization of the New York area, the stock market crashed, and the bust of the late 1920's gave way to bread lines in the early 1930's.

Initially, the 1929 stock market crash had little impact on employment of Ironworkers. From July 1, 1929, to June 30, 1930, the Union added 3,440 new members to its ranks, a gain comparable to the fiscal year preceding the crash. Financially the Union also prospered. On July 1, 1928, there was a total of approximately $647,000 in the treasury and approximately $652,000 four years later on July 1, 1932. While other international unions were experiencing wage reductions of 50 percent, the average reduction of all Ironworker locals amounted to 15.9 percent. Finally, the Iron Workers managed to secure two important working agreements. It appeared that the long struggle in the Metropolitan District of New York might be leading towards a settlement. A Union agreement for all bridge and structural steel erection was negotiated. A year later a Bridge Erector's Agreement went into effect covering the nation-wide jobs of fair contractors in the Structural Steel and Bridge Erectors' Association. Ironworkers took a wage reduction and worked six days a week so that these fair employers could compete with unfair contractors.

Depression and unemployment finally caught up with the Iron Workers within two years after the crash as building construction nearly came to a halt. Of course, all labor organizations suffered during this time, especially in the building trades. The Iron Workers lost nearly 50 percent of their paid membership, dropping to 14,504 men in good standing. Such a loss completely offset any gains made during the massive organizing campaign in the late 1920's. In spite of the deadly effects of the depression, nearly every Iron Worker local remained intact while the International sought work for them everywhere possible.

One of the largest projects under construction as the depression hit was the Merchandise Mart in

Cyclone Roller Coaster being erected at Palisade Park, Palisade, N.J., by members of Locals No. 11 and 42 in 1927.

Members of Local No. 27, Salt Lake City, who are erecting the Bannock Hotel, Pocatello, Idaho.

Member of Local No. 17 welding straps to steel window frames and overhead beam on Union Station in Cleveland, Ohio.

Fifty-four-ton generator being installed in Philadelphia, Pa., with members of Local No. 161.

Members of Local No. 7 working on the Mystic Dock job at Charlestown, Massachusetts.

Merchandise Mart being erected in Chicago by members of Local No. 1. This was the largest office building in the world.

Vault door being installed by York Safe and Lock Co. at Norristown, Pa., by members of Local No. 161.

Chicago, being built by Marshall Field & Company. It would be designed for Field's wholesale and manufacturing divisions which would occupy half of the building's 4 million square feet, equal to 100 acres. The company bragged that it would be the largest office building in the world, with the largest restaurant and radio station in the world (WBBM of NBC). More than 60,000 tons of structural steel was to be used in the structure, 29 million bricks, 5,500 windows, 1,350,000 cubic feet of concrete, and 200,000 square feet of Bedford stone and granite.

Members of Local No. 97, Vancouver, B.C. who topped out the Empress Hotel in Victoria, B.C. International General Organizer W.L. Yule is standing at the far right.

The structure would be built on 458 caissons over a site formerly occupied by the Northwestern Railroad Company.

The planning for the building began in March of 1927. Members of Local 1 would work on the construction which began on August 16, 1928. The country was still in a boom period at the time. Marshall Field & Company bragged that the cost of the building would be 35 million dollars. *The Bridgemen's Magazine* reprinted an article on the structure in October of 1929, the same month in which the economy would collapse.

"'*Wheelbarrows, shovels, handsaws, planes, chisels, and other builders' tools have succumbed to the mighty onslaught of the faster and more efficient products of the mechanistic age in the erection of the Merchandise Mart, the world's biggest business building, now being erected at Wells Street and the Chicago River.*"

"*Machines have displaced man power and hand tools, and as a result probably the greatest assortment of modern building equipment ever assembled on one building operation is employed on this great Chicago project.*"

A total of 2,500 workers were employed on this job, and they planned to have the building ready for its first occupants by May of 1930. There was no celebration when the building was finished. With an 18 million dollar mortgage the building and Marshall Field's wholesale business would lose money throughout the 1930's and early 1940's. In 1945, a combine headed by Joseph P. Kennedy would purchase the building, and it is still owned by the Kennedy family today.

As appeared in the October, 1995 issue of the IRONWORKER magazine

Eugene Debs-
A Fearless Leader
1855-1926

U.S. Labor Leader and
Socialist Candidate for President

This Fall marks the anniversary of the death of Eugene Victor Debs. Those who knew and worked with him in the American labor and socialist movements before World War I are now largely gone as well. And the nation's schoolbooks rarely treat his life in great detail.

In his own era, Deb's fame rested on two separate jail sentences he served in defense of his political principles. The first occurred in 1895 when Debs spent six months in jail after leading railroad workers during the great Pullman strike of 1894.

Debs's second term in jail occurred more that twenty years later.

Indicted and later convicted on charges of violating the Espionage Act of 1917, Debs served three years of a ten year sentence in Atlanta Federal Penitentiary. In 1920, while still in jail, Debs ran for the fifth time as the Socialist Party's presidential candidate. On a testament of support and affection for the working class activist, nearly a million Americans cast their ballots for the imprisoned Debs.

Debs was born in Terre Haute, Indiana on November 5, 1855 and grew to adulthood in a society that proclaimed equality of opportunity for all, regardless of family position. His early involvement with the craft unions among railroad workers seemed to encourage that promise.

In his own day, of course, most workers did not follow Debs in the socialist movement. Yet he remained a key figure for workers, applauded both for his willingness to defend workers' rights and to speak frankly of problems within working-class organizations.

Addressing the difficulties facing workers in his day, Debs stated before a Utah audience that he would not want working people to follow him blindly. He insisted: "You must use your heads as well as your hands, and get yourselves out of your present condition." That ultimate faith in the effectiveness of an active and energetic union membership remains one of Eugene Debs' greatest legacies.

Chapter Six

The Depression and a New Deal For Labor 1930-1940

At first the Crash of 1929 had little impact on our Union because many construction jobs were still in demand for Ironworkers to complete jobs. While Wall Street was referring to the collapse of the economy as a "Wall Street Readjustment" many workers were seeing their wages cut by as much as 50%, however, our members only had their wages cut by 15.9%. The prediction of 1930 was that there would be nine billion dollars worth of new construction with two billion of this being in the public sector. However, by 1931, two years after the crash, construction stopped and our membership dropped by 50 percent. Only 14,504 members remained in good standing.

On November 30, 1930, famous labor crusader "Mother" Jones died at the age of 100. She was a very close friend of the Iron Workers. During her entire lifetime she was in the forefront of labor struggles, cheering and inspiring men and women to fight for the cause of organized labor. Her motherly interests were for the rights of the coal miner, and her protest was against the abuses to which they were subjected under the old company store system. Mine operators, with this system placed in their hands, had complete control over the coal miner's personal, family, educational and spiritual affairs. She was also a member of the Knights of Labor. In 1891, at the age of 61, she participated in a mine strike where she saved a miners' organizer and herself from the company gunmen who were going to kill them. "Mother" Jones, using her Irish wit, convinced the gunmen to let them go.

Members of Local No. 63, Chicago, Illinois, working on the Navy Pier job.

"Mother" Jones

"Mother" Jones' career traces nearly every page of the tough struggles of the American Labor movement. Ludlow, Colorado, Cabin Creek, West Virginia, the American Railway Union Strike, Homestead, all tragedies of the American working class, saw her in the fray. The great steel strike of 1919 was her last great venture, when she was one of a hundred organizers thrown into the fray against the steel trust. She was nominated to be one of "the 12 greatest women in the United States," and sponsored as one of the "six greatest women the world had ever known."

Passage of the Davis-Bacon Act

In the March, 1931 issue of the *Bridgemen's Magazine* the heading on the title page read, "Government Approves Prevailing Wage Rate." This was the Davis-Bacon Act that provided for the payment of prevailing wages to our members and all other workers employed by contractors or subcontractors on public construction. The conservative President Hoover signed this bill, which continued to be supported by both Republican and Democratic presidents until 1995 when

Labor officials meet with President Hoover at the White House in 1931. General President P.J. Morrin is **shown 2nd from right.**

Reading from left to right are John Dempsey, Jr., business agent, Local No. 44 and future General Treasurer of the International Association; J.W. Smith, general superintendent for Sterrett; John Finn, general foreman of rod work, and Organizer Luchsinger. They were at the Carew Tower job on May 13, 1930 to make sure the Ironworkers returned to work after a strike.

it would be under attack by conservative Republican members of Congress.

John P. Frey, Secretary-Treasurer of the Metal Trades Department of the A.F. of L. wrote the following, which appeared in the *Bridgemen's Magazine:*

> *"If some of the money now being given as charity to the unemployed had been placed in the pay envelopes where it properly belonged, there would be much less unemployment and fewer soup lines."*

President Morrin and the other members of the Executive Council of the Building Trades Department of the A.F. of L. conferred with President Hoover. They urged the President to maintain the present wage scales in the country against the attempts of management to decrease wages. They presented a letter stressing that the purchasing power of the public must not be impaired. William Green, President of the A.F. of L., also urged at this time that legislation be passed for the 5-day week. Even William Randolph Hearst was proposing that with the demand and supply of manpower out of balance, American industry should immediately consider ways and means of adjusting itself to the six-hour day.

By October of 1931 the situation was becoming even worse with an estimated 7 million unemployed. The Executive Council of the A.F. of L. urged that wage levels be maintained, that workers be given shorter hours, that jobs be created through public works, that employment agencies be set up,

The Bridge Men's Magazine

Vol XXX   APRIL, 1930   No. 4

Published by
The International Association of
Bridge, Structural & Ornamental
Iron Workers

Canadian Bank of Commerce, Toronto, Canada.

and that young people should be kept in school longer.

An article in the *Bridgemen's Magazine* suggested that the unemployment situation among Ironworkers could be solved by building elevated highways over the railways in congested sections of major American cities such as Detroit, Chicago, Buffalo, and New York. A "National Elevated Toll Highway System" would be financed by the sale of bonds similar to those "Liberty Bonds" sold during World War I.

In March of 1932, it was announced that the Iron Workers and 43 other International Unions of the A.F. of L. along with the American Legion and other organizations had formed the United Action for Employment Campaign. Also in 1932, the International announced that it was successful in getting almost all the former members who were associated in the "white-card" movement back into membership.

During this period of such mass unemployment the Carpenters Union announced they were breaking their agreement with the Iron Workers. This agreement regarding jurisdiction had been entered into back in January of 1920. The Carpenters announced that beginning July 1, 1931 the agreement was no longer in effect. Our International did reach an agreement with the Elevator Constructors' International Union.

By June of 1932 the *Bridgemen's Magazine* reported that the country's unemployment rate had reached 11 million. By this time thousands of homes across the country were being sold to cover unpaid taxes. The Iowa State

Members of Local No. 12, Albany, New York, working on the National Savings Bank Building.

Members of Local No. 32 working for Kansas City Bridge Co. at Duluth, Minnesota in 1930.

Federation of Labor postponed its 1932 convention until 1933 since they felt the money could be better spent to give relief to the unemployed. The California State Building Trades Council decided not to have their convention for the first time in 31 years in order to save money. William Green, AF of L President, was concerned that many unions were planning to abandon regular Labor Day parades, meetings, and addresses in 1932. Green felt such events must take place to help the public to learn labor's story. At the same time, the *Bridgemen's Magazine* printed a story in July of 1932 about the wealth of one family alone...the Mellons. Their wealth of 8 billion dollars was greater than all the money in the United States Treasury.

In order to create jobs, our union recommended the repeal of Prohibition and the Volstead Act which limited the alcoholic content of beer. Seven breweries in St. Louis said they were prepared to spend 10 million dollars on

The welding crew.

Members of Local No. 424, erecting a storage building in 1930, for General Electric in Bridgeport, Connecticut. This is a five story job where Ironworkers welded all the steel - no rivets were used. Two-thirds of the steel was fabricated on the job.

new construction and re-employ 6,000 men if the law was repealed.

The **Twenty-Fourth Convention** of the Iron Workers was held September 19-24, 1932 in St. Louis, Missouri at the Jefferson Hotel. General President P.J. Morrin, General Secretary W.J. McCain and General Treasurer J.H. Lyons were reelected to office. Also nine General Vice Presidents were elected.

The delegates adopted a new Pension and Disability plan at the Convention since the funds were almost depleted. The action of the convention was necessitated by the fact that our organization could no longer pay the pension benefits provided by the old law without financial disaster to the organization as a whole. The important features of the new pension law were as follows:

1. The Pension Fund shall consist of monies collected from the sale of monthly pension fund stamps to all of our members at the rate of 50 cents each.

2. The payment of pension benefits from this fund shall be divided equally each month among members eligible to receive them. In other words, the pension fund will be pro-rated and only the amount of receipts collected from the sale of pension fund stamps will be paid out in pension benefits.

3. In order to be eligible to apply for old age pension benefits a member has to be sixty-five years of age and have twenty-five years continuous membership in our organization.

4. In order to be eligible to apply for disability pension benefits a member has to have twenty years continuous membership in our organization and has to be permanently disabled.

5. No member on the pension roll shall receive over $1,000 in pension benefits. When that amount has been received by a member he is automatically retired from the pension roll.

6. Any member who is able to work, whether at the iron workers' trade or at any occupation, is not eligible to receive pension benefits.

7. Any member whose revenue from any source

Ironworkers at the Overland Construction Company job in Toledo, Ohio, 1930.

Bart Foley, *member of Local No. 396, St. Louis, Missouri, is shown with all-leather bolt bag which he was making for the brothers around St. Louis, Missouri in November, 1930.*

Another safety measure used exclusively by "The Overland Construction Company" who has the patent on this device. They advertised in the Bridgemen's Magazine that there will be no more kinking of column slings, no more cutting of slings on sharp edges of columns, no more climbing of columns to release slings - always safe - always sure - column always hangs plumb.

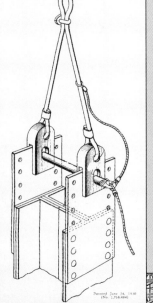

Cedar St. Bridge job at Peoria, Illinois by members of Local No. 112 in September, 1930. The total length is 2071 feet, 10 inches.

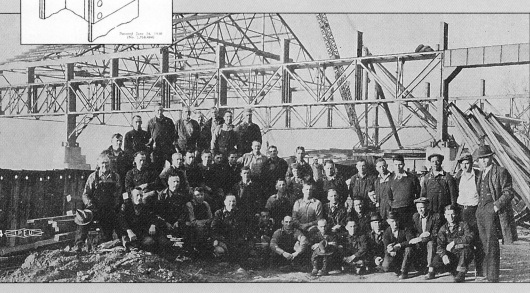

E. Meade Johnson river Rail Terminal job in 1930, being erected by members of Local No. 103. C.H. (Memphis) Kelly, general steel foreman; Harry Juncker, derrick foreman; J.T. Craven, pile driver foreman; C.A. Benderman and J.W. Morgan in charge of filling in and detail gangs. L.G. Williamson, steward on the job.

Delegates attending the Twenty-Fourth International Convention September 19-24, 1932 at St. Louis, Missouri.

whatever amounts to $30.00 or more per month is not eligible to receive pension benefits.

Among the important actions taken by the 24th Convention was to increase the initiation fee for membership from $25.00 to $100.00 except ex-members and applicants who have been guilty of infractions of trade union rules, and principles and conditions, in which case a special initiation fee may be provided not to exceed a maximum of $200.00.

In his report to the convention, President Morrin pointed out that the American Federation of Labor had decided that each trade should do the welding in connection with its own work, and that if the Ironworkers were going to keep pace with the times, it was up to the International to see that affiliate local unions were in a position to furnish capable and competent men that knew how to weld.

Conditions In Canada For Iron Worker Locals

President Morrin in October of 1932 reported that the conditions for Canadian workers at this time were as difficult as those in the United States. The International Association exempted the members of the Canadian

1932 Convention Badge.

local unions, whose wage scale was less than $1.00 per hour, from paying the International $2.00 assessment. The non-union steel erecting firms in Canada had reduced the wages of Ironworkers, which the International and the Canadian local unions resisted in every way possible even to the extent of appealing to the Provincial Government officials against the unfair tactics of these non-union firms. These reductions necessarily affected the fair Canadian firms because they continued to pay the union scale of wages and, in doing this, placed themselves in a position where they were unable to compete on a fair basis with non-union firms in securing work for the members of the Iron Workers.

Norris-LaGuardia Act of 1932

Until the signing of this Act, an employer experiencing a strike or picket line or demonstration against them on their property, had only to state his case to a Judge and the Courts would blindly issue an "Injunction" against Labor. This Act greatly narrowed the courts' ability to prohibit "peaceful picketing, peaceable assembly, organizational picketing, payment of strike benefits, and a host of other economic weapons that were almost illegal up until then." The Act

P.J. Morrin,
General President

William J. McCain,
General Secretary

John H. Lyons,
General Treasurer

Ironworkers Ride the Rails

In 1976, Brother R.E. "Dick" Gautney, Local No. 477, Sheffield, Alabama wrote to the editor of The *Ironworker Magazine* (formerly the *Bridgemen's Magazine*) about Ironworkers during the "Great Depression" of the 1930's. During this period, the magazine contained a complete list of all the jobs in the United States. It gave the name of the erector, the total tons, cost, and job location. He said "this information was a lifesaver for a large segment of our membership in those days."

Local Unions were scattered in those days, sometimes 800 miles apart. Most business agents worked on a job. A few of the members owned a Model A or T Ford, but usually could not afford gas, therefore, they used the "Oklahoma Courtesy Card," namely a siphon hose. This name was given the siphon hose by the Okies who migrated to California following the great dust storms of the thirties.

Most of the Ironworkers did their traveling by **freight train** which was very hazardous - they "Rode the Rails." Most or all structural steel was riveted at that time. A riveting gang usually traveled together. A gang was composed of four men. Others traveled in pairs. The usual procedure for seeking a job was to consult *"The Bridgemen's Magazine"* and pick a place to work. After deciding, they made their plans for an extended stay. They would carry their "suitcase" on their back. That is, they would wear all the clothes they owned. These consisted of a pair of khaki pants, a white shirt worn under a blue denim shirt, blue overalls, and a blue denim jumper or coat. If they found a job, the khaki pants and white shirt would be their dress clothes, the rest their work clothes.

The Ironworkers would walk to the nearest railroad. Most of the trains ran on steam, therefore the engines had to have water. So the Ironworkers would make their way to the water tank, being very careful to stay out of sight. Usually they hid in the weeds that grew beside the track. It seemed as if the Lord provided for his own by placing those weeds beside all railroad tracks. The reason they were so careful to stay hidden was there were some thoroughly bad "Railroad Bulls," slang for Railroad Police. Some of these men enjoyed beating up a hobo. There was "Texas Slim," "Hardrock Hardin," "Frisco Kid," "Big Charlie," and a host of others just as tough.

Besides the railroad police, Ironworkers had to dodge a host of sheriffs and town marshals. Most all states and towns recruited the labor for their farms, roads and chain-gangs off the railroads. If the men caught the train, and were lucky enough to get inside an empty car, they would have some protection from the rain and cold. One thing a man had to watch when he was "riding the rails" was his company. Sometimes there were murderers, cutthroats, prostitutes, pickpockets and honest working men all in the same car.

Upon reaching their destination, they learned the job was a short distance from town. They knew they would find a meal that night. All "Hobo Jungles" or "Camps" always had a pot of stew on the fire which was free to all. The ingredients were usually bummed. Usually the folks working on the job furnished the smoking tobacco. Even when getting to the job-site, the Ironworker boomer, in many instances, had to wait to go to work until someone got fired or fell. They would continue to camp on the river bank as long as there was hope of going to work. They used the river for their laundry, a campfire for a dryer. If it was cold they wrapped themselves in newspaper to sleep. If it rained, they would sleep under a bridge. If it snowed, they usually would seek asylum in the nearest jail.

Once an Ironworker got a job, the pay was usually low and the accident list was high. Some of the larger companies did not allow smoking on their jobs. They would fire a man for smoking about as quick as they would for not working. The "New Deal" dams had their own camps, often called "slab towns." They got their name because they were made of slabs of lumber. Gamblers, bootleggers and prostitutes followed the large construction jobs. The young members of today should know about the tough times the Ironworkers had during the "Great Depression" when many of them had to "Ride the Rails."

End view of U.S. Dirigible hanger being erected at Sunnyvale, California, with excellent view of portable derrick in center. This hanger was being erected by members of Locals No. 377 (San Francisco) and 378 (Oakland).

also outlawed "yellow dog" contracts which required workers to swear they would not join a union before being hired.

It was the first great piece of federal legislation for unions. It did not do much to demand that employers recognize the collective bargaining system, but it surely set the tone that it was now necessary for Congress, in the future, to guarantee "full freedom of association, self-organization, and designation of representatives of his or her own choosing, to negotiate the terms and conditions of his or her employment..free from interference, restraint, or coercion of employers."

Conditions Grow Worse in Early 1933

President Franklin Delano Roosevelt would not take office until March 4, 1933. During January and February, while Hoover was still President, the situation got worse with over 15 million workers unemployed and the International membership dropped to 10,318. When Roosevelt was sworn into the Presidency, he immediately went into action. What would follow were the famous "Hundred Days" (March 9 to June 16, 1932).

Among early measures FDR introduced was the **National Industrial Recovery Act,** generally called the NRA, which sought to stabilize industry under a system of fair wage and price codes. The object of the law was to halt the downward economic cycle which fed on price and wage cutting. Section 7(a) of the NRA gave workers the legal right to organize into unions of their own selection. While the section had no real legal teeth and employer resistance soon developed, Section 7(a) was instrumental in setting the stage for dramatic advances for working people.

Frances Perkins, Secretary of Labor

"Madame Perkins," as she was known, was appointed on March 4, 1933 as Secretary of Labor. This was the same day that Roosevelt took the oath of office. She would be the first woman ever appointed to a presidential cabinet. Labor was at first concerned since she was not out of the labor movement. She had been a social worker and later an industrial commissioner of the State of New York.

What a Secretary of Labor she became! In early 1934 she would make her recommendations to Congress and the *Bridgemen's Magazine* printed them in February of that year. Among the things she suggested were an employment service, a mediation service, unemployment insurance, low cost housing, more concern for worker safety, old-age insurance, higher wages, an end to child labor and the right of workers to organize. Some of these things had been established as temporary measures. Secretary Perkins wanted them to be permanent. Labor Secretary Perkins was instrumental in the passage of the **Wagner-Peyser Act** which created the United States Employment Service in the Department of Labor. In early 1934 she sent a letter of appreciation to General President Morrin and the readers of the *Bridgemen's Magazine* for the support given her.

The General Executive Council of the International Association, because of the Depression, took action to lower the Standard Initiation Fee and Reinstatement Fee from $100.00 to $25.00 effective July 1, 1933. General President Morrin stated that "due to unemployment a large number of members of our organization have permitted their cards to lapse, many through no fault of their own, as they were unable to secure work at our trade during the terrible dull period from which we are now emerging." This action was in effect until December 31, 1933.

Ironworkers, especially President Morrin and General Counsel Frank P. Walsh, were leaders in New

"DON'T TELL ME IT ISN'T WORKING."

NRA

SECRETARY PERKINS
REPORTS
$40,000,000
GAINS IN WEEKLY
PAYROLLS

2,2000,000
PUT BACK TO WORK
IN LAST 5 MONTHS.

750,000
RETURN TO
JOBS DURING
AUGUST.

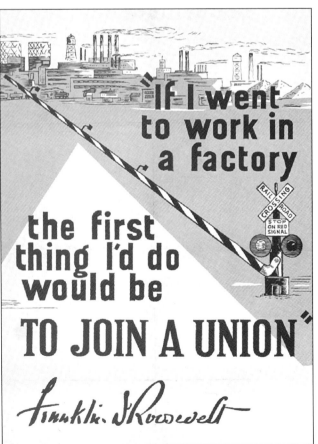

"If I went to work in a factory

the first thing I'd do would be

TO JOIN A UNION"

Franklin D Roosevelt

Deal efforts to get labor back on its feet again. On July 10, 1933, the Executive Board renewed the Bridge Erectors' agreement and revised it to cover building and other forms of iron and steel erection. This revised agreement served as a model for a proposed "Code for the Structural Steel Fabrication and Erection Industries" under provisions made by the National Recovery Administration in 1933. The Code, if passed, would have unionized the steel industry at a critical time, but apparent pressure from anti-union forces prevented formal action.

General President Morrin was so impressed with Roosevelt that he wrote a column in the August, 1933 issue of the *Bridgemen's Magazine* titled the "Nation Should Rise Up as One Man in Support of the President." It praised him for the National Recovery Act, especially that part which stated that workers had:

> "...the right to organize and bargain collec-
> tively through representatives of their own
> choosing and shall be free from interference,
> restraint or coercion of employers of labor or
> their agents...."

In another editorial in February of 1934, Morrin pointed out the difference between Hoover and Roosevelt. While Hoover had given money to the big corporations through loans from the RFC, Roosevelt provided funds from the bottom to the workers to increase buying power and to get the factories running again.

On April 30, 1934, the International Association granted a charter for Local No. 454, Casper, Wyoming because of the enormous work that was going on or pending in the uranium and oil industries. The original signers were from Casper, Wyoming with Paul Morgan as the first President and Roy C. Koenig as the first Business Agent of Local No. 454.

The Century of Progress Exposition: Chicago, 1933

Although unemployment was bad in Chicago, many Chicago building trades workers had been busy since 1928 on construction of the "Century of Progress Exposition." The *Bridgemen's Magazine* for several years had been printing articles by the Chicago Federation of Labor telling workers from other parts of the country not to come to Chicago, because there was only enough work for their men. In 1931 and 1933, the only construction going on in Chicago was the World's Fair Building and the Field Building in the Loop. The Century of Progress opened on May 27, and would remain open until November 1933. At the request of President Roosevelt it was reopened again in 1934.

Building Trades Board

On January 31, 1934, General President P.J. Morrin was appointed to the Construction Industry Planning and Adjustment Board which was considered one of the most important agencies set up under the construction industry code. This board was charged with responsibility for the planning and the development of policies that embraced the broad spirit of cooperation and good will in the promotion of better relations between employers and employees within the industry, and the furtherance of other matters of mutual employer-employee interest.

President Roosevelt suggested that the Board make a study of trade jurisdictional disputes, their causes and origins, and methods for their prevention and amicable solution. Its findings and recommendations were to be submitted to the President for consideration and appropriate action.

When the Supreme Court declared the National Industrial Recovery Act unconstitutional on May 27, 1935, the General Executive Board, through Representative Reuben T. Wood of the Sixth Missouri District, a former President of the State Federation of Labor for 25 years, introduced House Bill 12499 to the Seventy-fourth Congress. The bill was intended "to stabilize the structural steel fabricating and erection industry; to prevent monopoly conditions and practices therein; to provide for the general welfare; and for other purposes." This bill, however, was apparently held up in the Committee on Interstate and Foreign Commerce, and Congress adjourned before action could be taken. Meanwhile, other government projects, such as the Tennessee Valley Authority (TVA) and public works projects, put many unemployed Ironworkers back on the job, increasing wages as well as membership. By 1935 the Iron Workers had at least partially recovered from the terrible depression.

In the mid-1930's a "kick-back" racket was investigated by the Committee on Education and Labor. It was discovered that contractors were evading the law by forcing the worker to pay for his job by making deductions directly from his pay envelope. A worker on the Chicago Post Office construction project had to "kick-back" $472.50 in order to hold his job.

Finally, Congress passed the "Anti-Kick-Back Law" which provided a fine of not more than $5,000 or imprisonment for not more than five years, or both. But it would not be until May of 1935 that the first twelve contractors on government jobs would be found guilty.

Works Progress Administration (WPA) April 5, 1935

By February of 1936, 12.5 million would be employed on Federal jobs under the WPA program. Harry L. Hopkins, WPA Administrator, stated that "not one worker in a hundred has shown preference for relief rather than work."

The National Labor Relations Act or Wagner Act

The National Labor Relations (Wagner) Act, which passed on July 5, 1935, guaranteed the right of certain employees to freedom in self-organization, the designation of representatives of their own choosing for the purpose of collective bargaining.

In addition, it prohibits employers from interfering with the right of employees to join a union, interfering with any labor organization, to discriminate in hiring or firing, or to refuse to bargain collectively. The provisions of this act were amended in 1947. As early

as 1934, Senator Wagner saw the need to put teeth in the labor provisions of the National Recovery Act. A group of 58 lawyers working for the pro-management "Liberty League" called the Wagner Act unconstitutional. The bill passed the Senate after two days of debate by a margin of 63-12. There was an attempt by Senator Tydings of Maryland for an amendment to allow company unions but it was defeated 50 to 21.

First Shopmen's Local Union Organized on West Coast

On August 9, 1935, a Charter was granted to Shopmen's Local No. 472, San Francisco, California. This was the first shop local on the West Coast. It was organized by General Organizer Charles (Doc) Lyon, who would become the semi-official head of the Shop Division, even before the Shop Division was formally organized at Headquarters in 1950.

Social Security Act Passed on August 14, 1935

This act and its subsequent amendments provide insurance to certain wage earners for loss of income due to unemployment or old age, and provides certain benefits for the protection for their families in the event of death. The employer and the employee make equal contributions to provide for these benefits under the act. Twelve regional offices were set up. It would not be until May 24, 1937 that both the old age annuity and the unemployment insurance sections of the law would be declared constitutional by the Supreme Court. Before this Federal legislation, only one state, Wisconsin, provided unemployment insurance.

The Founding of the Congress of Industrial Organizations (CIO)

The Committee for Industrial Organization (later the Congress of Industrial Organizations) was formed on November 9, 1935 by several AF of L International unions and officials to foster industrial unionism.

On August 5, 1936 the Executive Council of the AF of L called upon the organizations holding membership in the CIO to make their choice within 30 days as to whether they would withdraw from affiliation with the AF of L or discontinue their membership in the Committee for Industrial Organization. On Sept. 5, 1936 they recognized the CIO as a rival to the AF of L. There were 102 Internationals still remaining in the AF of L. Just as the steel companies had been hostile to the Iron Workers over the years, they continued to be hostile to this new labor organization.

The **Twenty-Fifth International Convention** was held September 21-26, 1936 at the Jefferson Hotel in St. Louis, Missouri. Once again, P.J. Morrin was reelected General President, W.J. McCain was reelected General Secretary and J.H. Lyons was reelected General Treasurer. The following individuals were elected General Vice President:

J. Arthur Evensen	First Vice-President
William H. Pope	Second Vice-President
John T. Fitzpatrick	Third Vice-President
Dan M. Gayton	Fourth Vice-President
William F. Bauers	Fifth Vice-President
Thomas L. Chambers	Sixth Vice-President
Joseph F. Boyen	Seventh Vice-President
Gay Borrelli	Eighth Vice-President
B.A. Murray	Ninth Vice-President

At the convention, the delegates unanimously adopted a resolution which provided that all corrugated sheeting be handled by **apprentices** from unloading point to the mechanics.

In his report to the 25th Convention General President P.J.Morrin stated that, "In spite of the unemployment condition we were successful in increasing our total membership for the four-year period ending June 30, 1936, to 17,222 members, or a gain of 2,718 members during that period. When it is taken into consideration that the depression continued severely during the first three years, I consider that we have made good progress as it has only been during the past year that our members have become fairly well employed. If working conditions improve, I feel that by carrying on an aggressive effort to organize the capable and competent men of our trade and to bring about the reinstatement of former members that we shall be able to build up our organization considerably." The International funds had been $651,704 in 1932 and had gone down $10,240. Morrin considered that the organization was holding its own financially.

While Iron Workers had agreed at the worst time in the depression to take less wages (an average of 15.9% cuts) hoping this would help the situation, it had only made things worse. In 1936, the convention felt the work week should be shortened and wages go up. They were hoping for the passage of the Black Bill which mandated a "thirty-hour week"

The officers of the Union had also taken a 20% pay cut by putting that amount into the Pension and Death Benefit Funds. But even then this fund was being depleted and changes were made. By 1936 things were better.

The International launched a campaign to organize the shopmen in the bridge, structural steel and ornamental iron shops, but they had to fight the big steel companies that feed propaganda to the workers in these shops. General President Morrin determined that shop

Convention Badge delegates wore at the 1936 International Convention.

ironworkers needed a different dues schedule since wages were low. He pointed out that the International laws, constitution, regulations, initiation fees, per capita tax and benefits, as well as rules, were all designed for those engaged in field and construction work. General President Morrin recommended to the delegates attending the 25th Convention that a Conference for Shop Representatives be held in order to discuss Constitutional changes relative to shop Ironworkers. The delegates concurred with President Morrin's recommendation and unanimously adopted Resolution No. 25 which authorized the International Association to hold such a Conference.

Then came the CIO which also wanted to organize the shopmen. Morrin wrote letters protesting to John L. Lewis of the CIO, M.F. Tighe, President of the Amalgamated Association of Iron, Steel, and Tin Workers, and AFL President William Green. In his letter to the Mine Workers he pointed out how they had given aid to workers in the 1919 steel strike, and that the Iron Workers had been suffering for years from U.S. Steel and Bethlehem Steel.

At a Conference held for 150 General Organizers and Special Representatives, the International Association decided to challenge the CIO and agreed to launch a campaign to organize shop workers beginning April 1, 1937. General President Morrin stated "While there had never been a let-down in our organizing work, both among the structural workers and in the fabricating shops, we are confident that the time has now arrived for an intensive campaign to organize the 75,000 or more men employed in fabricating shops all over the country, and it has been decided to send 100 organizers into this field. These organizers are bona-fide members of our International Association and the only aid we expect from outside of our own ranks will be the assistance that has been volunteered to us by William Green, president of the American Federation of Labor; John P. Frey, president of the Metal Trades Department, and James W. Williams, president of the Building Trades Department."

By the end of April, 50 shop locals were chartered and by the end of July the number grew to 72. The campaign was later extended to the end of the year. In January, 1938 the organizing campaign was going so well it was extended for 6 more months. Morrin reported that, "It was decided to spend approximately 750,000 dollars to carry out the program."

National Apprenticeship Law is Enacted

On August 16, 1937 Congress passed the National Apprenticeship Act commonly known as the "Fitzgerald Act". The purpose of the Act is "to promote the furtherance of labor standards of apprenticeship...to extend the application of such standards by encouraging the inclusion thereof in contracts of apprenticeship, to bring together employers and labor for the formulation of programs of apprenticeship, to cooperate with State agencies in the formulation of standards of apprenticeship."

The Fitzgerald Act of 1937 set the pattern for today's system of Federal Government assistance in apprenticeship programs. The Federal Committee on Apprenticeship was organized to include equal representation of employers, labor and public members. The Apprentice Training Service (now the Bureau of Apprenticeship and Training) was established as the national administrative agency in the Department of Labor to carry out the objectives of the law, guided by the recommendations of the Federal Committee on Apprenticeship. General Vice President Raymond J. Robertson was appointed by three Secretaries of Labor (Elizabeth Dole, Lynn Martin and Robert Reich) to serve on the Federal Committee on Apprenticeship. He was elected as Labor Vice Chair of the Committee and in 1996 he is still serving in that capacity.

The Fair Labor Standards Act or Wage and Hours Law

This legislation passed on June 25, 1938 provided for most employees of firms engaged in producing goods for interstate commerce a minimum hourly wage, and time and one half the minimum hourly rate for all hours worked in excess of forty per week. The act prohibited the employment of children under the age of sixteen by industries considered to be engaged in interstate commerce.

Delegates attending the Twenty-Fifth International Convention, September 21-26 at St. Louis, Missouri., in 1936.

Postmaster General James A. Farley congratulating General President P.J. Morrin on eve of his departure for Blackpool, England where he will serve as delegate from the AFL to the British Trades Union Congress.

William J. McCain, who passed away September 8, 1939

Local No. 44, Cincinnati, Ohio, for 10 years, as General Treasurer. These appointments received the unanimous approval of the General Executive Council.

In February, 1940, President Morrin advised the membership through the *Bridgemen's Magazine* that the Public Works Administration (PWA) was drawing to a close and urged the members to write to their Senators and Congressmen to appropriate additional monies to keep this program going. It was pointed out that over six billion dollars had been spent to provide highways, bridges, schools, hospitals and other construction projects. Over 7,500,000 unemployed workers were given jobs under the PWA.

The **Twenty-Sixth International Convention** was held September 16-21, 1940 at the Hotel Jefferson in St. Louis, Missouri. P.J. Morrin was reelected General President. General Secretary John H. Lyons and General Treasurer John J. Dempsey, who were appointed in 1939 after the death of General Secretary McCain, were elected to these positions. General President Morrin reported to the delegates that the situation during

General Treasurer John H. Lyons Appointed General Secretary

The International Association sustained a desolating loss on Friday morning, September 8, 1939, when the word came to International Headquarters in St. Louis of the death of General Secretary William J. McCain. Inasmuch as the General Executive Council was then in formal session in St. Louis from September 12-18, 1939, inclusive, having returned from Brother McCain's funeral, President Morrin decided it would be best to fill the vacancy caused by General Secretary McCain's death at once. After giving the matter full consideration and acting under his authority, provided under Article IX, Section 20 of the International Constitution, President Morrin appointed General Treasurer Lyons as General Secretary (effective on October 1, 1939). Lyons resigned as General Treasurer at which time, President Morrin appointed **John J. Dempsey**, who had been the business agent of

John H. Lyons

100

The Death of
General Counsel Frank P. Walsh

Frank P. Walsh, the first General Counsel for the Iron Workers died on Tuesday May 2, 1939 at the age of 75. President Morrin said, "The International Association in particular and the American Labor Movement in general has suffered, through his passing, the loss of a man, whom I firmly believe did more during his lifetime to advance the cause of the working man than any other outside the Union Labor Movement itself. Mr. Walsh served the International for almost twenty years.

Frank P. Walsh,
General Counsel of the
International Association, 1918-1939

Frank Walsh was appointed by President Wilson to serve as Chairman of the United States Industrial Relations Commission. He served on the War Labor Board as joint chairman with former President William H. Taft."

The International Association has had three General Counsels between the years 1919 and 1996. Their role in representation of the International Union has not been the same because of the tremendous change in all aspects of life in the United States and Canada during this period. As an example, when Frank Walsh assumed the duties of General Counsel, the population was much less than it is today. At that time there were virtually no laws dealing with labor management in either country except those that were repressive of union activities and, indeed, in many areas of both countries, unions were illegal and were considered to be criminal enterprises.

At the beginning of the Walsh era, a very substantial proportion of the population of both countries worked on the farm and lived in rural communities. Under these circumstances, the activities of the General Counsel were to guide the Union in its internal institutional legal needs and to be conversant with criminal laws, constitutional matters and contract law.

The subsequent history of North America saw the great depression, World War II, labor shortages, several post war depressions, two major wars...Korea and Viet Nam and the enormous change in Eastern Europe which took place in the 1990's. The impact on the labor movement is reflected in the legal structure of the two countries with the passage of the social legislation of the 1930's including the Wagner Act, the Norris-LaGuardia Act and the National Recovery Act, followed by anti-repressive and anti-labor legislation such as Taft-Hartley and Landrum-Griffin and an absolute technological revolution which has transformed North America.

Thus, General Counsels had to become specialists in all the statutory labor law at the Federal, State and Provincial levels; international labor laws, including matters dealing with NAFTA and GATT, constitutional contract and criminal laws and laws dealing with trust funds before and after ERISA. Today the population of the United States and Canada is much greater and the workforce has been fed by internal growth and immigration from other countries.

Against this background a brief history of the two General Counsels that followed Frank Walsh is set forth below:

After the death of Frank Walsh in 1939, General President Morrin retained Harold Stern, born July 20, 1902 in New York City. He was admitted to the New York Bar on October 9, 1924. In 1925 General Counsel Frank Walsh invited Mr. Stern to join him in his law practice. Through his association with Mr. Walsh's law firm, Harold Stern began to work for the Iron Workers. During his long and distinguished career as an attorney, Mr. Stern exclusively represented labor unions. In addition to representing this International Association, he represented many of the Building Trades Unions in the New York City area and in particular Local Union No. 3 of the IBEW. One of his greatest accomplishments was his role in the Alan Bradley case which he tried before the United States Supreme Court and is recognized as a landmark decision in law school textbooks. After a long

Harold Stern,
General Council,
1939-1982.

and distinguished career, Mr. Stern was forced to retire on October 1, 1982 due to ill health and on November 27, 1983 he died at the age of 81.

Upon the retirement of General Counsel Stern, General President John H. Lyons, Jr. retained Attorney Victor Van Bourg as General Counsel in 1982. Mr. Van Bourg, the son of Russian trade unionist immigrant parents, was born in 1931 in New York City. Later, during the Depression, the family moved to California, where he resides today. Being from a poor family, Mr. Van Bourg worked as a truck driver, painter, hotel houseboy and at various other jobs. He was admitted to the bar in the State of California in 1956 after receiving his law degree from the Boalt School of Law at the University of California at Berkeley.

Victor Van Bourg,
General Council,
1982 to the present

General Counsel Van Bourg was retained to represent the District Council of California in 1958 and since that time he has spent his career practicing labor law, ERISA law, and trial law. He is the founder and senior partner of his firm. He represents many unions in the construction industry and other unions including the Farm Workers. He also represents Taft-Hartley Trust Funds. General President Juel D. Drake and General President Jake West, appreciating his talent, continued to retain Mr. Van Bourg and as we celebrate our 100th Anniversary he is our General Counsel.

the period from 1936-40 was far better for our organization than the 1932-36 period. Membership was up to a new high of 41,259. This was the result of the organizing campaign which had been authorized at the previous convention.

He stated to the delegates that "the passage of the Social Security Act is a great benefit to our members. When they have 40 quarters of coverage they will be 'fully insured' and able to retire with monthly benefits at 65 years of age." Morrin also pointed out that "the United States Housing Authority is a subject of deep interest to the members of our organization for it has provided a considerable amount of work..." Already these low income housing projects had provided 143,000 homes to rehouse 576,000 people who had been living in slums. Morrin was concerned that the housing program would be set aside for the national defense program.

General President Morrin pointed out that the "Wage and Hour Law" which was passed in 1938 would go into a new phase on October 25, 1940. At that time all workers engaged in interstate commerce would receive the 40 hour week, a minimum wage of 40 cents an hour, and not less than time and a half for overtime.

In 1940, our International was still having jurisdictional problems with some of the other building trades. Since our International was affiliated with both the Building Trades and Metal Trades Departments of the AF of L, we were able to adjust differences with the Bricklayers, Boilermakers and Elevator Constructors Union. However, General President Morrin pointed out the following:

"While numerous conferences have been held with the Machinists, Building and

John J. Dempsey, Business Representative, Local No. 44, Cincinnati, Ohio was appointed General Treasurer on October 1, 1939. He was born in Cincinnati, July 5, 1898. He became an Ironworker in Local No. 44 in 1916 and a journeyman in 1917.

Badge worn by delegates to the Twenty-Sixth International Convention in 1940.

Common Laborers, Sheet Metal Workers and Lathers, we have not been able to definitely harmonize all of our differences with those trades. However, we intend to continue our efforts with their officials in the hope we may be able to bring about a complete understanding of any differences that may exist."

National Defense was one of the main subjects covered at the 26th Convention. President Morrin said "today, practically all of Europe is engulfed in a war which has already destroyed the liberties of most European countries with their democracies either wiped out or threatened with destruction and their rights trampled underfoot. We in America who have enjoyed the rights and liberties granted to us under our constitution can scarcely realize the extent to which this invasion of countries may reach. Today and for the past few months our country is carrying on a stupendous war defense program. This is a colossal task on account of the vast shore and boundary lines of the United States and its possessions which must be defended in the event of invasion. These are not dreams or idle thoughts; they are not possibilities but realities, if we are to be guided by the total disregard of the rights of European democracies by the world's most heinous war monster, Adolf Hitler."

President Morrin recommended that all International Representatives as well as local union officers do everything in their power to provide, through agreement with employers, that all members of the International who are called into military service, be restored to their former positions at the end of such service.

Delegates to the Twenty-Sixth International Convention held September 16-21, 1940, in St. Louis, Missouri.

Labor Day parade in 1939. Leading the Ironworkers delegation was the Iron Workers District Council of New York. Shown in automobile are General President P.J. Morrin, General Secretary John H. Lyons and General Vice President Joseph F. Boyen who is President of the New York Council.

Members of Local No. 361, Brooklyn made a fine showing at the 1939 Labor Day parade.

A majority of members of Local No. 40 were on hand to march and were greeted with cheers as they proceeded up Fifth Avenue.

Members of Local No. 40 line up for 1939 Labor Day parade. Standing 3rd from left in first line is James V. Cole, business representative of Local No. 40, New York, N.Y..(later Mr. Cole would become General Treasurer of the International Association)

Members of Shopmen's Local No. 455, who turned out in large numbers to participate in the great parade.

Members of Local No. 580, formerly Local No. 447, New York City as they marched up Fifth Avenue in the parade.

Adolf Hitler ascends stairs to the podium at a Third Riech rally in 1939.

America Prepares for War

Hitler had come to power in Germany at the same time that Roosevelt was elected President. Both Germany and the United States were in the grips of a depression, but the way we solved our problems compared to Hitler's Germany were like night and day. Hitler had solved his economic problem by building up the military; we had "The New Deal" to help build up the nation and give jobs to workers.

Italy also had economic problems and, in 1935, Mussolini picked a quarrel with Ethiopia and invaded that African nation.

Japan had also developed a military machine, and in 1931 invaded Manchuria and went to war with China in 1933. Then in 1936, Germany and Italy took the side of the dictator, Franco, in Spain and civil war broke out. In that same year Hitler invaded the demilitarized Rhineland in violation of the treaty that ended World War I.

A speech Roosevelt gave on October 5, 1937 is known as the "Quarantine Speech." Roosevelt was particularly concerned with the aggressive policies of Germany in Europe, and of Japan in the Far East. Roosevelt said:

"It seems to be unfortunately true that the epidemic of world lawlessness is spreading. And mark this well! When an epidemic of physical disease starts to spread, the community approves and joins in a quarantine of the patients in order to protect the health of the community against the spread of this disease......War is contagious, whether it be declared or undeclared."

Roosevelt went on to say we wanted peace but we had to be prepared. An increase in military spending was passed by Congress. Many of our members were able to get jobs as riggers in various navy yards on both coasts.

By March of 1938, Hitler had annexed Austria. In September of that year he took over Czechoslovakia. On September I, 1939 Germany invaded Poland and on September 3rd England and France declared war on Germany. The Second World War had begun.

Although the United States declared neutrality on September 5, 1939 by June 27 of 1940, the United States declared a national emergency. On September 16, 1940 the Selective Training and Service Act was approved, and a month later men between the ages of 21 and 35 were required to register for selective service.

The nation and the labor movement still divided in 1940 over what role we should play in this world-wide conflict, but the attack on Pearl Harbor at the end of 1941 would unify the nation.

Apprenticeship Training

In his report to the delegates, President Morrin pointed out that the International Association consistently advocated and encouraged a form of apprenticeship over the years, so that the organization, as an integral part of the steel industry, would be provided with an even, continuous supply of men versed and trained in the particular and special skill of the trade. Ironworker Apprenticeship Standards that each affiliate local union could use were introduced.

Organizing Navy Yard Riggers

With an increase in ship building both by the U.S. Navy, as well as private shipyards who were building merchant ships, President Morrin said "Our International Association has always been recognized as having jurisdiction over shipyard riggers, and accordingly in the past has issued charters to this classification of workers where unionization of shipyards has been affected. The shipbuilding industry, however, as is well known, has been on the decline since the close of the last World War, and a great number of the yards operating at that time have since been closed up - a number being abandoned entirely, while the yards remaining in operation are doing so on part time with a very small force."

Morrin also stated that, "This is an important branch of our trade as the nature of the work in the various government navy yards requires highly skilled riggers, especially in the placement of machinery, heavy guns and gun mounts, some of which run as high as 135 tons. On work of this kind it is absolutely necessary to use skilled riggers not only for the safety of such machinery or equipment but for the men employed on such vessels. It is necessary that these men be experienced riggers, and especially cable splicers in order to insure the safe handling and rigging of heavy equipment used on the ships which also require experienced loftmen in performing the necessary ship rigging."

Since the United States Navy was now busy doing construction in Hawaii and other U.S. possessions in the Pacific, Morrin felt we needed to see to it that only union workers were employed. He warned members thinking of doing this work to check first with contractors regarding wages and working conditions rather than being surprised when they got there. Many who went to work on Guam and Wake Island would be trapped when the war began. Many Ironworkers went to work in Alaska and in Panama on the Canal.

General Vice-Presidents Boyen, Pope, Borrelli, Gayton and Murray and General Organizers Hurley and Myers were assigned to organize the shipyards in their respective territories. General Vice-President Evensen and General Organizers Tobin, Strickland and Brignac were later assigned to similar duties as conditions in their territories warranted. Our representatives worked closely with the officers of the Metal Trades Department.

Golden Gate Bridge opened to traffic on May 28, 1937.

The Golden Gate Bridge

Along with the Brooklyn Bridge, the Golden Gate Bridge is one of the world's best-known bridges and a civil engineering masterpiece. Construction was officially begun January 5, 1933 and the ground-breaking ceremony was held on February 26, 1933. The opening of the bridge to traffic was on May 28, 1937, however, the day before was designated "Pedestrian Day" when thousands of people enjoyed exclusive use of the new bridge. Joseph B. Strauss was the chief engineer. The 4,260 foot center span superseded the span of the George Washington Bridge. More than 100, 000 tons of steel, 693,000 cubic yards of concrete, and 80,000 miles of wire cable were used in the bridge's construction. Steel for the Towers was delivered to the erector in barge loads of about 500 tons each, which was the limit of storage at the tower pier. An 85 ton stiffleg derrick, with a 100 foot boom, unloaded the barges and rehandled the steel as necessary to serve the erection traveler.

Rivets in vertical seams of the tower were not driven until all horizontal joints below had been riveted. There were about 600,000 field driven rivets in each tower. The rivets were heated in coal-burning forges located on scaffolds outside the tower and passed to crews within the tower by pneumatic rivet-passers through holes 6-1/2 inches in diameter and left in the tower webs for that purpose. Special provisions were made for the safety of the men during the erection. Every man was

1936

1991

Hard Hat worn by Ironworker during construction of the Golden Gate Bridge.

continued

Al Zampa, Local No. 377, San Francisco who worked on the Golden Gate Bridge and the San Francisco-Oakland Bay Bridge in 1936. **At right,** *Al Zampa in 1991.*

The Golden Gate Bridge, *continued*

required to wear a hard hat to minimize head injuries from falling objects. The hard hats were primitive - made out of leather, similar to a football helmet. Because of the confined space within cells, extra precautions were taken against lead poisoning. This ailment was suspected in several workmen and as soon as its likelihood was discovered, all men were examined physically every two weeks and blood counts taken. All riveters were required to wear respirators, and provisions made so that hands could be kept clean to prevent hand to mouth infection. As a result of this experience on the Marin Tower, the paint on the splices of the San Francisco Tower,

then in the process of fabrication, was changed from red lead to iron oxide.

The cable wire was drawn and galvanized in the New Jersey plants of the John A. Roebling's Sons Company (same company that did the cables for the Brooklyn Bridge). A great aid to the speed of erection was the use of a safety net. This net made of manila rope, 3/8 inches in diameter and 6 inch square mesh, was placed progressively under the suspended structure as the latter was erected so that eventually it extended under the bridge its entire length between pylons and was wide enough to extend ten feet outside the trusses on both sides. This

In the foreground, strand shoes of Golden Gate Bridge are shown just forward of the eye-bars, in position to receive the wire.

Ironworkers install cable formers with vertical separators which keep strands in vertical rows during erection of Golden Gate Bridge.

Ironworkers wrapping the cable. This machine, as it whirls around the cable, covers it with a tight spiral wrapping of wire.

In the photo at left, Ironworkers International General President Paddy Morrin, left, and General Secretary Billy McCain at the top of the 746-foot San Francisco Tower for the inaugural of the bridge in 1937. At right, their successors, General President Juel Drake and General Secretary Jake West stand in the same spot fifty years later during the golden anniversary celebration.

Conditions In Canada In 1940

The following report was made by General President Morrin at our 26th convention:

"On account of the scarcity of work in Canada during the many years of the depression, most of our Canadian local unions were unable to survive. Conditions have been very dull throughout Canada in the past decade. The International in every way possible endeavored to sustain our local unions but were

106

safeguard was required by the Chief Engineer. In addition to saving 19 lives during the construction, there is no question but what the men worked faster and more efficiently since they felt the protection of the net below them and were able to move about more freely.

One of the Ironworkers that fell and was saved by the net was General Vice President Dick Zampa's father, Al Zampa. Al fell on October 20, 1936 when he slipped on a wet girder on the Marin side of the span. He broke three vertebrae and injured his pelvis because his weight sagged the net to the ground, only 25 feet below. The 19 men that fell, formed the "We Fell Off the Bridge Club," which they shortly renamed "the Halfway To Hell Club." In fifty-two months, 11 workers on the bridge would die. Many Ironworkers were employed during the construction of the bridge and since its completion in 1937, Ironworkers have been steadily employed in maintaining the bridge.

The San Francisco-Oakland Bay Bridge

The San Francisco-Oakland Bay Bridge was started in 1933 and completed in November, 1936. Ironworkers from Local No. 377 and Local No. 378 worked on this bridge. The construction of the bridge required enough timber to build houses for a town of 15,000 people, and enough concrete and reinforcing steel to rebuild downtown San Francisco. The concrete and steel in the bridge would build 35 skyscrapers.

This bridge contains fabricated steel equal in tonnage to 18 per cent of all the steel fabricated in the United States in 1933. The 71,000 miles of wire in the cables would reach three-tenths of the distance from the earth to the moon. A rise of one degree in temperature increases the total length of this wire by nearly half a mile. The elastic stretch of the wire from the weight of the bridge alone has increased its total length 140 miles.

The completed stiffening trusses of the San Francisco-Oakland Bay Bridge. The derrick on the upper deck is placing the floor steel.

The East Bay crossing of the San Francisco-Oakland Bay Bridge. The main span is 1400 feet which was the longest span in the United States in 1936.

unable to do so. Recently, however, construction has picked up some on account of the present war conditions and it is reported in the press that a considerable amount of construction is contemplated. If so, the International will try in every way possible to assist our Canadian local unions in getting reestablished in the principal centers in that country."

Organizing was one of the main subjects discussed at the 26th Convention. It was pointed out that twenty-seven outside local unions were organized since July 1, 1936 and by June 30, 1940 there were 10,000 more members affiliated with the outside local unions. By 1940 there were ninety-one shop local unions. Total membership, outside and shop, had grown to 62,651.

The National Election of 1940

Roosevelt received the nomination on the first ballot when the Democratic Party met in Chicago from July 15-18 at the Chicago Stadium. His running mate for Vice President this time would be Henry Wallace, an agriculturalist from Iowa and a former U.S. Secretary of Agriculture.

The Republican Candidate would be Wendell Willkie, a New York attorney who later became president of the Commonwealth and Southern Corporation. His firm opposed the creation by the Federal Government of the Tennessee Valley Authority. After he lost the election to Roosevelt by about five million votes and our nation went to war, Willkie would become a supporter of Roosevelt's war policies and the author of a book supporting the United Nations titled *One World.*

Okay, boys, you asked for it !

Chapter Seven

World War II and the Post War Struggles 1941-1952

The year 1941 opened with the world at war but the United States still at peace. All that would change on December 7th, 1941 when the Japanese bombed Pearl Harbor. For the next four years the labor movement would dedicate itself to the winning of the war. Workers would work long hours without any vacations, be relocated far from their hometown, live in poor housing, and experience high prices while their salaries were frozen. Yet with the exception of one major labor strike, union workers stayed on the job.

Yet during the war, anti-labor newspapers spread rumors about workers striking in great numbers. Businessmen were crying for repeal of the Wagner Act, the Wage and Hour Law, and even child labor legislation. One pro-labor writer wrote that management was more afraid of the union movement in America and more anxious to fight that war than to fight Germany and Japan.

Then, when the war ended, instead of rewarding labor with those things that were promised to them during the war, such as a national plan for free medical care, higher wages and shorter hours, and better housing and schools, Congress passed anti-labor legislation such as the Taft-Hartley Act which President Truman vetoed, but his veto was overridden by the Republican Congress.

Before we could even enjoy the fruits of peace we found ourselves involved in the cold war and the Korean conflict. President Truman, who had finished President Roosevelt's fourth term, would be attacked by Republicans and some Democrats but he would successfully be reelected in 1948 after a successful campaign.

Preparing for National Defense

With France conquered and England under attack, President Roosevelt was able to convince Congress to agree on the draft and a Lend-Lease program to aid Great Britain. Although America still had about 8 million workers unemployed, the war in Europe was producing more and more jobs. Many defense plants were now producing at full capacity, and many workers were working overtime under the new wage and hour laws receiving time and a half and double time on Sundays. Management was making big profits on defense contracts but didn't want to pay higher wages. The skills of the Ironworkers were in great demand. Most of the plants that produced products for domestic use needed to be converted to producing war material and equipment, therefore, these plants had to be renovated.

Management complained to Colonel Philip B. Fleming, the wage and hour administrator. His reply to

Executive Council of the Iron Workers International in 1941. **Left to right: Seated** *- Vice President William H. Pope, General Secretary John H. Lyons, General President P.J. Morrin, General Treasurer J.J. Dempsey, Vice President J. Arthur Evensen. Standing - Vice Presidents Gay Borrelli, Benjamin A. Murray, Dan M. Gayton, William F. Bauers, E.M. Woods, C.F. Strickland and Joseph F. Boyen.*

management was printed in the January, 1941 issue of the *Bridgemen's Magazine*.

"If there are to be days of sacrifice ahead, such sacrifices should be borne equally by all classes, so far as possible. It seems reasonable to me, that if we are going to ask labor to sacrifice some of its leisure time in the interest of national defense, we have a right to ask capital to make a corresponding sacrifice in terms of slightly higher labor cost."

"While it may be true that compulsion may be the most expeditious method of settling a labor dispute, it is not the true corrective method or the one that, in the final analysis, will prove effective in producing stability in the relationship between labor and industry."

Mounting attention was being directed toward apprenticeship, as a result of the efforts to solve the problem of training skilled workers for defense industries. A survey conducted in early 1941 by the Department of Labor revealed that the number of apprentices in training in all apprenticeable trades, including the Ironworkers, had jumped by approximately 20 percent. There were 125,000 apprentices, however, Labor Secretary Perkins said the number, based on demands, should be 1,500,000.

Anti-Labor Actions In Canada

Canada had entered the war with Great Britain in 1939, and until 1941 the situation for labor was bad. Although over a million Canadian men and women were engaged directly in war industry and production was high, wages were still low. In 1941, 32.9% of Canadian workers were earning less than $450 per year, and only 6.8% were earning over $1,949.

Until 1941, union membership in Canada was below what it had been in 1919. Canada did not have a "New Deal" in the 1930's like that in the United States. Workers were also divided into three large organizations. The Trades and Labour Congress of Canada (TLC) included unions affiliated with the A. F. of L. In 1940, the Canadian Congress of Labour (CCL) was founded, and it included many of the unions that were affiliated in the U.S. with the CIO. Lastly, in Quebec as well as other parts of Canada workers were organized into the Canadian and Catholic Confederation of Labour (CCCL).

However, the war gave labor an opportunity to make demands for higher wages and the right to organize the unorganized. By 1941 membership finally was greater than it had been in 1919. There were some strikes in Canada while the war was on and there was debate in the House of Commons in Ottawa to pass anti-labor bills, but Mr. McLarty, the Canadian Federal Minister of Labour, ended the debate by saying these words:

The *Bridgemen's Magazine* pointed out at this time that with the bombs dropping on England, workers still had the right to strike. In 1942 Britain had 29% more strikes, involving 61% more workers and causing 7% more worker lost days then in the United States. The Conservative Prime Minister, Winston Churchill, appointed a great labor leader, Ernest Bevin, as Minister of Labour. This had helped to bring harmony in wartime to that country. The *Bridgemen's Magazine* felt that America could learn a lesson from Britain and Canada if war came to the United States.

The Attack on Pearl Harbor: The War Begins for the United States

On December 7, 1941 the Japanese attacked Pearl Harbor. On the following day, December 8, 1941, the same day that General President Morrin wrote to the President of the United States, he sent the following message to all affiliated Local Unions. It stated the position we would take throughout World War II.

St. Louis, Mo., December 8, 1941

All Affiliated Local Unions:

Inasmuch as our country has been unjustifiably attacked by Japan, our International Association, through its officers, has pledged our complete cooperation and support to President Roosevelt, our commander-in-chief. In fulfillment of this pledge to the President of the United States and of the publicly established policy of this Association by delegates to our last convention to cooperate with the National Defense Commission to bring the national program to a successful conclusion, I as General President must insist that there shall be no strikes or stoppages of work by any local union, its officers or members of this Association during this national emergency.

P.J.MORRIN
General President

International Association of Bridge, Structural and Ornamental Iron Workers

St. Louis, Mo., December 8, 1941

Honorable Franklin D. Roosevelt,
President of the United States,
White House
Washington, D.C.

The International Association of Bridge, Structural and Ornamental Iron Workers, through its officials, pledges to you, our commander-in-chief, our full cooperation and support in all of your efforts to defend and protect our country against the unwarranted and unjustifiable attacks of Japan or any other nation which challenges the principles of freedom and democracy for which our country stands.

P.J.MORRIN
General President

THE WHITE HOUSE

December 9, 1941

P.J.Morrin, Esq.,
General President,
International Association of Bridge,
Structural and Ornamental Iron Workers,
St. Louis, Missouri.

My dear Mr. Morrin:

Permit me, in the President's name, to thank you and your association for your telegram. The pledges of patriotic support which have been received from the many, many loyal citizens in all parts of the country have given the President strength and courage to carry out the will of the American people.

For the splendid assurance conveyed in your message he is more appreciative than he can say.

Very sincerely yours,
STEPHEN EARLY
Secretary to the President.

International Association of Bridge, Structural and Ornamental Iron Workers

In the January, 1942 issue of the *Bridgemen's Magazine* the opening story dealt with the fact that the A.F. of L. through all of its affiliates pledged to purchase one billion dollars worth of United States Defense Bonds. At the same time our International Association subscribed for $100,000 worth of Defense Bonds, as well as $180,000 worth of United States Treasury Notes to help win the war. Before the war was over the government had six "War Loan Drives" and our Union and other unions invested to help end the war.

Early Fighting in the Pacific

Many members of our Union and other construction workers were working at the time of the early Japanese attacks in the Pacific. There were 10,000 A.F. of L. members working in Hawaii, 700 stationed on Midway, 400 at Guam and a small number on Wake Island.

"Far out in the Pacific Ocean, on tiny island outposts of America's vital defenses, hundreds of courageous American Federation of Labor members flung down the tools of their trade, picked up whatever weapons were at hand and fought valiantly side by side with American Marines and soldiers against the treacherous and deadly attacks of vastly superior Japanese forces."

Ironically, the Ironworkers and other construction workers captured by the Japanese on Wake Island at first received no compensation. While the government passed a bill covering the families of soldiers captured, nothing was done for the workers captured. The A.F. of L. found that their families were in a terrible state and asked Congress for legislation to cover them. After the A.F. of L. called this to the attention of the government a bill was passed to pay 70% of their salary to their families and the rest placed in a fund for them upon their liberation, however, this payment was only retroactive to January 4, 1944. Finally Congress passed legislation in November of 1945 that gave them their pay retroactive to January 1, 1942.

Many Ironworkers not only would serve in all branches of the military, but they would serve in the "Seabees." The fighting, never-say-die spirit of America's workers was exemplified in the South Pacific,

"Rosie-the-Riveter." During World War II more than half the workers in defense plants were women - a proud testament to their skills. Rosie and her friends built 12,000 ships, 300,000 planes, 87,000 tanks and hundreds of thousands of cannons, machine guns, rifles and other fire arms.

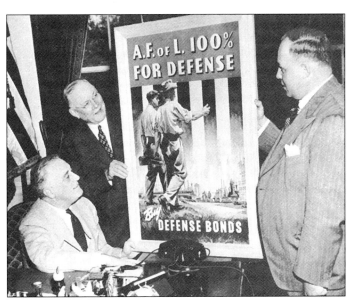

when a battle-scarred U.S. aircraft carrier was made ready for further battle by the "Seabees," who made emergency repairs at sea while the carrier was steaming to the scene of another action. Part of the repairs was actually completed while the ship was in battle. "Seabees" were men recruited for the Navy principally through the cooperation of A.F. of L. building trades unions. They were all volunteers, forming the Navy's construction battalion, trained to work and fight.

Reorganizing for War

After Pearl Harbor Congress passed the "War Powers Act" giving extraordinary powers to the President. Roosevelt would set up various Federal Agencies and distribute various wartime tasks to them. One of the agencies created was the War Production Board (WPB) with a Labor Production Division headed by a labor representative. The purpose of this division was to set up joint labor-management committees and to take suggestions from workers on how the war plant could operate more efficiently. Although this was denounced by industry as socialism and as a "foolish experiment," over 5,000 factories would take part, and production increased.

Another problem was manpower. Before the war

In 1943, General President Morrin joins A.F. of L. President Green, A.F. of L. Secretary-Treasurer Meany and other labor leaders at the home of the Armored Command at Fort Knox to discuss the labor skills required by Army mechanization and the problems of pre-induction training.

General Executive Council in 1944. **Sitting, left to right:** J.A. Evensen, J.H. Lyons, P.J. Morrin, J.J. Dempsey and W.H. Pope. **Standing, left to right:** D.M. Gayton, W.F. Bauers, E.M. Woods, C.F. Strickland, J.F. Boyen, B.A. Murray and G. Borrelli.

ended 11 million men and women would enter the armed forces. Of this number about 60% or about 6.5 million were taken from industry and the building trades. In 1941 there were still 8 million unemployed in spite of Roosevelt's New Deal. Some of them went into the war plants but many went into the military service. New war plants located in rural areas recruited farmers. Many senior citizens went back to work, and child labor legislation was relaxed to allow 2 million older teenagers to work. However, one of the largest sources of new labor was the 6 million women who entered the workforce. Known as "Rosie the Riveter" they helped to build 12,000 ships, 300,000 planes and 87,000 tanks from 1941 to 1945.

How the New Deal Projects Helped Us Win the War

When the war began the Tennessee Valley Authority (TVA) was quickly converted to war needs. Early in 1941 twelve large dams and a steam generation station were under construction. Our members and other building trades workers completed them in record time. One of the dams, Douglas, was constructed in twelve months and nineteen days. A large block of electrical power centers was built: new plants sprang up, and old plants were renovated. Half of the aluminum needs during the war came from plants supplied with electricity from the TVA. Not a single plant stopped or slowed down for want of power. The TVA ran munitions plants and even produced fertilizers that were sent to England to help them grow more food.

Delegate's badge to the 27th International Convention. Note: badge made out of cardboard and cloth because of the war effort.

Health and Safety During the War

Ironically, while management was attacking labor regarding time lost on strikes they were not publicizing the time lost from industrial accidents that were caused by unsafe conditions in the factories and on the work sites that management failed to correct. Secretary of Labor Francis Perkins estimated in 1943 that the sum total of production losses arising out of deaths and injuries to be 274 million worker-days lost as compared to a maximum of 13.9 million from strikes. In other words, accidents and deaths time lost was 20 times greater than time lost from strikes.

In late 1943, casualties to the U.S. armed forces since Pearl Harbor were 20,104 dead, 28,226 wounded, 32,905 missing, and 23,970 imprisoned - a total of 105,205. Casualties to American workers through accidents since Pearl Harbor were 80,000 dead and 7,000,000 injured, on and off the job. These figures were from the National Safety Council. The theme of the Congress was "Stop Accidents - Speed Victory."

The **Twenty-Seventh International Convention** would be held September 18-23, 1944 at the Jefferson Hotel in St. Louis, Mo. General President P.J. Morrin, General Secretary John H. Lyons and General Treasurer John J. Dempsey would be reelected. The convention dealt with many subjects related to the war. President Morrin

P.J. Morrin, General President, 1944.

The Bridge Men's Magazine

Vol. XLIV   SEPTEMBER, 1944   No. 9

CONVENTION NUMBER

HOTEL JEFFERSON, SAINT LOUIS, MO.

Convention Headquarters

1896 · · · 1944

reported that he visited shipbuilders even before Pearl Harbor and got them to see how they could benefit with recognition of our Union. He reported that there were 16,149 Ironworkers serving in the Armed Forces. Twenty were killed in action, twenty-one died from natural causes, five were missing in action and fifteen were prisoners of war. He pointed out the dues of all service men were suspended at the 1940 convention.

It was also reported that Staff Sgt. Ray L. Bowen, member of Local No. 24, Denver, Colorado, won the Bronze Star while fighting in the Solomons. He killed 15 Japanese soldiers that had ambushed a group of American soldiers and protected his 12-man patrol when they came under fire and had to withdraw. There were many Ironworkers who were heroes in World War II.

President Franklin Delano Roosevelt and Robert Hannegan, chairman of the Democratic National Committee, expressed themselves as being highly pleased with the announced policy of the International Association with regard to the nation's war effort. In personal letters addressed to General President Morrin, President Roosevelt warmly praised the no-strike pledge adopted by the delegates attending the Twenty-Seventh Convention and commended the International for its public reiteration of the no-strike pledge made to him on December 8, 1941, the day following Pearl Harbor.

Shop Organizing Campaign

In his report to the convention General President Morrin pointed out the tremendous increase in "Shop Membership." While there were only 17,140 members in our shop local unions in June of 1940, by June of 1944 we had a shop membership of 49,956. The International Association had signed agreements with 819 shops in 1940 and by 1944 there were 1,075 signed agreements. There was also a great improvement in the fact that few of the shops had vacations with pay in 1940, but by 1944, 563 shops had won this fringe benefit.

Another factor was the increase in pay for fabricated structural and ornamental metal work. In 1937 the average pay was 63.5 cents per hour. By 1940 it had increased to 74.1 cents, and in 1944 the average pay was $1.13 per hour.

In 1944, an investigation to determine lead poisoning hazards in structural steel operations and to discover preventive measures was begun by the New York State Labor Department. Field investigations were made in the demolition of the sheds at the Manhattan and Brooklyn approaches to the Brooklyn Bridge and in the demolition of portions of the elevated structures in Brooklyn. Tests were made to determine the amount of lead fumes to which Ironworkers were exposed. The test showed that 18 Ironworkers contracted lead poisoning chiefly when cutting painted beams with a torch.

An Advisory Committee was appointed by the Labor Commissioner of New York, to draft rules relating to the protection of workers from lead poisoning in connection with bolting, riveting and cutting of structural steel. Representing labor on the Committee was: General Vice-President Joseph F. Boyen, James V. Cole, business agent, Local No. 40, New York City; Paul Rockhold, business agent, Local No. 361, Brooklyn; and Michael F. Pinto, an attorney representing House Wreckers Union No. 95 of New York City.

On September 20, 1944 President Morrin was honored at a banquet in the Gold Room of the Hotel

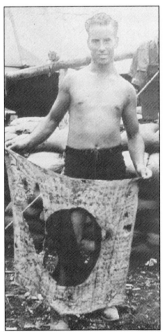

Daniel S. Wambolt, member of Local No. 607, Charlestown, Massachusetts, found a battle-torn Japanese flag on Morotai Island in 1944 when he was serving with the 31st Division during World War II. In the 1960's Wambolt, who was a District Representative for the International Association, returned the flag to the widow of the Japanese soldier who was killed on Morotai Island during the action.

Banquet in honor of P.J. Morrin held during the 1944 International Convention.

September 21, 1944

My dear Mr. Morrin:

I want to assure you and your associates
of my heartfelt appreciation of the promise of support conveyed by the resolution embodied in your inspiring telegram of September eighteenth, on behalf
of the International Association of Bridge, Structural
and Ornamental Ironworkers. In this crisis in world
affairs, it is a source of strength to have such an
assurance of faith.

The pledge which your membership assumed
voluntarily in 1941 to maintain full employment for
the duration -- and which you have kept faithfully --
exemplifies a fine spirit of patriotism and I want
all of you to know that your steadfast determination
has cheered and encouraged me for the tasks ahead.

Very sincerely yours,

Franklin D. Roosevelt

Mr. P. J. Morrin,
General President,
International Association of Bridge
   Structural and Ornamental Ironworkers,
St. Louis,
Missouri.

Letter from President Roosevelt to Morrin, September 21, 1944.

Election of 1944

As the 1944 Presidential Election approached, the attacks on labor and President Roosevelt increased. In June of 1944, the Vice President of the United States, Henry A. Wallace, spoke out against what he called "American Fascists." Wallace said that "if a small but powerful group, which put money and power first and people last, have their way, the four freedoms, for which we are fighting will become empty phrases and America will find itself 'back in the good old days' when there was plenty for the few and scarcity for the many."

Although the Democratic Party Platform did not have a separate labor plank in 1944, the Democrats did support some of the major demands of the American Federation of Labor. They did not agree to the specific repeal of the Smith-Connally Act, however, they did favor the Wagner Act which gave workers the right to decide for themselves which union should represent them in collective bargaining. The A.F. of L. wanted the Wagner-Murray-Dingell Bill which would expand the Social Security System to cover medical costs, something that was already passed in both England and Canada at that time.

The Democratic Convention met at the Chicago Stadium July 19-21, 1944. Although the A.F. of L. still did not believe in giving money directly to one party, they continued to follow Gompers' philosophy of "Reward your friends and defeat your enemies." General President P.J. Morrin sent a letter to President Roosevelt pledging the International's support to him for a fourth term in office. Morrin received a response from President Roosevelt dated September 21, 1944.

Roosevelt Dies and Truman Becomes President

President Roosevelt died on April 12, 1945. Vice President Harry Truman assumed the office of President. Because Truman had only been Vice President for a few months, many workers did not know how he stood on labor questions. Our magazine ran a story pointing out that Truman had almost a 100% record on labor issues.

When the Pacific war ended on VJ Day, August 14, 1945, the government was not prepared for peacetime. Military advisors to the President had estimated that

Jefferson for 25 years as President of the International Association. William Green, President, A.F. of L., and George Meany, Secretary-Treasurer, A.F. of L., spoke at the banquet. They both praised President Morrin and paid tribute to him for his achievements. Secretary Meany said "President Morrin had always been an aggressive and fearless leader and named him as one of the union leaders who never laid back when there was work to be done to advance the cause, not only of his own membership but that of all workers in the A.F. of L."

the war against Japan would last at least two more years. The atomic bomb changed all that.

President Morrin sent out Circular Letter No. 517 on November 27, 1945 to all local unions that effective December 1, 1945, all affiliated outside erection local unions of the International Association should return to their former procedure and hold regular membership meetings and Executive Board meetings in accordance with the practice and custom that was in effect prior to the war emergency.

The Taft-Hartley Act (Labor Management Relations Act-1947)

There is no doubt that Taft-Hartley was a serious blow aimed at the American trade union movement. It remains today the most serious legislative bar to the organization of workers, particularly in those states where the so-called "right-to-work" laws exist, which Taft-Hartley made possible.

The Act gives employers the right to conduct captive audience anti-union sessions on company time, without equal rights of unions. The National Labor Relations Board was seriously weakened by converting it into a quasi-judicial agency. The General Counsel of the

Canadian Ironworkers employed by Dominion Bridge in 1946.

Board was made independent and given broad powers to determine whether or not complaints would be heard. All elected labor officials – but not management – were required to file affidavits testifying that they were not members of the Communist Party. Unions were permitted to negotiate for the union-shop only after members approved in time-consuming special NLRB elections.

For years, unions had employed the "secondary boycott" in support of strikes. This took the form of refusal by union members to handle or process "hot" materials – goods processed or handled elsewhere under strike conditions. While the "secondary boycott" may have been abused in some instances, it was an important basic weapon against employers seeking to maintain substandard conditions. Taft-Hartley outlawed it.

IS A GESTAPO COMING TO THE U. S. A.?

SWEATSHOP

YOU'RE UNDER ARREST!

DEMAND UNION GOODS AND USE UNION SERVICES

PROPOSED ANTI-LABOR LAWS

UNION LABEL TRADES DEPT. A.F.L.

Keep Punching!

REPEAL

LABOR

TAFT-HARTLEY LAW

Copyright 1948
THE MACHINIST—I.A.M.

Taft-Hartley also restored the use of federal injunctions in strikes, outlawed in 1932, by giving the federal government the power to determine "national emergency strikes" and to halt them for periods up to 90 days. The law also banned the closed shop which required the employer to hire only union members. There are many other provisions of the law that are detrimental to the Labor Movement and the Ironworkers. The debate over Taft-Hartley took place between May and June of 1947. The President vetoed the bill but Congress passed it over his veto. A Gallup Poll showed voters opposed Taft-Hartley. This law gave many lawyers jobs, and the NLRB had to conduct some 10,000 elections in the building and construction industry that would cost the government millions of dollars.

The **Twenty-Eighth International Convention** was held September 20-25, 1948 at the Statler Hotel in St. Louis, Missouri. Paul J. (Paddy) Morrin who had been General President since 1918 for a total of 30 years decided to step down. The delegates to the 28th Convention unanimously adopted a resolution creating the office of "President Emeritus" and elected "Paddy" to that office for life beginning on January 1, 1949. It was

P.J. Morrin
General President retires. Delegates to the 28th Convention adopted a resolution making P.J. Morrin "President Emeritus."

pointed out in the resolution that the organization grew from a union of some 18,000 members and a negligible treasury when he took office in 1918 to the highest standing in the labor movement with a membership in excess of 100,000 and a treasury of more than eight million dollars.

The delegates elected **John H. Lyons Sr.** to succeed General President Morrin. He had no opposition. It was pointed out that Lyons was well qualified to step up in the ranks due to his admirable record, during the past nine years as General Secretary and his eleven years as General Treasurer. President Lyons would become the first individual to serve in all three top offices in the history of the International Association (General President, General Secretary and General Treasurer). This record still remains in 1996. Lyons was initiated into Local No. 9, Niagara Falls, New York in January of 1916. He later transferred to Local No. 17, Cleveland, Ohio where he was elected to several offices. In May, 1928, he was appointed General Organizer and later that year was elected as the first General Treasurer of the International Association at the 1928 convention.

The delegates elected James R. Downes to the office of General Secretary. President Lyons nominated him for that position. James R. Downes served as business agent of Local No. 550, Canton, Ohio from 1941-1946, at which time he was

JUEL D. DRAKE
Local #229

DELEGATE
TWENTY-EIGHTH
CONVENTION
INTERNATIONAL
UNION OF
THE STRUCTURAL
AND ORNAMENTAL
IRON WORKERS
SEPT. 1

Delegate's badge to the 28th International Convention in 1948.

117

appointed General Organizer. President Morrin assigned him to unionize and organize the Roanoke, Virginia area and after being successful he did the same thing in North and South Carolina. James W. Lowe of Local No. 11, Newark, New Jersey was also nominated, however, he lost the election. Downes received 377 votes. Lowe received 150 votes.

In a contested election, John J. Dempsey easily beat William Smorra, Local No. 378 (465 to 60 votes) for the office of General Treasurer.

James R. Downes
elected General Secretary at the 28th Convention.

Dempsey was first elected General Treasurer at the 1940 Convention. General Vice-Presidents reelected were: J. Arthur Evensen, Local No. 1; Dan M. Gayton, Local No. 3; William F. Bauers, Local No. 6; Gay Borrelli, Local No. 405; Benjamin A. Murray, Local No. 58; C.F. Strickland, Local No. 387; E.M. Woods, Local No. 377 and William J. Reynolds, Local No. 7.

The delegation stood and bowed their heads in silent tribute to those of the International Association who made the supreme sacrifice in World War II. In the first year of the war, 18,179 members of the International Association were engaged in the war effort in one of the services including the Merchant Marine and Sea Bees. This figure grew steadily until a peak of 30,052 was reached. Seven of the 202 men listed as having made the supreme sacrifice were missing in action while 35 were taken prisoners of war. Of those taken prisoner, 32 had been repatriated, according to records at headquarters.

President Morrin said "As I see the picture today, we are standing at the cross-roads. The post-war administration made a sharp turn away from the policies that had been established during the regime of the late President Roosevelt and it is now entirely up to us of the labor movement to exert every lawful means at our command to hold the gains that we had realized."

The Truman-Dewey Election of 1948

Our Union and the entire labor movement did everything in its power to get out the vote for Truman and liberal Senators and Congressmen. Truman called his

policies the "Fair Deal." After Truman's victory, the Iron Workers and other labor organizations continued to demand the repeal of the Taft-Hartley Act.

General President Lyons Takes Office

On January 1, 1949, John H. Lyons became General President.

The new administration presented to its members a modern and stream-lined version of *The Bridgemen's Magazine* which henceforth would be known as *"The Ironworker."* The official legal title of the publication would remain *"The Bridgemen's Magazine"* as provided in the International Constitution, but the pen name, *"The Ironworker"* as shown on the front cover has been adopted as a more appropriate title and one that more clearly describes the work of all the men of the trade. *The Ironworker* had many new features, for example, The President's Page, listing of local unions geographically and alphabetically instead of numerically, current schedule of wage rates, a new style of type which would make the magazine more legible, reports from General Vice-Presidents, General Organizers, and Shop

John H. Lyons
elected General President at the 1948 28th International Convention. He became the seventh International President since 1896.

General Executive Council in 1948. **Sitting left to right:** *D.M. Gayton, J.R. Downes, J.H. Lyons, J.J. Dempsey, J.A. Evensen, Attorney H. Stern.* **Standing left to right:** *J.F. Boyen, W.F. Bauers, E.M. Woods, C.F. Strickland, W.J. Reynolds, B.A. Murray and G. Borrelli.*

Delegates to the 28th International Convention, September 20-25, 1948.

General President John H. Lyons as he assumed the duties of his new office on January 1, 1949 surrounded by the flowers from his many friends and associates who sent him their congratulations.

in order to meet our foreign commitments and raise the standard of living at home, we must accord all possible governmental, management and labor support to the apprenticeship program of the country."

On March 15, 1949 an Ironworker-Boilermaker national joint committee was established to review jurisdictional disputes between the two organizations and to study possible changes and modifications to the Ironworker-Boilermaker agreement. In May, 1949, a "memorandum of understanding," amounting to a wage agreement, was consummated between the International Association and the Tennessee Valley Authority.

In 1949, President Truman was able to get a bill through Congress to raise the minimum wage from 40 to

Representatives. Also featured was the beginning of a blueprint course.

The January, 1949 issue of *The Ironworker* magazine featured a story and pictures on video (television) towers and a public utilities switching sub-station that members of the International Association were erecting. It was pointed out that all work of this nature including electric transmission line towers properly comes under the jurisdiction of the Ironworkers.

The average scale of wages for Ironworkers in 1949 was approximately $2.05 per hour for structural and ornamental ironwork and $1.87 per hour for rodmen. The following District Councils were listed in 1949: Greater New York & Vicinity; Chicago & Vicinity; St. Louis & Vicinity; Philadelphia, Pa. & Vicinity; Northern New Jersey; Bay District Council of San Francisco; Washington, D.C., Baltimore, Md. & Vicinity; Michigan; Kansas City & Vicinity; and Fort Worth and Dallas, Texas District Council.

In 1949, the Federal Committee on Apprenticeship recommended a draft deferment for apprentices who were under 24-1/2 years of age and who had as much as 6 months training under the Federal or State standards of apprenticeship. The FCA felt this was necessary in order to develop the skilled manpower called for in the national defense program. Labor Secretary, Maurice J. Tobin, said, "if we are to stiffen our industrial structure to secure increased productivity of the American worker

75 cents an hour. This was the first increase since 1938. Truman was also able to get the Senate to hike Social Security payments. The labor movement pledged that they would elect liberals in 1950 since conservatives of both parties were preventing the repeal of the Taft-Hartley Act.

In March, 1950, General President John H. Lyons advised the membership that a new International "seal or logo" was designed and appeared on the back cover of the March, 1950 issue of *The Ironworker*. The new seal portrays the work of the bridgeman, structural steel erector, derrickman, reinforcing Ironworker, ornamental Ironworker, machinery mover and rigger. He said, "the old seal which we have been using for the past forty or fifty years, has long since outgrown its usefulness as a symbol of the work of our trade. It is our intention to use this seal as the union label for our craft. At the present time we have over forty thousand members employed in the fabricating industry, and it is my considered opinion that the work fabricated by our members should leave the shops bearing our union label."

In her daily column, published throughout the nation, Mrs. Eleanor Roosevelt, widow of the late President, gave considerable space to the work of the Ironworker in 1950. She described her reaction to the hazards encountered by the men who erect the steel in skyscrapers. She noted their operations when sitting in a dental chair in New York City and looking out an eighteenth-floor window:

"How much we usually take for granted about the work of our fellow human beings! Somehow I had always thought of these huge skyscrapers as they are when finished, and had never before seen the skilled work and calm courage that goes into putting up the framework.

Ironworkers erecting Transmission Towers in 1949.

Clockwise, Ironworker members of Local No. 40 drape United Nations flag over the first girder set into the foundation of the United Nations Building. Members of Local No.'s 40, 580 and 197, New York City, completing the United Nations Building. Cornerstone is laid for United Nations Building. Albin Olsen, Membership No. 126091, Local No. 197, is guiding cornerstone into position.

Just walking across from one beam to another is an amazing acrobatic feat of balance with sure death below if you lose your head for a minute. The workers don't wear belts and are not hooked to anything, yet they behave just as though theirs was any ordinary occupation with the ordinary risks which all of us take in our daily work.

"I have long known what it means to be a miner, and I can well understand the responsibilities and risks of a pilot or of the men in the Army and Navy in various branches of the service. But here were men doing work that goes on day in and day out and is part of our daily lives, and I had never given a thought to the extraordinary skill and physical ability required to carry it through successfully. I was overcome at my own lack of imagination and understanding; *but I shall be grateful to these men in the future, and have a better understanding of what this kind of work requires."*

The Korean War

The Korean war began in July of 1950 and three months later China became involved. General Secretary James R. Downes sent Circular Letter No. 497 to all affiliated local unions. A portion of the letter reads as follows:

"Owing to the emergency that now exists which has again cast war clouds over our country it becomes neces-

Members of Shopmen's Local No. 473 of Chicago, donated food for the families of their fellow members engaged in a strike against one of the fabricating plants in Chicago in 1950.

International Representatives in 1950 attending the Union Label Industries show in Philadelphia. **From left to right:** General Organizers Leslie L. Myers and Thomas A. Lenehan, General Secretary James R. Downes, General President John H. Lyons and General Vice President Gay Borrelli.

sary to call to the attention of the officers and members of all of our local unions Section 9 (a), Article 17 of our International Constitution, which reads as follows:

"All members rendering military services to our Government, upon submitting satisfactory proof to the General Executive Board that they are paid up within the current month and are actually engaged in rendering military services to our Government during the present emergency shall be exempt from the payment of all dues and assessments during the duration of such military service and the General Secretary shall issue special stamps without charge to be inserted in the membership book of such members engaged in military service for the period so engaged."

General President Lyons asked members to examine the idea of joining the volunteer Seabees Reserve due to the fact that they would need 70,000 skilled construction workers. President Truman would ask for a repeal of the Capehart/Herlong Amendment which passed on all higher costs to the consumer and guaranteed management pre-Korean profits.

In 1950, Shopmen's Local Union No. 473 of Chicago began a concerted effort to organize the unorganized plants in their vicinity and to obtain satisfactory agreements covering the employees in such plants. In this effort, it was necessary to strike one plant for a period of three weeks. Each week during this time, the members of Local No. 473

New International "seal" introduced in March, 1950

generously donated food for the families of their fellow members engaged in that strike. Agreements were reached with a number of plants during this organizing campaign.

In February, 1951, twenty-five "outside" local unions showed substantial increases in wage rates. Local No. 321, Little Rock, noted a 12-1/2 cent across the board raise, giving the structural and ornamental men $2.25 and the rodmen $2.00 per hour. Local Unions No. 118, Sacramento, No. 155, Fresno, No. 377, San Francisco, and No. 378, Oakland reported a 7-1/2 cent increase making the wage rate of the structural and ornamental Ironworkers $2.57-1/2 cents per hour and the rodmen $2.32-1/2 cents per hour. The wage increases varied from 7 cents to 25 cents per hour.

In March, 1951, International Headquarters moved from the Syndicate Trust Building to the Continental Building, 3615 Olive Street, St. Louis, Mo., which provided more offices and necessary space to carry out the business of the International Association.

General President John H. Lyons stated in a Labor Day article appearing in *The Ironworker* magazine that, "As I see our situation today, Labor Day, 1951, there are clouds of oppression hanging over our heads. It is natural that we should hate war and the untold suffering it brings to so many of our people, but we hate oppression even more, so we must resolve ourselves to make whatever sacrifices are necessary to establish peace – everlasting peace – and resist with our every effort any further threats to our free way of life. We have

General President Lyons in 1951 at his desk in the new International Headquarters.

International Headquarters, 300 Continental Building, St. Louis, Mo.

General Secretary James R. Downes at his desk.

General Organizer Ed Glazner, who handles Shop local union affairs.

General Treasurer John J. Dempsey.

THE BRIDGEMEN'S MAGAZINE

Official Organ of

The **Ironworker**

Vol. LI   AUGUST, 1951   No. 8

Published Monthly by
The International Association of Bridge, Structural and Ornamental Iron Workers

Pat Corbett and his son Ray, Business Representative of Local No. 40, New York City, working on the 222 foot television tower on top of the Empire State Building in 1951.

Reception room where receptionist at switchboard greets visitors as they arrive in the office.

Ironworkers booth at the Union Label Industries show.

come a long way through the many years of our struggles and we dare not relinquish the gains that we have made, but must continue to strive for further progress in our national economy. We know that we can get no place standing still. We must fight to get ahead and we know that only in unity is there sufficient strength to maintain the higher standards of living and other gains won by our forbears who sacrificed themselves for our benefit and the benefit of those who will succeed us."

On August 24, 1951, President Emeritus Paul J. (Paddy) Morrin died at his home in St. Louis, Mo., after being ill for more than a year. He was buried at Calvary Cemetery, St. Louis. The General Executive Council in Executive session adopted a resolution of condolence. A few months later, Joseph E. McClory, a member of Local No. 17, who served as General President from 1914 to 1918 died in Cleveland on December 9, 1951. He was 74 years of age.

In the February, 1952 issue of *The Ironworker* magazine, General Secretary James R. Downes advised the membership that the International Association was formulating an Apprenticeship Program. He said, "While we have always been fully aware of the extreme importance of Apprenticeship Training in our field, the subject has been driven home with more than usual force by the enormous increase in work opportunities for our membership during the recent war (Korean) and present defense program. Our present plan for the training of apprentices does not seem adequate today. The very existence of our International Association depends upon

P.J. Morrin -
1879-1951
General President, 1918-1948
President Emeritus, 1949-1951

Joseph E. McClory,
1877 - 1951
General President, 1914-1918

the training of men to take the place of those who are dropped out of the field because of physical imparities and advanced years."

Later in 1952, at the Twenty-Ninth Convention, the delegates amended Article XXI of the International Constitution by adopting Apprenticeship Standards for Ironworkers, making it mandatory that each outside affiliated local union establish an Apprenticeship Program that complies with the Standards. Just before the International Convention in August, President Truman agreed that the government would give apprentices exemption from military service since college students already had it.

On February 6, 1952 the Iron Workers International and the Sheet Metal Workers International reached a jurisdictional agreement. The purpose of the agreement was to improve relations between the two trades, to establish procedures for the settlement of jurisdictional disputes directly between the two trades and to mutually assist each union to secure work coming within its recognized jurisdiction.

On July 3, 1952, General President Lyons advised all affiliated local unions that the date of the International Convention would be changed from September 15, 1952 to October 27, 1952 due to the fact that the American Federation of Labor had scheduled their convention during the September dates. The General Executive Council passed a resolution to that affect.

Two hundred and thirty-six ton press erected for the Air Force by members of Local No. 575, Detroit Michigan.

"The Ironworker" magazine circa 1951-1952.

Members of Local No. 716, Philadelphia Navy Shipyard Riggers lowering fabricated 30 foot addition into the submarine U.S.S. Ray in 1951.

Members of Local No. 3, Pittsburgh, erecting the 30 story Aluminum Company of America skyscraper. At that time, it was the only office building in the country to have a stamped aluminum panel curtain wall. The structure also contains reversible aluminum windows and aluminum column covers.

U.S. Postal Service stamps featuring bridges erected by Ironworkers

Chapter Eight

The Ironworkers Grow in the 1950's

The **Twenty-Ninth International Convention** was held October 27-31, 1952 at the Hotel Jefferson in St. Louis, Missouri. General President John H. Lyons, General Secretary James R. Downes and General Treasurer John T. Dempsey were reelected. J. Arthur Evensen, William Bauers, Joseph F. Boyen, Gay Borrelli, Benjamin A. Murray, C.F. Strickland, E.M. Woods, John L. McCarthy and E.G. Glazener were elected General Vice Presidents.

The delegates adopted a progressive form of a Shopmen's Agreement, participation of Shopmen in the Death Benefit Fund, the approval of the Bridge and Iron Workers Staff Retirement Plan, provision for the inclusion of Special Representatives in the Bridge and Iron Workers Staff Retirement Plan; and adjustment in the compensation of the International Officers and General Organizers to meet the increased cost of living since the last four years.

Other subjects such as safety, jurisdiction, working rules, local elections, death benefits and amendments to the constitution were covered at the Convention.

On November 21, 1952, A. F. of L. President William Green passed away. The Executive Council of the A. F. of L. elected Secretary-Treasurer George Meany to succeed William Green on November 25, 1952. Meany became the 4th president of the A. F. of L. in its 72 year history. At a press conference, Meany revealed that he urged President-elect Eisenhower to appoint a Secretary of Labor selected from the ranks of the trade union movement.

Joe Ironworker

Badge worn by delegates to the 29th International Convention.

On January 20, 1953, Dwight D. Eisenhower took over the presidency from Harry Truman. Therefore as the year 1953 opened there was new leadership both for labor and the nation. President Eisenhower heeded President Meany's recommendation and appointed Martin Durkin, General President of the United Association of Journeymen Plumbers and Steamfitters of the U.S. and Canada as Secretary of Labor, however, in September, 1953, Durkin would resign after a dispute with the President on amendments to the Taft-Hartley Act.

Early Policies of the Eisenhower Administration

Eisenhower, as a general of the army, had never served in any public office. There were even questions at the time whether he had previously been a Democrat. But like so many other times when they needed a strong candidate the Republican Party chose a war hero. During the election campaign, Eisenhower had

George Meany, President of the A.F. of L. and William Green.

THE BRIDGEMEN'S MAGAZINE
Official Organ of

The Ironworker

Vol. LIII   JUNE, 1953   No. 6

IRON WORKERS — ALL!

Published Monthly by
The International Association of Bridge, Structural and Ornamental Iron Workers

*June 1953 The Ironworker
magazine cover.*

promised that he would not "turn back the clock." Eisenhower also promised labor that he would repeal parts of the Taft-Hartley bill such as 14B, the so-called "Right-to-Work" section. When he addressed the A. F. of L. convention in 1952 he said:

"I have talked about the Taft-Hartley Act with both labor and industry people. I know how the law might be used to break unions. That must be changed. America wants no law licensing union busting, and neither do I."

It soon became obvious that Senator Taft and Representative Joseph Martin, the Republican Speaker of the House, would not permit this to happen. Taft opposed the types of programs that both Roosevelt and Truman had supported. He announced that social legislation is "primarily a state and local government responsibility." However, Taft and the Conservative Southern Democrats and conservative Republicans proposed a pension scheme for doctors, lawyers, dentists, and accountants that would permit self employed persons to invest in a private trust fund and not have to pay taxes on that money. This would cut back on funds to Uncle Sam and increase the nation's debt.

Jobs, the Economy and Workers

While many things were looking good an article appeared in *The Ironworker* magazine which stated that while productivity had increased since 1949 by 13%, workers' wages had only increased 7%.

"George Meany, A. F. of L. president, said this lag in purchasing power must be corrected if the nation's industries are to continue to expand. If wages fail to keep pace with productivity, he said, workers will not

have enough to buy the goods, markets will collapse, factories will be closed, mass unemployment will follow, and a depression will result."

Meany in a report by the A. F. of L. pointed out that when the Korean War ended defense spending would go down and that we needed to direct ourselves to civilian projects. The Korean war ended on July 27, 1953 with the signing of the armistice calling for a demilitarized zone and voluntary repatriation of prisoners.

On September 23, 1953, the Iron Workers entered into a "Memorandum of Agreement" with the Boilermakers. This "Memorandum of Agreement" between the two organizations supplements and interprets the agreement of October 15, 1928, between the two organizations and the decision of record of May 19, 1947. The agreement dealt with wire mesh, derricks, precipitators, overhead supporting steel for steam generators, the erection and repair of blast furnaces, forced and induced draft fans, catwalks, platforms, stairways and ladders.

The first industry-wide Pension Plan for shopmen Ironworkers was formally inaugurated on March 11, 1954. The Pension Plan provided three types of Pensions - a normal pension, reduced pension and a disability pension.

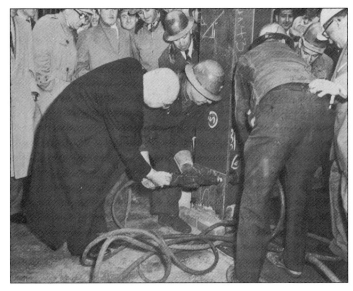

His Eminence Francis Cardinal Spellman, of New York as he drove a commemorative rivet into the steel framework of a 23 story building at 51st Street and Madison Avenue in 1953. Just before the Cardinal took the riveting gun in hand to drive the rivet he was made an honorary member of Local No. 40, New York City.

Delegates to the 29th International Convention held October 27-31, 1952, in St. Louis, Missouri, November, 1952.

General Executive Council in 1953. *Seated from left foreground,* General Vice Presidents E.G. Glazner, C.F. Strickland, Benjamin A. Murray, J. Arthur Evensen, General Counsel Harold Stern, General Secretary James R. Downes, General President J.H. Lyons, General Treasurer J.J. Dempsey and General Vice Presidents John L. McCarthy, William F. Bauers, Joseph F. Boyen, Gay Borrelli and E.M. Woods.

Ironworker members of Local No. 580, New York City enclosed a 22 story building in one day on June 21, 1954. At 6:00 A.M., Norman Tishman, President of the Tishman Realty & Construction Company, blew the whistle which was the signal for forty members of Ornamental Local No. 580 to begin the installation of the prefabricated aluminum building panels which were to cover the two facades plus setbacks of the 22-story office building known as the "Marion Davies" building at 460 Park Avenue, New York City. From this moment on, the accomplishment of such a goal, which might be considered the most revolutionary single development in commercial building construction in the past half century, was in the hands of the "Ironworkers." Ten hours later, at 4:00 P.M., the last of 676 panels were bolted into place completing the job.

On August 3, 1954, J. Arthur Evensen, First Vice President, passed away. He was 69 years of age at the time of his death. He was born in March, 1885. He became a member of Local No. 1 of Chicago, on March 27, 1913. Brother Evensen was elected business agent of Local No. 1 in 1920 and in 1924 he was elected Vice President of the International Association.

What Was the Condition of the Economy by 1955?

The Ironworker magazine reported that in the year and a half after the Korean War ended the economy prospered and there was less inflation. The Bureau of Labor Statistics stated that during the year 1955 prices were more stable than at any time since monthly pricing of items was begun in 1940. At the time the hourly wages of Ironworkers in the United States were from $3.00 to $3.20 per hour and $2.20 to 2.30 per hour in Canada.

One of the reasons why the economy was good was stated by Eisenhower's Secretary of Labor, James P. Mitchell:

December, 1954
The Ironworker magazine cover.

"...the average employed factory worker actually had more take home pay in the final months of 1954 than ever before, and he could get more with his pay envelope than in any earlier peacetime period."

George Meany had another theory about the prosperity of this period. He pointed out in an article in the *Philadelphia Inquirer,* which was mentioned in *The Ironworker* that this prosperity resulted from wage increases won by unions for millions of workers and

Norman Tishman blows whistle at 6:00 A.M. to start job... Job passes halfway mark... Aluminum walls are in place and job completed at 4:00 P.M. by members of Local No. 580, New York, N.Y.

Some of our Indian members - participants in a parade held on the Indian reserve Caughnawaga, Quebec, Canada. Among those pictured are Mike Montour, President Branch 219, Frank Stacey, Business Agent, Special Representative Paul Mercure and Commander-in-Chief, Harry "Cyclone" Taylor.

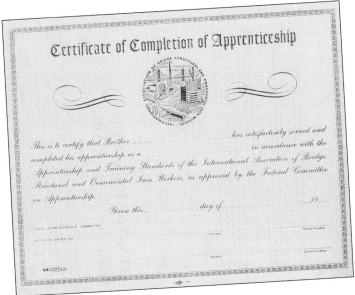

The National Association of Manufacturers and the U.S. Chamber of Commerce still wanted to turn back the clock twenty years or more. They were opposed to any increase in the minimum wages and even wanted the Fair Labor Standards Act repealed entirely. Unfortunately, conservatives in Congress only increased the minimum wage to $1.00, and there was no reduction in the hours for a week's work. The National Planning Association at this time was recommending higher wages and the lowering of prices in order to keep the economy moving.

Instead of lower prices the natural gas companies were conducting a million and a half dollar campaign at this time to convince the public of the need to deregulate prices in order to be able to charge an additional $200-$400 million dollars more to the public. *The Ironworker* magazine printed part of a speech by A. F. of L. President George Meany to a group of employers. He said,

"The wealth of America lies in the living standards of the people and business must have customers. You can't destroy those customers by destroying their unions and have prosperous business."

from wider employment. However, the labor movement continued to fight, as it had before the Second World War, for shorter hours and a higher minimum wage which was only $.75 at this time. The labor movement proposed an increase to $1.25 and to extend coverage to an additional 9 to 12 million workers. The plan also was to provide for a 37 1/2 hour week in 1957 and then to 35 hours in 1959. The Bureau of Labor Statistics pointed out that the lowest annual income for a family of four to maintain "health, efficiency, nurture of children...and self-respect" was $3,812 a year. A $1.25 wage would only mean $2,500 a year.

Ironworkers in 1953, jumping a 100 foot derrick during the construction of a new office building at 477 Madison Avenue in New York City.

Certificate of Completion of Apprenticeship was developed in 1955 and since then has been available to members who graduate to "Journeyman" classification after completing their apprenticeship.

Pensioners of Local No. 455, New York, N.Y. who received their pension under the first Industry-Wide Pension Plan. Guests and Pensioners, **Top Row, left to right:** Isaac Wollicover, Pensioner; Nicholas Danilik, Pensioner; John Voparil, Pensioner; Stanley Kryza, Pensioner; Isaac Steingart, Pensioner; Jacob Kaminsky, Pensioner; Charles Cambria, Pensioner. **Center Row left to right:** Harold Stern, Attorney; Frank Haas, Union Trustee; Martin Segal, Consultant; Robert Tilove, Martin Segal & Company; Louis Birnbaum, Pensioner; Morris Kleiman, Pensioner; William Steinbrenner, Pensioner; Ernest Sparks, Union Trustee. **At Table, left to right:** John Ruksteus, Pensioner; Morris Ginsberg, Pensioner; Frank Kohm, Union Co-Chairman; W. K. Ross, Employer Co-Chairman; Joseph F. Boyen, International Vice President; Mike Sadorowitz, Pensioner; and, Frederick Bruninger, Pensioner.

Interstate Highway Legislation and a Building Boom

General President J. H. Lyons wrote a letter on January 3, 1955 to all the affiliated local unions with an optimistic picture for the coming year. He pointed out that 90 billion dollars had been allocated by Congress for highway construction over the next ten years. Also, a commercial building boom which had started in New York City in the early 1950's had spread to Chicago.

The first new 41-story Prudential Life Insurance building was being erected. This would be the first such building built in Chicago in over 30 years. The last had been the Field Building, which Roosevelt had pointed to

General Organizer Hugh Williamson and Business Agent Jack Martin, Local No. 66, San Antonio, Texas congratulates Brother Fred Fishback as he retires from Local No. 66 in 1955.

John W. "Bill" Hardestey Appointed

On November 8, 1955, General President John H. Lyons appointed John W. "Bill" Hardesty as a General Organizer to serve in the capacity of Apprenticeship Director. He was assigned to assist in adjusting any problems which might arise concerning the proper administration of existing apprenticeship programs. Director Hardesty was the former President and Business Agent of Local No. 25, Detroit, Michigan.

John W. "Bill" Hardesty
Appointed General Organizer and first Apprenticeship Director of the International Association on November 8, 1955.

as the only private structure being built at the worst point in the depression. Ironworkers were looking forward to plenty of new jobs through a 9 billion dollar program to be completed over ten years in the Pacific Northwest. This included power plants as well as new dam construction. Also, employment opportunities were increasing through the Atomic Energy Construction Program.

The A. F. of L. Builds a New Building

The May, 1955 issue of *The Ironworker* magazine reported the laying of the cornerstone of the new home of the A. F. of L.. The building had been two years in the planning stage and it was designed to accommodate a unified AFL-CIO in the future. This building was to replace the former headquarters which had been built in 1916 and dedicated on July 4th by Samuel Gompers and President Woodrow Wilson. As the corner stone was laid the steel framework had already been completed by the Ironworkers. The 3 1/2 million dollar structure was located on 16th and H streets just across Lafayette Park from the White House.

In June of 1955, the International Association established an official office in Washington, D.C. General President Lyons pointed out in *The Ironworker* magazine that this office would allow International officers to meet with other labor leaders, management representatives and legislators.

Washington, D.C. branch office of the International Association opens in 1955. General President Lyons meets with other International representatives.

Committees Meet to Study the Merger of the A. F. of L. and CIO

Since both Phil Murray of the CIO and William Green of the A. F. of L. had died in 1952, and both organizations now had new leadership, there was for the first time in many years a chance for unity. Previous meetings had been held over the years going back to 1937, but they all failed. This would be the first meeting since 1950. The new leaders did not have the personal prejudices towards each other that had been built up by raids on each other's organization, and strong public statements about each other. Both organizations agreed to no prior conditions. They issued the following statement:

> *"We met today in good faith to try to achieve labor unity. Both sides came into the meeting with no prior conditions. ....There was a general discussion of all phases of the problems. In particular, the conference gave consideration to the problems of 'raiding' which, it was agreed, is not conducive to unity."*

The founding of the American Federation of Labor and Congress of Industrial Organizations (the AFL-CIO) on December 5, 1955, brought into one center unions representing approximately 16 million workers - over 85 percent of the membership claimed by all unions in the United States. The last conventions of the separate organizations, held on December 1 and 2, approved the merger agreement, a new constitution, and an implementation agreement designed to combine the two federations without dissolving either organization. The first convention of the AFL-CIO elected George Meany

George Meany and Walter P. Reuther, heads of the AFL-CIO, symbolize labor's new unity through merger on December 5, 1955.

President and William F. Schnitzler, Secretary-Treasurer. They also elected 27 Vice Presidents, 17 of whom had been proposed by the A. F. of L. and 10 by the CIO. Under the constitution, these 29 officers constitute the Executive Council and the governing body between the biennial conventions.

Juel D. Drake Appointed

General Organizer Juel D. Drake was appointed to the office of Ninth General Vice President on March 15, 1956 by General President John H. Lyons. General Vice President Drake would later become General Secretary and General President.

In order to establish and promote an adequate Apprenticeship Training Program for Shopmen, the General Executive Board on November 22, 1955, adopted Standards of Apprenticeship for Ornamental Metal and Structural Steel Fabricators which were subsequently approved by the General Executive Council. In order to promote such a training program, General President Lyons appointed General Organizer Charles L. (Doc) Lyon Director of Shopmen's Apprenticeship Training. General Organizer Lyon worked under the direction of Apprenticeship Director Hardesty.

Juel D. Drake appointed Ninth General Vice President on March 15, 1956.

Charles L. "Doc" Lyon General Organizer appointed Director of Shopmen's Apprenticeship Training on November 22, 1955.

First Standards of Apprenticeship For Structural Steel Fabricator

Shopmen's Local No. 491 of the San Francisco Bay Area in California had operated successfully an Apprentice Training Program for Structural Steel Fabricator apprentices since March, 1946. More than one hundred apprentices had been indentured, of which sixty-seven satisfactorily completed their apprenticeship training, and were issued Certificates of Completion by the Apprenticeship Division of the State of California. Their certificates were presented at banquets sponsored by the State of California. Among the prominent speakers that addressed the apprentices were Governor Earl Warren (who became Chief Justice of the Supreme Court), Secretary of Labor Maurice Tobin and Assistant Secretary of the Navy, Mark Andrews.

Members of Shopmen's Local No. 491 Joint Apprenticeship Committee, with the assistance of General Organizer Charles L. "Doc" Lyon, Apprenticeship Director-Shop Division and Apprenticeship Director J.W. "Bill" Hardesty, had been successful in negotiating revised Standards of Apprenticeship for the training of Structural Steel Fabricators, which standards conformed to the International's uniform apprenticeship training program. The new Standards were signed at a ceremonial dinner held in Oakland, California on Tuesday, August 21, 1956.

The Thirtieth International Convention was held October 22-26, 1956 at the Hotel Statler in Washington, D.C. General President John H. Lyons, General Secretary James R. Downes and General Treasurer John J. Dempsey were reelected by acclamation. All the incumbent General Vice Presidents were elected by acclamation. General Vice President Juel D. Drake who was also President of the Iron Workers District Council in Washington, D.C., Baltimore, Maryland and Vicinity opened the Convention. It was reported that as of June 30, 1956 the International Association had 139,469 members.

A total of 128 resolutions were considered and acted upon. Predominant among these resolutions were many covering the same subject - increase in Pension and Death Benefits. Many speakers addressed the delegates during the convention, such as, AFL-CIO President George Meany, Professor John T. Dunlop, Chairman of the National Joint Board for the Settlement of Jurisdictional Disputes, Metal Trades Department President James A. Brownlow and Secretary of Labor, James P. Mitchell. General Council Harold Stern addressed the delegates and explained in detail the status of the "Taft-Hartley Law" and the so-called "Right-to-Work Laws."

Delegates badge worn at the 30th International Convention held in Washington, D.C.

Delegates attending the 30th International Convention from October 22-26, 1956 in Washington, D.C.

On June 21, 1955, the first Annual Commencement Dinner given by Local No. 1, Chicago in co-sponsorship with the Association of Steel Erectors of Chicago was held, at which time fourteen apprentices were certified as journeymen.

Members of Local No. 7 working on Boston's Central Artery pledge lifesaving blood to the Red Cross. Workmen, left to right, are Angus Patterson, John McKenzie, John E. Buckley, Marvin G. Isenberg and Phil Kennedy.

Seated from left to right: Charles E. Hills, Jr. Recording Secretary, Local No. 491; Jack Bagnall, Secretary-Treasurer of Steel Fabricators Council, Director of Industrial Relations for Moore Dry Dock Company; Richard Murphy, JAC committee member for Judson Pacific Murphy Corp.; Frank Silva, President, Local No. 591. *Back Row, left to right:* Walter E. Siegel, Director of Industrial Relations, Soule Steel Company and Chairman, Steel Fabricators Council; Clyde Hammer, class instructor; Henry J. Figueira, Chairman, JAC and Assistant Business Agent, Local No. 491; Charles L. Lyon, Apprenticeship Director, Shop Division; Ernest Richards, JAC member for Herrick Iron Works; Anthony J. Chiappe, Business Agent, Local No. 491 and JAC member; John Sequeira, JAC, Moore Dry Dock Co.

Members of Local No. 433 erect 450 tons of structural steel for new ride and monorail system at Disneyland. The structure will reproduce, to exact scale, the famous Matterhorn Mountain of Switzerland. Two bobsled runs were also erected.

General Executive Council elected at the 30th International Convention.

133

It was reported at the convention that the Iron Workers International Association reached jurisdictional agreements with the Sheet Metal Workers (February 6, 1952); International Union of Elevator Constructors (May 26, 1953); Carpenters (June 3, 1953); Boilermakers (September 23, 1953); Plumbers and Pipe Fitters (October 8, 1953); Machinists (March 22, 1955) and the Electrical Workers (May 5, 1955 and Interpretation March 15, 1956). It was also reported that, as of June 30, 1956, eight hundred three (803) International agreements had been consummated.

George Meany
AFL-CIO President addressed the delegates to the 30th International Convention.

On November 26, 1956, General President Lyons was appointed by Secretary of Labor James Mitchell to serve on a committee to develop specific recommendations to President Eisenhower for the amendment of the Taft-Hartley Act with reference to its application to the building and construction trades. On December 26, 1956, Local No. 17, Cleveland, Ohio, honored General President Lyons who was also a member of Local No. 17. To emphasize their recognition of the work he had done on behalf of the International and his local union he was presented with an honorary life membership card engraved in gold. His services were further recognized by the presentation of a

Delegate George Melcher, Local No. 40, wearing the same shirt he wore at the 1907 Convention when it was Local No. 2.

beautifully engraved diamond ring. The presentation was made by President George Darling and Business Representative Thomas E. McDonald in St. Louis.

On January 4, 1957, General President Lyons sent a letter to all affiliated Shopmen local unions. He stated that, "Without fear of contradiction, I am of the confirmed opinion that the progress which we made in 1956 is greater than any year since our Shopmen Organizing Campaign was initiated in April, 1937 and, in

Vice President Juel D. Drake as President of the Washington/Baltimore District Council turning gavel over to President Lyons to officially open the 30th International Convention.

Lifetime membership Gold Card presented to President Lyons from Local No. 17, Cleveland, Ohio.

this connection, I can point with pride to the fact that: (1) our Organizing Campaign has progressed satisfactorily; (2) the agreements which were negotiated in 1956 are far superior to those negotiated in previous years; (3) new Welfare Plans have been established and the benefits provided for in existing plans have been greatly improved; and (4) the affairs of our Shopmen's Local Unions, as a whole, are being conducted with a higher degree of efficiency than at any time heretofore. In addition to obtaining in our new collective bargaining agreements provisions providing for greater protection for our members, we were also able to obtain wage increases averaging approximately 11-1/2 cents per hour."

On March 12, 1957 the Iron Workers International entered into an agreement with the Brotherhood of Painters, Decorators and Paperhangers of America for the purpose of improving relations between the two trades, facilitating the settlement of jurisdictional disputes and establishing an understanding that would mutually assist each union to secure and to perform work coming within its recognized jurisdiction on new construction work.

Business Manager Thomas E. McDonald (right) and President George Darling (left) of Local No. 17 present gold card to General President Lyons (center) on December 21, 1956.

134

First Joint Apprenticeship Class, Ironworkers Local No. 97, Vancouver, B.C., Canada in March, 1957.

The Ironworker Magazine Changes Size

The July, 1957 issue of *The Ironworker* magazine changed size from 10" x 6-1/2" to 11-3/4" x 8-1/2." On July 1, 1957, General President Lyons pursuant to the authorization given him by the General Executive Council, appointed General Organizer Stanley Rounds as **"Special Assistant to the President in Charge of Jurisdiction."** Unfortunately, Special Assistant Rounds would die a few years later on September 7, 1959. General Organizer C.G. Hungate would be appointed on October 1, 1959 to fill the vacancy created by the death of Brother Rounds.

*Size of **The Ironworker** magazine changes, July 1957 cover.*

James V. Cole Appointed General Treasurer

The sudden death of General Treasurer John J. Dempsey, Jr., on December 20, 1958, created a vacancy among the fiscal officers of the International Association. General President Lyons appointed James V. Cole, membership No. 80814, a member of Local No. 40, New York, N.Y., as General Treasurer effective

James V. Cole appointed General Treasurer effective January 1, 1959.

January 1, 1959. Brother Cole was born in Newfoundland, Canada, January 22, 1899 and came to the United States in May, 1919 at which time he became a member of Local No. 267, Camden, New Jersey. When the charter for this local was picked up in 1920 he transferred into Local No. 361 in Brooklyn, N.Y., where he established his home. The following two years he spent as a member of Local No. 13 in Philadelphia, Pa., and then in 1923 transferred into Local No. 40, New York, N.Y. He was elected to the Executive Board and became Business Agent of Local No. 40 in 1935 in which capacity he served until January, 1951 when he was appointed General Organizer.

The net proceeds from a dinner held in honor of General President John H. Lyons on November 29, 1958 were used to establish the John H. Lyons Scholarship Fund. This Scholarship Fund which is still in existence today has helped many children of members of the International Association.

Labor-Management Reporting and Disclosure Act of 1959

The Eighty-Sixth Congress passed the "Labor-Management Reporting and Disclosure Act of 1959," which became a law on September 14, 1959 when President Eisenhower signed the law. This law is designed to eliminate improper activities by labor or management. The Act provides certain protection for the rights of labor organization members; provides for the filing of reports describing the organization, financial dealings, and business practices of labor organizations, their officers and employees, certain employers, labor relations consultants, and unions in trusteeship; safeguards union election procedures; sets standards for the handling of union funds; amends the Taft-Hartley Law to eliminate the "no-man's land" in NLRB cases; closes previously existing loopholes in the protection against secondary boycotts; and limits organizational and jurisdictional picketing.

In 1960, members of Local No. 37, Providence, Rhode Island erected the first fully mechanized post office building in the United States.

135

First graduating apprentice class of Local No. 24, Denver was held in early 1960.

death benefit stamps. Members of Shopmen local unions and Navy Yard Rigger local unions would pay $1 a month per capita tax, 50 cents above the present amount.

A number of amendments were made to the International Constitution in order to clarify sections of the Constitution and to revise some other sections. This was done on advice of General Counsel Harold Stern and to comply with provisions of the Labor-Management Reporting and Disclosure Act of 1959, commonly known as the Landrum-Griffin Law.

Other subjects covered at the 31st Convention were Apprenticeship Progress, Jurisdictional Agreements with other International Unions, Bonding, Metal Curtain Wall Construction, Missile Base Construction, the Shopmen Division and financial matters. General President Lyons reported that during 1960 Shop representatives made 3,282 visits to unorganized shops - contacted 7,576 unorganized workers at their homes - attended 842 organizational meetings and as a result were successful in organizing 105 unorganized shops.

The **Thirty-First International Convention** was held October 17-21, 1960 at the Statler Hotel in Washington, D.C.. There were 816 delegates in attendance making it the largest convention in the history of the International. General President Lyons, General Secretary Downes and General Treasurer Cole were reelected. William F. Bauers, Joseph F. Boyen, Gay Borrelli, John L. McCarthy, E.G. Glazener, Juel D. Drake, John H. Lyons, Jr., LaVern Smith and Robert V. Poole would be elected as General Vice Presidents.

There were 220 resolutions presented at the convention. The delegates voted to raise the per capita tax for the first time since 1932 and to up the pension and death benefit assessments. For the members of outside locals, the convention adopted a $2 package increase in monthly payments, including a 75-cent hike in per capita from $2 to $2.75, a $1 increase in the pension fund payments and a 25-cent raise in the cost of monthly

General President Lyons congratulates General Secretary James R. Downes on his election to a new term at the 31st Convention.

General Vice President John H. Lyons, Jr. (right) and General President John H. Lyons, Sr., congratulate each other on their reelection at the 31st International Convention.

General Organizer Les Myers presents General President Lyons with a century-old wrought iron bolt removed from the Capitol dome during the repair work performed by Local No. 5 members in 1959.

General President Lyons pictured in the colorful Indian headdress presented to him by delegates Frank Stacey and Joseph Stacey of Local No. 711, Montreal, Canada. Mr. Lyons was made a blood brother of the Mohawk Reserve of Caughnawaga Canada and was given the name Ritotowanna, which means Brave Group Leader.

Friday, August 5, 1960 was a red-letter day for Local No. 201, Washington, D.C. That's the day the members celebrated by burning the mortgage on their new office and meeting hall at 1507 Rhode Island Avenue, N.E. General Vice President Lyons and General Organizer Robert Cooney attended the ceremonies along with General Treasurer James V. Cole.

John F. Kennedy's Election as President of the United States

What did the election mean? First of all, it had great meaning in the recognition of the role which organized labor played before and during the presidential campaign. President Kennedy had the support of most of organized labor, while in contrast, Nixon had the overwhelming support of business groups. Organized labor participated both in the formulation of the Democratic platform and in the practical work of electing the candidate.

This period in history would begin on a very cold January 20, 1961, as John Fitzgerald Kennedy assumed the office of President of the United States. Although the day was cold, the nation was optimistic about the future. It finally looked as if all the problems we had been sweeping under the rug would finally be looked at and solved.

In a column in *The Ironworker* magazine by John Herling, "Washington Observations," Mr. Herling compares the beginning of Kennedy's administration to the "First 100 Days" of the

Roosevelt administration in 1933. As Eisenhower left office and Kennedy became President the nation had more than five million unemployed. Kennedy knew he had been elected over Nixon with the help of labor, minority groups in the cities, and the poor of Appalachia. When the economic situation did not improve, Kennedy met with organized labor and they were impressed at how well aware of the situation he was. Kennedy was later quoted by President Lyons as saying:

Local No. 396, St. Louis, broke ground for their new union meeting hall, offices and apprentice school on December 2, 1960. General Vice President John McCarthy **(third from right)** and Joe Cousins, St. Louis Building Trades, get ready to turn over the first spadeful of dirt. Interested onlookers are **(left to right)** Assistant Business Agent John Miles; President John Rollings, Missouri State Labor Council, AFL-CIO; Business Agent Joseph Hunt; Local Union President Robert Nimmo; Architect Karl Nicoloff.

General Vice President John H. Lyons joins other labor union officials at a briefing held before touring the TITAN ICBM sites at Beale Air Force Base, Marysville, California. The Ironworkers had a great deal of work on these sites.

Iron Workers sign agreement on February 22, 1961 with Glaziers and Glazing Employers. General President Lyons is shown signing the agreement for the Iron Workers and General President L. M. Raftery signed for the Painters.

watched a long time dream come true as construction of their new hall and school began. The air conditioned brick and cut stone building would accommodate 350 members in the meeting room and two adjoining classrooms could be opened to seat an additional 150 people.

On January 19, 1961, the National Joint Board for the Settlement of Jurisdictional Disputes reaffirmed its July 28, 1960 job decision relative to the Lowry Missile Base which read as follows: "The loading, unloading and handling with power equipment of dust collectors, fans, blowers and other equipment is governed by the decision of record of October 1923, and shall be assigned to the Iron Workers."

On February 22, 1961, General President Lyons and L.M. Raftery of the Brotherhood of Painters, Decorators and Paperhangers of America signed the Iron Worker-Glazier Agreement. Other important documents signed at the time were: an agreement between the International Association and the National Joint Trade Board of the Glass and Glazing Industry guaranteeing work assignments in accordance with the Iron Worker-Glazier Agreement.

At a testimonial dinner held on May 13, 1961, honoring General Treasurer James V. Cole, the "James Vincent Cole Scholarship Fund" was established. The Fund provides a four-year scholarship annually to a deserving son or daughter of a Local No. 40 member. The first $4,000 scholarship was awarded to Edward Nicholson. Through the years, this Scholarship has benefitted many sons and daughters of Local No. 40 members who would not have had the opportunity to go to college.

"Our labor unions are not narrow, self-seeking groups. They have raised wages, shortened hours and provided supplemental benefits. Through collective bargaining and grievance procedures they have brought justice and democracy to the shop floor. But their work goes beyond their own jobs and even beyond our borders."

The need was to have a larger liberal majority in the House and Senate and labor pledged their support to do this in the elections of 1962. *The Ironworker* magazine reported that as Kennedy tried to pass important legislation for unions and the masses, he was constantly blocked not just by Republican "enemies" but by Democrats, many of them Southern Dixiecrats. Kennedy, like Roosevelt, was an expert at reaching the public. He would use a press conference to condemn the steel companies.

In the 1960's, many of the Iron Worker local unions would begin building their own union halls and schools. Some of the affiliates had the finances to either build their own building or to buy a building and convert it into offices, union hall and in some cases where there was enough room, they could also have an apprenticeship school. For example, on Saturday, December 2, 1960, members of Local No. 396, St. Louis, Mo.,

The James Vincent Cole Scholarship Fund is established at testimonial dinner honoring General Treasurer Cole.

138

THE IRONWORKER   NOVEMBER, 1961
VOL. LXI • No. 11

John H. Lyons, Sr.
1891-1961

GENERAL PRESIDENT JOHN H. LYONS
1891-1961

The Death of
General President John H. Lyons Sr.

John H. Lyons would die in his sleep on October 26,1961 at the Barnes Hospital in St. Louis while convalescing from a lung operation that had been performed three weeks earlier. General President Lyons served as head of the 140,000 member International Association for thirteen years. As pointed out earlier in this book, he had the unique distinction of being the only man to be elected to all three of the Iron Worker top offices, a record that still holds as we celebrate the 100th Anniversary of the Union's existence. President Lyons was initiated into Local No. 6, Niagara Falls and later transferred to Local No. 17, Cleveland, Ohio where he held several offices. In 1928, he was appointed General Organizer and in September of that year was elected the First General Treasurer of the International Association. In 1939, President Lyons was appointed General Secretary and at the 1940 International Convention he was elected to that office. In 1948, he was elected General President and took office on January 1, 1949.

A message was received from Secretary of Labor Arthur Goldberg:

> *"I am deeply grieved by the death of my good friend John H. Lyons...He was one of the most highly talented and dedicated labor statesmen I have had the good fortune to know during my association with the labor movement. Besides his consuming interest in the welfare of workers, he gave freely of himself to public service and community interest..."*

John H. Lyons, Jr.
Elected General President

The day after the late General President John H. Lyons Sr. was laid to rest the members of the General Executive Council met to select his successor in accordance with Article XII, Section 3 of the International Constitution. After pointing out all his qualifications, the General Executive Council elected John H. Lyons, Jr.,age 42, as General President.

President Lyons was initiated as an apprentice Ironworker by Local No. 17, Cleveland, Ohio in 1937. He later transferred to Local No. 392, East St. Louis, Illinois and continued working at the trade during summers while attending college. He received a bachelor of science degree in mechanical engineering from the University of Missouri School of Mines and Metallurgy in 1942.

After his honorable discharge from the U.S. Army Air Corps in August 1946, General President Lyons, Jr. was employed by one of America's largest ornamental companies, General Bronze Corporation and later became one of the leading experts in curtain wall construction. He was appointed General Organizer in 1954 and in 1955 was named to head the branch office of the International in Washington, D.C. at which time he transferred his membership to Local No. 5 of that city.   On April 28, 1958 he was appointed General Vice President and was elected to that office at the 1960 International Convention. On April 15, 1961, General Vice President John H. Lyons, Jr. was named Executive Assistant to the General President after the General Executive Council adopted a resolution authorizing General President John H. Lyons, Sr. to create this office.

John H. Lyons, Jr.,
elected General President by the General
Executive Council on November 1, 1961.

John H. Lyons
General President

Chapter Nine

John H. Lyons Jr. Elected President

It was immediately apparent when General President John H. Lyons, Jr. assumed office that he was destined to become an active and effective labor leader. At the AFL-CIO Convention held in Miami Beach in December, 1961, President Lyons was elected tenth vice president of the Building and Construction Trades Department, AFL-CIO and vice president of the Metal Trades Department, AFL-CIO. George Meany, President, AFL-CIO appointed President Lyons to serve on a Mediation Panel to solve internal disputes with the AFL-CIO.

Robert E. P. Cooney Appointed General Vice President

Prior to the AFL-CIO Convention, the General Executive Council of the International Association met on December 6, 1961, at which time President Lyons appointed General Organizer Robert Cooney, member of Local No. 17, Cleveland as Eighth General Vice President. He was the President of the Iron Workers District Council of the Mid-Atlantic States. He also represented the International Association on the executive board of the Maritime Trades Department, AFL-CIO. He has served as a board member for three years.

Robert E. P. Cooney
Appointed
General Vice President

Prior to his service with the U. S. Navy during World Ward II, Vice President Cooney was initiated by Local No. 17. He received an honorable discharge in 1945 after a 3-year hitch which included sea duty in the Pacific theater. He immediately returned home to resume work at his trade as a structural Ironworker.

The late General President Lyons appointed him an acting general organizer in June 1956, after having served his local in various offices. On July 1, 1957 he was named a general organizer. He retired in 1985.

Hugh Williamson Appointed General Vice President

Also appointed was General Organizer Hugh Williamson, member of Local No. 84, Houston, Texas as Ninth General Vice President. General Vice President Williamson was president of the Iron Workers District Council of the State of Texas. He was appointed an acting general organizer February 1, 1955 and named general organizer effective July 25, 1955. He previously served as business agent of Local 84 for six years and headed the Houston Building and Construction Trades Council for an unprecedented five terms. He was initiated in May 1942 by Galveston Local No. 135 and transferred to the Houston local in 1944. During his years

Hugh Williamson
Appointed
General Vice President

with the tools, he worked at all phases of the craft and furthered his technical knowledge by attending college engineering night classes. He retired in 1986.

John H. Lyons Jr. would see great changes in the role of the General President. He would be expected to take part in many government committees and commisions. For example, on January 21, 1962, he was appointed by Attorney General Robert F. Kennedy to serve on the 21-member Citizens' Advisory Council to the President's Committee on Juvenile Delinquency and Youth Crime. On November 1, 1962, Secretary of Labor Wirtz appointed President Lyons a member of the Federal Advisory Council to the Bureau of Employment Security. On

Iron Workers sign International Agreements with American Bridge Company and Bethlehem Steel Company. Signing for the International Association are: **Seated (second from right)** General President Lyons and **(left)** General Secretary Downes; Vice President Jack Wagner **(second from left)** signs for Bethlehem Steel and vice President Porter signs for American Bridge. **Standing (left to right)** are: General Treasurer Cole, General Counsel Stern; and General Vice Presidents Glazener, Williamson, Borrelli, Drake, Poole, Smith, Boyen, Cooney and McCarthy.

Martin Plattner, past president of Local No. 63 **(second from right)** receives 50-year pin from General Treasurer Cole **(right)**. General Organizer Leslie Myers **(left)** and Business Agent Math Martin also took part in the ceremony to pay tribute to the guest of honor, Mr. Plattner, and the forty-four other 50 year members of Local No. 63.

June 4, 1963, he was appointed by President Kennedy as a labor representative to the National Labor-Management Panel established by the Taft-Hartley Act and on August 12, 1964, President Johnson appointed him to the National Advisory Council to the Human Rights Commission.

New Agreement With American Bridge & Bethlehem Steel Companies

In 1905 the existing agreements between the International Association and most of the major steel erectors in the nation were torn up and they commenced operating on an open-shop basis. In 1937 after 32 years of virtual open warfare, a verbal settlement was reached and a harmonious relationship was resumed. It remained, however, as an objective of the International Association to again have a written signed document evidencing such agreement.

In March 1962, the General Executive Council, meeting with the top officers of the major steel companies, signed an International Agreement with the American Bridge Company, the Bethlehem Steel Company and all of the remaining unsigned major steel erectors in the nation. After 32 years of strife, and after 25 years of verbal understandings, relationship between our International Association and all steel erectors was once again formalized within a written agreement.

Legislation Affecting Labor Under Kennedy

The Kennedy Administration was attacked from all sides by conservatives that said he was too pro-labor and anti-business. In the John Herling column in

The Ironworker, Herling said, "...the Kennedy Administration was bothered and bombarded by anti-labor groups with such vehemence and hostility that there is no precedent for it short of the anti-Roosevelt campaign during the 1930's." One of the pieces of legislation that was supported by labor and was defeated was medical care for the aged under Social Security.

The Davis-Bacon Act was extended to provide prevailing wages at Minuteman Missile Site Facilities. A bill was also introduced to require builders entering into leasing agreements with the Post Office Department to comply with the provisions of the Davis-Bacon prevailing wage act. President Kennedy supported the liberalization of the National Labor Relations Board and appointed General President Lyons to the National Labor-Management Panel, which was designed to work out meth-

International Representatives attend a special staff conference at St. Louis, Missouri in 1963.

Ironworkers working on the "Skyway" Bridge at St. Catharines, Ontario in 1962.

General President Lyons meets with President Kennedy and other labor leaders to discuss various labor issues. (President Lyons is shown to the left and behind President Kennedy, center).

ods for making free collective bargaining work better.

General Secretary James Downes reported that attempts were being made to pass the Martin Bill, which limited collective bargaining to one union and one employer. This would nullify any International agreements or any multi-employer agreements at the local level. Members were encouraged to write, telegraph, and phone their representatives to stop this anti-labor legislation.

The fight was on again to change the Taft-Hartley Act, especially the so-called "right-to-work" clause, 14B. George Meany said at this time, "The power given states to bar union shops, under 14B, bestows on them greater power than belongs to the federal government."

On December 14, 1962, General President Lyons and General President Murphy of the Bricklayers International finalized the last of the series of numerous meetings by affixing their names to an agreement between the two crafts. The agreement applied to the installation and erection of all types of precast, pre-stressed concrete stone or imitation stone or other fabricated masonry units when installed as wall panels by means of bolting and/or welding to structural steel or concrete frame construction.

On May 27-28, 1963, the first staff meeting of all International Representatives was held in St. Louis, Mo.. In the two days a tremendous number of subjects were analyzed, with a total of fifteen subjects being discussed in joint session and a dozen other subjects being covered in each of the separate sessions. Some of the

subjects covered were the Taft-Hartley and Landrum-Griffin Laws; new techniques and processes relating to our trade; jurisdictional relationship with other trades; shop organization campaigns; shop negotiations; and NLRB decisions.

On November 23, 1963, General President Lyons had the distinct honor of unveiling a bronze plaque in memory of his father. The site of the memorial plaque is the International Bridge between Lewiston, New York and Queenstown, Ontario. Measuring 23" x 40" the plaque honors not only former President Lyons, Sr., but also all Ironworkers from both sides of the border.

The Assassination of President Kennedy

On "The President's Page" in the December, 1963 issue of *The Ironworker*, General President Lyons would write the following.

> "A warped mind and a mail order rifle costing a paltry twelve dollars has removed from the midst of this great nation a great and beloved President, John F. Kennedy.

> "Never before in the history of civilization has one individual done so much harm to so many, Lee Harvey Oswald lived a virtually useless and worthless life. Nowhere can there be found evidence of his having contributed anything to the welfare of his fellow man. Yet,

1891 1961

JOHN H. LYONS

THIS STRUCTURE CONNECTING TWO GREAT NATIONS AND ERECTED BY AMERICAN AND CANADIAN IRONWORKERS EXEMPLIFIES THE SKILL, ABILITY AND INGENUITY OF JOHN H. LYONS, WHO WAS AN IRONWORKER FOR MORE THAN 45 YEARS. HE BEGAN HIS CAREER IN NIAGARA FALLS AS A MEMBER OF IRONWORKERS LOCAL UNION NO. 9, WHOSE MEMBERS, TOGETHER WITH THE MEMBERS OF IRONWORKERS LOCAL UNION NO. 736, HAMILTON, ONTARIO, ERECTED THIS BRIDGE. AT THE TIME OF HIS DEATH, OCTOBER 26, 1961, HE WAS GENERAL PRESIDENT OF THE INTERNATIONAL ASSOCIATION OF BRIDGE, STRUCTURAL AND ORNAMENTAL IRONWORKERS, ONE OF THE PIONEER ORGANIZATIONS OF THE TRADE LABOR MOVEMENT. THIS SPAN OF STEEL ERECTED BY HIS FELLOW-CRAFTSMEN PORTRAYS ONE OF HIS LIFE-LONG OBJECTIVES, THE ELIMINATION OF BARRIERS BETWEEN PEOPLE.

Memorial to former General President John H. Lyons, Sr.

General President Lyons meets with President Johnson for a formal White House dinner.

A "slip form" method of pouring concrete for the inner core of a 270 foot office building in suburban St. Louis. The picture taken at night indicates that around-the-clock operation was necessary for this unique method of construction. Controlled from a central point, 67 hydraulic jacks raised the form, including a 22-ton Linden Crane, and 37 Ironworkers from Local No. 396, St. Louis, Missouri, at the rate of 1/8 inch per minute, or 15 feet per day. Fruin-Colnon were the contractors.

Members of Local No. 433 erect a unique monorail system for the Los Angeles County Fair. They not only erected the structural steel but in addition erected and secured the fourteen individual cars making up the system.

Fifty year members of Local No. 7, Boston were presented 50-year pins by General President John H. Lyons on May 9, 1962.

Members of Local No. 3, Pittsburgh in 1962, erecting the IBM building in that city. The frame is designed as a truss wall carrying the load to two points of ground contact on each side. There are no interior vertical columns.

incredible as it seems, this nonentity within a few seconds was able to destroy one of the outstanding leaders in history, thereby influencing beyond calculation the course of future events. The value that each American citizen as an individual, this country as a nation, and the world as a whole, would have derived in benefits from the life of John F. Kennedy, had he lived to his normal end, is beyond calculation."

To the surprise of the labor movement President Johnson dedicated himself to carrying out many of the unfinished programs started by President Kennedy including civil rights legislation, tax cuts for the middle and low income groups, and a medical care bill. On the evening of Monday, May 4, 1964 President Johnson invited sixty labor leaders to the White House for a formal dinner. Mr. & Mrs. Lyons were among the guests and Mrs. Lyons was seated at the table with the President.

On July 2, 1964 President Johnson signed H.R. 6041, an Act to amend the prevailing wage section of the Davis-Bacon Act. This bill brought the law up to date. Thirty years before, fringe benefits were unknown. The new law sensibly provided that wage determinations shall, in addition to cash wages, take account of prevailing benefits such as medical and hospital care, pensions and workmen's compensation, unemployment insurance, vacations, holidays and other such factors. General President Lyons was present at the historic signing and was presented with one of the pens used in the signing.

The **Thirty-Second International Convention** was held at the Hilton Hotel in San Francisco from October 12-16, 1964. General President Lyons, General Secretary Downes, General Treasurer Cole and all the General Vice Presidents were reelected. General President Lyons reported that the membership of the International had been growing steadily since 1962. General Vice President Juel D. Drake, who was also President of the State of California District Council, opened the Convention.

Some of the issues discussed were revision of the transfer system, increasing the funding for old age and disability funds. Changes were needed as membership increased and the number of older members were retiring. The small amounts paid into these funds were only enough to keep them solvent until 1972. The Death Benefit Fund and other funds were established at a time when the United States had no Social Security System. Also discussed were the salaries of full time officers which had not been increased in eight years.

Reports were made by the Credentials, Rules, Constitution, Grievance, Organization, Resolutions and Officers' Report Committees. Finances, Political Activity, Legislation, Relationships with Employers, Research and Organization, Apprenticeship, Shop Division, National Joint Board for Settlement of

Badge worn by delegates to the 32nd International Convention.

Ironworker members of Local No. 433 erected the structural steel for the Los Angeles Federal Building in 1963-64. Two hugh stiff-leg derricks that rolled on steel tracks were used to erect the structural steel. Some of the Ironworkers on the job: **Left to right** *- Sam Dickey, Job Steward; Wylie Mumper, R.B. Crump, Howard Northwood, Jake West, Business Agent, Local No. 433; Bob C. Varroll, S.W. "Tex" Williams, Business Agent, Local No. 433; Mike Murphy, P.O. "Whitey" Adams, Superintendent, American Bridge Co.; Leo Berg, Jim Sevas.*

Jurisdictional Disputes and Litigated Matters, among other subjects, were covered at the Convention.

It was announced that a new department was established by the International, a Department of Research and Organization. This was needed because of all the new methods of fabrication, prefabricated metal buildings, and other changes that were affecting our industry.

Ironworkers and the Space Program and Missile Programs

From the very beginning our Union was an important partner in the 3 billion dollar space program. President Kennedy in the first year of his presidency issued an Executive Order to establish an eleven-member Missile Site Labor Commission to have the power to settle disputes. Two years later at our 32nd Convention President Lyons would report the following:

"This committee concentrated on the missile site projects and accomplished almost incredible results in the protection of our work jurisdiction and the improvement in employment opportunities involving tens of thousands of Ironworkers during each of the past four years.

Ironworkers build Intercontinental Ballistic Missile silos in 1962 at 165 separate locations in Missouri.

Some of these projects have had as many as 1,500 Ironworkers employed at one time."

The year before, General President John H. Lyons had received unanimous approval to appoint a missile committee for the purpose of handling all problems involving our International Association at the various missile sites. This would be the beginning of our Union's involvement in the space program and the landing on the moon.

The **CIVIL RIGHTS ACT** was passed in 1964 which makes it unlawful for an employer to discriminate in his hiring practice because of race, color, religion, sex or national origin. The law places certain responsibilities on employers, unions, joint labor-management committees, and joint apprenticeship committees.

In 1964, the Johnson-Humphrey ticket won by the greatest landslide since Roosevelt won in 1936. The Johnson ticket also helped to increase the pro-labor vote in the House and Senate. John Herling in *The Ironworker* wrote "...it looks as if the country will have the strongest pro-labor Congress in 30 years." The Democratic platform called for the repeal of Section 14-b of the Taft-Hartley Law, and it looked as if finally this would happen, and the workers in the 20 states that outlawed the right for true collective bargaining would be organized.

In his State of the Union Address on January 4, 1965, Johnson would introduce his program called "The Great Society." It called for a continuation of many of

Joseph F. Boyen, General Vice President member of Local No. 580, New York City, passed away on January 23, 1965.

the New Deal ideas plus civil rights legislation, a war on poverty, funding for education, and job training programs, to name only a few of his fourteen-point program.

On January 23, 1965, First General Vice President Joseph F. Boyen died. At the 32nd Convention, Boyen was elected to an eighth consecutive term as General Vice President. Vice President Boyen was initiated May 14, 1920 in Local No. 52, New York City, which later became Local No. 580. Vice President Boyen's daughter Dorothy was married to General President John H. Lyons, Jr.

The Tenth National Legislative Conference was held in the spring of 1965 by the Building and Construction Trades Department. There were 4,500 delegates in attendance, many from the various Iron Worker local unions throughout the country. President Johnson and Vice President Humphrey, as well as a number of Senators and Congressmen, addressed the delegates. Some of the subjects covered were amendments to Taft-Hartley, Landrum-Griffin Act, Davis-Bacon Act, Fair Labor Standards Act and the Social Security Act. Taxes, Civil Rights, Public Works Programs, Military Construction, Housing, Education, and Federal Standards for Unemployment Compensation were also on the program. The Legislative Conference has continued over the years, including 1996.

On August 9, 1965, eight Ironworker members of Local No. 321, Little Rock, Arkansas died when an explosion and flash fire deep in the cavernous site of a Titan II missile silo occurred at Searcy, Arkansas. They, along with 45 other building tradesmen, who also lost their lives, were engaged in the modifying of the missile

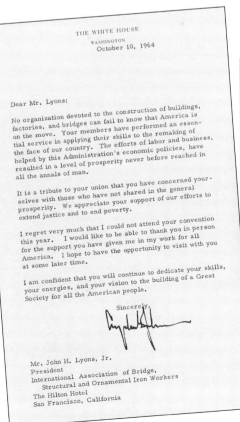

THE WHITE HOUSE
WASHINGTON
October 10, 1964

Dear Mr. Lyons:

No organization devoted to the construction of buildings, factories, and bridges can fail to know that America is on the move. Your members have performed an essential service in applying their skills to the remaking of the face of our country. The efforts of labor and business, helped by this Administration's economic policies, have resulted in a level of prosperity never before reached in all the annals of man.

It is a tribute to your union that you have concerned yourselves with those who have not shared in the general prosperity. We appreciate your support of our efforts to extend justice and to end poverty.

I regret very much that I could not attend your convention this year. I would like to be able to thank you in person for the support you have given me in my work for all America. I hope to have the opportunity to visit with you at some later time.

I am confident that you will continue to dedicate your skills, your energies, and your vision to the building of a Great Society for all the American people.

Sincerely,

Mr. John H. Lyons, Jr.
President
International Association of Bridge,
Structural and Ornamental Iron Workers
The Hilton Hotel
San Francisco, California

Delegates attending the 32nd Convention, October 11-17, 1964 in San Francisco, California.

146

General President Lyons attends historic signing of H.R. 6041, an Act to amend the prevailing wage section of the Davis-Bacon Act.

Quarterly meeting of District Council of Eastern Canada in 1966.

General President Lyons, receiving the gavel from temporary Chairman Juel D. Drake at the 32nd Convention.

George Meany, President of the AFL-CIO receiving congratulations from General President Lyons, General Secretary Downes and General Treasurer Cole after addressing the delegates to the 32nd Convention.

Members of Locals No. 40, New York City and 361, Brooklyn, N.Y. erecting the Unisphere for the New York World's Fair in 1963.

Vehicle Assembly Building, Merritt Island, Florida erected by members of Local No. 808, Orlando, Florida and fabricated by members of Local No. 698, Miami, Florida in 1965. The building is 525 feet 10 inches high, 716 feet 6 inches in overall length, and 518 feet in overall width. It has a 57,000 ton structural steel framework.

St. Louis Arch erected by members of Local No. 396, St. Louis, Missouri.

complex. Building Trades President Haggarty emphasized that all possible hazards must be removed from the numerous ICBM installations where thousands of construction workers are engaged in making similar modifications.

John F. Walsh Appointed

On July 8, 1966, General President Lyons appointed General Organizer John F. Walsh General Vice President, filling the vacancy created by the death of General Vice President Boyen. General Vice President Walsh was business agent of Local No. 272, Miami, Florida before being appointed General Organizer. Since 1958, he had been President of the Southeastern States District Council. General Vice President Walsh was closely associated with activities of the Kennedy Space Center. He retired on July 31, 1985.

On September 12, 1967, General President Lyons was the first General President of the Iron Workers to be appointed to the Executive Council of the AFL-

John F. Walsh
Appointed
General Vice President

CIO. He was appointed by AFL-CIO President George Meany.

By 1968 the nation was divided over the Vietnam War. With the decision of President Johnson not to run in 1968, Hubert Humphrey became the candidate. Humphrey, a true friend of labor, was endorsed by our Union and the entire AFL-CIO, and General President Lyons was a delegate to the Democratic Convention. The anti-war demonstrations in Chicago during the 1968 Democratic Convention that were shown on television damaged the Humphrey campaign. Nixon promised he had a way of ending the war and became the Republican nominee for President and the winner in what turned out to be a surprisingly close race.

The **Thirty-Third International Convention** was held October 7-11, 1968 at the New York Hilton Hotel in New York City. General President Lyons, General Secretary Downes, General Treasurer Cole and the incumbent General Vice Presidents were elected. General Organizer Thomas Clarkson, President of the Greater New York and Vicinity District Council, opened the Convention as temporary Chairman.

AFL-CIO President George Meany addressed the delegates. He said, "Let me say at the outset that I want to congratulate Jack Lyons and the officers of this organization and the delegates to this convention because you represent a modern American trade union dedicated to the welfare of its membership and making its contribution to the welfare of the community as a whole.

Members of Local No. 6, Buffalo, N.Y. erected two 250-ton basic oxygen furnaces at the Lackawanna plant of Bethlehem in 1965.

A group of Ironworkers employed on the Lackawanna plant's basic oxygen furnaces building. In the front row are several Union officers which included Business Manager James J. Willis and General Organizer Bannister.

148

Delegates attending the 33rd International Convention in New York City from October 7-11, 1968.

President Lyons acknowledges the delegates' ovation on his reelection at the 33rd Convention.

AFL-CIO President George Meany **(right)** talks with General President Lyons **(left)** and General Secretary Downes at the 33rd Convention.

Business Agent Jake West, Local No. 433, Los Angeles **(left)** travelled throughout the country with Gene Muskie, also a member of Local No. 433 and the brother of Vice Presidential candidate Edmund S. Muskie, in order to meet with officers and members of Iron Worker Local Unions to impress upon them the importance of the 1968 elections. General President Lyons **(3rd from left)**, General Secretary Downes **(4th from left)** and General Organizer Ralph Larkin, a member of Local No. 433 meet with Jake West and Gene Muskie to discuss the schedule.

Delegate's badge worn at the 33rd Iron Workers International Convention in 1968.

General Treasurer Cole **(left)**, General President Lyons **(center)** and General Secretary Downes showing unity at the 33rd Convention.

General Executive Council in 1964.

Members of Local No. 563, Duluth, Minnesota as well as members from Locals No. 103, 577 and 793 working on the expansion of the Taconite Industry on the 100 mile long Mesabi Iron Range in 1966.

Local No. 396 member James P. Mulherin helping to evacuate children from a Viet Cong village in 1966.

Ironworkers Robert Weidlich, Local No. 197 and Robert Hammock, Local No. 482, were serving in the SeaBees in Viet Nam in 1966.

Over the years, the Ironworkers have given concrete proof of the fact that collective bargaining under the American system can provide economic justice for members of the union and their families, and at the same time make a contribution to the advancement and welfare of the society of which you are a part."

As in past conventions many subjects were covered and voted on. General Secretary Downes reported that the organizing campaign which had been conducted in the Dominion of Canada for a number of years, involving the installation of Shopmen or Outside Erection Local Unions, had been successfully continued, with outstanding results.

He also reported that on September 10, 1966, the Iron Workers District Council of the Mid-Northern States was chartered and installed in St. Paul, Minnesota. The affiliates of the district council are located in Minnesota, Northern Michigan and North Dakota. At that time there were twenty-one district councils in the United States and Canada. It was also reported that seventeen new local union charters were issued and installed during the four-year period beginning July 1, 1964 and ending June 30, 1968. During that same period, seven local union charters were revoked. At that time there were 182 Outside Erection Local Union charters and 141 Shopmen Local Union charters, making a total of 323 local unions affiliated with the International Association. The total membership record as of June 30, 1968 was 164,902.

Other subjects, such as Apprenticeship Progress, Wage Increases, International Agreements, Amendments to the International Constitution, Finances, Death Benefit Fund, Old Age and Disability Pension Fund, Safety and many more subjects were covered.

President Lyons meets with Astronaut Buzz Aldrin after he came back from the Moon.

Victory in Space

President Nixon had been in office only six months when the Space Program launched by President Kennedy proved successful. On July 20, 1969 Neil Armstrong and Edwin Aldrin reached the moon in Apollo 11. Our Union, especially Local No. 808, had been active in the construction part of the U.S. Space Program and General President Lyons served on the Missile Advisory Board.

The Need To Repair
The Nation's Bridges

Even before Nixon took office it became obvious that America's infrastructure was in need of repair. In 1967, the Silver Bridge at Point Pleasant, West Virginia collapsed killing 46 people. The government was finally beginning to realize the need to replace "critically deficient" bridges throughout the nation. Reports published by our Union showed that out of the 563,500 bridges in the United States about 88,900 were in need of repair. Our International would continue to call attention to this issue in *The Ironworker* magazine as well as in the halls of Congress from the late 1960's until the present day. One of the bridges being repaired on a continual basis was the Golden Gate Bridge which was built by our members in the early 1930's. Members of Locals No. 377 and No. 378 were replacing the suspension cables on the bridge in 1974.

The Nixon years would also be a period of major new bridge construction. By November of 1969, members of Local No. 229 in San Diego were involved in the construction of the beautiful Coronado Bridge. Other bridges constructed at this time by our members included the Newport Bridge across Narragansett Bay, and by December of 1972 members of Baltimore Local No. 16 were working on the New Chesapeake Bay Bridge. New bridges were also being built by our members as a part of the Interstate Highway System which was started

during the Eisenhower years. By 1971, a total of 42,500 miles of highway had been completed or 75% of the proposed system.

National Iron Workers Contractor Associations Formed

In 1969, General President Lyons appointed a special ad hoc committee consisting of General Organizers Raymond J. Robertson and Ralph Larkin to travel throughout the United States to meet with Union Iron Worker contractors in order to determine whether these contractors would be interested in forming a National Iron Worker Contractors Association. The committee reported to President Lyons and then the General Executive Council in St. Louis. It was determined that the Ironworking Industry would be best suited by having four distinct National Contractor Associations covering Structural, Ornamental, Reinforcing and Rigging. At that time the International did not have a formal employer group to work with on a national basis. The primary problem in those days was the high level of activity at the National Joint Board for "Settlement of Jurisdictional Disputes." There was no National Iron Workers' Employers' group in existence to assist the Iron Workers International Union Representatives in their efforts to preserve their traditional jurisdictional claims at the Board level.

These contractors that took part in the meetings were advised of the International Association's recommendations and as a result, a meeting was held in 1969 in St. Louis, Missouri, between the Iron Workers International Association and various national contractors that represented each facet of the trade. This meeting resulted in the contractors forming The National Association of Miscellaneous, Ornamental and Architectural Products Contractors, The National Association of Reinforcing Steel Contractors and The National Erectors Association. The final organization that was involved was already in place, which was

John Hancock Center, Chicago, Illinois. Structural Steel erected by members of Local No. 1 and Curtainwall and Ornamental work erected by members of Local No. 63 in 1969.

Local No. 1 Business Agent, Joe Frankovic meets with Ironworkers on the John Hancock Center project. **Left to right:** Bill Bullard, Len Campbell, Joe Frankovic, Dody Cryder, Jack Bullard.

Local No. 1 connectors William Stone **(left)** and Robert W. Eldredge **(right)** at the top of the 100-story John Hancock Center, bolt the final ceremonial steel beam into place.

The structural framing of the exterior walls of the towers of the World Trade Center.

Over 525 Ironworkers of Local No. 40, New York City and No. 361, Brooklyn erected 210,000 tons of structural steel for the Twin Towers 110-story World Trade Center in New York City. Local No. 580 had 357 of their members erecting the skin of the building. Members of Shopmen's Local No. 455 fabricated the grillages for the Towers.

152

the Specialized Carriers and Rigging Association. From that time until the present day, these organizations have played an important role in issues confronting the Ironworking Industry.

New Building Construction

The late 1960's and 1970's was a time when many of our members were busy with the construction of major buildings. In early 1969, Local No. 1 "topped-out" the 100-story John Hancock Center in Chicago. In Albany, New York, in the State Capital, the entire center of town was leveled for the South Mall Project which was pushed by Governor Nelson Rockefeller. This state project was similar to the privately built Rockefeller Center development built by Governor Rockefeller's father in the 1930's. A total of 270,000 tons of steel was erected by our members.

By July of 1971, the twin towers of the World Trade Center in New York City were nearing completion. The "topping out" ceremony would take place on July 19th with General President Lyons taking part. At the time of peak employment, 525 Structural Ironworkers dispatched from Local No. 40 were working on the towers. For a short time these would be the world's tallest buildings.

Then in early 1971, Sears, Roebuck and Company announced plans to build the world's tallest building in Chicago. It would also be constructed by our members. The 1,454 foot high Sears Tower would be "topped out" on May 3, 1973. By July of 1971, nearly 1,000 Ironworkers were on the job in Orlando, Florida constructing Walt Disney's Magic Kingdom. Members of Local No. 808 were also working on the construction of a unique monorail at that site.

Plans were also underway for "Expo 74" in Spokane, Washington. The construction of this fair would provide hundreds of construction jobs for Ironworkers from Locals No. 14 and No. 511. These workers also constructed the Washington State Pavilion with a 2,700-seat theater and 75,000 square feet of exhibition halls.

Member of Local No. 1, Chicago welding on the world's tallest building, the Sears Tower, in 1973.

Below, Members of Local No. 1 who erected Structural Steel on Sears Tower.

Ironworkers position a heavy column during the Tier 1 construction phase of the Sears Tower.

Iron Workers General President John H. Lyons (right) greets Chicago Mayor Richard J. Daley during the topping out ceremonies for the Sears Tower; Iron Workers out of Local 1, Chicago, are seen in the background.

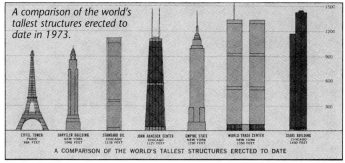

A comparison of the world's tallest structures erected to date in 1973.

A COMPARISON OF THE WORLD'S TALLEST STRUCTURES ERECTED TO DATE

153

The Walker Johnson Building at 18th Street and New York Ave. and houses in Washington, D.C., that occupied the space where the Ironworker Headquarters is to be built.

Excavation completed and reinforcing steel being placed by members of Local No. 201, Washington, D.C.

Connectors who secured final beam of the United Unions Building.

Members of Reinforcing Local No. 201 at garage level of the United Unions Building.

Ironworkers setting precast units for International Headquarters.

"Topping Out"

Members of Local No. 5, Washington, D.C. who worked on the "United Unions Building" gathered at the "topping out" ceremony with International Officers and representatives of other International Unions who will own the building with the Ironworkers.

General President John H. Lyons signs his name on last beam to be erected at topping out ceremonies of International Headquarters.

AFL-CIO Secretary-Treasurer Lane Kirkland who would later become AFL-CIO President signing name on last beam.

The International Moves To Washington D.C.

When the International was first established the headquarters were located wherever the Secretary-Treasurer lived. By the time of the McNamara incident International Headquarters would be in the American Central Life Building in Indianapolis. In 1920, General President Morrin moved headquarters to the Syndicate Trust Building in St. Louis. Then, at the time of the 29th Convention the International moved to new head-quarters in the Continental Building in St. Louis. However, more and more International unions were relocating in Washington, D.C.. It was becoming necessary to protect the interests of our membership against anti-labor legislation. In July of 1955, the International Association rented office space in Washington, D.C., where a branch office was opened.

It would be at the 33rd Convention in 1968 that a resolution was passed to move the International Headquarters to a site in Washington D.C.. An ideal situation developed when several other Internationals wished to do the same thing at the same time. Accordingly, United Unions, Inc., was formed, consisting of the Iron Workers International, the International Brotherhood of Painters & Allied Trades, the International Association of Firefighters, the Sheet Metal Workers International Association and the International Brotherhood of Bookbinders.

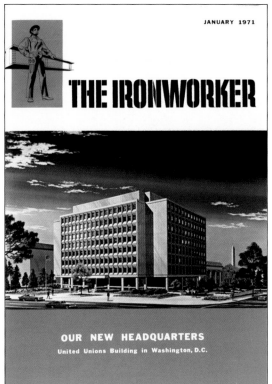

The site selected was both ideal and historic. It is only a short distance southwest of the White House and the Headquarters of the AFL-CIO. Across the street on New York Avenue is the Octagon House, which was used by President Madison and his wife Dolly as a temporary White House after the burning of the city by the British during the War of 1812.

Later, the site of the United Unions Building would be used by the National Federation of Women's Clubs in 1923 for the construction of a model home known as "The Little House." It was supposed to set the standard for good family housing in America. The house was patterned after the house in Easthampton, New York about which John Howard Paine wrote "Home Sweet Home." In 1924 this structure was turned over to the Girl Scouts of America and used as a hospitality center from 1924 to 1955. A plaque telling this story was later placed in the lobby of the United Unions Building.

It would be in October of 1970 that the ground breaking ceremony took place. Later, the tradition of the "topping out" ceremony would take place on August 2, 1971 with General President Lyons signing his name on the final beam. On September 15, 1972 our International staff moved into offices on the fourth and seventh floors of the new United Unions Building.

155

The National Shopmen Pension Fund issued its first pension check on May 20, 1970 at the regular meeting of Shopmen's Local No. 521, Scranton, Pa.. **Standing, from left to right:** District Representative Sam Spadea; Carl Guzzi, receiving check from Trustee Spadea; Executive Board Member Basil Bagen; Recording Secretary Henry Laskosky; President Peter Kervalavich; General Organizer William J. Modell; Financial Secretary-Treasurer Nicholas Jadick.

The Growth of Labor Education and Apprenticeship

As anti-unionism grew during the late 1960's and 1970's the labor movement and our International saw the need to reach more members through education programs. Also, the new technology which was developing at this time demanded more training.

In February of 1968, the AFL-CIO announced plans to establish a Labor Studies Program. The program began in 1969 and operated out of temporary offices in Washington D.C. and in 1971 the AFL-CIO purchased a 47-acre site in Silver Spring, Maryland. General President Lyons would be present at the dedication of the campus in late 1974. In August of 1975, two ironworkers, Richard Eyeston, Local No. 8 and Alfred Strayer, Local No. 395, were among the first to graduate. Later, the center's name would be changed to The George Meany Labor Studies Center.

In the summer of 1970, our International signed a 1.2 million dollar pact with the U.S. Department of Labor to train 600 members of minority groups as Journeymen Ironworkers. This would be the beginning of the National Ironworkers and Employers Training Program. This program was somewhat successful, however, it was the local union apprenticeship programs that adopted an Affirmative Action Plan under Federal Regulation 29.30 that really helped bring in more minorities and women.

Leonard P. Mahoney Appointed

Leonard P. Mahoney
Appointed
General Vice President

General Organizer Leonard P. Mahoney, former Business Agent of Local 401, Philadelphia, was appointed General Vice President on May 15, 1970, filling the vacancy created when General Vice President Gay Borrelli retired. He became the president of the Philadelphia and Vicinity District Council. General Vice President Mahoney began his career in Local No. 40, New York City and later transferred to Local No. 401 in 1939. In 1951 he was elected Business Agent and was appointed General Organizer in 1962. He retired on January 31, 1984.

In the February, 1976 issue of The Ironworker magazine the International listed all the training materials available to the local union apprenticeship and training programs throughout the United States and Canada.

General Secretary James R. Downes Retires

*James R. Downes
General Secretary
retires.*

On December 31, 1970, General Secretary James R. Downes ended his career after serving 22 years as General Secretary.

Secretary Downes was initiated in Local No. 550, Canton, Ohio on September 1, 1938 as a Journeyman Ironworker. In 1942 he was elected Business Agent of Local No. 550 and in 1946 was appointed General Organizer. He was elected General Secretary at the 1948 Convention, and took office on January 1, 1949.

Juel D. Drake Appointed General Secretary

*Juel D. Drake
takes over as
General Secretary.*

General Vice President Juel D. Drake upon the retirement of Downes was appointed General Secretary by General President Lyons. General Secretary Drake's appointment, which was approved by the General Executive Council, became effective January 1, 1971. A member of the International Association for 32 years, and a member of the International staff for more than 22 years, General Secretary Drake was initiated as a Journeyman Ironworker in Local No. 229, San Diego, California, on August 4, 1939.

In 1942, General Secretary Drake was elected Conductor and in 1943 he was appointed Executive Board member of Local No. 229. In 1945 he was elected Business Agent. In 1946 and 1947 he served as President of the Building and Construction Trades Council of San Diego County. Secretary Drake was appointed General Organizer on August 23, 1948. He was elected General Vice President in 1956. He also served as Acting President of the District Council of Washington, D.C., Baltimore, Maryland and Vicinity, 1954 through 1958. General Secretary Drake was elected President of the District Council of Iron Workers of the State of California and Vicinity in December, 1959.

A. S. Goodwin Appointed General Vice President

A. S. Goodwin, Executive Director of the Shopmen's Division of the International Association, was appointed General Vice President on December 21, 1970.

President Lyons made the recommendation to the General Executive Council in December and the nomination was approved unanimously. General Vice President Goodwin had been a General Organizer since 1954, and since May, 1970 had headed the Shopmen's Division. He was initiated into Shop Local No. 526, Chattanooga, Tennessee. He helped to organize and became a charter member of Shopmen's Local No. 733, Nashville, Tennessee. He retired on February 1, 1988 and passed away on March 13, 1989.

*A. S. Goodwin
General Vice President*

Members of the International Association were involved in virtually every nuclear power plant built in the United States and Canada. From fabrication, to rod work, to erecting structural steel, to rigging. During 1970, electric utilities made known plans for 13 nuclear power plants. In this period, the utilities ordered 14 reactors with a total capacity of about 14,336,000 kilowatts. As of December 31, 1970 there were 20 nuclear power plants in operation, 53 more being built and 36 planned.

Atomic Reactor for the Oyster Creek Nuclear Power Station is rigged into place by members of Local No. 350, Atlantic City, New Jersey in 1968.

Members of Local No. 433, Los Angeles erect Goldstone Deep Space Antenna for NASA in 1966.

Union Oil off shore drilling platform built by members of Local No. 433, Los Angeles was completed in the Santa Barbara Channel in October, 1968.

Members of Local No. 75, Phoenix, Arizona erect support structure and dome for a 150-inch stellar telescope in 1969.

The "Haystack" a Satellite communications antenna is erected by members of Locals No. 7, Boston and 351, Lawrence, Massachusetts in 1965.

Jumbo Jet Doors are erected by Local No. 63, Chicago, at O'Hare International Airport in 1968 for United Airlines. The overhead doors weigh 80 tons. Work consisted of complete assembly of doors in the field and welding of all connection points prior to erection. Total weight consisted of 510 tons of door materials, 410 tons of counterweights and 24 tons of 7/8" rigging cable.

Local 63 crew, **top row, left to right:** *Allan Simcox, Jim Culp, Joe Schuch, Ron Florio, Don Florek, Vic Wallenberg.* **Second row, left to right:** *Allen Douglas, Fin. Sec. Treas.- Bus. Agt., John Lawlor, Foreman, Tony Deters, Steward, Jacob Merkle, Foreman, Joe Muff, Business Agent, Helmer Ringstrom, Appr. Coordinator, A. E. Witter, President, Byrne Door, Inc., Walt Dombrowski, Supt., Local 25, Paul Foester, Local 25, George Butz, Bus. Agent, Ray Ptak.*

Members of Local No. 84, Houston, Texas, **(shown below)** erect the Domed Stadium in 1963.

Members of Local No. 8, Milwaulkee, Wisconsin set 260-ton Atomic Reactor generating station at Point Beach, Wisconsin in 1970.

159

The 75th Anniversary of Our International

The year 1971 marked the 75th Anniversary of the founding of the Union on February 4, 1896. Beginning in January, *The Ironworker* magazine was completely reorganized. Many features which had disappeared over the years reappeared including "For the Ladies," "Indoor-Outdoor Rambling," "Shanty Talk," and a history section called "Yesterday in the Ironworker" was introduced and ran for several years. The size of the magazine was also standardized to 9 x 12 inches. Also, a series of pictures of famous bridges, waterways and canals, buildings, dams, national monuments, interstate highways, and defense and space projects that we had constructed were published.

Renewed Attention to Health and Safety Issues

Our International has always been concerned with safety issues. Early issues of *The Bridgemen's Magazine* are filled with lists of Ironworkers who were killed on the job site. Early statistics showed that the average Ironworker could expect to work 10 years on the job before he was killed or seriously injured. One of the reasons our members first organized was to provide burial money and death benefits to the wives and children of members.

In 1969, General President Lyons endorsed the Congressional legislation known as the Construction Safety Act of 1969, which lead to the passage of the Occupational Safety and Health Act of 1970 (OSHA). On April 28, 1971 OSHA officially became the law.

OSHA did a study of the things that were most often violated in the construction industry. They were in the following order based on the numbers of cited violations: guardrails; handrails; scaffolding; ladders; gas welding and cutting; cranes and derricks; housekeeping; flammable and combustible liquids; general electrical; electrical equipment installation; fire protection; and trenching. Most of the items on this list would be items of concern to our members.

Ironworkers became aware for the first time, in October, 1973, of a new danger to their health. An unpublished government study hinted that common asbestos might be dangerous to the public health and cause cancer. Studies had shown that a large percentage of asbestos workers had died of asbestosis.

A "Rigging" Agreement between the Ironworkers and Carpenters (Millwrights) was entered into on May 1, 1971. This Agreement provided that all contractors be required to make assignments between Millwrights and Iron Workers on rigging in accordance with the terms of the Agreement.

Members of Local No. 808, Orlando, Florida and other members from around the country erect monorail system at Disney World in Orlando, Florida. They also built trees, castles, an Alpine Chalet and modular hotel units for the theme park. Over 1,000 Ironworkers were employed on the project.

Dale M. Ray Appointed

On May 15, 1971, Dale M. Ray, Executive Director in charge of Jurisdiction for the International Association was appointed Ninth General Vice President at which time he became President of the California and Vicinity District Council. In 1942, he was initiated as an apprentice in Local No. 378, Oakland, California and later became Business Agent before being appointed General Organizer in 1963. On July 23, 1983, General Vice President Dale Ray passed away at 58 years of age.

*Dale M. Ray
Appointed
General Vice President*

Robert McVay Appointed

*Robert McVay
Appointed
Executive Director*

When General Vice President Ray left to take over the California and Vicinity District Council, President John H. Lyons appointed General Organizer Robert McVay to the position of Executive Director in charge of Jurisdiction. Executive Director McVay had worked with General Vice President Ray for a number of years in the jurisdictional office. Executive Director McVay was former Business Agent of Local No. 67, Des Moines, Iowa. He retired in 1986.

General President Lyons joins Labor leaders in White House meeting with President Nixon on the Wage Price Freeze.

Inflation and the Economy Under Nixon

Unlike World War II when the government established a way of controlling prices through the Office of Price Administration (OPA), nothing like this was done during the early Vietnam War period. Our Union and the entire labor movement became concerned over runaway inflation.

One area that was particularly hit by inflated prices was the housing and construction industry. While the wages of our members had not increased enough to keep up with the rising cost of living, the real increases had been caused by higher land value, higher interest rates, and higher prices on building materials. Nixon and conservative republicans launched a campaign to convince the public that the wages of building trades workers were the reason for higher building costs. The media reported the hourly wages of construction workers and then computed them based on a 40-hour week throughout the year. They paid no attention to the fact that our outside men did not work throughout the year and that it was a seasonal business. Then on February 23, 1971, President Nixon issued a proclamation suspending the Davis-Bacon Act claiming it was inflationary.

The Building and Construction Trades Department and many in Congress protested the suspension of the Davis-Bacon Act. On March 29, 1971, President Nixon issued a wage stabilization plan and the establishment of the Construction Industry Stabilization Committee (CISC) for the construction industry and reinstated the Davis-Bacon Act.

On August 15, 1971, President Nixon proclaimed a Phase I freeze on wages and prices to be followed 90 days later with Phase II. For many unions that had recently negotiated contracts this amounted to the voiding of the negotiated pay increases. In a way the entire system of collective bargaining was voided as far as union contracts were concerned. All other types of corporate business contracts were not affected.

A year later on March 22, 1972, the AFL-CIO made a decision that all their representatives should resign from the Pay Board since it was designed to favor "Big Business" and not workers! By late 1972 the Department of Labor Statistics reported that food prices alone had increased in one month by 5.7%, the largest single month increase in 26 years.

In January of 1972, the International Association entered into an agreement with the Department of Interior, Bureau of Indian Affairs and the Federal Highway Administration sponsoring the National Iron Workers Training Program for American Indians. There have been three training centers. The first was in Antigo, Wisconsin, the second in Local No. 395 apprenticeship school near Hammond, Indiana and the third at the apprenticeship school of Local No. 63, Chicago.

Signing of contract to begin the training of American Indians at Antigo, Wisconsin. **Seated, left to right**, are Harrison Loesch, Assistant Secretary, Department of Interior; Louis R. Bruce, Commissioner of Indian Affairs; and General Secretary Juel D. Drake. **Standing, left to right**, are Interior Department Deputy Under-Secretary William L. Rogers, Bureau Contract Specialist R. W. Crammer, Bureau Vocational Guidance Specialist J.C. LaSalle, General Organizer Raymond J. Robertson, Executive Director of Apprenticeship and Training J.W. Hardesty, and General Organizer C.L. Walker.

This program is still in existence and has trained over 2,000 American Indians. The Indian program has had four Directors, Robert Zimmerman, Local No. 8, Steve Canty, Fran Shea and Robert Mitacek, Local No. 63. General Vice President Raymond J. Robertson is chairman of this program and is responsible for contract negotiations.

During the construction of the Trans-Alaska Pipeline, the American Indian program established a satellite school for Alaskan natives in Kenai, Alaska. The program has also worked closely with the Navajo tribe at Window Rock, Arizona.

The **Thirty-Fourth International Convention** was held August 28 through September 1, 1972 at the Americana Hotel in Bal Harbour, Florida. There were 1,036 delegates present. General President Lyons, General Secretary Drake and General Treasurer Cole and all the General Vice Presidents were reelected.

General President Lyons outlined past, present, and future issues facing the Union. They included the problems of the growth of the "Open Shop" movement. He said:

> *"One of the major problems which has beset the construction industry since the close of our last convention has been the phenomenal growth of the non-union contractor successfully performing the principal types of construction which we, as an International Association, engage in, namely the industrial, large commercial, and monumental types of construction."*

Another issue discussed was the economy. Prior to President Nixon taking office our members had enjoyed 92 months of consecutive economic growth and prosperity. But since Nixon froze wages the profits of American corporations were larger than at any period in American history, while workers' wages had stayed the same.

In his opening address to the convention, General President Lyons pointed out the need for legislative changes. One of the major pieces of legislation mentioned at this time was the need to pass the Burke-Hartke Trade Bill which would remove the incentives for U.S. corporations to manufacture overseas. This was the beginning of the importing of fabricated steel, which would eventually result in the loss of many of our shop locals. General President Lyons would warn about the "dumping" of foreign steel and other items on the American market. Realizing the importance of political action and because of the Campaign Reform Law of 1972, our Union set up the Ironworkers Political Action League (IPAL) in order to support our friends and defeat our enemies.

The keynote speaker at the 34th Convention would be George Meany, who was upset with the way the Democratic Party Convention a few weeks before had been organized,

Badge worn by delegates to the 34th International Convention.

Badge worn by guests to the 34th International Convention.

Final beam is hoisted.onto the "United Unions Building" at the "topping out" ceremony in September 1971.

Topping Out

"Topping out," the celebration of which is so cherished by Ironworkers, is a ritual based on centuries old traditions, customs and legends. "Topping out" needs no explanation to the Ironworker but for the benefit of those not familiar with the term, it means the placement of the topmost member of a steel structure, whether it be a bridge or skyscraper.

It doesn't matter where the structure is being topped out. It could be a bridge across a canyon or river in an isolated area miles away from human habitation, or in the heart of a business district in a large city. In any case, Ironworkers attach the Stars and Stripes, Canadian flag or an evergreen tree to the topmost member either before it is raised to its position or, in some cases, after the member is placed.

The nice thing about "Topping Out" is that no two ceremonies are exactly alike. For some, the evergreen symbolizes that the job went up without a loss of life, while for others it is a good luck charm for the future occupants. For some, the flag signals a structure built with federal funds but for others it suggests patriotism or the American or Canadian dream.

Thus, the "Topping Out" ceremony, like all rich traditions, does not seem to consist of rules and strict ritual. But tradition does run deep, and Ironworkers, who of course deny they are superstitious, say it brings "good luck."

Delegates attending one of the sessions at the 34th International Convention held August 28 through September 1, 1972 at the Americana Hotel in Bal Harbour, Florida.

failing to give labor its rightful position. General President Lyons was a member of the committee to reform the rules of the Democratic Party after the 1968 Convention, and he too was upset with the changes. Therefore labor would not endorse Senator George McGovern in 1972.

It was reported at the 34th International Convention that in November of 1971 our International Association along with the carpenters and laborers signed a joint agreement covering the construction of chimneys, silos, stack and hyperbolic cooling towers.

On October 6, 1972, Second Vice President Laverne Smith was killed in an automobile accident near Baton Rouge, Louisiana. He was 56 years old. He was initiated into Local No. 584, Tulsa, Oklahoma in January, 1939 and later became Business Agent. In 1952 he was appointed General Organizer and in 1959, General Vice President.

Matthew Taylor Appointed

On February 9, 1973, General President Lyons appointed General Organizer Matthew Taylor to fill the vacancy created by the death of Laverne Smith. General Vice President Taylor was initiated into Local No. 3, Pittsburgh, Pa., in January, 1942. After serving as an officer of Local No. 3, he was appointed General Organizer in 1959. He retired on January 10, 1986.

Matthew Taylor
Appointed
Second Vice President

The Presidential Election of 1972 and its Aftermath

In the election of 1972 Nixon would carry 49 states with a total of 521 electoral votes. George McGovern would carry only one state with 17 votes. Nixon's election would receive 61% of the popular vote to 38% for McGovern. This would be the most lop-sided election since Alfred Landon lost to Roosevelt in 1936.

Ironically, it was only ten months after Nixon took office that Watergate and its cover-up resulted in our International and the AFL-CIO calling for the resignation or the impeachment of the President. By the end of 1973, Vice President Spiro Agnew was forced to resign and was replaced by Gerald Ford. Ford had a terrible COPE record having voted "right" only seven times on issues important to labor and "wrong" 102 times.

THE IRONWORKER

OCTOBER 1972

1896 1972

ernational Association of Bridge, Structural, and Ornamental Iron Workers

JOHN H. LYONS
General President

JUEL D. DRAKE
General Secretary

JAMES V. COLE
General Treasurer

Robert A. Georgine
*elected President,
Building & Construction
Trades Department.*

George Meany
AFL-CIO President .

James V. Cole
General Treasurer.

John McKean
*General Organizer elected General
Treasurer on January 9, 1974 by
the General Executive Council.*

General President Lyons called for the passage of legislation for the development of the Alaskan oil fields, since this would help to solve the nation's energy problems. It would also provide jobs for our members in the construction of 33 new U.S.-flagged tankers, the fabricating of pipes, plus construction jobs in Alaska. Although our Union was an early supporter of the environment, we were concerned that environmental groups were blocking the development of the Alaskan oil fields. Finally, in May of 1974 work began on the Trans-Alaska pipeline. By the summer of 1975 a total of 18,000 construction workers were on the job. The government pledged 3,500 jobs to native Alaskans and among those that would be employed were graduates from our Alaskan Indian training program.

General Treasurer James V. Cole retired in January, 1974, culminating a distinguished career during which he was General Treasurer for 15 years, an officer of Local No. 40 for 24 years and an Ironworker for 55 years. General Organizer and President of the Rocky Mountain District Council, John McKean was named General Treasurer to succeed Treasurer Cole. General Treasurer McKean was initiated into Local No. 27, Salt Lake City, Utah on February 2, 1934. He was born September 17, 1909.

In 1974, a memorable chapter in American Labor history was closed out by the Cigar Makers, the union that gave Samuel Gompers to the trade union movement, when delegates to a special convention voted to merge with the Retail, Wholesale and Department Store Union.

On June 1, 1974, Robert A. Georgine was elected president of the Building and Construction Trades Department, replacing Frank Bonadio who retired. President Georgine was formerly president of the Lathers International Union and Secretary-Treasurer of the Building and Construction Trades Department at the time of his election. Through the years he has been a good friend of the Ironworkers having worked as an Ironworker for a short period of time before joining the Lathers Local No. 74 in Chicago. In 1995 he became a member of the IABSOIW.

Strikes and Demonstrations During the Nixon Years

While hundreds of our union members were serving their country in Vietnam, companies back home were trying to break our Union as well as other unions within the AFL-CIO. By December of 1969, 150,000 General Electric workers were on strike. Our International and

Detroit building tradesmen picket meeting of Associated Builders and Contractors. 49 Ironworkers were arrested during the peaceful demonstration.

164

the entire labor movement supported these workers against the anti-union policies of General Electric. The company would be found guilty on 19 Federal counts of price fixing on a billion dollars worth of equipment a year. In the construction industry some companies began to pursue a policy known as "Double-Breasting." A company would set up dual companies, one union and one non-union.

Other anti-union contractors would contribute money to the union-busting efforts of the Associated Builders and Contractors (ABC). In the fall of 1973 when the ABC was having a meeting at the Club Venetian in the Detroit area, Ironworkers joined in a peaceful demonstration. Suddenly police officers wearing battle-type helmets, carrying gas masks on their belts and carrying clubs, arrested 73 union members including 49 Ironworkers. They were held in jail from 7 p.m. until 2 a.m. and then charged with loitering and released on $100 personal bonds. Republican Congressman Robert Huber was the ABC speaker that day. He was quoted as saying that when he got back to Washington he was going to sponsor, "...restrictive labor legislation."

J.W. Merritt Appointed

General Organizer J.W. Merritt was appointed Ninth General Vice President on March 18, 1974. He was initiated into Local No. 79 in Norfolk, Va., as a journeyman on April 29, 1941. He later transferred to Local No. 601, Charleston, S.C. In May, 1947, Local No. 709, Savannah, Ga., was chartered and J.W. Merritt was appointed Charter President and then elected Business Agent. General Vice President Merritt was appointed General Organizer on August 7, 1961. He retired on September 1, 1989 and passed away on December 25, 1995.

J.W. Merritt
Appointed
Ninth General Vice
President.

President Nixon Resigns and Gerald Ford becomes President

On August 9, 1974, Richard Nixon became the first President of the United States to resign from office. AFL-CIO President George Meany expressed the feelings of many when he said, "I'm not interested in seeing the President of the United States go to jail. I just want to see him go away." After the long ordeal of Nixon and Watergate it seemed that things might improve with the administration of President Ford. Prior to the 1974 Congressional elections, President Ford called a series of mini-summits as well as a Summit Conference on September 27 at the Washington Hilton Hotel. General President Lyons would participate in these meetings as well as meetings with President Ford in the White House. The issues discussed were homebuilding, transportation, and the construction of both public and private buildings. While our Union and others in the building trades pointed out that high interest rates were

one of the problems, President Ford paid no attention to this. General President Lyons would say the following about these meetings:

> *"It does not get to the true sources of inflation; it does not present a short range approach to solving unemployment; it does not present a positive approach to the energy crisis; it does not present a direct solution to the homebuilding and housing depression; and most unfortunately, in seeking additional federal revenue, it does not even commence to shift the tax burden from the backs of the average working family to be one equally shared by workers and corporations."*

Gay Borrelli and James R. Downes Pass Away

Gay Borrelli, retired General Vice President, passed away on September 8, 1974 at 74 years of age. He was a member of Local No. 405, Philadelphia, Pa. He was appointed General Vice President in 1936 and elected to that position by the delegates at the 1936 through 1968 International Conventions. Also, on March 19, 1975 former General Secretary James R. Downes passed away. He was a member of Local No. 550, Canton, Ohio.

Jack Martin Passes Away

On January 24, 1975, General Organizer Jack Martin passed away at 67 years of age. Brother Martin was initiated into Local No. 66, San Antonio on May 27, 1930. The Governor of Texas appointed General Organizer Martin to the Texas Industrial Commission for two terms. He represented Labor as an emissary of President Lyndon B. Johnson at the dedication of the Mangla Dam in Pakistan.

Jack Martin
General Organizer,
passed away on
January 24, 1975.

General Vice President Robert E.P. Cooney was sworn in for his second term as a member of the U.S. Advisory Committee on Construction Safety and Health in 1974. At that time General Vice President Cooney served as chairman of the National Iron Workers Safety Committee.

Unemployment and Inflation

By January of 1975, unemployment was increasing by 1% a month, meaning that an additional one million workers were claiming unemployment insurance. Plus inflation was causing real buying power to decrease. President Lyons wrote the following on his "President's Page" in the March, 1975 issue of *The Ironworker*:

> "Fifteen percent of the nation's construction workers are unemployed...I am sure that many local unions of this Association would be relatively happy if they could report that only 15% of their locals were unemployed. For those of you whose local unions are still experiencing relatively good employment and are unaware of the situation existing in many other local unions, let me advise you that some of our local unions are experiencing unemployment percentages as high as 50%."

An Action Program to put America Back to Work

General President Lyons and other members of the Executive Board of the AFL-CIO along with representatives of the 115 affiliated International Unions met to discuss the nation's problems and outlined an "Action Program to Put America Back to Work." By now our Union and the entire AFL-CIO were disappointed with the performance of President Ford. President Lyons would say: "President Ford, after starting out last fall with an air of openness and candor that brought forth the summit conferences, has moved quietly into the back rooms where big business influences prevail."

Despite the "Action Program" Ford wanted to create a federal deficit of 60 billion dollars. Although Franklin Roosevelt had wanted a balanced budget in 1933, he realized that feeding people and getting them back to work was more important. On May 29, 1975, Ford even vetoed the "Emergency Employment Appropriations Act" which had been passed by both the House and Senate. Ford said it was not "an effective response to the unemployment problems."

Ford Vetoes the Situs Picketing Bill

Since many contractors used subcontractors that were non-union the building trades wished to have the right to picket them on the common construction site. However, in a controversial 1951 decision of the U.S. Supreme Court this was prohibited as an illegal secondary boycott under the Taft-Hartley Act.

A great deal of time was spent by Secretary of Labor John T. Dunlop, meeting with both unions and contractors, and an agreement was worked out. The bill was known as the "Common-Situs Picketing Bill" or "The Equal Treatment for Construction Workers Bill." It was passed by the House and then by the Senate by 52-45. Everyone thought that President Ford would sign it but on December 22, 1975 he vetoed the bill.

Secretary of Labor Dunlop was horrified that Ford didn't sign this bill since he had promised to do so and that building trades unions had given concessions that were "hard to swallow." Dunlop was so angry that Ford had double-crossed him that he resigned as Secretary of Labor.

Construction in Canada and the United States

In September of 1974 *The Ironworker* magazine ran a story about the involvement of our members in the building of five earth stations to link the Westar space satellite for the Western Union Corporation. Stations were located at Glenwood, N.J, Estill Fork, Alabama, Lake Geneva, Wisconsin, Steele Valley, California, and Cedar Hill, Texas.

In **Canada** Ironworkers were building new structures as well as restoring the old. Members of Local 759 at Thunder Bay, Ontario were restoring Old Fort William which is one of the early trading posts used by the North West Company in 1801 and later the Hudson Bay Company, two of the charter companies that settled Canada. In November of 1975, the world's tallest freestanding structure had its "topping out." It was the 1,815 foot high Canadian National Tower which was built by members of Local 721.

In March of 1976, members of Local 711 in Montreal were constructing buildings for the 1976 Summer Olympic Games. About 750 members were busy building the stadium and another 250 on the Velodrome, an air-conditioned area that would hold 10,000 people.

THE IRONWORKER
NOVEMBER 1975

CANADIAN NATIONAL TOWER: THE WORLD'S TALLEST

166

General Organizer Joseph F. Maloney Elected Secretary-Treasurer

Joseph F. Maloney was elected Secretary-Treasurer of the Building and Construction Trades Department.

In October, 1975, General Organizer Joseph F. Maloney was elected as Secretary-Treasurer of the AFL-CIO Building and Construction Trades Department. General Organizer Maloney was Business Agent for Local No. 7, Boston, Massachusetts before being appointed as General Organizer in 1960. He was assigned to work in the Washington, D.C. office where he became active in negotiating national agreements and contract maintenance. His new office required him to leave the International Association. After a long, distinguished career servicing the Ironworkers and the Building and Construction Trades Department, Joe Maloney retired on December 31, 1995.

In October of 1975, a list of the types of accidents experienced by Ironworkers was compiled. The list included such things as back problems, resulting from overexertion; slips and falls or being struck by moving objects; contact with dust, chemicals or smoke in fabricating shops. A study indicated that Ironworkers are more conscientious about wearing protective equipment than other crafts in heavy industrial construction, but adequate head, hand and foot protection cannot be emphasized enough for all workers.

Another study was reported in the June, 1976 issue of *The Ironworker* magazine. It dealt with lead poisoning. Ironworkers faced this problem when burning, and especially when they were taking down the 3rd Avenue "EL" in New York City. Congressman David Obey of Wisconsin was furious when he found that

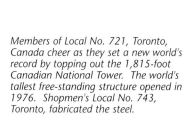

Members of Local No. 721, Toronto, Canada cheer as they set a new world's record by topping out the 1,815-foot Canadian National Tower. The world's tallest free-standing structure opened in 1976. Shopmen's Local No. 743, Toronto, fabricated the steel.

General Motors had refused to release a report on the effects of lead on workers in the workplace. He said: "Ironworkers endangered by lead poisoning, as well as other workers, deserve to know the facts of such a study to make the workplace safer. The symptoms range from kidney ailments to brain damage."

On October 31, 1975, General Vice President John L. McCarthy retired after 46 years of service. In 1930 he became Business Agent for Local No. 392, East St. Louis, Illinois and in 1937 was elected President of the St. Louis and Vicinity District Council. In 1949 John was appointed "Acting" General Organizer and in 1952 he was elected General Vice President at the 1952 Convention. He passed away on March 30, 1977. Just before John McCarthy died, General Organizer Raymond J. Robertson met with him at his home at which time John presented the International Association with all of his convention badges (Ironworkers, AFL-CIO, Building Trades and Metal Trades) from 1932. These badges are now part of the historical display of the International Association.

Thomas Clarkson Appointed General Vice President

General Organizer Thomas Clarkson was appointed General Vice President on March 13, 1976. At the time of his appointment he was the President of the District Council of Greater New York and Vicinity. He was Assistant Business Agent and Financial Secretary of Local No. 40 before being appointed General Organizer. His grandfather drove rivets on the Brooklyn Bridge and his father started as an apprentice on the Singer Building in New York City in 1906. He retired on April 30, 1988.

Thomas Clarkson, General Organizer, appointed General Vice President.

The **Thirty-Fifth International Convention** was held August 23-27, 1976 at the San Diego Convention Center, San Diego, California. The theme of the convention was "80 Years Building for America." General President John H. Lyons, General Secretary Juel D. Drake and General Treasurer John McKean along with the nine General Vice Presidents were elected to serve a five year term. At the 35th Convention a resolution was passed to hold future conventions every five years rather than every four years. It was determined that going to five years would save a tremendous amount of money. Also, that by going to five years, the 39th Convention would be held in 1996, the 100th Anniversary of the International Association. The 35th Convention was the first International convention to introduce multimedia presentations and a "Historical" display area which enhanced the convention proceedings.

Delegates attending meetings at the 35th International Convention in San Diego, August 23-27, 1976.

craft form of organization, the relatively short duration of construction jobs, often in remote locations, the necessarily migratory nature of many contractors and our members who follow the work, and the changing methods and materials used in construction. While jurisdictional questions thus inevitably arise in construction operations, it is a measure of both a local union and an international union to establish orderly procedures and policies for the prompt settlement of these disputes."

Other subjects covered at the 35th Convention were the highlights of Shopmen Activities, Apprenticeship and Training, Educational and Training Aids, District Councils and Regional Conferences, American Indian Training Program, Safety, National Shopmen's Pension Fund, the National Economy and Jobs, Pension Plan Legislation and Maintenance.

Badge worn by delegates to 35th International Convention.

President Lyons reported that one of the more undesirable and regrettable developments that had taken place was the placing of the Old Age and Disability Pensions on a revolving basis in accordance with the Constitution of the International Association. The defeat of the Situs Picketing Bill and the growth of the non-union contractor were main topics covered at the convention.

A review of Canadian operations was another important topic covered at the 35th Convention. President Lyons reported that, for a dozen or more years during the 1950's and the first year or so of the 1960's virtually every local union in Canada was receiving financial subsistence without which they would have been unable to operate. In the beginning of the 1960's, the wage rates in the outside local unions and in the shops in Canada were all within the lowest twenty-five percent of the wage rates of all of the local unions. In the early 1960's, the efforts of the previous decade to turn this around began to bring results. At that time, the financial security of the local unions was such that all International subsistence was stopped and virtually every local union in Canada since that time has been financially self-sustaining.

In reference to Jurisdictional Disputes, President Lyons stated that "in this industry, jurisdictional disputes are deeply ingrained in the very nature of construction operations: competition among contractors, the

General President seconds endorsement of Carter-Mondale ticket for AFL-CIO Executive Council in 1976.

Labor Endorses Jimmy Carter for President

The International and the entire AFL-CIO endorsed Jimmy Carter in the Presidential election of November, 1976. He won largely through the efforts of organized labor. Labor made the difference with 70% of union members voting for Carter. Union households made the difference.

168

John H. Lyons
General President

Juel D. Drake
General Secretary

John McKean
General Treasurer

For the first time in many years labor saw a chance to repeal 14B of Taft-Hartley, pass a National Health Bill, solve our energy problems, give attention to our transportation needs, and put our members back to work on public projects.

At the 35th Convention the delegates enthusiastically supported Martin T. Byrne who was running for Congress from the 2nd District of the State of Rhode Island. At that time he was Business Agent of Local No. 37, Providence, Rhode Island and the President of the Central Body of the AFL-CIO. Although he failed to win election he was appointed by President Carter to be Assistant to the Secretary of Transportation in Washington, D.C. Later, President Lyons, recognizing his abilities, appointed Martin T. Byrne as General Organizer.

General President Lyons testified before the House Labor Committee on pension reform in 1976.

Chapter Ten

The Tradition Continues 1977-1988

With the election of President Carter a less formal and more down-to-earth attitude seemed to prevail. The "Imperial Presidency" of Nixon and the "Caretaker Administration" of Ford were over. Union members and all Americans felt a breath of fresh air had come to Washington, D.C. and to the White House.

The issues that our Union and the other members of the Building and Construction Trades Department, AFL-CIO, saw of major importance for passage by the 95th Congress and this new President were strengthening of the Davis-Bacon Act, federal funding for all types of transportation—rail, air, and highways, a solution to the energy crisis, cleaning up the environment, enforcing OSHA, and legislation to protect union pension funds.

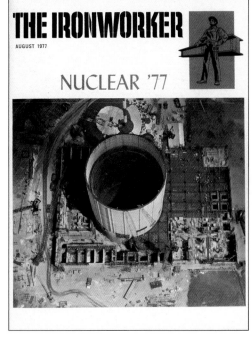

The year 1977 started out to be a good year for offshore drilling, beginning a new era in North American energy development. On the West Coast, an eight-year delay in offshore drilling for oil and natural gas was ended as drilling resumed off the shores of Southern California and Alaska. Anticipating the work opportunities for organized labor in this expanding field, seven building trade unions, including the Ironworkers, ironed out a milestone West Coast agreement with the offshore industry's prime contractors.

The model agreement, which went into effect January 1, 1977 for two years, had been adapted for East Coast operations as well. General President John H. Lyons served on the President's Offshore Construction Committee and General Organizer Jake West served as Chairman of the Agreement's Policy Committee. At that time, with no-strike and no-lock-out guarantees, Ironworkers were on the rigs for 14 days and off seven days.

About 20 miles out from Santa Barbara stood the world's largest offshore drilling structure, the "Hondo,"

"Hondo"
Drilling Platform

The 7,000 ton bottom half of the "Hondo" platform glides by the San Francisco waterfront on its way to Southern California.

Spanish for "The Deep," requiring over a million man-hours to build and erect with members of Local No. 378 of Oakland and Local No. 433 of Los Angeles. Hondo can house 44 workers. The platform jacket or substructure weighs approximately 12,000 tons, has eight main legs, and is framed with X and diagonal bracing.

Solar Energy and Wind Energy were among President Carter's more important programs in 1978. The Department of Energy explained that solar energy research was largely proven and that solar technology was ready to move into the market place. One of the more ambitious and promising large-scale solar projects involved members of Local No. 495 in Albuquerque where they erected the tallest solar tower in the world at the Solar Thermal Test Facility in New Mexico.

Sticking out of the desert is a 430-foot tower surrounded by 1,700 mirrors, called "heliostats." The

Ironworkers from Local No. 495, Albuquerque erect 430 foot tower which will be surrounded by 1,700 mirrors, called "heliostats."

heliostats track and reflect the sun, bouncing the solar rays onto a single collection panel mounted on a boiler or steam generator atop the tower. The steam which is generated in the tower is then piped down the concrete tower to two locations. One head of steam runs a turbine in an electrical power generation plant on the ground. The rest of the steam runs to a nearby thermal storage system designed to supply the steam needed to run the 10 Megawatt electric generator during the night or during cloud cover.

Members of Local No. 63, Chicago, Illinois erected 8,000 square feet of solar panels at Navy Pier. The solar panel framing system is constructed from extruded aluminum structural members. The solar panels themselves consisted of extruded aluminum and galvanized iron, preglazed with two lites of 1/8" tempered glass and an inner core of radiator-type material with copper tubing. Also, members of Local No. 408, Amarillo, Texas erected a 93-foot tower and a 200-kilowatt wind generator in Clayton, New Mexico. The "windmill" produces enough electricity to run 60 homes.

In 1978, members of Local No. 16 constructed an "L" blast furnace at Bethlehem Steel's Sparrows Point Plant. The new furnace has four times the original designed capacity of a "K" blast furnace which began operations in 1957. This furnace produces 8,000 tons of iron per day, and has a hearth diameter of 45 feet and a

Members of Local No. 408, Amarillo, Texas erected a 93-foot 200-Kilowatt wind generator in 1977.

Members of Local No. 63, Chicago, install 8,000 square feet of solar panels at Chicago's old Navy Pier in 1978.

Ironworkers top out new steel furnace at Sparrows Point Plant in 1978.

Members of Local No. 16, Baltimore, constructed an "L" blast furnace at Bethlehem's Sparrows Point Plant

THE IRONWORKER

APRIL 1978

Steel Plant Modernization

In 1978, 125 Ironworkers from Local No. 736, Hamilton, installed and erected 21,300 tons of steel for a basic oxygen furnace and melt shop in Hamilton, Ontario, Canada.

working volume of 130,000 cubic feet. The total tonnage of structural steel erected in the construction of the "L" furnace, stockhouse, coke receivers, including conveyors, was 22,000 tons. Total reinforcing rod tonnage was 1,438 tons and 85 tons of wire mesh.

Also in 1978, members of Local No. 736, Hamilton, Ontario modernized Dofasco Steel Mills. At the peak, there were 125 Ironworkers employed to erect the 21,300 tons of steel for a basic oxygen furnace and melt shop. A 240-ton basic oxygen furnace with a 175-ton trunnion ring was installed. The melt shop to house this operation is four levels, a thousand feet long and 225 feet high.

Charles R. Anding Appointed

In September, 1978 General Treasurer John McKean announced his retirement. General President Lyons appointed General Organizer and President of The Mid South District Council Charles R. Anding to fill the vacancy. General Treasurer Anding was initiated into Local No. 135, Galveston, Texas in January, 1946. He transferred his membership to Local No. 710 where he was elected Business Agent.

Charles R. Anding
General Treasurer

Anti-Unionism Continues To Grow

The efforts by anti-union forces to destroy unionism in America became well organized in the early 1950's by using newspapers, the radio and television, and even films to show unions in a bad light. One of these groups was **"The Business Roundtable,"** whose members

considered union hiring halls and even the federal government to be "arbitrary outside influences."

Another force against labor was **"The New Right."** In the 1976 election they used classic techniques to defeat the liberal Senator Frank Moss of Utah and replace him with the ultra-conservative, anti-labor Orrin Hatch. Colorado brewer, Joseph Coors, was a member of the **"New Right"** and for years he used union-busting techniques against Ironworkers, brewers, and other building tradesmen. In the *Ironworker Magazine* of October of 1978, John Lyons wrote:

"The main theme of all these New Right organizations, as well as a growing number of industry associations and corporations, is the crippling and eventual destruction of organized labor. Let's face it. The only thing standing between an employer's greed and the rights of workers is the union. Without the union and its negotiated contract there is no protection. The worker without

Members of Local No. 301, Charleston, West Virginia erect world's longest main arch span bridge in Fayette County, West Virginia. The main arch stretches 1,700 feet across the New River gorge.

a union has no voice, no right; he is absolutely defense-less at the job site. That's the way the New Right would want it, and that's what they are working so hard for. I can't prevent that, but we can."

A third anti-union group was the so-called *Associated Building Contractors (ABC)*. General President Lyons at our 35th International Convention in 1976 spoke about this organization that was trying to restore "the open shop." This group represented a growing number of non-union contractors as well as miscellaneous individuals and small companies who were out to destroy unions. The ABC in Utah tried to repeal the "Little Davis-Bacon Act." Governor Scott Mattheson, a Democrat, vetoed the legislation saying it would destroy the buying power of the construction workers of the state. In 1977 the Building and Construction Trades Department of the AFL-CIO adopted a special assessment to be used to fight "the open shop movement."

In July of 1980, an article titled "Tale of Two Sites" appeared in *The Ironworker*. Two power plants were being built in towns near Houston, Texas; one union, and the other by Brown & Root with non-union labor. The union built power plant in Richmond, Texas was completed in 29 months, while the non-union plant at Bay City was four years behind in construction.

A New Organizing Campaign For Shop Ironworkers

It was not just the "open shop" policies of the ABC and other union busting companies that were taking jobs away from the shop locals of the International. It was also resulting from the importation of fabricated structural steel from Japan and Korea.

At the San Diego Convention in 1976, a resolution was passed to have a series of Shop Organizing Conferences. This would be similar to the organizing campaign in the 1930's when Morrin was the General President. As a result of this action conferences were held in the summer of 1977 in New Orleans, White Haven, Pennsylvania, and Chicago. This organizing campaign was conducted over 18 months and resulted in additional members and shops being organized.

On March 24, 1979, President Lyons testified before the ad hoc Select House Committee on the Outer Continental Shelf regarding an estimated multi-million-dollar loophole in our trade policies that allowed companies like Brown & Root to fabricate off-shore drilling platforms overseas.

More than 150 Shop delegates from the Middle Atlantic and Northeast areas and Eastern Canada attended the second of four organizing conferences in 1977. The conferences were held following convention action in 1976.

Ship Construction and Our International

One of the issues discussed at the mid-winter meeting of the AFL-CIO at Bal Harbour, Florida in 1979 was an issue important to our International, our Maritime Industry. Only 550 ships were carrying the American flag at this time, and we had come from first place to tenth place as a maritime power.

Not only were we losing members in Shop Locals but also in locals involved in ship building such as Local No. 627 at the National Steel and Shipbuilding Co.(NASSCO) in San Diego, California. In October of 1979 this was the largest shipbuilding company on the West Coast with a total of 5,000 workers, half of whom were Ironworkers. At this time they were building much needed oil tankers to be used in the shipment of Alaskan Pipeline oil. They worked as welders, burners, fitters, chippers, riggers, and on some Navy vessels as riveters.

But ever since World War II, the United States had been slipping in the building of ships. In 1978 U.S.-flagged ships carried only 2% of our own exports and imports. In 1978 the United States built only 15 ships, while the Japanese built 502 ships in 1975 alone.

Ironworkers in American shipyards were laid off. For example, Bethlehem closed down its shipyards at Sparrows Point, Maryland and 2,000 workers lost their jobs. Bethlehem then upgraded its plant in Singapore. Another 2,000 shipyard workers at the Brooklyn Navy Yards were also temporarily laid off at this time. In April of 1979 shipyard workers at Newport News Shipbuilding and Dry Dock Company were clubbed by the police. Although they had won a union election for recognition the company refused to recognize the union.

Ironically it was our own policies after 1945 that caused this situation. We gave nearly 4 billion dollars to 11 nations, including Japan and Korea to fund the development of steel making and shipbuilding.

Launching a Campaign For Labor Law Reform

With a Democrat in the White House our Union and the entire AFL-CIO hoped that we would finally be able to pass legislation that would enable the labor movement to operate on a level playing field. A bill was passed in the House of Representatives by a margin of 94 votes designating October 4, 1977 as **"Labor Law Reform Day"** throughout the nation.

The 2.5 million "Hanford Giant" derrick gently lifts the 966-ton nuclear reactor vessel into the containment shell in 1977 at the Hanford No. 2 Power Station using members of Local No. 14, Spokane, Washington.

General President Lyons spoke in favor of trying again to pass the "Common Situs-Picketing Bill" which had been vetoed by President Ford. President Lyons also called for strengthening of the Wagner Act and called on contractors that supported the Iron Workers Union to get behind labor reform legislation. One of these pieces of legislation that was supported by all the building trades unions was "The Federally Funded Construction Contract Act of 1979," which would establish a minimum wage on all federal construction. This would be an effective way to fight low wage contractors like Brown and Root.

The Building and Construction Trades Council hoped to repeal 14B of the Taft-Hartley Law which allowed states to pass so-called "Right-to-Work" laws. At this time anti-labor forces launched open

Members of Local No. 498, Rockford, Illinois built a Segmental Bridge in 1978. Working each side of a pier to ensure balance, the precast segments are joined and secured. At mid-points between the piers, a shorter concrete section is reinforced, cast in place and post-tensioned to complete another leg of the project.

shop campaigns in 9 states. All but one of these was defeated, raising the number of states with a "Right-to-Work" law to 21.

By April of 1978 the Labor Reform Bill had still not passed. Groups such as the anti-union National Action Committee, the National Association of Manufacturers, the Associated General Contractors, and the National Right-to-Work Committee spent ten times more money than the AFL-CIO to defeat this legislation. The bill was eventually defeated as the result of a filibuster in the Senate by conservative Republicans and Dixiecrats. Pro-labor Senators needed 60 votes to break the filibuster but they only had 59. President Lyons believed that if they could have broken the filibuster, 70 out of the 100 Senators would have supported the legislation, and the labor movement would have a chance to again grow as it had under Roosevelt's New Deal.

Occupational Safety and Health under Carter

There were attempts under Nixon and Ford to dismantle OSHA. Stories were released to the media that OSHA was spending all of its time and money looking into split toilet seats and the height on the walls of fire extinguishers. In 1975, there was a slight drop in job related deaths and injuries. However, 5,300 deaths and

Safety Advisory Committee consisting of members of the International Association and Contractor Associations in 1977.

29.8 million workdays lost to injuries was an absolutely intolerable situation in a civilized country.

In 1976 a total of 70 Ironworkers lost their lives as a result of on-the-job accidents. In the first half of 1977 another 26 were killed. President Carter and Secretary of Labor Ray Marshall would try to strengthen OSHA. At this time our Union and others in the building trades would work to get grants to train 180 additional tradesmen and management representatives in health and safety. A government report showed that construction had the highest rate of safety hazards (16%), with manufacturing second (13%), and mining last (11%).

OSHA also began to move against the dangers from lead poisoning and asbestos. Violations of OSHA would continue. On April 27, 1978, fifty-one workers, including 11 Ironworkers, were killed in the construction of a cooling tower at the Willow Island, West Virginia power plant. This would be the worst construction disaster in 52 years!

Although Ironworkers had completed 36 similar cooling towers in the preceding years, there had been very few mishaps. OSHA found 10 willful violations and 10

175

For over three hours in 1978, Ralph A. Winner Jr., of Local No. 3, Pittsburgh who was working on the demolition of the old Brady Street Bridge in Pittsburgh became wedged between some beams. One leg was freed, however, the other leg had to be amputated by a young surgeon using a thin piece of wire. "The courage he displayed was beyond belief," his fellow Ironworkers said. Brother Winner recovered and in 1996 is an Honorary member who attends the union meetings regularly.

Members of Local No. 17, Cleveland, Ohio lower the 840-ton reactor pressure vessel into place inside the containment building at the Perry Nuclear Power Plant in Ohio. In 1978 only two reactors were ordered compared to 41 ordered in 1973.

serious violations by the contractors. This time the total fine was set at $108,300. It seems that the scaffolding was not properly bolted to the tower, and they had not tested whether the concrete was properly cured.

Disaster in the field of Nuclear Power

Since many Ironworkers were employed in the building of nuclear power plants, General President Lyons wrote in August of 1978 his concern with environmental problems that were causing nationwide debates over the Seabrook Power Plant in New Hampshire as well as the Clinch River Breeder Reactor in Tennessee. But jobs were not the only reason for our concern. Nuclear power would also make us less dependent on foreign oil, and help to solve our foreign trade balance.

Then on March 28, 1979 our worst commercial nuclear accident took place at Three Mile Island, Pennsylvania. Although members of Local No. 404 would eventually get the plant working again, this would slow up the building of additional nuclear plants and make us even more dependent on foreign oil. By April of 1980 50% of our oil would be imported and 70% of this would come from the Persian Gulf countries.

Another safety problem was the deplorable condition of bridges in the United States. As early as 1977 our International began stressing the need to rebuild the nation's infrastructure, especially our bridges. It was pointed out in *The Ironworker* that the average bridge was designed to last 40 years, yet three-fourths of America's half million bridges were more than 45 years old.

The Economy in Canada and the United States

At the time that President Carter took office in 1977, as we were coming out of the recession of the Nixon/Ford years, General President Lyons wrote:

"In Canada we see a similar situation. Anti-inflation efforts have pushed the unemployment rate in Canada to its worst level in 15 years. Real income for Canadian workers actually dropped in 1975 because of a severe loss in purchasing power."

Although the Canadian government was reporting that construction industry unemployment was at 15.4% it was actually more like 27%. However, many of our members in Canada did find employment in building structures for Olympics '76, which was held in Montreal.

Just as in the United States, right-wing political groups were fighting the union movement. In the *Canadian Report* in *The Ironworker* magazine in the December 1979 issue it was pointed out that Canadian businessmen were crying for "de-regulation," which also meant getting rid of unions. This was based on the view that legal regulations were an unfair burden on business, and therefore should be repealed or watered down wherever possible.

In the United States during the Carter years inflation continued at a very high rate. Business kept raising prices in fear that President Carter would slap on

Willow Island, West Virginia. Described as the worst construction fatality in American history, 51 workers, including 11 journeymen Ironworkers, plunged 170 feet to their death as scaffolding peeled away from the top of a cooling tower on April 27, 1978.

General President Lyons met with Ironworker Business Agents in Ottawa, Canada while attending the National Canadian Conference in 1977.

At the chartering of Local No. 46 Metallic Lathers and Reinforcing Ironworkers are General Vice President Thomas Clarkson, Local No. 46 Business Manager Jim Maher, General President John H. Lyons, General Organizer Mickey Brennan, and Business Agent Jim Maloney. In back are Local 46 Business Agent Ed O'Connell, Recording Secretary Fred Lemoine, Business Agent John Ryan, Business Agent Pete McGovern and Local No. 46 President John Williams.

price controls. The AFL-CIO was still recovering from the so-called wage/price controls under Nixon, which turned out to be just wage controls. They were against any similar program. Yet profits for companies at this time were 15.5% after taxes.

One of the ways our Union and other members of the Building and Construction Trades Council were working to provide more jobs was the **J for Jobs Program** in cooperation with the Union Labor Life Insurance Company. Our Union had been one of the founders of this insurance company in the 1920's, and all of our General Presidents has served on its board of directors. Now this company was loaning money for union construction projects to help the economy and provide jobs for our members. The J for Jobs Program would only finance projects that were guaranteed to be 100 % union.

Raymond J. Robertson Appointed Director of Apprenticeship and Training

In the October 1979 issue of *The Ironworker* magazine it was announced that General Organizer Raymond J. Robertson would replace J.W. Hardesty as the Director of Apprenticeship and Training. General Organizer Robertson had worked out of the Chicago and Vicinity District Council from 1967 through 1979 where he handled jurisdictional disputes in a four state area and also processed all Ironworker-Glazier disputes in the United States and Canada. One of his primary assignments during this period of time was to work on matters pertaining to apprenticeship and training. From time to time, during this period, he worked in the Apprenticeship and Jurisdictional Departments at International Headquarters in St. Louis and Washington, D.C. He was eventually appointed Executive Director of Apprenticeship and Training by President Lyons.

Raymond J. Robertson
Apprenticeship Director

A Historical Event

By the summer of 1979, the Lathers International Union no longer existed as an International union of the AFL-CIO since its membership had declined. The remaining locals were given the opportunity to vote to become a part of another International. Although most of the locals voted to join the Carpenters Union, Lathers Local No. 46 of New York City voted on July 28, 1979 to join the Iron Workers International.

In 1917 when our International was expelled from the AFL, the Lathers and other Internationals wanted jurisdiction over iron and steel work. Although our original jurisdiction over this work was restored in 1920, the Metallic Lathers Local No. 46 kept jurisdiction in New York City over installing reinforcing rods in building construction in that city. This was something our International had to live with for over 60 years. However, with the decline of the Lathers as the result of factory produced wallboard and fabricated systems it was agreed that this local, which was doing totally different work, could separate from all the other locals and vote separately on what International to join. General President Lyons proudly attended the meeting of this new local to welcome them into our International.

Counterfeit Bolts

In 1979, the International Association urged markings on bolts, nuts and rivets. While some contractors were bidding construction jobs with American materials and admittedly substituting cheap import fasteners, General President Lyons asked the Commissioner of Customs to enforce a law which required markings from the country of origin. President Lyons said the Ironworker deserves to know, for his own safety, where the bolt was milled. Quite by accident, a worker on the Wolf Creek Nuclear Power Project in Kansas reported that he discovered an anchor bolt stripped clean and loose, apparently after someone forced it several turns. The bolt is said to have been on the nuclear containment structure, a critical area, and was manufactured in a foreign country.

George Meany Passes Away

President Lyons praised George Meany for his years of service to the men and women of the Labor Movement. AFL-CIO President Lane Kirkland said: "His life works would do honor to a dozen men." George Meany was a good friend of the Ironworkers. On January 10, 1980, former AFL-CIO President George Meany passed away just eight weeks after making his retirement speech at the AFL-CIO 1979 convention. He died sixty-three years to the day after his admission, as a journeyman plumber, into Local 463, New York City, N.Y. He was a controversial figure from the beginning, with more than a dash of vitriol--a burly Irishman from the Bronx, who made up his mind in the early 1920's that he would make a career of labor leadership.

George Meany
President, AFL-CIO

His career was unparalleled in American Labor histo-

Crystal Cathedral near completion in 1980.

The Crystal Cathedral Local No. 433 crew with Rev. Schuller at topping out ceremonies in 1980.

ry. Besides dealing with eight U. S. Presidents, he knew scores of world political and labor leaders, hundreds of members of Congress and thousands of American union officials. He chatted with Popes, royalty, sports and media figures.

From business agent, Meany rose through leadership roles in New York City labor to the presidency of the New York State Federation of Labor. In 1940 he went to Washington as secretary-treasurer of the AFL; he moved up to the presidency in 1952. Three years later he brought about the merger of the AFL and CIO after convincing powerful union chiefs in both organizations that they had to end the internecine war that had been underway for twenty years. Then he struggled for more than a decade to prevent a new split threatened by the United Auto Workers' Walter P. Reuther.

Crystal Cathedral

In 1980, the Ironworkers fabricated and erected the "Crystal Cathedral" in Anaheim, California. It stands as a monument to the skills and know-how of Shop and Outside Ironworkers who labored diligently on the construction of a steel pipe and glass "space frame" which is taller and longer and wider than the Notre Dame Cathedral in Paris. Shopmen's Local No. 624, Fresno, California fabricated 30,000 pipe members with 27,000 steel gussets to form the 150-ton steel pipe frames. Local No. 433, Los Angeles, erected the steel and installed a total of 10,661 reflective glass panes. Local No. 433 Business Manager C.W. "Red" Lansford and Business Agent Joe Ward were frequent visitors to the project during construction.

The Presidential Election of 1980

In January, 1980, President Lyons pointed out that under President Carter the largest expansion of the economy took place in a two and a half year period. Both President

President Carter waits with General President Lyons to deliver his speech to the BCTD delegates attending the Legislative Conference in Washington, D.C., in 1980.

Carter and Secretary of Labor Ray Marshall had listened to almost every point presented to them by labor. The Administration had also moved forward with a jobs program to solve the 25% unemployment rate in the construction industry and they were 100% in support of the Davis-Bacon Act. Accordingly, the International Association decided to support the re-election of President Carter.

However, Reagan would win with just over half of the popular vote and an overwhelming amount of the electoral votes. The voter turnout was very poor. Although the Republicans claimed a mandate for change, this was hardly justified. The House of Representatives would remain Democratic, but the Senate went to the Republicans. Orrin Hatch would take over the Senate Labor and Human Relations Committee. His immediate goal was to reduce the minimum wage for young people and allow them to work in stores and fast-food outlets at 14 years of age.

Tragedy and Heroism in Las Vegas

Shortly after the elections, on November 21, 1980 a fire broke out in the MGM Grand Hotel in Las Vegas. Ironworkers were working nearby and came to the rescue. Eighty-eight members of Local No. 433 helped to save hundreds of lives, although 84 people died and 500 were injured. One of the heroes of this event was 72-year-old Lou Hillegass, who had worked on the building and knew the layout. He would later be honored for his bravery. This Ironworker hero had been an Olympic Gold Medal winner in the 1924 Olympic Games along with another member of the team, Johnny Weissmuller, later of Tarzan movie fame.

In the book *The Politics of Rich and Poor* by Kevin Phillips the author compares three periods in American history when the rich became richer and the union movement was put down. The first of these three periods was the so-called "Gilded Age" when

178

The MGM Grand Hotel casino was consumed by flames and black toxic smoke in minutes, causing 84 deaths and over 500 injuries. Ironworker members from Local No. 433, Los Angeles, who were working at an additional building for the hotel, rushed to save lives even before the fire department arrived.

Some of the 88 Ironworkers from Local No. 433 who rescued hundreds of victims on November 21, 1980.

our Union was first being organized. This was the time of Haymarket and the Homestead Strike. The second period was the "Roaring Twenties" when taxes on the rich were reduced from 73% to only 25%. This was the period of Harding, Coolidge, and Hoover when union contracts were being broken by the Landis Awards.

The third and most recent period was the 1980's under Reagan and Bush when taxes on the rich were reduced from 70% to 28% and for the first time since the 1930's companies began using so-called "replacement workers" whenever unions went out on strike. During the 1980's the percentage of unionized workers decreased each year, and it became more and more difficult to organize.

Although Reagan had only won 50.8% of the popular vote in the 1980 election, he felt he had a mandate for change or what he called an "era of national renewal."

Lou Hillegass, 72 years young, accepts a commemorative plaque with all 88 names engraved from Local No. 433 Business Manager C.W. Lansford on behalf of the Local No. 433 rescue team at the MGM Grand Hotel fire.

The Democrats still controlled the House of Representatives by 243 to 192, but the Republicans had gained control of the Senate by 53 to 46.

The period known as the era of Reaganomics began on January 20, 1981 as Ronald Reagan was sworn in as the 40th President of the United States. It was a bright and sunny day with balmy temperatures. The ceremony was very formal in contrast to the Carter inauguration. To play to the television cameras, for the first time the ceremony took place on the West Front of the Capitol with a great view toward the Washington Monument.

After speaking for twenty minutes, President Reagan made his surprise announcement. After 444 days in captivity the 52 American hostages in Iran would be freed. Soon afterwards the public found out that a deal had been made to restore some $8 billion in Iranian funds in American banks to the Iranian leader, Khomeini.

When the returning hostages flew into Andrews Air Force Base near Washington D.C., they were greeted by the "Great American Flag." The flag, which was as large as two football fields, had been laid out near the runway by 300 volunteers who were members of Local 5 and 201. It was the first thing the former hostages saw as they returned.

An Assassination Attempt on the President

On March 30, 1981, President Reagan spoke to 5,000 delegates and guests at the Legislative Conference of the Building and Construction Trades Department of the AFL-CIO in Washington, D.C.

Only five minutes after leaving the ballroom of the

In 1981, the International Association made hard hat, bumper and windshield stickers available to members of the Association.

Some of the volunteers who gave the returning Americans their "biggest welcome home."

Hundreds of Ironworkers and members of the Washington Building Trades volunteered to unfold the Great American Flag along the runway to greet the former hostages. It took four hours to unfurl all 86,379 square feet of Old Glory.

Washington Hilton, President Reagan was shot and wounded, along with his press secretary, a Secret Service officer, and a policeman, by a deranged assassin. The second and third day of the conference were canceled out of respect for the wounded President. Vice President Bush temporarily took over the responsibilities of the President, who recovered in a remarkably short time. His press secretary, James Brady, was paralyzed for life. The attempted assassin was John W. Hinckley, Jr., an unemployed drifter who would later plead insanity. Many of the Ironworker delegates were at the scene of the assassination attempt seconds after it happened. One of the Building Trades delegates was credited with knocking Hinckley down to the ground.

In July, 1981 the "Gemini" computer system was launched. Financial Secretaries and their office personnel from 44 of the largest outside and shop locals spent two full days getting acquainted with a mini-computer system - "Gemini," General Membership Information Network for Ironworkers. The local office mini-computers were designed to have resident files of all the pertinent data that is required for reporting to the International Association such as member information, payment information, local information, statistical information and accounting detail. Using a display terminal,

the local union officer is able to inquire into files, apply payment, initiate activities and automatically produce receipts. By 1996, the Gemini program would be upgraded several times. Gemini classes have been held on a continual basis since 1981.

The **Thirty-Sixth International Convention** was held August 10-14, 1981 at the Diplomat Hotel in Hollywood, Florida. General President John H. Lyons, General Secretary Juel D. Drake and General Treasurer Charles R. Anding were reelected along with the nine General Vice Presidents. President Lyons reported to the delegates that organizing campaigns relative to the Shop Division revealed that 12,413 employees were contacted at the plants where they were employed and 6,682 employees were contacted at their homes. He also reported that since the last convention, 2,724 collective bargaining agreements were negotiated for an average of 549 per year. Even with this impressive record, the shopmen membership decreased by 4,894 members, caused by the influx of imported steel.

President Lyons reported that from July 1, 1976 through June 30, 1981, International Headquarters processed 9,076 jurisdictional disputes. President Lyons reported on the "Institute of the Ironworking Industry" which is a non-profit corporation organized under

Delegates' badge worn by the delegates at the 36th International Convention.

Financial secretaries, local representatives and International staff at the GEMINI seminar held in 1981

The delegates to the 36th International Convention reelect General President John H. Lyons (left), General Secretary Juel D. Drake (middle) and General Treasurer Charles R. Anding.

the laws of the District of Columbia. The Institute was established to protect, promote, foster, and advance the interests of its sponsors as fabricators and erectors of structural steel, reinforcing steel, precast concrete, miscellaneous and architectural metals, rigging and precision placing and all other products fabricated or erected by the Ironworking Industry. The Institute employed John McMahon, member of Local No. 5 and former contractor, as Director.

President Lyons pointed out the importance of the Ironworkers Political Action League (IPAL) headed up by General Organizer Michael Brennan who was named Political Director. He also pointed out that "Politics" has become so important to our issues and interests that if we do not do everything possible to get our message across, then the concerns of working people will be ignored.

Another important subject covered at the convention was "Contract Maintenance." It was pointed out that

the purpose of having Maintenance contracts is to cover continuing supplemental repair, renovation, alteration, and modification of existing plants and facilities. In 1981, there were 921 maintenance agreements that were administered from the General Secretary's office. President Lyons advised the delegates that he had appointed General Organizer James J. Willis as Director of the Maintenance Department to assist General Secretary Juel D. Drake in handling maintenance contracts.

The importance of Apprenticeship and Training was stressed at the 36th Convention as well as Safety and the Canadian Labour Congress. There were at this time 165 Apprenticeship Programs with 9,342 apprentice members. This was an increase of 43% since the previous convention. General Counsel Harold Stern, General Secretary Juel D. Drake and General Treasurer Charles R. Anding made detailed reports to the delegates on the activities of their offices. Over 70 resolutions were submitted to the 36th Convention covering a variety of subjects.

Reports from the convention showed that the total membership of the International at this time was 182,046, and during the period from 1976 to 1981 the average wage of an Ironworker had increased by 39.5%.

Solidarity Day, 1981

On September 19, nearly 500,000 workers marched on Washington, D.C. in what was the largest demonstration in American history. They came by bus, train, and car, but not by plane, to protest the treatment of the PATCO workers.

General President Lyons thought that without being able to travel by air, there would be a poor turnout, with

Ironworkers for Solidarity Day.

Ironworkers for Solidarity Day.

less than 1,000 Ironworkers in attendance. As he drove into D.C. that day he was thrilled to see people everywhere. Instead of the 1,000 Ironworkers some 6,500 participated, coming from all parts of the country. One Ironworker from Indiana said he was there because he was "ticked off at OSHA and the lack of enforcement of the Davis-Bacon Act."

The Reagan Recession and The Economy

Late in 1981 the nation went into a severe recession. General President Lyons would testify before the U.S. Congress on December 4, 1981. He pointed out that unemployment was the worst since the 1930's with 9 million people out of work, 1 million discouraged workers, and 5 million only working part time.

"But in construction the recession has been compounding for nearly two years, as construction employment is down by 230,000 with an alarming unemployment rate of 18 percent. That's almost one out of every five construction workers without a job."

The "Reagan Recession" would continue throughout his first four years in office. One of the industries to suffer was steel, which was our most basic industry. By December of 1981, McDonald's was employing three times as many employees as the U.S. Steel Company at its peak.

Union-Busting Under Reagan

Beginning with the Reagan years a new type of union-busting began. Management seminars with titles like "Making Unions Unnecessary" or "How to Stay Non Union" taught management how to rid their company of unions and achieve a "Union Free Environment." An excellent article about this appeared in the January, 1981 issue of *The Ironworker*. Part of the article read as follows:

"Union-busting is as old as the labor movement itself. In earlier days, however, fear of workers' rights led employers to guns, goons, injunctions, lawsuits, anything--legal or not legal--just to keep unions out. The tactics have changed and have become less obvious. Modern union-busters use psychological manipulation, emotional intimidation or 'preventive unionism' as their anti-union weapons. George Meany said: 'Today's labor relations consultants carry briefcases instead of brass

knuckles and they leave no visible marks on their victims. But their job is the same--frustrate human hopes and nullify human rights."

But some of the old kinds of union-busting were still going on! In the 1980's a Michigan security force named NUCKOLS was involved in labor disputes, and they were using handguns, handcuffs, billy clubs, mace and a "SWAT" vehicle.

Members of Local No. 704, Chattanooga and Local No. 384, Knoxville, Tennessee, erected more than 640 tons of structural steel for the five level steel-framed globe atop the Sunsphere for Energy Expo '82 in Knoxville.

Reciprocity Seminar for Pension & Health & Welfare

In April, 1982, more than 75 Ironworker Business Agents who also served as Trustees on their respective pension and welfare plans came together at the George Meany Center to evaluate fully all aspects of reciprocity. The meeting resulted in an agreement that would assure a benefit upon retirement for every Ironworker member participating in one or another pension plan, despite changes of employment. President Lyons opened the meeting by giving a brief history of the Ironworkers' pension coverage. "We have had 'boomers' as long as we have had Ironworkers." General Organizer Martin T. Byrne who was appointed Chairman of the Committee by President

Reciprocity Seminar–General President Lyons speaks to the delegates after being introduced by General Organizer Martin T. Byrne who organized the Seminar.

Lyons introduced a panel of pension and welfare experts at the four-day seminar. As we go into 1996 the International has almost 100 percent reciprocity participation.

Shopmen fabricate first "Bulkhead Flatcar." Members of Local No. 508, Detroit, Michigan built 100-ton, 74 foot flatcar at the Paragon Railcar Operation facility in Novi, Michigan.

Foreign Fabricated Steel and the Loss of Our Jobs

It was mentioned at the 36th Convention that fabricating shop locals were closing and we were losing members because of the importation of fabricated steel during the Reagan years. One example of this was the Star Iron and Steel Works of Tacoma, Washington. This company and its shopmen had been engineering and fabricating custom-built shipboard and portside cranes since 1933. But a National Defense Department order in 1982 went to the Japanese. A second blow to the company and our Union workers was when the Port of Seattle also allowed a major order for a large electric container crane to go to the Japanese.

Another of our Union fabricating plants in Seattle would close in 1983, Isaacson Steel, which had been in operation for 76 years. During World War II, the company employed 1,200 workers and built vital ship castings that helped win the war.

Members of Local No. 378, Oakland, California moved and placed a giant 375-ton "Superconducting Magnet" into the Mirror Fusion Test Facility in 1982.

THE IRONWORKER
SEPTEMBER 1982

Ironworker members of Local No. 808, Orlando, build the 18 story "Spaceship Earth" at Disney World in Orlando. The geodesic dome involved approximately 50,000 man hours to complete.

A 21,000-pound cap piece is set atop the Spaceship Earth Geodesic dome by members of Local No. 808.

Some of the Ironworkers along with Bob Clark Sr., President of Tampa Steel Erecting, at topping out ceremony of the Spaceship Earth Geodesic dome.

In November of 1984, General President Lyons reported on a letter he had received from Ed Porter, the Mayor of Bessemer, Alabama. It seemed that Bristol Steel, a union fabricating plant, which had been operating in Bessemer for many years, was going out of business. The Mayor wanted President Lyons to solve the problems by making all kinds of wage and working condition concessions to keep it open. President Lyons pointed out that the Mayor should contact Congress to change the laws. He pointed out that Korean fabricated steel was now replacing the Japanese imports. While the Koreans had only 13.9% of imported steel in 1983, by 1984 it had 52.6%.

Our International urged Congress and the White House, as well as the Labor Department, to address the growing import problem. One by one, our fabricating shops were either working at half-capacity or going out of business. By 1986, we were facing competition from imported steel from South Africa, Brazil, and even Great Britain.

Rebuilding An Old Bridge

Built too early for the use of photography to record the Ironworker's craft going into it, the Wheeling Suspension Bridge is the oldest bridge of its type in the world. Built in 1849, and the first to cross the Ohio River without touching the water once, the bridge was rehabilitated by members of Local No. 549, Wheeling, West Virginia in January, 1983. Ironworkers building the bridge in 1849

had pioneered a new method of suspending the bridge using materials and techniques that had never been used before. Abandoning the custom of using chain links, which had the potential of dropping the whole bridge if one link broke, Ironworkers used some of the first wrought iron wire to make cables for supporting the bridge. Not only did the cables prove to be stronger, but they also had the advantage of stretching, instead of breaking, with the bridge's normal movement.

In 1849, the threads on support rods were hand scored, wire cable was hand wrapped, and all of the other bridge workings hand forged. The object of the work in 1983 was to maintain the authenticity of the bridge while rehabilitating it. Ironworkers from Local No. 549 were commended for the work they did on the bridge.

Retired Former General Treasurer James V. Cole Passes Away

*James V. Cole
General Treasurer
1899-1983*

On April 30, 1983 retired General Treasurer James V. Cole passed away at 84 years of age. General President Lyons delivered the Eulogy. He noted that Brother Cole was a man who had done great things for the International Association through total dedication and hard work.

John T. Traylor Appointed

On July 1, 1983, General Treasurer Charles R. Anding resigned as General Treasurer. President Lyons noted that General Treasurer Anding expressed a desire to return home to Louisiana to represent the International Association as President of The Mid-South District Council. To fill the vacancy, President Lyons with the approval of the General Executive Council appointed General Organizer John T. Traylor to be General Treasurer. General Treasurer Traylor, a member of Local No. 16, Baltimore, Md. had worked 9 years in the Jurisdictional Department.

*John T. Traylor
General Treasurer*

The Great American Flag

About 110 Ironworkers and volunteers from the Washington Building Trades Council unfurled the Great American Flag one last time before it became the official property of the U.S. Government on Flag Day, 1983. "Over the years we have come to love this flag," said President Lyons at White House ceremonies, "all seven tons of it, all two acres of stars and stripes." President

The old Wheeling Suspension Bridge is rebuilt by members of Local No. 549, Wheeling, W.V.

Reagan accepted the flag on behalf of the American people and circled around the flag on the Ellipse in a helicopter on his way to Tennessee.

Ironworkers involvement in the project began on June 28, 1976, when New York Ironworkers hoisted a smaller version of the Great American Flag on the Verrazano Narrows Bridge as a bicentennial tribute. Due to high winds, the flag was ripped to shreds in eight hours. By 1980, Flag Day, the new Great American Flag was ready for display beneath the Washington Monument, unfurled by the Washington, D.C. Ironworkers and International staff personnel. Then out to Andrews Air Force Base for the biggest welcome home for the American hostages from Iran, and finally to New York's Central Park. Each time, Ironworkers volunteered and unfurled the flag.

Jake West Appointed

Jake West,
General Vice President

On September 30, 1983 President Lyons appointed General Organizer Jacob F. West as General Vice President to fill the vacancy created by the death of General Vice President Dale Ray. He started out in Local No. 301 of Charleston, West Virginia in 1948. In 1951 he became a member of Local No. 433, Los Angeles and was elected Business Agent in 1961 and Business Manager in 1970. With this appointment General Vice President West took over as President of the District Council of Ironworkers of the State of California and Vicinity.

At the end of 1983, with the federal Bureau of Apprenticeship crippled by cuts of more than half of its staff and numerous positions, including the directorship, left unfilled, the U.S. House Subcommittee on Employment Opportunities cranked up hearings to examine forecasts of skilled craft shortages. Reagan Administration budget cuts and both neglect and disorder in the U.S. Department of Labor had led to the decline and even death of viable apprenticeship and training programs, Congress was told.

Representing the Building Trades - Metal Trades Joint Apprenticeship Committee as Chair, Executive Director of Apprenticeship and Training Raymond J. Robertson outlined to the Employment Opportunities Subcommittee of the U.S. House Education and Labor Committee, the qualities of union apprenticeship and suggested several possible ways the federal government could and should assume a more important role.

The first meeting of the Board of Trustees of the National Ironworkers and Employers Apprenticeship Training and Journeyman Upgrading Fund took place on February 7, 1984 in Washington, D.C. General President John H. Lyons met with the trustees and gave some background regarding the fund. General Secretary Drake also spoke with the trustees. One of the first actions taken by the trustees was to establish an annual Ironworker Instructor school and to develop a number of video training modules for the participants of the fund.

Lial Field Appointed

Lial Field
General Vice President

Following the retirement of General Vice President Leonard P. Mahoney, General Organizer Lial Field, member of Local No. 392, East St. Louis, Illinois was appointed General Vice President by President Lyons on March 19, 1984. At the time of his appointment, he remained a Vice President until the middle of 1985 and later retired on March 1, 1990.

The Presidential Election of 1984

In January of 1984, Reagan announced that he would run for a second term in spite of the nation's economic situation. In August at the Republican

General President John H. Lyons spoke on the lawn of the White House: "Mr. President, with the presentation of the world's largest flag to the U.S. government today, on Flag Day, 1983, our patriotic role sadly comes to an end. Our great flag now has a home. We are most grateful to the muscle and sweat of our volunteers whose efforts have, in the past and now today, assisted our fund raisers to make these several patriotic tributes to 'the land of the free and home of the brave.'"

International Representatives and some of the Washington, D.C. Ironworkers who met at the White House.

Executive Director of Apprenticeship and Training Raymond Robertson (sitting, right) testified on behalf of the Building Trades - Metal Trades Joint Apprenticeship Committee before the Employment Opportunities Subcommittee of the U.S. House Education and Labor Committee in 1984.

Presidential candidate Walter F. Mondale meets with General Secretary Juel D. Drake and General President John H. Lyons at the 15th Constitutional Convention of the AFL-CIO in 1984.

Convention in Dallas, Texas he was nominated by his party as their candidate. Reagan received the support of 2,235 of the delegates with only 2 voting against him.

General President Lyons had been elected as co-chair of the Democratic Platform Committee. He did not support Gary Hart, but did support Walter Mondale. On the "President's Page" in the June issue of *The Ironworker* he listed why our members should not support Reagan for a second term. He pointed out that the nation's greatest need was to create new jobs. Reagan had given a $750 billion tax break to big corporations, but this had not created any new jobs. The American dollar had increased in value by 57% in just 3 1/2 years, making it impossible to sell our goods overseas. The minimum wage of $3.35 which was set in 1978 had dropped in real value to $2.08, and it would have to be raised to $4.29 to have the same value as it had in 1978.

President Lyons also pointed out that Reagan had packed the National Labor Relations Board with anti-union members, fired OSHA inspectors, and packed the Civil Rights Commission as well as the Equal Employment Opportunity Commission.

At the Democratic Convention in San Francisco in July the nomination went to Walter Mondale and Geraldine Ferraro as his running mate. They received the support of Ironworker delegates to the convention from Locals, l, 21, 89, 396, 451,and 495.

A meeting of the National Ironworkers and Employers Apprenticeship Training and Journeyman Upgrading Fund was held on February 7, 1984. Seated, left to right: George Weiland Jr. and Mike Newington, Employer trustees; General President John H. Lyons and General Secretary Juel D. Drake. Standing, left to right: Clyde Quick, Employer trustee, William Costello, Attorney, Executive Director of Apprenticeship and Training Raymond J. Robertson, General Vice President Thomas Clarkson and General Vice President Jacob West, Union Trustees.

On election night Reagan received 58.8% of the popular vote and 525 electoral votes. Mondale received only 13 electoral votes carrying only his home state of Minnesota and the District of Columbia. However, Reagan would lose his majority in the Senate. Now both Houses of Congress were in the hands of the Democrats.

Roosevelt Remembered

In late 1984, workers looking for a way to commemorate the golden era of labor legislation under the Roosevelt Presidency found a way by restoring F.D.R.'s favorite retreat - the U.S.S. Potomac. Congress pledged $2.5 million in matching funds to restore the "floating White House." The U.S.S. Potomac would be a floating museum of labor history, showing F.D.R.'s commitment to trade unions to an estimated half-million school children at ports-of-call each year. On March 29, 1941 President Roosevelt broadcast from the Radio Room of the "floating White House."

Throughout the war, the U.S.S. Potomac served President Franklin D. Roosevelt well as an asylum from raging battles overseas and enormous sacrifices at home. Here is where he came to rest or relax, write speeches and plan strategy. Some of the famed "Fireside Chats" were composed here, some even delivered from the Radio Room of the U.S.S. Potomac. The Ironworkers District Council of the State of California and Vicinity and its affiliates played an important role in the ship's restoration.

General President John H. Lyons Resigns

Five months after President Reagan took office for the second time, General President John H. Lyons, after serving 24 years as General President, was forced to resign on June 2, 1985 because of ill health. President Lyons would not recover from his illness and on October 26, 1986, only three days before

John H. Lyons General President Emeritus, retires.

Restoration of the "U.S.S. Potomac"

President Franklin D. Roosevelt on the Presidential Yacht "The U.S.S. Potomac."

The U.S.S. Potomac was also a place to honor and entertain foreign statesmen, such as the Royal Family of England in 1939.

The U.S.S. Potomac was a decoy for F.D.R.'s clandestine meeting with Churchill aboard H.M.S. Prince of Wales on August 10, 1941.

General Vice President Jake West, who was also President of the California District Council in 1985, received a unanimous vote from the delegates to assist in the U.S.S. Potomac restoration project.

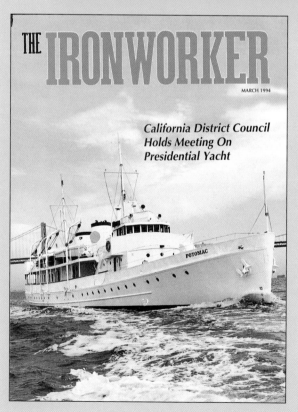

THE IRONWORKER

MARCH 1994

California District Council Holds Meeting On Presidential Yacht

Members of Local No. 606, Wichita, Kansas topped out a $9 million expansion of the Century II Civic Center in 1985.

General President Juel D. Drake is sworn in by General Vice President Hugh Williamson on June 6, 1985.

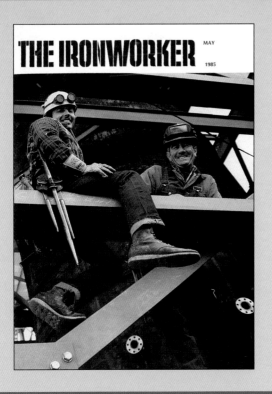

his 67th birthday, he would pass away.

The democratic tradition that began with the founding of the International Association in 1896 continued when General Secretary Juel D. Drake was elected on June 6, 1985 by the General Executive Council to succeed John H. Lyons.

General President Juel D. Drake had served as General Secretary since January 1, 1971. He had been a member of the International Association for 46 years (Local No. 229, San Diego, California) and a member of the International staff for more than 36 years. One of President Drake's first actions was to appoint John H. Lyons General President Emeritus which was approved unanimously by the General Executive Council and later by the delegates at the 37th Convention in 1986.

Jake West Appointed General Secretary

Jake West
General Secretary.

To fill the vacancy created by his election on June 6, 1985, General President Drake appointed General Vice President Jake West as General Secretary. General Secretary West said, "Teamwork and dedication are my goals. I sense deeply the obligation and trust bestowed on me by General President Drake as I assume the office of General Secretary. The membership can be assured that I will work diligently to create the teamwork necessary to serve the membership in accordance with our Constitution and in the review of our contracts and agreements. I am aware of the problems of the construction industry and will be working with each local union and District Council to solve these problems. My major concern is to protect the future of each and every member of this International Association and their families."

LeRoy E. Worley Appointed

General Organizer LeRoy E. Worley was appointed General Vice President by acting General President Juel D. Drake effective June 2, 1985. General Vice President Worley was initiated into Local No. 29, Portland, Oregon in 1961 where he served a three year apprenticeship. He was Business Agent and Financial Secretary-Treasurer before being appointed General Organizer in 1981.

LeRoy E. Worley,
General Vice President

James E. Cole Appointed

James E. Cole, Executive Assistant to the General President, was appointed General Treasurer on August 13, 1985 by President Juel D. Drake, with the unanimous approval of the General Executive Council. He was initiated into Local No. 40, New York, N.Y., in June of 1964 where he worked as a Journeyman Ironworker. Prior to 1964, General Treasurer Cole served as an apprentice for the Harris Structural

James E. Cole,
General Treasurer

Steel Company in New York City, received a Bachelor of Science in Economics from Fordham University, and served in the U. S. Army as an officer. He also received a Doctor of Jurisprudence by Fordham University School of Law and thereafter was admitted to the Bar in New York State. On January 10, 1971, he was appointed General Organizer. He worked at International Headquarters in St. Louis and when International Headquarters moved to Washington, D. C. he assisted General Secretary Juel D. Drake and General President John H. Lyons before being named General Treasurer. General Treasurer Cole attended the Harvard Trade Union program. He also serves on the Ironworkers joint labor management safety committee for the industry. His father, James V. Cole, served as General Treasurer of the International Association from 1960 to 1974.

William H. Sullivan Appointed

General Organizer William H. Sullivan was appointed General Vice President on August 1, 1985. In 1951, he began his apprenticeship in Local No. 3, Pittsburgh. From 1965 through 1975 he served as Business Agent and in 1975 was appointed General Organizer. He was president of the District Council of Eastern Ohio, Western Pennsylvania and Northern West Virginia for sixteen years. General Vice President Sullivan retired on February 1, 1995.

William H. Sullivan,
General Vice President

James J. Willis Appointed

On August 13,1985, General President Drake appointed James J. Willis, Executive Director in Charge of Maintenance, as General Vice President. Brother Willis became an apprentice in Local No. 6, Buffalo, New York in May, 1945. He held several offices including Business Agent in Local No. 6 before being appointed General Organizer in 1967. At the time of his appointment, General Vice President Willis had been representing the International Association on a number of committees, such as the National Erectors Association, National Maintenance Agreements Policy Committee, Specialized Carriers and Rigging Association, Associated Maintenance Contractors and the National Council of Erectors, Fabricators and Riggers.

James J. Willis,
General Vice President

Martin T. Byrne Appointed

General President Juel D. Drake announced the appointment of General Organizer Martin T. Byrne, a member of Local No. 37, Providence, Rhode Island, as Executive Assistant to the General President effective February 1, 1986. It was noted that

Martin T. Byrne,
Executive Assistant to the
General President

In 1985, the First Annual Ironworker Instructors Training Program was held at the University of California-Berkeley. More than 100 Ironworker Instructors attended the program. President Drake said, "The future of this great organization depends on the success of the National Fund and its goal, which is to standardize training and provide employers with the highest skilled work force possible." The purpose of the program is to: Assure that every instructor is fully qualified in teaching techniques; help keep instructors current with technological changes as they occur in the industry; and provide a forum for instructor colleagues to exchange ideas and standardize training for Ironworkers from coast to coast.

1st Annual Ironworker Instructors Training Program

Certificate of Completion

This is to certify that

has successfully completed the National Ironworker
Instructors Training Program at

The University of California-Berkeley

on this date _____ **June 21, 1985**

Chairman

Secretary-Treasurer

NATIONAL IRONWORKERS
AND EMPLOYERS
APPRENTICESHIP TRAINING
AND JOURNEYMAN
UPGRADING FUND

CENTER FOR LABOR RESEARCH AND EDUCATION

Institute of Industrial Relations   University of California, Berkeley

This certifies that

has successfully completed

FIRST ANNUAL IRONWORKER
INSTRUCTORS' TRAINING PROGRAM
at
Berkeley, California
June 16-21, 1985

Sponsoring Organization

General Secretary Jake West **(right)** and Executive Director Raymond Robertson at the 1st Annual Ironworkers Instructors Training Program.

Management trustee Clyde Quick attends one of the classes with Ironworker Instructor students.

Executive Assistant Byrne represented the International Association on various committees, including the Iron Worker International Reciprocal Agreement, AFL-CIO Building Trades Market Recovery Program, National Building Trades Project Review Committee, General Presidents Offshore Committee, and since July of 1985 has been Editor of *The Ironworker.*

James A. Martin Appointed

On February 1, 1986, General Organizer James A. Martin was appointed General Vice President by General President Drake. Brother Martin joined Ironworkers Local No. 66, San Antonio, Texas, in 1958. Before he was appointed General Organizer in 1973, he served as Business Manager and Financial Secretary of Local No. 66. General Vice President Martin was also former President of the San Antonio Building Trades and at the time of his appointment was serving on the Executive Council of the Texas State AFL-CIO. He also worked at International Headquarters for a period of time in the General Secretary's Office before returning to Texas to take over as President of the State of Texas District Council.

*James A. Martin,
General Vice President*

O.C. Yancy Appointed

On March 17, 1986, General Organizer and President of the Rocky Mountain District Council O.C. Yancy was appointed General Vice President by General President Drake. Brother Yancy started his career as an Ironworker in 1947 when he became a member of Local No. 14, Spokane, Washington. He also held memberships in Local Unions No. 86, 377, 263, and 24, Denver. He was a Business Agent for Local No. 263, Fort Worth, Texas before he was appointed General Organizer in 1965. General Vice President Yancy retired on January 1, 1994.

*O.C. Yancy,
General Vice President*

Fhane B. Jones Appointed

General President Juel D. Drake appointed General Organizer Fhane B. Jones as General Vice President on March 17, 1986. General Vice President Jones was elected President of the District Council of Philadelphia and Vicinity in 1984. He was initiated into Local No. 399, Camden, New Jersey where he served his apprenticeship from 1961 to 1963 before becoming a journeyman. Brother Jones was elected Business Manager of Local No. 399 in 1969 and in 1984 he was appointed by General President Lyons as General Organizer. General Vice President Jones also served as President of the Camden Building Trades from 1971 to 1985.

*Fhane B. Jones,
General Vice President*

Vincent B. Ryan Heads Up Jurisdictional Department

Robert McVay, after serving 21 years in the Jurisdiction Department, the last 16 years as Executive Director, retired on May 1, 1986. On May 12, 1986, General President Drake appointed Vincent B. Ryan, Business Agent of Local No. 229, San Diego, California, as General Organizer to head up the Jurisdiction Department and on September 1, 1986 he was appointed Executive Director in charge of Jurisdiction.

*Vincent B. Ryan, Executive
Director in charge of
Jurisdiction*

In January, 1986 in Becancour, facing Trois-Rivieres, on the south shore of the St. Lawrence River, halfway between Montreal and Quebec City, members of Montreal Local No. 711 completed the erection of an aluminum smelter, one of the largest projects in Canada.

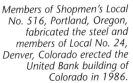

THE IRONWORKER
JANUARY 1986

Members of Local No. 580 who worked on the Statue of Liberty in 1985 and 1986.

*Inside, at the torch, **front row, from left**: General Vice President Thomas Clarkson; General Secretary Jake West, John McGibney, Financial Secretary, Local No. 580; General President Juel D. Drake, Frank Leone, President, Local No. 580; William McNulty, Business Agent and Dennis Milton, Recording Secretary, Local No. 580; **Back row, from left**: Thomas McGowan, Business Agent; Daniel Monaghan, Business Agent; Daniel Butler, Executive Board; Harold O'Shinsky, Sergeant at Arms, Local No. 580; General Treasurer James E. Cole, Joe Nolan, Vice President, Local No. 580 and James Gavin, Trustee, Local No. 580.*

Members of Shopmen's Local No. 516, Portland, Oregon, fabricated the steel and members of Local No. 24, Denver, Colorado erected the United Bank building of Colorado in 1986.

The 37th Convention of Our International

The **Thirty-Seventh International Convention** was held August 4-8, 1986 at the Bally MGM Hotel in Las Vegas, Nevada. This was the same hotel that had burned on November 21, 1980, and where members of Local 433 had gone in with their faces covered with moist towels to save the lives of hundreds of people.

General President Juel D. Drake was reelected. During his keynote address, he said, "I'm proud to be an Ironworker, and I'm honored to be your President." General Secretary Jake West and General Treasurer James Cole were also reelected by the delegates.

General President Drake reported that although this convention was opening at a time of relatively fair employment in field construction and maintenance renovation, the shop membership was still going down because of foreign imports. Also, the employment situation during the previous five years and the loss of membership had caused a drop in the Per Capita Tax and the Convention Fund Assessment which would have to be raised.

During the period since the 1981 Convention Ironworkers had seen a slight increase in wages and fringe benefits for both outside and shop workers. Drake also stated that we need to reaffirm our commitment to the apprenticeship program.

Delegates' badge to the 37th International Convention.

The 254 organizing campaigns to bring in more shop workers had been successful with 193 firms being organized. This was a 76% success rate at a time when the rest of the labor movement was only having 48% success rate in organizing. However, because of foreign fabricated steel forcing the closing of many other union shops, our shop membership had dropped from 56,315 to 37,691.

Delegates attending one of the sessions at the 37th International Convention held August 4-8, 1986 in Las Vegas, Nevada.

At the Convention, a report on the Market Recovery Program for Union Construction was presented to the delegates in detail. The Market Recovery Program was designed to retain and recapture construction work for union contractors.

Astronaut Lt. Col. Jerry Ross is escorted to the podium at the 37th International Convention. Col. Ross was made an honorary member of the Ironworkers after he assembled a metal frame in space in preparation for the future space station.

One of the special guests at the convention was Lt. Colonel Jerry Ross, an astronaut. It was fitting since our International had been active in the Space Program since its inception. Colonel Ross had walked in space and helped construct a long tower to simulate the future construction of the space station. The International Association made him an Honorary Member.

There was also a ceremony at the time of the convention to honor the Ironworkers who had saved so many lives at the MGM Hotel six years before. At the Convention, there was an elaborate historical display which included old badges, pictures and other items of historical significance to the Ironworkers.

stand tall among us. His place in the history of the Iron Workers, and the Labor Movement in general, will be one for Ironworkers' children and their children to commemorate reverently in the future of the Iron Worker organization. Jack Lyons was a union man through and through. He lived and breathed this Union. Everything he did, every working hour he spent was devoted to us. Devoted to the Ironworker hanging off a beam twenty stories high; to the Ironworker fabricating a half-ton I-beam in a shop; to the Ironworker setting rebar one hundred feet below the ground in a tunnel."

The Bridgeport Tragedy

On April 23, 1987, 28 workers were killed in the collapse of the L'Ambiance Plaza Complex which was under construction in Bridgeport, Connecticut. Among the twenty-eight dead were seven Ironworkers from Locals 424, New Haven, Connecticut and 66, San Antonio, Texas. Ironworkers from Locals No. 7, Boston, Ma.; 12 Albany, N.Y.; 15, Hartford, Connecticut; 37, Providence, Rhode Island; and 357, Springfield, Ma., as well as hundreds of other union volunteers rushed to the scene as the tragedy unfolded. Members worked around the clock in shifts searching for the injured and the dead.

Ironworker General President Drake announced that a special fund of $10,000 would be sent to assist in expenses for the rescue operation. A special "Family

General President Emeritus John H. Lyons Passes Away

On October 26, 1986 General President Emeritus John H. Lyons passed away. He was born on October 29, 1919. General President Juel D. Drake said: "It was with deep regret and profound sorrow that your General Executive Council received the news of the death of General President Emeritus John H. Lyons. He will always

John H. Lyons
October 29, 1919 -
October 26, 1986

Scores of Ironworkers and hundreds of other union volunteers search for the bodies entombed by the collapse of the L'Ambiance Plaza complex in Bridgeport, Connecticut.

Displays

Historical display of old badges and pictures at 37th International Convention.

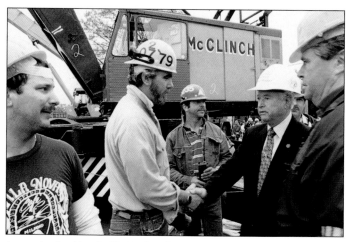

Ironworker President Juel D. Drake talks with rescue worker at Bridgeport site.

Senator Lowell Weicker, a liberal Republican of Connecticut, was so angered by this event that he introduced legislation to establish a trust for the families of the 28 dead workers from the $5 million dollars in fines collected. Senator Weicker felt that OSHA had failed and that "the failure of a federal agency to do its job should not result in a boon to the U.S. Treasury."

On Labor Day, in 1987, a monument was unveiled to the memory of the 28 construction workers who lost their lives in the Bridgeport tragedy of April 23, 1987. The monument also honored those who had risked their lives to save the injured.

Donald W. O'Reilly Appointed

Donald W. O'Reilly, General Vice President

On February 1, 1988, General Organizer and Executive Director of Canadian Operations Donald W. O'Reilly was appointed General Vice President by General President Juel D. Drake. General Vice President O'Reilly was initiated into Local No. 97, Vancouver, British Columbia as a Journeyman Ironworker in 1957. He was elected Business Agent of Local No. 97 in 1964. He was appointed General Organizer by General President John H. Lyons in 1971.

Victims Benefit Fund" was set up by Local 424.

When the tragedy occurred workers were using a method known as "lift slab construction," in which concrete slabs are cast on the ground and then hoisted into place. This technique had been used since the 1950's with only one other non-fatal mishap. The five companies involved in this tragedy were later fined $5 million by OSHA. It was announced in August of 1988 that the Texstar Construction Company of San Antonio, Texas, that was the lift-slab builder at Bridgeport, declared bankruptcy after they were fined $2 million by OSHA.

Both General President Drake and General Secretary Jake West would testify before the House Subcommittee on Health and Safety over this event. The Local 424 Business Agent, Joseph Egan, also testified and he would point out the following:

> *"...the untold story was that the rescue effort was organized, run and staffed almost entirely by union volunteers."*

It seemed that unlike airline crashes, OSHA had no power to seize control of the site so that evidence would not be damaged. Egan also pointed out that there were only two OSHA inspectors in the entire State of Connecticut.

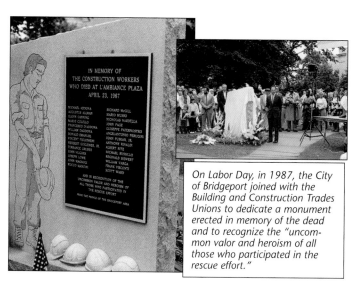

On Labor Day, in 1987, the City of Bridgeport joined with the Building and Construction Trades Unions to dedicate a monument erected in memory of the dead and to recognize the "uncommon valor and heroism of all those who participated in the rescue effort."

Dennis Toney Heads Up Shop Division

Also on February 1, 1988, President Drake appointed General Organizer Dennis R. Toney Executive Director of the Shop Division. Executive Director Toney was initiated into Shopmen's Local No. 493, Des Moines, Iowa in 1962. He was elected to several offices in Local No. 493 before being appointed District Representative in 1979 at which time he serviced Shopmen's Local Unions in the Western New York and Vicinity District Council area. In June, 1985, he was appointed General Organizer assigned to International Headquarters.

Dennis R. Toney, Executive Director of the Shop Division

It took a four-month strike at AMOCO Oil Company's Whiting, Indiana, refinery, but the solidarity of Ironworkers Local No. 395 of Hammond, Indiana, along with other members of the Northwestern Indiana Building Trades Council, finally resulted in victory over the giant oil company. The issue

195

General Treasurer James E. Cole **(left)**, General President Juel D. Drake **(middle)** and General Secretary Jake West announce the new Iron Workers' Master Card program in June, 1987.

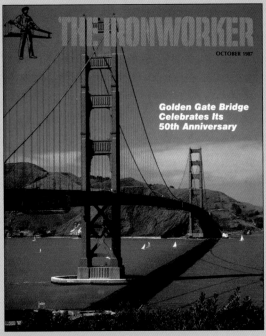

THE IRONWORKER

OCTOBER 1987

Golden Gate Bridge Celebrates Its 50th Anniversary

HAPPY BIRTHDAY GOLDEN GATE BRIDGE!
From the men who built you
ironworkers Local Union 377 San Francisco

This billboard greeted residents and visitors to downtown San Francisco as the city prepared for the 50th year celebration of the Golden Gate Bridge.

General President Paddy Morrin **(left)** and General Secretary Billy McCain **(left picture)** in 1937 when the Golden Gate Bridge opened and General President Juel D. Drake **(left)** and General Secretary Jake West in 1987 during the celebration of the bridge's 50th birthday.

Members of Ironworkers Local No. 395, Hammond, Indiana, and family and friends march through downtown Whiting, Indiana, as part of a rally to protest the actions of Amoco Oil Company.

was Amoco's decision to hire non-union contractors for major maintenance work at the refinery, despite the fact that the Building Trades unions built the facility and have been responsible for maintaining it in the past.

The company did not take into account the solidarity that made organized labor what it is. On Sunday, October 18, 1987, more than 5,000 building tradesmen and their families and friends staged a rally that was the kick-off to a nationwide boycott of Amoco Oil products.

Late in 1988, the National Ironworkers, and Employers, Apprenticeship Training and Journeyman Upgrading Fund held special classes on caulking and sealants for Local No. 86, Seattle, Washington in Seattle. General Vice President Worley who was also the President of the Pacific Northwest District Council said that there is a need to train more of our members in caulking and sealants. General Vice President Worley pointed out that curtain wall, window wall and precast concrete companies are requesting our affiliates to provide them with additional members who are qualified in the application of caulking and sealants.

Ironworker members from Chicago Local No. 1, and Local No. 63, erected the world's tallest and fastest super steel roller coaster at Six Flags Great America in Gurnee, Illinois in 1988. The track length is 3,900 feet and riders experience one 130-foot high vertical loop, two 116-feet loops, a corkscrew and two boomerang loops during the two and a half minute ride.

Ironworkers from Locals No. 1 and 63, Chicago erected a super steel roller coaster in Gurnee, Illinois in 1988

Ironworkers who erected the roller coaster, *from left to right, front row:* Bill Hoth, Rick Mitchell, Joel Torola, Paul Sonnenberg, Al Duburg, Ron Stonebreaker, Frank Brazcenski and Don Nettnin, lying in front. *Standing:* Local No. 1 Business Agent Ted Trzaskowski, Frank Mizzio, Chuck Funston, Dave Murray, Rich Brown, Rade Pankovich, Bob Williams, Ron Baringer, Raul Garza, Bill Gluckman, Bill Froelich, Local No. 63 Business Agent Dan DeJohn, John Martin and Tom Shervino.

Local 3 Ironworkers *front row, left to right:* Jim Long, Operating Engineer Jack Verab, Dale Margus, Stan Yendell, Tom Gasior John Steele and Jim Urlakis. *Second row, kneeling, from left, are:* Ed Thomas, Mark Saftner, Dan Mace and Terry Miller. *Third row, from left:* Paul Farabaugh, James Sobrasky, Len Jones, Dennis Benson, Dave Shack, Rodger Brown, Dave Gibbons, Kevin Carlson, Cary Heard, Tom Knaus, George Seekford, Superintendent Tim Quail and Ed Conway. *Back row, from left:* Bill Kunz, Joe Rozanc, Peter Paris, Jim Oler, Mark Thomas, Dave Cameron, Ed Mackiewicz, John Heinlain, Steve Barko and Mack McGuffey. The Ironworkers were employed on the Fifth Avenue Place project in downtown Pittsburgh by the American Bridge Company, Pittsburgh Plate Glass and Blazing Granite Company

Pacific Northwest District Council in conjunction with the National Ironworkers and Employers Apprenticeship Training and Journeyman Upgrading Fund held caulking and sealant classes at Local No. 86 Apprentice School in Seattle, Washington in 1988.

Teachers and observers included, *from left to right:* Robert Heider, Sealants and Coating Systems Co.; Frank Cusma, Pacific Northwest District Council Apprentice Administrative Coordinator; Fran Shea, of Local 63, Chicago; Raymond J. Robertson, Executive Director of Apprenticeship and Training; Local 86 Business Agent Doug Glockner, Local 86 Coordinator Mike Asper, and General Vice President LeRoy Worley, President of the Pacific Northwest District Council.

Members of Local No. 736 in Hamilton, Ontario, Canada erected the Burlington Skyway over the Burlington Bay in Hamilton.

General President Juel D. Drake, *right,* and Executive Assistant to the General President Martin T. Byrne, also Editor of THE IRONWORKER magazine, admire the plaque that accompanies the Second Award for General Excellence in the International Labor Communications Association 1988 Journalistic Awards Contest. THE IRONWORKER was cited by the judges for its mixture of Washington news and achievements by Ironworker Local Unions.

Chapter Eleven

Pathways to the 21st Century Under The Leadership of General President Jake West

O n January 28, 1989, only eight days after the inauguration of President Bush, General President Juel D. Drake resigned after a long and distinguished career as an Ironworker. His achievements were many; he worked in the field as a journeyman, he held several elected offices in Local No. 229, San Diego, including Business Agent, and was President of the San Diego Building Trades Council. President Drake was a General Organizer, General Vice President, President of two District Councils, General Secretary and General President. President Drake had held the office of General President for three and a half years, taking over the post when John H. Lyons was hospitalized and was too ill to continue on as General President. President Drake was subsequently elected as General President at the 37th International Convention in 1986.

After his resignation, the General Executive Council elected General Secretary Jake West to replace Juel D. Drake in the Office of General President. The first official act of the new General President was to appoint his predecessor to the position of General President Emeritus. This had been the custom since the retirement of the former General President P.J. "Paddy" Morrin in 1948. President Emeritus Juel Drake would only enjoy a little over two years of retirement. He passed away on April 5, 1991 at the age of 77.

At his swearing-in ceremony, General President West said:

> "I promise the membership of our International Association that I will do everything in my power to protect the welfare of every Ironworker and their families and that I will be looking ahead to keep us secure in the

General President Jake West, center, raises his hand to take the Oath of Office from retiring General President Juel D. Drake, with the members of the General Executive Council looking on. President Drake was later voted to the office of General President Emeritus by the Council.

future. I am well aware of the problems that we are facing in our industry and will work with the District Councils and local unions to help solve these problems."

General President West began his career as an Ironworker when he joined Local No. 301, Charleston, West Virginia in 1948, after serving three years with the U.S. Merchant Marines and with the U.S. Army. In 1951, President West boomed out and became a member of Iron Workers Local No. 433, Los Angeles, California.

He was elected Business Agent of Local No. 433 in 1961 and was reelected to that position until he was elected Financial Secretary Treasurer/Business Manager in 1970. He served in that position until his appointment as a General Organizer on February 15, 1971. General Organizer West worked the geographic area of the District Council of Ironworkers of the State of California and Vicinity. In 1971 he was also elected

First Vice President of the District Council, a position he held until the death of District Council President Dale Ray. Then, First Vice President West succeeded Dale Ray and became Council President in 1983.

General President West was Chairman of the California Field Ironworkers Local Unions Negotiating Committee and a member of the Board of Trustees on the California Field Ironworkers Pension, Welfare, Vacation, Annuity and Apprenticeship Trust Funds. In 1978 he was selected as National Chairman of the General Presidents' Onshore-Offshore Construction Work Group.

On September 30, 1983, then General President John H. Lyons appointed General Organizer Jake West as General Vice President of the International Association. In the same year he was appointed to serve on the National Ironworker-Carpenter Joint Committee.

From his early years on the West Coast, from 1967 until its discontinuation in 1983, General President West served as a member of the Board of Publishers for the Los Angeles Citizen labor newspaper. He was also a trusted member of California Governor Edmund G. Brown, Jr.'s group of labor advisors, serving on various committees and appeal boards during Governor Brown's incumbency between 1975 and 1982.

In 1980, President West was an alternate delegate to the Democratic Party Convention in New York City. In 1985, he was appointed to serve on the Executive Board of the AFL-CIO Maritime Trades Department. At the time of his election as General President, Jake West had already had a distinguished career as an Ironworker and a labor leader. He was definitely the person to lead the International Association toward the 21st Century.

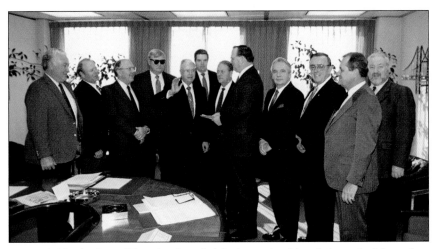

Surrounded by the General Executive Council of the International Association, retired General President Juel D. Drake takes the Oath of Office of General President Emeritus.

General Vice President LeRoy E. Worley Becomes General Secretary

Shortly after General President West took office he appointed General Vice President LeRoy E. Worley as the new General Secretary of the International Association. This appointment was approved by the General Executive Council and became effective February 3, 1989. At the time of his appointment, General Secretary Worley already had a distinguished career with the International Association. He was initiated into Local No. 29, Portland, Oregon as an apprentice in 1961 after serving in the U. S. Navy. In 1964, he became a journeyman Ironworker after completing his apprenticeship.

General Secretary Worley served as an Assistant

LeRoy E. Worley
General Secretary

Business Representative with Local No. 29, Portland, Oregon and was then elected to three consecutive terms as Business Representative and Financial Secretary-Treasurer. He was appointed a General Organizer in 1981 and was assigned to International Headquarters in Washington, D.C. In 1983, he was elected President of the Pacific Northwest District Council, headquartered in Portland, Oregon. On June 2, 1985, he was appointed as Ninth General Vice President by General President Juel D. Drake which was approved by the General Executive Council on June 6, 1985. General Secretary Worley is an alumnus of the prestigious Harvard University Trade Union Program, which he attended in 1983.

After he was sworn in, General Secretary LeRoy E. Worley commented: "I am indeed honored and proud of the confidence that you have entrusted in me today. I pledge my continued support to General President Jake West, the General Executive Council and the entire membership of this International Association. And, I will strive to carry out the duties of the office of General Secretary to the best of my abilities. The trust that has been placed in me by your actions today leaves me with a feeling of great pride and determination and makes me determined to do my utmost for the benefit of the membership of this great International Association and their families."

President Bush Appoints a New Secretary of Labor

The tradition of appointments to the office of Secretary of Labor under Democratic presidents had been to select someone from the labor movement or someone who had worked with labor. However, this had not always been the tradition under Republicans. President Bush's selection for Secretary of Labor would be Elizabeth Dole. Her appoint-

Elizabeth Dole
Secretary of Labor

ment was praised at the time by the AFL-CIO and its President, Lane Kirkland. Senator Edward Kennedy, chairman of the Senate Labor and Human Resources Committee said Elizabeth Dole is "an excellent choice for the Labor Department."

In accepting the nomination, Secretary Dole said she pledged to "promote and protect the welfare of America's working men and women." Secretary Dole, who is married to Senator Robert Dole (R-Kansas), began her public career as an aide in Lyndon Johnson's White House. She also served on the Federal Trade Commission and was the Secretary of Transportation under President Reagan. Secretary Dole would work very closely with labor and on many occasions she supported labor on a number of issues.

In 1989 she was part of a Presidential Mission with AFL-CIO President Kirkland and BCTD President Georgine to Poland which led to the establishment of two craft training centers in Warsaw and Gdynia, Poland in conjunction with five international building trades unions which included the Iron Workers and the Solidarity Union headed up by Lech Walesa. The person in charge of this effort under the direction of General President West was General Vice President Raymond J. Robertson who worked closely with Secretary Dole, Building Trades President Robert Georgine and Solidarity President Lech Walesa and later his successor, Marian Krzaklewski, to make these programs a success.

Solidarity President Lech Walesa leads Poland to Democracy and works with the Building & Construction Trades Department, Iron Workers and other international unions in establishing construction craft training centers to help in the rebuilding of Poland after 50 years under communism.

Michael Brennan Appointed

On March 17, 1989, General President Jake West appointed General Organizer Michael Brennan as Executive Director of the Legislative Department. Executive Director Brennan was a member of Lathers Local Union No. 46, New York City; where he served as Business Agent and later was elected to the office of General Secretary-Treasurer of the Lathers International Union in 1972. Lathers Local No. 46 historically performed the placing of reinforcing rods in New York City, therefore, that Local Union merged with the

Michael Brennan, Executive Director, Legislative Department.

Iron Workers International in 1979. All the other Lathers locals merged with the Carpenters.

Richard "Dick" Zampa Appointed

On May 22, 1989, General President Jake West appointed General Organizer Richard "Dick" Zampa as General Vice President. General Vice President Zampa became an apprentice member of Local No. 378, Oakland, California in 1956 and became a journeyman in 1959. He held several local union offices before being appointed General Organizer on September 1, 1985. General Vice President Zampa was instrumental in building Local No. 378's Apprentice and Training facility in Benicia, California. He is also President of the District Council of Ironworkers of the State of California and Vicinity.

Richard "Dick" Zampa, General Vice President

Ironworkers Build Monuments

Members of our International have always shown an interest in our communities, states, and country. They have always been the first to volunteer for public service and to honor great citizens, workers, and veterans of our wars. During the Bush years a number of events took place of this kind.

On the same day, January 28, 1989 that our new General President Jake West took office, members of Ironworkers Local 272 unveiled a monument which they had erected as a memorial to America's Challenger Seven Astronauts. The monument stands in Bayfront Park in Miami. It was unveiled exactly three years to the date, hour, minute, and second that the tragic explosion killed the seven astronauts, including the school teacher, Christa McAuliffe.

Beginning in 1989, the American Federation of Labor designated every April 28th as "Workers' Memorial Day."

*Members of Local No. 272, Miami, Florida erect Challenger Memorial. **Left to right:** Local No. 272 Business Agent Leighton "Skip" Warner, General Organizer Billy Joe Walker, Ironworking Institute Deputy Director John Schlecht and Ralph H. Clark Jr., Local No. 272 Business Agent.*

Toronto's Local 721 Builds SkyDome

MAY 1989

DIRECTORY ISSUE

Members of Local No. 721, Toronto, Canada, erected the Toronto SkyDome in 1989. It is close to the CN Tower also erected by members of Local No. 721.

Two groups of Ironworker members of Local No. 721 who erected SkyDome.

Ironworkers from Local No. 103, Evansville, Indiana, held a memorial dedication ceremony on Workers Memorial Day in honor of "those killed in the forgotten environment, the workplace." Pictured at the dedication are, **from left to right: Front row:** Don Whalen, Bob Wheatley, Vince Hill, Bill Garrett and Bill Garrett III. **Back row:** Tom Sherrill, Paul Helfert, Local No. 103 Business Manager Billy Curtis, General Organizer Charles Hill and Carl Wallace.

A group of Ironworkers stand before the inner skeleton of the Vietnam Veterans Memorial that they erected in 1992, Suffolk County, N.Y. Ironworkers representing Locals No. 361, 580, 46 and Shopmen's Local No. 455, volunteered their time and skills in the effort to build the monument.

On this day we are to pay tribute to the 100,000 workers killed and injured nationwide in workplace accidents each year. Our Ironworkers began a tradition that continues to this day of locals dedicating monuments in their communities to workers who have lost their lives on the job. One such monument was unveiled by Local 103 in Evansville, Indiana in 1991.

Ironworkers representing Locals 361, 580, 46, and Shopmen's Local 455, volunteered their time and skills to build a Vietnam Memorial in Suffolk County, New York. Local communities donated money for the project and school children, senior citizens, and local businessmen conducted fund raisers for the project. The monument was dedicated on Veterans Day, November 11, 1991 with thousands present.

Raymond J. Robertson Appointed

On August 14, 1989, General President West appointed Executive Director Raymond J. Robertson as Eighth General Vice President. General Vice President Robertson was initiated as an apprentice into Local No. 63, Chicago in 1956 and in 1959 became a journeyman. He worked on numerous projects in Chicago and surrounding local unions as a journeyman, foreman and superintendent. He was an apprentice and journeyman instructor and a member of the JAC/TRUST of Local No. 63.

Raymond J. Robertson, General Vice President

General Vice President Robertson wrote several training manuals used by affilliates to train apprentices. After being elected to two terms on the Examining Board of Local No. 63, he became Apprenticeship Coordinator and Assistant to Local No. 63 Business Manager Matt "Moon" Martin where he handled Local Union jurisdictional disputes and presented cases before the Chicago Joint Conference Board for the Settlement of Jurisdictional Disputes. He was appointed General Organizer on May 1, 1967 where he worked 12 years out of the Chicago & Vicinity District Council, and during this time processed special assignments from International Headquarters both in St. Louis and Washington, D.C.

Local No. 424 Ironworkers Scott Mucherino and Mark Graham set "Old Glory" in place at the topping out of the R.D. Scinto/Enterprise Tower Project in Shelton, Connecticut in 1989.

Alan Simmons Appointed

On September 1, 1989, General President West appointed General Organizer Alan Simmons as Ninth General Vice President. He was initiated into Local No. 361 apprenticeship program in 1955. After serving in several local union offices which included the Executive Committee, President and Business Agent and Business Manager, Financial Secretary Treasurer, he was appointed General Organizer in April, 1988 and elected President of the Greater New York and Vicinity District Council. He also served as President of the Building and Construction Trades Council of Nassau and Suffolk Counties as well as other Councils in the New York City area. He represents the International Association on several committees.

Alan Simmons, General Vice President

Leadership into the Nineties and the 21st Century

The Iron Workers International Association concluded four highly successful Regional Conferences in 1989. These Regional Informational Conferences were established years ago in order to bring about a direct line of communication between the International, the local union officers and members. The sessions covered dozens of topics of value to the delegates in attendance. The conferences reviewed all of the daily activities that were taking place within the International Association. They brought about a hands-on approach to a wide variety of issues that Ironworker local union officers and members are concerned about. District Council Presidents in the United States and Canada gave a comprehensive report to the delegates on every issue that was taking place in their Council. Delegates received a Reference Manual that included information on each Department at International Headquarters. This Reference Manual is of valuable assistance to the officers of each local union.

In addition to the Regional Conferences over two hundred International and local union officers from the United States and Canada attended a series of Ironworker meetings in conjunction with the AFL-CIO winter meetings. These meetings took place in early

Reference Manual given to each delegate attending Regional Conferences.

THE IRONWORKER

OCTOBER 1989

Local 17 Ironworkers Top Out World's Fastest Roller Coaster

Ed Thomas, **left**, and Chris Catri, Local No. 17, erecting the roller coaster.

Local No. 17 Ironworkers who erected the world's highest, fastest and longest roller coaster at Cedar Point, Ohio, included, **from left to right: Front row:** Steward Bob Nolf and John Karadimas. **Second row:** Dick Schultz, Wayne Miller, Operator Bill Krinek, Business Agent Buddy Bianchi, Foreman Chuck Catri, Lloyd Bonderer, Chris Catri, Mark Outland and Tom Menzies. **Third row:** Dan Myers, Operator Paul Soisson, Operator Gregg Dauch, Company Owner Gail Duach, Pat Finnegan, Ed Thomas, Gail Dauch, Jr., Paul Brown, of Local No. 15.

Ironworkers from Local No. 17, Cleveland, Ohio, erected the World's Fastest Roller Coaster at the Cedar Point Amusement Park. Riders will reach speeds of over 70 miles per hour during the ride and descend from a 201-foot hill.

THE IRONWORKER

NOVEMBER 1989

Ironworkers Erect Huge Hotel/Casino in Las Vegas, Nevada

In 1989, members of Local No. 416, Los Angeles, California placed the reinforcing steel for the Mirage Hotel/Casino in Las Vegas, Nevada.

Below: Members of Local No. 711, Quebec, Canada use new safety cable system during the erection of the General Motors plant in Boisbriand, Quebec, Canada. Six crews erected the steel and installed all the cables. The connectors tied themselves to the vertical cables installed in the columns and, after having connected the horizontal pieces, installed the horizontal cables permanently. This way, the Ironworkers and Welders were tied to the cable permanently wherever they had to walk and work. The large crew of Ironworkers get together for a group photo at the site.

Delegates attending Regional Conferences.

General President Jake West, General Secretary LeRoy E. Worley and General Treasurer James E. Cole address the Local Union Officers attending the winter meetings in early 1990.

Local Union District Council Advisory Committee appears before Local Union Officers.

1990. These meetings took place in early 1990. General President Jake West appointed General Secretary LeRoy E. Worley to chair these meetings while he attended the AFL-CIO Executive Council meetings. General Secretary LeRoy E. Worley chaired these meetings. General President Jake West and General Treasurer James E. Cole addressed the delegates. Every department head at International Headquarters made a report on the activities of their department. General Counsel Victor VanBourg also brought the delegates up to date on legal matters affecting the International Association and affiliated local unions.

Ironworkers to the Rescue

During the time of the Bush Administration Ironworkers would be faced with helping the public during two natural disasters. The first of these was **Hurricane Hugo** which hit Charleston, South Carolina with 100 mph winds on September 21, 1989. Members of Local 601 successfully anchored a section of the new Cooper River Bridge, which was under construction, and saved it from destruction. Local 601 also volunteered their union hall to be used as a Disaster Relief Center by the Red Cross. Red Cross workers and volunteers spent long hours handling emergencies from Local No. 601's office and meeting hall. Less than a month later on October 17, 1989 a 7.1 earthquake hit the San Francisco Bay Area. Again our Ironworkers, as well as other members of the building trades, responded. Members of Locals 378 and 377 worked around the clock along with Pile Butts, Carpenters, and Operating Engineers to remove sections of highways that had collapsed.

General President West in writing about the Ironworker volunteers said that "...you have given honor and respect to our organization and all other unions."

Retired Ironworker Draws the Tasks of Our Trade - Retired Ironworker Blair Kennedy, Local No. 736, Hamilton, Ontario, Canada, still had Ironworking in his blood. The talented retiree uses the tasks of an Ironworker as the subject of drawings he does.

Legislation Before Congress During the Bush Era

Although George Bush had won the Presidential race he was unsuccessful in winning a Republican House and Senate in either the 101st or 102nd Congress. However, the Democrats never had more than 57 votes in the Senate, and therefore, the Republican Senators could block any legislation with a filibuster. Sixty votes are needed to cut off debate of this kind.

General President Jake West would urge members to get involved politically with these words:

> *"The pressing need for Ironworkers to become involved with politics reminds us once again of the tightly-knit relationship between organized labor and the workings of the American government."*

One of the bills before Congress at this time which was important to our members and the entire labor movement was **The Worker Replacement Bill.** The bill was introduced into the House of Representatives by William Clay, a Democrat from Missouri. After President Reagan had replaced the 12,000 striking gov-

Politics is a necessary part of the life of any labor union in the United States and Canada. The Ironworkers Political Action League (IPAL) works with our legislators to help American workers. In the photo, General President Jake West, **center**, meets with House Majority Leader Richard A. Gephardt (D-Missouri), **left**, and House Speaker Thomas S. Foley (D-Washington) during a conference in Washington, D.C.

General President Jake West meets with President George Bush to discuss matters of concern regarding the construction industry and the Ironworkers in general. In reference to the "Gulf" war, President West assured President Bush that, "The American labor movement stands in full support of our country and of the men and women in our armed forces."

ernment PATCO workers, the private sector unions saw this as a signal that they could now face the same thing.

There was a loophole in the 1935 National Labor Relations Act. Since Senator Wagner wrote the bill to guarantee workers the right to organize and promote collective bargaining, there was no protection for workers who struck over wage issues. Therefore the Supreme Court ruled that workers could not be replaced during an organizing campaign, but they could be replaced during a strike over wages or benefits. When the labor movement was strong right up until 1981, not many employers had ever taken advantage of this loophole in the law.

Suddenly companies tried to provoke strikes over wages and fringe benefits. This happened to workers at Phelps Dodge, TWA, Continental Airlines, International Paper, and Greyhound to name only a few. Replacement workers were then brought in.

The importance of the Ironworkers Political Action League (IPAL) was continually expressed by General President West as well as all the General Officers. General President West stated: "It can not be overstated how important it is to have our voice heard by the nation's decision makers. For only pennies a day we can support pro-labor candidates who will defend our livelihoods in return. Let us not forget that we work too hard to be ignored by the government we work to support. The decisions made in Congress and state legislatures impact our lives as much as the collective bargaining process. As working people we must be more concerned about who makes the decisions and how they are made."

The Ironworkers across the country have been a big part of the fund raising activities on DAD's Day (Dollars Against Diabetes) that funds diabetes research. General President West and Billy, the poster child for the 1990 DAD's Day, are shown together in President West's office in Washington, D.C.

Ironworkers' Skills, & Pension Funds go to work in Times Square

In 1990, Ironworkers from Locals No. 40, 46L, and 580, New York City, used their skills to construct a 44-story, $155 million Embassy Suites Hotel over the Manhattan Palace Theater in New York's Times Square, which is designated as a historical landmark. In order to build the hotel, it was necessary to erect two three-story high, 130 feet long steel trusses encased in concrete which is three feet thick. Each truss weighs 25 tons and is supported at each end by a 145-foot tall super column. The International Union's Pension Plan in the AFL-CIO Building Trust provided part of the construction and permanent financing for the project.

The officers of the International traveled to New York in 1990 to review the progress of the challenging construction project in Times Square. Pictured in front of the Embassy Suites site are: **From left to right:** General Treasurer James Cole; Peter Brennan, President of the Building & Construction Council of Greater New York; General President Jake West; General Secretary LeRoy E. Worley and Mike Arnold, Director of Investor Relations for the AFL-CIO Housing and Building Investment Trusts.

Ironworker Locals No. 25 & 700 renovate the Ambassador Bridge in 1990. The 60-year old suspension bridge between Detroit, Michigan and Windsor, Canada opened in 1929.

206

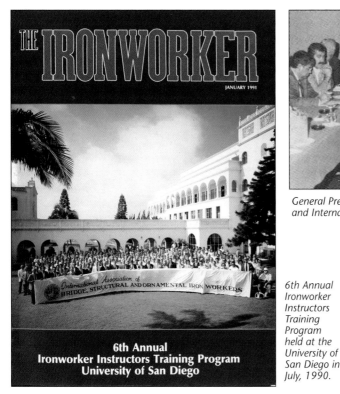

6th Annual
Ironworker Instructors Training Program
University of San Diego

General President Jake West & Vice-President Don O'Reilly chair meetings of Business Agents and International Representatives in Quebec City.

6th Annual Ironworker Instructors Training Program held at the University of San Diego in July, 1990.

Business Agents and International Representatives during Quebec City meetings.

Instructor Training

The National Ironworkers and Employers Apprenticeship Training and Journeyman Upgrading Fund held its 6th Annual Ironworker Instructors Training Program at the University of San Diego in July, 1990. Each year, this program expands and provides a variety of courses in order to keep Ironworker Instructors up-to-date on technological changes occurring in the Ironworking industry.

The purpose of the program is to standardize training for Ironworkers from coast to coast in the United States and Canada, assure that every instructor is fully qualified in teaching techniques and to provide a forum for instructor colleagues to exchange ideas. One of the courses introduced at the 6th Annual Program was "Hazardous Material Training." There were 34 courses in all that were offered. General President Jake West said: "Our forefathers would be proud of the achievements made by the International Association in the area of training as we move toward our 100th year as an organization."

Canadian Business Agents' Meeting

On September 15, 1990, the third annual meeting of Business Agents from across Canada was held in Quebec City. These meetings were very informative and gave the Canadian local unions an opportunity to express their views and problems directly to International Headquarters. A number of subjects were covered that pertained to both the outside and shop local unions in Canada. General President West and General Vice President and Executive Director of Canadian Operations, Don O'Reilly, chaired the meeting. In attendance were 31 local union officers representing 19 local unions.

General President Jake West Named to ULLICO Board

General President Jake West was named to the Union Labor Life Insurance Co. (ULLICO) Board of Directors in April of 1990. "Jake West brings a solid union background and a profound commitment in improving the quality of life for working men and women in this country," said ULLICO President and CEO Daniel E. O'Sullivan. "His expertise and life-long dedication to the labor movement will be put to good use on the ULLICO Board." Also in 1990, President West was appointed to the National Building Museum Board. The museum is dedicated to preserving and showcasing the American construction industry, with its many innovations over the past century.

In 1990, the highly skilled Ironworkers of Local No. 401 & 405 successfully completed the structural and reinforcing steel on the Mellon Bank Center Building in Philadelphia, then again displayed their outstanding skills erecting the $20 million curtainwall.

THE IRONWORKER

JUNE 1991

Newfoundland
Giant Offshore
Oil Platform

Ironworkers from Local No. 764, in Newfoundland, Canada and others building a massive oil drilling platform in the Hibernia Oil Field.

Ironworkers in Newfoundland Build Giant Offshore Oil Platform

On July 5, 1990 a Project Agreement was signed by Local No. 764, St. John's, Newfoundland, and the International Association, along with all other Building Trades unions for the six year construction and placement of a massive drilling platform, 315 kilometers out at sea on the Hibernia Oil Field. The Hibernia Oil Field has proven and probable reserves estimated at between 525 million and 650 million barrels of oil.

It is located in about 80 meters of water on the continental shelf in the northeast corner of the Grand Banks

off Newfoundland. Full field development is expected to require 83 wells. The number of Ironworkers used on this project is in the hundreds and as we approach the 100th anniversary of the International Association, the project is still under construction.

Steve Cooper Appointed

On October 4, 1990 General President Jake West appointed General Organizer Stephen D. Cooper to the position of Executive Director of Safety and Health for the International Association. Executive Director Cooper is responsible for all safety and health issues of the membership and reports directly to the General President. In 1960 Executive Director Cooper was initiated as an apprentice member of Local No. 24, Denver, Colorado and became a journeyman member in 1963. For a number of years Executive Director Cooper served as chairman of the Statewide Colorado Apprenticeship Program in Colorado.

*Steve Cooper,
Executive Director
of Safety*

*Pictured at the signing of the Project Agreement for the Hibernia Development Project are, from **left to right**: **Seated**: James Kenny, Chairman of the Negotiating Committee of the Hibernia Employer's Association, Inc.; Ironworkers General Vice President Donald O'Reilly; Ironworkers Local No. 764 Business Agent/FST David Wade and David Fagan, Coordinator of Site Negotiations. **Standing**: Ironworkers General Organizer James Phair; Local No. 764 President Thomas Woodford and Ironworkers General Treasurer James E. Cole.*

Hostage Released

In 1990, Jack Frazier, member of Local No. 433, Los Angeles, California was released after spending almost three months as a hostage in Iraq. He credited his release by Iraqi strongman, Saddam Hussein, to a campaign by his old friend from Local No. 433, General President Jake West. "After hearing of Jack's situation, I immediately had our political people call the State Department to find out what they could do," said General President West. The Ironworkers Political Action League (IPAL) then pursued its legislative contacts. IPAL Executive Director Michael Brennan and Legislative Assistant Frank J. Voyack contacted Montana Senator Max Baucus and Representative Pat Williams who were invaluable in securing Jack's release. (Jack was a native of Montana). President West also wrote a letter to the Iraqi ambassador in Washington, D.C., appealing to him on behalf of the International Association.

The Ironworkers International Headquarters team that organized the political and diplomatic efforts to win freedom for Brother Jack Frazier got together with him during his visit to Washington, D.C. **From left to right**: General Treasurer James E. Cole, Political and Legislative Director Michael Brennan, Brother Frazier, Political and Legislative Assistant Frank J. Voyack and General President Jake West.

At the Festival of the Building Arts, the column climbers *from left to right:* Joe Windsor, John Sinkovits, Brian McMahon, Bobby Young, Jack Carter, General President Jake West, Russell Boggs, Jerry Eddy, Larry Morris, Tom Trigger, an unidentified Local 16 member and Pee Wee Hanks.

The Ironworkers who erected the steel building at the National Building Museum in Washington, D.C. *From left to right:* *Front row:* Pee Wee Hanks, Russell Hanks, Russell Boggs, Brian McMahon, Jack Carter, Frank Hooks, Jr., and Eugene Brooks. *Back row:* Bill Moon, Royce Briley, General Treasurer James E. Cole, General President Jake West, Institute of the Ironworking Industry Executive Director John McMahon, General Vice President James J. Willis, John Schlecht, Larry Morris, Bobby Sweeney and Kenny Waugh, Jr.

The Local No. 201 "Rod Busters" also participated in the demonstrations at the Festival of the Building Arts. *Pictured from left to right:* Local No. 201 Business Manager George Hindle, Coordinator Gaither Musgrove, General Vice President James J. Willis, General Treasurer James E. Cole, General President Jake West, Greg Hatley, Willie Lewis III and John McMahon, Institute of the Ironworking Industry.

Festival of the Building Arts

On Sunday, May 5, 1991, the National Building Museum in Washington, D.C. celebrated its 1st Annual "Festival of the Building Arts." Ironworkers Local No. 5, erected a 6-bay steel building which was fabricated by members of Shop Local No. 486. There was an open competition in a 40 foot column climbing contest. The competition was extremely close with just one second each separating the first five spots; the winner was Russell Boggs, a 48-year old journeyman Ironworker from Local No. 5. General President Jake West presented Brother Boggs with an Ironworker watch for his winning time in the column climb.

Rodbusters Local No. 201 also had an exciting presentation, with an exhibit of cad welding, tying floor mats and column cages. The Ironworker exhibits were the hit of the festival, which also included 16 other exhibits of building tradesmen skills.

Lead Poisoning in the Ironworking Industry

Throughout the history of the Iron Workers International and its affiliated local unions, a very serious problem has continued to confront the Ironworkers in North America when they are cutting, welding or exposed to sandblasting when working on metal structures that are painted with lead based paint. Poisoning normally occurs by inhalation of fumes allowing direct access into the blood stream. Ingestion of lead dust and particles causes those foreign bodies to get trapped in the mucous lining of breathing passages. Dust and particles are eventually swallowed and then absorbed into the blood stream. The past practice of having lead-exposed workers drink milk was an effort to "coat" the stomach so as to minimize the absorption of lead.

Skin absorption may also allow a small amount of lead to pass through the skin to cause additional exposure problems. Once in the blood stream, lead goes with the blood to the kidneys and other organs. Lead can be stored in the kidneys, liver and fatty tissue including the fat surrounding nerve cells and lead stored in the bones can be kept for months and even years after initial exposure. Screening members for lead poisoning in various local unions, such as Local No. 16, Baltimore, Maryland was con-

Gateway Arch Anniversary - The world-famous Gateway Arch in St. Louis, Missouri, celebrated its 25th anniversary in October of 1990. It was built by members of Local No. 396, St. Louis and fabricated by members of Shopmen's Local No. 493, Des Moines, Iowa. The first photo shows the keystone section being lifted into place. The second photo shows some of the Ironworkers who came to the celebration of the anniversary. *From left to right:* *front row:* Fred Morris, Jim Thompson, Gil Penfold, Robert Boulware, Sam Myers and Albert Perkins. *Second row:* Marshall Chapel, Charlie Smalley, Pat Brown, Jack Gross, Dean Sample, St. Louis Mayor Vince Schoemehl, Wayne Newell, District Council President Joe Hunt, Jerry McDowell and Francis Markwell.

ducted in 1990 and 1991. Under the direction of General President West, the International Association was successful in developing an OSHA lead standard for the construction industry.

The Safety Department headed up by Executive Director Steve Cooper has worked very closely with the Apprenticeship Department and the National Fund to develop "Lead Hazard Training" programs throughout North America. By the end of 1995 there were over 100 certified Ironworker Instructors that were qualified to teach lead hazard training by the National Fund to members of the International Association. The National Fund provides all the necessary equipment, such as respirators and instructional booklets, to all affiliated local unions requesting lead hazard training classes.

Thirty-Eighth International Convention

The **Thirty-Eighth International Convention** was held August 5-9, 1991 at Bally's Hotel in Las Vegas. General President Jake West would be reelected to serve for another five years. In his keynote address to the delegates he would state:

> "We are assembled here this week to represent all of our members to the best of our ability. We have a solemn responsibility to make decisions that will make our International Union and all of our local unions the strongest and most progressive in North America."

General Secretary LeRoy E. Worley and General Treasurer James E. Cole would be reelected as well as the incumbent General Vice Presidents, William H. Sullivan, James J. Willis, James Martin, O.C. Yancy, Fhane B. Jones, Donald W. O'Reilly, Richard Zampa, Raymond J. Robertson and Alan Simmons.

It has been the practice in recent conventions to have the delegates' pictures taken from the various District Councils. Because this was the last convention before the 100th anniversary of the International Association it was decided that this History Book should show those officers and members who were responsible in laying out the path the International Association would take during the five years leading up to the 100th year of this great organization under the leadership of General President Jake West.

At this time there were 174 Outside Local Unions and 102 Shopmen Local Unions or a total of 276 local unions affiliated with the International Association. On June 30, 1991 the total membership of the International Association was 140,898.

There were many topics and issues that were discussed at the 38th International Convention. Every delegate was urged to dedicate him or herself to carrying out the objective to organize

Badge worn by delegates to the 38th International Convention held in Las Vegas, Nevada.

SEPTEMBER 1991

"We are a strong union, with a glorious history; it is my commitment to keep us strong and united forever."
Jake West

General President Jake West, General Secretary LeRoy E. Worley, General Treasurer James E. Cole and the General Executive Council members were all reelected to serve a five year term at the 38th International Convention. Former General Vice President Joe Merritt administered the oath of office to the newly elected General Officers.

the unorganized workers in our trade and also to convey this message to the membership of each local union. A summation of the efforts the International Association and its Shop affiliates made with respect to organizing campaigns during the preceding five years was presented. Organizing campaigns during this period were conducted among employees of 203 firms, of which 142 were organized. This reflects that the International Association was successful in 70 percent of these organizing campaigns, compared to about 48 percent experienced by all other labor organizations as reported by the National Labor Relations Board.

In the organizing campaigns conducted by International General Organizers and District Representatives, it was reported that 14,623 employees were contacted at their workplace and 6,452 employees were met in their homes. General President Jake West said: "We must not, nor

General Vice President Richard "Dick" Zampa, President of the California District Council who opened the 38th International Convention hands over the gavel to General President Jake West to officially start proceedings of the Convention.

Ironworker District Councils - 1991

Delegates, by District Council, who attended the 38th International Convention in 1991 at the Bally's hotel.

Canada

Western New York and Vicinity

Greater New York and Vicinity

Tennessee Valley and Vicinity

The Michigan-Great Lakes and Vicinity

Chicago and Vicinity

The Mid-Atlantic States

The State of Texas

Philadelphia and Vicinity

The Pacific Northwest

Ironworker District Councils 1991 - *continued*

The Rocky Mountain Area

St. Louis and Vicinity

Eastern Ohio, Western Pennsylvania and Northern Virginia

Southern Ohio and Vicinity

North Central States

The Southeastern States

The New England States

Northen New Jersey

The State of California and Vicinity

212

will we, allow the accomplishments of the past 55 years to be obliterated by today's anti-labor political philosophy which permeates our government structure. I have every confidence that we will succeed in our efforts."

General President West made some key points relative to organizing, such as, Legal Methods, Targeting, Joint Organizing efforts between Shop Local Unions and Outside Local Unions, Double Breasted Contractors and Reorganizing of previously organized Ironworkers.

Many other subjects, such as Lightweight Steel Framing, Safe Bolts and Nuts, Standing Seam Metal Roofing, Apprenticeship and Training, Jurisdiction, Political Action, Legislation which included Davis-Bacon were brought before the delegates.

Highlights of Canadian operations were reported on by President West. It was pointed out that Ironworkers in Canada, like all other Building Trades members, are in most matters governed by Provincial Labour Codes with the exception of the Northwest and Yukon Territories which are governed under the Canada Labour Codes, or what is referred to as the National Labour Act. The Canada Labour Code has responsibility for workers in federally regulated industries, specifically: International and Interprovincial railways, highway transport, telephone and telegraph systems, pipelines, canals, ferries, tunnels and bridges, shipping and shipping services, air transport and airports, nuclear facilities and uranium mining.

General Secretary LeRoy E. Worley made a detailed report on such subjects as Membership Statistics, Wage Increases, Apprenticeship Progress, International Agreements and a Summary of Cases considered by the General Executive Council and the General Executive Board.

General Treasurer James E. Cole made a detailed report concerning the Finances of the International Association, Per Capita Tax and International Assessments, Defined Benefit Pension Plan, Local Union

Various views of the Historical Display set up for the delegates attending the 38th International Convention.

Solidarity Day '91 held on August 31, 1991 in Washington, D.C.

Audits, Data Processing, Bonding, Death Benefit Fund, Convention Fund and other subjects.

At the time of the convention our Union honored all those who fought in the Gulf War. Delegate James Berta of Local 229, who was also a U.S. Navy Reserve Master Chief Petty Officer, had served in the Persian Gulf. He thanked the Ironworkers for their patriotic support.

Solidarity Day II

On August 31, 1991, after eleven years of the Reagan/Bush Administration, the AFL-CIO called for another "Solidarity Day" like the one that had taken place ten years before. Our Ironworkers and other trade unionists and their friends came to Washington, D.C. to tell President Bush and Congress that they were fed-up with policies that were hurting middle

Local No. 401 Ironworkers came down from the City of Brotherly Love, Philadelphia, to show their concerns about the Bush Administration's policies.

Rodman's Local No. 201, Washington, D.C., brought a strong contingent to the march.

class and poor Americans. "We came here because we wanted to warn our leaders that we have had enough of their neglect of working men and women," said General President West. The Ironworker contingent, with General Secretary LeRoy E. Worley and General Treasurer James E. Cole joining President West in the lead, carried placards to let the media and general public know why they felt that they had to return to Washington ten years after the original Solidarity Day demonstration in 1981.

The main issues of the march were the need for affordable health care, the need to rebuild the nation's infrastructure, and the need for "fair trade" and not "free trade." A total of 325,000 people marched in 96 degree heat. Over 2,000 Ironworkers from across the United States attended the march.

Ironworkers answering the call of the International Association and the AFL.-CIO throughout the United States came by bus, car and train to support Solidarity Day '91.

Local No. 790 Shopmen fabricated large girders for the California Plaza Hotel in 1991. Shop Ironworker Chuck Rosario welds chain tie-downs to the trailer before a huge girder is sent to the project.

*Local No. 790 Shop members who fabricated large girders include, **from left:** S.A. Wahlen, R. Schei, R. Covello, R. Dickerson, C. Blois, R. Leiva, M. Gray, R. Ortiz, B. Fisher, Y. Nam and R. Favelo.*

About 170 Ironworkers from Fort Worth, Texas, Local No. 263 and some boomers from all across the United States worked to erect the world's largest cantilever hangar at Alliance Airport in Fort Worth. The hanger is designed to house seven wide-bodied commercial airliners during maintenance.

Roy Williams Heads Up Department of Ornamental, Architectural and Miscellaneous Metals

In early 1992, after lengthy discussions and review of the technological changes that had occurred in the iron-working industry, it was determined that ornamental, architectural and miscella-neous metal work had been affected more profoundly by technological changes than other facets of the ironworking trade. Accordingly, President West decided that the appropriate direction to take in maintaining this very active and fast chang-ing part of the trade was to establish a new department which would intelligently address the problems experienced by Iron Worker affili-ates in North America, when dealing with this type of work.

Roy Williams
heads up new Department

Curtain wall and window wall systems had changed radically by 1992. Today, these systems include many different combinations of materials. The units may be delivered to the project prefabricated and preglazed, or may require extensive assembly on the jobsite. There is a variety of high tech caulking and sealants used that require different types of electrical, air and manual caulking guns. Other work falling under the Department of Ornamental, Architectural and Miscellaneous Metal (DOAMM) are elevator fronts, doors of all types, entrances, stairs, ladders, railings, fencing, sub-framing, jail and detention equipment, atri-ums, conveyor work, metal studs, metal windows, sky-lights, high slope architectural metal roofing and many other categories of work.

President West appointed Roy Williams, former Financial Secretary, Treasurer and Business Manager of Architectural and Ornamental Iron Workers Local No. 63, Chicago to head up this department. General Organizer Roy Williams brings with him 35 years' experience as an Architectural Ironworker, along with his 27 years as an officer and 16 years as a full time salaried officer of this specialty local union. On April 1, 1994 General Organizer Williams was appointed Executive Director by President Jake West. The Department operates directly under General Secretary LeRoy E. Worley's office.

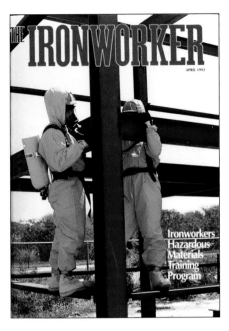

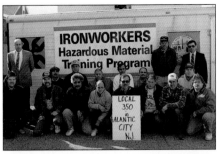

Pictured are some of the over 2,000 Ironworker members who received training and were certified to work on sites containing hazardous materials, featured in the April, 1992 issue of The Ironworker magazine.

Hazardous Material Training Moves Forward

By April, 1992, the National Ironworkers and Employers Apprenticeship Training and Journeyman Upgrading Fund in conjunction with the International Association had over 150 local union Ironworker Hazardous Material Training instructors certified to conduct classes in all parts of the United States. Over 2,000 Ironworker members had received training and were certified to work on sites designated as hazardous. General Vice President Raymond J. Robertson who chairs the National Fund said, "it is very important that our affiliates, Joint Apprenticeship Committees and contractors understand that in order for Ironworkers to perform any type of work on a site that has been designated as hazardous, the members must have a certification card stipulating that he or she completed a 40-hour OSHA approved course. In fact, no person can get through the gate on these sites unless they have a certification, and that includes business representatives and contractors."

General President Jake West said, "the training received in Haz/Mat, Lead Hazard and Asbestos Abatement not only means more jobs for our members, but also provides the knowledge they need to protect themselves when performing work on projects that may have hazardous materials."

James Phair Appointed

On April 20, 1992 General Vice President Donald W. O'Reilly, who was also Executive Director of Canadian Operations, retired from the International Association. General President

James Phair,
General Vice President

Jake West appointed General Organizer James Phair General Vice President and Executive Director of Canadian Operations on April 20, 1992. General Vice President Phair was initiated into Local No. 700, Windsor, Ontario in 1965 and held local union office before being appointed General Organizer by General President John H. Lyons in 1979.

Members of Local No. 721 who erected Canadian Tire Distribution Centre in Toronto, Ontario, Canada in 1992.

We Must Protect Our Future

As the Iron Workers and other unions prepared for the 1992 Presidential and Congressional elections in the United States, President West stated that "IPAL is the only way we can survive in the political and legislative arena." It was pointed out that as the cost of running a modern day political campaign spirals upward, Ironworker contributions to IPAL during this construction depression lagged too far behind. To become a powerful voice in the political area we need every working member to check-off a deduction of only pennies a day for our IPAL Program.

It was also pointed out that the Reagan-Bush Administrations opposed anti-strikebreaker legislation,

General President Jake West joins with thousands rallying for "Safe Jobs Now," at the U.S. Capitol. Speaking in the background is BCTD President Robert Georgine.

About 200 Ironworker foremen and officers attended the first Foreman Training Seminar in Toronto, Canada in 1992. They represented Ironworker Locals No. 721, 736, 700, 765 and 786.

attempted to gut and repeal Davis-Bacon prevailing wage laws, thwarted efforts at strengthening construction occupational safety and health measures, continuously attempted to tax the Ironworker fringe benefits and raid Ironworker pension funds, ignored the mounting cost of health care, offered protection to the double-breasted contractor, handed down devastating regulations by way of the Department of Labor in order to attack Ironworker apprenticeship programs, and nominated anti-worker appointees to the National Labor Relations Board.

National Ironworkers Welding Certification Test Program

The International Association in conjunction with the National Ironworkers and Employers Apprenticeship Training and Journeyman Upgrading Fund established the National Ironworkers Welding Certification Test Committee in 1992. It was the committee's goal to have all Ironworkers who pass the certification test be recognized on projects throughout North America without the necessity of retaking a test every time they change employers or jobs. "The key to this program will be to certify Iron Worker training facilities which will allow the facility to administer the certification test in accordance with AWS standards" said General Secretary LeRoy E. Worley.

General President Jake West stated at the Committee meeting that "the International Association and National Fund are strongly committed to the establishment of a National Ironworkers Welding

Both labor and management participated in the Foreman Training Seminar in Toronto. Pictured from left: Bill Jemison, Ontario Employers Association; LeRoy E. Worley, General Secretary and James D. Phair, General Vice President and head of Canadian Operations, International Association.

Certification Test Program." In implementing the Program, the International Association announced the publication of 10 Welding Training Manuals for Ironworkers that were written by Ironworker Certified Welding Inspectors, Coordinators and Instructors.

In addition to the Welding Program, the National Fund continued holding Foreman Training Seminars in the United States and Canada. The topics covered were: Roles and Responsibilities of the Foreman; Job Planning; Maintaining Payroll and Cost Records; Jobsite Safety and Health; Effective Communication Skills for the Foreman; Team Building: The Foreman's Role; and Time Management for the Foreman. One such seminar was held for approximately 200 Ironworker foremen in Toronto, Canada in 1992. At the time of our 100th Anniversary, this program is still very active and will continue to provide the information our foreman need to be more proficient in their duties.

In 1992 the National Welding Certification Test Committee meet in Washington, D.C.

General President Jake West's Labor Day Message in 1992

"Throughout history, from the days of the craft guilds in old Europe, organizations of workers have acted to represent their own members, as well as society in general. Labor organizations united the population to work for better conditions from whomever happened to be the

Local No. 387 members, Atlanta, Georgia, topping out the Nations Bank Building which was the tallest building in the southeastern U.S. in 1992. *From left to right:* Billy Stewart, Lewis "Sparky" Bryson, Floyd "Tex" Struckmeyer, James Haynes and Russ Lowery.

and roads and bridges that make our two nations what they are. But, there are those who want to destroy our pride and replace our solidarity, so that they can benefit their corporate greed.

"Let us make a point this Labor Day, to think before we vote in our local, state or provincial, and national elections, and do what we can to elect those who believe in the rights of workers. Let us ensure that our families and friends are aware of the political threats to our way of life and vote to elect pro-worker candidates."

Ironworkers and AFL-CIO Support for Governor Clinton

After the Democratic Convention of 1992, Governor Clinton would appear before the AFL-CIO General Board meeting, which had endorsed the Clinton-Gore ticket. Present at this meeting were the leaders of the Iron Workers International Association. Governor Clinton spoke of the need to provide jobs, the need to repair and maintain the infrastructure of the nation and the need

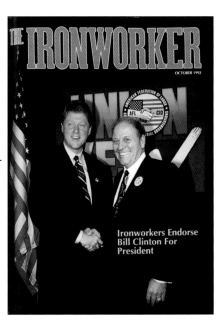

to invest in transportation, housing, and research. General President West would pledge full support for Governor Clinton and Senator Gore because:

"...they are the candidates who can put America back to work and who will listen to the needs of American workers."

ruler. The guilds used their solidarity to win concessions from European monarchs centuries ago, and the guild's successors, labor unions, have worked to make life better for us all.

"When we think of all they have done - the 40-hour, five-day work week, pension plans, health programs and safety on the job, we can see their benefits for the unionized workers. But, the influence of labor unions go further; they pioneered development of such things as universal public education, social security benefits, Medicare and Medicaid and other programs that benefit all citizens, whether or not they are union members.

"To me, this is what the Iron Workers International Association, and the rest of the labor movement in the United States and Canada, is all about - helping people. We have so much to be proud of; let's face it, we built the buildings

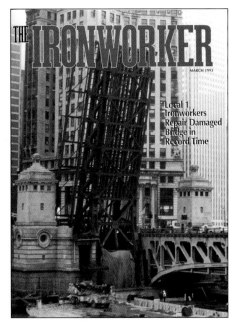

Local No. 1 Ironworkers repair bridge in record time. On September 20, 1992, the southeast leaf of the Michigan Avenue Bascule Bridge over the Chicago River came loose from its rear locks and came smashing down into the counterweight pit. The momentum was so great that the resulting force ripped the bridge trunnion girder from its foundation.

Members of Local No. 1 who worked on Michigan Bascule Bridge.

The AFL-CIO General Board meeting had only one item on the agenda: whether or not to endorse a ticket for President of the United States. The delegates voted overwhelmingly to endorse the Clinton-Gore Democratic ticket. Pictured at the meeting are, **from left:** Executive Assistant to the General President Martin T. Byrne; General Vice President Raymond J. Robertson; Ironworkers Legislative Director Michael Brennan; General Secretary LeRoy E. Worley; General Treasurer James E. Cole and Mid-Atlantic District Council President Carroll Allison.

With the election of William Jefferson Clinton in 1992 as the 42nd President of the United States, the labor movement felt good again. The President would have a Democratic majority of 259 to 175 in the House and a 57 to 42 majority in the Senate during his first two years; however, this was not enough to stop a filibuster. Many of the Southern Democrats were really Dixiecrats who voted with the Republicans on labor and liberal issues. Although he received no credit for it from the media, President Clinton cut the deficit for the first time since the huge increase in the deficit under Reagan and Bush.

Robert Reich Appointed Secretary of Labor

The appointment of Robert Reich, a key advisor to President Bill Clinton for many years, as Secretary of Labor in the new administration won the praise of the trade labor movement. The AFL-CIO praised his selection and described him as "exceptionally well qualified to participate as a full partner in the economic decision-making of the Clinton administration." General President West noted that Secretary Reich "has always been sympathetic to the economic problems that are faced by working Americans and should be understanding to the needs of America's unionized workforce."

Robert Reich, Secretary of Labor

President Clinton Revokes Executive Orders

On February 3, 1993, General President West advised all affiliated local unions in the United States that President Clinton took two actions to restore a much needed balance in America's workplace. First, President Clinton revoked Executive Order No. 12818. This order, issued on October 23, 1992 by President Bush in a desperate attempt to appease the right wing of the Republican Party, "prohibited contractors that have entered into project agreements with unions from bidding on federal construction contracts." By revoking Executive Order No. 12818, such project agreements will again be allowed in federal construction contracts.

Second, President Clinton also revoked Executive Order No. 12800, issued on April 13, 1992 by President Bush. This order "required unionized federal contractors to post a notice in the workplace that workers are not required to join or support a union and threatened sanctions against contractors who did not comply." In rescinding this order, President Clinton said that "the effect of this order was distinctly anti-union as it did not require contractors to notify workers of any of their other rights protected by the National Labor Relations Act, such as the right to organize and bargain collectively. By revoking this order (and ending any postings), I today end the Government's role in promoting this one-sided version of workplace rights."

New York City Ironworkers Called Into Action

Terrorists blew it apart, and Ironworkers put it back together again. Over 100 Ironworkers, most from Local No. 40 and others from Locals No. 361, 580 and 46, worked for several weeks in the dark dusty hole which was once four interior stories of the World Trade Center complex in downtown Manhattan. Two shifts of Ironworkers, laboring night and day, worked 10-hour days, six days a week for The Karl Koch Erecting Company, Inc. The Ironworkers braced the interior temporarily until the permanent restoration work could be started.

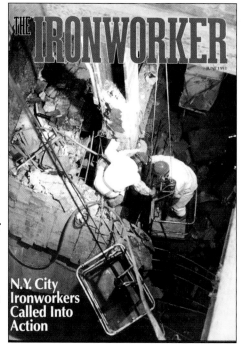

While engineers and police officials determined that the bomb itself was detonated next to one of the exterior

The extensive amount of damage done to the World Trade Center hotel parking garage area is evident in this dramatic photo. The two-and-one-half foot square structural steel columns with X-bracing are credited with successfully withstanding the tremendous force of the blast. Members from Locals No. 40, 361, 580 and 46 worked on two shifts, six days a week.

columns of the 110-story World Trade Center Tower A in a sub-basement, there was no significant structural damage to the tower itself. Apparently the two-and-a-half foot square structural steel column with an X-brace was able to withstand the tremendous force of the February 26, 1993 blast.

Koch's rehabilitation of the building included the removal of super heavy machinery destroyed by the blast and the installation of replacement equipment. To perform the technical rigging that was needed, they brought in the highly skilled Ironworker riggers from Local No. 40, working for the Gerosa Rigging Company. Ironworkers from Local No. 46, installed reinforcing on the floor slabs damaged by the explosion and Local No. 580 members repaired the exterior wall system and architectural metal damage. Once again, the highly skilled and well trained Ironworkers came to the rescue and performed courageously.

A Historical Rigging Job

Ironworkers from Washington, D.C., Local No. 5 were the heart of the rigging team that moved a famous and familiar national treasure from atop the dome of the United States Capitol Building for cleaning and restoration. The Statue of Freedom, a 19-1/2 foot, 14,985 lb., hollow cast-bronze statue symbolizing America, was removed on May 9, 1993, for the first time since it was put in place in 1863, 130 years before. The statue, which was originally installed in five sections raised by a hand-powered pulley and then bolted together on top of the Capitol dome, had started to deteriorate with age and badly needed cleaning, repair and a protective coating for the future.

Union Industries Show

For many years, the International Association, District Councils and affiliated local unions have been involved in setting up an Ironworker exhibit at the AFL-CIO

Union Industries Show in various cities throughout the United States. An estimated 180,000 people filed through the Cervantes Convention Center in St. Louis, Mo., May 14-17, 1993, taking stock of more than 300 union exhibits. The District Council of St. Louis and Vicinity, officers and members of Locals No. 396, St. Louis, Mo., and Local No. 392, East St. Louis, Illinois and the Joint Apprenticeship Committees joined with the Institute of the Ironworkers Industry (III) and several contractors and companies in setting up an outstanding display. The AFL-CIO Union Label and Service Trades Department is responsible for putting on this show.

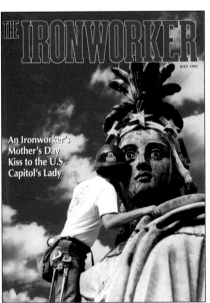

The Statue of Freedom, a 19-1/2 ft., 14,985 lb., hollow cast-bronze statue symbolizing the United States, was moved for the first time since it was put in place in 1863 (33 years before the Iron Workers Union was established) by members of Local No. 5, Washington, D.C. An S-64 Skycrane helicopter was used to lower the statue to the ground below where it would be cleaned and renovated.

The Ironworker crew is pictured in front of the Statue of Freedom following the completion of its removal from atop the U.S. Capitol dome in Washington, D.C. **Left to right:** Carroll Allison, President of the Mid-Atlantic States District Council; Charles Hill, General Organizer; Members of Local No. 5 Tim Levy, Charles Blake, Megal DePanza, Jeff Grooms, and Mike Sandlin; and General Treasurer James Cole. **Kneeling, left to right:** are members of Local No. 5 Robert Jackson, John Hunt, and Kenny Waugh.

Pictured next to the Ironworkers Exhibit at the AFL-CIO Union Industries Show in St. Louis, Missouri are, **left to right**, General Secretary LeRoy E. Worley, General Treasurer James E. Cole, General Organizer Roy Williams, Joe Hunt, President of the St. Louis and Vicinity District Council and General Organizer Charles Hill, along with officers of the District Council.

NAFTA - We Fought a Good Fight

The House of Representatives approved NAFTA 234-200 on November 17, 1993. The Senate quickly followed suit with a 61-38 vote. Representatives and Senators from most industrialized states voted to block the so-called free trade deal with Mexico and Canada that President Bush negotiated before he was voted out of office in 1992. Opponents had warned that NAFTA threatens good-paying U.S. jobs and would undercut wages as more U.S. corporations move plants and production to Mexico.

Following the House vote, AFL-CIO President Lane Kirkland said NAFTA's approval "is a bitter disappointment and defeat for millions of working Americans." He saluted the efforts of affiliated unions and their members for conducting a valiant grass-roots campaign against passage of the NAFTA legislation.

Ironworkers Sworn To Secrecy

Throughout history, Ironworkers have been involved in many different types of work that have had an impact on the security of their country. In earlier chapters the work that the Ironworkers did during the MX Missile program was highlighted. Ironworker members of Local No. 155, Fresno, California, were instrumental in the fabrication, erection and rigging of the many facilities necessary for the use and testing of the F-117A Stealth Fighter Aircraft at the Tonopah Test Range in Nevada.

Sworn to secrecy, the Ironworkers of Local No. 155 were proud of the role that was required of them through the years of testing at the Tonopah Test Range. The F-117A Stealth Fighter was unveiled to the public in April, 1989 and permanently relocated to another base in May, 1992. The aircraft was a major force in Panama and in the Persian Gulf War Operation Desert Storm. The article involving the Stealth Fighter could not appear in *The Ironworker* magazine until October, 1993 because of security reasons.

On November 19-20, 1992 Business Agents from the California District Council attended a Training Seminar held by the International Association. General President Jake West, General Secretary LeRoy Worley and General Treasurer James Cole joined other International Representatives in making presentations on a variety of subjects.

Joe Hunt Appointed

On January 1, 1994, General President Jake West appointed General Organizer Joseph J. Hunt General Vice President. A third generation Ironworker, General Vice President Hunt became an apprentice member of Local No. 396, St. Louis, Missouri in 1962. He was elected to several offices including Business Manager of Local No. 396. In 1983, he was appointed

Joseph J. Hunt,
General Vice President

General Organizer and was assigned to work at International Headquarters as Assistant to the Director of Jurisdiction and Research. He then became Assistant to the General Treasurer. In 1990 General Vice President Hunt returned to St. Louis to become the President of the

In front of an F-117A Stealth Fighter are the men of different crafts: Local No. 155 Ironworkers Ron Pierce, **kneeling, third from left**; Bill Clay, foreman, **kneeling fourth from left**; Nephi Pagan, steward, **kneeling, ninth from left**; and superintendent Dan Morrell, Reynolds Electrical and Engineering Company, Inc., **standing, first from left**.

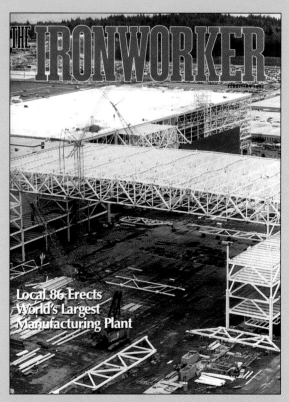

THE IRONWORKER

FEBRUARY 1993

Local 86 Erects World's Largest Manufacturing Plant

In 1884, a Soldier's Monument was erected at Monument and Main Streets in Dayton, Ohio, which sat in the middle of the intersection for a period of 64 years. Then in 1948, the historic statue was dismantled, moved and re-erected in Sunrise Park by Dayton Local No. 290 Ironworkers, working for Foreman Machinery Movers.

It remained in that spot for 44-years, until in March 1991, the monument was again dismantled, moved, and erected within a half-block of its original position. The second move was done by Local No. 290 Ironworkers working for Omega Rigger in 1991.

Members of Local No. 86, Seattle, Washington and other members from Ironworker Local Unions throughout the United States working for Baugh Industrial Contractors erected the iron for an addition to the Boeing Airplane Company's new 777 production complex at Everett, Washington in 1992.

The Ironworker crew erecting the Boeing 777 High Bay Assembly Building.

Topping out ceremony of the Denver Airport Terminal Building in 1993. Members of Local No. 24 erected the last big beam for the terminal. **In the middle of the front row, left to right,** are Local No. 24 President/Business Agent Joseph L. Trujillo, General Vice President O.C. Yancy, and Local No. 24 FST/BM Howard A. Rathe.

District Council of St. Louis and Vicinity. He is a member of several committees for the International Association.

Steel Erection Negotiated Rulemaking Advisory Committee (SENRAC)

In 1988 OSHA announced that it was their intention to rewrite the Federal OSHA Standards concerning steel erection. It was clear that OSHA's intention was to require 100% fall protection at heights six feet above any surface, under all circumstances. Through the efforts of General President Jake West a meeting was held at International Headquarters with the head of OSHA, Assistant Secretary of Labor Gerry Scannell. The meeting resulted in a jobsite review of six structural jobs in Chicago, conducted by President West and attended by Scannell and his staff, the Ironworkers Labor and Management Safety Committee, and Local Union and District Council officials.

This two day review of jobsites was the first time a top OSHA official had ever come to a construction site to review the practicality of present and proposed safety standards. This inspection of jobsites with the head of OSHA resulted in a review of national jobsites and a final recommendation to initiate negotiated rule making.

Since OSHA had grappled with the issue for nearly twenty years, the Secretary of Labor, then Lynn Martin, approved the initiation of an industry wide Steel Erection Negotiated Rulemaking Advisory Committee (SENRAC) and appointed labor, management, Government and other groups to develop a standard by consensus.

This twenty person committee had their first meeting in June, 1994 to develop a new OSHA Safety Standard (Sub-part R - Steel Erection). General President Jake West appointed General Treasurer James E. Cole, also Co-Chairman of the Safety Advisory Committee of the Structural, Ornamental, Rigging and Reinforcing Industry; Executive Director of Safety, Steve Cooper; and General Vice President Alan Simmons to represent the International Association. Iron Worker Erectors are represented by John Murphy, President of Williams Enterprises of Georgia and NAMOA; Bill Brown, President of Ben Hur Construction, Inc.; Eric Waterman, Safety Director, NRA; and Fred Codding, Executive Vice President of NAMOA and NARSC. Other organizations that played important roles in the negotiations included the Institute of the Ironworking Industry (III); the Allied Building Metal Industries, Inc., of New York City; and the Ironworkers Employers Association of Western Pennsylvania.

The Committee held hearings throughout the United States. During the eighteen (18) months of hearings, labor and management experts discussed ways to improve Ironworker safety. SENRAC reviewed the causes of collapses, injuries and fatalities resulting from falls.

On December 1, 1995, after 18 months of deliberation an agreement was reached by all parties on regulations in which the structural steel industry would be regulated. Not only did SENRAC establish the explicit jobsite activities to be governed it also established standards mandating that controlling contractors perform activities assisting the steel erector. In addition, SENRAC established regulations governing the fabrication and manufacturing of structural products. Due to the efforts of General President Jake West and SENRAC, a great deal was accomplished on improving the safety of all Ironworkers while performing their daily tasks.

COMET Program - Fred Summers Heads Up Department of Organizing

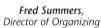

In the April, 1994 President's page of *The Ironworker,* General President Jake West stated that the Construction Organizing Membership Education and Training (COMET) program could be the most timely and rewarding organizing effort in the long history of organizing by our International Union. President West appointed Fred Summers, former Business Agent of Local No. 395, as Director of Organizing, to head up this important program. His job is to travel from council to council, from local to local to help define and set up a COMET program. Director Summers was assigned to explain the goal of COMET which is to regain control of the skilled labor supply.

Fred Summers, Director of Organizing

General President West said: "Yes, I know how hard it is to organize when you have unemployment, but the reason we have unemployment is because unscrupulous non-union contractors are underbidding our fair contractors who are paying decent wages. When the economy expands there will be a need for hospitals, schools, water treatment plants, power plants, and the rebuilding of our infrastructure. We want these jobs to be union jobs for our membership. And that is what the COMET program is all about."

Diabetes Research Institute

The dedication of the Diabetes Research Institute on February 23, 1994 marked the high point of the Building and Construction Trades Department's "Blueprint for Cure" campaign. "This is a great day for labor and a great day to eradicate the disease," AFL-CIO President Lane Kirkland told an audience of approximately 900 in Miami, Florida. The construction

Exterior view of the Diabetes Research Center at the University of Miami, Florida. It was the Ironworker members along with other building tradesmen that raised the money for this center, mainly on "DAD's" day.

General President Jake West, **right**, attends dedication of Diabetes Research Center with Dr. Daniel Mintz, Scientific Director and Chief of the Academic Office of the Institute, **center**, and AFL-CIO Building Trades Department President Robert Georgine.

of the 87,000 square foot building, the most comprehensive diabetes research facility in the world, would not have been possible without the hard work and dedication of the labor community.

General President West thanked all the Ironworker members from the United States and Canada for working the street corners and having all types of functions to raise money for diabetes research and this building. The Ironworkers have always been leaders when they are called on to help others.

Construction in Canada Continued to Slide in 1994

Unemployment among construction workers in Canada stood at depression levels in January, according to figures released in May by StatsCan. The 189,000 jobless construction workers amounted to 22.9 percent of the industry, and 12 percent of Canada's 1.6 million unemployed. Though Canada's recession is supposed to be over and the nation enjoying a "slow recovery," construction jobs declined by 48,000 between January, 1993 and January, 1994 - an 8 percent drop.

In the July, 1994 issue of *The Ironworker* magazine there was an important message from General President Jake West to the membership regarding "Ironworkers' Job Line." The message read as follows: "Starting July 1, 1994 the Iron Workers International Union contracted with AT&T for a service which I believe will be a great benefit to our membership. It is called 'Voice Com,' and it will provide job opportunity information for Ironworkers through a toll free 800 number. This innovative program could not have come at a better time. We are beginning to see signs of increased employment in our industry and many local unions need Ironworkers. This toll free number will tell you which locals need workers, type of work and, who to contact. I will keep you updated on this exciting program. The toll free 'Job Line' number is 1-800-369-Jobs (5627)."

Ironworkers Memorial– Second Narrows Crossing Bridge

On June 17, 1958, 18 men working on the construction of the Second Narrows Crossing Bridge in Vancouver, British Columbia, including 13 Ironworkers, died in the horrible collapse of the structure. An additional four Ironworkers lost their lives before construction was ultimately completed. In human terms, this was an horrendously expensive bridge project.

Thirty-six years to the day later, June 17, 1994, fellow Ironworkers from Local No. 97, survivors and families of the deceased, the Premier of the Province of British Columbia Mike Harcourt, the Minister of Transportation and Highways Jackie Pement, General Secretary LeRoy E. Worley, and invited guests participated in a ceremony honoring "the people who helped build this province and those who lost their lives during the construction of the Second Narrows Crossing Bridge on June 17, 1958."

Local No. 97 Business Manager and Financial Secretary Gary Short recalled the tragedy and read the names of the men who were killed. Brother Short said, "Ironworkers will remember this dedication with pride."

Ironworker Instructors and Observers attending the 10th Annual Ironworker Instructors Training Program in 1994.

10th Annual Ironworker Instructors Training Program

Approximately 400 Ironworker Instructors and Observers attended the 10th Annual Ironworker Instructors Training Program at the University of San Diego. There were 32 courses offered. Emphasis was placed on architectural and ornamental ironwork and the Certified Welding Inspectors course. The trustees of the National Fund expressed their appreciation to all the teachers and staff for the outstanding job they did in presenting courses. General President Jake West stressed the importance of this program in providing instructors with the latest technology in the ironworking trade. President West said "the success of our future depends on the skilled workforce we provide to our contractors."

Ironworkers signed an historical agreement for Tappan Zee Bridge reconstruction. **Left to right:** John Mills, Attorney for Local No. 40, New York City; General Vice President Alan Simmons; Gary Gaydos, FST/BA, Local No. 417, New York City; John Kelly, President/BA, Local No. 40; General President Jake West; Ray Mullett, FST/BM, Local No. 40; General Treasurer James E. Cole; Edward Walsh, RS/BA, Local No. 40; Walter Lofink, President, Local No. 417; and Dennis Milton, BA, Local No. 580, New York City.

Ironworkers Sign Historic Agreement for Tappan Zee Bridge

Shortly after Labor Day 1994, Union Ironworkers began the reconstruction of the Tappan Zee Bridge under the terms of a progressive project labor agreement between the New York Building Trades Council and the New York State Thruway Authority. This new agreement provided four years' work for nearly 100 Ironworkers and many other members of the other building trades unions.

The outstanding apprentices representing their District Councils who participated in the First National Ironworkers Outstanding Apprenticeship Contest, which was one of the highlights of the conference, are pictured with General President Jake West, General Secretary and Conference Chairman LeRoy E. Worley, General Treasurer James E. Cole, General Vice President and Honorary Chairman Raymond J. Robertson, General Vice President William H. Sullivan and Billy Joe Walker, President of the Southeastern States District Council.

Eric Costa of Local No. 397 representing the Southeastern States District Council was awarded first place in the First National Ironworkers Outstanding Apprenticeship Contest held during this conference.

The bridge was erected by members of Iron Workers Locals No. 40 and 417 from 1951 through 1955. The agreement represents the first time a government agency of New York State entered into a union pre-hire agreement allowed under the March, 1993 U.S. Supreme Court Boston Harbor Decision. The work includes structural steel repair, ship collision protection, redecking, substructure repair, dredging, pile replacement and repairs to the bridge superstructure. General President Jake West and General Treasurer James E. Cole were present at the signing. At the completion of the ceremony, General President West noted, "This is truly a great day for organized labor and for the Ironworkers in particular. This agreement is a prime example of how well our American system of collective bargaining works for the best interests of everyone."

Ironworkers & Employers Apprenticeship & Training Conference of North America

The International Association held the first Ironworkers and Employers Apprenticeship and Training Conference of North America in Pittsburgh, Pennsylvania in October, 1994. Over 200 management and labor delegates attended from the United States and Canada. The very informative Conference was highlighted by the First National Ironworkers Outstanding Apprenticeship Contest which was held on Saturday and Sunday preceding the main meetings. Local No. 3, Pittsburgh, hosted the contest.

The Conference Chairman was General Secretary LeRoy E. Worley. There were general sessions held each day. Regional workshops were also held. Paul Songer, President of the National Erectors Association was Co-Chairman and General Vice President Raymond J. Robertson was Honorary Chairman. General President Jake West was the keynote speaker at the opening session. He stressed the importance of training a skilled workforce through the Local Union Joint Apprenticeship Training Programs. President West congratulated the Outstanding Apprentices who competed in the National Apprenticeship Contest. In October of 1996, this conference will be held again in Vancouver, British Columbia.

Over 200 attendees from the United States and Canada consisting of contractors, apprenticeship committee members, Outstanding Apprentices, Local Union and International Officers participate in the first Ironworkers and Employers Apprenticeship and Training Conference of North America.

225

Charles W. Hill Appointed

On October 26, 1994, General President Jake West appointed General Organizer Charles W. Hill as Executive Assistant to the General Secretary. Executive Assistant Hill is a member of Local No. 103, Evansville, Indiana and was the Business Manager of that local before coming with the International Association. He had worked out of the General Secretary's office for a number of years prior to being appointed.

Charles W. Hill
Executive Assistant to
the General Secretary.

Government Plaza in Mobile, Alabama

Ironworkers from Local No. 798, Prichard, Alabama, working for International Steel Industries, Inc. and Harmon Contract Company, Inc. erected the Government Plaza building in 1994. The main plaza trusses, weighing up to 51.4 tons per truss, were erected in three sections. The triangle shaped truss sections were erected first and were carefully adjusted on false-work, before setting the larger truss sections. The main plaza roof consisted of 75 truss-full-penetration welded splices of which no deficiencies were noted during testing. The endwall and elevator pipe framing also contained 189 full-penetration welded splices. The Ironworkers working on the wall panels and windows demonstrated their training skills and did an outstanding job for Harmon Contract Company.

World's Tallest, Fastest Roller Coaster

Ironworkers from Local No. 433, Los Angeles, California erected the world's tallest and fastest roller coaster in 1994 at the Prima Donna Corporation's new Buffalo Bill's Casino at Jean, Nevada on the California-Nevada state boundary line. In order to meet the critical opening date, the contractor employed 35 Ironworkers on a twelve hour work schedule for approximately 80 days straight during a record heat wave which had temperatures above 110 degrees for at least 10 days straight.

The mammoth roller coaster has the steepest and longest drop of any coaster in the world. The unique design of the pipe rail tracks provides the 220' high coaster with its extremely smooth riding characteristics. All the tackwelds were either x-rayed or ultrasonically tested to the most stringent standards.

Joseph M. Quilty Appointed

General President Jake West appointed General Organizer and President of the New England States District Council, Joseph M. Quilty as General Vice President on February 1, 1995. He was initiated into Local No. 7, Boston, Massachusetts as an apprentice member in 1956 and became a journeyman in 1958 where he worked in all facets of the trade. In 1976 General Vice President Quilty was elected to the

Joseph M. Quilty,
General Vice President

Members of Local No. 798 and boomers who worked on the Government Plaza project in Mobile, Alabama. Pictured is the Ironworker crew who worked on the job: Marvin Turner, Shawn Smith, Scott Alford, Ford Spencer, Billy Kennedy, Nat O'Cain, Kenny Malone, Lewis Harville, Steve Danley, Jim Matthews, Jimmy Owens, Bill McClure, Albert Likely, Steve Kelly, Mack Corley, Wayne Jackson, Bill Nichelson, Curtis Edwards, Horace Eubanks, George Ragains, L.L. Crager, Evan Allen, Tim Crager, Stephen Crager, Todd Cole, Willie Powe, V.H. Urban Jr., Carey Howard, Jerry Hartline, Darrell Alford, Earl Whittington, James H. George, Gene Mann, Ronnie Whittington, Charles McClure, James W. Smith, Vance Davenport, J.C. Scott, Ricky Miller, Darrell Lawshe Jr., P.C. Stewart III, Ben Taylor, Thomas Caylor, James Wade. Boomers include: Lenny Hollaway, Eric Nash, Ralph Linsey, Floyd Carpenter, Thomas Kurns, Stony Allen, Niles Rubar, Darrell Lawshe Sr., Robert Stacy, Dale Hamrick, Eugene Jowers, Len Prichet. Project managers: Dan Gillooly and Adam Sizemore. Superintendent: Tim Gillooly, Local 798 Business Agent Ray S. Helton

Local 798 Ironworkers
Erect Government Plaza
In Mobile, Alabama

THE IRONWORKER

JANUARY 1995

Local Union 433 Erects
World's Tallest, Fastest
Roller Coaster

Members of Local No. 433 who worked on the world's tallest and fastest roller coaster in 1994. **Kneeling, left to right:** *Charles Trotman, Scott Lathery, Steward Jim Larson, Mike Lathery, Jr., Enrique Mejia, Richard Crowe, and Don Luster.* **Standing:** *Superintendent Mike Lathery, Sr., Jerry Kossuth, VP Coast Engineering & Mechanical Co., BA Max Price, Ian Coleman, Terry Lathery, Tom Parson, Dale Brasket, Ron Hudson, John Putney, Jr., Ed Williamson, Dick Marriott, Steve Hayes, Joe Jones, Jessie Tapia, Dean Ward, Rick Hudson, Mike Palenko, Hector Hernandez, Paul Bissett, Matthew Moore, and Bob Johnson.*

Executive Board of Local No. 7 and later was elected Business Agent. In December, 1985, General Vice President Quilty was appointed General Organizer by General President Juel D. Drake.

Ironworkers Hold Informational Seminar

As the International Association began its 99th year as an organization, local union officers from the United States and Canada gathered in Miami, Florida, February 21-22, 1995 for a full schedule of meetings. General President Jake West, General Secretary LeRoy E. Worley, and General Treasurer James E. Cole spoke to the delegates along with all the department heads at International Headquarters. There were other speakers, such as John McMahon, Executive Director of the Institute of the Ironworking Industry, Guy Dumoulin, Executive Secretary, Canadian Building & Construction Trades Department, Congressman Martin D. Frost, U.S. Congressman (D-Texas) and James Stanley, Deputy Assistant Secretary of OSHA.

These types of meetings allow the International Association to communicate directly with the Business Agents and other local union officers on important issues that are currently confronting the affiliates. General President West thanked Secretary Worley for chairing the meeting and doing an excellent job. President West thanked the delegates for their attentiveness and participation. He also brought the delegates through all the activities relative to the Davis-Bacon Act. "This law keeps our union contractors competitive on government projects," President West said, "therefore we must do everything in our power to save this law."

General President Jake West, General Secretary LeRoy E. Worley and General Treasurer James E. Cole as well as all Department Heads made presentations to the delegates attending the Informational Seminar.

Delegates from the United States and Canada attending the annual Ironworkers Informational Seminar held February, 1995 in Miami, Florida.

Ironworkers Volunteer in Rescue Efforts in Oklahoma City

On April 19, 1995, the most disastrous domestic terrorist attack in history occurred in Oklahoma City, Oklahoma when the Alfred P. Murrah Federal Building, located in the heart of downtown Oklahoma City was targeted and bombed at 9:02 a.m. while over 500 federal employees were starting their routine work-day. The fatality count from the explosion was 168. Volunteers from Ironworkers Local No. 48 gathered at the site minutes after the explosion.

Oscar J. Boldt Construction Company set up a fabricating yard a short distance from the explosion site. Fabrication of supporting material was per-formed in this area by Ironworkers, then trucked to the site, unloaded by crane for shoring and bracing of the dam-aged structure. Clad in hard hats, T-shirts, jeans and White Mule gloves, the guardian angels (Ironworkers) came from their jobs and homes April 19 to wade amid the carnage in the ruins of the federal building and make it safe for fire fighters and recovery teams.

As rubble was removed from the pit area, the exist-ing concrete columns had to be supported with 4" and 6" pipe running horizontally and diagonally through the structure to prevent the slabs from collapsing on the rescue workers. Some of the bracing was 42 feet long and took 40 men to hand carry it into the pit area.

Ironworkers rigged chainfalls and erected support bracing in critical areas to protect rescue workers. The process went on around the clock until workers reached the basement floor. The rigging skills of the Ironworkers were utilized to their fullest potential in

Rescue workers, including members of Local No. 48, Oklahoma City, Oklahoma, are searching for survivors at the Alfred P. Murrah Federal Building.

removing hazardous debris, not only to protect the lives of the rescue workers, but also to insure the safety of the many victims still trapped within the building. General President West sent a letter to Business Agent John A. Hunter, expressing his sincere appreciation to the members of Local No. 48 and other locals that participated in the rescue efforts.

Jim Minx, Executive Director of the Oklahoma State Fire Fighters Association, had high praise for Ironworker members. He said, "We couldn't have done our jobs if it hadn't been for these very brave and very skilled construction workers."

International Association of
Bridge, Structural and Ornamental Iron Workers

JAKE WEST
GENERAL PRESIDENT

LeROY E. WORLEY
GENERAL SECRETARY

JAMES E. COLE
GENERAL TREASURER

SUITE 400
1750 NEW YORK AVE. N.W.
WASHINGTON, D.C. 20006
202 383-4800

Affiliated with AFL-CIO

Mr. John A. Hunter, FST/BA
Local Union No. 48
617 SW 29th Street
Oklahoma City, OK 73109

May 3, 1995

Dear Sir and Brother:

This letter is to express to you and the membership of Local Union No. 48 the most sin-cere appreciation I can offer for the noble and heartwarming acts of heroism on the part of those Local Union No. 48 members who volunteered their skills and labor to save lives in the horrible terrorist bombing of the Alfred P. Murrah Federal Building in Oklahoma City.

No other act by our members could merit a greater degree of pride than what I feel in being your General President. I also know that people from all over the United States envy the Ironworkers Union for the quality of their membership both in skill of craftsmanship and in their eagerness to serve the community in which they live and work.

Our members, throughout the 100 year history of this International Union, have always exhibited heroism and gallantry above the call of duty in every war and conflict on behalf of our national defense whenever they have been called upon to serve. Today's battlefield is in the cities of our great country. Cowardly terrorists are killing innocent citizens and destroying the monumental structures which represent our Democratic Government. As always, in a time of a national emergency our members are the first to volunteer to do their part to help their community and our great nation.

With the unselfish example being set by our members at the Oklahoma City catastrophe, future generations of Ironworkers will naturally follow in their shoes as our nation calls them to action to protect the population of our country, as well as the ideals and principles upon which it was founded.

Again, please extend my deepest appreciation on behalf of all our Ironworkers, because we want those who served so heroically in Oklahoma City to know that they have brought great pride to all of our members and to the International Association.

With best wishes and kind personal regards, I am

Fraternally yours,

Jake West

GENERAL PRESIDENT

Left to right: Local No. 48 Ironworkers Floyd Parker, BA John Hunter, Mark Pierce, and Jack Ross, along with Operating Engineers BM David Farris, and Allen Farris at disaster site in Oklahoma City.

Ironworkers in the pit area of the Federal Building.

President Bill Clinton received a lengthy standing ovation from the more than 3,000 delegates attending the recent AFL.-CIO Building Trades 1995 National Conference in Washington, D.C. General President Jake West is fifth from the President's left.

AFL-CIO Union Industries Show of 1995

The Michigan-Great Lakes and Vicinity District Council hosted the AFL-CIO Union Industries Show in Detroit, Michigan in May, 1995. General Secretary LeRoy E. Worley who is also a Board member of the Union Label and Service Trades Department, and General Treasurer James E. Cole were on hand to greet the visiting Ironworkers and their families. General President West congratulated District Council President Harold Cooper, along with the entire District Council, for their dedication and their award winning exhibits.

President West also expressed special thanks to the Shop Department, Institute of the Ironworking Industry, The National Training Fund, Apprenticeship Coordinators, Business Agents, and all the journeymen and apprentices who worked so diligently during the week to coordinate, assemble, and manage the Ironworkers' displays.

Capitol Hill Rally - Thousands of building tradesmen listened to Department President Robert Georgine speak at a rally on Capitol Hill in support of Davis-Bacon. General President Jake West is pictured second from the right with other General Presidents.

*AFL.-CIO Union Industries Show - **Pictured from left to right:** John Kontich, Nick Seifert, Business Agents, Gregory Hicks, FST and Business Manager, Local 25, Detroit, Michigan; General Vice President Ray Robertson; General Treasurer James E. Cole; Harold Cooper, President of The Michigan-Great Lakes District Council; Nick Seifert, Jr.; General Secretary LeRoy E. Worley; James Wood, member from Local 15, Hartford, Connecticut; Jack Koby, President and Business Agent, Local 25; John Schlecht, Deputy Director, I.I.I.; Charles Most, Natural Training Fund; Bruce Hawley, FST and Business Manager, Local 340, Battle Creek, Michigan.*

A Tribute to Korean War Veterans

America's forgotten war was remembered on July 27, 1995 when the Korean War Veterans Memorial was dedicated. The memorial located within view of the Lincoln Memorial and directly across the mall from the Vietnam Veterans Memorial, honors America's veterans who served in Korea from June of 1950 through the official cease fire at 10:00 a.m. on July 28, 1953. There were 54,246 Americans killed in action, 8,177 still listed as missing in action, 103,284 wounded, and 7,140 individuals taken as prisoners of war.

Ironworker members of Local No. 5 erected the statues for the new Korean War Memorial. The statues are cast stainless steel and weigh 1,000 pounds each. "Let's look with hope that this outstanding Memorial will help us remember the forgotten heroes of this bloody conflict. Many Ironworkers participated in the Korean War and some lost their lives. This Memorial will be a remembrance of their great courage," said General President Jake West.

On July 27, 1995 the Korean War Memorial was dedicated in Washington, D.C. Members of Local No. 5 erected the 19 statues.

*Ironworkers from Local No. 5, Washington, D.C., erected the statues for the new Korean War Memorial in the nation's capital, working with Superior Iron Works. The statues are cast stainless steel and weigh 1,000 pounds each. They are bolted to stainless steel pads. **Left to right:** Dan McGraw, Don Kaetzel, Bob Murphy, and Foreman John Morris.*

Newly Elected Local Union Officers Attend Training Seminar

A very successful program that was established by the International Association a few years before, continued to be a huge success for the newly elected officers of the various affiliates attending the training seminar for newly elected local union officers in October of 1995. General President Jake West appointed General Secretary LeRoy E. Worley to chair the daily sessions.. All the department heads at International Headquarters including General Treasurer James E. Cole, gave detailed reports on the activities of their departments. General President West reported to the officers as a group and talked to each officer personally to make them aware that they are only a telephone call away from getting any assistance that they may need to perform their duties.

Bernie Evers, BA, Local 7; Billy Burns, FST-BR, Local 14; Pete Oresky, BA and Shorty Gleason, BA, Local 25; Michael Ruggieri, BA, Local 37; Steve P. Canty, FST-BM, Eric M. Dean, BA, and Richard Rowe, BA, Local 63; Mike Cox, VP-Ass't BA, Local 67; Jim Murphy, FST-BM, Local 118; James F. Jordan, III, Acting BA, Local 161; Pasquale "Pat" Manzi, P-Ass't BA, Local 172; Dave DeCarolis, FST-BM, Local 348; Jerry Wakefield, FST-BA, Local 492; Richard Frahm, BA, Local 512; Jerry D. Wilson, FST-BA, Local 710; Pierre Desroches, BA, Local 711; Aaron Murphy, FST-BM, Local 721; and Bert Royer, FST-BA, Local 771.

Members of Local No. 396 who built the St. Louis Stadium in 1995.

What is more important is that each participant receives a reference manual that the local union officer can use in carrying out his or her daily activities. Such important issues as jurisdictional disputes, safety, financial matters, organizing, apprenticeship and many more subjects are covered. In order for the participants to understand how International Headquarters operates, they are taken on a tour of headquarters where they see first hand what each department does. The department heads answer questions that the local union officer may have concerning the operation of the department.

General President Jake West Elected AFL-CIO Vice-President

Ironworkers were well represented at the 21st AFL-CIO Convention held October 23-26, 1995 in New York City, by a delegation led by General President Jake West, General Secretary LeRoy E. Worley and General Treasurer James E. Cole. General President Jake West was elected a Vice President of the AFL-CIO Executive Council by the more than 1,000 delegates in attendance representing the 13 million members of the affiliated unions.

In the forty year history of the AFL-CIO, President West is only the second Ironworker's General President to serve on this prestigious board. President John H.

The fight to save the Davis-Bacon Act which preserves local area wages and labor standards is carried out by the Ironworkers and the Building Trades. General President Jake West expressed his concerns relative to the Davis-Bacon Act and other legislation that affects Ironworkers to President Bill Clinton and Vice President Al Gore at a Labor Council meeting in 1995.

Lyons, Jr. was the first. General President West's election to this influential board will only enhance his ability to help Ironworkers. President of the United States Bill Clinton congratulated General President West on his election to the AFL-CIO Executive Council.

John J. Sweeney was elected AFL-CIO President by a 1.6 million vote margin out of 13 million votes cast. Delegates also elected Sweeney's running mates, Mine Workers President Richard L. Trumka as Secretary-Treasurer of the AFL-CIO and Linda Chavez-Thompson,

Ironworker delegates at 65th Convention of the Building and Construction Trades Department held August 29-31, 1995 in Chicago.

231

Ironworker delegates to the AFL-CIO Convention, **first row, left to right:** Jerry L. Hufton, FST/BA, Local 79, Norfolk, Virginia; General Vice President Joe Hunt, General Treasurer James E. Cole, General President Jake West, General Secretary LeRoy E. Worley, General Vice President Ray Robertson, and Executive Assistant Martin T. Byrne. **Second row, left to right:** Gordon McDonald, President of the Nebraska State AFL-CIO; Michael Fitzpatrick, President, District Council of Western New York; Frank Caine, BA, Local 416, Los Angeles, California; General Vice President Fhane Jones, General Vice President Joe Quilty, and General Vice President Allan Simmons.

General President Jake West was elected AFL-CIO Vice President at the 21st AFL-CIO Convention in New York City. President Bill Clinton who addressed the delegates congratulated President West immediately following the election.

Newly elected leaders of the AFL-CIO, **left to right:** President John J. Sweeney, Executive Vice President Linda Chavez-Thompson and Secretary-Treasurer Richard L. Trumka.

American Federation of State, County and Municipal Employees to the newly created office of Executive Vice President.

Canadian District Councils Joint Conference

On the 2nd, 3rd and 4th of November, 1995, the three District Councils in Canada (District Council of Western Canada, District Council of Ontario and the District Council of Eastern Canada) attended joint meetings at the Empress Hotel in Victoria, British Columbia. This conference, the first of its kind, was held to discuss the numerous problems facing

Ironworkers across Canada. At the same time ideas were exchanged by those in attendance as to how to deal with problems such as non-union and labour legislative changes.

General President West who chaired one of the meetings addressed the delegates on the current status and future direction of the International as it pertains to the strengthening of the Iron Workers Union. Informative reports were also given by General Secretary LeRoy E. Worley and General Treasurer James E. Cole. Further reports were given by department heads of the International Association and District Council Presidents. The key thrust of the conference was communication and therein lies its success. By communicating and working together at all levels, we can as

Picture includes the attendees at the Canadian Conference: **Left to right 1st row:** Marty Byrne, Assistant to President West; Bill Howard, Asst. B/A, LU 700; Michael Brennan, Ex. Director, IPAL; Jim Willis, VP; James Cole, General Treasurer; Jake West, General President; Steve Cooper, Ex. Director, Safety; Jim Phair, VP; Vince Ryan, Ex. Director of Jurisdiction; Charles Hill, Assistant to General Secretary; Fred Summers, Executive Director of Organization; Don Beley, B/A, LU 728; Graham Donaldson, B/A, LU 643. **Left to right 2nd row:** Rene Wattell, Assistant B/A, LU 712; Gus Zaba, Retired G.O.; Donald O'Reilly, Retired VP; David Wade, B/A, LU 764; Dennis Toney, Ex. Director of Shopmen's Division; Greg Zaba, G.O.; Donald Oshanek, G.O.; Rod MacLennon, B/A, LU 752; Don Fortin, G.O.; Egbert Basque, B/A, LU 842; Roy Williams, Ex. Director, DOAMM; Stephen Allen, Pres., LU 643. **From left to right 3rd row:** Tom O'Neill, Asst. B/A, LU 712; Don Melvin, B/A, LU 765; Frank Knutsen, Retired Dist. Rep.; Perley Holmes, LU 97; Sherridan Godwin, Pres., LU 771; Glen Shauf, Pres., LU 838; Jim LaJeunesse, Pres., LU 786; Gord Verdecchia, B/A, LU 786; John Sciandra, G.O.; Robert Stoppell, Pres., LU 759; Glen O'Neill, B/A, LU 725; Jacques Dubois, B/A, LU 771; Darrell Donecz, Pres., LU 720; Bruce Madoche, B/A, LU 720. **From left to right back row:** Mike Clark, Dist. Rep.; Bob Scott, Pres., LU 805; Wayne Foot, Pres., LU 97; Roger Booth, Ontario T.I.; Ted Rignanesi, B/A, LU 805; Robert Beller, FST, LU 838; Gary Caroline, Ontario District Council Lawyer; Gary Short, B/A, LU 97; Aaron Murphy, B/A, LU 721; Bert Royer, B/A, LU 771; Greg Michaluk, B/A, LU 700; Roger Bernier, Ex., LU 771; Fred Marr, G.O.

Ironworkers overcome all adversity. This will ultimately result in the certain growth and strengthening of the Ironworkers trade and our International Union.

Some Legal Observations as We Move Into the 2nd 100 Years.

Victor Van Bourg, General Counsel for the International Association had some observations as the Iron Workers Union completed 100 years as an organization. He said, "The beginning of the tenure of President West occurred at the time when the labor laws of the United States as they affect collective bargaining, organizing and labor management relations, were at their most regressive anti-union and pro-management level since the New Deal Days of the 1930's. Functionally, the National Labor Relations Board became irrelevant to the real world of the work place. The First Amendment rights to freedom of speech and the peaceful dissemination of ideas was severely trampled when it came to rights of unions and union members.

"The technological revolution and the 'global economy' combined with an almost complete breakdown of job protection allowed many corporations to replace workers with technological changes and wholesale exportation of jobs to low wage countries on an unprecedented vast scale. At the same time, the productivity of American workers improved on a similar unprecedented and vast scale while their real wages suffered a reduction of from

4 to 10 percent per annum. Neither workers nor their unions could look to the labor laws to protect them during their fall from the 'middle class' to a 'class' as yet unnamed.

Victor VanBourg
General Counsel

"Even though we start the second 100 years with the most anti-union federal government in more than 60 years, this International Association led by General President Jake West and its legal staff have undertaken an aggressive program, in cooperation with other unions and the AFL-CIO, to seek repeal of the Taft Hartley Act and a recognition that laws prohibiting a peaceful secondary boycott are immoral, unjust and unconstitutional. In addition, laws will be sought and interpretations will be urged which will return jobs to the United States, prohibit runaway shops and repeal those provisions of NAFTA, GATT and other agreements which encourage the runaway shop.

"Finally, part of the legal program of the International Association is to develop new and more aggressive methods of organizing which fall beyond the scope of legal prohibition. Part of this organizing program includes a strategy dealing with expanded steel export and realistic limitations on steel imports so that 'fair trade' becomes a reality. This legal strategy for the United States and Canada is based upon a firm belief that Ironworkers (and all other North American workers) can compete with anyone in the world on a level playing field and on the notion that it is perfectly legal to boycott foreign goods or domestic goods produced by child labor, convict labor and sub-standard wage labor. This legal strategy recognizes that today labor laws in Canada and most of its Provinces are less anti-union than the laws of the United States, but Canadian corporations are very anxious to be just as anti-union as the United States and we will resist that ambition to the best of our ability."

One Hundred Years of Our Proud History

This book has not only taken the reader through 100 years of struggles and accomplishments of the International Association of Bridge, Structural and Ornamental Iron Workers, AFL-CIO, but the earlier years that led up to the formation of this great organization. General President Jake West, in the President's page of the January, 1996 issue of *The Ironworker* magazine very eloquently summarized the history of this great organization.

"One hundred years later we must reflect back to the sixteen brave delegates who formed this great Union on February 4, 1896. As we look back through our distinguished history, there's no doubt you will realize as I do that our Union's struggle for recognition and respect involved tremendous personal sacrifice by our forefathers who had to overcome never-ending incredible obstacles. We are truly standing on the shoulders of these giant men and women who risked everything, even their lives when necessary, so that we may today enjoy the fruits of our labor.

"Some of our younger members, as well as our own children, may not be aware of the historical contributions that were made by our progressive union members

Jake West,
General President

in the United States and Canada to keep our two great nations economically strong and constitutionally free. Our old timers and straight line ancestors fought the wars, built the skyscrapers and bridges, and manned the picket lines to protect freedom for our nations as well as their work sites.

"Our forefathers suffered the blows of Pinkerton detectives and other hired thugs that the robber barons of the corporate monopolistic trusts were using to crush unions. These brave men are the reason we enjoy the lifestyle we have today. Labor has correctly been described as the stabilizing force that is preventing our society from being divided into the very rich and the very poor. The gains that unions have been able to achieve have brought benefits, direct and indirect, to the entire public as a whole, regardless of personal union membership.

"As we look to a new century, the goals we have achieved and the challenges we must face will only be accomplished through union solidarity. Where we have gone as an organization, and what we have painstakingly accomplished in the past one hundred years, will chart the path for the future. The groundwork has been laid; our task now is to continue the benefit programs that the Ironworkers before us so courageously fought for, which we enjoy today. As we enter our second century let us continue to rally around this great organization like never before.

"We need to keep telling our friends and enemies alike that organized labor represents the best hope for making both our nations, the United States and Canada, greater than ever before. I know there are many challenges ahead and that we face much uncertainty, but as long as we stick to the traditions of the trade union movement that made us strong throughout the past one hundred years, we will triumph. Let's stand proud of the legacy that was passed on to us, and draw from that raw strength for the encouragement to carry their work forward into the Iron Workers International Union's second century."

THE IRONWORKERS

A 100th Anniversary

1896 1996

INTERNATIONAL ASSOCIATION OF BRIDGE, STRUCTURAL AND ORNAMENTAL IRON WORKERS

A Gallery
of
International
Officers

1896 - 1996

General Presidents

Edward J. Ryan
Local No. 7
Boston, MA
1896 - 1899

John T. Butler
Local No. 6
Buffalo, NY
1899 - 1900

Frank Buchanan
Local No. 1
Chicago, IL
1901 - 1905

Frank M. Ryan
Local No. 1
Chicago, IL
1905 - 1914

James E. McClory
Local No. 17
Cleveland, OH
1914 - 1918

Paul J. Morrin
Local No. 18
St. Louis, MO
1918 - 1948

John H. Lyons, Sr.
Local No. 17
Cleveland, OH
1948 - 1961

John H. Lyons, Jr.
Local No. 5
Washington, D.C.
1961 - 1985

Juel D. Drake
Local No. 229
San Diego, CA
1985 - 1989

Jake West
Local No. 433
Los Angeles, CA
1989 -

Secretary-Treasurers

James G. Crowley
Local No. 1
Chicago, IL
1896- 1897

William E. Barry
Local No. 2
New York, N.Y.
1897 - 1898

J.W. Prayle
Local No. 3
Pittsburgh, PA
1899 - 1900

D.F. McIntyre
Local No. 3
Pittsburgh, PA
1901- 1902

J.W. Johnston
Local No. 2
New York, N.Y.
1902 - 1903

J.J. McNamara
Local No. 17
Cleveland, OH
1904 - 1912

H.S. Hockin
Local No. 25
Detroit, MI
1911 - 1912

J.E. McClory
Local No. 17
Cleveland, OH
1912 - 1913

Harry Jones
Local No. 40
New York, N.Y.
1913 - 1925

W.J. McCain
Local No. 10
Kansas City, MO
1925 - 1928

General Secretaries

W.J. McCain
Local No. 10
Kansas City, MO
1928 - 1939

John H. Lyons, Sr.
Local No. 17
Cleveland, OH
1939 - 1948

James R. Downes
Local No. 550
Cleveland, OH
1949 - 1971

Juel D. Drake
Local No. 229
San Diego, CA
1971 - 1985

Jake West
Local No. 433
Los Angeles, CA
1985 - 1989

LeRoy E. Worley
Local No. 29
Portland, OR
1989 -

General Treasurers

J.H. Lyons Sr.
Local No. 17
Cleveland, OH
1928 - 1939

John H. Dempsey
Local No. 44
Cinncinati, OH
1939 - 1958

James V. Cole
Local No. 40
New York, NY
1959 - 1974

John McKean
Local No. 27
Salt Lake City, UT
1974 - 1978

Charles Anding
Local No. 710
Monroe, LA
1978 - 1983

John Traylor
Local No. 16
Baltimore, MD
1983 - 1985

James E. Cole
Local No. 40
New York, NY
1985 -

General Vice Presidents

John Brady
Local No. 2
New York, NY
1896 - 1902

No
Photo
Available

M. Hanna
Local No. 6
Buffalo, NY
1896 - 1901

C.F. Lyons
Local No. 17
Cleveland, OH
1901 - 1902

J.T. Butler
Local No. 6
Buffalo, NY
1902 - 1906
1909 - 1913

Ernest L. Warden
Local No. 15
Hartford, CN
1902 - 1904

Wm. J. McCain
Local No. 10
Kansas City, MO
1903 - 1904

J.J. McNamara
Local No. 17
Cleveland, OH
1903 - 1904

E.A. Clancy
Local No. 377
San Francisco, CA
1904 - 1911

J.H. Barry
Local No. 18
St. Louis, MO
1906 - 1909

H.S. Hockin
Local No. 25
Detroit, MI
1911 - 1912

J.E. McClory
Local No. 17
Cleveland, OH
1913 - 1914

P.J. Morrin
Local No. 18
St. Louis, MO
1913 - 1914

General Vice Presidents

J.A. Johnston
Local No. 11
Newark, NJ
1914 - 1924

W.J. McCain
Local No. 10
Kansas City, MO
1914 - 1928

Ben Osborn
Local No. 29
Portland, OR
1914 - 1924

Frank McKinney
Local No. 75
Phoenix, AR
1914 - 1916

D.J. O'Shea
Local No. 7
Boston, MA
1914 - 1930

P. Vaughn
Local No. 78
San Francisco, CA
1914 - 1917

John McMullen
Local No. 1
Chicago, IL
1915 - 1924

Thos. Scahill
Local No. 377
San Francisco, CA
1917 - 1924

Michael C. Artery
Local No. 136
Chicago, IL
1922 - 1932

P.L. Arci
Local No. 274
Brooklyn, NY
1922 - 1924

D.J. Brophy
Local No. 307
Montreal, Que; CAN
1922 - 1924

No
Photo
Available

Theo. M. Brandle
Local No. 45
Jersey City, NJ
1924 - 1927

George McTague
Local No. 377
San Francisco, CA
1924 - 1936

J. Arthur Evensen
Local No. 1
Chicago, IL
1924 - 1954

William H. Pope
Local No. 7
Boston, MA
1924 - 1947

George Ashley
Local No. 347
Windsor, Ont; CA
1924 - 1928

Ben C. Pitts
Local No. 84
Houston, TX
1924 - 1935

John M. Schilling
Local No. 52
New York, NY
1928 - 1936

John T. Fitzpatrick
Local No. 387
Atlanta, GA
1928 - 1944

B.J. Hiscock
Local No. 307
Montreal, Que; CN
1928 - 1932

William P. McGinn
Local No. 301
Charleston, WV
1932 - 1934

Dan M. Gayton
Local No. 3
Pittsburgh, PA
1932 - 1952

William F. Bauers
Local No. 6
Buffalo, NY
1932 - 1961

Thomas L. Chambers
Local No. 377
San Francisco, CA
1936 - 1937

General Vice Presidents

Joseph F. Boyen
Local No. 580
New York, NY
1936 - 1965

Gay Borelli
Local No. 405
Philadelphia, PA
1936 - 1969

Benjamin A. Murray
Local No. 58
New Orleans, LA
1936 - 1959

Clyde F. Strickland
Local No. 387
Atlanta, GA
1940 - 1958

E. M. Woods
Local No. 377
San Francisco, CA
1940 - 1960

William J. Reynolds
Local No. 7
Boston, MA
1948 - 1956

John L. McCarthy
Local No. 392
East St. Louis, IL
1952 - 1975

E.G. Glazener
Local No. 539
Birmingham, AL
1952 - 1970

Juel D. Drake
Local no. 229
San Diego, CA
1956 - 1970

John H. Lyons Jr
Local No. 5
Washington, D.C.
1958 - 1961

LaVerne Smith
Local No. 48
Oklahoma City, OK
1959 - 1972

Robert V. Poole
Local No. 340
Battle Creek, MI
1959 - 1974

244

General Vice Presidents

Robert E.P. Cooney
Local No. 17
Cleveland, OH
1961 - 1985

Hugh Williamson
Local No. 84
Houston, TX
1961 - 1986

John F. Walsh
Local No. 272
Miami, FL
1966 - 1985

Leonard Mahoney
Local No. 401
Philadelphia, PA
1970 - 1984

A. S. Goodwin
Local No. 620
Tulsa, OK
1970 - 1988

Dale M. Ray
Local No. 378
Oakland, CA
1971 - 1983

Matthew Taylor
Local No. 3
Pittsburgh, PA
1973 - 1986

J.W. Merritt
Local No. 709
Savannah, GA
1974 - 1989

Thomas Clarkson
Local No. 40
New York City, NY
1976 - 1988

Jake West
Local No. 433
Los Angeles, CA
1983 - 1985

Lial Field
Local No. 392
East St. Louis, MO
1984 - 1985

LeRoy E. Worley
Local No. 29
Portland, OR
1985 - 1989

General Vice Presidents

William H. Sullivan
Local No. 3
Pittsburgh, PA
1985 - 1995

James J. Willis
Local No. 6
Buffalo, NY
1985 -

James Martin
Local No. 66
San Antonio, TX
1986 -

O.C. Yancy
Local No. 24
Spokane, WA
1986 - 1994

Fhane B. Jones
Local No. 399
Camden, NJ
1986 -

Donald O'Reilly
Local No. 97
Vancouver, B.C.
1988 - 1992

Richard Zampa
Local No. 378
Oakland, CA
1989 -

Raymond J. Robertson
Local No. 63
Chicago, IL
1989 -

Alan Simmons
Local No. 361
Brooklyn, NY
1989 -

James D. Phair
Local No. 700
Windsor, ON
1992 -

Joseph J. Hunt
Local No. 396
St. Louis, MO
1994 -

Joseph M. Quilty
Local No. 7
Boston, MA
1994 -

One Hundred Years of Proud History

Local Union
Directories
of
Yesteryear

CORRESPONDENCE.

The Bridgemen's Magazine Disclaims Responsibility for Opinions Expressed by
: : : Correspondents. : : :

SECRETARY McINTYRE'S LIST.

DUQUESNE, PA., March 13.

Editor Bridgemen's Magazine:

As it is now drawing towards the first of May, and consequently increasing the work of this office, you will excuse any lengthy communication at this time. As yourself and the secretaries are asking for a list of the Locals and their secretaries' addresses I will furnish you with what I have at hand, as I believe this will be as interesting as anything I could write for you and the members in general.

Local No. 1, Chicago—President and business agent, W. E. Francis; secretary, N. J. Darragh. Address 198 East Madison street. Meets every Wednesday at 198 East Madison street.

Local No. 2, New York—President, Robert E. Neidig; secretary, R. B. Davison. Address 147 West Thirty-second street. Meets every Friday at 147 West Thirty-second street.

Local No. 3, Pittsburg, Pa.—President, John Eder; secretary, John McCabe, 510 Wylie avenue. Meets every Thursday at 510 Wylie avenue.

Local No. 4, Boston, Mass.—President, J. Franklin Carr; secretary, Ed J. Ryan, 9 Blue Hill avenue. Meets second and fourth Tuesdays at Carroll Hall.

Local No. 5, Washington, D. C.—President and business agent, Charles W. Winslow; secretary, Charles E. Barbour, 1212 Potomac street. Meets every Friday.

Local No. 6, Buffalo, N. Y.—President, D. Gallagher; secretary, Ed Liptrott, 189 Cedar street. Meets every Friday at Council Hall, Huron and Ellicott streets.

Local No. 7, Boston—President and business agent, F. C. Webb; secretary, M. Connolly, No. 2 Willow court, Dorchester, Mass. Meets every Monday at 45 Elliott street.

Local No. 8, Milwaukee, Wis.—President, John Duhig; secretary, M. J. Shea, 918 Clybourn street. Meets every Friday at 413 East Water street.

Local No. 10, Kansas City, Mo.—President, William E. Wise; secretary and business agent, W. J. McCain, 823 Central street. Meets every Friday at 823 Central street.

Local No. 11, Newark, N. J.—President, James Bannister; secretary, Joel A. Giles, 67 Summit street. Meets every Friday at 94 Market street.

Local No. 12, Albany, N. Y.—President, R. S. Niblock; secretary, Guy Ross, 66 Livingston avenue. Meets first, second and third Mondays at Grand Army Hall, Broadway and Hudson avenues.

Local No. 13, Philadelphia—President, James Wright; secretary, Moulton H. Davis, 1502 Swain street. Meets every Thursday at 707 North Broad street.

Local No. 16, Baltimore, Md.—President, Frank Lee; secretary, James N. Orr, 2658 Bernard street. Meets every Monday at 702 East Baltimore street.

Local No. 17, Cleveland—President, ————; secretary, John H. Keith, 63 Hurd street. Meets every Monday at Arch Hall, 393 Ontario street.

Local No. 18, St. Louis, Mo.—President, ————; secretary, John P. Finnegan, 1423 North Twenty-fourth street. Meets first and third Tuesdays at 640 Market street.

Local No. 19, Minneapolis—President and business agent, James G. Williams; secretary, Thomas G. McCurrin, 1823 Jackson street, N. E. Meets first and third Fridays at 36 Sixth street, South.

Local No. 20, Wheeling, W. Va.—President, John Taylor; secretary, Howard F. Smith, 4100 Water street. Meets every Wednesday at Odd Fellow's Hall.

Local No. 21, Omaha, Neb.—President, Thomas J. Kennedy; secretary, Howard Eliason, 2880 Binney street. Meets every Tuesday at Fifteenth and Dodge streets.

Local No. 22, Indianapolis — President, Samuel D. Ray; secretary, Charles E. Covert, 728 Germania avenue. Meets every Monday at 247 East Washington street.

Local No. 23, Scranton, Pa.—President, Joseph Donohue; secretary, Michael Hannon, 710 Stone avenue. Meets second and fourth Thursdays at 316 Washington avenue.

Local No. 24, Colorado Springs, Col.—President and business agent, P. L. Beck; secretary, F. T. Kiser, 23 West Rio Grande avenue. Meets every Monday.

Local No. 25, Detroit, Mich.—President, ————; secretary, John T. Lee, 255 Beaubien street.

Local No. 26, San Francisco—President, D. McEatchen; secretary, W. C. Allen, Fruitvale, Alameda county. Meets every Sunday at 2:30 p. m. at 46 Stewart street.

Local No. 27, Salt Lake City—President, Clarence Walton; secretary, A. H. Taylor, box 212, Salt Lake City. Meets second and fourth Saturdays at Labor Hall.

Local No. 28, Richmond, Va.—President, Joseph C. Reid; secretary, John J. Campodonico, 104 South Eighth street. Meets every Thursday.

Local No. 29, Portland, Ore.—President, ————; secretary, F. H. Taylor, 850 Corbett street.

Local No. 30., Des Moines, Iowa—President, F. J. Page; secretary, Charles N. Arnfield, 1413 Grand avenue.

International executive board:—President, Frank Buchanan, 464 Racine avenue, Chicago; vice president, John Boday, 155 Court street, Brooklyn, N. Y.; Wm. McIlwaine, 726 Moore street, Philadelphia, Pa.; John H. Carr, 17 Cottage Terrace, Boston, Mass.; George Flears, 803 8th street South, Minneapolis, Minn.; James Trainer, 3301 La Salle street, St. Louis, Mo.; John McCabe, 523 8th avenue, Homestead, Pa.

OFFICIAL DIRECTORY
International Association of Bridge and Structural Iron Workers

Headquarters, Rooms 422-424 American Central Life Building, Indianapolis, Ind.
Long Distance Telephone, Main 4014

OFFICERS

F. M. RYAN, President, American Central Life Building, Indianapolis, Ind.
J. E. McCLORY, First Vice-President, 4721 Franklin Ave., N. W., Cleveland, Ohio.
P. J. MORRIN, Second Vice-President, 13th and Chouteau Ave., St. Louis, Mo.
HARRY JONES, Secretary-Treasurer, American Central Life Building, Indianapolis, Ind.

EXECUTIVE BOARD

P. Vaughan, 80 Mizpah Ave., San Francisco, Cal.   Frank McKinney, Box 93, Clarkesdale, Ariz.
J. A. Johnston, 103 Market St., Newark, N. J.   D. J. O'Shea, Ericson Place, Niagara Falls, N.Y.

DISTRICT COUNCIL OF SAN FRANCISCO AND VICINITY

J. D. Barnes, President.   W. O. Bjerke, 395 Capp St., Secretary-Treasurer.
Local No. 31—San Francisco, Cal.   Local No. 78—San Francisco, Cal.
Local No. 77—San Francisco, Cal.   Local No. 117—Oakland, Cal.
Local No. 118—Sacramento, Cal.

LOCAL UNIONS

P, President; R S, Recording Secretary; F S, Financial Secretary; T, Treasurer.

1, Chicago, Ill.—Meets Thursday evenings at Hod Carriers' Hall, 814 W. Harrison st., Tel. Mon. 3643.
Robt. L. Jahncke...................P
Michael McDonald..................R S
R. H. Houlihan, 814 W. Harrison st....F S

3, Pittsburg, Pa. (Bridge, Structural and Ornamental)—Meets Monday evenings at 111 Smithfield st.
Jas. Conway.......................P
Wm. Dolbow.......................R S
John Corcoran, 909 Lamond st..........F S

4, Toronto, Ont.—Meets first and third Tuesdays at Labor Temple.
A. Wilson.........................P
W. B. Gracie......................R S
P. Smithson, 297 Symington ave....F S & B A

5, Washington, D. C.—Meets every Friday night at Costello's Hall, 610 G st. N. W.
William Carpenter.................P
C. R. Rudasill....................R S
Chas. Sherrier....................T
J. Enoch Phillips, 1010 7th st. S. W....F S

6, Buffalo, N. Y.—Meets Friday evenings at Council Hall, cor. Ellicott and Huron sts.
Michael Meegan...................P
Alfred Wright.....................R S
A. C. Bannister, 19 Columbus Place....F S

7, Boston, Mass.—Meets every Monday at 386 Harrison ave.
J. J. Hurley......................P
H. B. Sullivan....................R S
Richard Grant, 189 Sheridan ave., Medford, Mass..........................F S

8, Milwaukee, Wis.—Meets every Tuesday evening at Labor Temple, Brisbane Hall, 6th and Chestnut sts.
F. H. Kolas.......................P
Adam Sladky......................R S
John Wallace, 528 Chestnut st.....F S & B A

9, Niagara Falls, N. Y.—Meets every Monday night at C. M. B. A. Hall, 217 Falls st.
J. T. Butler......................P
W. Patterson......................R S
Dan J. O'Shea, City Line..........F S & T

10, Kansas City, Mo.—Meets Wednesday evenings at Labor Temple, 14th and Woodland.
Geo. Steffe.......................P
J. G. Williams....................R S
Wm. T. Sheehan, Labor Temple, 1400 Woodland ave...............F S & B A

11, Newark, N. J.—Meets Friday evenings at 66 So. Orange ave.
Wm. Brown........................P
Chas. Becker......................R S
John A. Johnston, 103 Market st.......F S

12, Albany, N. Y.—Meets second and fourth Monday evenings at 67-69 S. Pearl st.
J. J. Carroll.....................P
Joe Keefe.........................R S
Bert Hall, 708 State st...............F S

13, Philadelphia, Pa.—Meets Thursday evening at Lenar's Hall, 9th and Springarden sts. Office 1134 Vine st., Bell Phone Walnut 2145.
Thos. Malone......................P
James Gallamore...................R S
Wm. Smith, 1134 Vine st..........F S & T

14, Spokane, Wash.—Meets every Wednesday night at Waiters' Hall, 722 1st ave.
Levy Mitchell.....................P
T. A. Weaver......................R S
Chas. Sears, Box 419...........F S & B A

15, Hartford, Conn.—Meets second and fourth Wednesdays at 11 Central Row.
J. Brennan........................P
E. J. O'Neil......................R S
Sam Carlisle, P. O. Box 1083.F S & T & B A

16, Baltimore, Md.—Meets Friday evenings at 1023 E. Baltimore st., Phone St. Paul 7613.
Thos. E. Grove....................P
David Hennebery...................R S
J. J. Walker, 827 So. Milton ave...F S & T

17, Cleveland, O.—Meets Tuesday evenings at 310 Prospect av. S.E., Phone, Bell, Main 2419.
Chas. McCabe......................P
Frank Lynch.......................R S
Chas. Smith, 310 Prospect ave. S. E....F S

18, St. Louis, Mo.—Meets at new Club Hall 31st st. and Chouteau ave., every Friday evening. Phone Olive 1510, Kin. Cent. 5622.
John Rau..............................P
F. D. Hall............................R S
D. A. Cowan, 13th st. and Chouteau ave.
    F S & T

19, Minneapolis, Minn.—Meets first and third Friday nights at 26 Wash. ave. So.
Mike Keenan...........................P
J. T. Turner..........................R S
Thos. Kelly, 26 Wash. ave. So....F S & B A

20, Wheeling, W. Va.—Meets every Tuesday at Ohio Valley Trades and Labor Assembly Hall, 1515 Market st.
H. S. Calvert.........................P
S. J. Cuddihy, 216 So. 7th st., Martins Ferry, Ohio....................F S & T

21, Omaha, Neb.—Meets every Tuesday evening at Bartenders' Hall, 214 So. 14th st.
R. B. Donahoe.........................P
A. Black..............................R S
E. F. Voboril, 1211 Arbor st......F S & T

22, Indianapolis, Ind.—Meets Friday evening at 138 West Washington st.
F. J. Sherman.........................P
L. M. Shepherd........................R S
Al Mundee, 138 W. Wash. st......F S & B A

23, Scranton, Pa.—Meets every 1st and 3rd Tuesday evening at 226 Wyoming ave.
Thos. McLaughlin......................P
W. H. Tennis..........................R S
John McConnell, 821 Hemlock st.......F S

24, Denver, Colo.—Meets first and third Wednesday evenings at Room 103 B T Club.
W. J. Hamilton........................P
M. H. Ryan............................R S
M. H. Ryan, 147 Osceola st.......F S & T

25, Detroit, Mich.—Meets Monday evening at 140 First st.
Sam Tobin.............................P
Jno. Gazley ....R S
L. A. Noel, 249 12th st............F S & T

27, Salt Lake City, Utah.—Meets second and fourth Wednesday at Labor Temple.
Edw. Hagerty..........................P
D. M. Fowler..........................R S
W. O. Shope, Labor Temple......F S & B A

28, Richmond, Va.—Meets every Monday evening at Labor Temple Hall, cor. Sixth and Marshall sts.
J. G. Thomas..........................P
John C. Smith.........................V P
Chas. F. Maynes, 516 N. 6th st....R & F S

29, Portland, Ore.—Meets Tuesday evenings at 162½ Second st.
J. E. Fitzgibbons.....................P
Chas. Barrett.........................R S
Ben Osborne, 162½ Second st.....F S & B A

31, San Francisco, Cal. (Bridge and Structural Iron Workers, Riggers and Machinery Movers).—Meets Monday evenings at Metal Workers' Hall, 224 Guerrero st.
A. Olson..............................P
J. I. Petrie..........................R S
Paul Abel, 209 A. Guerrero st.........F S

32, Duluth, Minn.—Meets second and fourth Wednesday evenings at Sloan's Hall.
Wm. Furvey............................P
J. A. Webber..........................R S
Peter G lant, 813 Fifth ave., East.....F S

33, Rochester, N. Y.—Meets every Tuesday night at 18 Andrew st.
John Fraynor..........................P
Wm. Irwin.............................R S
J. P. Cary, 42 Exchange st........F S & T

34, Atlanta, Ga.—Meets 1st and 3rd Monday nights at Cumberland Hotel, cor. Broad and Marietta sts.
Robt. Rains...........................P
D. V. Allen...........................R S & B A
Robt. Rains, Box 338..............F S & T

35, Brooklyn, N. Y.—Meets every Friday night at Arcanum Hall, 407 Bridge st.
Thomas Joy............................P
J. P. Gillen..........................R S
Robert Hart, 100 6th st., Union Course..F S

36, Easton, Pa.—Meets second and fourth Sundays at Journal bldg., 234 Church st.
John Coyle............................P
A. W. Smith, R. F. D. No. 5...........F S

37, Providence, R. I.—Meets first and third Thursdays at 72 Weybossett st.
Wm. J. Powers.........................P
J. O'Rourke...........................R S
H. W. Potter, 51 Leonard ave., East Providence, R. I....................F S & T

40, New York, N. Y.—Meets Wednesday evening at 154 E. 54th st.
Thomas Nolan..........................P
W. E. Quinn...........................R S
Martin Callon, 154 E. 54th st...........F S

41, New Orleans, La. (Piledrivers).—Meets 2nd and 4th Thursdays at 128 Exchange Place.
Jesse Clark...........................P
M. Powers.............................R S
V. Cassreino, 2824 St. Thomas st....F S & T

43, St. Louis, Mo. (Piledrivers).—Meets every Thursday evening at 13th st. and Chouteau ave.
Sam Robertson.........................P
Frank Harris..........................R S
J. H. McFarland, 1418 St. Louis ave..F S & T

44, Cincinnati, O.—Meets every Monday night at Central Turner Hall, 1407 Walnut st.
Peter J. Clinton......................P
Joe Anslinger.........................R S
Chas. Mueller, 318 Central ave........F S

45, Jersey City, N. J.—Meets Friday evenings at Hawkes Hall, 13th and Erie sts.
Joe Bradley...........................P
Thos. Dodge...........................R S & T
Dan Unix, 32 W. 44th st., Bayonne, N. J...F S

46, Springfield, Ill.—Meets second and fourth Wednesdays at 210½ S. 5th st.
L. A. Nunes...........................P
Frank Wilson, 311 Logan ave...........F S

47, Milwaukee, Wis. (Piledrivers, Machinery Movers and Derrickmen).—Meets first and third Mondays at Harmonie Hall, 387 First ave.
Ed. Daly..............................P
P. O'Connor...........................R S
Walter Bogs, 610 Hanover st.......F S & T

49, Utica, N. Y.—Meets fourth Thursday evening at Labor Temple, cor. Charlott and Deveran sts.
Edw. Cassidy............................P
John Giffons............................R S
E. A. Connolly, Oxford Road, New Hartford, N. Y............................F S

51, Los Angeles, Cal.—Meets every Tuesday evening at Labor Hall, 538 Maple ave.
Bert Kolburn............................P
E. G. Brown ....T
M. L. Holmes, 540 Maple ave............F S

52, New York, N. Y. (Finishers).—Meets Friday evening, Labor Temple, 243 East 84th st. Day Room, 201 East 44th st.
Wm. O'Rourke............................P
Henry C. Wolf............................R S
John Schilling, 201 East 44th st.........F S

53, Ft. William, Ont.—Meets first and third Friday, Trades and Labor Hall, May st.
Angus McLeod............................P
Rod Young............................T
Wm. Preston............................R S
Wm. Higgins, 116 South Brodie st........F S

55, Toledo, O.—Meets Monday evening at Central Labor Hall, 314 Cherry st.
Wm. Moore............................P
Frank Carraher............................R S
A. Fryman, 242 Dearborn ave.....F S & T

57, Worcester, Mass.—Meets first and third Thursday at 419 Main st.
Wm J. O'Donnell............................P
Harry Howarth, 511 Southbridge st....R S
W. S. DeLany, 8 Ashton st............F S

58, New Orleans, La.—Meets every Wednesday at 8 p. m., 407 Carondelet st.
John Teuteberg............................P
J. P. Eden............................R S
Jno. W. Meyer, 2239 St. Philip st........F S

59, Dallas, Tex.—Meets every Thursday in Electric Workers' Hall.
A. W. Yount............................P
J. A. Harnell............................T & R S
Chas. A. Theime, 1608 Patterson av..F S &BA

60, Syracuse, N. Y.—Meets first and third Friday evenings at Smith Hall, 312 S. State st
Frank Shea............................P
Pred Ebersole............................R S
Joseph Teatom, 307 Gifford st.....F S & T

63, Chicago, Ill. (Architectural Iron Workers).—Meets every second and fourth Thursday at 365 W. Madison st.
Edw. Ryan............................P
Richard Hedberg............................R S
Ed. Tolf, 3007 Edgewood ave...........F S

66, San Antonio, Tex.—Meets every second and fourth Sundays at 9 a. m. at Trades Council Hall.
W. R. Conway............................P
W. R. Tomlinson............................R S
W. J. Manger, R. F. D. No.1,Box 141.F S & T

67, Des Moines, Ia.—Meets second and fourth Wednesday, 411 Eighth st., West City.
Al Way............................P
Silas Taft............................R S
D. W. Miller, 1646 Maple st......F S & T

68, Trenton, N. J.—Meets first and third Wednesday at Ribsom Bldg.
Jos. McNerney............................P
Wm. Hogan............................R S & B A
Frank Miller, 1108 Lamberton st.....F S & T

70, Louisville, Ky.—Meets 2nd and 4th Mondays at Beck's Hall, 1st and Jefferson sts.
J. Edlin............................P
Wm. Donovan............................R S
J. B. Potts, Room 16, Kenyon Bldg..F S & T

75, Miami, Ariz.—Meets every Tuesday night at Miami Hall.
O. K. McLindon............................P
John Kelley............................T
G. F. S. Caswell............................R S
King Pittman, Box 1081..........F S & B A

77, San Francisco, Cal. (Piledrivers and Bridge and Structural Iron Workers).—Meets every Wednesday evening at 457 Bryant st.
Don Cameron............................P
A. L. McDonald............................R S
A. L. McDonald, 457 Bryant st....F S & T

78, San Francisco, Cal. (Finishers).—Meets Wednesday evening at 200 Guerrero st.
John A. Hoffman............................P
Ben C. Williams............................R S
Thos. Scahill, 200 Guerrero st..........F S

79, Norfolk, Va.—Meets every Thursday evening at Plumbers' Hall, 427 Williams st.
G. A. Burke............................P
F. E. Lawless............................R S
P. C. Carlisle, 219 Arlington Place..F S & T

81, Anaconda, Mont.—Meets every second and fourth Friday nights at 7:30 p. m., at Moose Hall, 124 E. Commercial.
L. B. Crosswhite............................P
Lee Johnson............................R S
H. Bothwell, 600 Cedar st..........F S & T

82, Winnipeg, Man.—Meets second and fourth Wednesdays at Labor Temple, James st.
A. Young............................P
Jas. Dixon............................R S
Wm. H. Blow, Box 924..........F S & B A

84, Houston, Tex.—Meets every Wednesday at A. O. U. W. Hall.
L. W. Francis............................P
J. U. Riley............................R S
R. L. Blades, Capitol Hotel............F S

86, Seattle, Wash.—Meets every Thursday evening at Labor Temple, Sixth and University.
H. Pullum............................P
Geo. Balbaugh............................R S
Scoty Hofeditz, Labor Temple....F S & B A

89, Cedar Rapids, Ia.—Meets Thursday nights at Federation Hall.
Harry White............................P
Wm. Bluski............................R S
B. T. Flaherty, 1812 6th st. East........F S

92, Birmingham, Ala.—Meets every Wednesday night at 8 p. m., 2008½ Third ave.
N. A. Campbell............................P
A. G. Kelly............................R S & T
E. S. Ingram, Box 490..........F S & B A

93, Montreal, Canada.—Meets every Monday at Labor Temple, 301 St. Dominique st. Phone, Bell, East 5633.
A. Binnette.................................P
D. Duval..................................R S
Jos. M. Belanger, 279 First ave., Vianville
................................F S & T

94, St. Paul, Minn.—Meets second and fourth Friday evenings of each month at Federation Hall, 309 Wabasha st.
Mike Broderick...........................P
Sam Dahlquist...........................R S
Walter Bock, 756 Jessamine st., Tri-State phone 21380...................F S

97, Vancouver, B. C.—Meets every Monday night at Labor Temple.
W. G. Cawley.............................P
Pete Neilson.............................R S
Wm. L. Yule, Box 1196...........F S & T

98, Pueblo, Colo.—Meets 1st and 3rd Thursday, at B. T. C. Hall.
P. H. O'Neal...............................P
H. G. Brosius............................R S
W. E. Palmer, 2405 Osman ave...F S & B A

99, Seattle, Wash. (Finishers).—Meets first and third Friday evenings at Labor Temple.
Roy McElhowe............................P
Arthur Boncher.........................R S
L. Lang, 3205 Nineteenth ave. So....F S & T

101, New York, N. Y. (Foremen).—Meets first and third Thursdays at 300 Eighth ave.
Wm. Ritchie..............................P
O. N. Lowe..............................R S
Wm. Becker, 104 E. 124th st...........F S

102, San Diego, Cal. (Bridge, Structural and Atchitectural Iron Workers).—Meets every Thursday at 8 p. m. at Labor Temple.
F. Fisher................................P
G. S. Darling...........................R S
C. F. Sandberg, Box 880...............F S

103, Evansville, Ind. (Bridge and Structural Iron Workers).—Meets every Wednesday night at Lovejoy's Hall, 5th and Sycamore sts.
R. C. Grimes.............................P
Oley Flagler..............................T
F. J. Guth, 1008 Third ave.............F S

107 Butte, Mont. (Bridge and Structural Iron Workers, Piledrivers and Machinery Movers).—Meets every Monday night at Carpenters Union Hall.
S. Noah..................................P
Joe O'Gorman...........................R S
E. A. Storvik, 320 N. Main st..........F S

109, San Jose, Cal.—Meets Tuesday evenings at Labor Temple.
E. L. Sanders...........................P
Cal Humphrey, 77 Lenzen ave..........F S

111, Rock Island, Ill., Moline, Ill., and Davenport, Iowa.—Meets second Wednesday at Danish Brotherhood Hall, 609 W. Fourth st., Davenport, Iowa.
Geo. Bixby, phone North 1154X.........P
Lon McCandless.........................R S
H. B. Knowles, 2818 Boies st., Davenport, Ia....................F S & T

112, Peoria, Ill.—Meets first and third Tuesdays at Iron Workers' Hall, Main and Washington sts.
H. A. Kloppenburg.....................P
Elmer Blythe...........................R S
Albert Ulrich...........................T
Robert Evans, 4221 S. Adams st........F S

114, Tacoma, Wash. (Piledrivers and Builders Wooden Bridge).—Meets every Tuesday night at 1916 Jefferson ave.
Robert Kerr.............................P
Martin McDounagh......................R S
M. Johnson, 1712 So. Yakima ave.......F S

117, Oakland, Cal.—Meets first and third Mondays at 470 Twelfth st.
Thos. Horrigan..........................P
Tony Quintal............................R S
Paul G. Reimer, 2811 Atwell ave.......F S

118, Sacramento, Cal.—Meets every Wednesday, Hall No. 6, at Labor Temple, 8th and Eye sts.
J. T. Foley..............................P
W. J. Leflar.............................R S
Chas. Ertell, Labor Temple, Box 68......F S

119, Montreal, Quebec, Canada.—Meets every Monday night at Labor Temple.
Duncan Paul.............................P
J. Neil..................................R S
F. D. Scullin, 187 Murray st............F S

123, Lincoln, Neb.—Meets second and fourth Thursday at Labor Temple.
J. J. Flynn..............................P
F. E. Swenson, 2814 F st............F S & T

125, Port Arthur, Tex.—Meets first and third Sundays at Carpenters' Hall.
John Dunnigin..........................P
Thos. Palmer...........................R S
W. H. Coughlin, 704 Fourth st..........F S

126, Calgary, Alberta, Canada.—Meets every Thursday evening at Labor Temple.
Jas. Burns..............................P
Wm. Finlay.............................R S
Thos. Frame, Box 2026.................F S

128, Caughnawaga, Quebec, Can.—Meets every Sunday at Town Hall.
Mike Stalk..............................P
P. T. Angus............................R S
J. M. Jocks, P. O. Box 102..........F S & T

129, Edmonton, Alberta, Canada.—Meets first and third Thursdays at Moose Hall, cor. Fraser and Isabella sts.
Geo. Wilson............................P
Claude Metzger.........................R S
J. R. MacDonald, Box 264....F S & T & B A

132, Chicago, Ill. (English)—Meets first and third Tuesday at 630 W. Lake st.
Anthony Rehna..........................P
E. L. Cory.............................R S
Hans Dystrup, 2320 W. Belmont ave....F S

133, Chicago, Ill. (German).—Meets every first and third Wednesday at 630 W. Lake st.
Henry Osterloh.........................P
Wm. Schenker..........................R S
Wm. Stahlheber, 5631 S. May st.......F S

134, Chicago, Ill. (Bohemian).—Meets every first and third Wednesday at 630 W. Lake st.
Albert S. Konpy..........................P
Norbert Honsmicht.....................R S
Frank Rada, 1917 Blue Island ave.....F S

135, Galveston, Texas (Structural Iron Workers, Piledrivers and Wooden Bridgemen).—Meets first and third Fridays at Cooks and Waiters' Hall.
John Larssen..............................P
H. L. McInturff.........................R S
Ed. Schwarz, 4024 Avenue M...........F S

136, Chicago, Ill. (Machinery Movers and Riggers).
Thos. F. Kelly............................P
R. Remington............................R S
Michael Artery, 732 Madison st....F S & B A

138, Chicago, Ill. (Piledrivers).—Meets second and last Thursday of month at Bricklayers' Hall.
Thos. Driscoll...........................P
Joe McMullen...........................R S
David Hackett, 912 W. Monroe st.......F S

139, Toronto, Ont. (Shopmen).—Meets second and fourth Friday at Labor Temple, Church st.
W. E. Brown.............................P
C. Bell...................................R S
A. B. Pilliner, 14 Dean st..............F S

143, Cincinnati, Ohio (Inside Bridge, Structural and Ornamental Iron Workers; Shopmen).—Meets every first and third Tuesday at Central Turner Hall, Walnut st.
Chas. Vorbach..........................P
H. Moeller.............................R S
John C. Ahr, 3137 Imperial.............F S

145, Montreal, Que. (Foremen).
J. B. Johnston...........................P
Joseph Caron............................T
Peter D. Elmes, 68 Dagenais st........F S

146, Newark, N. J. (Shopmen).—Meets every Monday night at Zimmerman's Hall, 66 So. Orange ave., cor. Broome.
M. Hershkovitz...........................P
Wm. Rosenfield.........................R S
Wm. Rosenfield, 28 Avon Place.........F S

147, Ft. Wayne, Ind.—Meets every first and third Thursday at 1022 Calahound st.
L. Offerle................................P
Carl Jamison............................R S
Ora Gilliland, 446 Elizabeth st........F S

149, El Dorado, Ark.
L. S. Crawford...........................P
H. McKinzie, Box 91....................F S

150, Great Falls, Mont.—Meets every Sunday at 3 p. m., Independent Plumbing Co.
Louis Ludvar............................P
W. Plant.................................R S
E. J. Turner.............................T
F. J. Keenan, Box 1613..................F S

151, Indianapolis, Ind. (Shopmen).—Meets first and third Tuesday nights, Columbus Hall, McCarty and S. Delaware sts.
Earl C. Rozell...........................P
J. Silvernagle..........................R S
Chas. Seib...............................T
Orel Ruffin, 319 Bicking st.............F S

152, Kansas City, Mo. (Shopmen).—Meets first and third Thursdays at Labor Temple, 14th and Woodland ave.
N. P. Nelson.............................P
Merritt Burns...........................R S
Chas. Stevenson.........................T
LeRoy Old, 2432 Quincy.................F S

153, Kansas City, Mo. (Piledrivers).
R. R. Sims, 416 Kansas ave., Kansas City, Kans. ....F S

154, Boston, Mass. (Inside).—Meets every first and third Tuesdays at 995 Washington st.
Louis Peterson..........................P
A. Dawson..............................R S
Benard Boettger.........................T
H. J. Boynton, 10 Ames st., Somerville, Mass...............................F S

155, Fresno, Cal.
L. R. Boltinghouse......................P
John Crabb.............................R S
Paul Kidd, R. R. 1, Box 41.............F S

156, Vancouver, B. C., Canada (Piledrivers).—Meets second and fourth Friday at room 204 Vancouver Labor Temple.
Henry J. Wagner.........................P
Angus McDonald........................R S
William Eastman, 242 Georgia st....F S & T

157, Stockton, Cal.—Meets every Wednesday night at Bldg. Trades Temple, 19 N. Hunter street
A. H. Taylor.............................P
S. A. Lowe.............................F S & T

158, Binghampton, N. Y.—Meets every second and fourth Friday at 77 State st.
F. M. Birney............................P
Harold Mann............................R S
Joe P. Quinn, 126 Water st.........F S & T

Constitutions, By-Laws, Stationery, etc., printed by Harrington & Folger, Printers, 316 Century Building, Indianapolis, Ind.

OFFICIAL DIRECTORY
International Association of Bridge, Structural and Ornamental Iron Workers

---

Headquarters, Rooms 1615-16-17-18-19, Syndicate Trust Building, 915 Olive Street, St. Louis, Mo.

OFFICERS

P. J. Morrin, President, 1615 Syndicate Trust Bldg., 915 Olive St., St. Louis, Mo.

Wm. J. McCain, First Vice-President, 1615 Syndicate Trust Bldg., St. Louis, Mo.

D. J. O'Shea, Second Vice-President, 32 Erickson Pl., Niagara Falls, N. Y.

Michael C. Artery, Third Vice-President, 738 West Madison St., Chicago, Ill.

Theo. M. Brandle, Fourth Vice-President, Jersey Journal Bldg., Sip Ave., Jersey City, N. J.

Geo. McTague, Fifth Vice-President, 200 Guerrero St., San Francisco, Calif.

J. Arthur Evensen, Sixth Vice-President, Room 307, 184 W. Washington St., Chicago, Ill.

Wm. H. Pope, Seventh Vice-President,104 Windsor Rd., Medford, Mass., Mystic 4457-M.

Geo. Ashley, Eighth Vice-President, 400 Chatham St. West Windsor, Ont., Canada.

Ben C. Pitts, Ninth Vice-President, Box 687, Houston, Texas.

W. J. McCain, Acting Sec'y-Treas., 1615 Syndicate Tr. Bldg., 915 Olive St., St. Louis, Mo.

DISTRICT COUNCIL OF CHICAGO AND VICINITY
Meets the first Thursday evening of each month at 179 W. Washington Street.
Room 603.   Tel., Central 1137.

Edw. Ryan, President.   John Drexel, Secy.-Treas., 508 W. 32nd St.
Local No. 1   Local No. 63   Local No. 136   Local No. 179

DISTRICT COUNCIL OF ST. LOUIS AND VICINITY

P. J. Brice, President.   J. H. Barry, Secretary-Treasurer, 305 Collinsville Ave., East St.
Local Union No. 396.   Local Union No. 203   Louis, Ill.
                                                                       Local Union No. 392
                                                                       Local Union No. 211

DISTRICT COUNCIL OF CINCINNATI, OHIO, AND VICINITY
Meets the first Wednesday of each month at 1322 Walnut Street.

Sol. White, President   J. A. Anslinger, Secretary-Treasurer, 1424 Republic St
Local No. 372.   Local No. 44

STATE COUNCIL OF TEXAS
Oscar Nelson, Secretary-Treasurer, 1212 M½ St., Galveston, Tex.

Local No. 66—San Antonio	Local No. 84—Houston.	Local No. 59—Dallas.
Local No. 125—Port Arthur	Local No. 135—Galveston.	Local No. 174—El Paso
Local No. 263—Ft. Worth.		

DISTRICT COUNCIL OF NEW YORK AND VICINITY
Office; 1261 Broadway, Room 918 Martin Building.   Phone: Penn. 4379

T. M. Brandle, President.   T. M. Brandle, Secy.-Treas.

Local No. 11—Newark, N. J.	Local No. 170—New York, N. Y.	Local No. 361—New York, N. Y.
Local No. 40—New York, N. Y.	Local No. 187—Brooklyn, N. Y.	Local No. 373—Perth Amboy, N. J.
Local No. 45—Jersey City, N. J.	Local No. 197—New York, N. Y.	Local No. 391—Jersey City, N. J.
Local No. 52—New York, N. Y.	Local No. 217—New York, N. Y.	

DISTRICT COUNCIL OF WESTERN NEW YORK
H. Bauers, Pres.   Jerry Ryan, V-Pres.   Jos. Teatom, Sec.-Treas., 476 S. Salina St., Syracuse, N. Y.
L. U. 6, 9, 33, 60, 158.

TWIN CITY DISTRICT COUNCIL OF ST. PAUL-MINNEAPOLIS AND VICINITY
C. E. Carlson, President, 418 N. Franklin St.   C. M. Mahoney, Fin. Secy. & Treas., 2301 17th Ave.
St. Paul, Minn.   So., Minneapolis, Minn.
Earl Peck, Business Agent,   J. P. Johnston, Rec. Secy.
Labor Temple, Minneapolis, Minn.

LOCAL UNIONS

P, President; R S, Recording Secretary; F S, Financial Secretary; T, Treasurer; B A, Business Agent. Mixed, means local controls all branches of trade.

1. Chicago. Ill. (Structural).—Meets every Monday at 178 W. Washington st.
Levi Mitchell ....P
Geo. Fitzgerald.........................R S
J. F. McDougall, Room 29-30,
112 N. LaSalle st......................F S & T
A. Evenson, Room 29-30, 112 N. LaSalle st.B A
Jos. Corr, Room 29-30, 112 N. LaSalle st..B A

3, Pittsburgh, Pa. (Mixed).—Meets every Thursday at Morehead's Hall, 2nd and Grant sts.
J. E. Conway, 516 54th st.................P
Thos. McShane, 306 Miltenburg st..........R S
J. P. Kelly, Morehead's Hall,
2nd and Grant sts, Res., R. R. No. 1,
Mars, Pa...............................F S & T
M. J. Flaherty, Morehead's Hall,
2nd and Grant sts., Res. 1918 5th ave.,
Bell Phone, Grant 6629..................B A

4, Toronto, Ont. (Structural).—Meets every 1st and 3rd Tuesday at Labor Temple, Church st.
A. Wilson, 250 Semcoe st.................P
L. Lynch................................R S
L. E. Bowring, 47 Nickle ave.,
Mt. Dennis.......................T, F S & B A
Financial Secretary at Labor Temple every Sunday afternoon.

5, Washington, D. C. (Structural and Ornamental).—Meets every Thursday night at 430 Ninth st., N. W.
W. A. Carpenter..........................P
L. L. Meyers............................R S
Wm. Kholerick, 824 9th st., N. W....F S & T
D. Southern, 430 9th st., N. W.,
Phone West 2587........................B A

6, Buffalo, N. Y. (Mixed).—Meets Tuesday evenings at 351 Broadway.
Wm. Finnegan ....P
Geo. Larson............................R S
J. Anson, 3 Prospect ave..............F S & T
Wm. Bauers. 184 Kilhoffer st............B A

7, Boston, Mass. (Mixed).—Meets every Monday at 386 Harrison ave. Tel. Beach 7600.
Dan McLean, 135 Cedar st., Roxbury.
Tel., Roxbury 3166-M....................P
John E. Dolan, 41 Everett st., Jamaica Plain.
Tel., O. 170 Jam.......................R S
Hugh Ferris, 122 Falcon st.,
East Boston, Mass.......................T
M. J. Crump, 386 Harrison ave.
Res. 8 Elder st., Dorchester, Mass......F S
Jas. J. Murphy, 386 Harrison ave.........B A

8, Milwaukee, Wis. (Mixed).—Meets every 2nd and 4th Monday evening at Lipp's Hall, Third and Prairie sts. Office, Brisbane Hall, 6th and Chestnut sts. Phone Grand 7500.
Gust. Damke ....P
Edward Kloman ....T
H. G. Van Loghem ....R S
W. E. Reddin, 528 Chestnut st.......F S & B A

9, Niagara Falls, N. Y. (Mixed).—Meets 1st and 3rd Thursday at Trades & Labor Council Hall, 2103 Main st.
F. H. Fairburn.............................P
Matt Cussac................................R S
Frank McCombs, River rd.,
Box 404. LaSalle. N. Y........F S, T & B A

10, Kansas City, Mo. (Mixed).—Meets Wednesday evenings at Labor Temple, 14th and Woodland.
W. R. Paris, 3223 Brown av.,
Kansas City, Kan.........................P
Geo. R. Steffe, 2225 Chelsea av...........R S
W. F. McCoy, Labor Temple, 1400
Woodland av.
Res., 5006 Wabash av........F S, T & B A

11, Newark, N. J. (Mixed).—Meets Friday evenings at 66 S. Orange ave.
J. O'Neil, 159 Steuben st., E. Orange, N. J...P
Paul Van Eastern, 190 Dewey st......T & R S
J. Cowan, 39 Lincoln pl., Irvington, N. J....F S
Wm. Sherlock. 74 Market st..............B A

12, Albany, N. Y. (Mixed).—Meets 2nd and 4th Tuesday evenings at Labor Temple, 87 Beaver st.
Jas. Mullen, 87 Beaver st................P
Bert Hall, 72 B. Morris st.
Office Tel., Main 2029,
Res. Tel., West 6047......R S, F S, T & B A

14, Spokane, Wash. (Mixed).—Meets every Tuesday night, 819½ Riverside ave.
Chas. Mairet ....P
J. L. Utterberg...........................F S
J. J. Laurence, Box 419............R S & B A

15, New Haven, Conn. (Mixed).—Meets 4th Friday of month, Trades Council Hall, 215 Meadow st.
D. McCormack, 136 Holmes st.,
Stratford, Conn. ....P
E. J. O'Neil, 16 Webster st.............R S
M. J. Louden, Box 768.........T, B A & F S

16, Baltimore, Md. (Mixed).—Meets every Friday at 509 E. Baltimore st. Day office, 509 E. Baltimore st. Phone, Calvert 3359.
M. J. Reynolds, 37 S. Highland av.........P
J. F. Rausch, 241 East Franklin ave.....R S
Dan Scanlon, 509 E. Baltimore st.
Office Tel., Calvert 3359.
Residence, Park Heights and Rogers av.
Residence Tel., Liberty 4311....F S, T & B A

17, Cleveland. Ohio (Mixed).—Meets every Thursday evening at Insurance Center Bldg.
L. C. Murphy, 3235 Prospect av............P
John Ingram, Insurance Center Bldg........R S
John O'Brien, Insurance Center Bldg.;
Res. 9516 Orleans ave...................F S
Jno. Keenan, Insurance Center Bldg........T
Thos. McDonald, 4111 Whitman av.
Office Tel., Main 4322..................B A

19, Minneapolis, Minn. (Mixed).—Meets 1st and 3rd Friday nights at 601 4th ave., So.
Victor Johnson, 3107 N. E. Johnson st.....P
Cecil Mahoney, 2301 17th ave., S.........R S
Otto Peterson, 5116 31st ave., S.
Office, 601 4th ave., S..............F S & T
Fred W. Huston, 165 14th ave., N. E......B A

20, Wheeling, W. Va. (Mixed).—Meets every Monday at Union Labor Temple Hall, 1506 Market street.
Sam McCeary ....P
A. H. Ingram............................V. P.
A. E. Donnelly. Labor Temple.B A, F S, R S & T

21, Omaha, Neb. (Mixed).—Meets 1st and 3rd Wednesday evening at Hall No. 3, Labor Temple.
Clarence Gordan, 1920 Ames ave............P
Chas. Fay, 228 Dorcas st.................R S
Bert Grimes, 3157 Grand ave.........F S & T
F. K. Painter, Res. 2314 Dewey ave.,
Tel. Jackson 0531; Labor Temple,
Tel. Jackson 6571.......................B A

22, Indianapolis, Ind. (Mixed).—Meets at 537½ East Washington st., 1st and 3rd Thursday.
T. J. Gillespie...........................P
Clyde Cline.............................R S
Herman Manthey ....T
J. J. McNamara, 537½ East
Washington st.......................F S & B A

23, Scranton, Pa. (Mixed).—Meets every 1st and 3rd Saturday at 521 Lackawanna ave.
John Stanco, 922 Jefferson ave.
Phone 22006.......................F S & P
Jos. Walton, 722 Hampton st.............R S
Thos. McLaughlin, 1349 Albright ave.
Phone 22724.............................T
Joe Downs, 521 Lackawanna ave.
Res. Tel., 7-7448. Office Tel., 6975.......B A

24, Denver, Colo. (Mixed).—Meets 1st and 3rd Wednesday evenings at 1923 Curtis st.
J. F. Cole, 4575 W. 6th ave..............P
G. B. Henderson, 41 Madison st..........R S
O. H. Black, 1216 E 17th ave.............T
E. S. Kinsley, 3151 Stout st.
Tels., Office, Charpa 9221;
Res., Charpa 5837................F S & B A

25, Detroit, Mich. (Structural and Ornamental).—Meets Wednesday, 8 p. m., 911 Gratiot st.
Earl Rudell, 5909 Cooper st..............P
Jas. Stewart, 1816 Second ave............R S
Thos. Taylor, 1312 St. Jean st............T
Earl Remington, 911 Gratiot st..........F S
M. J. Conley, 911 Gratiot st,.
Res., 438 Henry st......................B A

27, Salt Lake City, Utah (Mixed).—Meets 2nd and 4th Wednesdays at Labor Temple.
Ed. Sherrin, Labor Temple................P
O. E. Pattie, Labor Temple...............R S
J. E. Munsey, Labor Temple.
Tel., Was. 6258. Res., 2734 Edison st.
Tel., Hy. 1556-J...............T, F S & B A

28, Richmond, Va. (Mixed).—Meets every 1st and 3rd Monday evenings at Arcade Bldg., Foushee st., between Grace and Broad sts.
Geo. C. Clarke..P
R. W. Aley...V-P
Geo. Brown, 1803 E. Main st.,
　Phone Randolph 4185-W.........R S & F S

29, Portland, Ore. (Mixed).—Meets every Thursday evening at Labor Temple, Hall D.
E. Dilthey, 408 E. 32nd st. Tel. East 7070....P
Del Lafrances, 841 E. 7th st.......................R S
Ben Osborne, Room 201 Labor Temple,
　Tel. Atwater 4501; Res., Hamilton Hotel,
　Tel. Main 6152...................F S, T & B A

32, Duluth, Minn. (Mixed).—Meets 1st and 3rd Monday evenings at Glencoe Hall, 224 W. 1st st.
Axel Bergaline, 2005 Lackawanna ave.,
　Superior, Wis.......................................P
Julius Brahus, 1020½ E. 4th st.,
　Duluth, Minn.......................................R S
Guy E. Larson, 213 E. 3rd st........F S & T

33, Rochester, N. Y. (Mixed).—Meets every Tuesday night at 38 Exchange st.
L. H. Young, 38 Exchange st.....................P
M. J. Byrne, 38 Exchange st.....................R S
F. L. Reiter, 38 Exchange st.
　Office Tel., Main 5160.
　Residence, 156 N. Union st.
　Residence Tel., Stone 5080-X....T, F S & B A

36, Easton, Pa. (Mixed).—Meets 1st Sunday at Eagles' Hall.
Wm. Burns, 250 Madison st.........B A & P
Frank Kane, So. Main st., Phillipsburg, N. J.......................................T & R S
John Coyle, 355 Thomas st.,
　Phillipsburg, N. J..............................F S

37, Providence, R. I. (Mixed).—Meets every Tuesday at 399 Eddy st.
Geo. Burdick, 47 Dartmouth ave............P
J. J. White, 90 Elm st..............................R S
M. McGrath, 34 Perry st.............F S & T

40, New York, N. Y. (Structural).—Meets Tuesday evenings at 209 East 124th st. Tel., Harlem 7197.
Wm. Fay, 209 E. 124th st........................P
John Moran, 209 E. 124th st.....................R S
James Hays, 209 E. 124th st.......F S & T
Chas. Massey, 209 East 124th st............B A
Chas. Johnson, 209 E. 124th st.
　Res., 504 Bergen ave., Bronx, N. Y......B A

44, Cincinnati, Ohio (Structural, Ornamental, Riggers & Machinery Movers).—Meets every Monday night at 1322 Walnut.
Thos. Gearns, 1622 Walnut st..................P
C. N. Stringfellow, 1619 Moore st............R S
J. A. Anslinger, 1424 Republic st.,
　Phone Canal 4509-L.................F S & T
Wm. Knox, 338 Oregon st.,
　Phone Canal 5411...............................B A
　Office: 1619 Moore st.

45, Jersey City, N. J. (Structural).—Meets Monday evenings at Hawkes Hall, 13th and Erie sts.
John E. Delaney, Jersey Journal Bldg.,
　Phone Bergen 2000.............................P
Jos. F. Bradley, 13th and Erie sts.....R S & T
Dan Unix, 39 W. 43rd, Bayonne, N. J.,
　Phone Bayonne 4166..........................F S
Theo. M. Brandle, 583 Summit ave. Phones, Bergen 2000 and 2001.............................B A
John E. Delaney, Jersey Journal
　Building ....Asst. B. A.

46, Springfield, Ill. (Mixed).—Meets 2nd and 4th Tuesday at Allen's Hall, 7th and Washington sts.
Mack O'Conner.....................................P
Harry Gilbertson.....................................R
Ray Heffner, 805½ East Washington st.
　Bell phone Capital 3171.......F S, T & B A

48, Oklahoma City, Okla. (Mixed).—Meets every Tuesday at 8½ S. Robinson st.
E. B. Cook...P
Theo. Basedow, R. No. 6, Box 246..F S, B A & T

51, Los Angeles, Cal. (Mixed).—Meets every Tuesday evening at Labor Temple Hall, 705 Maple ave.
Carl Keyes, 1219 S. Bonnie Baerd pl
　Tel., Angeles 0933...............................P
Wm. Burkett, 365 Amalia st.....................R S
Geo. J. Greene, 215 Labor Temple.
　Tel., Main 2183-2184.........F S & T B A

52, New York, N. Y. (Ornamental).—Meets every Friday evening at Labor Temple, 243 E. 84th st. Day room, 604 3rd ave. Tel. Caledonia 7514.
Edward Coleman, 604 3rd av....................P
Chas. Sheridan, 604 3rd ave.
John Schilling, 604 3rd ave ....F S & T
Henry C. Wolf, 604 3rd ave...................B A

53, Port Arthur, Ont., Canada (Mixed).—Meets 2nd and 4th Friday in Trades and Labor Hall.
Angus McLeod, 344 Dufferin st..............P
J. McKeenan..R S
Rod Young, 119 Pine st., Port Arthur, Ont...F S & T

55, Toledo, Ohio (Mixed).—Meets every 1st and 3rd Thursday evening at Labor Temple, Jeff. and Mich streets.
Harry Turner, 2019 Idaho st....................P
Chas. F. Vogt, 2206 Broadway..................R S
James Dunn, 315 10th st........F S, T & B A

57, Worcester, Mass. (Mixed).—Meets 1st and 3rd Monday at 554 Main st.
Gerald Matte..P
Frank Guertin...R S
Anthony Gardella, 143 Pilgrim ave.........T
Wm. Spooner, 105 Pleasant st......F S & B A

58, New Orleans, La. (Structural and Ornamental).—Meets every Thursday at 721 Poydras st.
Joe Romeo, 721 Poydras st......................P
Frank Herron, 1324 Congress st.............R S
Dan Hickey, 721 Poydras st.
　Res. 443 Bolivar st............F S & T, B A

59, Dallas, Texas (Mixed).—Meets every Thursday in Labor Temple.
Chas. Bradley...P
E. H. Morrow..R S
Sam McGregor, Labor Temple..F S & B A

60, Syracuse, N. Y. (Mixed).—Meets 1st and 3rd Friday evenings at Smith Hall, 312 S. State st.
Clarence King, 709 Wolf st......................P
John Erion, R. F. D. No. 1, Marcellus, N. Y..R S
Joseph Teaton, 476 S. Salina st.,
　Phone 25526.　Home Address Mail,
　R. F. D. No. 2, Liverpool, N. Y.
　Phone Baldwinsville 8-F-11...F S, T & B A

63, Chicago, Ill. (Architectural Iron Workers).—Meets every 2nd and 4th Thursday at 180 W. Washington street.
Edward Ryan, 3841 W. Monroe st...........P
Jas. Sweetman, 5323 Adams st................R S
Wm. Clark, 4100 W. 24th pl....................T
Ed. Tolf, 179 W. Washington st.,
　Room 506..............................F S & B A

66, San Antonio, Texas (Mixed).—Meets 2nd and 4th Sunday at 10:00 a. m. at Labor Temple.
T. F. Hart, Labor Temple........................P
W. F. Mylius, 104 Webb st.......................R S
Fred Fishback, Box 204. Office phone,
　Crockett 1268. Res., 114 Atlantic st.,
　Harlandale Add. Tel., Travis
　8740-W...............................F S, T & B A

67, Des Moines, Iowa (Mixed).—Meets 2nd and 4th Thursdays, 106 6th ave.
D. W. Miller, 1646 Maple st.....................P
Clyde Judkins, 1242 W. 5th st.................R S
John Graham, 944 West 18th st..F S, T & B A

68, Trenton, N. J. (Mixed).—Meets 1st and 3rd Wednesdays, 703 S. Broad st.
Jos. McNerney, 408 Clymer ave.,
　Morrisville, Pa....................................P
Frank J. Walsh, 144 W. Hanover st........R S
M. Walsh, 34 Beaver st.,
　Trenton, N. J......................F S & T
Wm. E. Hanford, R. F. D. 3.
　Tel., Rural 4873 R4.............................B A

70, Louisville, Ky. (Mixed).—Meets every 2nd and 4th Thursday evening at Labor Temple, 133 W. Market st.
Joe Underwood ....P
J. H. Staten, 2641 Bank st.......................R S
J. E. Hunter, 303 Labor Temple,
　127 W. Market st.............F S & T, B A

75, Miami, Ariz. (Mixed).—Meets every 1st and 3rd Wednesday at Labor Temple.
Horace Y. Brown, Box 1997.....................P
J. J. Soeder, Box 1997..............F S & T

79, Norfolk, Va. (Mixed).—Meets 2nd and 4th Thursday in the Eagles' Home, Church st., at 8 p. m.
C. B. Spruill..P
P. C. Carlisle, Box 1274; Residence 112
　W. 10th st. Phone Dial 39441...F S, T & R S

81, Anaconda, Mont. (Mixed).—Meets every 1st and 3rd Saturday night at 7 p. m., at Musician's Hall. Chestnut st.
Andrew Thorson, 714 Ash st....................P
Chas. J. Mihelic,
　312 Washington st..............F S & T, R S
A. Hedge, P. O. Box 1234...........V P & B A

82, Winnipeg, Man. (Mixed).—Meets 2nd and 4th Wednesdays at Labor Temple, James st.
R. E. Johnson..P
B. Petrie...R S
B. J. Hiscock, 1574 Elgin ave....F S, T & B A

84, Houston, Tex. (Mixed).—Meets every Friday night at 910½ Preston ave.
L. Sapp, Box 687 ....P
J. L. Simmons........................R S
Mandy Lane ....T
B. C. Pitts, Box 687 ....F S & B A

86, Seattle, Wash. (Mixed).—
Jerry Cunningham, 1433 W. 51st st.
　Telephone, Sunset 3118...............P
Jos. Clements, 1819 W. 50th st.
　Telephone, Sunset 1945..........R S, F S-T

89, Cedar Rapids, Iowa (Mixed).—Meets every 1st and 3rd Thursday night at Federation Hall.
John Krabacher ....P
C. J. Faltison........................R S
Albert Holcomb, 1007 S. 3rd st.
　East ....F S, T & B A

92, Birmingham, Ala. (Mixed).—Meets Monday nights at Ironworkers' Hall, 2119½ 1st ave.
H. R. Jones..............................P
J. C. Burt............................R S
J. W. Oakley, Box 490.......F S & T & B A

94, St. Paul, Minn. (Mixed).—Meets 1st and 3rd Monday evening of each month at St. Paul Labor Temple, 418 N. Franklin st.
C. E. Carlson, 259 McBoal..............P
Kenneth Diegnan, 957 E. 3rd st ....R S
Henry Stahl, 986 E. 3rd st......F S & T. B A

97, Vancouver, B. C. (Mixed).—Meets every Monday night at 811 Holden Building.
Jas. F. Burns, 2833 Furner st.,
　Tel. Highland 3562-L...................P
Paul Lauret, Maple Hotel,
　Tel. Seymour 4848-O.................R S
W. J. Cook, Box 302. Res. 4058 Perry Rd.
　Tel. Fairmount 4772-Y, S. Vancouver.
　B. C....................F S. T & B A

103, Evansville, Ind. (Mixed).—Meets every 1st and 3rd Tuesday at Bricklayers' Hall, 5th and Locust st.
Arthur Muth.............................P
Louis Deissler, 1423 Grand ave.,
　Phone M4950............R S, F S, T & B A

107, Butte, Mont. (Mixed).—Meets 2nd and 4th Tuesday at Norway Hall, 51 West Copper st.
Ed. Graff, 515 E. Mercury. Tel., 6564-J......P
John Mathison, 740 W. Park.
　Tel. Park 692 ....R S-T
Jas. Peters, 2121 Oak st. Tel. 1415-M......F S

109, San Jose, Cal. (Mixed).—Meets 1st and 3rd Tuesday evening at Labor Temple.
Cal. Humphrey, 77 Lenzen ave.............P
J. C. Lally, 42 Porter ave................F S-T

111, Rock Island, Ill.; Moline, Ill., and Davenport, Iowa (Mixed).—Meets 2nd and 4th Tuesday at Industrial Hall, Rock Island, Ill.
Tony Peterson ....P
Wm. Maynard........................R S
Earl Wivinis ....T
Chas. Dobbler, 318 10th st., Rock Island, Ill..F S

112, Peoria, Ill. (Mixed).—Meets 1st and 3rd Thursday at 301 Lincoln ave.
Geo. Cordts............................B A & P
A. Strope...........................R S
F. J. Tieman. 214 Kane st.............F S & T

114, Tacoma, Wash. (Mixed).—Meets every Tuesday, Carpenters Hall, 1012½ Tacoma av.
Jerry L. Condon, 3001 Grand View av.......P
R. W. Edwards, Regents Park P. O........R S
J. J. Hurley, Box 448, Tel., Office, Main 4997.
　Res., 316 S. 35th st.
　Res. Tel., Mad. 1044.............F S & B A

115, Sacramento, Cal. (Mixed).—
W. J. Leflar, Labor Temple.................S

122, Lincoln, Neb. (Mixed).—Meets 1st and 3rd Tuesday at Labor Temple.
Wm. Foster, 217 N. 11th st..............P
W. C. Swanson, 2324 Que st...........R S
F. E. Swenson, 2325 S. 11th st....B A, F S & T

125, Port Arthur, Texas (Mixed).—Meets 1st and 3rd Tuesday at Eagles' Hall.
R. A. Allen..............................P
W. C. Keller........................R S
W. H. Caughlin, 704 4th st........F S & T

126, Calgary, Alberta, Can. (Mixed).—Meets 1st and 3rd Monday at Labor Temple.
Jas. A. Chisholm, 1310 18th ave., N. W......P
Thos. G. B. Scott......................V-P
Wm. Chisholm, Labor Temple............R S
Jas E. Worsley, 1006-18th ave.,
　East ....F S, T & B A

135, Galveston Texas (Mixed).—Meets 1st and 3rd Friday at Carpenters' Hall.
A. E. Erickson, 1212 Ave. C ....P
Oscar Nelson, 1212 M½ st...........R S
Aug. Gustafson, 1423 M ½ st....F S, T & B A

136, Chicago, Ill. (Machinery Movers, Riggers, House Movers.
Frank Biller............................P
F. A. Bayer ....R S
Michael Artery, 738 W. Madison st....F S & T
C. J. Malone, 738 Madison st...........B A

147, Ft. Wayne, Ind. (Mixed).—Meets 1st and 3rd Thursday at Painters' Hall, Columbia and Barr sts.
J. C. Murray, 1901 Ascher ave............P
F. Farra, 1029 Cochrane st.............T
J. Stephens, 1803 Monroe st...........R S
R. H. Dunlap, 909 Barr st..........B A & F S

155, Fresno, Cal. (Mixed).—Meets 1st Friday of month at Union Hall, 1139 Broadway.
O. M. Brockless, 727 Agusta st...........P
W. H. Sturtevant, 1109 Howard ave........R S
F. C. Littlefield, 3553 Iowa ave............F S

158, Binghamton, N. Y. (Mixed).—Meets 1st and 3rd Thursday at Central Labor Union Hall, 53 State st.
P. A. Eipur, 11 Blanchard ave..............P
F. J. Hogan.............................V-P
J. Ryan, 53 State st..............F S & T
Jos. P. Quinn, 118 Oak st..............B A

161, Philadelphia, Pa. (Riggers and Machinery Movers).—Meets 1st and 3rd Thursday night at Labor Lyceum, 6th and Brown sts.
J. Nyhuis, 2337 S. 8th st...............P
Parcival Grahl, 1424 S 4th st.............T
F. Mehlman, 146 Watkins st...R S, F S & B A

167, Memphis, Tenn. (Mixed).—Meets every Tuesday at Labor Temple, Beak and Lauderdale.
W. D. Adams.............................P
Wm. Barry...........................R S
J. R. Williams, R. R. No. 1,
　Box 439B..............F S & T & B A
Send telegrams to 1056 Parkway E.

170, New York City, N. Y. (Riggers and Machinery Movers).—Meets every Monday of each month at 70 South st. Phone, John 1846.
D. Baxter...............................P
J. J. Harkin........................R S
Harry Ostling, 70 South st......F S, T & B A

172, Columbus, Ohio (Mixed).—Meets every Thursday, 68½ E. Long st.
E. L. Bierce, 1527 E. Main st.............P
J. A. Casey........................R S
Nelson Wells, Box 202...........F S & T
F. B. Conklin, 1563 Worthington st........B A

174, El Paso, Texas (Mixed).—Meets every 2nd and 4th Monday at Labor Temple.
Guy Price ....P
A. L. Wimber, Box 255.......R S, B A & F S

179, Chicago, Ill. (Stone, Derrickmen and Riggers).—Meets every 1st and 3rd Wednesday of each month at 180 W. Washington st.
John Drexel, 508 W 32nd st..............P
William Taylor, 3325 N. Halstead st....R S
Wm. Hammond, 6234 S. Hermitage ave.F S & T
John Drexel, 508 W. 32nd st.
　Tel., Yards 2458....................B A

184, Sioux City, Iowa (Mixed).—Meets every 1st and 3rd Thursday at Labor Temple, 6th and Neba sts.
Jack Douglas, 613 7th st...............P
M. Johnson, Auto Phone 66246,
　1000 Corneilla st....................R S
Ray G. Allen, 2023 N. Howard st......F S & T

186, Hamilton, Ontario, Can. (Mixed).—Meets every 2nd and 4th Tuesday at 137½ King st.
Charles Gracie...........................P
Wm. Burkholder.......................R S
A. R. Irvine, 136 Sanford ave., N......F S & T

187, Brooklyn, N. Y. (Navy Yard Riggers).—Meets every 3rd Tuesday of month at 182 Clermont ave.
Valentine Remz, 333 Menahan st...........P
Frank Penner, 962 55th st.............R S
M. L. Andress, No. 1 Slocum st.,
　Evergreen, L. I., N. Y...........F S & T
John Hogan, 272 Vanderbilt ave...........B A

191, Tulsa, Okla. (Mixed).—Meets every Friday night at Court House.
Ferd Graham............................P
E. I. McPherson.......................R S
Fred Graham, 124 S. Main st.........F S & T

195, Portland, Maine (Mixed).—Meets 1st and 3rd
Monday at Farrington Block.
Walter S. Cushing.............................P
H. T. Gillis.................................T
Wm. C. Smart...............................R S
John F. Foley, 51 Tyng st..................F S

197, New York City, N. Y. (Stone Derrickmen).
Wm. Brander, 472 60th st., Brooklyn, N. Y..P
James Fagan, 1624 3rd ave.............R S & T
Wm. Hilbert, 1737 Ave. A..................F S
Owen J. O'Brien, 320 E. 83rd st............B A

198, Douglas, Ariz. (Mixed).
L. Sanders...................................P
Karl Meroney, 823 20th st............F S & T

200, Rockford, Ill. (Mixed).—Meets 1st and 3rd
Sunday, 10 a. m., 118 S. Wyman st.
Henry Noreen, 825 Island av.................P
Milton Haight, 820 Kishwaukee st. F S & B A

201, Washington, D. C. (Reinforced Concrete Iron
Workers).—Meets every 2nd and 4th Thursday
in each month at 720 5th st., N. W.
J. E. Davis..................................P
Frank D. Lapp, 1404 Girard st., N. W.......R S
E. E. Dobyns, 1619 H st., S. E.......F S & T
Frank Biggs, 1348 D st., N. E..............B A
Phone: Lincoln 2322-W; Franklin 2058.

203, St. Louis, Mo. (Stone Derrickmen).
Walter Sullivan..............................P
P. J. Brice, 4440A Chouteau ave....R S & B A
M. L. Monahan, 1209 Grattan st.........F S-T

207, Youngstown, Ohio (Mixed).—Meets every Fri-
day night at 338½ W. Federal st.
Jas. Higgins................................P
Geo. Lundy...........................T & R S
John Foley, 338½ W. Federal st....F S & B A

211, St. Louis, Mo. (Shopmen).—Meets 2nd and 4th
Tuesday at Druids Hall, 9th and Market sts.
Louis Maurath...............................P
Henry Fritchie............................V-P
G. M. Banks, 4530 Newport ave.......F S & T

227, Mobile, Ala.—
Ed J.Siuria, Room 16 Mobile Labor Temple. P
A. E. Mobley, 115 N. Catherine st........R S

228, Portsmouth, Va. (Norfolk Navy Yard Riggers).
—Meets every 4th Thursday at 417 Jefferson st.
Thos. A. Wood, 417 Jefferson st.
Tel. Portsmouth 1298-W.................P
W. H. Clark, 510 4th st..........F S, T & R S

229, San Diego, Cal. (Mixed).—Meets every Thurs-
day night at Labor Temple, 621 Sixth st.
Frank J. Castro, 621 6th st................P
E. A. McLean, 621 6th st..................R S
B. G. Thomas, 621 6th st.,
care Labor Temple.........F S, T & B A

243, Charlestown, Mass. (Navy Yard Riggers).—
Meets every 2nd and 4th Friday night at 5
p. m., at Roughan's Hall, City Square.
Thos. A. Smith.............................P
Leslie A. Chapman, 192 Rock Island rd.,
Quincy, Mass.............................R S
Geo. M. Duke, 79 High st.............F S & T

263, Fort Worth, Texas (Mixed).—Meets at 104½
E. Weatherford St. every Wednesday night.
J. G. Garret................................P
W. G. Baumes, 200 W. Bluff st............R S
A. D. Moore, 716 Louisiana st.......F S & T
C. A. Perkins..............................B A

272, Miami, Fla. (Mixed).—Meets every Tuesday at
Building Trades Hall, 927 N. E. First ave.
J. H. Greider, 925 N. E. 1st ave...........P
I. Kent, 925 N. E. 1st ave................R S
R. L. Harris, 925 N. E. 1st ave......T, F S
Pat. McDonald, 925 N. E. 1st ave..........B A

290, Dayton, Ohio (Mixed).—Meets every Tuesday
evening at Bricklayers' Hall, 801 E. 5th st.
Michigan Cardwell, Dayton, O., R. R. 1.....P
L. L. Ross, 2553 Mundale av.,
Dayton, Ohio............................R S
W. A. J. Smith, 208 Linwood st.....F S & T
Woodford Riley, 840 So. Main st..........B A
Office, 801 E. 5th st.

292, South Bend, Ind. (Mixed).—Meets 1st and 3rd
Monday evening at Labor Temple, 315 S. Michi-
gan st.
W. H. Goucher..............................P
Fred Davidson, R. R. No. 1,
New Carlisle, Ind.......................R S
John Wilkening, 319 Hydraulic ave.,
South Bend, Ind..............B A, F S & T

301, Charleston, W. Va. (Mixed).—Meets every Sat-
urday at 118 Anderson st., at 8:00 p. m.
Al Watts, St. Albans, W. Va. Phone D-9441..P
Harry White, So. Charleston, Box 355.....R S
Richard Couch, Box 82..............F S & T

307, Montreal, Que., Canada (Mixed).—Meets 1st
and 3rd Monday at 417 Ontario st., East.
Val Langevin................................P
Samuel Doyle..............................R S
A. Langevin, 329 Delanaudiere st..B A. F S & T

308, Pana, Ill. (Shopmen).—Meets 2nd and 4th
Thursday night at P. of P. Hall, 117 S. Lo-
cust st.
Otto Glick..................................P
Chas. Metzger.............................R S
C. C. Kirkpatrick, 715 Jefferson st....F S & T

315, Niagara Falls, Ont., Canada (Mixed).—Meets
1st and 3rd Wednesday at Bamfield's Hall, Erie
ave.
C. B. Eastabrook.....................B A & P
C. Oldfield...............................R S
Thos. J. Whiteside, 35 Maple st.........F S-T

321, Little Rock, Ark. (Mixed).—Meets every 1st
and 3rd Monday at Labor Temple, corner 6th
and Scott.
C. C. Darrett..............................P
R. W. Upson..............................R S
Frank Woodall, Box 1081............F S & T

347, Windsor, Ont., Can. (Mixed).—Meets 2nd and
4th Monday at 61 Pitt st., E.
C. Forest..................................P
Geo. Ashley..............................R S
E. Whickes, 13 Salter st...........F S & T

348, Erie, Pa. (Mixed).—Meets every Thursday at
1701 State st.
Fred Ames, 1120 Plum st. Tel. Mut. 58-434....P
F. H. Morton, 1130 E 27th st.
Tel. Mut. 02317........................R S
Wm. Whitford, 1321 State st.
Tel. Mut. 22-582................F S & T
Mike Espline, 635 E. 10th st.
Tel. Mut. 23597........................B A

350, Atlantic City, N. J. (Mixed)—Meets every
Tuesday evening at Red Men's Hall, Michigan
and Atlantic ave.
John Burke.................................P
Frank Costello...........................V P
Wm. Raws, 116½ N. New Hampshire
ave. Phone, Marine 4230......R S, T & F S
John Burke, 122 Seaside ave.
Phone Marine 7963.....................B A
502 Freeman Bldg., 1516 Atlantic ave.

351, Lawrence, Mass. (Mixed).—Meets 2nd and 4th
Friday at Loomfixers' Hall.
Thos. Fowler...............................P
J. Douglas, 297 Water st..................T
J. H. Sullivan, 156 Margin st............F S
John McGrail, 296 Prospect st......R S & B A

357, Springfield, Mass. (Mixed).—Meets at Central
Labor Union Hall, 2nd and 4th Friday.
Thos. Dunn, 75 Bradford st.................P
E. B. Burke, 115 Wilbur ave..............R S
J. W. McGuire, 20 Van Horn place....F S & T
Daniel Linnehan, 17 Holyoke st...........B A

361, Brooklyn, N. Y. (Structural).—Meets every
Wednesday at Columbus Hall, Court and State
st., 3rd floor. Phone, Main 7149. Office, 571
Pacific st. Phone, Cumberland 0189.
John Kane, 200 W. 96th st., N. Y...........P
Fred Walters, 340 Gates ave.,
Brooklyn, N. Y..........................R S
Earl Calvert, 1054 Simpson st., New York
City. Phone Dayton 0593......F S, T & B A

368, Topeka, Kan. (Railroad Bridgemen), Santa Fe
System.—Meets 1st and 3rd Thursday at Santa
Fe Headquarters, Topeka, Kan.
J. C. Isaac................................P
R. C. Morse, Box 442, Hutchinson, Kan..F S & T

369, Coffeyville, Kan. (Mixed).—Meets 4th Thurs-
day at Eagles Hall.
Fred Joyce.................................P
T. R. Gann...............................R S
H. C. Gray, 606 Beech st.................F S

372, Cincinnati, O. (Reinforced Concrete Steel
Workers).—Meets 1st and 3rd Tuesday at Labor
Temple, 1314 Walnut st.
Del F. White, 816 Thornton st., Dayton, Ky...P
Carl Ludwig, 3433 Corlerain ave..........R S
Jas. Obermeyer, Office 301 W. Liberty st.
Tel. West 292 and 2908. Res. 3436
Colerain ave. Tel. Park 2039-L.F S & T, B A

373, Perth Amboy, N. J. (Mixed).—Meets every
Tuesday night, Columbia Hall, 387 State st.
Harry Johnson, 354 Market st..............P
John G. Reichardt, 82 Fayette st..R S, F S & T
F. McCormick, 151 Market st..............B A

374, Chicago, Ill. (Railroad Bridgemen).—Rock Island R. R. System.—Meets last Friday night of each month at station members are employed.
Dewey Watkins, 218 Merchant st.,
  Emporia, Kan. ....P
Fred Hinrichs, 540 35th st.,
  Rock Island, Ill...........................V-P
Vernon Merrick, Miller, Mo.........F S & T

377, San Francisco, Cal. (Mixed).—Meets 1st and 3rd Wednesday of each month at 200 Guerrero st.
Wm. G. Swicegood, 1058 27th st...........P
H. A. Hawkins, 1362 Vermont st..........R S
Geo. McTague, 200 Guerrero st.,
  Res., 1481 8th ave...........B A, F S & T

378, Oakland, Cal. (Mixed).—Meets 2nd and 4th Thursday of each month at Labor Temple, 480 20th st.
Asa Bennett, 705 25th st..................P
J. T. Fahey, Hotel Vernon,
  11th and Franklin sts.........F S. T & R S

379, Lafayette, Ind. (Mixed).—Meets 1st and 3rd Tuesday of month at Labor Temple, 5th and Columbia sts.
Frank Taylor, 1310 S 4th st................P
F. E. May, 239 Pierce st.,
  West Lafayette, Ind...........R S, F S & T

380, Champaign, Ill. (Mixed).—Meets 2nd and 4th Tuesday of month at Labor "Hall"
J. W. Richter, 105 E. Church st.P, R S & B A
Michael M. McCabe. Box 257..............F S

381, Bremerton, Wash. (Navy Yard Riggers).—Meets 3rd Tuesday at Labor Temple.
Chas. Biquette, 819 Park av..............P
G. A. Ring, 1058 6th st., Charleston, Wash..R S
C. R. Winn, 814 Washington ave.....F S & T

382, Shreveport, La. (Mixed).—Meets 2nd and 4th Wednesday at Central Labor Union Hall, 216½ Texas st.
Jos. Sowell.............................P
F. Eubank, 410 Allen av.................R S
Jim Tucker, 1455 Abbie st.
  Phone 1773-J Old.............F S, T & B A

383, Madison, Wis. (Mixed).—Meets 2nd and 4th Thursday at Madison Labor Temple.
H. C. Tiedeman, 938 E Dayton st..........P
Dewey Dilley, Labor Temple.........F S & T
A. R. Lang, 502 W. Mifflin st.............R S

384, Asheville, N. C. (Mixed).—Meets every Friday, 7:30 p. m., at Labor Temple, 222 Patton ave.
Geo. E. Willis, 26 Highland st.............P
W. H. Davis, 112 Park ave................R S
T. C. Caldwell, 425½ Depot st.........F S & T

386, La Salle, Ill. (Mixed).—Meets 2nd and 4th Wednesday at Slovenski Dome, La Salle and First st.
Neil C. Baxter, 320 E. St. Paul St.,
  Spring Valley, Ill.....................P
Fitz Victory ....R S
Jas. Savage...............................T
Neil Wilson, 1815 8 st., Peru, Ill.......F S

387, Atlanta, Ga. (Mixed).—Meets every Monday at Labor Temple, 112 Trinity ave.
J. T. Fitzpatrick, Box 299..............P T
R. R. Vogh, Hapeville, Ga........R S & B A
Wm. Van Houten, Labor Temple,
  112 Trinity ave.; Phone Hem. 4878-J....F S

388, Nashville, Tenn. (Mixed).—Meets 2nd Monday each month at Labor Temple, Hall 31, at 7:30 p. m.
J. L. Lynch, Labor Temple................P
R. B. Bean, Labor Temple................R S
W. V. McMahan, 232 Shelby ave.F S, T & B A

391, Jersey City, N. J. (Stonederrickmen).—Meets at 583 Summitt ave.
Arthur Bolton, 108 Van Wagner ave..P & B A
John Dowd, Jr., Box 121, Lawrence ave.,
  Dumont, N. J............................T
Peter Fisher, 497 Liberty ave...........R S
Wm. Murray, 410 Cleveland ave.,
  Harrison, N. J...........................F S

392, East St. Louis, Ill. (Mixed).—Meets every 1st and 3rd Thursday at 305 Collinsville ave.
Smith Morgan ....P
John Shovlin..............................R S
J. H. Barry, 305 Collinsville ave..F S. T & B A

393, Aurora, Ill. (Mixed).—Meets 1st and 2nd Tuesday at 22 S. River st.
P. W. Majerus, 485 High st.; Tel. 1792.B A & P
Roy Reed, 278 Watson st.; Tel. 3310-W....R S
Mike Pamson, 779 New York st.; Tel 5204.F S
Nick Kettenhofer, 237 Liberty st.;
  Tel. 3718-W..............................T

394, Allentown, Pa. (Shopmen).—
D. M. Gayton, 635 N. 5th st.............F S

395, Hammond, Ind. (Mixed).—Meets 2nd and 4th Tuesday at Labor Temple, Sibley st. and Oakley ave.
Mike Madura, 436 Roberts ave.,
  Whiting, Ind...........................P
Wm. Curtin, 1141 Indianapolis blvd.,
  Whiting, Ind. ....R S
John Dunne, Labor Temple.
  Res., 911 Calumet ave.,
  Hammond, Ind. ....F S. T & B A

396, St. Louis, Mo. (Mixed).—Office. 307 N. Garrison ave. Phone, Jefferson 1318.
J. H. James, Res. 4720 Kennerly ave.;
  Tel. Cabany 5155-M.....................P
B. K. Fisher, Res. 3257 So. Jefferson ave.;
  Tel. Sidney 2732-M....................R S
Walter Weaver, 307 N. Garrison ave.; Office
  Tel., Jefferson 1318; Res., 3731 Blow st.;
  Tel. Riverside 2328-J.............F S & T
Lon Morgan, 307 N. Garrison ave.; Res.,
  805 Clarkson Pl.; Tel. Lindell 3076-R....B A

397, Tampa, Fla. (Mixed).—Meets every Saturday, 7:30 p. m., 713½ Franklin st.
A. B. Grant, 713½ Franklin st............P
M. W. Thompson, 230 Third ave.,
  St. Petersburg, Fla....................R S
R. T. Richie, 713½ Franklin st., Tampa,
  Fla. Phone 3182. Res., 653 6th ave
  South, St. Petersburg, Fla. Phone
  72473....................F S, T & B A

398, Casper, Wyo. (Mixed).—Meets 1st Monday of each month at Labor Hall.
Porter K. Davis, 304 East A..............P
C. C. Campbell, 1204 N. Derbin......B A & R S
H. M. Davis, 716 So. Ash st.........F S & T

399, Camden. N. J.—Meets every Thursday evening at Second and Market sts., Camden, N. J.
Christian Borden, care Buil Shaw,
  National Park, N. J....................P
Eugene McGonigal, 1435 Shink st.,
  Philadelphia, Pa................R S, F S
Chas. Munsdorf, 1713 Spring Garden st.,
  Philadelphia, Pa.......................T

400, Santa Barbara, Cal. (Mixed).—Meets every Monday night at 1104 Santa Barbara st.
S. J. Dean, 423 Chapala..................P
L. F. Blackburn, 310 De La Vina st..F S & T

401, Philadelphia, Pa. (Mixed).—Office 5th floor Grand Fraternity Bldg., 1626 Arch st.
Wm. P. McGinn, 5th floor Grand
  Fraternity Bldg.........................F S

402, West Palm Beach, Fla. (Mixed).
T. H. McLain, Box 3604..............F S-T

403, Jacksonville, Fla. (Mixed).
Geo. M. Park, Phoenix Park..............P
J. C. Young, 1143 E. 15th st............R S

May 1936

OFFICIAL DIRECTORY

International Association of Bridge, Structural and Ornamental Iron Workers

---

Headquarters, Room 1615-16-17-18-19, Syndicate Trust Building, 915 Olive Street, St. Louis, Mo. Telephone: GArfield 2454-55-56.

INTERNATIONAL OFFICERS

P. J. Morrin, General President, 1615 Syndicate Trust Bldg., 915 Olive St., St. Louis, Mo.

Wm. J. McCain, General Secretary, 1615 Syndicate Trust Bldg., St. Louis, Mo.

J. H. Lyons, General Treasurer, 1615 Syndicate Trust Bldg., St. Louis, Mo.

First Vice-President (deceased).

J. Arthur Evensen, Second Vice-President, 6104 Bernice Ave., Chicago, Ill.

Wm. H. Pope, Third Vice-President, 34 Royall St., Tel. Mystic 3498-M, Medford, Mass.

Fourth Vice-President, deceased.

Fifth Vice-President (vacant).

J. T. Fitzpatrick, Sixth Vice-President, 1615 Syndicate Trust Bldg., St. Louis, Mo.

Seventh Vice-President (vacant).

Dan M. Gayton, Eighth Vice-President, Hamilton Hotel, Washington, D. C.

Wm. F. Bauers, Ninth Vice-President, 12 Olcott Place, Station E., Tel. Filmore 5138, Buffalo, N. Y.

TWIN CITY DISTRICT COUNCIL

Chas. Carlson, 785 Jefferson Ave., St. Paul, Minn., President; Carl O. Olson, 3701 40th Ave. So., Minneapolis, Minn., Tel. Drexel 2834, Financial Secretary, Treasurer and Recording Secretary. Meets odd months in Labor Temple, St. Paul, even months at 614 First Ave., No., Minneapolis, Minn. Meets first Thursday of every month.

DISTRICT COUNCILS

DISTRICT COUNCIL OF GREATER NEW YORK

Patrick Waters, 221 E. 84th St., New York City, President.

Charles McNamara, 529 W. 135th St., New York City, Recording Secretary.

Walter Gorman, 332 E. 54th St., Brooklyn, N. Y., Financial Secretary and Treasurer.

Local No. 40—New York, N. Y.	Local No. 170—New York, N. Y.	Local No. 197—New York, N. Y.
Local No 447—New York, N. Y.	Local No. 455—New York, N. Y.	Local No. 361—Brooklyn, N. Y.

DISTRICT COUNCIL OF CHICAGO AND VICINITY

Meets the first Thursday evening of each month at 806 W. Washington St. Office, Rooms 7-8. Tel., Monroe 5823.

Michael Artery, President; R. P. McInnis, Vice-President; John Innes, F. S., T., R. S.. Res., 7733 Fielding Ave., Office, Rooms 7-8, 806 W. Washington St., Chicago, Ill.

Local No. 1   Local No. 63   Local No. 136   Local No. 179

DISTRICT COUNCIL OF MONTREAL, CANADA, AND VICINITY

Local Union No. 307—   Local Union No. 418—
Montreal.   Montreal.

Meets last Wednesday of month at 8:30 p. m., 415 St. Catherines St., East, Montreal, Que., Can.

J. A. Charron, President, 1675 Valois Street. Tel.: Frontenac 7737.
Oscar Johanson, Secretary, 6363 Chateaurriand Avenue, Montreal, P. Q., Canada.

DISTRICT COUNCIL OF ST. LOUIS AND VICINITY

P. J. Brice, President; Frank J. Lahey, Secretary-Treasurer, 307 North Garrison Avenue, St. Louis, Mo.

Local Union No. 396.   Local Union No. 203.   Local Union No. 392.   Local Union No. 211.

DISTRICT COUNCIL OF PHILADELPHIA, PA., AND VICINITY

E. R. Lewis, President,   Gay Borrelli, Recording Secretary,
Res. 33 Avan Ave., So., Westville, N. J.   Res. 2044 So. 18th St., Philadelphia, Pa.

Francis A. Mehlmann, Treasurer, Res. 146 Watkins St., Philadelphia, Pa.

DISTRICT COUNCIL OF CINCINNATI, OHIO, AND VICINITY

Meets the first Wednesday of each month at 1322 Walnut Street.
President: J. A. Anslinger, Secretary-Treasurer, 1424 Republic St.

Local No. 372   Local No. 44

DISTRICT COUNCIL OF JERSEY CITY, N. J., AND VICINITY

Meets second and fourth Wednesday of each month at 583 Summit Ave, Jersey City, N. J.

Local No. 11—Newark, N. J.   Local No. 45—Jersey City.   Local Union No. 391—
                                                                  Jersey City, N. J.

Local No. 373—Perth Amboy, N. J.

BAY DISTRICT COUNCIL OF SAN FRANCISCO AND VICINITY

Meets first and third Friday of each month,

Martin Conley, President; Edward Lewis, Secretary

Local No. 377   Local No. 378   Local No. 472.

LOCAL UNIONS

P, President; R S, Recording Secretary; F S, Financial Secretary; T, Treasurer; B A, Business Agent. Mixed, means local controls all branches of trade.

1, Chicago, Ill. (Structural).—Meets every Monday night at 948 W. Madison.

John Von Allman, off. 948 W. Madison St.
Tel. Monroe 2328.
Res. 3007 N. Halsted st.
Tel. Wellington 7051...................P
Roy Rogers, off. 948 W. Madison St.
Tel. Van Buren 9785.
Res. 269 North Crawford Ave........R S
J. J. Walt, off. 948 W. Madison St.
Tel. Monroe 2328.
Res. 2306 Calumet Ave.
Tel. Victory 4495..................F S, T
John Callahan, off. 948 W. Madison St.
Tel. Monroe 2328.
Res. 2122 Orchard St.
Tel. Lincoln 2841....................B A
Jean McDougall, Office 948 W. Madison st.
2nd Fl. Tel. Monroe 2328.
Res. 3840 Palmer st.
Tel. Spaulding 2461.....Acting F S & T
Joseph P. Corr, office 948 W. Madison st.
Tel. Monroe 2328.
Res. 4957 N. Kilbourn ave.
Tel. Pensacola 5089..................B A

3, Pittsburgh, Pa. (Mixed).—Meets every Tuesday at 1345 Fifth Ave.

Matthew Gorman, 5467 Rosetta st.
Tel. Emerson 0918.....................P
Fred McCall, 843 Peralto st.
Tel. Cedar 8047......................R S
J. P. Kelly, 1345 5th ave.
Office Tel. Atlantic 3745.
Res. R. D. No. 1, Mars, Pa.
Tel. Mars 40, Ring 4.............F S & T
M. J. Flaherty,
Res. 1727 Fifth Ave.
Tel. Atlantic 3482...................B A

4, Toronto, Ont. (Structural). — Meets First and Third Wednesday night at Labor Temple, Church st.

L. Lynch, 30 Millicent st.
Tel. Elgin 4661......................P
Al. Wilson, Labor Temple,
Church st. Tel. Elgin 6998.
Res. 332 Dundas st., East.
Tel. Ra 5845................R S-T-F S
George Parker, Labor Temple, Church st.
Tel. Elgin 6998.
Res. 2879 Dundas st., West.
Tel. Ju 9106......................B A

5, Washington, D. C. (Structural and Ornamental).—Meets every Thursday night at 704 Sixth St., N. W.

H. Erkenbrach, 926 5th st. N. E.
Tel. Metropolitan 5259...............P
Jas. C. Harris, 1414 Maryland ave.
N. E.................................R S
W. E. Griffith, 2117 Branch ave. S. E.
Tel. Lincoln 7919-W..................F S
E. G. Myers, 2808 26th st. N. E.
Tel. Potomac 2682....................T
Leslie L. Myers, off. 908 D st., N. W.
Tel. Metropolitan 5259.
Res. 9 Glendale ave.
Alexandria, Va. Tel. Alex. 988-W....B A

6, Buffalo, N. Y. (Mixed).—Meets every Thursday night at 475 Franklin St.

Martin Spencer, off. 475 Franklin st.
Res. 79 Troup st.....................P
Fred Phillips, off. 475 Franklin st.
Res. 719 Hopkins st.................R S
Geo. W. Brown, Office, 475 Franklin st.
Tel. Grant 1083. Send all mail to Res.
100 Ladner st. Tel. Abbott 2760. F S T
& B A.

7, Boston, Mass. (Mixed).—Meets every second and last Saturday of each month at 10:00 A. M. at 9 Appleton St. Tel. Liberty 7036.

Jas. A. McDonald, 9 Appleton st.
Tel. Lib. 7036. Res. 11 Queensbury st.,
Tel. Kenmore 1786...................P

John E. Dolan,
Off. 9 Appleton St. Tel. Liberty 7036.
Res. 41 Everett St., Jamaica Plain,
Mass. Tel. Jamaica 1715-R.........R S
Frank Moriarty,
Off. 9 Appleton St. Tel. Liberty 7036.
Res. 89 Wellsmere Rd., Roslindale.
Tel. Parkway 3629-M...........F S & T
Wm. J. Reynolds,
Off. 9 Appleton St. Tel. Liberty 7036.
Res. 33 Spring Park ave., Jamaica Plain,
Mass. Tel. Jamaica 0515.............B A

8, Milwaukee, Wis. (Mixed).—Meets every 2nd and 4th Tuesday evening at Office, Dorsen Bldg., 2218 N. 3rd, Room 407-9. Marquette 4332.

Gus H. Damske, res. 408 N. 40th St.
Tel. 3014M ....P
Edw. K. Preuss, off. Dorsen Bldg.,
2218 N. 3rd, Room 407-9.
Tel. Marquette 4332.
Res. 3251 N. 11th st.................R S
Chas. T. Link, off. Dorsen Bldg.,
2218 N. 3rd, Room 407-9.
Tel. Marquette 4332.
Res. 1131 S. 19th st.................T
Herbert J. Mueller,
Off. Dorsen Bldg., 2218 N. 3rd,
Room 407-9. Tel. Marquette 4332.
Res. 5330 N. 34th St.
Tel. Hilltop 8372................F S, B A

9, Niagara Falls, N. Y. (Mixed).—Meets 1st and 3rd Thursday at 2124 Main St.

Emil Hasley, 527 7th st.............P
C. Randolph, 458 5th st. Tel. 2007-M....R S
D. J. O'Shea, 184 57th st.
Tel. 441-R................F S, T & B A

10, Kansas City, Mo. (Mixed). — Meets Wednesday evening at Labor Temple, 14th and Woodland.

Fred Decker, res. 2300 Oakley.
Tel. Benton 0297.....................P
P. D. McElroy, office, Labor Temple,
14th and Woodland. Tel. Harrison
4880. Res. 2739 Chelsea. Tel.
Linwood 0030 ....F S-T & B A
Ralph M. Hankins, res. 2318 Lawrence ave.
Tel. Humboldt 0173-W...............R S

11, Newark, N. J. (Mixed).—Meets Thursday evenings at 59 Beacon St.

Patrick Sweeney, off. 59 Beacon st.
Tel. Market 2-8177.
Res. 106 7th st., Harrison, N. J........P
Ralph Golden, Newark, N. J.
Off. 59 Beacon st. Tel. Market 2-8177.
Tel. Essex 2-3125...............F S-R S
Jay D. Cowen, 39 Lincoln place,
Irvington, N. J......................T
Off. 59 Beacon st. Tel. Market 2-8177.
John A. Johnston, Off. 59 Beacon st.
Tel. Market 2-8177...................B A

12, Albany, N. Y. (Mixed).—Meets 2nd Tuesday of each month at Labor Temple, 87 Beaver St.

Roy Carroll, 20 Genesee st. Tel. 3-7284...P
Joe Keefe, Res., 571 N. Pearl st., Albany,
N. Y. Tel. Dial 4-7428,
Albany..............F S, T & B A-R S

14, Spokane, Wash. (Mixed).—Meets every Wednesday at 8:00 P. M., Fraternal Hall, 305½ W. Riverside ave.

Chas. A. Mairet, Res. 3128 Ferrall St.
Tel. Lakeview 0756R.................P
Olsie S. Bro. All mail to Box 419.
Res. 1204 W. Carlisle.
Tel. Broadway 1103......F S & T, B A
Con Johnson,
Res. Temple Court Hotel,
Tel. Riverside 2087.................R S

15, Hartford, Conn. (Mixed).—Local Union meets every 4th Wednesday of month; Executive Board meets 2nd and 4th Wednesday at Labor Temple, 97 Park St., Hartford, Conn.

E. B. Blackwilder, Res. 14 Groten st.
Tel. 7-6013 ....P
Raymond J. McGinnis, Res. 35 Owen st.
Tel. 2-5987 ....F S-T
Henry Hagey, Res. 24 Saunders st.,
East Hartford, Conn. Tel. 8-3261.....B A
Bernard Reynholds, 28 Midian ave.,
Windsor, Conn. Tel. Windsor 249-2...R S

16, Baltimore, Md. (Mixed).—Meets every Tuesday night at 360 N. Gay St. at 8 p. m.

Thomas Mowbary, off. 360 N. Gay st.
Tel. Plaza 5646.
Res. 1703 E. 29th st......................P
J. T. Walker, off. 360 Gay st.
Tel. Plaza 5646, 3605 Belair road.....R S
D. J. Scanlan, 360 N. Gay st.
Tel. Plaza, 5646. Res. 13 E. Franklin st.
Tel. Vernon 7192..............F S-T-B A

17, Cleveland, Ohio (Mixed).—Meets every Thursday evening at 2111 Prospect ave.

Joseph Keenan, off. 2111 Prospect ave.
Tel. Prospect 5558.
Res. 3194 W. 110th st. ....P
Dan Monahan, Res. 1439 W. 54th st.
Tel. Melrose 6710-W.................R S
Thos. Lenehan, 2111 Prospect ave.
Tel. Prospect 5558. Res. 1070 East
171st st. Tel. Kenmore 3021-J........F S
Louis Fay, off. 2111 Prospect ave.
Tel. Prospect 5558.
Res. 1665 Wyandotte ave., Lakewood,
Ohio. Lakewood 6058-J. ....Acting F S-T
John L. Kelly, off. 2111 Prospect ave.
Tel. Prospect 5558. Res. 1864 E. 73rd
st. Tel. Endicott 1246.................B A

19, Minneapolis, Minn. (Mixed).—Meets 2nd and 4th Tuesday nights at 601 4th ave., S.

Earl Martin, off. 24 N. 8th st.
Tel. Geneva 2452. Res. 3119
Sheridan ave., No. ....P-B A
Carl O. Olson, 24 North 8th st. Tel.
Geneva 5528. Res. 3701 40th ave. So.
Tel. Drexel 2834 ....R S
John Lindberg, 24 North 8th st. Tel.
Geneva 2452. Res. 3710 Washburn
ave. No. Tel. Hyland 0089........F S-T

20, Wheeling, W. Va. (Mixed).—Meets every Monday at Union Labor Temple Hall, 1506 Market St.

Jas. A. Campbell, Bellair, Ohio, Route 3.P
Frank McNeil, off. 1506 Market st.
Tel. Wheeling 318. Send all mail to
Res., 100 Kenney st.
Tel. 957-J ....R S-F S-T, B A

21, Omaha, Neb. (Mixed).—Meets 1st and 3rd Wednesday evening at Hall No. 3, Labor Temple.

John P. Shipley, 5339 No. 25th ave...F S-T
F. K. Painter, 1342 S. 27th st..........B A

22, Indianapolis, Ind. (Mixed).—Meets first and third Tuesday of each month at 411 Transportation Building.

Carl Vestal, off. 411 Transportation Bldg.
Tel. Lincoln 1816. Res. 426 N. Tibbs st.
Tel. Belmont 3208...........P-F S-B A

Al Sparks ....R S
Gustave F. Mayer, off. 411 Transportation
Bldg. Tel. Lincoln 1816.
Res. 1431 Congress ave.
Tel. Talbott 1332.......................T

24, Denver, Colo. (Mixed).—Meets every 2nd Wednesday evening at 1021 17th St., Day Hall, at 1425 Curtis St.

John Bagan, 684 S. Washington st.......P
Paul Spoor, 1721 E. 32nd ave............R S
E. S. Kinsley, 3155 Stout st.
Tel. K. E. 9215..............F S & T-B A

25, Detroit, Mich. (Mixed).—Meets every Monday, 8 p. m., at 69 Erskine St.

R. M. Anderson, off. 69 Erskine st.
Tel. Temple 1-8139. Res. 13329
Rosemary. Tel. Pingree 7912...........P
Jos. N. Cummings. 69 Erskine st.
Tel. Temple 18139. Res. 1009 Columbia
road, Berkley, Mich. Tel. Royal Oak
1067-W ....B A-F S-T
A. Hoobing, off. 69 Erskine st. Tel.
Temple 1-8139. Res. 1567 Delamore
st. Tel. Madison 7131.................R S

27, Salt Lake City, Utah (Mixed).—Meets 2nd and 4th Wednesdays at Labor Temple.

Edward Ruben, Res. 5591 State st.
Tel. Murray 51.........................P
P. W. Jacobs, 2023 S. 8 East st........R S
Paul Hagerty, off. Labor Temple.
Tel. Was. 6258. Res. 1534 Park ave.
Tel. Hy. 3019M.........................T
R. H. Hopley, off. Labor Temple.
Tel. Was. 6258. Res. 241 So. State st.
Tel. 10040 ....F S-B A

28, Richmond, Va. (Mixed).—Meets every 1st and 3rd Tuesday evenings at 1803 East Main St.

Geo. Brown, 1803 E. Main st. Phone
Dial 3-2459 ....F S-T & B A

29, Portland, Ore. (Mixed).—Meets every 1st and 3rd Thursday evening at Labor Temple, 4th and Jefferson Sts., Hall H, 4th floor, 8 p. m.

Edward R. Hein,
Res. 721 N. E. Roselawn st............P
C. R. Munstedt, 201 Labor Temple.
Tel. Atwater 0171, 1114 N. E. Winona
st. Tel. Walnut 7091..................R S
John O'Neill, Res. 5765 N. E. Cleveland,
Tel. Wa. 4501. Off. 201 Labor Temple,
Tel. Atwater 0171. Res. 6524 Missouri
ave. ....F S-T-B A

33, Rochester, N. Y. (Mixed).—Meets every Tuesday at 91 State St.

H. Hyland, off. 91 State st.
Tel. Main 5402.
Tel. Glenwood 2753-J...................P
P. J. Denison, off. 91 State st.
Tel. Main 5402.......................R S
Harry E. Keys, off. 91 State st.
Tel. Main 5402. Res. 770 Monroe
ave. ....F S-T
J. D. Earnest, off. 91 State st.
Tel. Main 5402. Res. 533 Meigs st.
Tel. Monroe 2715.....................B A

36, Easton, Pa. (Mixed).—Meets last Sunday at Peinningest Hall.

John Sheehan, 205 S. 16th st.,
Allentown, Pa. Tel. 8919.........P-B A

37, Providence, R. I. (Mixed).—Meets every 2nd and 4th Thursday at 201 Union St.

Γ. E. Carroll, 39 Lawrence st.,
Arlington, R. I. ....P
M. M. McGrath, 34 Perry st.
Tel. Plantations 8142.................R S
Jos. Daylor, Office 201 Union st.
Tel. Plantations 8142. Send all mail to
Roseland ave., Hillsgrove, R. I. Res. Tel
Greenwood 1986............F S & T-B A

40, New York, N. Y. (Structural).—Meets 2nd and 4th Tuesday evenings at N. Y. Labor Temple, 243 E. 84th St. Executive Board meets first and third Fridays.

Edw. Leary, off. 221 E. 84th st. Tel.
Regent 4-5562. Res., 330 E. 65th
st. ....P
James J. O'Connor. Send all mail to Res.
Off. 221 E. 84th st. Tel. Regent 4-5562.
Res. 62-84 60th Place, Ridgewood, L. I.,
N. Y. Tel. Heq 3-9254..............R S
Joseph Hild, 221 E. 84th st.,
Res. 2551 Aqueduct ave., Bronx..F S & T
Patrick Waters, 221 E. 84th st........B A
Val Schneible, off. 221 E. 84th st.
Tel. Regent 4-5562.................B A

44, Cincinnati, Ohio (Structural, Ornamental, Riggers & Machinery Movers). —Meets every Friday night, 7:30 P. M., at Liberty and Clay Sts. Executive Board meets first and third Friday at Business Office, 119 E. Liberty St. Tel. Cherry 5411.

Thomas Gearns. 2669 Bellevue ave., Mt.
Auburn, Ohio. Tel. Avon 1016-W.....P
Chas. Rapp, 1783 Sycamore st.........R S
J. A. Anslinger. Send all mail to 3597
Haven st. Tel. Avon 8562-M....F S & T
John Dempsey, Jr., 119 E. Liberty st.
Tel. Cherry 5411. Res., 2542 Cypress Way,
Pleasant Ridge. Cincinnati. Ohio....B A

45, Jersey City, N. J. (Mixed).—Executive Board meets every Tuesday evening at Orpheum Bldg., 583 Summitt Ave., Jersey City, N. J.

John Dornbierer, 583 Summitt ave.
Res. 1022 Boulevard, Bayonne, N. J....P
Dan Unix ....F S
Edward Cumesty. Off. 583 Summitt ave.
Res. 46 Harrison ave.
Tel. Delaware 3-1973.................B A
Harry Kegelman. Off. 583 Summitt
ave. Res. 269 Jewett ave..........R S-T
Dan Unix, 39 W. 43d st., Bayonne, N. J.
Phone Bayonne 3-4166................F S

46, Springfield, Ill. (Mixed).—Meets 2nd and 4th Tuesday at Painters' Hall, 214½ S. 6th St.

Jas. S. Reid, 500 W. 4th st............R S
C. T. Turner, 205½ E. Washington st....P
Chas. Kastner, 1013 S. 13th St.
Tel. Cap. 2715.............F S-T & B A

48, Oklahoma City, Okla. (Mixed).—Meets 2nd and 4th Friday at Labor Temple, 426½ W. 2nd St.

W. L. Collins, Box 4119, Capitol Hill Sta.,
Oklahoma City, Okla. ....P
Joe McElroy, 536 S. W. 9th st.......R S-B A
J E. Reardon. 1408 N. Blackwelder ave.
Tel. 5-2245 ....F S-T

55, Toledo, Ohio (Mixed).—Meets every Thursday evening at 524 Front St., Room No. 4.

I. J. Barrett, 1018 Radcliff Dr.............P
Jack Walters, 1402 Ironwood ave......R S
Fred Middaugh, Walbridge, Ohio.........T
Earl Scofield, 524 Front St. Tel. Taylor
1096. Send all mail to Box 28,
Sta. A ....F S-B A

57, Worcester, Mass. (Mixed).—Meets second Saturday of each month at 10:00 a. m. at Labor Temple, 100 Portland St.

Wm. F. Riordan, 65 Eureka st.
Tel. 57118.....................P B A
J Kelleher. 905 Main st...............R S
Henry Hedge, 7 Wall st.............F S-T

58, New Orleans, La. (Mixed).—Meets second and fourth Thursday night, at 528 Bienville St. Send all mail to 540 S. Genois St.

J. P. Serio, Off. 528 Bienville st.
Res. 717 Barracks st.
Tel. Main 0121....................P
E A. Chaix, Off. 528 Bienville st.
540 S Genois st.
Tel. Galvez 7768............F S-T, R S
B. A. Murray, Res. 3600 Cleveland ave.
Tel. Galvez 5212...................B A

60, Syracuse, N. Y. (Mixed).—Meets 4th Friday evenings.

Clarence King, 709 Wolf st. Tel. 22545....P
Joseph Burns, 132 Elmwood ave........R S
Joseph Teatom...............F S, T & B A
Send all mail to Home Address, Route 3,
Baldwinsville, N. Y.......F S, T & B A

63, Chicago, Ill. (Architectural Iron Workers).—Meets every 2nd Thursday at 123 W. Madison St., 16th floor.

Edward Ryan, off. 123 W. Madison st.,
Room 1820. Tel. Central 3385.........P
Gus Kreutz. 3733 No. Troy st.
Tel. Keystone 6417..................R S
Wm. Clark. 1419 So. Grove ave.,
Berwyn, Ill. Tel. Berwyn 5086-W....T
M. H. Martin. off. 123 W. Madison st.,
Room 1820. Tel. Central 3385.
Res 1506 N. Laramie ave.
Tel. Merrimac 2213...........F S & B A

66, San Antonio, Texas (Mixed).—Meets 2nd and 4th Tuesday night at 7:30 p. m., at Labor Temple.

Jack Martin, off. Labor Temple. Tel.
Garfield 3581. Res. 504 Carson st.......P
W. E. Sonc, Labor Temple.
Tel. Garfield 3581..................R S
C. G. Passmore, Labor Temple.
Tel. Garfield 3581 ....T
Fred Fishback, Labor Temple.
Send all mail: P. O. Box 204, San
Antonio, Tex. 126 North st.
Office phone Garfield 3581. Res.
114 Atlantic st. No mail delivery.
Tel. Lambert 21982.................B A

67, Des Moines, Iowa (Mixed).—Meets 2nd and 4th Thursdays, 3rd and Locust Sts.

Silas Taft, R. R. 1, Valley Junction, Ia.
Tel. 5-3617 ....P
W. H. Tassau, 401 E. 6th st. Tel. 3-1837. R S
J .W. Davidson, Polk City, Ia.
Tel. Polk City 1752..........F S-T-B A

68, Trenton, N. J. (Mixed).—Meets 1st and 3rd Wednesdays, at Labor Lyceum, 159 Mercer St., 4th Floor.

A. Cunningham, 370 Newkirk ave.
   Tel. 86036 ....P
Frank J. Walsh, R. D. No. 2,
   Marshall ave., Trenton, N. J.
   Tel. 8-6594 ....R S-B A
John R. Davis, 115 Mary st.
   Tel. 8-6594 ....F S-T

70, Louisville, Ky. (Mixed).—Meets every
1st and 3rd Tuesday evening at Labor
Temple, 127 W. Market St.
   Joseph Underwood, off. 926 Tyler Hotel.
      Tel. Wabash 3745.
      Res. 1727 Crop st. ....P
   H. P. Bruck, off. 926 Tyler Hotel.
      Tel. Wabash 3745.
      Res. 171 Wellington st.
      Tel. Magnolia 0804-J.........F S-T-B A
   Reed Bunch, off. 926 Tyler Hotel.
      Tel. Wabash 3745.
      Res. 3833 Washington st.,
      St. Mathews, Ky. ....R S

75, Phoenix, Ariz. (Mixed).—Meets every
1st and 3rd Wednesdays at Labor Temple.
   Joe M. Smith, Route 7, Box 542.........P
   C. E. Gould, 2145 West Adams st..F S & T

79, Norfolk, Va. (Mixed).—Meets 2nd and
4th Thursday in the Eagles' Home,
Church St., at 8 p. m.
   C. B. Sprulll, R. F. D. No. 2,
      Box 350, Portsmouth, Va.............P
   B. C. Cook.......................R S
   O. J. Evenson, 3122 Tait Terrace,
      Tel. 32592 ....F S-T

81, Anaconda, Mont. (Mixed).—Meets every
3rd Wednesday night at 7 p. m., at Pay
Office Hall, 121 Main St.
   Ray Reardon, 517 E. Commercial st..P-B A
   Joe Hedge. Res. 721 Birch
      st ....F S-T R S

84, Houston, Tex. (Mixed).—Meets first and
third Friday night at 509 Louisiana St.
Tel. Preston 1667.
   R. L. Shoemake, Off. 509 Louisiana st.
      Tel. Beacon 30403. Res. 4909 Eigel.
      Tel. 1909......................P
   Geo. Livington, send mail to P. O. Box 687.
      Office 509 Louisiana ave. Tel. Beacon
      30403. Res. 7818 Williford st. Tel.
      Wayside 8812 ....F S-T-B A
   Frank De Wees, Off. 509 Louisiana st.
      Tel. Preston 1462. Res. 1614 Scott st.
      Tel. Fairfax 5702.................R S

86, Seattle, Wash. (Mixed).—Meets Room
318 Labor Temple, 1st and 3rd Tuesday
night.
   Paul Fredrickson, off. 202 Labor
      Temple. Tel. Elliott 2424.
      Res. 2353 W. 70th st. Tel. Su. 4287.....P
   Richard Tracey, off. 202 Labor Temple.
      Tel. Elliott 2424; Res. 2709 44th ave.
      S. W. Tel. West 3109....F S-T, B A, R S

89, Cedar Rapids, Iowa (Mixed).—Meets
1st and 3rd Thursday night at Federa-
tion Hall.
   Carl Stickley, res. 423 8th ave., S. E.
      Tel. 24925 ....P
   Chas. Berger, res. 1302 L ave., N. E.
      Tel. 24727 ....R S
   C. J. Faltinson, 916 E ave., N. W.
      Tel. 2-4983 ....F S & T

92, Birmingham, Ala. (Mixed). — Meets
every 2nd and 4th Thursday night at
7:30 p. m., 1823½ 5th Avenue North.
   W. A. Gilmore, 2351 Ave. P.
      Tel. 6-6189 ....P
   F. C. Golden, 950 N. 48th st.
      Tel. 9-9750 ....R S

W. O. Hare. Send all mail to Box 490.
   Office 212 Fox Bldg.
   Tel. 7-3038. Res. Tel. 6-2359..F S-T-B A

94, St. Paul, Minn. (Mixed).—Meets 2nd
and 4th Friday evening of each month
at St. Paul Labor Temple, 418 N. Franklin St.
   Chas. Carlson, 785 Jefferson ave.
      Tel. Elkhurst 2302 ....P
   Paul E. Kohls, 719 Blair st.
      Tel. Elkhurst 3504. ....F S & T
   Wm. O'Connell, 691 Jefferson ave.
      Tel. Elkhurst 3913.................R S

97, Vancouver, B. C. (Mixed).—Meets every
2nd and 4th Wednesday night, Hall 2,
Labor Headquarters, Beatty Street.
   Bryce Phillip, off. 531 Beatty st.
      Tel. Seymour 7495.
      Res. 2248 Triumph st.
      Tel. Highland 611L.................P
   W. J. Cook, off. 531 Beatty st.
      Tel. Seymour 7495.
      Res. 3526 Rumble st.
      Tel. Carleton 980L-2.................R S
   J. P. Rankin, Office, Labor Temple.
      531 Beatty st. Tel. Seymour 7495.
      Res. 52 11th ave. West.
      Tel. Fairmount 346-Y......F S & T, B A

103, Evansville, Ind. (Mixed).—Meets every
1st and 3rd Wednesday at Labor Forum,
8th and Main Sts.
   Ed Jung, Office 615 N. W. First St.
      Tel. 20996. Res. 612 N. W. High st.P-B A
   James B. Bulger,
      Res. 24 W. Delaware St.
      Tel. 2-0996.................F S-T-R S

107, Butte, Mont. (Mixed).—Meets 1st and
3rd Monday at Carpenters' Union Hall,
156 W. Granite.
   John Powers, res. 1630 Phillips Ave......P
   F. E. Carlson, res 1530 Warren Ave.
      Tel. 2-2563 ....R S-T
   James Peters, 2121 Oak st.
      Tel. 4569 ....B A-F S

111, Rock Island, Ill.; Moline, Ill., and Dav-
enport, Iowa (Mixed).—Meets 2nd and
4th Wednesday at Industrial Hall, Rock
Island, Ill.
   Harry Passmore, 2204 41st.
      Rock Island, Ill. ....P
   Fred Hinrichs, 1434 41st st., Rock Island,
      Ill. Tel. Rock Island 5517. Off. 202
      Labor Temple Bldg., Rock Island, Ill.
      Tel. 578 ....F S-B A
   W. Maynard, 1805 6th ave.,
      Rock Island, Ill. Tel. R. I. 6096........T
   Peter P. Stauduhar, P. O. Box 405,
      Rock Island, Ill.................R S

112, Peoria, Ill. (Mixed).—Meets 1st and 3rd
Wednesday at Labor Temple.
   Herod Gorsage, Off. Building Trades
      Council, Labor Temple. Tel. 9340
      Res. 1219 Broadway, Pekin, Ill.
      Tel. 1151A Pekin, Ill..............P-B A
   Benj. Neavea,
      Res. 209 Cynthiana St., Pekin.
      Tel. 1599-B ....F S-T
   Elmer Blythe,
      Off. 400 N. Jeff St. Send mail to this
      address. Tel. 9340.
      Res. 210 Samford St. Tel. 7498........R

114, Tacoma, Wash. (Mixed).—Meets 1st and
3rd Monday at 740½ Broadway in Build-
ing Trades Hall.
   James McInnis, 901 East Morton St.
      Tel. Main 6801....................
   A. J. LaFramboise,
      6320 S. D. st...........R S, T, B A, F
   Address all mail to residence. Tel.
      Garland 2903-R.

118, Sacramento, Cal. (Mixed).—Executive Board meets every Thursday night, 7:00 P. M. at Labor Temple.

Thos. McEwen, send mail to Labor
   Temple. Res. Route 9, Box 2087........P
W. J. Leflar, Labor Temple. Tel. M-440.
   Res. 2317 13th st.
   Tel. M-5128-J ....R S, F S & T

125, Beaumont, Texas (Mixed). — Meets every Tuesday at Carpenters' Hall, Pine and Feres Sts.

R. Gooch, 1143 Laurel ave...............P
R. W. Picken, 2475 Primrose st........R S
Robert Bailey, 520 Shamrock st.
   Tel. 6567-W.................F S, T, B A

135, Galveston, Texas (Mixed).—Meets 2nd and 4th Wednesday at Cooks and Waiters' Hall, 309½ 23rd St.

A. E. Erickson,
   Lamarque, Tex. ....P
Sigvert Hansen,
   2802 Ave. M.....................F S, T

136, Chicago, Ill. (Machinery Movers, Riggers, House Movers).—Meets 1st and 3rd Tuesday of each month at 777 West Adams St.

F. Wilbern,
   Res. 2110 Warren ave..................P
G. Townsend,
   Res. 2316 Monroe st..................R S
Michael Artery, Rm. 7, 806 W. Washington blvd. ....B A
T. Kelly, off. 4881 St. Paul ave.
   Tel. Monroe 3487.
   Res. 212 Whiting st...........F S & B A
   Send all mail to 4881 St. Paul ave.,
   Chicago, Ill.

147, Ft. Wayne, Ind. (Mixed).—Meets 1st and 3rd Thursday at Labor Temple, 209 W. Berry St.

Send all mail to Walter Fiedler, Waynedale, Ind., until further notice.
Frank J. Farrar, res. 2721 Abbott St.
   Tel. H. 10915.........................P
Walter Fiedler, res. Waynedale, Ind.
   Tel. H. 40665.......................R S
Walter Fiedler, R. R. 4,
   Ft. Wayne, Ind. ....T, F S, B A

155, Fresno, Cal. (Mixed).—Meets first Friday of month at Labor Temple.

Pete Cavalla,
   R R 9, Res. 403 B....................P
Jas. E. Welden, 2028 Clay ave.
   Tel. 2-8269 ....R S & F S B A

158, Binghamton, N. Y. (Mixed).—Meets 1st and 3rd Thursday at Central Labor Union Hall, 93 State St.

Fred M. Birney, 93 State st. Tel. 24833.
   Res. 156 Oak st.......................P
J. Ryan, 93 State st. Tel. Binghamton 24833. Res. 31 Walnut st.
   Tel. Binghamton 41436.....R S, F S & T
F. J. Hogan, 93 State st. Tel. 24833.
   Res. 14 Parsons st. Tel. 20464......B A

161, Philadelphia, Pa. (Riggers and Machinery Movers).—Meets 1st and 3rd Thursday night at Labor Lyceum, 6th and Brown Sts.

Daniel Stewart, 1435 N. 62nd st.
   Tel. Allegheny 8332..................P
Edwin G. Kleckner, Labor Lyceum Hall,
   6th & Brown st. Tel. Market 4649.
   Home 3305 No. Grausback st.
   Tel. Garfield 7165..................R S
F. Mehlman, office Labor Lyceum Hall.
   Tel. Market 4649. Res. 118 Watkins
   st. Tel. Fulton 1891. Send all mail
   to Res. address...........F S, T & B A

167, Memphis, Tenn. (Mixed).—Meets every second and fourth Friday at Labor Temple, Beale and Lauderdale Sts.

H. P. Hough, 1151 Coker st.
   Tel. 6-6442R ....P
J. R. Williams, 1056 So. Parkway E.
   Tel. 3-3990 ....F S-T
Wm. M. Barry, 596 Malcomb
   Tel. 2-4475 ....B A

170, New York City, N. Y. (Riggers and Machinery Movers).—Meets 1st Wednesday of each month at 105 Broad St. Telephone, Bowling Green 9-6652.

Fred Wilhelmson, off. 105 Broad St.
   Tel. Bowling Green 9-6652.
   Res. 1884 55th St., Brooklyn. Tel. Beachview 2-1491 ....P
Daniel Maher, off. 105 Broad St.
   Tel. Bowling Green 9-6652.
   Res. 417 25th St., Union City, N. J...R S
Chas. Kleppe, off. 105 Broad St.
   Send mail to res. 753 55th St.,
   Brooklyn. Tel. Sunset 6-0965........B A
Louis Kelter, address all mail to
   residence, office 105 Broad st.,
   N. Y.
   Tel. Bowling Green 9-6652.
   Res. 509 26th st.,
   Union City, N. J..................F S-T

172, Columbus, Ohio (Mixed).—Meets every Friday night, 141½ S. Third St., 7:30 p. m.

Tom Boyhan, Res. 819 No. 4th st..........P
Wm. Fickenger, res. 1149 N. Peters
   ave. ....F S, T
R. A. Friedsam. Office 141½ S. 3rd st.
   Tel. Adams 0555. Res. 62 S. Richardson
   ave. Tel. Un. 9015..................B A
Oscar Barclift, Res. 240 S. Ogden ave.
   Tel. Ra. 4933.......................R S

174, El Paso, Texas (Mixed).—Meets first and third Wednesday of each month at Labor Temple, 223 So. Oregon St.

H. L. Thompson, Gen. Del.,
   Fort Bliss, Tex......................P
E. E. Boedeker, 4117 LaLuz.
   Main 8704-W ....R S
G. H. Moore, 4017 Moorehead....F S-T-B A

179, Chicago, Ill. (Stone, Derrickmen and Riggers).—Meets every 1st and 3rd Wednesday of each month at 30 N Wells St.

Wm. Hammond, 6934 S. Loomis blvd.
   Tel. Republic 2731.............F S & T
John Innes, 7705 Normal ave.........R S
John Grier, 4427-25 No. Racine ave.
   Tel. Ardmore 2123..............P-B A

184, Sioux City, Iowa (Mixed).—Meets every 2nd Tuesday at Union Label Hall, 410 Fifth St.

Frank H. Jenner, 1419 W. 21st st....P-B A
Wm. Fehrman,
   Res. 1402-22nd st..........F S & T-R S

197, New York City, N. Y. (Stone Derrickmen).—Meets 2nd and 4th Tuesday of each month at 162 E. 23rd St.

Wm. Brander, 162 E. 23rd st.
   Tel. Gramercy 5-3925.
   Res. 471 60th st., Brooklyn, N. Y....P
Walter J. Gorman, 162 E. 23rd st.
   Tel. Gramercy 5-3925. Res. 332 E. 54th
   st., Brooklyn N. Y.
   Tel. Dickens 6-2663.......F S-T-R S-B A

John Thompson, off. 162 E. 23rd st.
Tel. Gramercy 5-3925.
Res. 167D Edgewater Park.
Bronx, N. Y., tel. Talmadge 2-6878...B A

201, Washington, D. C. (Reinforced Concrete Iron Workers).—Meets every 1st and 3rd Friday in each month at 423 G St., N. W., in Typographical Temple at 8 p. m.

R. O. Boyd, res. 1835 California st.,
N. W., tel. Potomac 3084.............P
J. E. Davis, res. 4013 4th st., N. W.,
tel. Columbia 7558..................R S
Claude A. Rogers, off. 631 Penna. ave.,
N. W., tel. Metropolitan 8886. Res.
6426 Brooks Lane, tel. Wisconsin
3622-J ....B A

203, St. Louis, Mo. (Stone Derrickmen).— Meets 1st and 3rd Friday at Italian Fraternal Bldg., 626 N. Vandeventer Ave.

M. Syron, 4319 Laclede Ave.
Tel. Jeff. 9786.......................P
P. J. Brice, 5206 Holly Hills.
Tel. Flanders 1365.....F S-T, B A & R S

207, Youngstown, Ohio (Mixed). — Meets last Friday night of each month at 124 So. Champion St.

Roy Williams, 631 Alice st..............P
Geo. Lundy, Res. 729 Mahoning ave.
Tel. 78654......................T & R S
John Foley, send all mail to
Res. 729 Marshall st.
Tel. 73304....................F S & B A

227, Mobile, Ala.

A. N. Schaffer, 105 Grand
Blvd. ....P, F S-T, B A
Wm. Patterson, 106 Kate st.,
Pritchard, Ala. ....R S

228, Portsmouth, Va. (Norfolk Navy Yard Riggers).—Meets every 1st Thursday at 417 Jefferson St.

Thos. A. Wood, 417 Jefferson st.
Tel. Portsmouth 404-W...............P
Charles W. Benninghove, 732 Grayden
Park, Norfolk, Va. Tel. Nor. 44085..F S-T
Wm. Jordan, 37 Virginia Road,
Portsmouth, Va. ....R S

229, San Diego, Cal. (Mixed).—Meets first Thursday night of each month at Labor Temple, 621 Sixth St.

T. L. Vellner.........................P
Geo. Harbs, 621 6th st................R S
A. S. Terhaar, 621 6th st.............T
E. C. Fox, 621 6th st. Tel. M-7716.
Res. 592 D st., Chula Vista, Calif....F S
B. G. Thomas, 621 6th st.
Tel. Main 7716.......................B A

263, Fort Worth, Texas (Mixed).—Executive Board Meets at Labor Temple every Tuesday night at 7:00 P. M.

W. E. Crawford........................P
Clifton Brignac, 1440 Spurgeon
Tel. 6-2712.............R S-F S T-B A

272, Miami, Fla. (Mixed).—Meets 2nd and 4th Friday of each month at Labor Temple, First Ave., 925 N. E.

W. Perkins, Rt. No. 1, Box 717,
Hileah, Fla..........................P
E. M. Nicard, Rt. 1, Box 633,
Miami, Fla. Tel. 2-7343........F S-B A
Ike Matthews, 224 N. E. 21st st.,
Miami, Fla. ....R S

290, Dayton, Ohio (Mixed).—Meets every Tuesday evening at Bricklayers' Hall, 5th and Walnut Sts.

F. C. Doane, 3801 Woodbine.............P
John L. Metzler, 4032 Germantown st..R S
Woodford Riley, Off. Labor Headquarters,
202 S. Ludlow st. Tel. Fulton 2681.
Send all mail to Res. 840 S. Main
st., Tel. Fulton 1776......F S & T. B A

292, South Bend, Ind. (Mixed).—Meets 1st and 3rd Monday evening at Labor Temple, 103 W. La Salle Ave.

Edw. Salisbury, 103 W. LaSalle st.
Phone 3:0826.
Res. 1209-25th st. ....P
S. A. Sweeney, 731 Harrison ave.,
So. Bend, Ind., Tel. 3-5523..........R S
R. Cook, 444 Wellington st.
Tel. 4-7591.......................F S, T
Thos. Minnus, 103 W. LaSalle ave.
Tel. 3-0826.
Res. R. R. 2, Box 65, Niles, Mich....B A

301, Charleston, W. Va. (Mixed).—Meets every Friday at 18½ Alderson St. at 7:30 p. m.

C. F. Schrimpf, Box 82.................P
O. P. Mangus, Box 82..................R S
Harry White. Send all mail to Box 82.
Res. Tel. So. 42885..........F S, T & B A

307, Montreal, Que., Canada (Mixed).—Meets every 2nd and 4th Friday, at 415 St. Catherine's St., East.

Gerald Winson, Room 21-7 Craig st. E.
Res. 7914 Lajeunesse st.
Tel. Calumet 8224-W..................P
J. A. Charron. Tel. Lan. 9745.
Send all mail to res. 1675 Valois st.
Tel. Frontenac 7737........F S-T-B A

321, Little Rock, Ark. (Mixed).—Meets every first and third Tuesday at 213½ W. 2nd St.

Joe Strohm, 507 Parker st.
Tel. 4-4046 ....P
Frank Woodall, off., Labor Temple.
Res. 1834 Park st.
Tel. 4-3571 ....R S-F S-T-B A

340, Battle Creek, Mich. (Mixed).—Meets second and fourth Friday at 8 P. M., at 2 E. Michigan Ave.

Roy Hamilton, 54 Riverside Drive........P
Floyd Hess, 85 Harris st. Tel. 3873....B A
H. R. Lutz, 9 Highland Ave............R S
Jas. Gaines, 14½ Capital Ave., S. W.
Tel. 8322 ....F S & T

348, Erie, Pa. (Mixed).—Meets every 2nd and 4th Thursday night at C. L. U. Hall, 1701 State St.

Harold McAdoo, Belle Valley, Pa.........P
Michael B. Espline, 1701 State st.,
Tel. 2-2367 ....R S
C. V. Myers, Office 1701 State st.
Tel. 22357. Send all mail to Res.
21 Metz st. Tell 23722......F S & T-B A

350, Atlantic City, N. J. (Mixed).—Executive Board meets every Wednesday night at 8:00 p. m., at 152 S. Chalfonte Ave.

Louis J. Moser, 152 S. Chalfonte ave.
Tel. 4-4492........................P-B A
Charles J. Meloncy, 19A Irving ave.,
Atlantic City, N. J.................R S

351, Lawrence, Mass. (Mixed).—Meets 2nd and 4th Tuesday, Building Trades Hall, 96 Concord St.

J. Douglas, 397 Water st. Tel. 31404.....T
J. H. Sullivan, 36 Monmouth st.
    Tel. 27956..... ....F S, B A R S

357, Springfield, Mass. (Mixed).—Meets at Central Labor Union Hall, 21 Sanford St., 2nd and 4th Friday.
    J. W. McGuire, 73 Governor st.
      Tel. 2-7942.................P, F S, T, B A
    Hiram Fox, 136 Nelson st. West.
      Springfield, Mass. Tel. 3-0997........R S

361, Brooklyn, N. Y. (Structural).—Meets every Wednesday of each month, 550 Atlantic Ave. Tel. Main 4-7909. The Executive Board will meet Friday following each 1st and 3rd Wednesday.
    James F. Keenan, off. 550 Atlantic ave.
      Tel. Main 4-7909. Res. 394 Bergen st...P
    Henry Dedow, off. 550 Atlantic ave.
      Tel. Main 4-7909. Res. 1041 74th st.
      Tel. Shore Road 5-1706..............R S
    Jas. Baird, 550 Atlantic ave.
      Tel. Main 4-7909. Address all
      mail to Res. 2044 East 37th st.
      Tel. Dewey 9-1403..........F S. T & B A

368, Topeka, Kan. (Railroad Bridgemen), Santa Fe System.—Meets 1st and 3rd Thursday at Santa Fe Headquarters, Topeka, Kans.
    Louis Bucking, c/o Eagles Club,
      Fort Madison, Iowa.................P
    V. E. Groce, Bucklin, Mo.
      Box 251 ....F S & T

372, Cincinnati, O. (Reinforced Concrete Steel Workers).—Meets 2nd and 4th Friday, Room 307, Brotherhood of Railway Clerks Bldg., Court & Vine Sts.
    Jos. Obermeyer, office 308 Brotherhood
      Bldg., Court and Vine sts.
      Tel. Parkway 4207-7088.
      Res. 742 Woodlawn ave.
      Tel. Wabash 4921-W.............P-B A
    Carl Ludwig, 1648 Cooper st...........R S
    Sam Fisher, 7405 Forbes Rd.,
      Fernbank ....F S-T

373, Perth Amboy, N. J. (Mixed).—Meets every Tuesday night, Columbia Hall, 387 State St.
    Harry Johnson, 258 Elm st.
      Tel. 1520-W ....P
    Cliff Zehrer, 397 Compton ave......F S, T
    Wesley Hanson, 101 State st.
      Tel. Perth Amboy 4-1495.............B A
    John Wade, 313 Washington st.
      Tel. 4-2291W ....R S

377, San Francisco, Cal. (Mixed).—Meetings held 2nd and 4th Fridays of each month at 200 Guerro, S. P., Building Trades Temple.
    Ed Lewis, Off. 200 Guerrero st.
      Tel. Hemlock 8577.
      Res. 2665 Franklin st.
      Tel. Graystone 3975.................P
    Loyd A. Fox, 200 Guerrero st. Tel.
      Hemlock 8577. Res. 227 Pierce st.
      Tel. Underhill 1066.................R S
    T. L. Chambers, 200 Guerrero st. Tel.
      Hemlock 8577. Res. 1075 Ellis st.
      Tel. Tuxedo 1763...........F S-T-B A

378, Oakland, Cal. (Mixed).—Meetings held first and third Friday of each month at Carpenters' Hall, 761 12th St., at 8 P. M.
    C. F. Jackson, 1327 60th ave. Tel.
      Trinidad 8981 ....P
    J. L. Fahey, off. Carpenters' Hall,
      761 12th St. Tel. Lakeside 7985.
      Res. 140 Breed ave., San Leando,
      Calif. Tel. Trinidad 6923....F S, T, B A

Arthur Frost, 677 Sycamore st.
    Tel. Higate 2107.....................R S

379, Lafayette, Ind. (Mixed).—Meets 1st and 3rd Tuesday of month at Labor Temple, 5th and Columbia Sts.
    Willard Wampler, 105 Lincoln st....P-B A
    Richard Wampler,
      105 Lincoln st.........B A-Acting F S-T

380, Champaign, Ill. (Mixed).—Meets 2nd and 4th Tuesday of month at Labor Hall.
    Wm. Giesler, 726 S. Randolph st.,
      Champaign, Ill. ....P-B A-F S

382, Shreveport, La. (Mixed).
    The books of this local union are at International Headquarters. Members should send their money for dues to Treasurer J. H. Lyons, 1615 Syndicate Trust Bldg., St. Louis, Mo.

383, Madison, Wis. (Mixed).—Meets 2nd and 4th Thursday at Madison Labor Temple.
    Russell Oxnem, 2244 Rugby Row.
      Tel. Badger 3718.................P
    Orla V. Coleman. Res. 19 N. Brearly St.
      Tel. Badger 1226..............F S, T
    H. C. Tiedeman, 933 Edgewater Court.
      Tel. Fairchild 1443....................B A
    John Ulrich, Rt. 6................R S

384, Knoxville, Tenn. (Mixed).—Meets 1st Thursday 8 P. M. at 311 Morgan St. Meets 2nd and 4th Thursday at 8 P. M. at Norris, Tenn.
    G. C. Monroe, Rt. 1, Coal Creek, Tenn....P
    Bob Everhart,
      Clinton, Tenn. ....R S
    Stanley Rounds. Res. 111 Granger st.
      Tel. 2-9942. Send all mail to P. O.
      Box 332 ....F S-T, B A

386, La Salle, Ill. (Mixed).—Meets 2nd and 4th Wednesday at Slovenski Dome, La Salle and First Sts.
    Evan Thomas, Tel. 154-L-1.
      R. F. D. No. 1,
      Spring Valley, Ill....P, F S, T, B A
    John Navin. Res. 108 N. Dakota st.,
      Spring Valley, Ill.................R S

387, Atlanta, Ga. (Mixed).—Executive Board meets 2nd and 4th Friday of each month at 354 Hurt Bldg., at 7:30 P. M.
    C. F. Strickland, 663 W. Peachtree st....P
    W. E. Knox, 282 Atlanta ave., S. E....R S
    W. Allanson. Rt. No. 2, Box 378-A.
      College Park, Ga. ....F S-T
    Dick Hudson, 720 Hill st.
      Res. Tel. Main 9057.
      Off. 354 Hurt Bldg.
      Tel. Main 1491....................B A

391, Jersey City, N. J. (Stone Derrickmen).—Meets first Thursday of each month at 583 Summitt Ave.
    James Boyd,
      310 Danforth Ave.................P, B A
    George Gray, 235 Linden ave..F S, T, R S

392, East St. Louis, Ill. (Mixed).—Meets every 1st and 3rd Thursday at 647a Collinsville Avenue.
    Frank McCarthy, Res. 216 Julia ave.,
      Signal Hill, E. St. Louis, Ill.
      Tel. Express 876....................P

John L. McCarthy, Res. 1311 Nectar ave.,
East St. Louis, Ill. Tel. East 6376.
send all mail to 647a Collinsville ave.
Tel. East 163.
Tel. East 6376.................T-B A-F S

Alby Pritchard, Res. 5164 N. 59th st.
Tel. East 5164.......................R S

393, Aurora, Ill. (Mixed).—Meets 2nd and
4th Wednesday, 7:30 p. m., Labor
Temple, 141 Main St.

Charles L. Garbe, R. R. No. 3,
Aurora, Ill. Tel. 85426.................P

Mike Frass. 324 Rosewood ave.
Aurora, Ill. Tel. 2-2566.............F S

Geo. Brown, R. R. 1, Box 70,
N. Stoddard ave., Wheaton, Ill........

Nick Kettenhofen, 427 Liberty st.
Tel. 2-3789 ....T

Oscar W. Pederson, Off. Labor Temple.
Tel. 2-7516; Res. 916 Liberty st. Tel.
9673 ....B A

395, Hammond, Ind. (Mixed).—Meets 1st and
3rd Tuesdays at Labor Temple, Sibley
St. and Oakley Ave.

N. E. Jensen, Off. Labor Temple.
Tel. Hammond 471; 819 Truman ave....P

John McCooley, Off. Labor Temple.
Tel. Hammond 471; Res. 9949 Exchange ave., So. Chicago, Ill..........R S

Frank W. McCoy, office Labor Temple.
Tel. Hammond 471, Res. 5433 Tell st.,
Hammond, Indiana,
Tel. Hammond 424.............B A-F S-T

396, St. Louis, Mo. (Mixed).—Office, Forest
Park Hall, 4514A Manchester Ave.
Meets last Friday of each month. Tel.
FRanklin 7404.

John E. Craven, Off. Forest Park Hall,
4514a Manchester ave. Res. 4020 Peck ave.
Tel. Colfax 8214R.......................P

Lon Morgan, 4514-A Manchester ave.
Tel. Franklin 7404. Res. 805 Clarkson Place. Tel. Franklin 1427........B A

Joe Cousins, 4514A Manchester ave.
Tel. Franklin 7404; Res. 4621 West-
minster. Tel. Forest 9007 ....R S

Walter Weaver, Office, Forest Park Hall,
4514-A Manchester ave.
Tel. Franklin 7404. Res. 3731
Blow st. Tel. Riverside 6681....F S & T

397, Tampa, Fla. (Mixed).—Meets every
Wednesday at 206 S. Franklin St.

Frank Weathers, 2810 Clark st.
Tel. Y-4142 ....P

H. E. Marchant, 206 So. Franklin st...F S
J. C. Bass, Res. 8207 Shaw Ave.
Tel. 5-3872 ....Acting B A

399, Camden, N. J.—Executive Board meets
every Monday evening at Labor Temple,
Camden, N. J.

Frank Mahoney, 503 Trenton ave.........P
Thomas Kelly, 1233 Chase st..........R S
Wm. Banke. 311 Hudson st.,
Gloucester, N. J.
Tel. Gloucester 811.............F S, T

A. J. Vollmer, Labor Temple,
Camden, N. J. ....B A

400, Santa Barbara, Cal. (Mixed).—Meets
every 1st and 3rd Monday night at 1104
Santa Barbara St.

B. Hardison. Send mail to 809 Castillo st.,
Santa Barbara, Calif.
Tel. 21309..............P, R S, F S & T

401, Philadelphia, Pa. (Structural and Ornamental).—Office Room 227 Plaza
Bldg., 1505 Arch St. Executive Board
meets every Monday night, 8 p. m.

Chas. Maslow, off. 1924 Springarden st.
Tel. Fremont 3734.
Res. 2713 No. 9th.......................P

Harry H. Boyle, off. 1924 Springarden st.
Tel. Fremont 3734.
Res. 3029 Agate st.....................R S

Wm. Joyce, off. 1924 Spring Garden st.
Tel. Fremont 3734. Res. 6556 Winsor
ave. Tel. Saratoga 8603.....F S, T, B A

402, West Palm Beach, Fla. (Mixed).—Meets
at Labor Temple, 414 So. Rosemary,
W. Palm Beach, Fla., second Friday of
each month, 7:30 p. m.

F. Springberg, 438 12th st...............P
S. B. Crabtree, 3414 Broadway.
Tel. 2-3817....................R S, F S, T

404, Harrisburg, Pa. (Mixed).—Meets last
Thursday at 208½ Strawberry St.

Winifred B. Wagner, 221-223 Market st...P
John Boughter, 1235½ Bailey st..........T
E. T. Heckert, Res. 2034 Fulton st.....R S
John A. Myers, Res. 226 Reily st.,
Tel. 2-0465 ....F S

W. S. Jones, Res. 624 Oxford st.,
Tel. 22848 ....B A

405, Philadelphia, Pa. (Reinforced Concrete
Iron Workers).—Meets every Wednesday at 8 p. m. at Southeast corner Clear-
field St. and Frankford Ave.

John Petrino, Res. 2131 So. 11th st.,
Phila., Pa. Tel. Dewey 3539...........P

Gay Borrelli, office 1334 Spring
Garden st. Tel. Stevenson 2968.
Send all mail to
Res. 2323 So. 11th st.
Tel. Fulton 3166...............F S-T-B A

A. J. Clark, 3212 N. Fairhill st.
Tel. Nebraska 4170...................R S

408, Amarillo, Texas (Mixed).—Meets 1st
Wednesday evening of each month at
Carpenters Hall, 207 W. 7th St., at 8
p. m.

John Rochelle,
517 Pierce st.............................P
H. C. Gray,
312 E 24th st...............R S, F S & T

410, Great Falls, Mont.

W. M. Keller, 1024 8th ave.,
So. Great Falls, Mont..............F S-T

413, Charlotte, N. C. (Mixed).—Meets Fridays at G. A. Smith Bldg., 14 S. Church
St., at 7:30 p. m.

M. A. Saine, 1608 The Plaza....F S & T P

414, Wilkes Barre, Pa. (Mixed). — Meets
1st and 3rd Thursday night, 8:00 p. m.,
41 E. Market St., 3rd floor.

Charles Williams. 106 So.Meade st........P
Harry Royal, Sr., 76 Willow st.
Tel. W. B. 25410................F S & T
Harry J. Royal, Jr., 76 Willow st.
Tel. W. B. 25410...................R S-B A

416, Los Angeles, Cal. (Reinforced Concrete Steel Workers). Executive Board meets every Monday night, 8:00 p. m., Room 214, Labor Temple, 532 Maple Ave.

Geo. W. Davis, 3724 Maple ave..........P
Geo. Stein, 1017 Esperanza st...........R S
David G. Mitchell,
   Office, 214 Union Labor Temple.
   Tel. Mutual 3593.............F S, T-B A

417, Newburgh, N. Y. (Mixed).—Meets 1st Tuesday of each month in Labor Temple. Executive Board meets 3rd Tuesday of each month.

A. J. Zenowitch, 80 S. Water st.
   Tel. Newburgh 3165.................P
Chas. T. Shea, Labor Temple.
   Res. 328 W. 113th st., New York, N. Y.
   Tel. University 4-8245.............R S
Geo. Commo. 11 Gate st., Poughkeepsie,
   N. Y. Tel. Poughkeepsie, 1467R.F S-T-B A

420, Reading, Pa. (Mixed).—Meets fourth Thursday of each month in Plumbers' Hall, 4th floor, at Reed and Courts Sts.

Dewey Downey, Res. 33 So. Wyomissing
   ave. Tel. 41459....................P
John C. Sauer, 744 N. 12th st..........R S
John Pinkerton,
   2202 Raymond Ave., Northmont.
   Reading, Pa. Tel. 2-5945.....F S-T-B A

424, New Haven, Conn. (Mixed).—Meets Fourth Friday night at Trades Council Hall, 215 Meadow St. Tel., 7-3665.

D. McCormick, 136 Holmes st.,
   Stratford, Conn. Tel. Bpt. 7-2199.......P
Lawrence Neary, 620 Washington ave.,
   Bridgeport, Conn. Tel. Bpt. 3-1942....R S
J. R. Thompson. Send all mail to Box 1311,
   New Haven, Conn. Res. 56 Sea View
   ave., West Haven, Conn.
   Tel. N. H. 9-4102............F S-T, B A

426, Detroit, Mich. (Reinforced Concrete Steel Workers).—Meets 2nd and 4th Wednesday of each month at 907 Hoffman Bldg.

J. G. Coleman, 907 Hoffman Bldg.
   Tel. Randolph 1121. Res. West Marga-
   ret. Tel. Townsen 6-2368..............P
Sam Olney, 907 Hoffman Bldg.
   Tel. Randolph 1121. Res. 4022 Ho-
   garth. Tel. Euclid 8286........F S-T-B A

433, Los Angeles, Calif. (Structural, Ornamental Iron Workers, Riggers and Machinery Movers). Tel. Madison 3264. Ex. Board meet every Tuesday night at Labor Temple.

W. J. Starr, 616 Keenan st..............P
H. W. Rehfeldt, 2334 Crenshaw blvd.
   Tel. Parkway 2439...................R S
F. B. Johnson, Office 210 Labor Tem-
   ple. Tel. Madison 3264. Res. 3011 West
   62nd st. Tel. Thornwall 1426..F S-T, B A

436, Elmira, N. Y. (Mixed).—Meets first and third Thursday at 114 Lake St.

John Koch, 459 Franklin st. Tel. 2708....P
Daniel J. Culliney, 120 W. Miller st....R S
Edward Koch, office 143½ Water st.
   Send all mail to Res. 459 Franklin st.
   Tel. 2-2708 ....F S-T

439, Terre Haute, Ind.—Meets every Tuesday night 8:00 p. m. at Labor Temple.

C. J. Townsend, 402 Mullberry st........P
L. A. Morrison, 2137 Hendriks ave......R S
J. A. Ligett, 330 S. 6th st.,
   West Terre Haute, Ind.......F S-T-B A

440, Utica, N. Y. (Mixed).—Meets 4th Friday of each month at Labor Temple, 714 Charlotte St.

Martin J. Walter, 805 Buchanan rd.,
   Frankfort, N. Y. Tel. 4-1858...........P
Thos. M. Entwistle, 1535 Seymour ave.,
   Frankfort, N. Y......................R S
Frank J. Hauser, Route 2, Frankfort, N. Y.
   Tel. Utica 1F-33.............F S, T, B A

443, Wichita, Kansas (Mixed).—Meets 1st and 3rd Friday night at Labor Temple.

C. A. Russell, 1301 S. Moseley.
   Tel. 4-1268 ....P-B A
R. B. Kline, 605 South Ash st.
   Tel. 4-4998 ....R S F S-T

444, Joliet, Ill., (Mixed).—Meets 1st and 3rd Tuesday at 127 E. Jefferson St.

John J. Smith, Off. 127 E. Jefferson
   st. Tel. 6406; Res. 115 Cleveland ave...P
J. C. McDonald, 436 Henderson ave.
   Tel. 2-0612 ....R S-B A
Axel Martinson, office 127 E. Jef-
   ferson st. Tel. Joliet 6406.
   Send all mail to Res. 125 Willow ave.
   Tel. Joliet 2-9013...................F S-T

447, New York, N. Y. (Ornamental).—Regular meeting held every 2nd Friday of each month at Labor Temple, 243 E. 84th St., Room 10, at 8 P. M. Executive Board meets 4th Wednesday of each month at Headquarters, 150 W. 28th St., at 8 P. M. Room 603, Tel. Chickering 4-1447. Send all mail to 150 W. 28th St.

Henry C. Wolf, off. 150 W. 28th st., tel.
   Chickering 4-1447 ....P-F S-T
D. K. Miller, off. 150 W. 28th st., tel.
   Chickering 4-1447 ....R S
Joseph F. Boyen, Off. 150 W. 28th st.,
   Room 603. Tel. Chickering 4-1447.
   Res. 51-53 47th st., Woodside, L. I...B A
Edward Cline, off. 150 W. 28th st., tel.
   Chickering 4-1447 ....B A
Harry Howard, off. 150 W. 28th st., tel.
   Chickering 4-1447. Res. 117-23 195th
   st., St. Albans, L. I..................B A

449, Ottumwa, Iowa (Mixed).—Meets every Wednesday night at Labor Hall.
Clell Lynch, 1701 West Main st........P
Leroy Ream, 324 North st.............R S
Paul J. Ream, 146 South Elm st..F S-T-B A

451, Wilmington, Delaware.—Meetings held every Wednesday night at Eden Hall, 10th and Orange.

Eric R. Johnson, 1125 E. 13th st...........P
William E. Denny.
   Res. 830 W. 6th St...................F S
Walter Denny, res. 302 W. 7th st.
   Tel. 8953 ....R S
Geo. W. Foreaker, res. 832 W. 6th st....T

452, Green Bay, Wis. (Mixed).—Meets 1st and 3rd Tuesday of each month at Labor Temple.

Anthony Legener. Res. 712 Chicago st.
   Off. Labor Temple. Tel. Howard 3056..P
Frank McKowski, 1004 Dousman st.
   Adams 5303 ....F S
Albert Schmitt, 811 9th st. Tel.
   Adams 5868 ....R S

454, Casper, Wyoming (Mixed).

Wm. Vogler, 106 W. 11th st.............P
Chas. C. Campbell, 737 E. 4th st.
   Tel. 1465-W ....F S-T-R-S, B A

455, New York City (Shopmen).—Meets 2d and 4th Friday at 7 E. 15th St., Room 508.

Max Karasik, Off. 7 E. 15th St.
Tel. Gramercy 7-5537.
Res. 1069 Tiffany St., Bronx..........P
Chas. Isaacs, Off. 7 East 15th st.
Tel. Gramercy 7-5537.
Res. Apt. 2C, 1370 5th ave............R S
Leon L. Smetana, Off. 7 E. 15th st.
Tel. Gramercy 7-5537
Res. 34 Hillside ave
Tel. Loraine 7-9511................F S-T

459, Roanoke, Va. (Shopmen).—Meets 15½ Franklin Rd., S. W., 2d and 4th Friday each month.

Wm. M. Williams, res. 1608 Kenwood
blvd., S. E............................P
Brady G. Woolwine, 2406 Orange ave..R S
Harry W. Haynes, 1807 10th st., N. W..F S

460, St. Joseph, Mo. (Mixed).

Joe B. Arvin, Off. Labor Temple. Tel.
61107; Res. 623 No. 12th st. Tel. 8138...P
Geo. S. Randle, 415½ S. 15th st.
Tel. 8302 ....F S-T-R S

463, Rankin, Pa. (Shopmen). Meets 1st and 3rd Thursday of each month at 318 Braddock Ave., Braddock, Pa.

Geo. McAchern. Off. 318 Braddock ave.,
Braddock, Pa.   Res. 301 Talbot ave.,
Braddock, Pa. Tel. Brandywine 2443...P
Charles Tomesic. Off. 318 Braddock ave.,
Braddock, Pa. Res. 316 Third st.
Tel. Brandywine 1281...............T-F S
Homer Roberts. Off. 318 Braddock ave.
Res. 2222 Columbia ave.,
Swissvale, Pa. ....R S

464, Rochester, N. Y. (Shopmen).—Meets first and third Friday of each month at Carpenters' Hall, Fitzhugh St.

George S. Cooper, Off. 344 West ave.
Tel. Genesee 3454. Res. 31 Savannah
st., Rochester ....P
Howard Mossbrooks, 360 West ave.....F S
Henry Whiteside, Off. Carpenters' Hall,
Fitzhugh st. Res. 7 Clarence Park....R S

465, Kankakee, Ill. (Mixed).

W. O. Cook, Res. 806 So. Elm ave.......P
A. V. Davidson, Res. 343 So. May ave..F S
Frank Saltzgiver, Res. 645 Osborne ave.R S
R. Walker ....B A

468, Cleveland, Ohio (Shopmen).—Meets first and third Monday at 2106 Prospect Ave.

Albert Schwartz, Jr., Res. 10406 Jasper
ave. ....P
Robert Gray, 9362 Amesburg ave......R S
Fred J. Bernard, 1347 Payne ave......F S
Alex Y. Dawson, Res. 3402 East blvd.....T

469, Gulfport, Miss. (Mixed).—Meets 2nd and 4th Thursday each month.

Charles Waller, 1633 25th ave...........P
Curtis Hill, Mississippi City, Miss......R S
W. Harris, 918 33rd ave........F S-T-B A

470, Jamestown, N. Y. (Shopmen).—Meets 2nd and 4th Monday nights at the Industrial Union Hall, 40-42 So. Main St.

Harold C. Kofod, Res. 63 Meadow Lane...P
G. C. Yernberg, 80 Durant ave........F S
J. Paul Ice. Res. 35 Flagg ave........R S

471, Milwaukee, Wis. (Shopmen).—Meets 2nd and 4th Thursday at Metropolitan Hall, 6th and Clark Sts.

Ervin Schenk, 3139 N. 42nd st............P
Chris Bonerz, 4746 No. 35th st.
Tel. Hilltop 5445..................F S, B A
Clarence Henning, 2617B No. Pierce st..R S
Emil Sonntag, 2239 No. 11th st.
Tel. Conc 1386 ....T

472, San Francisco, Calif. (Shopmen).— Meets 2nd and 4th Wednesday of each month in Friendship Hall, Building Trades Temple, 200 Guerrero St.

Matthew A. Casey, Res. 1482 46th st.
Tel. Montrose 7884....................P
William J. Bohm, 200 Guerrero st.
Tel. Market 1806. Res. 1453 Church
st. Tel. Valencia 1074..............R S
William Barca, 200 Guerrera.
Tel. Market 1806.
Send all mail to residence.
655 Naples ave.
Tel. Elkridge 1375.................F S-T
Fred L. O'Hara. off. 200 Guerrero st.
Tel. Market 1806. Res. 788 8th st.,
Oakland, Calif. Tel. Lakeside 0902...B A

473, Chicago, Ill. (Shopmen).—Meets 1st and 3rd Friday at 8 P. M. at 2700 So. Turner Ave. Tel. Rockwell 5244.

Emil W. Lestina, 2838 So. Springfield
ave. ....P-B A
John Glaw, 3814 Broadway............R S
Vincent Severa,
Off. 2700 S. Turner ave.,
Tel. Rockwell 5244,
Res. 3012 S. Parnel ave. ....F S-T

474, Manchester, N. H. (Mixed).—Meets 1st and 3rd Friday of month at Labor Temple, 788 Elm St.

Forest A. Worthen, Res. 345 Gofftown rd.,
Rt. No. 4. Tel. Manchester 3469-R......P
Peter Jarosz, 71 Nashua st.,
Manchester, N. H........R S-F S-T
Bernard H. Cowette, Merril rd.
Tel. Manchester 3478-M..............B A

476, Muskogee, Okla. (Shopmen). — Meets first and third Monday of each month at Woodmen of the World Hall, at 8 P. M.

Lee Bruton, Res. 341 Okmulgee......P-B A
Don Johnston, 406 Lawrence..........R S
Byron B. West, 111½ S. C st........F S-T

477, Sheffield, Ala. (Mixed). — Meets every 2nd and 4th Sunday at W. O. W. Hall, at 4th St. and Montgomery Ave., except each third Sunday when meeting is held at Pickwick Dam.

W. D. Adams, 501 Howell st.,
Florence, Ala. ....P
Robt. Lanier, Tel. 222.
1209 Dover ave.
Send all mail to P. O. Box 408.
Tel. 222 ....F S-T-B A
E. S. Peacock, 109 East Jackson st.....R S

478, Birmingham, Ala. (Shopmen).—Meets 2nd and 4th Friday of each month.

J. L. Ward, 3212 N. 32nd st.............P
Clarence Meeks, 1011 So. 68th st......R S
C. T. Stephens, res. 1626-4 Ave. W.
Tel. 6-5965 ....F S-T-B A

479, Toronto, Ont., Can. (Shopmen).—Meets 2d and 4th Tuesday of each month at Labor Temple, 167 Church St.

Wm. Underdown, Res. 211 Gilbert ave.
Tel. Kenwood 1409....................P
Geo. H. Cross, Res. 247 Caledonia rd.F S-T
Frank Cordner, Res. 68 Franklin ave...R S

OFFICIAL DIRECTORY

International Association of Bridge, Structural and Ornamental Iron Workers

---

Headquarters Room 1624 Syndicate Trust Building, 915 Olive Street,

St. Louis (1), Mo. Telephone: GArfield 2454-55-56. L. D. 322.

INTERNATIONAL OFFICERS

P. J. MORRIN, General President, 1624 Syndicate Trust Bldg., 915 Olive St., St. Louis (1), Mo.

J. H. LYONS, General Secretary, 1624 Syndicate Trust Bldg., St. Louis (1), Mo.

J. J. DEMPSEY, General Treasurer, 1624 Syndicate Trust Bldg., St. Louis (1), Mo.

J. ARTHUR EVENSEN, First Vice-President, 6104 Bernice Ave., Chicago (34), Ill., Tel. Palisades 1977.

DAN M. GAYTON, Second Vice-President, 1624 Syndicate Trust Bldg., St. Louis (1), Mo.

WILLIAM F. BAUERS, Third Vice-President, 15 Olcott Place, Station E. (11), Tel. Humboldt 5138, Buffalo, N. Y.

JOSEPH F. BOYEN, Fourth Vice-President, 265 W. 14th St., New York (11), N. Y., Tel. Watkins 9-4766.

GAY BORRELLI, Fifth Vice-President, 2329 S. 11th St., Tel. Fulton 9-3166, Philadelphia, Pennsylvania.

BENJAMIN A. MURRAY, Sixth Vice-President, 2239 Pauline St., Tel. Crescent 7383, New Orleans, La.

C. F. STRICKLAND, Seventh Vice-President, 3842 Bakers Ferry Road, S. W., Atlanta, Ga., Tel. Amhurst 1314.

E. M. WOODS, Eighth Vice-President, 600 Hillcrest Blvd., Millbrae, Calif.

WILLIAM J. REYNOLDS, Ninth Vice-President, 33 Spring Park Avenue, Jamaica Plain, Mass., Tel. Jamaica 4-0515.

DISTRICT COUNCILS

DISTRICT COUNCIL OF GREATER NEW YORK AND VICINITY

Office, 265 W. 14th St., Zone 11. Tel. Watkins 9-4766. Meets second and fourth Thursday of each month. Business Agents meet each Monday at 11:00 A. M.

Joseph F. Boyen, President.

Charles McNamara, Recording Secretary.

Wm. Brander, Financial Secretary.

Paul S. Rockhold, Treasurer.

Local No. 40—New York, N. Y.	Local No. 455—New York, N. Y.	Local No. 417—Newburgh, N. Y.
Local No. 580—New York, N. Y.	Local No. 197—New York, N. Y.	Local No. 424 — New Haven, Conn.
Local No. 170—New York, N. Y.	Local No. 361 — Brooklyn, N. Y.	

Mail to Delivery District—New York (11).

DISTRICT COUNCIL OF CHICAGO AND VICINITY

Meets the third Friday evening of each month at Room 1219, 130 No. Wells St., P. O. Station 6.

J. A. Evensen, President; Frank McCoy, 503 Sibley St., Hammond, Ind., Vice-President; C. E. Foxworth, F. S., T., R. S., 130 No. Wells St. Tel. Franklin 4791.

Rt. 1, Box 393, Melrose Park, Ill. Tel. Franklin Park 3455-R.

Local No. 1.	Local No. 63.	Local No. 136.	Local No. 393, Aurora, Ill.
Local No. 395, Hammond, Ind.		Local No. 444, Joliet, Ill.	
Local No. 465, Kankakee, Ill.		Local No. 473, Shopmen, Chicago, Ill.	
Local No. 498, Mixed, Rockford, Ill.		Local No. 524, Shopmen, Waukegan, Ill.	
Local No. 590, Shopmen, Aurora, Ill.		Local No. 650, Rockford, Ill.	

Local No. 654, Hammond, Ind.

DISTRICT COUNCIL OF ST. LOUIS AND VICINITY

Meets first Thursday of each month at 8:00 p. m. Tel. FR-0730.

President, John McCarthy, Local 392, 1207 Missouri Ave., E. St. Louis, Ill., Tel. East 163.

Recording Secretary, Arthur A. Zeis, L. U. 518, 2345 Lafayette Ave., St. Louis 4, Mo. Tel. PR. 6690.

Financial Secretary-Treasurer, Joe Cousin, L. U. 396, 7405 Rupert Ave. Tel. HIland 7382.

Local Union No. 396	Local Union No. 203	Local Union No. 392
Local Union No. 513	Local Union No. 518	

DISTRICT COUNCIL OF PHILADELPHIA, PA., AND VICINITY

Meets second and fourth Friday of each month at 1803 Spring Garden St.

Board of Business Agents Meeting every Monday morning at 10:00 a. m., in Council Office, 1031 City Center Bldg., 121 No. Broad St., Philadelphia (7).

Tel. Rittenhouse 6-7835 and 6-7836.

Gay Borrelli, President.   Arthur Lee, Secretary-Treasurer.

Send all mail to 1031 City Center Bldg., Zone 7.

Local Union No. 36	Local Union No. 405	Local Union No. 565
Local Union No. 68	Local Union No. 420	Local Union No. 572
Local Union No. 161	Local Union No. 451	Local Union No. 579
Local Union No. 350	Local Union No. 502	Local Union No. 599
Local Union No. 399	Local Union No. 519	Local Union No. 664
Local Union No. 401	Local Union No. 544	Local Union No. 670
Local Union No. 404	Local Union No. 548	Local Union No. 681
		Local Union No. 692

DISTRICT COUNCIL OF NORTHERN NEW JERSEY

Meets second and fourth Monday of each month at the Hotel Robert Treat, Newark, N. J.
J. W. Lowe, President, 852 S. 15th St. Tel. Essex 2-8370.
John McCarthy, Fin. Sec.-Treas., Recording Secretary, 255 Vermont Ave., Irvington, N. J.
Tel. Essex 3-1082.

Local No. 11—Newark, N. J.   Local No. 45—Jersey City
Local No. 373—Perth Amboy, N. J.
Local Union No. 480—Elizabeth, N. J.
Local Union No. 483—Hackensack, N. J.
Shopmen's Local Union No. 545—Newark, N. J.

BAY DISTRICT COUNCIL OF SAN FRANCISCO AND VICINITY

Meets first Saturday of each month, alternating meetings in San Francisco, Oakland.
Sacramento and Fresno. For further information see E. M. Woods, 200 Guerrero St.,
San Francisco. Tel. Hemlock 4736.

E. M. Woods, President, 600 Hillcrest Blvd., Millbrae, Calif.
Jos. R. Costa, Local 491, Vice-President, 1518 13th Avenue, Oakland, Calif.
C. R. Burton, Local 118, Secretary-Treasurer, P. O. Box 1061, Sacramento. Calif
Tel. 2-8870.

Local 118 and Local 504, Sacramento; Local 378, Oakland;
Local 377, Local 472 and Local 491, San Francisco, Calif.;
Local 155, Fresno, Calif.; Local Union 624, Fresno, Calif.

DISTRICT COUNCIL OF WASHINGTON, D. C., BALTIMORE, MD., AND VICINITY

Meets first Tuesday of each month, alternating between Washington, D. C., and
Baltimore, Md.
President, L. L. Meyers; Vice-President, John C. Finck, Jr., Local 657; Recording Secretary,
Edw. T. Smith, Local Union No. 16; Financial Secretary, C. B. Reynolds, Local Union
No. 5; Sergeant-at-Arms, Harry Haynes, Local Union No. 5.

DISTRICT COUNCIL OF MICHIGAN

Meets third Tuesday of each month at Iron Workers' Labor Temple, 3126 Parke Ave.
Office: 3126 Park Ave.
President, Samuel P. Tobin, Local 25.
Recording Secretary, Financial Secretary and Treasurer, Paul C. Allen, Riggers'
Local No. 575, 8213 Woodward Ave. Tel. Trinity 2-4110, Detroit, Mich.
Vice-President, C. W. Pascoe, Local No. 426.
Sgt.-at-Arms, H. O. Poole, Local No. 340, Battle Creek, Mich.
Structural Local No. 25; Rodmen's Local No. 426; Riggers' Local No. 575;
Mixed Local No. 340; Battle Creek, Mich.; Shopmen's Local No. 508;
Shopmen'sLocal No. 615, Muskegon, Mich.,
Shopmen's Local No. 688, Grand Rapids, Mich.

DISTRICT COUNCIL OF KANSAS CITY AND VICINITY

Meets first Monday of each month in offices: 2906 Brooklyn Ave.; Tel. Lo. 2526
Perrin D. McElroy, 5410 Wabash St.; Tel. Delmar 1125, President.
Ralph G. Amberger, 715 Cleveland Ave.; Tel. Benton 1739, First Vice-President.
John Bell, 1423 Olive St., Leavenworth, Kans., Second Vice-President.
Earle J. Ferguson, 4334 Summit St.; Tel Logan 0486, Recording Secretary,
Financial Secretary-Treasurer.

Local No. 10—Kansas City, Mo.   Local No. 582—Kansas City, Kansas.
Local No. 520—Kansas City, Mo.   Local No. 660—Leavenworth, Kansas.

DISTRICT COUNCIL OF FT. WORTH AND DALLAS, TEXAS

Clifford Brignac, 3418 No. Crump St., Ft. Worth, Texas, President; Elbert Wickham,
Local 481, Dallas, Texas, Vice-President; W. R. Easter, Local No. 263,
Ft. Worth, Texas, Recording Secretary, Financial Secretary-
Treasurer.

Local No. 263—Ft. Worth, Texas (Mixed).   Local No. 563—Dallas, Texas (Shopmen).
Local No. 481—Dallas, Texas (Mixed).   Local No. 543—Ft. Worth, Texas (Shopmen).

LOCAL UNIONS

P, President; R S, Recording Secretary; F S, Financial Secretary; T, Treasurer;
B A, Business Agent.   Mixed, means local controls all branches of trade.

1, Chicago, Ill. (Structural).—Meets every Monday night at 2754 W. Madison St. Executive Board meets every Monday night at 2754 W. Madison St., Zone 12.

John Von Allmen, 3203 N. Clark St.,
Tel. Diversey 9261........................P
Geo. Fitzgerald, 3512 W. Hirsch St.
Tel. Spaulding 5670......................R S
Elmer E. Lane, off. 2754 W. Madison
St., Zone 12. Tel. Sacramento 6466.
Res. 3000 W. Palmer Sq.
Tel. Spaulding 6366.............F S-T
William Currier, Res. 4337 Berkley Ave.
Tel. Atlantic 7757..................B A
Joseph Denight, 3251 N. Osage Ave.
Tel. Tuxedo 9549.......................B A
Send all mail to office, 2754 W. Madison
St., Zone 12.

3, Pittsburgh, Pa. (Mixed).—Meets every Tuesday at 1213 Penn Ave., Zone 22, Tel. Atlantic 9806.   Executive Board meets every Tuesday.

James P. Conway, 322 Stanton Ave.,
Millvale, Pa. Tel. Millvale 1484-J......P
Matthew Gorman, 327 Lehigh St.
Tel. Emerson 0918...................F S-T
All mail to Office, 1213 Penn Ave.,
Zone 22. Tel. Atlantic 9806.
Charles E. Boyle, Off. 1213 Penn Ave.,
Zone 22. Res. 826 North Ave.,
No. Braddock, Pa. Tel. Brandywine
9041 ....R S
O. J. Royer, Off. 1213 Penn Ave,
Res. 1524 Creedmore St., Brookline,
Pittsburgh, Pa. Tel. Fieldbrook 5383..B A
Edw. Conway, Off. 1213 Penn Ave.
Res. 318 Stanton Ave., Millvale, Pa.
Tel. Millvale 1417....................B A

4, Toronto, Ont. (Mixed).—Meets first and third Wednesday night at Labor Temple, Church St. Send all mail for Local 4 to E. Larson, 73 Gladstone Ave.

E. Larsen, 520 Watson St.,
Fort Whitby, Ont.................P-F S-T

5, Washington, D. C. (Structural and Ornamental).—Meets every Thursday night at 405 9th St., N. W. Tel. Met. 5259. Executive Board meets first and third Thursdays.

Ted C. Harris, 1362 Oak St., N. W.
Tel. Adams 3317...........................P
Geo. R. Murphy, 6406 45th Place,
Riverdale, Md. Tel. Warfield 8705....R S
Frank Herron, 154 11th St., N.E.,
Zone (2). Tel. Franklin 5906..........F S
E. L. Pierpont, 1121 New Hampshire
Ave. Tel. Republic 0636, Ex. 102........T
C. B. Reynolds, off. 405 9th St. N. W.
Res. 2804 Myrtle Ave., N. E.
Tel. North 8153 ....B A

6, Buffalo, N. Y. (Mixed).—Meets every Friday night at 475 Franklin St. (2). Tel. Garfield 4146.   Executive Board meets every Friday night.

Jos. B. Masterson, off. 475 Franklin St.
Res. 147 Roosevelt Ave. (15).
Tel. Parkside 9271...................R S
Geo. J. Bannister, 1034 Kenmore Ave.
Tel. Ri-5723...............................P
James Brisson, 475 Franklin St.,
Zone (2). Tel. Ga. 4146...........F S-T
Elmer J. Hoffman, Res. Elks Club,
211 Delaware Ave. Tel. Cleveland 1690.
Off. 475 Franklin St...................B A

7, Boston, Mass. (Mixed).—Meets last Sunday afternoon of each month at 2:00 p. m., at 390 Tremont St. Executive Board meets Tuesday before fifteenth of month and Tuesday before last Sunday. Tel. Liberty 7036.

Daniel McLean, Off. 390 Tremont St......P
Fred Campbell, 390 Tremont St..........R S
Frank J. Moriarty,
Off. 390 Tremont St. Tel. Liberty 7036.
Res. 62 Landseer St., West Roxbury,
Mass. Tel. Parkway 4727..........F S & T
Wm. J. Reynolds,
Off. 390 Tremont St. Tel. Liberty 7036.
Res. 33 Spring Park Ave., Jamaica
Plain, Mass. Tel. Arnold 0515........B A

8, Milwaukee, Wis. (Mixed).—Meets second and fourth Tuesday evening at Sokol Hall, 1309 W. Walnut St.

Gus H. Damske, Res. 235 N. 39th St.,
Zone 13. Tel. West 6745-R.............P
Edw. K. Preuss, Res. 2813 W. Wright St.,
Zone 10. Tel. Hopkins 9685-J.........R S
James P. Hamill, Res. 4915 W. National,
Zone 14. Tel. Orchard 0916-J...........T
Herbert J. Mueller,
Off. 1012 N. 3rd. Room 214, Zone 3.
Tel. Daly 5490. Res. 5330 N. 34th St.
Zone 9. Tel. Hilltop 8372..........F S-B A

9, Niagara Falls, N. Y. (Mixed).—Meets fourth Thursday night in Eagles' Home, 1103 Main St., Tel. 8249. Executive Board meets second and fourth Thursdays.

Alfred J. Sample, Res. Randolph, N. Y.....P
Charles S. Harvey, Off. Eagles Club.
1103 Main St., Niagara Falls, N. Y.
Tel. 8249, Ex. 2, Res. 23 Woodland,
R.F.D. No. 1, Tel. 2-0104........F S-T-B A
F. H. Fairburn, Off. 1103 Main St.
Tel. 8249, Res. 9147 Buffalo Ave.........R S

10, Kansas City, Mo. (Mixed).—Meets second and fourth Wednesday evenings at office, 2906 Brooklyn (3). Tel. WA-0565.

Geo. Steffee, 3554 E. 23rd St.
Tel. BE-8925...........................P
Send mail to residence.
Homer Sexton, off. 2906 Brooklyn Ave.
Tel. Wabash 0565. Res. 3705 Bales
Ave. Tel. Armour 0624...............R S
W. R. Buchanan, 11211 Winner Rd.,
Independence, Mo.
Tel. Clifton 5549...............F S-T-B A
All mail to office.

11, Newark, N. J. (Mixed).—Meets first and third Thursday evenings at 34 Park Place, Zone 2.

Victor Woodall, Off. 34 Park Pl.
Tel. MA. 2-8177.........................P
Ralph Golden, Newark, N. J.
Off. 34 Park Place, Zone 2.
Tel. Market 2-8177...............F S-R S
Wm. J. Norris, 12 Walnut St.
Tel. MA-3-1163...........................T
J. W. Lowe, Off. 34 Park Place, Zone 2.
Tel. Market 2-8177.
Res. 852 S. 15th St. Tel. ES. 2-8370....B A

12, Albany, N. Y. (Mixed).—Meets second Tuesday of each month at Labor Temple, 87 Beaver St. (10).

Joseph L. Bannon, 437 Third Ave.,
Watervliet, N. Y. Tel. 1419-W.........P
Joe Keefe, Res. 571 N. Pearl St.,
Albany (4), N. Y.
Tel. Dial 4-7428...............F S-T-B A
Robt. Healey, 106 1st St., Watervliet,
N. Y. Tel. Watervliet 903-W.........R S

14, Spokane, Wash. (Mixed).—Meets fourth Thursday at 8:00 p. m., West 104 Third Ave. Zone 8. Executive Board meets second and fourth Thursdays.

Edgar C. Bryan, 11315 E. 12th Ave.,
Opportunity, Wash. Tel. W-3073......P
James B. Hill, R.F.D. No. 9,
Spokane 15, Wash. Tel. W-4477..Act R S
Geo. H. Holland, Res. 4323 2nd Ave.
Off. West 104 Third Ave., Zone 8.
Tel. R-7037. Res. Tel. LA-2535..F S-T-B A

15, Hartford, Conn. (Mixed).—Local Union meets second and fourth Thursday nights of month at Labor Temple, 95 Park St. Executive Board meets first and third Thursday nights at 327 Trumbull St., Zone 3. Tel. 6-3675.

Joseph Clancy, Res. 8 Columbia St.
Tel. 6-7085..............................P
Alv Latourette, Res. 41 Lake St.,
Norwich, Conn. ....R S
Frank E. Connor, Res. 241 Franklin Ave.
Tel. 6-3380. Off. 327 Trumbull St.
Tel. 6-3675 ....F S-T-B A

16, Baltimore, Md. (Mixed).—Meets every Friday night of each month at 360 N. Gay St., Zone 2, at 8 p. m. Executive Board meets second and fourth Saturday at 9 a. m. Off. Tel. Plaza 5646.

Edw. T. Smith, 20 S. Arlington Ave.
Tel. Lexington 4929....................P
Sinclair Sylvester, Res. 620 N. Monroe
St., Zone 17.
Tel. Edmondson 0315-W............F S-T
Nick Lister, 8210 Long Point Road,
Dundalk, Md. ....B A
John D. Hurtt, 2305 Aisquith St.,
Zone 14.................................R S

17, Cleveland, Ohio (Mixed).—Meets every Friday evening at 1544 E. 23rd St., Zone 14. Executive Board meets every Friday.

Joseph Keenan, Off. 1544 E. 23rd St.,
Zone 14. Res. 3194 W. 110th St.
Res. Tel. Clearwater 3030.................P
Arthur R. Waters, 17701 Puritas Ave.
Tel. Orchard 1710........................R S
Geo. A. Solomon, Off. 1544 E. 23rd St.,
Zone 14. Tel. Prospect 5558-5454.
17503 Puritas Ave.
Tel. Orchard 7423....................F-S
Thomas McDonald, 1544 E. 23rd St.
Tel. Prospect 5558.
Res. Tel. Atlantic 1919................B A
John K. Ingram, 2545 Carnegie Ave.
Tel. Prospect 2791......................T

21, Omaha, Neb. (Mixed).—Meets first and third Wednesday evening at Hall No. 3, Labor Temple, Zone 2.

F. K. Painter, Res. Congress Hotel.
Tel. Jackson 7676.
Send mail to Labor Temple, Zone 2.
Tel. Jackson 6571....................P-B A
Larry Glynn, 2811 Fort St.
Tel. Ke. 2339. Send all mail to Labor
Temple, Zone 2................F S-T-R S

22, Indianapolis, Ind. (Mixed).—Meets every Tuesday night of each month at 423 Transportation Building, Zone 4. Tel. Franklin 1286. Executive Board meets second and fourth Tuesdays.

A. C. Hoyt, Jr., Off. 423 Transportation
Bldg. Res. 2033 Houston St.
Res. Tel. Cherry 4854-W................P
Gustave F. Mayer, 1431 Congress Ave.
Tel. Talbot 8247.......................T
W. N. Hazelwood, 423 Transportation
Bldg. Res. R.R. L, Box 350.
Res. Tel. GA-1592................F S-B A
R. A. Hendricks, Off. 423 Transportation
Bldg. Res. 3341 E. Michigan St.......R S

24, Denver, Colo. (Mixed).—Meets first and third Thursday evenings at 1947 Stout St., Zone 2. Tel. CH-8273. Executive Board meets first and third Thursday.

John Bagan, Off. 1947 Stout St.
Res. 684 So. Wash St.
Res. Tel. PE-4933.......................P
Wm. H. Bowman, Off. 1947 Stout St.
Res. 336 Elita St.
Res. Tel. Pearl 5310................F S-T
J. Harold Smith, Off. 1947 Stout St.,
Res. 1530 Downing St.
Tel. Ch. 8374.........................B A
John J. Wiegeman, 4401 S. Elastic St.,
Englewood, Colo. Tel. ENG. 1271-R....R S
Send all mail to 1947 Stout St., Zone 2.

25, Detroit (1), Mich. (Structural and Ornamental).—Meets second and last Monday, 8 p. m., at 3126 Park Ave., Zone 1. Tel. Temple 1-0312. Executive Board meets every third Monday.

Alex Strong, 3126 Park Ave., Zone 1........P
Samuel B. McKinney, 3126 Park Ave.,
Zone 1.................................R S
T. Pasell, 3126 Park Ave., Zone 1,
Res. 408 Temple St..............F S-T-B A
Elinor Simstad, 3126 Park Ave.,
Zone 1 ....Asst B A

27, Salt Lake City, Utah (Mixed).—Meets third Friday night at 308 Labor Temple. Tel. 3-9991. Executive Board meets first and third Fridays.

Herbert L. Clark, 2054 Crystal Ave.
Tel. 7-8864 ....P
Clifford A. Langford, 308 Labor Temple,
Res. 1420 Crandall Ave.................R S
John McKean, 608 Wilson Ave.
Tel. Ph. 6-4800. Off. Tel. 3-9991.F S-B A-T
Send all mail to 308 Labor Temple.

28, Richmond, Va. (Mixed).—Meets every first and third Thursday at 8:00 p. m. in Labor Temple, 1013 E. Marshall St. Tel. 2-6837. Executive Board meets second and fourth Mondays.

O. E. Howerton, 2305 E. Broad St..........P
James R. Hairfield, 510 So. Pine.
Tel. 3-7994. Off. 1013 E. Marshall St.,..B A
J. F. Wilkerson, 719 Northside Ave.
Tel. 3-0603 ....F S-T
J. F. Wilkerson, Jr.,
719 Northside Ave. ....R S

29, Portland, Ore. (Mixed). — Meets every second and fourth Friday evening at Labor Temple, Fourth and Jefferson Sts., Hall K, fourth floor, 8 p. m. Executive Board meets second and fourth Friday.

Jerry McCabe, Off. 203 Labor Temple.
Off. Tel. Atwater 0171....................P
C. R. Mungstedt, 1114 N.E. Winona St.
Tel. WE-6308.........................R S
John O'Neill, Off. 203 Labor Temple,
Zone 4. Tel. Atwater 0171.
Res. 5765 N. E. Cleveland.
Tel. Murdoch 4561...............F S-T-B A

33, Rochester, N. Y. (Mixed).—Meets second and fourth Tuesday nights at 8 p. m., 360 Plymouth Ave. So. Executive Board meets second and fourth Tuesdays at 7 p. m.

Daniel J. McCarten, 16 Boothe St.
Tel. Monroe 1896-J.......................P
Seymour McDonald, Res., 214 Meigs St.
Res. Tel. Monroe 8202-J.................R S
Harry E. Keys, Res. 25 Wilmington St.
Tel. Monroe 2034-R.
Off. 360 Plymouth Ave., S. (8).
Tel. Main 5402................F S-T-B A

36, Easton, Pa. (Mixed). — Meetings held third Sunday of each month at 2 p. m., Central Labor Union, 214 Northampton St., Easton, Pa. Executive Board meets first and third Sunday of each month at 2 p. m and 1:30 p m., respectively, Central Labor Union, 214 Northampton St., Easton, Pa.

Wm. Burns, 147 James St., Easton........P
Edward F. Storm, Res. 716 Davis St......R S
Michael F. Foley, 104½ N. Second St.,
 Allentown, Pa. Tel. 26326..............B A
Kenneth L. Reed, Off. 514 N. 5th St.,
 Allentown, Pa. Tel. Allentown 7446....F S
Henry Miller, Box 53, Cementon, Pa.
 Tel. 7582, Northampton, Pa.............T

37, Providence, R. I. (Mixed).—Meets second and fourth Thursday night at 8 p. m., at 37 Clemence St. Executive Board meets first and third Thursday.

Thos. Stevens, 194 Grand Ave.,
 Cranston, R. I.........................P
Benjamin F. Sullivan, Cedar Avenue,
 Island Park, Portsmouth, R. I.........R S
John J. White, Off. 56 Washington St.,
 Zone 3. Tel. Dexter 2862. Res. 12
 Granger Court, Hoxie, R. I.....F S-T-B A

40, New York (Zone 3), N. Y. (Structural). Office, 80 East 11th Street, Room 207, Tel. Orchard 4-1241-2.—Regular meeting will be held second and fourth Tuesday evenings at Werdermann's Hall, 160 Third Ave. (near E. 16th St.). Executive Board meets first and third Tuesday evenings at 80 East 11th St.

Patrick Magone, Off. 80 E. 11th St.,
 Room 207, Zone 3.
 Tel. Orchard 4-1241-2.
 Res. 415 E. 154th St., Bronx, N. Y........P
Charles Pankuch, Off. Room 207,
 80 East 11th St. Tel. Orchard 4-1241-2.
 Res. 142 Kamda Blvd., New Hyde Park,
 L. I. Tel. Floral Park 8781...........R S
David Mansfield, Off. 80 E. 11th St.,
 Room 207, Zone 3.
 Tel. Orchard 4-1241-2...............F S-T
James Cole, Off. 80 E. 11th St.,
 Room 207, Zone 3.
 Tel. Orchard 4-1241-2...............F S-T
 Tel. Windsor 5-3768................B A
 Res. 238 Senator St., Brooklyn, N. Y.

44, Cincinnati, Ohio (Structural, Ornamental, Riggers & Machinery Movers). —Meets first and third Friday night, 7:30 p. m., at 1411 Walnut St. Executive Board meets first and third Friday at Business Office, 1411 Walnut St. Tel. Cherry 5411.

Thos. Braley, 2325 Vine St. Tel. Un. 1347—.P
Chas. Rapp, 6031 Plainfield Road.
 Tel. Me. 8982, Silverton 22, Ohio......R S
J. A. Anslinger. Send all mail to 3597
 Haven St. (20). Tel. UN. 6783.....F S & T
Lonnie Shrader, Off. 1411 Walnut St.
 Tel. Cherry 5411.
 Res. Rt. 2, Batavia, Ohio.
 Tel. Williamsburg 4834................B A

45, Jersey City, N. J. (Mixed).—Meets second and fourth Tuesday evenings. Executive Board meets first and third Tuesday evenings at Central Hall, 574 Newark Ave., Zone 6, Jersey City, N. J.

Daniel J. Trainor, 674 Newark Ave.,
 Jersey City 6, N. J. Tel. Journal
 Square 2-3365. Res. 136 Highpoint
 Ave., Weehawken, N. J. Tel. Union
 7-6609...............................P
Wm. Wancura, 574 Newark Ave.,
 Jersey City 6, N. J. Tel. Journal
 Square 2-3365. Res. 717 16th St.,
 Union City, N. J.....................R S

John Boyle, Off. 574 Newark Ave.,
 Jersey City 6, N. J. Tel. Journal
 Square 2-3365. Res. 189 Harrison
 Ave. Tel. Bergen 4-0692..............B A
Peter Arci, Off. 574 Newark Ave., Tel.
 Journal Square 2-3365. Res. 107-28,
 104th St., Ozone Park, N. Y.........F S-T

46, Springfield, Ill. (Mixed).—Meets second and fourth Tuesday nights at Building Trades Council, 216⅓ E. Monroe St.

John Wheeling, Off. 216⅓ E. Monroe
 St. Res. 107 N. Grand Ave., West.
 Tel. 3-1219..........................P
Dewey F. Hicks. Off. 216⅓ E. Monroe
 St. Tel. 2-4232. Res. 3939 S. Douglas,
 Tel. 3-4132....................F S-T-B A
Paul Reimer, 216⅓ E. Monroe.
 Res. R. R. No. 5.....................R S
All mail to office, 216½ E. Monroe St.
 Tel. 2-4232.

48, Oklahoma City, Okla. (Mixed).—Meets every Monday at 7:30 p. m., at Office, 105 W. Grand, Room 301, Zone 2. Executive Board meets first and third Mondays. Tel. 7-8942.

A. W. Spence, Off. 105 W. Grand.
 Res. 2904 S. W. 29th St., Rt. 6, Box 42.
 Res. Tel. 6-4915.....................P
Clovis G. Bowman, Off. 105 W. Grand.
 Res. Rt. 9, Box 491-X.
 Res. Tel. 6-5339.....................R S
Russell B. Elliott, Off. Room 301, 105
 W. Grand, Zone 2. Tel. 7-8942. Res.
 15 S. W. 23rd St. Tel. 2-8037....F S-T-B A

55, Toledo, Ohio (Mixed.) — Meets third Tuesday evening in Labor Temple, 912 Adams St. Tel. Main 9101. Executive Board meets first and third Tuesday evenings.

Stanley R. Walters, 603 Robindale St.
 Tel. Talyor 6724.....................P
D. B. Hipkiss, Jr., off. 912 Adams St...F S-T
I. G. Barrett, Box 399, R-1 Woodville
 Rd. Zone 5...........................B A
Send all mail to Central Labor
 Union, 912 Adams St. Zone 2.

57, Worcester, Mass. (Mixed). — Meets second Friday of each month at 8 p. m., at Labor Temple, 62 Madison St.

Frank Guertin, 9 5th Ave.,
 Shrewsbury, Mass. ....P
Roland Bourque, 8 5th Ave.,
 Shrewsbury, Mass. ....F S-T
Patrick Kelliher, 257 Chandler St.
 Tel. 28217...........................R S
Thos. F. Dey Negro, Off. Labor Temple,
 Tel. 3-9652. Res. 159 Eastern Ave.
 Tel. 6-0554..........................B A
Send all mail to residence.

58, New Orleans, La. (Mixed). — Meets second and fourth Thursdays at 8 p. m., at 836 Carondelet St. Tel. RA-7436. Executive Board meets second and fourth Thursdays. Send all mail to 836 Carondelet St. (Zone 13).

Eugene LeFevre, Off. 836 Carondelet.
 Tel. RA-7436. Res. 6435 Milne St.
 Tel. GA-6135. ....P
E. C. Grandin, Off. 836 Carondelet.
 Tel. RA-7436. Res. 2335 Painters St.
 Tel. By-6675........................F S-T
Raymond L. Church, Jr.,
 Off. 836 Carondelet St. Tel. Ra. 7436.
 Res. 1559 N. Miro St.. Zone 19.
 Tel. Crescent 8122...................R S
Wm. O. Hunt. Off. 836 Carondelet St.
 Res. P. O. Box 112, Harahan, La......B A

60, Syracuse, N. Y. (Mixed).—Meets second and fourth Friday evenings at 309 So. Franklin St. Executive Board meets second and fourth Fridays.

James K. Hughes, 517 N. Townsend St.
Tel. 3-5302 ....P
Wade H. Burns, 709½ E. Fayete St....R S
Jos. Burns, 132 Elmwood Ave. (7).
All mail to 309 S. Franklin.
Tel. 2-3363 ....F S-T-B A

63, Chicago, Ill. (Architectural Iron Workers).— Meets last Friday night at 160 N. Halsted Ave., Zone 6. Executive Board meets second and last Fridays. Tel. Monroe 7751.

J. Ziska, 6250 N. Winthrop Ave.
Tel. Ambassador 4607................P
Geo. Bishop, 1532 Barry Ave.............R S
M. H. Martin, Off. 160 N. Halsted Ave.,
Zone 6. Res. 3606 North
Francisco Ave. ....F S-B A
Charles Corinth, Off. 160 N. Halsted Ave.,
Zone 6. Tel. Monroe 7751.
Res. 7326 W. Summerdale Ave.,
Zone 31. Tel. Newcastle 6953...........T

66, San Antonio, Texas (Mixed).— Meets fourth Tuesday at 8:00 p. m., at Labor Temple. Executive Board meets first Saturday and fourth Tuesday.

W. Z. Keeney, 648 Avondale.
Tel. Lambert 2-6991 ....P
Harold Goodman, 1807 San Pedro.
Tel. P2-0593 ....R S
Fred Fishback, 114 Atlantic St.
Tel. Garfield 3581. Res. Tel.
Lambert 2-1982.
Send all mail to P. O. Box 204...F S-T-B A

67, Des Moines, Iowa (Mixed). — Meets second and fourth Tuesday nights, 204 7th St., Zone 9. Tel. 4-9742. Executive Board meets first and third Tuesdays.

Richard Garn, 16 S.E. Broad St.
Tel. 24129 ....P
Lee Gregory, 1915 Tichinor St...........R S
Sam Turk, Off. 204 7th St., Zone 9.
Tel. 4-9742.
Res. 1110 29th St. Tel. 5-3061.....F S-B A
Send all mail to office, 204 7th St., Zone 9

68, Trenton, N. J. (Mixed). — Meets third Wednesday night at Labor Lyceum, 159 Mercer St., first floor. Executive Board meets first and third Wednesdays.

Thomas Warwick, 163 Beal St.
Tel. 25301 ....P
Frank J. Walsh, R. D. No. 2.
Marshall Ave., Trenton, N. J.
Tel. 2-2683 ....R S
John R. Davis, 115 Mary St.
Tel 6878 ....F S-T
Wm. E. Hanford, 1 Herbert Ave.,
Hamilton Sq. Tel. 28048...............B A

70. Louisville, Ky. (Mixed). — Meets every fourth Friday evening at 128 E. College St., Zone 2. Tel. Wabash 5713. Executive Board meets second and fourth Fridays.

Fred L. Green, Off. 128 E. College (2)......P
Geo. V. Fritsch, Off. 128 E. College.
Zone 2. Res. Rt. 5. Salem, Ind........R S
J. G. Glenn Inman, Off. 128 E.
College (2). Res. 568 Lilly Ave.......F S-T
James M. Foster, Off. 128 E. College St.
Tel. WA-5713. Res. 615 N. 29th St.
Tel. SH-2672 ....B-A

75, Phoenix, Ariz. (Mixed).—Meets second and fourth Fridays at A. F. of L. Bldg., 300 W. Washington St. Tel. 30402.

W. J. Gilson, 3005 E. Washington St.......P
E. T. Sexton, Res. 1730 W. Maricopa St...R S
Ralph C. Shobe, 3915 S. Second St.
Tel. No. 4-6745.................F S-T-B A
Send all mail to P. O. Box 1409.

79, Norfolk, Va. (Mixed).—Meets first and third Wednesdays in Moose Hall, 812 Freemason St., at 8 p. m. Executive Board meets first and third Wednesdays.

David H. Kimberlin, 1616 Laurel Ave.,
Portsmouth, Va. Tel. 6853-W..........P
Frank Freeman, 4333 Peterson St.,
Tel. Norfolk 50320 ....F S-B A

81, Anaconda, Mont. (Mixed).—Meets every third Tuesday at 7 p. m., at Mill and Smeltermen's Hall, 111 Main St.

Fred Watts, 820 Birch............ ....P-B A
James J. Murphy, 802 Mt. Haggin
Homes ....F S-T

84, Houston, Tex. (Mixed). — Meets second and fourth Friday nights at 2309 Austin. Tel. Preston 5442. Executive Board meets first and third Friday.

W. R. Conway, Off. 2309 Austin.
Res. 7842 Ave. F. Tel. W-62355.......P
J. G. Martindale, Off. 2309 Austin St.
Res. 8137 Detroit.
Res. Tel. W-91488 ....F S-T
I. Deslattes, Off. 2309 Austin St.
Res. 7442 Dallas...................B A
F. W. Garren, Off. 2309 Austin St.
Res. 6617 Ave. K. Tel. W-68910........R S

86, Seattle, Wash. (Mixed).—Meets Hall 5, New Labor Temple, 2800 First Ave., second and fourth Thursday nights. Executive Board meets second and fourth Tuesdays.

Walter Elliott, 13442-6th Ave. S..........P
Joe Strong, 4437 38th Ave. S...........R S
A. H. Guiberson, Off. 2800 1st Ave.
Tel. Elliot 2424, Ex. 41.
Res. 1628 41st No.............F S-T-B A
Send mail to office, New Labor
Temple, 2800 1st Ave., Zone (1).

89, Cedar Rapids, Iowa Mixed). — Meets first and third Thursday nights at Federation Hall. All mail to 90 First Ave., N. E. Executive Board meets first and third Thursdays.

Donovan Tharp, Off. 90 First Ave., N.E...P
John W. Sullivan, Off. 90 First Ave., N.E.
Tel. 3-1729. Res. 1416 32nd St., N.E.
Tel. 7084.....................F S-T-B A
Richard Walsh, 108 29th St., N.E.
Tel. 2-3587 ....R S

92, Birmingham (1), Ala. (Mixed). — Meets every first and third Friday at 7:30 p. m., 112½ N. 24th St. Tel. 3-2746. Executive Board meets first and third Wednesdays at 6:30 p. m.

Alando C. Bonner, off. 112½ N. 24th St.....P
J. W. Rutherford, Jr., 112½ N. 24th St.
Res. Rt. No. 1, Box 65. Cleveland.
Ala. ....F S-T-B A
F. C. Golden, off. 112½ N. 24th St.
Res. Rt. 6, Box 444. Tel. 9-4179........R S

97, Vancouver, B. C. (Mixed).—Meets every second and fourth Wednesday night, in Room 215 Dawson Bldg., 193 E. Hastings St.

J. E. Fitzpatrick, Off. Room 216
Dawson Bldg., 193 Hastings St., East.
Tel. MA-0940. Res. 1229 E. 11th Ave.
Tel. FA-4650-R.....................P
Ernest G. Cook, Off. Room 216
Dawson Bldg., 193 Hastings St., East.
Tel. Ma. 0940. Res. 1175 Woodland Dr. Tel. Hastings 5348-R..F S-T-B A
John Marcus, Off. Room 216 Dawson
Bldg., 193 Hastings St., East.
Res. 195 22d Ave., East.
Tel. Fair 2790-L..................R S
Send all mail to Office.

103, Evansville, Ind. (Mixed). — Meets every second and fourth Wednesday nights at C. L. U. Hall, 210 N. Fulton Ave. Tel. 3-4619. Executive Board meets second and fourth Wednesdays.

Louis Duncan, off. 210 N Fulton Ave.
  Res. 19 S. Bedford Ave.
  Tel. 32306 ....F S-T-B A
Arthur Oldham, off. 210 N. Fulton Ave.
  Res. 21 E. Chandler Ave.................P
J. W. McDevitt, 210 N. Fulton Ave.....R S

107, Butte, Mont. (Mixed). — Meets second and fourth Monday nights at Carpenters' Union Hall, 156 W. Granite. Executive Board meets first and fourth Mondays.

Joseph Cappa, 531 S. Idaho St. Tel. 24288...P
Reginald Peters, 2616 Harvard Ave.
  Tel. 6320 ....F S-B A

111, Rock Island, Ill. (Mixed).—Meets first and third Monday nights at 1512 Fourth Ave., Rock Island, Ill. Executive Board meets first and third Mondays. Tel. 578.

Geo. L. Crum, off. 1512-4th Ave. Tel.
  578, Res. 3202 Harrison St., Daven-
  port, Ia. ....P
Robert Fancher, Off. 1512-4th Ave.
  Res. 615-17th St.
  Tel. R-1-7152 ....F S-T-B A
Mike M. Quinn, off. 1512-4th Ave.
  Res. 325 S. Lincoln St., Davenport, Ia.
  Tel. 7-9883.........................R S
Send all mail to Office.

112, Peoria, Ill. (Mixed). — Meets first and third Wednesday nights at Labor Temple. Executive Board meets first and third Wednesday nights.

A. W. O'Dell, Washburn, Ill. ....P
Edward McDonnell, Labor Temple,
  400 N. Jefferson St. Send all mail to
  Labor Temple. Tel. Peoria 4-8559.
  Res. 609 Center St., East Peoria.
  Tel. 3-1795 ....F S-T-B A
Geo. Breedlove. Off. 400 N. Jefferson St.
  Res. No. 1 Kenmore Ct., Pekin, Ill.
  Tel. 1725 ....R S

114, Tacoma, Wash. (Mixed).—Meets second and fourth Tuesdays of each month in Labor Temple. Executive Board meets second and fourth Tuesdays. Tel. Main 1166.

A. H. Sonn, 6215 McKinley Ave.
  Tel. Ga. 4618.........................P
Einar Nelson, Off. 228 Labor Temple.
  Tel. MA-1116. Res. 2910 S. 13th St.
  Tel. MA-7938 ....F S-T-B A
Allen D. Fisher, Off. 228 Labor Temple...R S
  All mail to 228 Labor Temple.
  Tacoma (3).

118, Sacramento, Calif. (Mixed). — Meets at 8:00 p. m., first and third Fridays in Labor Temple. Executive Board meets on first and third Thursdays each month at 8:00 p. m., in Local Union office.

O. D. Reasor, Box 1061, Off. Tel. 2-8870.
  Res. 2422 Hackberry, Stockton, Calif.
  Tel. 2-4065 ....P
C. R. Burton, P. O. Box 1061.
  Tel. 2-8870. Res. 3257-10th Ave.
  Tel. 5-2921 ....F S-T-B A
William B. Goode, Box 1061. Tel. 2-8870.
  Res. 3325 43rd St. Tel. 6-0011...........R S

125, Beaumont, Texas (Mixed).—Meets second and fourth Fridays of each month at 8:00 p. m., Labor Temple, 650 Franklin St. Executive Board meets first and third Fridays.

Roy Muench, Rex Hotel, 450½ Bowie St.
  Tel. 9662..............................P

James C. Peake, off. P. O. Box 2232,
  Beaumont, Tex. Res. 903 Newell
  Court, Orange, Texas..................R S
H. H. Matthews, P. O. Box 2232.
  Off. Tel. 1845.................F S-T-B A
Send all mail to P. O. Box 2232.

135, Galveston, Texas (Mixed) — Meets second and fourth Fridays at 8:00 p. m., at office, Labor Temple, 214 23rd St., Tel. 2-3932. All mail to P. O. Box 831. Executive Board meets second and fourth Fridays at 7:00 p. m.

A. J. Day, Off. 208 Labor Temple.
  Tel. 2-3932. Res. Apt. No. 45, 3rd
  Ave., Villas, Texas City. Tel. 1885-J....P
R. W. Cochran, 208 Labor Temple........R S
J. W. Allison, Off. P. O. Box 831. Tel.
  23932. Res. 3518 Ave. Q.
  Tel. 2-9207..................F S-T-B A

136, Chicago, Ill. (Machinery Movers, Riggers, House Movers).—Meets third Wednesday night of each month at 15 North Halsted St., Zone 6. Executive Board meets first and third Wednesdays.

John Artery, 2547 Washington...........R S
L. J. Tuttle, 2038 Rice St.
  Tel. Monroe 3420.............F S-T-B A
Send all mail to 15 N. Halsted St.,
  Chicago, Ill., Zone 6.

147, Ft. Wayne, Ind. (Mixed). — Meets first and third Thursday nights at 212½ W. Main St., Zone 2. Tel. Anthony 8494. Executive Board meets first and third Thursdays.

Wm. C. Hockemeyer, 1437 Lillie St.
  Tel. E-1019 ....P
Eugene C. Fleckenstein, 1339 Huestis Ave.
  Tel. Harrison 59613..................R S
Walter F. Fiedler, Off. 213½ W. Main
  St., Zone 2, Res. 727 Home Ave.,
  Zone 6. Tel. Harrison 44644....F S-T-B A
Send all mail to office.

155, Fresno, Calif. (Mixed — Meets fourth Friday night of each month at Labor Temple. Executive Board meets second and fourth Fridays.

O. E. Dahlgren, 3005 Adeline St............P
Shirley Everhart, Res. 844 S. 9th St.,
  Tel. 2-8421 ....R S
Wm. J. Dawson, off. 1035 Broadway.
  Tel. 31237. Res. Star Rt., Box 15,
  Fresno. Tel. 48379............F S-T-B A

158, Binghamton, N. Y. (Mixed).—Meets first and third Thursday nights at Central Labor Union Hall, 221 Washington St.

Fred M. Birney, Res. 160 Oak St..........P
Francis J. Hogan, 7 Park Ave. Tel.
  No. 2-6621 ....F S-T-B A

161, Philadelphia, Pa. (Riggers and Machinery Movers).—Meets first and third Thursday nights at Labor Lyceum, Sixth and Brown Sts. Tel. Market 7-8836. Executive Board meets first and third Fridays.

Joseph Scully, Off. 809 No. 6th.
  Res. Gilbert Ave., South Westville,
  N. J. Res. Tel. Woodbury 2-632-R......P
Geo. H. K. Smith, Jr., Res. 200 Wash-
  ington Ave., Clifton Heights, Pa.
  Tel. Decatur 3360-M. Off. 809 No.
  6th ....R S-T
Thos. Druding, Off. 809 N. 6th St. Tel.
  Market 7-8836. Res. 306 Fitzgerald
  St. Zone 48. Tel. Howard 8-8663.
  Send all mail to residence.............F S
Edwin Kleckner, Off. 809 No. 6th St.
  Res. 3305 Gransback St. Res. Tel.
  4-7165 ....B A

167, Memphis, Tenn. (Mixed).—Meets every first and third Thursday nights at Labor Temple, Beale and Lauderdale Sts., Tel. 8-5891.

John F. Moriarty, Off. Labor Temple.
   Res. 1588 Netherwood St.
   Tel. 36-4873 ....P
E. C. Weber, Off. 565 Beale Ave.
   Tel. 8-5891. Res. 76 E. Mallory Ave.
   Tel. 35-6970 ....B A
W. R. Dodson, 2396 Hubbard Ave.
   Tel. 48-0374 ....R S
Jack A. Page, Off. Labor Temple.
   Res. 3655 Carnes Ave.
   Res. Tel. 4-5972. Send all mail
   to residence ....F S-T

170, New York City, N. Y. (Riggers and Machinery Movers). — Meets third Wednesday night of each month at 116 Broad St., Room 69, Zone 4. Telephone, Bowling Green 9-6652. Executive Board meets first and third Wednesdays.

Chas. McNamara, Off. 116 Broad St.
   Tel. Bowling Green 9-6652.
   Res. 161 W. 228th St..............P
Joseph F. Girard, Off. 116 Broad St.,
   Res. 35-05 30th St., Astoria, N. Y.
   Tel. Ravenswood 8-6798...........R S
Robert Hansen, Off. Room 69,
   116 Broad St., Zone 4. Tel. Bo 9-6652.
   Res. 317 W. 22nd St.
   Tel. Ch. 2-8717.................F S-T-B A

172, Columbus, Ohio (Mixed).—Meets second and fourth Fridays at 476 E. Rich St. (Zone 13), at 8 p. m. Tel. Adams 2632. Executive Board meets first and third Fridays.

R. O. Murphy, Off. 476 E. Rich.
   Res. Lilly Chapel, Ohio..........P
Thos. F. Boyhan, Off. 476 E. Rich.
   Tel. Adams 2632. Res. 96 W. First
   Ave. University 6863.............F S-T
Jay L. Tatham,
   Off. 476 E. Rich St............Act F S-T
Roy Zarabaugh, Off. 476 E. Rich.
   Res. Rt. 1, Groveport, Ohio......R S
Guy Morrison, Off. 476 E. Rich St.,
   Zone 13. Res. 738 S. Sixth St.
   Tel. GA-7993 ....B A
   Send all mail to office.

174, El Paso, Texas (Mixed)—Meets first and third Wednesday nights of each month at Labor Temple, 223 So. Oregon St. Executive Board meets first and third Wednesdays.

Aug. H. Bastian, 2425 Pittsburg.
   Tel. 5-4819......................P
Joe Bombach, 3001 Nashville.
   Tel. 5-7828......................R S
G. H. Moore, 4017 Morehead St.
   Tel. East 1005 ....F S-T-B A

184, Sioux City, Iowa (Mixed).—Meets every third Wednesday at 508 5th St.

Frank M. Smith, Dakota City, Neb.......P
John P. Sivill, 912 29th St..............R S
C. D. Holder, 4416 3rd Ave.
   Tel. 6-4996 ....B A
H. B. Dugan, P.O. Box 1165
   Res. 1209 W 2nd St. Tel. 5-5689.....F S-T

197, New York City, N. Y. (Stone Derrickmen).—Meets third Friday night of each month at 162 E. 23rd St. Executive Board meets first and third Fridays.

D. A. Gordon, Off. 162 E. 23rd St.
   Res. 51 Stockholm St., Brooklyn.
   Tel. Glenmore 27631..............P
Wm. Brander, Off. 162 E. 23rd St.
   Tel. Gramercy 5-3925, Res. Tel. 860 71st St.,
   Brooklyn. Tel. Beachview
   8-2385 ....F S-T-B A
Thos. P. Stevens, Off. 162 E. 23rd St.
   Res. 2320 Westchester Ave.,
   Bronx, N. Y., Zone 61............R S

201, Washington, D. C. (Reinforced Concrete Iron Workers).—Meets every first and third Friday night in each month at Iron Workers' Hall, 405 Ninth St., N. W., at 8 o'clock. Executive Board meets first and third Wednesdays.

Wm. M. Embrey, 636 Eye St., N. E.......P
Paul P. O'Dowd, 5600 36th Place, Hyatts-
   ville, Md. Tel. Warfield 1999...........R S
R. O. Boyd, 2900 Nash Pl. S.E.
   Tel. Atlantic 0872..............F S-T-B A

203, St. Louis, Mo. (Stone Derrickmen).— Meets second Friday night of each month at Swedish Hall, 1159 S. Kingshighway.

Walter Zinn, 2921 Brentwood Blvd.,
   Brentwood, Mo. Tel. Webster
   5366-W ....P-B A
Wm. L. Everding, 2533 Bacon St.........R S
A. Thom, 2632a Oregon Ave.
   Tel. Gr. 6845 ....F S-T

207, Youngstown, Ohio (Mixed). — Meets first and third Monday night of each month at 8:00 at 100 E. Rayen Ave. Tel. 38910. Executive Board meets second and fourth Mondays.

Wm. E. Thomas, Off. 100 E. Rayen Ave.,
   Zone 3, Res. 5368 Belmont Ave. Exp.
   Youngstown 4, Ohio. Tel. 4-4967........P
Jas. D. McCarthy, Off. 100 E. Rayen Ave.
   Zone 3, Res. 1914 Kensington Ave.
   Tel. 3-1207.....................R S
Thos. C. Kelly, Off. 100 E. Rayen Ave.,
   Zone 3. Tel. 3 8910. Res. Rt. No. 1,
   East Liverpool, Ohio...........F S-T-B A
Send all mail to office.

228, Portsmouth, Va. (Norfolk Navy Yard Riggers).—Meets every first Friday and third Tuesday at Gompers Hall, Middle and County Sts.

M. O. Davidson, Jr., 2 Stephen's Place,
   Cradock Gardens, Portsmouth, Va......P
Francis A. Dougherty, 310 Shafer St.,
   Norfolk 2, Va...................R S
Luther G. Hankins, 5911 Locust Ave.,
   Norfolk 2, Va...................F S

229, San Diego, Calif. (Mixed).—Meets first Friday night of each month at Labor Temple, 811 "F" St. Executive Board meets first and third Fridays.

E. A. McLean, 813 F St., Zone 1..........P
John Haning, Off. 813 "F" St.
   Tel. F-3385.....................R S
Juel Drake, 813 F St., Zone 1.
   Tel. F-0822.....................F S-T-B A

263, Fort Worth, Texas (Mixed). — Meets second and fourth Friday nights of each month at 1400½ Main St.

R. T. Noonkester, 1806 Highland St.,
   Zone 6. Tel. 6-4202.............P
T. J. Ingram, 1701 Roberts Cut-Off Rd.,
   Zone 7. Tel. 6-8201.............R S
Louis R. Robinson, 3012 S. Adams St.,
   Zone 4. Tel. 4-8911. Send mail to
   residence. Off. Tel. 2-6888.......F S-B A

272, Miami, Fla. (Mixed).—Meets second and fourth Fridays at 8:00 p. m., at Labor Temple, 925 First Ave., N. E. Tel. 2-2651. Executive Board meets at 8:00 p. m., each Friday.

E. J. Stephenson, Off. 925 N.E. First
   Ave. Tel. 2-2651. Res. Tel. 4-4639.......P
E. K. McCullough, 115 S.W. 18th Ave....R S
Chas. E. Johnson, Off. 925 N.E. First Ave.
   Tel. 2-2651. Send all mail to office.F S-B A
C. W. Warrington, Off. 925 N.E.
   First Ave.......................T

290, Dayton, Ohio (Mixed). — Meets every second and fourth Tuesday evenings at Labor Headquarters, 202 S. Ludlow St., Zone 2. Tel. Adams 3255. Executive Board meets first and third Tuesdays.

Fred Gage, Off. 202 S. Ludlow St.,
Zone 2. Tel. Adams 3255.
Res. 6 Abbot Dr., Zone 10.
Tel. KE-6581 ....F S-T
L. L. Ross, 202 W. Herman Ave., Zone 5.
Tel. Adams 7684 ....R S
Ray E. Armstrong, Off. 202 S. Ludlow
St., Zone 2. Tel. Adams 3255.
Res. 3420 Susannah St., Zone 5.
Tel. RA-7324 ....B A
Chas. E. Brown, 51 Costello St.,
Zone 8. Tel. FU-6008 ....P

292, South Bend, Ind. (Mixed).—Meets first and third Monday at 8:00 p. m., in Labor Temple, 103 LaSalle St. Tel. 3-9885. Executive Board meets first and third Mondays at 7:00 p. m.

Woodie D. Dolan, R.R. 2, Bourbon, Ind... P
Harvey E. Deacon, R.R. 2, Mishawaka, Ind.
Tel. 55785 ....R S
R. Zimmer, R.R. 19, Mishawaka, Ind.
Tel. 5-1050 ....F S-T-B A
All mail to 103 West LaSalle St. (6).

301, Charleston, W. Va. (Mixed). — Meets every Tuesday at Laborers' Temple, 615½ Tennessee Ave., at 7:30 p. m. Executive Board meets first and third Tuesdays. All mail to 120½ Washington St. W. Tel. 25-343.

Earnest R. Johnson, off. 120½ Wash-
ington St., W........................P
Leonard F. Crittendon, Off. 120½
Washington St. W. Res. Spring Fork,
W. Va. Tel. 52780 ....R S
Harry T. Emery, Off. 120½
Washington St. W. Res. 102½ Third
Ave., So. Charleston, W. Va.
Tel. 44-642 ....B A
Norman O. Reese, 3409 Piedmont Rd.,
Huntington, W. Va.................F S-T

321, Little Rock, Ark. (Mixed). — Meets second and last Fridays at 8:00 p. m. Executive Board meets every second and last Friday nights in Office, 1121½ W. Markham. Tel. 4-3583.

Thos. R. Gray, Res. 209 Booneville
Ave., Booneville, Ark. Tel. 4-4693,
Little Rock ....P
J. D. Grogan, Off. 1121½ W. Markham
St. Res. 4-5409 ....F S-T-B A
G. F. Ervin, Off. 1121½ W. Markham.
Res. Booneville, Ark. Tel. 395.........R S

340, Battle Creek (26), Mich. (Mixed). — Meets first and third Fridays at 8 p. m., at 11 Green St. Tel. 2-5043. Executive Board meets first and third Fridays.

Milton McClain, Off. 11 Green St. Res.
Rt. No. 1 Vicksburg, Mich.
Tel. Fulton 214 ....P
Robt. V. Poole, Off. 11 Green St. Res.
522 N. Washington Ave. Tel. 3-3627..R S
Herbert O. Poole, Off. 11 Green St.
Tel. 2-5043. Res. 9 Riverside Dr.
Tel. 6084 ....F S-T-B A
Send all mail to 11 Green St.

348, Erie, Pa. (Mixed).—Meets last Thursday night at C. L. U. Hall, 1701 State St. Executive Board meets every second Thursday night.

C. V. Myers, Off. 1703 State St.
Tel. 22-548. Send all mail to residence,
1612 State St. Tel. 63-209.............P
Frank R. Scalise, Off. 1703 State St.
Tel. 22-548. Res. West Springfield, Pa.
Tel. 1106 W. Springfield, Pa.....F S-T-B A
Ralph Leopold, Res. Girard, Pa.
Tel. 101-R..............................R S
Send all mail to 1703 State St.

350, Atlantic City, N. J. (Mixed).—Meets at Odd Fellows Hall, 30 S. New York Ave., first and third Wednesdays at 8:00 p. m. Executive Board meets first and third Wednesdays.

Edward Lind, 2905 Arctic Ave. ....P
Charles L. Barber, 10 South Texas
Ave. Tel. 4-1375 ....R S-F S-T
Terrence Norton, 418 N. Dover Ave.
Tel. 4-6313 ....B A

351, Lawrence, Mass. (Mixed).—Meets fourth Tuesday night, Building Trades Hall, 96 Concord St. Executive Board meets second and fourth Tuesdays at 7:30 p. m.

Harry Agnew, 421 Merrimack St.,
Methuen, Mass. ....P
J. Douglas, 297 Water St.
Tel. 31404 ....F S-T-B A-R-S

357, Springfield, Mass. (Mixed). — Meets at Central Labor Union Hall, 21 Sanford St., fourth Friday night. Tel. 69323. Executive Board meets second and fourth Fridays.

W. Coyle, Off. Central Labor Union
Hall, 21 Sanford St. Tel. 69323.
Res. 177 Winton St. Tel. 35351...........P
T. J. Crean, Off. Central Labor Union
Hall. Tel. 69323. Res. 13 Oakdale
Ave., Westfield, Mass.
Tel. 1054-J ....F S-B A
F. Capitanio, Off. Central Labor Hall,
21 Sanford St. Res. 119 South St.,
Agawam, Mass. Tel. 66484 ....R S
John Hamre, 20 Crane St. Tel. 7-2861 .....T

361, Brooklyn, N. Y. (Structural).—Meets every Wednesday night of each month, 550 Atlantic Ave. Tel. Main 4-7909. The Executive Board will meet Friday following each first and third Wednesday.

Jesse Butt, 9 Harbor Road, Amityville,
L. I., New York. Tel. Amityville
1625-W. Send all mail to office..........P
Paul Horn, 550 Atlantic Ave.
Res. 157 Clinton St. Tel. Main 4-0434...R S
All mail to office.
Paul S. Rockhold, 550 Atlantic Ave.,
Zone (17). Tel. Main 4-7909.
Res. 140 82nd St.
Tel. Shore Road 5-3688 ....F S-T-B A
Send all mail to 550 Atlantic Ave., Zone 17.

372, Cincinnati, O. (Reinforced Concrete Iron Workers). — Meets second and fourth Friday nights, Room 300, Brotherhood of Railway Clerks Bldg., Court and Vine Sts. Executive Board meets second and fourth Fridays.

James Keating, 805 E. 6th St.
Tel. Parkway 7465 ....P
Carl Ludwig, 2467 Seegar Ave.
Tel. WA-8202 ....R S
Joseph Obermeyer, Room 300, 1015 Vine
St., Zone 2. Res. Vogel Rd., Mt. Airy,
Cincinnati, Ohio. Tel. KI 5566..F S-T-B A
Send all mail to Room 300, 1015 Vine
St., Zone 2.

373, Perth Amboy, N. J. (Mixed). — Meets second and last Tuesday nights of month at 31 Smith St. Tel. Perth Amboy 4-1495.

Harry Christiansen........................P
John J. Wade, 36 Broadway,
Keyport, N. J. Tel. Keport 1240......R S
Geo. T. Nelson, Res. 31 Smith St.
Tel. Perth Amboy 4-3672-R.........F S-T
Send all mail to office.
Wesley Hansen, Off. 31 Smith St.
Res. 406 Nevil St.
Tel. Perth Amboy 4-1496.
Off. Tel. Perth Amboy 4-1495.........B A

377, San Francisco (3), Calif. (Mixed.)—Meetings held second and fourth Friday evening at 200 Guerrero St., Building Trades Temple. Executive Board meets first and third Friday evening.
John Ricketts, Off. 200 Guerrero St., Zone 3. Tel. Hemlock 1-4736. Res. 21 Naylor St. Tel. Juniper 5-7741........P
A. F. Mailloux, Off. 200 Guerrero St. Zone 3. Tel. Market 1-1806..........R S
Tel. Randolph 0656 ....R S
M. Fenton, Off. 200 Guerrero St. (3). Tel. Hemlock 1-4736. Res. 3905 Army St. Tel. Mission 5836............F S-B A

378, Oakland, Calif. (Mixed). — Meetings held third Friday night of each month at Labor Temple, 2111 Webster St., Zone 12. Executive Board meets first and third Wednesdays.
James Beal, Off. 2111 Webster St. Tel. Twinoaks 2262. Res. 470-38th St. Tel. Hum. 5490..................P
James Barrett, Res. 2921 61st Ave. Res. Tel. LO-8-4530 ....R S
Ralph G. Graham, Off. 2111 Webster St., Zone 12. Tel. Twinoaks 2262. Res. 1249 First Ave. Tel. Templebar 0362..................B A
Send all mail to 2111 Webster St., Zone 12.
L. L. Sorenson, Off. 2111 Webster St. Tel. Twinoaks 2262. Res. 20857 Birch St., Hayward, Calif..................F S-T

379, Lafayette, Ind. (Mixed). — Meets second and fourth Friday nights of month at Labor Temple, Fifth and Columbia Sts.
Herold Saeler, 332 S. 30th St. Tel. 46163....P
Fred L. Taylor, Route No. 4. Tel. 31-R.16 ....R S-B A
Frank Byroads, 809 Wabash Ave......F S-T

380, Champaign, Ill. (Mixed). — Meets second and fourth Tuesdays of each month at 7:30 p. m., at Labor Hall.
Carl Harmon, 513 S. Edwin St. Tel. 3065..................P
Clarence R. Phillips, 926 No. Collett St., Danville, Ill. Tel. 5178-J..............R S
Wm. Giesler, 303 West Clark St. Tel. 4796 ....F S-T-B A

383, Madison, Wis. (Mixed). — Meets second and fourth Fridays at Madison Labor Temple at 8 p. m. Executive Board meets second and fourth Fridays.
Send all mail to office, 115 W. Main St. (3). Tel. Gifford 5200.
Russell Oxnem, 10 Vista Rd. Tel. Badger 3718.
Vincent Hildebrandt, 2620 Chamberlain Ave. Tel. Gifford 2721..................R S
Orla V. Coleman, Off. 115 W. Main St. Zone 3. Res. Edwards Park, McFarland, Wisc. Tel. McFarland 48R15 ....F S-T-B A

384, Knoxville, Tenn. (Mixed). — Meets first and third Friday of month at 202 Caswell St., at 8 p. m. Executive Board meets first and third Fridays at 8:00 p. m., at 202 Caswell St.
Charles G. McDowell, 2736 Buffatt Rd. Tel. 3-0673. Knoxville (17). Tel. 4-1653....P
W. C. Burns, Off. 202 Caswell St........R S
Geo. A. Hines, Sr., Off. 202 Caswell St. Tel. 4-1653. Res. Woodlawn Pike, Rt. 10, Knoxville, Zone 15. Tel. 2-6949..................F S-T-B A
Geo. C. Wolff, 3300 Curtis St. Tel. 2-2994. Chattanooga, Tenn..............Ass't B A
All mail to 202 Caswell St.

386, La Salle, Ill. (Mixed).—Meets fourth Wednesday night at Slovenski Dome, First and Croset Sts. Executive Board meets second and fourth Wednesdays.
Clarence O. Nelson, Rt. No. 1, Spring Valley, Ill. Res. Tel. 149-L-1..........P

John Booker, Rt. No. 1, Spring Valley, Ill. ....R S
Burt Cooley, 247 Joliet St. Tel. 1505 ....F S-T-B A

387, Atlanta, Ga. (Mixed). — Meets second and fourth Friday of each month at Labor Temple, 91 Trinity Ave., S. W., Zone 3, at 7:30 p. m. Tel. Lamaro 2511. Executive Board meets first and third Fridays at 7:30 p. m.
L. W. Lynn, Off. 91 Trinity Ave., S.W. Res. 257 Macon Dr. Res. Tel. Calhoune 7686..................P
Guy C. Ivester, 10 Ellen St. Tel. Belmont 1380-J..................R S
Y. F. Geeslin, Off. 91 Trinity Ave., S. W. Tel. Lamaro 2511. Res. 245 Flat Shoals Ave., S.E. Tel. Lamar 7766..................F S-T-B A
All mail to 91 Trinity Ave., S.W., Zone 3.

392, East St. Louis, Ill. (Mixed). — Meets second and fourth Friday nights at 451 Collinsville Ave. Executive Board meets second and fourth Fridays.
Frank McCarthy, Off. 1207 Missouri Ave. Tel. East 163. Res. 327 N. 7th St. Tel. Hemlock 2014..................P
John E. Shovlin, Off. 1207 Missouri Ave. Tel. East 163. Res. 1409 Cleveland Ave. Tel. East 5841..................R S
John L. McCarthy. Off. 1207 Missouri Ave. Tel. East 163. Res. 626 Pershing Ave. Tel. Express 1114 ....F S-T-B A

393, Aurora, Ill. (Mixed).—Meets first and third Mondays, 7:30 p. m., Labor Temple, 213 Main St., Tel. 2-7516. Executive Board meets first and third Mondays.
Albert J. Ochsenschlager, Off. Aurora Labor Temple. Res. 356 South Ave. Res. Tel. 5587..................P
Jacob Maakestad. 139 N. Union St. Tel. 2-7762 ....R S
O. W. Pederson, 912 Liberty St. Tel. 9673..................F S-T-B A

395, Hammond, Ind. (Mixed). — Meets first and third Tuesday nights at Labor Temple, Sibley St. and Oakley Ave. Tel. Sheffield 424. Executive Board meets second and fourth Monday nights.
James Dugan, Off. Labor Temple..........P
Benjamin A. Michaw, 530 Florence St....R S
Frank W. McCoy, Off. Labor Temple. Res. 5433 Tell Ave., Hammond, Indiana. Res. Tel. 8709. Off. Tel. Sheffield 424. Send all mail to P. O. Box 67...B A-F-S-T

396, St. Louis, Mo. (Mixed). — Office, 618 N. Newstead Ave., Zone 8. Meets last Friday night of each month. Executive Board meets first and third Fridays of each month. Tel. FRanklin 0730.
John Burgdorf. R.R. 2, Florissant, Mo. Tel. OR-5693..................P
John S. Ware, 4935 Claxton Ave. Tel. Mulberry 6428..................R S
Henry Hessel, Off. 618 N. Newstead, Zone 8. Res. 4505 Minnesota Ave. Tel. Lockhart 3186..................F S-T
Joe Cousin, Off. 618 N. Newstead. Zone 8. Res. 7405 Rupert. Tel. Hi-7382.......B A

397, Tampa, Fla. (Mixed). — Meets second and fourth Friday nights at 1801 N. Franklin St., Zone 2. Tel. M-66834. Executive Board meets first and third Fridays.
H. O. Fletcher. 312 E. Selma Ave. Tel. M-64-501..................P
Gus Rodreguis. 2814 Jefferson St. (3)...R S
E. R. Minor, Off. 1801 N. Franklin St., Zone 2. Tel. M-66834. Res. R.R. No. 4, Box 532. Tampa 7. Fla. Tel. S-62274 ....F S-T-B A

399, Camden, N. J. (Mixed). — Meets fourth Monday evening at Labor Temple, Camden, N. J. Executive Board meets second and fourth Mondays.

Edward Brennan, Maple and Crestwood
　Aves., Somerdale, N. J.
　Tel. Laurel Springs 4-0858-M...........P
Thos. Kelly, Labor Temple. Tel. 2412.
　Res. 656 Washington St.
　Tel. Emerson 5-2698-M.................R S
L. M. Carroll, Labor Temple.
　Res. Hadonfield Rd. and Sherwood Ave.,
　Merchantville, N. J.
　Tel. Merchantville 2436-R...........F S-T
Wm. Banke, 212 White Horse Pike,
　Collingswood, N. J. Tel. 824 ....B A

401, Philadelphia, Pa. (Structural and Ornamental). — Meets third Friday of each month, 1620 N. Broad St., at 8:00 p. m. Executive Board meets first Friday of each month, 1924 Spring Garden Street, Zone 30, at 8:00 p. m. Also meets third Friday of each month after General Meeting at 1620 N. Broad St. (Steamfitters Hall).

Wm. J. Monahan, off. 1924 Spring Garden
　St. Tel. Locust 4-0458-59. Res. 2355 N.
　Laurence St. Tel. Regent 9-0837........P
Wm. B. Mansfield, Off. 1924 Spring
　Garden St. Tel. Locust 0-0458.....F S-T
Charles Coughlin, Res. 313 E. Sheldon
　St. Tel. Mich. 4-5497 ....R S
Leo McDonald, Off. 1924 Spring Garden
　St. Tel. Locust 4-0458.
　Res. 1426 E. Hunting Park Ave.
　Tel. Del. 6-1625 ....B A

402, West Palm Beach, Fla. (Mixed). — Meets at Labor Temple, 414 South Rosemary, West Palm Beach, Fla., second and fourth Fridays of each month, 7:30 p. m.

A. F. Flory, Box 323,
　Lake Worth, Fla. ....P-R S
E. L. Carpenter, Box 248,
　Riviera Beach, Fla. ....F S-T-B A

404, Harrisburg, Pa. (Mixed.) — Meets first and third Friday nights of each month at Union Labor Hall, 1219 N. Third St. Executive Board meets first and third Fridays.

Howard O. Heckert, Off. 267 Cumberland
　St. Res. 535 Woodbine St.............P
Earl T. Heckert, Off. 267 Cumberland
　St. Tel. 6-0921. Res. 2204 Logan St.
　Tel. 6-1453 ....F S-T
W. C. Weikert, 812 Packer St.
　Williamsport. Pa. ....R S
Joseph Harris, Off. 267 Cumberland
　St. Tel. 60921 ....B A

405, Philadelphia, Pa. (Reinforced Concrete Iron Workers). — Meets first and third Friday nights of each month at 1805 Spring Garden St., Zone (30). Tel. Locust 4552.

Nick Corbi, 1639 S. Isminger St............P
James Corbi, Off. 1805 Spring Garden
　St. Res. 1230 S. Juniper St.
　Tel. HO-2-5365.....................F S-T
Alfred J. Clark, Off. 1805 Spring
　Garden St. Res. 3840 N. 10th St..   R S
John Petrino, Off. 1905 Spring Garden St.
　Tel. Locust 4552. Res. 1329 Shunk St..B A

408, Amarillo, Texas (Mixed). — Meets second and fourth Sunday in W. O. W. Hall, 209 E. 7th St. at 2:00 p. m. Tel. 23000. Executive Board meets second and fourth Sundays of each month at 10:00 a. m.

C. E. Tate, 209 E. 7th, Tel. 2-3000.
　Res. 731 N. Aldridge, Tel. 2-4436.......P

C. T. Young, 209 E. 7th Ave., Tel. 2-3000.
　Res. 704 S. Lincoln St., Tel. 7459.....R S
F. H. Prock, Off. 209 E. 7th, Tel. 2-3000.
　Res. 803 Lincoln St.
　Tel. 23600 ....F S-B A

410, Great Falls, Mont. (Mixed).
Pete Likeness, 1815 7th Ave., No..R S-F-S-T

413, Charlotte, N. C. (Mixed). — Meets second and fourth Thursdays at 8:00 p. m. at Labor Temple, 317½ N. Tryon St., Tel. 4-1428.

J. E. McElduff, Mt. Holly, N. C.
　Tel. 225-M ....P
W. D. McKinna, 207 York Ave.,
　Rock Hill, S. C. ....Act. R S
J. A. Canida, 317½ N. Tryon
　St. ....Act. B A-F S-T

416, Los Angeles, Calif. (Reinforced Concrete Iron Workers). — Meets fourth Monday at 8:00 p. m., at 832 Figueroa St., Zone 14. Executive Board meets second and fourth Mondays at 8:00 p. m., 832 Figueroa St., Zone 14.

Clifford F. Brown, 832 S. Figueroa.
　Res. 1222 W. 93rd St. (44).
　Tel. Twinoaks-4185 ....P
Arthur E. Clawitter, 832 So. Figueroa....R S
Frank Vaughn, Off. 832 S. Figueroa,
　Zone 14. Tel. Tucker 7662. Res.
　2128½ Elsinore St...............F S-T-B A

417, Newburgh, N. Y. (Mixed). — Meets first and third Friday nights of each month in Labor Temple. Executive Board meets first and third Fridays of each month.

Claude Ballard, 83 Sherman Ave.,
　Walden, N. Y.
　Tel. Walden-2-1463 ....P
Michael J. Doyle, Off. 1 Washington
　Pl. Tel. Newburgh 2141. Res. 187
　Henry St., Kingston, N. Y.
　Tel. Kingston 1236 ....F S-T-B A
Chas. T. Shea, Vailsgate, N. Y.
　Tel. Newburgh 108-J-3 ....R S

420, Reading, Pa. (Mixed). — Meets fourth Thursday night of each month in Plumbers' Hall, fourth floor, at Reed and Court Sts. Executive Board meets second and fourth Thursdays.

Wm. T. Davis, 138 Vine St.
　Tel. Rdg. 3-9998 ....P
Edmond H. Pinkerton, 433 Fairview
　St., Hyde Park, Pa. Tel. 9-2638........R S
Harry M. Walters, 2202 Raymond Ave.
　Tel. 3-2950 ....F S-T
Dewey Downey, 605 Fern Ave.
　Tel. 3-7090 ....B A

424, New Haven, Conn. (Mixed). — Meets fourth Friday night at Labor Temple, 139 Goffe St. Executive Board meets second and fourth Fridays.

Wm. F. Hennessy, 319 Willow St.
　Tel. 7-2065 ....P
James Kavanaugh, 252 Putman St.
　Tel. 5-6919 ....R S
James O'Kane, 244 Stratfield Rd.,
　Bridgeport, Zone (4), Conn.
　Tel. Bridgeport 4-7546 ....F S-T-B A

426, Detroit, Mich. (Reinforced Concrete Iron Workers). — Meets first and third Friday nights at 3126 Park Ave., Zone 1. Tel. Temple 1-9612. Executive Board meets first and third Fridays.

W. R. Miller, Off. 3126 Park Ave., Zone 1..P
Byron Sparks, Res. 1164 Webb Ave.
　Tel. TO-54016......................R S
C. W. Pascoe, Off. 3126 Park Ave.
　Zone 1.........................F S-T-B A

433, Los Angeles, Calif. (Structural, Ornamental Iron Workers, Riggers and Machinery Movers). — Tel. Mutual 4388. Executive Board meets each Tuesday night at 536 S. Maple Ave., Room 601, Zone 13. Local meets second and fourth Tuesday night of each month at 536 S. Maple Ave., Room 601, Zone 13.

John R. Reasoner, Off. 536 S. Maple Ave., Room 601, Zone 13. Tel. Mutual 4388 ....P
James R. Shively, Room 601, 436 Maple Ave., Zone 13 ....R S
James F. Cheely, Off. 536 S. Maple Ave., Room 601, Zone 13. Tel. Mutual 4388. Res. 1024½ S. Westmoreland, Zone 6. Tel. Exposition 5785....F S-T-B A

436, Elmira, N. Y. (Mixed). — Meets first and third Saturday of each month at 10:00 a. m., at 143½ W. Water St.

Walter Burke, 440 Broadway. Tel. 6571 ....P
John A. Koch, Off. 143½ W. Water St. Res. 459 Franklin St. Res. Tel. 22708. Send all mail to 459 Franklin St. 6............F S-R-S-B A
Edw. Koch, 459 Franklin St. Tel. 22708.

439, Terre Haute, Ind. (Mixed). — Meets first and third Tuesdays at 8:00 p. m., 33 So. 4th St. Tel. C-5421.

Eugene Chambers, Off. 33 S. 4th St.......P
Edw. F. Jones, Off. 33 S. 4th St. Tel. Crawford 5421. Res. Box 207. R. R. No. 7........................F S-T
A. Fred Gard, Off. 33 S. 4th St. Tel. Crawford 5421. Res. Shelburn, Ind. Tel. 70-G........................B A
N. Hensley, 33 S. 4th St. Tel. H-4876 ....R S

440, Utica, N. Y. (Mixed). — Meets fourth Friday night of each month at Labor Temple, 714 Charlotte St. Executive Board meets second and fourth Friday at 7:30 p. m.

Matthew Kozlowski, 1213 Steuben St. Tel. 22211 ....P
James H. Donovan, 15 Church St., Chadwicks, N. Y. ....R S
Frank J. Hauser, R.R. 2, Frankfort, N. Y. Tel. Utica 4-7058........F S-T-B A

444, Joliet, Ill. (Mixed). — Meets second and fourth Monday nights at 465 Collins St. Tel. 23642. Executive Board meets second and fourth Mondays.

Salvatore Albert, 210 Pasadena Ave. Tel. 4338 ....P
Howard J. Loeffler, 415 Benton St. Tel. 2-8811 ....R S
Peter Cinotti, 322 Colburn Tel. 2-6986 ....F S-B A
Send all mail to 465 Collins St.

451, Wilmington, Delaware. (Mixed). — Meetings held every second and last Wednesday nights at office, 608 French St. Tel. 3-0946. Executive Board meets second and fourth Wednesday nights at 8:00 o'clock. Tel. 3-0946.

Clete Snavley, 2307 Tatnall St..Acting Pres.
Timothy D. Hartnett, 1311 N. Clayton St. Tel. 2-6651 ....F S-B A
All mail to P. O. Box 846.

454, Casper, Wyoming (Mixed). — Meets second and fourth Thursday of each month at 7:30 p. m., at 320 N. Wolcott St. Executive Board meets second and fourth Mondays at 7:00 p. m., at 737 E. 4th St.

Robt. R. Argo, 807 N. Beach St..........P
Chas. Campbell, 737 E. 4th St. Tel. 1154 ....R S-F S-T-B A
All mail to 737 E. 4th St.

455, New York City. (Shopmen). — Executive Board meets every Wednesday at 8:00 p. m., at 853 Broadway, Zone 3.

Rudolph Schaefer, Off. 853 Broadway. Tel. Gramery 5-2226. Res. 2554 Woodhull Ave., Bronx, N. Y....P
Irving Nussbaum, Off. 853 Broadway. Res. 29 Attorney St. ....R S
Murray Powell, Off. 853 Broadway, New York (3), N. Y. Off. Tel. Gramercy 5-2226-7. Res. 24 Attorney St. ....F S-T
Nat Tipelin, Off. 853 Broadway. Res. 500 Trinity Ave., Bronx, N. Y....B A
Max Karasik, Off. 853 Broadway. Res. 1717 Bryant Ave., Bronx, N. Y....B A

460, St. Joseph, Mo. (Mixed). — Meets first and third Thursdays at 8:00 p. m., at Labor Temple, Fifth and Edmond Sts. Tel. 2-2663. Executive Board meets first and third Fridays.

Homer Wheeler, RFD No. 1, Halls, Mo.....P
R. O. Vessar, R. R. 2 ....F S-T
Bert Cammack, 725 Alabama St. Tel. 8-1155 ....B A

464, Rochester, N. Y. (Shopmen). — Meets first and third Friday nights of each month at 360 Plymouth Ave., South.

Jos. Crowley, 85 Penrose St. Tel. Charlotte, 1065-W........................P
Alexander Cairns, 342 Cumberland St. ...B A
John Greer, 70 McEwen Rd. Tel. Charlotte 1521-W........................R S
Morris Sandgrund, 76 Lansdale St. Zone 7. Tel. Monroe 494-J..............F S

465, Kankakee, Ill. (Mixed). — Meets first and third Wednesday nights in Kankakee Federation of Labor Hall, 257 E. Court St. Executive Board meets first and third Mondays.

Robert H. Morrow, 338 N. Rosewood Ave. Tel. 3408-R2 ....P
Clyde M. Crawford, Aroma Park, Ill. Tel. 4937-R2 ....R S
Henry R. Stahl, 574 N. Union. Tel. Main 683..................F S-T-B A

468, Cleveland, Ohio. (Shopmen). — Meets first and third Monday nights at 1544 E. 23rd St. Zone 14. Tel.: Main 7524.

Albert Davis, Off. 1544 E. 23rd St., Zone 14. Res. 2081 W. 45th St. Tel. Atlantic 6048 ....P
Frank Csore, Off. 1544 E. 23rd St., Zone 14. Res. 12110 Buckeye Rd. Res. Tel. LO-4564 ....T
Clarence E. Greek, Off. 1544 E. 23rd St. Zone 14. Res. 5819 Superior. Res. Tel. Henderson 3222 ....F S
Fred Neumann, 3685 West Blvd. Tel. Woodbine 5871 ....R S
J. S. Mansbarger, Off. 1544 E. 23rd St. Tel. Main 7524, Res. 6209 Whittier Ave. Tel. EN 1391 ....B A

469, Jackson, Miss. (Mixed). — Meets second and fourth Tuesday nights each month at 130 Woodrow Wilson Ave. Executive Board meets second and fourth Tuesday nights.

C. H. McDonald, Off. 130 Woodrow Wilson Ave. Tel. 2-1790. Res. 719 W. Silas Brown St. Tel. 3-3664........F S-T-B A
W. L. Ford, 316 North St. Tel. 4-6422..................P
P. F. Burnside, 1112 Hunter St..........R S

470, Jamestown, N. Y. (Shopmen). — Meets second and fourth Tuesday nights at the Central Labor Council, Washington St.

Harold C. Kofod, Res. 287 Fairmount St..P
Carl A. Danielson, 412 Front St. ....R S
Clifford C. Tennies, 915 No. Main St.,
   Jamestown, N. Y. ....F S-T

471, Milwaukee, Wis. (Shopmen). — Meets second and fourth Thursdays at 8:00 p. m., at Metropolitan Hall, Sixth and Clark Sts. Tel. Concord 2900.

Ervin Schenk, 4359 N. 41st St., Zone 9.
   Tel. Hilltop 1216......................P
Lawrence Ruplinger,
   2030-A Farwell Ave. Zone 2........R S
Emil Sonntag, 2239 N. 11th St. (5).
   Tel. Concord 3271....................T
Chas. Waldow, 1105 W. North Ave.,
   Zone 5. Tel. Concord 2900. Res. 2839
   N. 21st St., Zone 6. Tel. Hopkins
   6046 ....F S-B A

472, San Francisco, Calif. (Shopmen).—Meets third Wednesday at Union Carpenters' Hall, 761 Twelfth St., Oakland, and fourth Wednesday night of each month in Brotherhood Hall, Building Trades Temple, 200 Guerero St. Telephone Market 1806 and 0455.

Ernst Poch, Hotel York, 580 Geary St.....P
Bruno Pruss, 801 Central Ave.,
   Alameda, Calif. ....R S
E. W. Schmitz, 200 Guerrero St. (3)....F S-T
Fred L. O'Hara, Off. 200 Guerrero St.
   Tel. Market 0455. Res. 806 Brush
   St., Oakland, Calif.
   Tel. Twin Oaks 0634................B A

473, Chicago, III. (Shopmen).—Meets second and fourth Friday at 8 p. m., at 5 N. California Ave. Tel. Kedzie 5953.

Richard W. Watson, Off. 2758 W.
   Madison St., Zone 12.
   Res. 5858 Waveland Ave..........P-B A
Wm. E. Cooney, 1808 Burlington Ave.,
   Lisle, Ill. ....R S
Wm. B. Ross, Off. 2758 W. Madison St.,
   Zone 12. Res. 3940 Thomas St.
   Tel. Spaulding 1643................F S-T
All mail to 2758 W. Madison St., Zone 12.

474, Manchester, N. H. (Mixed).—Meets third Sunday morning of each month at 10:00 A. M., 48 Manchester St. Executive Board meets third Sunday morning before regular meeting.

George Johnson, 34 Hospital Ave.
   Tel. 6053-J ....P
Edward Schunemann, 284 Silver St.
   Tel. 1156-M ....R S
Bernard H. Cowette, Off. 550 Elm St.
   Tel. Manchester 9871.
   Res. 1150 S. Willow St.
   Tel. 1856-R ....F-S-T-B A

476, Muskogee, Okla. (Shopmen). — Meets first and third Friday nights of each month at 226½ N. Second St.

Wm. D. Fillman ....P-B A
E. R. Lee, 208 Spaulding St..............R S
Woodrow H. Wilson,
   1202 E. Okmulgee..................F S-T

477, Sheffield, Ala. (Mixed).—Meets second and fourth Friday in Galloway Hall, at Fourth St. and Montgomery Ave., 8 p. m. Business Tel. 1538. Executive Board meets second and fourth Friday nights at 7 p. m.

C. W. Box, 2618-15th Ave., Tel. 2010-W...P
Clem P. Journey, 235 Wildwood Park Rd.,
   Florence, Ala. Tel. 1477-X-W.......R S
Robt. Lanier, 1212 Atlanta Ave.
   Tel. 222. Off. 401½ Montgomery Ave.
   Off. Tel. 1538.
   Send all mail to P. O. Box 671..F S-T-B A

480, Elizabeth, N. J. (Mixed).—Meets second and fourth Thursday evenings at 940 Elizabeth Ave. Executive Board meets first and third Monday evening. Tel. Eliz. 2-8245.

Thos. Burke, Res. 453 Devon St.,
   Kearny, N. J. Tel. Kearny-2-5408.......P
John Anderson, Off. 940 Elizabeth Ave.
   Tel. Elizabeth 2-8245. Res. 245 Rahway.
   Tel. Elizabeth 3-4216.................F S
David Williams, Off. 940 Elizabeth Ave.
   Tel. Elizabeth 2-8245. Res. 646.
   Jefferson Ave., Elizabeth, N. J.
   Tel. Elizabeth 3-7512.............T-R S
Wm. Dewald, Off. 940 Elizabeth Ave.
   Tel. Elizabeth 2-8245. Res. The Village
   Apt. 20-D, Magie Ave., Union, N. J.
   Tel. Elizabeth 5-2806.................B A

481, Dallas, Tex. (Mixed).—Meets in Labor Temple first and third Monday at 8 p. m. Executive Board meets first and third Friday at 5:30 p. m.

W. C. Galloway, Res. 2802 Alaska St.
   Res. Tel. Yale 2-5631..................P
D. G. Spradling, Res. 1810 Fourth Ave.
   Res. Tel. Harwood 7491................R S
L. E. Dilley, Res. Route 3, Box 22B.
   Res. Tel. 913-F-12. Off. Labor
   Temple, Dallas, Texas. Tel. Central
   4655. All mail to 1727 Young St.,
   Zone 1, Dallas.................F S-T-B A

482, Austin, Tex. (Mixed).—Meets in Labor Temple second and fourth Friday, at 8 p. m. Executive Board meets second and fourth Fridays.

Leonard Smith, Labor Temple.
   Zone 22. Tel. 88611.
   Res. Tel. 3839.................P-F S-B A
   Send all mail to L. A. Smith.
Monroe Smith, 4712 Ramsey Ave.
   Tel. 2-4644 ....R S

483, Hackensack, N. J. (Mixed).—Meets first and third Thursday evening at Carpenters' Hall, 36 Bergen St., Hackensack, N. J. Tel. Armory 4-554. Executive Board meets second and fourth Thursdays.

Jean F. Seymour, 149 Van Houten St.,
   Paterson, N. J., Tel. 4-0617-J..........P
James B. Stagg, Boulevard and Banta
   Ave., Pequannock, N. J.
   Tel. Mountain View 8-1195.........R S
J. D. Templeton, Jr., Res. 243 Burling-
   ton Ave., Paterson, N. J.
   Tel. Sherwood 2-1424...............F S-T
Jas. Leonard, Res. 129 20th St., Union
   City, N. J. Tel. Union 7-0383..........B A
Office of Local 483, 359 Van Houten St..
   Paterson, N. J. Tel. Armory 4-5544.

486, Washington (4), D. C. (Shopmen).—Meets second Tuesday night at 8 p. m., in Iron Workers' Hall, 405 Ninth St., N. W., Zone 4. Tel. Met. 5259. Executive Board meets fourth Tuesday at 8:00 p. m.

Harry Olshonsky, 6000 13th St. N.W.
   Tel. Taylor 7214........................P
Thos. R. Browning, 2147 O St. N.W.
   Tel. Michigan 7782...................R S
Henry Duckworth, Off. 405 9th St.
   N.W. Tel. Metropolitan 5259.
   Res. R. R. No. 2, Rockville, Md.
   Tel. Olympic 9107.............F S-T-B A
August Carabrese, 3935 A St., S.E.
   Tel. Franklin 8300. Ex. 350.....Ass't F S

487, Youngstown, Ohio. (Shopmen). — Meets second and fourth Monday nights at 1013 Albert St. Tel. 2-2448.

John J. Creighton, 1831 Warren Court.
Tel. 7-7277 ....P
T. P. Sweeney, 733 Cassius Ave.
Tel. 35747 ....R S
H. D. Kelly, 1661 Brownlee Ave.
Tel. 2-2448.
Off. 1018 Albert St..............F S-B A-T

489, Scranton, Pa. (Mixed). — Meetings held at 218 Adams Ave. on fourth Thursday night of each month.

Joseph L. Downes, Off. Room 312,
218 Adams Ave., Tel. Scranton 2-7353.
Res. 1911 Electric St., Dunmore, Pa.
Tel. 4-2091 ....P-B A-F S-T
Joseph G. Cawley, Off. 218 Adams Ave.
Tel. Scranton 4-2091.
Res. 2527 Birney Ave.
Tel. Scranton 3-5017 ....R S

491, Bay Area, San Francisco and Oakland, Cal. (Shopmen). — Meets every first Thursday at Building Trades Temple, 200 Guerrero St., San Francisco; every third Thursday at Building Trades Temple, 2111 Webster St., Oakland. Tel. Higate 4-6575. Executive Board meets second Friday in Oakland in office, Room 211, and fourth Friday in San Francisco, in Press Room, Building Trades Temple.

Frank Silva, off. 2111 Webster St.,
Oakland 12, Calif. Tel. Highgate 4-6575.
Res. 918 5th St., Zone 7, Tel.
Templebar 2-5389 ....P
Jos. R. Costa, 1518 13th Ave., Oakland.
Res. Tel. Kellogg 4-5308.
Off. Tel. Higate 4-6575 ....Asst' B A
Anthony J. Chiappe, 709 Albemarle St.,
El Cerrito. Res. Tel. Landscape 5-6130.
Off. Higate 4-6575. All mail to office,
2111 Webster St., Oakland.B A-F S-T-R S

492, Nashville, Tenn. (Mixed). — Meets third Wednesday night of each month at 7:30 p. m., in Labor Temple. Executive Board meets first and third Wednesdays. Office, 212 No. Eighth Ave. Tel. 5-9064.

J. M. Halliburton, Off. 212 8th Ave. N.
Tel. 5-9064, Res. 217 N. First St.
Tel. 6-4393 ....P
A. E. Yow, 212 8th Ave. N., Zone (3).
Res. Tel. Goodlettsville 2954..F S-R S-B A

493, Des Moines, Ia. (Shopmen).—Meets first and third Monday nights of each month at 204 W. 7th St., 3rd floor.

Gilbert Phillips, 1075 14th Place.
Tel. 3-0732 ....P
Harold Ordway, 1550 W. 13th St.........R S
Edwin Clarkson, 2915 E. Walnut..F S-T-B A

494, Cheyenne, Wyoming. (Mixed). — Meets second and fourth Monday of each month in Labor Hall, at 8 p. m. Executive Board meets every Tuesday.

Ralph E. Potter, 703 E. 6th St..........P
Harvey L. Brannick, 1606 E. Lincolnway.
Res. Tel. 5055 ....F S-B A
T. O. Mandery, Box 27-B., Meridan
Rt., Tel. 2-2247.................R. S.-T.
All mail to Box 814.

495, Albuquerque, N. M. (Mixed). — Meets first and third Friday nights of each month in K. of P. Hall.

Kenneth Miller, 517 N. 7th St...........P
Wm. Wedemeyer, Box 238 CC, Rt. 4.....R S
W. A. Walker, R. R. 2, Box 494.
Tel. 29131. Send all mail to
411 N. 2nd St.................B A-F S-T

496, Portland, Me. (Mixed). — Meets second and fourth Thursday at Labor Temple,

110 Exchange St., at 8 p. m. Executive Board meets second and last Thursday at 6:00 p. m., at office. Room 507, 22 Monument Square.

Ronald J. McIntyre,
Off. 110 Exchange St...............P
Wm. V. Sanphy, Off. 110 Exchange St.
Tel. 4-1406. Res. 1246 Broadway,
So. Portland, Tel. 4-8498.....F S-T-R S
M. D. Carey, Off. 110 Exchange St.
Res. 45 A St., So. Portland,
Tel. 2-6886 ....B A

498, Rockford, Ill. (Mixed). — Meets in Central Labor Temple, 212 So. First St., second and fourth Friday nights of each month. Executive Board meets second and fourth Fridays.

Carl Stromquist, Res. 607 No. London.
Off. 212 S. First St. Tel. 3-8463.
Tel. F-1873 ....P
Jos. Lambiotte, Off. 212 So. First St.
Tel. 3-8463. Res. 1222 Blaisdell
St. Tel. Blackhawk-7005..............R S
Hobart Hardy, Off. 212 S. First St.
Tel. 3-8463.
Res. Rt. No. 7, Prairie Rd.
Tel. Blackhawk 2936...........F S-T-B A

499, Toledo, Ohio, 912 Adams St. (Shopmen). —Meets third Sunday of each month at 9:30 a. m., in Hall D, Labor Temple.

Edw. Fleischman, 2903 Wayne St.,
Route No. 4 ....P
Herman Fineske,830 Tecumseh St.....F S-T
Harold A. Miller, 938 Toronto Ave.
Tel. Wa. 6860.......................R S

500, New Orleans, La. (Reinforced Concrete Iron Workers).—Executive Board meets first Thursday; regular meeting, third Thursday of each month at 836 Carondelet St., Zone 13. Tel. RA. 7436.

Al Keither, Off. 836 Carondelet St.
Tel. RA. 8072. Res. 210 S. Scott St.
Tel. AU. 2333 ....P
Al. Keither, Off. 836 Carondelet St.,
Zone 13. Res. 210 S. Scott St..........R S
Felix Blanchard, off. 836 Carondelet St.,
Zone 13. Tel. RA. 7436.
Res. 1824 Enterpe St...............F S-T
Harry Eskine. Off. 836 Carondelet St.,
Zone 13 ....B A

501, Boston, Mass., (Shopmen). — Meets first and third Friday nights of each month at 40 Prospect St., Cambridge, Mass., 8:00 p. m. Executive Board meets at 321 Tremont St., Boston, Wednesday nights, 8:00 p. m. Tel. Hubbard 9355.

Earl McMann, 113 DeForest St.,
Hyde Park, Mass.
Tel. Parkway 5473-W..............P-B A
Chas. H. Kelly, 862 Main St.,
Greenwood, Mass.
Tel. Crystal 1476-M..............F S-T
S. W. Morrill, 8 Herbert St.,
Everett, Mass. Tel. Everett 3529-J....R S

502, Philadelphia, Pa. (Shopmen). — Meets every first and third Friday nights of each month at 1803 Spring Garden St., Zone (30), at 8 p. m. Tel. Locust 7-3677.

Raymond C. Adams, 5014 Smedley St......P
Jos. A. Ecker, 2107 Stella St..............R S
William Modell, 1805 Spring
Garden St. Res. 838 Guenther Ave.,
Yeadon, Pa. Tel. Decatur
1907-J ....F S-T-B A
All mail to 1805 Spring Garden St.,
Zone (30).

504, Sacramento, Calif. (Shopman). — Meets first Monday of each month in Labor Temple, Eighth and Eye Sts., at 8 p. m. Executive Board meets first and third Mondays.

F. G. Kinz, 4044 4th Ave. Tel. 6-1113.....P
Al. Grenz, Rt. 1, Box 2103...............R S
Philip Ritthaler, 4932 T St., Zone 16.
Tel. 6-8235.........................F S

505, Mt. Vernon, Wash. (Mixed).—Meets first Friday of each month in Labor Temple, Mt. Vernon, Wash., and third Friday of each month in Labor Temple, Bellingham, Wash. Executive Board meets first and third Friday.

Tom E. Day, 2532 Superior, Bellingham,
   Wash. Tel. 5128-R..............P-B A
Julius Bloom, Off. Main and Gates.
   Tel. 5553. Res. Five Station.
   Tel. 1101....................R S
Cal Larson, Res. 3227 Laurelwood,
   Bellingham, Wash. Tel. 4158-J.....F S-T

506, Seattle, Wash. (Shopmen). — Meets second and fourth Monday nights of each month in Labor Temple.

Earl L. Lawrence, 5937½ 45th Ave.,
   S.W. Tel. West 5613.............P-F S-T
Tod Deems................................R S
   Send all mail to Labor Temple, Zone 1.

507, Denver, Colo. (Shopmen). — Meets every second and fourth Friday at 8 p. m., at Carpenters' Hall.

Lloyd Goodwin, Off. 1947 Stout St.,
   Zone 2. Tel. Tabor 4062. Res. 212 Hooker
   St. Tel. Glendale 3046..................P
Irven A. Jacobson, Off. 1947 Stout St.,
   Zone 2. Tel. Tabor 4062. Res. R. 2,
   Box 35, Arvada, Colo.
   Tel. Arvada 303-J............F S-T
M. G. Manfro, Off. 1947 Stout St., Zone 2.
   Res. 2333 W. 33rd Ave.
   Tel. Glendale 1064..............R S-B A

508, Detroit, Mich. (Shopmen). — Meets first and third Tuesday, at 8 p. m., at 3126 Park Ave. Tel. Temple 1-9611.

Walter Seymour, 3126 Park Ave., Zone 1..P
Frank Ross, 3126 Park Ave., Zone 1......R S
S. P. Tobin, 3126 Park Ave., Zone 1.
   Tel. Temple 1-9611..................Act F S
   Send all Local Union Mail to George
   W. Sucy, 3126 Park Ave., Zone 1.

509, Los Angeles, Calif. (Shopmen). — Meets fourth Wednesday of each month at Room 702, Labor Temple, 532 S. Maple Ave., Zone 13. Send all mail to office, Room 702 Labor Temple, 532 S. Maple Ave., Zone 13. Tel. Michigan 4520.

Herbert Olson, Room 702 Labor
   Temple, 532 S. Maple Ave. (8)..........P
Alvin Dively, 675 Oakford Drive,
   East Los Angeles (22)................R S
Harvey J. Miles, Off. 532 S. Maple Ave.
   (13). Tel. Michigan 452A.
   Res. 3869 E. 5th St.
   Tel. Angelus 3-4585 ....F S-T
John Hammock, Room 702 Labor
   Temple, 532 S. Maple Ave. (13)........B A

510, Corpus Christi, Texas, (Mixed). — Meets third Tuesday at 8 p. m., at 1824 Mesquite St. Office 2-9041. Executive Board meets first and third Fridays.

W. R. Flanagan, Off. 1824 Mesquite St.
   Res. 412 Elisa St........................P
M. M. Simmons, Off. 1824 Mesquite
   St. Res.
   1508-5th St. Tel. 2-4619.......F S-T-B A
John B. Kirton, Res. 216 Hughes St.
   Tel. 23155 ....R S

511, Spokane, Wash. (Shopmen). — Meets second Monday of each month at Labor Temple, West 104 Third Ave.

Carl Wibon, 416 E. Montgomery St.
   Tel. Glenwood 3827......................P
Carl Fetzner, 1316 N. Hollis St.F S-R S-B A
John H. Parker, 5917 N. Wall St...........T

512, Twin Cities, Minneapolis and St. Paul, Minn. (Mixed). — Meets second and fourth Tuesday at 2618 Territorial Rd., St. Paul 4, Minn. Off., 2618 Territorial Rd., Zone 4, St. Paul. Tel. Nestor 2122. Executive Board meets second and fourth Thursday.

James P. Lynch, 3606 6th St.,
   N. Minneapolis. Tel. Hyland 5579........P
J. H. Healey, 1220 W. Minnehaha,
   St. Paul, Minn. Tel. Nestor 9136.....R S
Clarence Bailey, Off. 2618 Territorial Rd.,
   Zone 4, St. Paul. Tel. Nestor 2122.
   Res. 1368 Galtier St., St. Paul.
   Tel. Humboldt 1805..............F S-T-B A

513, East St. Louis, Ill. (Shopmen). — Meets first and third Monday nights of each month at 449½ Collinsville Ave., East St. Louis.

Wm. Swager, Caseyville, Ill.,
   R. R. No. 2.........................P-B A
Melvin Dawson, 1403 Peabody Ct.
   St. Louis Mo........................F S-T
Wm. Ramacher, 3100 Converse Ave......R S

514, Peoria, Ill. (Shopmen).—Meets every fourth Wednesday night in Labor Temple at 8 p. m.

B. W. Miller, 903 Shipman St..............P
Ulfert R. Ideus, Endres Hotel.
   Tel. 3-3617 ....R S
Marion Sleister, 509 Garfield,
   Bartonville, Ill. ....F S-T

516, Portland, Oregon. (Shopmen). — Meets second and fourth Thursday night of each month in Labor Temple.

Gus Loprinzi, c-o M. Reuter & Sons,
   2230 S.E. Holgate (2). Res. 2234 S.E.
   30th Ave. Res. Tel. Vermont 2305.......P
Fred Moser, Jr., Off. 1130 S.W. 3rd Ave.,
   Rooms 15 and 16. Tel. Beacon 4627.
   Res. 3904 N.E. 42nd. Zone 13..........R S
Homer I. Park, Off. 15 Madison Bldg.,
   Off. 1130 S.W. 3rd Ave., Zone 4,
   Tel. Beacon 4627, Res. 6921 No.
   Leonard St. ....F S-T-B A

518, St. Louis, Mo. (Shopmen). — Meets first and third Fridays at 8 p. m., at office, St. Louis House, 2345 Lafayette Ave. Tel. PR-6690. (Send all mail to office.)

Wm. J. Myers, Off. 2345 Lafayette Ave.
   Res. 6725 Morganford. Tel. HU-7092..P
Henry Callahan, Off. 2345 Lafayette.
   Res. 7718 Michigan Ave.
   Tel. LO-7943 ....F S-T
Jerry Hajek, Res. 3113 Wyoming St.
   Tel. LA-9378.........................R S
Arthur A. Zeis, Off. 2345 Lafayette.
   Res. 4050 Quincy, Zone 16.
   Tel. Flanders 5088....................B A

519, Reading, Pa. (Shopmen).—Meets second and fourth Wednesday nights at Falcon's Hall, Spring Garden and Bingaman Sts.

Robt. A. Bicking, Res. 305 Fairview St.,
   Hyde Villa, Reading, Pa.
   Res. Tel. Laureldale 9-1976..............P
H. W. Trosky, Res. Stony Creek Mills,
   Pa. Tel. 38382.......................R S
William Guillette, 138 S. 8th St.
   Tel. 7695 ....F S-T

520, Kansas City, Mo. (Shopmen). — Meets first and third Wednesday of each month at 8 p. m., at 2906 Brooklyn Ave.

Dan Collins, 2262 Russell, Kansas City,
   Kan. Tel. Drexel 6754..................P
Thos. Francis, 4013 Charlotte, Kansas
   City, Mo. Tel. Valentine 6128.........R S
Cecil Randall, 3823 E. 39th St.
   Tel. Lin. 5789...................F S-T-B A

521, Scranton, Pa. (Shopmen). — Meets first and third Thursday nights at 116 Adams Ave.

Matthew Marcin, 827 Albert St.,
Dickson City, Pa.... P
William A. Cook, 215 S. Decker Ct...... R S
Nicholas Jadick, 1151 Amherst St., Zone 4.
Tel. 30406 ....F S-T

522, Cincinnati, Ohio. (Shopmen). — Meets every first and third Tuesday nights at Richfield Hall, Ninth and Plum Sts. Tel. Cherry 1077.

Kenneth A. Downer, Park St., Crescent
Springs, Ky. Tel. Dixie 7810-R..........P
Joseph E. Meister, 3215 Madison Rd......R S
Louis F. Moatz, 135 E. Court St.,
Court Hotel, Zone 2................F S-T

523, Providence, R. I. (Shopmen). — Meets first and third Tuesday nights of each month at 881 Eddy St. (1).

Edw. Parisee, Blossom Road,
Fall River, Mass.
Tel. Fall River 32837 ....P
Earle T. Herring, 75 Detroit Ave., Zone 7
Tel. ST. 2218 ....F S-T
Chas. G. O'Connell, Off. 56 Washington
St. ....R S

524, Waukegan, III. (Shopmen).—Meets first and third Friday nights of each month at 217 W. Washington St. Tel. Majestic 4925.

Geo. Van Treeck, Off. 217 Washington
St. Tel. Majestic 4925. Res. 12th St.
and Dugdale Rd. ....P-R S-T
Chas. E. Foxworth, 217 W Washington
St. Tel. Majestic 4925.............F S

526, Chattanooga, Tenn. (Shopmen). — Meets every first and third Tuesdays at 7:30 p. m., at 1426½ Dodds Ave.

Hugh D. Childress, 1018 E. 13th St.
Tel. 6-7275 ....P
Geo. Kelley, 2726 N. Chamberlain Ave.
Tel. 4-6676 ....R S
D. B. Springer, Res. 2407 Kirby Ave.
Tel. 41861 ....F S-T

527, Pittsburgh, Pa. (Shopmen).—Meets second and fourth Fridays of each month at second floor Rodger Bldg., 105-107 Federal St., North Side, Pittsburgh, at 8 p. m.

Thomas L. McGrail, 719 Ohio River
Blvd., Avalon 2, Pa. Tel. JU-6141.......P
Chas. Jacob, 1206 N. Murthland Ave.....R S
Severn Nedbaletz, 307 Robinson St.;
Oakland, Pittsburgh, Pa.
Tel. Mayflower 3967................F S-T

529, Indianapolis. (Shopmen). — Meets every second and fourth Fridays at 8 p. m., in Room 423, Transportation Bldg. Tel. Irvington 4572.

Waldo Driver, Box 92, Acton, Ind........P
Chas. W. Irish, 425 S. Noble St.
Tel. Fr. 6560 ....F S
Chas. McCurdy, 1587 E. LeGrande Ave...T
John T. Walker, 1738 Spruce St..........R S

530, Memphis, Tenn. (Shopmen). — Meets every second and fourth Wednesday in Memphis Labor Temple.

J. R. Shearon, Off. 565 Beale St.
Tel. 8-5891. Res. 222 Cosset . Tel. 51852..P
Paul H. Violette, Off. 565 Beale St.
Res. 374 Olive...................R S

Richard C. Cicalla, 567 S. Parkway E.....F S
Frank L. McGill, Off. 565 Beale St.
Res. R.F.D. No. 2, Box 376............T
F. L. Barclay, Off. 565 Beale St..........B A

531, Springfield, Ohio. (Shopmen). — Meets first and third Mondays at 7 p. m., in Labor Temple.

Lester Kitchen, R. R. 8................P
Chas. L. Doty, 419 Linwood Ave..........R S
Howard N. Mountcastle, R. R. 6..........T
Roy Jenkins, 1878 Malden Lane.
Tel. M-4256-M ....F S

532, New Haven, Conn. (Shopmen). — Meets second and fourth Monday nights at 137 Goffe St.

Frank J. Smee, 281 Cottage St.,
Zone 5, Bridgeport, Conn.
Tel. 3-1276 ....P-F S-T-B A
Charles E. Cullen, Res. 69 Hine St.,
West Haven, Conn. ....R S

534, Albany, N. Y. (Shopmen).—Meets third Monday in Labor Temple, 87 Beaver St.

Paul Berger, 282 Morton Ave..............P
Curt Luxenius, McClellan Rd.,
Nassau, N. Y..................F S-T-R S

535, Twin Cities, St. Paul and Minneapolis, Minn. (Shopmen). — Meets second and fourth Friday nights of each month at Ironworkers Hall, 2618 Territorial Road. All mail to office, 2618 Territorial Road, Zone 4, St. Paul, Minn.

Wesley Kvasnicka, 2349 James Ave.,
N. Minneapolis 11, Minn.
Tel. Aldrich 1283.................P
Alexander Burns, Off. 2618 Territorial
Road. Zone 4. Tel. Midway 0120.
Res. 4525 29th Ave., S., Minne-
apolis 6. Tel. Dupont 6903......F S T-B A
Albert F. Striebel, Off. 2618 Territorial
Road. Zone 4. Tel. Midway 0120.
Res. 1020 Barrett St., Zone 3.
Tel. Humboldt 6256..................R S

536, Dallas, Texas. (Shopmen).—Meets first and third Friday nights of each month in Labor Temple, 1729 Young St.

Chas. King ....P
J. L. Hartford, Rt. 2, Box 36,
Irving, Tex. ....F S-T-R S

539, Birmingham, Ala. (Shopmen). — Meets first and third Mondays at 10:30 a. m., and 7:30 p. m., at 1922½ N. Fourth Ave. Tel. 4-2496.

Carl M. Robinson, 1664 Alameda
Ave., S.W. ....P
Wm. L. Hayden, 803 Apt. D, Air-
port Hills ....R S
T. W. Odeneal, 936 N. 47th St.
Tel. 9-6609 ....F S-T
Send all mail to 1922½ N. 4th Ave.

541, Springfield, Mass. (Shopmen). — Meets second Tuesday of each month at 8 p. m., in Paliski Hall, Willimansett, Mass.

L. R. Chamberland, 143 Trilby Ave.,
Aldenville, Mass.
Tel. Holyoke 2-1361.................P-F S
Louis F. Forand, 622 High St.,
Holyoke, Mass. ....R S
Albert Brodeaur, 17 Charboneau Terrace,
Willimansett, Mass. Tel. Holyoke
2-2962 ....T

544, Spring City, Pa. (Shopmen). — Meets first and third Sunday at 2:00 p. m. in Liberty Fire Co., Hall St.

Ernest MacFarland, R. R. 1.............P
Lee Coupe, Main St., Royersford, Pa.....R S
John W. Ludolph, Rawn Ave.,
Graterford, Pa....................F S-T

545, Newark, N. J. (Shopmen).—Meets every first and third Friday nights of each month at 34 Park Place. Office Tel., Market 2-0176. All mail to office, 34 Park Pl., Zone 2.

Donald A. Nicholas, Off. 34 Park Place.....P
Michael McHugh, Off. 34 Park Place,
  Res. 111 66th St. W.
  Res. Tel. Union 3-8285..........R S-B A
Albert Shaffer, Off. 34 Park Pl., Zone 2.
  Tel. Market 2-0176, Res. 770 S. 13th St.
  Tel. Blg 2-6956.....................F S-T

546, Oklahoma City, Okla. (Shopmen). — Meets second and fourth Wednesday at 8 p. m., in Old City Hall Bldg., 105 W. Grand, 3rd Floor.

H. W. Miller, 1607 N. W. 6th St.,
  Tel. 2-6189 ....P
C. P. Jones, 2518 S. W. 33rd St.
  Tel. 6-3094 ....B A
Harry Briscoe, 3837 N. W. 24th St.
  Tel. 9-3770 ....R S
Jack Burch, 921½ N. W. 6th St..........F S

547, Wilkes-Barre, Pa. (Shopmen). — Meets first and third Tuesday nights of each month at Firemen's Hall, Luzerne, Pa.

Samuel Heydon, 69½ Oak St.,
  Forty Fort, Pa........................P
Francis Garrahan, 3 Webster St.
  Pringle Boro, Luzerne, Pa...........R S
John Grunert, 21 Mott St., Kingston,
  Pa. Tel. 76870 ....F S-T

548, Allentown, Pa. (Shopmen). — Meets first and third Friday at 7:00 p. m., at Harugari Home Assn., 180 Gordon St.

Michael Smicker, 907 3rd St.,
  Fullerton, Pa...........................P
John Bruchok, 705½ N. Front St........R S
John Sisnowski, 111 Tilghman St........F S

549, Wheeling, W. Va. (Mixed).—Meets second and last Friday night of each month in Labor Temple, 1506 Market St. Executive Board meets second and last Fridays.

D. J. Jones. Off. 1506 Market St.
  Tel. 1493. Res. 812 Pearl St., Martins
  Ferry, Ohio. Tel 324-W.................P
Cecil Hedrick, R. D. No. 1,
  Triadelphia, W. Va. Tel. 3634......R S-T
Arch Adams. Off. 1506 Market St.
  Off. Tel. Wheeling 1493.
  Res. R. D. No. 4, Cameron, W. Va.F S-B A

550, Canton, Ohio. (Mixed). — Meets fourth Friday evening of each month at 803 Tuscarawas St. Executive Board meets second and fourth Fridays.

Arthur G. Boyer, 323 Lincoln Ave.,
  N.W. Tel. 47473.........................P
Wm. L. Downes, Magnolia, Ohio, R. D.
  Tel. Magnolia 6052....................R S
H. Roy McKelvey, Res. 906 Essig Ct.,
  N. W., Zone 3. Res. Tel. 32747......F S-T
  Send all mail to residence.
Vernon J. Sherer, Off. 201 Second St.,
  N. E. Tel. 48664. Res. 1516 Second St.,
  S. E. Tel. 8971.........................B A

553, Omaha, Nebr. (Shopmen). — Meets at 8:00 p. m., fourth Tuesday nights of each month in Labor Temple, Nineteenth and Davenport Sts., Zone 2. Executive Board meets second and fourth Tuesday nights at 8:00 p. m.

Louis D. Jensen, 5019 Poppleton.
  Tel. GI-4490...........................P
Don H. Moore, 2304 Douglas St.........R S
Gordon C. Preble, Off. Labor Temple,
  Zone 2. Tel. Ja-6571. Res. 3620 No.
  34th St. Tel. Kenwood 6469...F S-T-B A

555, Hartford, Conn. (Shopmen).—Meets first and third Wednesday nights at 327 Trumbull St.

Stanley A. Zebrowski, 240 High St.,
  New Britain, Conn.
Everett Seaburg, 52 .Burnham St.,
  Kensington, Conn. ....F S-T

557, Jacksonville, Ill. (Shopmen). — Meets at 7:30 p. m., every second and fourth Mondays of each month at 360 N. Gay St. Executive Board meets first and third Wednesdays in Plumbers Hall, 1133 Hartford Ave.

David S. Dickerson, Off. 624 S. Prairie
  St. Tel. 655-Y.........................P
Oscar L. Kennedy, 721 E. Beecher Ave.
  Tel. 1388-Y ....F S-T
H. K. Decker, 721 S. Diamond St.......R S
L. V. Sweeney, 315-E Washington St....B A

558, Appleton, Wis. (Shopmen).—Meets third Tuesday in Labor Hall.

Allyn Seemann, 1617 N. Alvin...........P
Earl R. Vande Bogart,
  1210 W. Commercial St...............R S
Erwin Casey, 719½ N. Fair St........F S-T

560, Grand Coulee, Wash. (Mixed).—Regular meetings second and fourth Tuesday of each month. Executive Board meets second and fourth Tuesdays.

A. A. Nelson, Off. P. O. Box 426.
  Tel. 160. Res. Coulee Dam, Wash......P
K. C. Will, Off. Box 426. Tel. 160.F S-B A
S. C. Riggle, Electric City, Wash......R S
M. O. Baker, Res. phone 04-J..............T
  Send all mail to P. O. Box 426.

562, Salt Lake City, Utah. (Shopmen).—Meets first and third Thursday nights of each month at Labor Temple. Tel.3 -9991.

Orson Ross Lott, Res. 3267 South Second West St., Tel. 6-6678.................P
Glen Duane Davis, Res. 1523 East
  3045 South St........................R S
Lynn Gillett, Res. 751 7th Ave. Off.
  308 Labor Temple...................F S-T

563, Duluth, Minn. (Mixed). — Meets second and fourth Friday nights of each month in Labor Temple, 320 W. First St. Tel. Melrose 4404. Executive Board meets first and third Friday.

John Jenssen, 331½ W. Third St.........P
Richard J. Thomas, 1440 8th Ave., E.,
  Zone 5. Tel. Hemlock 6091......F S-T-B A
Francis Benoist, 1024 S. 72nd Ave., W...R S

565, Mechanicsburg, Pa. (Shopmen). — Meets second Wednesday in Rescue Hook & Ladder Co., No. 1 Hall, at 7:30 p. m.

Mervin Derrick, 19 E. Locust St..........P
Lawrence Fertenbaugh,
  318 W. Keller St......................R S
Lewis Smith, 115 E. Locust St.........F S-T
Robt. C. Kaley, 324 W. Allen St.........B A

568, Cumberland, Md. (Mixed).—Meets third Saturday night of each month at 123 Frederick St. Executive Board meets first and third Saturday of each month, at Building Trades Council Hall, at 723 Frederick St.

John Hertz, 123 Frederick St............P-T
Jas. W. Winsow, R. 4, Box 410.........R S
Edwin L. Simon, Res. R. 4, Box 410.
  Off. 123 Frederick St., Off. Tel. 2073.
  Res. Tel. 1891-R................F S-B A
  Send all mail to Route 4, Box 410,
  Cumberland, Md.

572, York, Pa. (Shopmen).—Meets second and fourth Mondays at 8 p. m., at 124 S. Pershing Ave.

James A. Wertz, 618 Cleveland Ave........P
Leroy H. Mayer, 770 Village Rd.
    Tel. 48228 ....R S-B A
    Send all mail to 770 Village Road.
Alfred S. Rooney, 634 E. Boundary Ave.....T
Leo J. Bowling, 935 E. Hay St............F S

573, Baltimore, Md. (Shopmen).—Meets first and third Mondays of each month at Lithuanian Hall, Hollins and Parker Sts.

Walter M. Brooks, 1906 Wilhelm St........P
Stephen Wendling, 2115 Maisel St.,
    Mt. Winans ....R S
Wm. Cooke,
    1446 Marshall St., Zone 30..........F S-T

575, Detroit, Mich. (Machinery Movers and Riggers).—Meets third Wednesday night of each month at 8213 Woodward Ave., Zone 2. Office, 8213 Woodward Ave., Zone 2. Tel. Trinity 2-4110 and 2-4111.

Richard Morrison, Off. 8213 Woodward
    Ave., Zone 2. Tel. Temple 1-7380........P
Paul C. Allen, 8213 Woodward Ave.,
    Zone 2. Tel. Trinity 2-4110...F S-T-B A
Henry J. Bushey, Off. 8213 Woodward
    Ave. (2) ....R S

576, Buffalo, N. Y. (Shopmen).—Meets second and fourth Friday at Ahls Hall, 634 Broadway. Tel. Madison 4118.

Peter Schalberg, Res. 23 Cherry Lane,
    Cheektowaga. Tel. Parkside 0016........P
Geo. E. Riedel, 104 Densmore St.
    Tel. Tr. 6072......................R S
Geo. E. Mintzer, 393 Glenwood Ave.,
    Zone 8. Tel. Ll. 3217.............F S-B A
    Send all mail to 320 White Bldg., Zone 2.

577, Burlington, Iowa. (Mixed). — Meets first and third Wednesday night of each month at 205 Labor Temple. Tel. 299. Executive Board meets first and third Wednesdays.

John H. Sullivan, Off. Labor Temple.
    Off. Tel. 299. Res. 505 May Ave.
    Tel. 5408-J ....P
E. J. Schreiner, 205 Labor Temple.
    Res. 2107 Connor Ave. Tel. 1039-W..F S-T
Roy Fitzpatrick, 3131 Sunnyside Ave.
    Tel. 5079 ....R S
T. J. Treharne, Off. 205 Labor Temple.
    Tel. 299. Res. 409 May Ave.
    Res. Tel. 5571-J....................B A
    All mail to 205 Labor Temple.

579, Trenton, N. J. (Shopmen). — Meets first Thursday night of each month at 159 Mercer St.

Leroy Hambright, Res. 991 So. Olden Ave...P
Tulli Rossi, 209 Greenland Ave............R S
W. L. Cook, Res. 211 Johnston Ave.,
    Zone 9..............................F S-T
John Mauer, 1606 Greenwood Ave.,
    Zone 9. Tel. Trenton 8744............B A

580, New York, N. Y. (Ornamental Iron Workers).—Regular meeting held last Friday of each month at Werdermann's Hall, 16th St. and 3rd Ave., at 8 p. m. Executive Board meets second Wednesday of each month at Headquarters, 234 W. 12th St., at 8 p. m. Tel. Chelsea 3-2676.

Frank Meenan, 1670 Woodbine St.,
    Brooklyn (27), N. Y....................P

Edw. J. Lynch, Jr., 108-14 Metropolitan
    Ave., Forest Hills, N. Y...............R S
Daniel P. Murphy, Jr., 60-71 55th St.,
    Maspeth, L. I., N. Y................F S-T
Charles Sheridan, 52-41 66th St.,
    Maspeth, L. I., N. Y................B A
Albert Mendes, 285 N. Fulton Ave.,
    Mt. Vernon, N. Y...................B A

581, Tacoma, Wash. (Shopmen). — Meets second and fourth Monday nights of each month in Labor Temple, Seventh and Pacific Ave.

Lloyd Hickok, 1611 S. L. St., Zone 3.......P
Jesse J. Johnston, 1115 N. L. St..........F S
William E. Durand, 404 N. G. St.,
    Zone 8. Tel. No. Br. 2682.............B A

582, Kansas City, Kansas. (Shopmen). — Meets first Wednesday at 8:00 p. m., Odd Fellows Hall, Twenty-first and Silver.

J. F. Wright, Off. 21st & Metropolitan.
    Tel. Fairfax 6020.
    Res. Room 36, Alta Vista Hotel,
    430 W. 11th St., Kansas City, Mo........P
Henry Larson, 1141 Metropolitan.
    Tel. DR 3148.......................R S
K. A. Wiyninger, Off. 21st & Metropolitan.
    Tel. Fairfax 6020.
    Res. 516 N. 13th St. Send all mail
    to residence ....F S-T

583, San Antonio, Texas. (Shopmen).—Meets second Tuesday of each month.

E. Y. Blount, 446 Drexel Ave.,
    Tel Lambert 23035....................P
Joseph A. Guirand, 106 Wyoming St.
    Tel. 5487..........................R S
R. P. Brown, Rt. 6, Box 852.
    Tel. L-2-5272 ....F S-T

584, Tulsa, Okla. (Mixed). — Meets third Friday. Executive Board meets first and third Friday a. m., at 432 N. Boston, Zone 6.

Hershell Litterell, Off. 432 N. Boston,
    Zone 6, Tel. 3-1933...................P
Wm. Willert, 432 N. Boston, Zone 6......R S
Laverne Smith, 432 N. Boston,
    Zone 6. Off. Tel. 3-1933,
    Res. Tel. 9-6509...............F S-T-B A

585, Vincennes, Ind. (Shopmen).—Meets first and third Mondays at 7:30 p. m., in Trades Council Hall, 414½ Main St.

Maurice Brown, R. R. No. 4................P
R. W. Crawford, 509 Maple St.,
    Lawrenceville, Ill. Tel. 839-M.......F S-T
Burl Deem, 1901 N. 2nd St..............R S

586, Manchester, N. H. (Shopmen). — Meets second Friday night of each month at 550 Elm St.

James White, 56 Eve St.................P
Joseph LaRose, 83 Ward St.,
    Tel. 3856-M ....R S
Arthur Auger, 69 Brunelle Ave.........F S
Alfred Champagne, 101 Putnam St.....B A

587, Akron, Ohio (Shopmen).—Meets second Wednesday and fourth Friday nights in German-American Hall, 834 Grant St.

S. L. Crute, Res. 1179 Laurel Ave.
    Tel. BL. 1009.......................P
Paul P. Helfrick, 522 East Ave......F S-T
Ralph Ballinger, 1135 Florida Ave.,
    Zone 14............................R S

588, Tampa, Fla. (Shopmen).

R. T. Richey, Off. 1801 N. Franklin St.,
    Zone 2, Res. 2717 N. A. St.,
    Zone 6........................R S-F S-T

589, Easton, Pa. (Shopmen).—Meets Wednesday nights at 8 p. m., in Bethlehem Twp. Roosevelt Democratic Club, Miller Heights, Easton, Pa.

James Sharkey, 209 Cattell St............P
Roy Schweitzer, Freemansburg, Pa...F S-T
Ellis Little, 314 So. 17th St.............R S

590, Aurora, Ill. (Shopmen). — Meets second and fourth Friday nights in Labor Temple, 215 Main St.

Stanley Seaton, Res. 567 Benton St.
   Tel. 2-3157 ....P
Willard Peterson, 137 N. 4th St..........R S
Gustav Pentek, 368 Beach St.........F S
Otto Reed, 78 N. Root St...............T

591, Shreveport (23), La. (Mixed). — Meets first and third Friday nights, 714½ Milam St. Executive Board meets second and fourth Monday. All mail to 714½ Milam St., Zone 23. Tel. 2-0875.

A. S. Palmer, 714½ Milam St., Zone 23.....P
R. C. Higginbotham, 714½ Milam St.....R S
H. S. Morgan, Off. 714½ Milam St.
   Tel. 20875 ....F S-T-B A

592, Wichita Falls, Texas. (Mixed).—Meets second and fourth Friday nights of each month in Labor Temple, 705 Travis St. Tel. 5662.

W. A. Keen, Rt. 1, Box 444-A.
   Tel. 25744 ....P
D. D. Bell, Box 261, Petrolia, Tex..F S-T-B A
All mail to Box 261, Petrolia, Tex.

593, Utica, N. Y. (Shopmen). — Meets second Thursday night of each month in Labor Temple, 714 Charlotte St.

Anthony J. Sandora, 72 Spruce St.,
   Ilion, N. Y., Tel. Ilion 530-J..........P
Frank J. Melchorre, 1010 Rutger St..F S-R S

594, Bethlehem, Pa. (Shopmen). — Meets second Monday at 8:00 p. m., at Grover Cleveland Democratic Club, 904 Main St.

Sterling J. Frey, R. D. No. 2............P
Edward E. Wesenberg,
   940 Delaware Ave...................R S
Russell R. Shaffer, 30 W. North St......F S

595, Paducah, Ky. (Mixed.) — Meets third Saturday night at 1023 Broadway. Executive Board meets first and third Saturdays.

Oscar Downey, 1023 Broadway............P
W. B. Sanders, 110½ S. 5th St. Tel. 745.
   P. O. Box 1019.
   Res. R. No. 4, Paducah, Ky.
   Tel. County 8706...............F S-T-B A

597, Jacksonville, Fla. (Mixed).—Meets first and third Friday nights of each month at 808 Main St. Send all mail to P. O. Box 3593. Tel. 5-4296.

J. R. McGill, 520 Talleyrand.
   Tel. 3-1650-M....................P
E. V. Thompson, 1639 Roosevelt Ave....R S
J. J. Gilday, Off. 808 Main St.
   Tel. 5-4296. Res. 1331 Ionia St..F S-T-B A

598, Kalispell, Mont. (Mixed).—Meets in Carpenters' Hall first of each month.

Francis E. Willits, Genl. Delivery,
   Belton, Mont. ....P
Ralph Laurich, 226 8th
   Ave., W. ....F S-T-R S-B A

599, Norristown, Pa. (Shopmen). — Meets 8:00 p. m., third Monday of each month at 46-48 E. Main St., 3rd Floor.

Walter Bechtel, 509 Haws Pl.............P
Clarence L. Mohn, 505 Noble St.,
   Tel. 7415 ....R S
Harold Kiemer, 2727 Nolan St.,
   Chester, Pa. ....F S-T

600, Mobile, Ala. (Mixed). — Meets fourth Wednesday night of each month at 8:00 p. m., at 54½ Dauphin St. Tel. 3-1162. Executive Board meets second and fourth Wednesdays.

C. W. McKnight, 54½ Dauphin St.........P
Edwin Bradley, 54½ Dauphin St.........R S
Jack H. Jones, 54½ Dauphin St........F S
S. A. Alsup, 54½ Dauphin St. Tel. 31162.
   Res. Rt. No. 4, Box 179-A.
   Tel. 61729 ....B A
Send all mail to P. O. Box 1226.

601, Charleston, S. C. (Mixed). — Meets first and third Friday at 8:00 p. m., 4 Broad St. Executive Board meets first and third Friday.

A. W. McLean, Off. 4 Broad St.
   Tel. 2-0011. Res. 102A Celtic St.,
   N. Charleston ....P
A. R. Cloud, Off. 4 Broad St.
   Res. Gen. Del., St. George, S. C.........R S
Geo. P. Simmons, Sr., Off. 4 Broad St.
   Tel. 2-0011. Res. 600B Lancaster St.
   N. Charleston, S. C...........F S-T-B A

606, Wichita, Kansas. (Mixed). — Meets first and third Wednesday nights of each month in Labor Temple. Executive Board meets first and third Wednesdays.

S. E. Ayers, Off. 417 E. English.
   Tel. 4-2424. Res. 408 N. Meridian.......P
Dewey B. Bryant, Off. 417 E. English.
   Tel. 4-2424. Res. 827 S. Estelle.
   Tel. 3-5438 ....F S-T-B A
A. W. Conklin, Mulvane, Kansas.
   Tel. 27-J ....R S

607, Charlestown, Mass. (Navy Yard Riggers.)—Meets third Friday at 8:00 p. m. at Parker House, Boston.

Matthew G. Vikre, 34 Matchett St.,
   Brighton, Mass. Tel. Stadium 7072.....P
Joseph Donahue, 7 Bay View St.,
   Revere, Mass. Tel. Revere 4455-W.F S-T
Edw. F. Hines, 1098 Hyde Park Ave.,
   Hyde Park, Mass. Tel. Hyde Park
   1728-R ....R S

611, Waukesha, Wis. (Shopmen).—Meets first and third Tuesdays of each month in Labor Temple, 324 West Ave.

Floyd Baltes, 204 Harrison Ave..........P
Alvin Betker, 1022 E. Main St..........R S
Kenneth G. Sickels, Rt. 1, Box 34,
   Hartland, Wis....................F S

612, Syracuse, N. Y. (Shopmen). — Meets fourth Tuesday of each month at Labor Temple, 309 S. Franklin. Executive Board meets second Wednesday of each month.

John J. Rowe, R. D. No. 1,
Jamesville, N. Y. ....P
Kenneth Beardsley, R. D., Brewerton,
N. Y. ....R S
Henry Darling, 309 S. Franklin St.
Tel. 3-4553 ....T
Geo. S. Cooper, Off. 309 S. Franklin.
Tel. 2-3363. Res. 619 E.
Fayette St. ....F S-B A

615, Muskegon, Mich. (Shopmen). — Meets second and fourth Wednesdays of each month at Labor Temple.

Frank Goldembieski, 1370 D Bellum Ave....P
Arthur Adamson, 315 Catawba Ave.
Tel. 246-255 ....F S
Merle Graves, 1214 Jarman St.,
Muskegon Hgts. ....R S

616, Atlanta, Ga. (Shopmen).—Meets second and fourth Tuesday nights in Labor Temple.

W. M. Wilson, 294 Cheshire Bridge Road,
Send all mail to office,
91 Trinity Ave., S.W. ....P
E. B. Evans, Off. 91 Trinity Ave.
Tel. JA-4880. Res. 15 Simpson,
S. N. W. ....R S
W. W. Hudson, 154 Warlick Ave.,
Live Oak Garden, College Park, Ga..F S-T

617, Pascagoula, Miss. (Shipyard Riggers).

L. V. Williamson, 1217 Adm. Dewey.......P
J. L. Williamson,
Res. 1314 14th St..............F S-T-B A
Edward O. Castona, Kreole, Miss........R S

619, New Orleans, La. (Shopmen). — Office 836 Carondelet St. Tel. Raymond 7436.— Meets second Tuesday at 8:00 p. m., and fourth Sunday at 9:00 a. m.

John H. Landry, 8420 Pontchartrain
Blvd. ....Act P
Thos. F. Millar, 3720 D'Hemecourt
St. Tel. AM. 3146 ....R S
Nick Tedesco, Off. 836 Carondelet St.
Tel. RA 7436.
Res. 3519 N. Tonti St............F S-T-B A
Send mail to residence.

620, Tulsa, Okla. (Shopmen).—Meets second and fourth Wednesdays of each month at Ironworkers' Hall, 17½ N. Lewis. Tel. 5-2851. All mail to 432 N. Boston, Zone 6.

Levi T. Rogers, Off. 432 N. Boston,
Zone 6. Tel. 5-2851.
Res. 1324 N. Santa Fe. Tel. 49802........P
Chas. M. Overton, Off. 432 N. Boston,
Zone 6. Res. 347 27th Pl., N.
Tel. 4-4026 ....R S
John Dugan, 432 N. Boston, Zone 6.
Tel. 5-2851. Res. 4716 E. 6th..F S-T-B A

621, Elmira, N. Y. (Shopmen).—Meets second and fourth Friday of each month at Union's Social Clubhouse, 118-120 Lake St., Elmira, at 8:00 p. m. Executive Committee meets first and third Mondays.

Stephen Collins, 151 E. 18th St.,
Elmira Heights, N. Y. ....P
Michael Watach, 215 Horseheads
Blvd., Elmira Heights, N. Y.........R S
Adelbert Southard, 506 Fitch St.
Tel. 9626 ....F S-T
Peter N. Whitcher, Hotel Langwell.
Tel. 7131 ....B A

622, Charleston, S. C. (Navy Yard Riggers).

C. E. Herman, Rt. 7, Box 466,
Navy Yard, S. C. ....P
Robt. C. Carnes, 1207 Wando Rd.,
Palmetto Gardens, North
Charleston, S. C. ....F S
Theodore R. Westervelt, Off. Charleston Naval Shipyard. Tel. 608.
Res. Rt. No. 4, Box 886, Tel. 3-2849.....R S

623, Baton Rouge, La. (Structural).—Meets first and third Wednesday night at 8:00 p. m., 2725 Seneca St. Executive Board meets first and third Wednesdays.

B. E. Shattuck, off. 2725 Seneca St.
Res. 1728 N. 24th St. Tel. 8423......P-F S
John M. Beysselance, off. 2725 Seneca St.
Res. 1142 North St. Tel. 3-9449........R S
C. J. Young, 2725 Seneca St.
Res. 2525 E. Montesano Ave............T
W. E. Melton, 2725 Seneca St.
Tel. 6407, Res. 3015 Spruce St.
Tel. 2-1649 ....B A
Send all mail to 2725 Seneca St., Zone 5.

624, Fresno, Calif. (Shopmen). — Meets first and third Thursdays in Building Trades Hall, 1035 Broadway.

Conrad Stumpp, 146 F St................P
William Johnson, 920 Klette Ave.,
Fresno 1, Calif. Tel. 43975......F S-T-B A

625, Honolulu, Hawaii, T. H. (Mixed).— Meets first and third Fridays at King and Alaeka Sts.

George Kauka, Off. 211 McCandless Bldg...P
Sadamu Fujikawa. Off. 211 McCandless
Bldg. ....R S
A. S. Relle, Off. 211 McCandless Bldg.
Tel. 65852 ....F S-T-B A

626, Columbus, Ohio. (Shopmen). — Meets second and fourth Sunday at 2:30 p. m. at 525½ N. Park St.

Leonard E. Frazier, 525½ N. Park St.
Res. 866 Kleiner Ave. Tel. WA. 61094....P
James W. Beller, Off. 525½ N. Park St.
Res. 3862 Cass Blvd., Grove City, Ohio.
Tel. FR. 66401 ....R S
D. A. Hart, Off. 525½ N. Park St.
Res. 148 S. Terrace Ave.
Tel. Randolph 7908................F S-T

627, San Diego, Calif. (Shopmen).—Meets first Monday at 811 F St., at 8:00 p. m.

Dewey Hamblin, 4272 Fairmount Ave.......P
James Parker, 4505 Cragie.............R S
Vernon Noland, 7412 Wellington,
Zone 11 ....F S-T
Juel Drake, 813 F St..................B A

629, Mobile, Ala. (Shipyard Riggers).—Meetings held second and fourth Sunday of each month at 2 p. m., 101 N. Royal St.

Office, 51 St. Francis St. Tel. Dexter 737.
N. J. Lambeth, 450 S. Dearborn St........P
W. F. Phillips, 307 St. Joseph St.........R S

630, Orange, Texas. (Shopmen).—Meets first and third Thursdays of each month at 7:30 p. m. Executive Board meets second and fourth Thursdays of each month. Both meet in Room 18 Petty Bldg.

Eugene Vanpelt, 908 3rd St.............P
Windell Cornier, 1102 17th St...........R S
Jack Peveto, Room 18, Petty Bldg.
Tel. 2524 ....F S-T-B A

632, Balboa, Canal Zone.—Meets first Friday of each month.

Merrill F. Will, Box No. 518.
Tel. 2-2783 ....P
Thomas Croom, Box 1650. Tel. 2-2929.
Balboa, Canal Zone.
Tel. 2-1328 ....F S-T-R S
L. A. Godby............................B A

633, Evansville, Ind. (Shopmen).—Meets first and third Tuesday night at 7:30 p. m., of each month at Room 104, C. L. U. Bldg., 210 N. Fulton Ave. Tel. 32632.

Joseph Lantz, 310 E. Columbia St.
  Tel. 2-5002 ....P
Max Doty, 1003 N. Elliott St...........R S
Chas. Orth, Off. Room 104, C. L. U.
  Bldg., 210 N. Fulton Ave. Res. 1741
  S. Morton Ave. Tel. 8818.......F S-T-B A
Send all mail to office.

636, Durham, N. C. (Mixed).—Tel. J-3321— Meets fourth Sunday of each month. Executive Board meets second and fourth Sundays.

C. F. Frye, Labor Temple. Res. Maple St...P
John M. O'Quinn, off. Labor Temple.
  Res. 609 Chapel Hill St...............R S
Julian F. Head, Off., Labor Temple.
  Res. Carrboro, N. C...........F S-T-B A

637, Decatur, Ala. (Shopmen).—Meets every Thursday at 7:00 p. m., at 402½ Second Ave.

J. R. Dobyns, 620 5th Ave., West..........P
R. J. Harwell, 1115 4th Ave., E..........R S
Thomas O'Neal McCarley,
  1121 4th Ave. E. Tel. 1789-XW....F S-T

640, Phoenix, Ariz. (Shopmen).

W. R. McDowell, Glendale, Arizona,
  Box 530 ....P
B. R. Wilson, 1305 E. Durango
  St. ....R S-F-S-T

642, Erie, Pa. (Shopmen).—Meets second and fourth Friday nights at Central Labor Hall, 1701 State St.

Cyril Bauers, 1843 Buffalo Rd., Apt. B-1....P
Edw. Budzinski, 632 E. 19th St...........F S
Frank Campana, 1833 W. 13th St.........R S

643, Victoria, B. C. (Shipyard Riggers).— Meets third Monday in Labor Hall, 602 Broughton St. Executive Board meets first and third Mondays.

A. G. Sainsbury, 837 Broughton St.
  Tel. E-4500 ....P
H. L. Ritchie, 2620 Quadra St.....F S-T-R S

646, Boise, Idaho. (Mixed).—Meets second and fourth Saturday of each month in Labor Temple. Executive Board meets first and third Thursdays.

Ralph L. White, 1717 Cleveland St.
  Tel. 154-J-2 ....P
Richard A. Murray, 403 N. 23rd Rd.
  Tel. 3052-M ....R S
J. H. Halsey, 2117½ Bannock St.
  Off. Tel. 4480. Res. Tel. 3007-J........F S

647, Clinton, Iowa. (Shopmen). — Meets first and third Wednesday of each month at 7 p. m.

Arthur Perryman, 105½ 2nd Ave., S.......P
Fred Orte, 410 Second Ave., S.
  Tel. 3138-W ....F S
Jerome Brown, 410 2nd Ave., S..........R S

648, Port Washington, Wis. (Shopmen).— Meets last Thursday at 318 Franklin St.

Reuben Krube, 535 Michigan St...........P
Felix S. Yankunas, Belgium, Wisc......R S
Fred Roedelbronn, 452 Michigan St.......T
Warren Klumb, 451 W. Chestnut.......F S

649, Martins Ferry, Ohio. (Shopmen).—Meets first and third Fridays of each month at Jr. O. U. A. Hall at 7:30 p. m.

William F. Mills, Market and Wilson
  St., Yorkville, Ohio..................P
Geo. Nicholaus, 238 29th St., Wheeling,
  W. Va. ....R S
Earl Cochran, 807 Vine St., Martins
  Ferry, Ohio ....T
Robert Summers, 88 New Jersey,
  Wheeling, W. Va. Tel. Wheeling
  4681-M ....F-S

650, Rockford, Ill. (Shopmen).—Meets second and fourth Wednesdays of each month.

John Moore, Res. 746 N. First St..........P
Chas. Wiler, Off., 1120 Harrison Ave.
  Off. Tel. Main 700. Res., 1319 Boilvin
  Ave. Tel. Main 4271-R3 ....R S
Delbert Kunz, Off., 3032 Parkside Ave.
  Tel. Blackhawk 3073..................V P
Adolph Keinz, Off., c-o A. C. Woods &
  Co. Res., 1902 Ivy Terrace..........F S-T

652, Little Rock, Ark. (Shopmen).

R. E. Bennett, 1911 Short 17th St.,
  North Little Rock....................P
A. D. George, R. R. 3, Box 205-A.........R S
W. E. Kooms, 1607 Maple St.,
  North Little Rock. Tel. 7344.......F S-T

653, Mt. Vernon, Ohio. (Shopmen). — Meets first and third Fridays at G.A.R. Hall.

Samuel B. Hoar, No. 13 Seeley.
  Tel. 1104-M.........................P
Ulysses Willisen, Res. 302 Calhoune St.
  Tel. 466-J ....R S
Clarence Butler, R. D. No. 3,
  Mt. Vernon, O. Tel. 2013-T........F S-T

654, Hammond, Ind. (Shopmen).—Meets fourth Tuesday at Labor Temple, 503 Sibley St.

H. A. Martin, 6121 Columbia Ave.
  Hammond, Ind.......................P
Ruth Ruebel, 4143 Grover Ave............R S
Arnold Gilbertson, 732 Indiana Ave....F S-T

655, Orange, Tex. (Shipyard Riggers).

J. H. Hernandez, Off., Room 18, Petty
  Bldg. Tel. 2524. Res. 807 College St.,
  Rt. 3, Box 33.........................P
F. Broussard, Off. Room 18, Petty Bldg.
  Res. 341 Rodgers Ct............R S-F S-T

657, Baltimore, Md. (Shopmen). — Vickers Bldg., Room 203, 225 E. Redwood St. Tel. Saratoga 7833. Meets at Lithuanian Hall, 2nd Monday at 8:00 p. m. and 4th Sunday at 10:30 a. m.

John C. Finck, Jr. Send all mail to
  Res. 3031 Matthews St., Zone 18.
  Tel. HO. 3293. Off. 202 Vickers Bldg.
  225 E. Redwood St. Tel. Saratoga 7833...P
Chas. F. Faber, Res. 832 Hartford
  Court, Res. Tel. Vernon 0132-W.
  All mail to 832 Hartford Court
  Baltimore 2, Md. ....F S
Robt. H. Newton, Res. 5331 Patrick
  Henry Drive ....T

660, Leavenworth, Kansas. (Shopmen). Meets second Wednesday of each month in Eagles Hall. Executive Board meets second and fourth Wednesdays.

Thos. E. Brown, 1218 Kenton.
  Tel. 142-W.........................P-B A
Robt. L. Donnelly, 217 Columbia.
  Tel. 2157-M ....R S
Henry L. Riepenkroger, 515 N. 5th.
  Tel. 3397-W.........................F S-T

662, Canton, Ohio. (Shopmen).—Meets first and third Thursdays at 7:30 p. m. at 803 Tuscarawas St., W.

Fred Hamilton, 4416 17th St., N. W.,
  Zone 7 ....P
Francis E. O'Brien, R. D. No. 2,
  Louisville, Ohio ....F S
Alvin Buhecker, 801 Third St., N. E.,
  Zone 4 ....R S

663, Jamestown, N. Y. (Shopmen).—Meets second and fourth Fridays at 8 p. m., at Nordic Temple Hall.

Lewis Vincent, 14 Dunn Ave.............P
Jack V. Wahlstrom, 45 Grant St.......R S
Sylvester Rickard 363½ E. Main St.,
  Falconer, N. Y. ....F S

664, Pottstown, Pa. (Shopmen). — Meets second and fourth Thursdays at 24 S. Charlotte St.

Joseph Kunkle, R. R. 4. Tel. 919R1.........P
Donald Kunkle, 328 Myrtle St.,
  Royersford, Pa..............................R S
Albert L. Wertz, 482 Penn St.,
  Spring City, Pa.............................F S
Lorin Buckwalter, 216 N. 3rd Ave.,
  Royersford, Pa. ....T

665, Madison, Wis. (Shopmen).

Karl Kruger, R. R. 4.........................P
Wm. Zingg, 3606 Wyotee St. Tel. F-1843..R S
Chas. O'Kroley, 1921 Fisher St.........F S-T

666, Nazareth, Pa. (Shopmen).—Meets fourth Sunday at Carlos Hall.

Frank R. Yeakel, 307 S. Green St.
  Tel. 677-J-1 ....P
Walter S. Miller, 161 S. Main St.......F S-T
James G. Hahn, 1417 E. Livingston St.,
  Allentown, Pa. ....R-S

667, Panama City, Fla. (Shipyard Riggers).—Office, 111 Harrison Ave. Tel. 132.

T. W. Campbell, 111 Harrison Ave.
  Res. St. Andrews, Fla. Tel. 1151.......P
J. W. Savage, 111 Harrison Ave.
  Tel. 132. Res. DeFuniak Springs,
  Florida. Tel. 16 ....R S
G. C. Mann. Off. 111 Harrison Ave.
  Res. St. Andrews, Florida,
  Box 562 ....F S-B A
  Send mail to 111 Harrison Ave.

668, Providence, R. I. (Shipyard Riggers).—Off. 56 Washington St. Tel. De. 2862.

Edward James Duffy. Off. 56 Washington
  St. Res., 82 West River St.
  Tel. DE 2862 ....P
John Helfant, 15 Burt St., Taunton,
  Mass. ....R S
W. H. Reardon, 244 Byron Bldg.
  Tel. Jasper 9832 ....B A
Eugene A. Banigan, 38 Booth Ave.,
  Pawtucket, R. I. ....F S-T
Andrew P. Forrest, 215 Hull St.,
  East Providence ....B A

669, Bedford, Ind. (Shopmen).—Meets first and third Fridays of each month at 7:30 p. m., Central Labor Union Hall, Sixteenth St.

Thos. Mason, Sr., 325 L St. Tel. 1229-W...P
Ralph Mikels, Res. 620 Q St............R S
Emery C. Turner, 1714-24th St.
  Tel. 1045-J..............................F S-T

670, Coatesville, Pa. (Shopmen).

Taylor Worth, 205 Main St.
  Parkersburg, Pa.......................P-B A
Grady Gidney, 107 Foundry St.,
  Coatesville, Pa........................F S-T
Joseph Knapp, R. D. No. 2,
  Coatesville, Pa........................R S

671, Dickson City, Pa. (Shopmen).—Meets first and third Thursdays in Borough Bldg., Boulevard Ave.

Henry Laskosky, Res. 830 Brook St.
  Res. Olyphant 1224 ....P
Francis J. Hungerbuhler,
  1433 Elizabeth St., Scranton 4, Pa...F S-T
Arthur Driscoll, Res. 539 N. Bromley
  Ave. ....R S
Joseph Downes, 116 Adams St.,
  Scranton, Pa. ....B A

674, Charleston, S. C. (Ship Riggers).—Office, 68 Society St. Tel. 20011.

L. E. Cribb, 101a Chase St.,
  St. Andrew's Homes, Zone 32.
  Off. Tel. 3-2561 ....P
V. J. Gonzalez, 23 Sorentrue Ave.
  Navy Yard 56, S. C...............R S-F S

678, Lake Charles, La. (Mixed). — Meets fourth Tuesday of each month at 932½ Bilbo. Tel. 7721. Executive Board meets second and fourth Tuesdays.

Henry S. Jackson, P. O. Box 1438.........P
Zachary B. Richard, Off. 932½ Bilbo St.
  Tel. 7721.
  All mail to Box 1438.
  Res. Rt. 3, Box 502.
  Res. Tel. 5182.............F S-T-B A
C. O. Redden, P. O. Box 1438............R S
  All mail to Box 1438. Tel. 7721.

680, Fond du Lac, Wisc. (Shipmen).—Meets every third Tuesday of each month at 7:30 p. m., at Labor Hall, 183 S. Main St.

Peter Langolf, 134 N. Brooke St.
  Tel. 1287 ....P
James Benson, 278 Rose Ave.
  Tel. 6550-R ....R S
Orren M. Burroughs,
  172 Ledgeview Ave. Tel. 2254.......F S-T

681, Royersford, Pa. (Shopmen).

J. W. Wenzel, Royersford, Pa.
  Tel. 42. Res. 370 Green St.
  Res. Tel. 401-W...........................P
Lewis Charles Hunsberger, Res. 434
  Queen St., Spring City, Pa.
  Tel. Royersford 68-J....................R S
Chester S. Fisher, Royersford, Pa.
  Tel. 42. Res. Douglassville, Pa........F S
Ralph C. Kochel, Res. 124 E. 3rd St.,
  Pottstown. Tel. 1139-M ....T

682, Louisville, Ky. (Shopmen).—Meets second and fourth Thursday of each month at Room 201, 307 S. 6th St. Tel. Jackson 6262.

Marcus F. Vitt, 1336 St. Anthony Pl.......P
Edgar Farmer, 1100 Algonquin
  Parkway ....R S
John H. Remfry, 948 Baxter Ave. ....F S-T
  Send all mail to Room 201, 307 S.
  Sixth St.

**683, Brooklyn, N. Y. (Navy Yard Riggers).—
Meets second Wednesday of each month.
Executive Board meets fourth Wednes-
day of each month at The Talyho, 29-31
Cumberland Ave.**

Jesse Ford, Jr., 780 McDonough St. ....P
George C. Hocter, 65 Bank St.,
  New York City ....R S
Joseph Marcelin, 635A Halsey St.,
  Brooklyn ....F S-T

686, Marion, Ind. (Shopmen).

James W. Barton,
  428 N. Washington St..................P
John R. Bradford, Van Buren, Ind......R S
Fred Henning, 4702 S. Race St.
  Tel. 3270-R ....F S

**688, Grand Rapids, Mich. (Shopmen). Meets
first Friday of each month at A. F. of L.
Labor Temple, 415 Ottawa, N.W. at
4:00 p. m.**

Theo. R. Case, 46-60th St., S.W.
  Tel. 394516 ....P
Coppins Carew, 528 Henry, S.E.
  Tel. GI-46450. ....R S
Andrew Ringewold, 721 Butterworth
  Ave. Tel. 85622.....................F S

**689, Covington, Ky. (Shopmen).—Meets first
Monday night at 808 Scott St. at 8:00 p. m.**

Chas. F. Meyer, 1437 Holman St. ....P
Oscar L. Marshall, 3910 Tracy Ave. ...F S-T
Lary Stolz, 812 Crescent Ave. ....R S

**690, Niles, Ohio. (Shopmen).—Meets first and
third Tuesday at Labor Hall, State St.**

Ralph Crytzer, R. D. No. 1,
  Mineral Ridge, Ohio ....P
Quentin R. Britton, 647 Woodbine Ave..
  Hubbard. Ohio ....F S-T-R S

**691, Rock Island, Ill. (Shopmen). — Meets
fourth Fridays at Ironworkers' Hall,
1512 Fourth Ave., at 7:30 p. m.**

Ray Henry, Res. 900 4th St.
  Tel. R. I. 8430 ....P
Clarence G. DeSmet, 728½ 15th St.....R S
Howard K. Walker, 2414 20th Ave.
  Tel. RI-6324 ....F S

**692, Atlantic City, N. J. (Shopmen).—Meets
second and fourth Wednesday.**

Robert Sampson, Off. Odd Fellows Hall,
  So. New York Ave. Res. 145 Collins
  Ave., Pleasantville, N. J.............P
Edw. Crosby, 112 N. California Ave.....R S
Joseph Sweeney, Off. Odd Fellows Hall,
  So. New York Ave.
  Res. 238 N. Missouri Ave...........F S-T

**693, Baltimore, Md. (Shopmen). — Meets
second and fourth Monday at Plumbers
Hall, Biddle and Alsquith Sts.**

C. M. Schulte, 610 S. Eaton St., Zone 24.
  Tel. Wolfe 5591.....................P
E. M. Wysocki, 4412 Kavon Ave., Zone 6..R S
John W. Hamilton, 143 N. Lakewood
  Ave., Zone 24 ....F S-T

694, Houston, Tex. (Shopmen).

Benny Lee Parnell, Off. 2309 Austin.
  Tel. Preston 5442. Res. Rt. No. 1,
  Baytown, Tex. Tel. Channelview 2181...P
D. A. Ferruggio, Res. 1701 Gano St.
  Tel. M-32738. ....R S
W. D. Best, Off. 2309 Austin. Tel.
  Preston 5442. Res. 105 Glen Park.
  Tel. V-2-1237.......................F S-T

**695, Quincy, Ill. (Shopmen). — Meets first
and third Wednesday at Labor Temple.**

Harvey Tipton, 329 Jersey St.
  Tel. 6734-J ....P
Orville K. Wilson, 319 Maertz Lane.....R S
Gerald Marshall, Off. 1110½ Chestnut.
  Tel. 6-098-W ....F S-T-B A

**696, Fort Smith, Ark. (Shopmen). — Meets
second and fourth Mondays of month at
Labor Temple, 109 N. 10th St., at 6:30
p. m.**

Fred C. Miller, P. O. Box 293,
  Greenwood, Ark. ....P
Clarence V. Barnard. Res. 1510
  Lexington Ave. Tel. 2-3359.........R S
A. L. Kendrick, Off. 1008 S. 20th St.
  Tel. 5401 ....F S-T

**697, Roanoke, Va.—Meets second and fourth
Saturday night each month at 8:00 p. m.
Executive Board meets second and
fourth Saturday night each month at
7:00 p. m.**

W. I. Belcher, Off. 305 Tazewell Ave.,
  S. E. Off. Tel. 3-8266. Res. White
  Sulphur Springs, W. Va. ....P
R. F. Groseclose, Off. 305 Tazewell Ave.,
  S. E. Tel. 3-8266. Res. White
  Sulphur Springs, W. Va..............R S
N. D. Sullins, Off. 305 Tazewell Ave.,
  S. E. Tel. 3-8266. Res. 1306 So.
  Jefferson St., Res. Tel. 7406....F S-T-B A

698, Miami, Fla. (Shopmen).

Max M. Heigel, 758 N. W. 74th St...........P
H. D. Martin, Box 3119, Rt. 1,
  Hialeah, Fla. ....F S
S. W. Godbee, 1827 N. W. 19th St..........R S

699, Fort Worth, Texas. (Shopmen).

K. T. Speaker, 211½ W. 13th St. Tel.
  2-6888. Res. 2501 McKenzie St...........P
Edward Doss, Off. 211½ W. 13th St.
  Tel. 2-6888. Res. 4006 Little John St.,
  Zone 5 ....F S-T
Send all local union mail to
  L. R. Robinson, 3012 S. Adams St., Zone 4

**700, Windsor, Ontario, Canada. (Mixed).—
Meets third Thursday of each month.**

John H. Rider, 1342 Wyandotte Ave., W.,
  Apt. 8 ....F S
W. J. Burkholder, 311 Chatham St., W.....P

**701, Joplin, Mo. (Shopmen).—Meets second
and fourth Thursday of each month at
1322 Main St.**

Russell Funk, 726 Sergeant Ave.
  Tel. 3277 ....P
Asa Ray Asher, 1718 Illinois.
  Tel. 4773-W ....R S
Carl M. Beaver, 118 E. 21st St..........F S-T

**702, Jackson, Miss. (Shopmen).—Meets first
and third Wednesdays of each month at
7:30 p. m. at 628 S. State Street. Tel.
2-1790.**

J. H. Hilton, 628 S. State St.
  Tel. 2-1790 ....P
Johnnie Puckett, 734 S. Congress St.
  Off. Tel. 2-1790. Res. Tel. 3-6302......R S
Zeno G. Riley, 781 Evergreen.
  Tel. 2-1790 ....F S-T

704, Chattanooga, Tenn. (Mixed). — Meets second and fourth Friday in Room 201 Labor Temple, 540 Vine St., at 7:30 p. m.

C. C. Hobbs, Off. 540 Vine St. Tel. 7-4334. Res. 1509 E. Ridge Ave. Tel. 2-1475 ....P
Everett D. Liles, Off. 540 Vine St. Res. Rt. No. 1, Hixson, Tenn...........R S
C. G. Hungate, Off. 540 Vine St. Tel. 7-4334. Res. 4726 Old Mission Rd. Tel. 2-8652 ....F S-T-B A

705, Greenville, S. C. (Shopmen).

Paul Rodgers, Rt. No. 1, Duncan, S. C. Tel. 605-R-2 ....P
John C. Langford, Rt. No. 2, Taylors, S. C. ....R S
Mitchell D. Howard, Rt. 2, Taylors, S. C. Tel. 5292-J ....F S-T

706, Savannah, Ga. (Shopmen). Meets second Wednesday of each month in Labor Temple.

Edw. H. Crawford, 521 E. Broughton.....P
H. L. Elmore, 232 A Garden Homes.....R S
Harvey B. Waters, 504 E. McDonough St. ....F S

707, Newcastle, Ind. (Shopmen).

Vern W. Bell, 210 S. 11th St. Tel. 2448-R....P
John Bach, Mt. Lawn, Newcastle, Ind. ...R S
Wm. Judkins, 129 Burgess Court......F S-T

708, Billings, Mont. (Mixed).

Clyde G. Medley, 315 N. 23rd St. Tel. 3616. Off. Tel. 8796....P-F S-T-B A
F. F. Griffin, 217 S. 30th St. Tel. 4492...R S

709, Savannah, Ga. (Mixed).—Meets every Friday 8:30 p. m., at office, 34 Drayton St. Tel. 3-5407.

J. W. Merritt, Rt. 4, Box 8.................P
C. L. Stratton, 2027 Hawthorne St. Tel. 2-6004 ....R S
J. W. Cain, 34 Drayton St. Tel. 3-5407 ....F S-T-B A
Send all mail to office.

710, Monroe, La. (Mixed).—Meets second and fourth Fridays at 7:30 p. m., at 108½ St. John St.

John Otis Brown, Off. 108½ St. John St. Tel. 5690. Res. Edgewater Gardens. Tel. 3806-J.................P
Frank F. Fontana, Off. 108½ St. John St., Res. Rt. No. 3, Monroe, La. Tel. 6164-W ....R S
Clyde Anderson, Off. 108½ St. John St. Tel. 5690, Res. 101 S. 6th St. Tel. 3356-M. Send mail to P. O. Box 686 ....F S-T-B A

711, Montreal, Quebec (Mixed).—Meets second and fourth Wednesdays at Carpenters Hall, 3560 St. Lawrence Blvd.

Armond Richard, 1450 Davidson St. Tel. Falkir 8186 ....P-B A
Paul Leduc, 1078 Amherst..............R S
Eugene Lajeunesse, 1880 Ste. Catherine St. Est. Montreal. Tel. FR- 3534....F S-T

712, Vancouver, B. C. (Shopmen).—Meets second and fourth Thursday in Labour Temple at 8:00 p. m.

A. D. McCameron, 2194 W. 20th Ave. Tel. Bay 8091-L.........................P
E. F. Chester, 3106 E. Broadway. Tel. Has. 0569-R.......................R S
V. E. Steers, 559 W. 19th Ave. Tel. Fair. 1075-R....................F S-T

713, West Bend, Wis. (Shopmen).—Meets first Thursday of each month at Barton Opera House, Barton, Wis.

Alex Pesch, R. No. 3, Kewaskum, Wis.....P
Ralph Dueiykel, Barton, Wis............R S
Daniel Krebs, Allenton, Wis............F S
Martin O. Wiltgen, West Bend, Wis. Tel. 1095-J-2............................T

Editor, Bridgemen's Magazine,
1615 Syndicate Trust Building,
St. Louis, Missouri.

REQUEST FOR CHANGE OF ADDRESS

It is important that you notify us of any change in your address, so that our MAGAZINE may reach you promptly. Fill out this blank and forward to the Editor, Bridgemen's Magazine.

OLD ADDRESS
(PLEASE PRINT OR TYPEWRITE)

NAME_____

STREET OR
P. O. BOX_____

CITY_____ ZONE_____STATE_____

NEW ADDRESS
(PLEASE PRINT OR TYPEWRITE)

STREET OR
P. O. BOX_____

CITY_____ ZONE_____STATE_____

PRINT SIGNATURE_____

LOCAL No._____ MEMBERSHIP No._____

At left, Ironworkers wearing white shirts, celluloid collars and neckties. At right, lowering a beam atop the Singer Building.

The Michagan Avenue Bascule Bridge, Chicago, Illinois during its renovation by Local 1, Chicago in April, 1957.

A "formal" lunchbreak during the construction of the Waldorf Astoria, circa 1930.

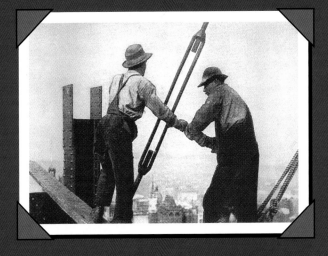

At left, two Ironworkers straightening a bent splice plate on the 47-story Singer Building in Lower Manhattan. *At right*, two Ironworkers tightening a turnbuckle. Note the absence of such safety equipment such as hardhats, gloves, and safety belts.

The End